Colorado

LITHO BY WALSWORTH PUB. CO., INC., MARCELINE, MO.

Colorado

ITS

GOLD AND SILVER MINES,

FARMS AND STOCK RANGES,

AND

HEALTH AND PLEASURE RESORTS.

—————

Tourist's Guide

TO THE

ROCKY MOUNTAINS.

—————

BY FRANK FOSSETT.

—
SECOND EDITION
—

New York:
C. G. CRAWFORD, PRINTER AND STATIONER, 49 and 51 PARK PLACE.
1880

637587

The Rio Grande Press, Inc.

GLORIETA, NEW MEXICO · 87535

SANTA CLARA COUNTY LIBRARY
SAN JOSE, CALIFORNIA

SANTA CLARA COUNTY LIBRARY

• 3 3305 00147 6419

©1976
The Rio Grande Press, Inc.,
Glorieta, NM 87535

Second edition from which this edition was reproduced
was supplied by
FRED ROSENSTOCK, Books,
1228 East Colfax Avenue,
Denver, Colo. 80218

Photographically enlarged in reproduction.

New scholarly introduction by Robert G. Huddleston, Denver, Colo.
New index of all mines, new index of all other places
and proper names by Katherine McMahon, Albuquerque, NM

The heretofore unpublished map of Leadville
Mining District, a map of Territorial
Colorado c. 1876, and a woodcut engraving Bird's
Eye View of Leadville c. 1882 supplied
by the
DENVER PUBLIC LIBRARY
Western History Department
Leadville Research by Robert G. Huddleston

Color photographs of Leadville, c. 1975, by
Robert B. McCoy

A Rio Grande Classic
First published in 1876

First Printing 1976

Library of Congress Cataloging in Publication Data
Fossett, Frank.
    Colorado, its gold and silver mines, farms and stock
ranges, and health and pleasure resorts.

    (A Rio Grande classic)
    Reprint of the 2d ed., 1880, published by C. G.
Crawford, New York.
    Includes indexes.
    1. Colorado. 2. Mines and mineral resources--
Colorado. I. Title.
F776.F76 1975   978.8   75-33701
ISBN 0-87380-109-1

The Rio Grande Press, Inc.
GLORIETA, NEW MEXICO · 87535

Publisher's Preface

Colorado!

The very name (which means "colored red") conjures up images of cloud-kissing mountains, vast panoramas of plains, peaks, meadows and foaming rivers. A pastoral paradise, as it were; a bucolic nostalgia, a dream of frontiers past and glamorous present, a glorious place to visit, a privilege to live in, a paragon of virtuous climate, a veritable bit of heaven on earth in just the right combination of good and bad everything . . . including people. Ah, yes! Call it Colorful Colorado, the Centennial State, the Midland Empire, the New Eldorado (or the old one—either applies); take note that if it were flattened out it would be bigger than Texas and Alaska put together. Call it beautiful. Call it great. Call it anything you wish, along these lines, and you are right!

All of its thousand peaks that tower and soar to elevations between 10,000 and 15,000 feet, and all of the vast meadowlands and parks and fertile valleys in the very heart of America became on maps the Colorado Territory in 1861. On August 1, 1876, as Americans celebrated their first national centennial, Colorado became the 38th state to be admitted to the Union. Today, natives call it the Centennial state, and because we are republishing this book a century later—as Americans celebrate our nation's second centennial—we take particular pride in designating *Colorado,* by Frank Fossett, as both a centennial and a bicentennial salute to Colorado!

Colorado, as a territory and as a state, has a fascinating and vivid history. In the few lines we have space for here, no writer could do justice to this magnificent portion of what is often referred to as ". . . the Old West". Author Frank Fossett was there in person, though, a hundred years ago, and in the unhurried 592 folio pages of this book, he leisurely examines Colorado thoroughly—as it was from 1876 to 1880. What he misses is hardly worth knowing about; what he wrote is a bonanza of source data unequalled in scope . . . and reliability.

We are using the 1880 edition for reproduction, instead of the 1876 edition, because a great deal happened in Colorful Colorado in those four years. In those pioneer, gold rusher and Indian days, the Rocky Mountains crawled with fortune hunters. Not a peak, no matter how tall or rugged, nor a valley, nor a stream, nor a watercourse, nor an arroyo, nor a gulley, nor a running rivulet—not a cliff face, not an escarpment, not a landfall or cave-in or avalanche, escaped the prying eyes of the grizzled prospector. The call of the wild was, in essence, the search for the beautiful metals. Lonely men wandered in lonely places, working in lonely labor, seeking their personal, their very own Eldorado.

Like the ubiquitous but synthetic "males" of today, they were men with poor personal hygiene, long hair and bushy mustaches, but by God in Heaven, in those days males were *MEN!* The evidence of their multitudinous passing is still visible all over the Colorado Rockies. One drives in ease and luxury over smooth and gracefully bending highways, in the valleys, through the canyons, over the passes—almost at every turn one can see the abandoned tipples, the dessicating flumes, the decaying and tumbled log shanties that sheltered the lonely men, the ore dumps, the settling ponds, the rip-rap logs shoring up the hillsides and the gaping holes in the earth that were mineshafts barely big enough to admit the miner and his tools.

Today's visitor can but view in awe the incredible, unbelievable labor, the uncounted man-hours of honest, dirty, hard, backbreaking toil that built those crumbling structures. It is easy to perceive the exploratory ore-dump, high on a mountain inaccessible to modern men, where one man or maybe two or three men, dug deep into the earth to see what was there. The larger workings (diggins') show that here and there were found good "color", and a mine was actually constructed. We at The Rio Grande Press, being ardent devotees of American history, look at all this mute evidence of the hope that springs eternal in the breast of man, and we can have nothing but respect for those boisterous, hardworking, hard-playing, vital, vigorous, daring, adventurous—yes, and philosophical—men of yesterday. With only their own resources, their own muscles, eyes, hands and feet, a pick, a shovel, an ax, a pan and a patient little burro to help (or maybe for company), these men gouged and ripped from a resisting earth their disappointment or their fortune.

Yesterday's failure might be today's bag of nuggets, or perhaps tomorrow's undoing. Yep. They were unwashed, unsanitary, unshaven and unclipped, but we repeat with emphasis—by God, they were *MEN!* They were men with a purpose. They knew what they wanted. They knew that the only way to get what they wanted was to work for it. There is no such thing as a "free lunch" (or anything else), and those men of yesterday knew it. We hail their memory with profound admiration.

Author Fossett focussed the 1880 edition of this book on the gold and silver strikes that built a lusty mining community into Colorado's second largest city in less than four years. At Leadville today, one can buy a little souvenir booklet entitled *The Leadville Story 1860-1960*, by Rene L. Coquoz, and two paragraphs therefrom tell the whole tale:

"*. . . It was shortly afterward that a wonderful new era started in Leadville, the country and the entire state. It was a preface to buried treasures under a crust of prophyritic rock and was in due time to place Colorado among one of the greatest mining regions of all time. The great treasures from the hills amazed the world as the fabulous fortunes poured out daily. It was as unbelievable as a modern fairy tale. The news of the huge treasures from the hills of Leadville was published in nearly all the papers in the country and abroad . . .*"

"*. . . There were four lines of Concord coaches arriving daily; each having two to four lines operating between here and Webster, located at the eastern part of Kenosha Pass, the terminal of the South Park Railway. Another line of coaches were operating by way of the Arkansas Valley. Each line was capable of accommodating 18 to 20 passengers. There was also a great number arriving by private hack and buckboard. By October, 1878, the population had reached the 8,000 mark; by the end of the year, Hall estimated 20,000; the Carbonate Chronicle in 1880 estimated 40,000. The streets were filled from curb to curb day and night and the confusion became even greater than it had been in 1879 . . .*"

The words are apocryphal, but perhaps hold the ring of truth: ". . . for every ounce of gold and silver mined out of Colorado until now, a million ounces are still to be found." If this be true of Colorado in general, it may be even more true of Leadville.

Leadville is not far from our base at beautiful Glorieta, where we live and work. We have been there often, and we like it. We went there for a visit in September 1975, and took the color photographs we have added to our bicentennial edition. We have not captioned the pictures precisely and accurately, as it was not our purpose to be definitive with them. What we simply wanted to show was some of the things the visitor to Leadville today might see. We think all visitors who see the vast ruins of yesteryear everywhere one looks will be saddened—as we were—by the rape of nature so eloquently visible, as it were. The lovely land has been torn, ripped and mangled beyond repair in the greed and indifference of those hectic years. A century later, only a little healing of the wounded earth can be seen. The visitor regrets this, but even as one cannot unscramble an egg, nothing can alter or change what happened yesterday.

Man is fundamentally a greedy creature, and even as men today are greedy and indifferent to the future, so were the men of yesterday. To say this in no way detracts from the splendid manhood of the Colorado treasure seekers. The difference, as is so often the case, lies in degree. The men of yesterday, for all their violent plundering of the slopes and heights around Leadville (and elsewhere) were destroying a relatively small area in the remote mountains which led, inevitably, to the construction of a great nation. In the milieu of those years, destruction of the natural environment was called "progress". These days, similar vandalism is called "recreation".

A number of our photographs show, on the slopes of the Continental Divide facing Leadville, a great ugly gash through the primeval pine forest. Here had fallen a host of giant trees that may have been mere seedlings when Hernando Cortez first set foot in the New World. Were those splendid products of a gracious and bountiful nature brought down in the name of "progress", or even for some worthy purpose?

No, they were not. They were destroyed, along with the lovely mountainside roundabout, to make a "ski playground" for adults. The hypocrisy, the ever-visible, ever-more-apparent double standard so prevalent among many young people today, is here glaringly obvious. It was ". . . terrible, outrageous, hideous, criminal . . ." (etc., etc., ad nauseum) for Colorado's early treasure seekers to so ruthlessly mutilate a breathtaking landscape in the search for such trash as gold and silver. But, like WOW! What a marvelous ski run (newly torn and ripped untimely from the living earth to make a profitable playground for the idle)! The early Coloradoans "vandalized" like Trojans, working incredibly hard to make a state and a nation; today's vandals hack out their destructiveness for nothing more than sheer, aimless, mindless pleasure and profit.

But our purpose in writing this commentary is mainly to present a perspective for our publication of this title. We have done that. Let us now offer thanks to our great and good friend, Fred Rosenstock of Denver, for allowing us to use his 1880 edition of this book to reproduce our edition. Fred doesn't always agree with what we write, but he likes what we do with our editions. It was Fred Rosenstock who, many years ago, planted the seed that germinated finally (in 1962) into The Rio Grande Press, Inc. We believe we have no better friend anywhere than this amiable, knowledgeable, gentle man. We greatly appreciate him and his friendship. We wish him the best of everything, always.

During the Rocky Mountain Book Fair in late April 1975, we exhibited our products to the interested public. Hardly had the show opened when a young man with a scholar's gleam in his eye visited our exhibit. He had learned from Fred Rosenstock, he said, that we were preparing to publish a new edition of this title, and he offered us some ideas we thought were good. That is how we met Robert G. Huddleston, a candidate for a Ph.D. degree (in Western American History, no less) at Denver University, and that is why we invited him to write a scholarly Introduction to this edition for us. He not only did that, and did it well (as the reader can determine for himself in the pages following ours), but with the help of the ever-accommodating Ms. Eleanor Gehres (head of the Western History Department of the Denver Public Library), he located three items we have added to our edition which were not in previous editions, namely: (1) a Map of the Leadville Mining District, c. 1880, (2) a Map of Territorial Colorado, c. 1876, and (3) a Photodiagram "Bird's Eye View of Leadville 1882". Item 1 is a gorgeous map of the Leadville Mining District, published here (with the permission of the Denver Public Library) for the very first time. All three of these items are printed as large as we could print them, and are folded into a pocket at the back of the book.

The 1880 edition's Table of Contents is a sort of index found on pages V, VI and VII, and on page VIII there is a semi-list of important mines. We have improved on that. We commissioned a professional index from our good friend and great lady (and expert indexer) Ms. Katherine McMahon of Albuquerque. She not only prepared a painstaking and meticulous index, but she indexed also (in a separate listing) all of the mines named in the book. The result, therefore, makes our *Colorado* a volume easy to use.

Lastly, or at least next to lastly, we invite the reader's attention to the dimensions of our edition. As with so many early books, small type was printed on small pages, perhaps for economy. In offset printing, there is no problem in enlarging the copy size during production, and we have done so. The 1880 edition's dimensions were 5 inches by 7 3/4 inches. Our edition has been enlarged to 8½ inches by 11 inches. This certainly enhances the book's readibility, but unfortunately, it has the effect also of enhancing whatever imperfections are to be found in the 1880 printing. If the letters appear a little fuzzy to modern eyes, squint a bit until the haziness disappears with familiarity.

It goes without saying, but we'll say it anyway, the enlargement improves also the clarity of the maps and engravings throughout the book. We believe it not unduly immodest to point out that, as of 1975, The Rio Grande Press is the only commercial reprint publishing house (that we know of) which goes to the lengths we do to improve our editions. We know of no other reprint publisher that, for instance, adds indexes or contemporary but germane color plates to a reprint edition, such as we have done here and with other titles. We do this whenever we can as a matter of course. Our efforts in this connection should not be interpreted as "updating" or "annotating" a reprint title. We call it "improving" a title with germane emendations, and that is all it is. Obviously, after doing so, our edition becomes an edition far more useful, per se, than the edition we started with (even if it was a first edition).

We regret very much that we have to impose such a formidable retail price on this title. Like the cost of everything else, all the components of book production have risen to allow the producer a margin of profit after his costs. It is our personal opinion that American citizens haven't seen anything yet, insofar as inflation goes. With an irresponsible and profligate government throwing our hard-earned tax money away by the billions of dollars, the price of everything we buy has no place to go but up—and the only end possible, in our opinion, is ultimate economic catastrophe. So, if you believe the list price of this book is too high, we're sorry. We invite you most cordially to place the blame exactly where it belongs—on the doorsteps of the White House, the Capitol and the misnamed "Supreme Court", where, collectively, hang out the nuttiest bunch of "leaders" ever to afflict any nation in history.

We salute Colorful Colorado on its centennial birthday, and we wish it well in the years to come. On the eve of its bicentennial, we salute America, too; it is our country, and we love what it once stood for deeply. What it represents now is anyone's guess. We don't know, and we know nobody who does.

Robert B. McCoy

John T. Strachan

Glorieta, New Mexico
October 1975

Introduction
by
Robert G. Huddleston

A mine is a speculative investment—the shaft following a rich vein of high grade ore, and then the next dynamite blast uncovers country rock and the glorious bonanza becomes a borrasca, not worth the expense of hauling the equipment out from the face of the vein.

To assist potential nineteenth century investors, the hard rock mining regions developed a number of experts, men whose reputations depended upon their ability to accurately examine and report on the present worth and future value of a mine. These mining engineers, primarily graduates of colleges such as the Colorado School of Mines at Golden, were in great demand by the large corporations. The eastern and European capitalists needed the professional engineers to guide them in the consolidation of mining claims and to testify as expert witnesses in the lengthy lawsuits which arose over land titles and the judicial interpretation of "apex" law.

But the services of the mining engineer were too expensive for the average investor—and perhaps the professionals' reports were too dry and technical to interest men who were certain that the Shining Mountains were glistening with precious stones. To satisfy the needs of these ambitious men, the shelves of Colorado bookstores were stocked with lavishly illustrated volumes describing in flowing words the wonders of the mining districts. Most of these works were so much pulp, but one or two stand out because their authors, journalists rather than geologists, made an effort to verify the data that they reported. Today these few are still avidly read by historians for the insights they offer into the Colorado mining experience. The outstanding volume in this regard is Frank Fossett's *Colorado*.

Of Fossett himself, almost nothing is known. Born in Rome, New York about 1843, he was trained as a newspaperman. About 1867 he felt the call of the west and moved to Colorado. New smelting techniques were being introduced into Gilpin County and Central City was coming out of its wartime doldrums when Fossett arrived and settled into a Spring Street room. He joined the staff, and later became the editor, of the Central City *Colorado Times* (which became the *Colorado Herald* in 1870), a newspaper "devoted to the advancement of the mining interests and general industries of the Territory, and to the dissemination of accurate information concerning all matters that interest the public at large, especially every thing pertaining to mines and mining." Like many another newspaper of early day Colorado, the *Herald* folded in 1875; it was described as being "ultra-Democratic" and perhaps its politics were unwelcome in Henry Teller's home town. Tragically for the historian, the files of the *Times* and the *Herald* were never collected and except for a few scattered issues, Fossett's newspapers have entirely disappeared.

Occasionally other newspapers around the state made mention of the comings and goings of their fellow editor from Central City (travels often made in connection with the activities of the territory's Democratic Party), but the only real news item that has survived concerns a brawl on the streets of Central City, gleefully reported by his Gilpin newspaper rival, the *Register*. However, Fossett was establishing a reputation as a mining reporter, serving as a roving correspondent for several eastern journals, including the New York *Mining and Engineering Journal*.

Following the collapse of the *Herald*, Fossett was able to devote full time to the writing of a book which he hoped would provide the definitive answer to questions concerning the gold and silver regions of the new Centennial State. *Colorado: A Historical, Descriptive and Statistical Work on the Rocky Mountain Gold and Silver Mining Regions* was printed in Denver in 1876 by the Daily Tribune Steam Printing House. The first edition concerned itself almost entirely with those areas with which Fossett was most familiar; the camps in Gilpin, Clear Creek, and Boulder counties. The present-day reader suspects, from the full account given three counties and the superficial treatment accorded the rest of the state, that Fossett originally planned to cover only this small, but at that time, very important part of the mining industry of Colorado. Perhaps the publisher changed Fossett's mind, and he hurriedly padded out the remainder of the book. In any event, the five hundred pages were a landmark of promotional literature and were well worth the purchaser's two dollars.

Although the book did not sell well, Fossett was encouraged by the professional reception that it received, and the new silver strikes in Aspen and Leadville provided additional fields for him to examine. In 1879 C. G. Crawford of New York published a completely rewritten and expanded study, *Colorado: Its Gold and Silver Mines, Farms, and Stock Ranches, and Health and Pleasure Resorts; Tourist's Guide to the Rocky Mountains.* Providing complete coverage not only of the expanding mining camps, but also the state's scenic attractions in recognition of the increasing value of the incipient tourist industry, the book was a tremendous success. A *Rocky Mountain News* reviewer commented that *Colorado* was not only interesting, "but what is of more value, entirely reliable." The paper went on to declare that no tourist should think of visiting the state, and surely, no capitalist should think of investing in Colorado, without consulting Fossett's book.

As a result of his fame and reputation, Fossett was called to New York where he became the editor of a mining newspaper with national circulation. The stocks of *Colorado* were quickly exhausted, and in 1880 Fossett brought out a revised edition, which included much new material on the development of the state in the year since the earlier edition had appeared. The major additions concerned the booming Leadville region.

Unfortunately, Fossett contracted tuberculosis. He returned to Colorado in an attempt to effect a cure, but even the dry climate did not help, and he died in his rooms in Denver's Windsor Hotel in the early hours of August 26, 1881. Fossett was buried the next afternoon in Riverside Cemetery. The life-long bachelor's only survivor was a sister in Massachusetts.

But, if little remains of Fossett the man, his reputation as an author and mining expert has been established. His honesty, combined with his readability, makes *Colorado* worth studying as well as enjoying a century after the publication of the first edition. In words still pertinent today, the *Rocky Mountain News* endorsed Fossett: "The chief merit of the book is its complete reliability."

Robert G. Huddleston

Denver, Colo.
July, 1975

LEADVILLE

Colorado

ITS

GOLD AND SILVER MINES,

FARMS AND STOCK RANGES,

AND

HEALTH AND PLEASURE RESORTS.

Tourist's Guide

TO THE

ROCKY MOUNTAINS.

BY FRANK FOSSETT.

SECOND EDITION

New York:
C. G. Crawford, Printer and Stationer, 49 and 51 Park Place.
1880

PREFACE.

THIS volume, as its name implies, is devoted to Colorado. Its contents are descriptive, statistical, and historical, and embrace a detailed account of the State's resources, productions, and progress. For general convenience it has been divided into four parts. The first of these will answer for a traveler's guide, and relates to routes of travel, health and pleasure resorts, scenic attractions, and climate. The second part is historical, and the third contains much information concerning the State at large and the farming and live stock interests. Part fourth is devoted to the mines. As mining is Colorado's main industry and source of wealth, it receives the space and attention its merits deserve. The statistics in this department are of the most elaborate character, and are as accurate as time, labor, and research could make them. The narrative of gold and silver mining possesses enough of romance and adventure to interest the general reader, and the descriptions of mines, and of mining and milling, together with statements of requisite outlays from beginning to end, will prove especially serviceable to investors or capitalists. The author has endeavored to furnish a compendium of useful and general information concerning Colorado, and trusts this book will meet the present requirements of the public in that respect.

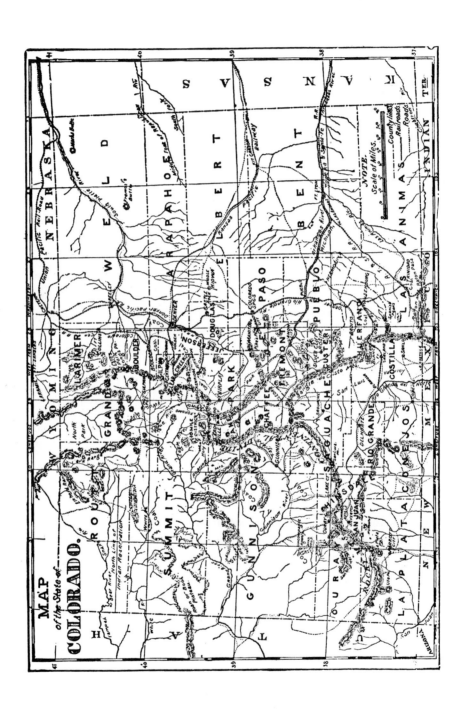

CONTENTS.

PART FIRST.

PART SECOND.

PART THIRD.

PART FOURTH.

APPENDIX.

LEADING MINES.

ALPHABETICAL LIST OF MANY PROMINENT MINES, AND NUMBER OF PAGE.

PART FIRST.

CHAPTER I.

THE GENERAL RECORD OF THE CENTENNIAL STATE—HER REMARK-
ABLE PROGRESS AND PROSPERITY—GEOGRAPHICAL FEATURES
AND NATURAL ADVANTAGES.

At the present time Colorado is attracting more attention than
any other one section of the country. This is true as regards moneyed
men as well as with the masses. The tide of emigration that is
setting so strongly in that direction, and a growing disposition
for mining investments, indicate a general belief in Colorado's superior prospects for labor and capital. So widely prevalent an opinion
can only be caused by continuous prosperity and great natural wealth.
That Colorado deserves the reputation and renown she is securing,
her present rapid advancement and growing productions attest.
Brilliant as her recent record has been, it is evident that it can bear
no comparison with that of the future.

It is generally admitted that Colorado is the most prosperous
division of the West, or of the whole country. This is due to her
varied and extensive resources, developed and taken advantage of by
an enterprising and intelligent population. It is fast being demonstrated as an established fact that Colorado's mineral resources exceed
those of any other western state or territory. These will soon be
developed so that she will surpass all other sections in production. Added to mountain locked treasure vaults of gold and
silver, and endless deposits of coal and many valuable minerals, are
agricultural and stock-growing lands of an extensive and most
productive character. To crown the whole are climatic advantages
that have made the State famous far and wide, and an empire of
scenic attractions, such as no other region in either hemisphere
can boast of. Thus, while her gold and silver veins are astonishing
the world and enriching her people as well as outside investors, and
her farms and stock ranges are extremely remunerative, her fine

climate and grand scenery attract as many health and pleasure seekers as her mines do settlers and investors.

Colorado is situated in the centre of that part of the United States lying between the Mississippi river and the Pacific ocean and British America and Mexico. The eastern section of the State embraces a portion of the great plains, while the central and western divisions are mainly composed of mountain ranges and their offshoots, with occasional valleys and plateaus of great extent. The Rocky mountains here attain their greatest elevation, and from their summits and slopes rivers flow to either ocean. Colorado has an area of 104,500 square miles, or more than any other state, excepting Texas and California. It lies between the thirty-seventh and forty-first parallels of north latitude, and extends from the one hundred and second to the one hundred and ninth meridians of longitude. It is almost square or rectangular in shape, having a width from north to south of very nearly two hundred and eighty miles and an average length of about three hundred and seventy miles from east to west. It is west of Kansas, north of New Mexico, east of Utah, and south of Wyoming.

The great plains rise gradually from the Missouri westward for six hundred miles to the base of the foot hills and spurs of the great mountain system. The elevation of the western limit of these plains is usually about one mile above sea level. This broad and level expanse is destitute of timber, except along the river bottoms, but is covered with nutritious grasses that afford excellent grazing for cattle and buffalo. What are known as the "foot hills" are the less elevated portions of the mountains. These gradually increase in altitude for a distance westward of from twenty to fifty miles, where they merge into the main or "snowy range." Some are smooth and rolling and others rugged masses of rock and earth, but all more or less heavily timbered. The "Continental Divide," or higher portion of the mountains, is usually from forty to sixty miles beyond the base of the hills first mentioned. The elevation of this divide is generally from 12,000 to 14,400 feet above tide water and several thousand feet above the line where timber and nearly all vegetation ceases. This has been termed the backbone of the American continent. From its eternal snows, crystal lakes, and sparkling rivulets, streams are formed that eventually unite and make great rivers. Here the Arkansas, Platte, Grande, and

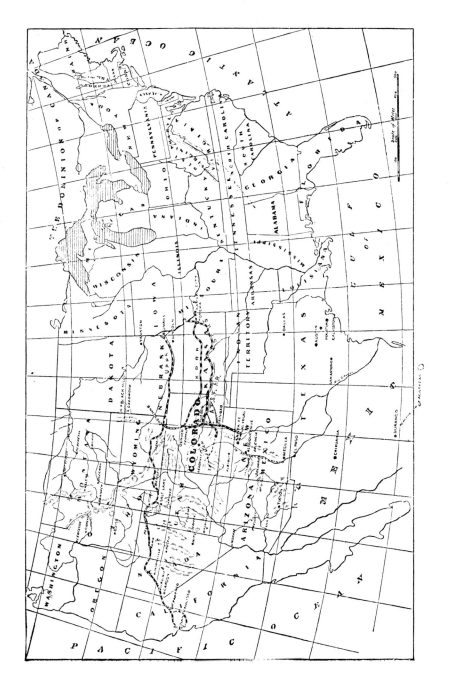

Colorado start on their long journeys of two thousand miles or more toward the Gulf of Mexico or California. Western Colorado is made up of mountains, hills, plateaus, valleys, and ravines, extending on to Utah or Arizona. The gold and silver bearing belts and districts are confined to these mountain chains, hills, and ravines. Most gold sections are of less average elevation than those of silver, although there is no great degree of regularity about this. Many silver lodes and deposits are situated on the highest peaks and near or above what is called "timber line."

The parks of Colorado are a distinct and remarkable feature of this mountain system. They are generally composed of level or rolling lands, covered with luxuriant grasses, and dotted here and there with groves of timber. They are firmly walled about with mountains grand and high, and are watered by streams of the purest character. It is evident that these parks were the basins of former lakes at an early period of the world's history, and that they were subsequently deprived of their water by volcanic agency, while their original outlines were retained. The largest of these are called San Luis, South, North, and Middle Parks. The mountains of Colorado are covered, up to elevations of from 10,800 to 11,800 feet, with pine, fir, spruce, aspen, and other forest trees. Above the region of timber all is bleak and barren rock and "slide," varied with the occasional presence of stunted grass and flowers.

CHAPTER II.

INFORMATION FOR THE TOURIST, TRAVELER, AND IMMIGRANT—WAYS OF REACHING COLORADO AND POINTS OF INTEREST, DISTANCES AND ELEVATIONS, CLIMATE AND SCENERY—HUNTING AND FISHING GROUNDS, AND MINERAL SPRINGS.

A trip to Colorado during the summer months is at once pleasant, interesting, and instructive in the highest degree. To all wishing to escape the confinement of city life, the heat of summer or the recurring monotony of eastern watering-places, or who would see something of life on the western prairies and among the gold and silver mines, the advice is tendered, Go to Colorado. It requires less time and money than to visit Europe, and will prove far more satisfactory than to remain at home. Take the western train, breathe the pure air of the mountains, feast your eyes on the picturesque features, the golden ores and silver bullion of this wonderland, and in a few weeks you can return, feeling better than you ever could do in the damp heavy atmosphere of a lower clime.

While the foundations of enduring wealth are secured by the mining, farming, and pastoral resources, Colorado offers a world of attractions and advantages, as beneficial to those who reside within her borders as to sojourners from abroad. Possessing a climate any land might envy, and surpassing all others in extent and beauty of her mountain ranges, one cannot do otherwise than admit that Nature has dealt with a lavish hand in this new land of the West. Thus it is that her balmy air, exhilarating atmosphere, health-restoring mineral waters, picturesque scenery, and unrivaled fishing and hunting grounds are bringing visitors or residents from almost the wide world over.

So vast is this land of mountain, park, and plain, that Switzerland is insignificant in comparison, and far behind in variety and attractiveness. Pen fails to do justice to the massive grandeur of the "Snowy Range," the majesty of its cloud-capped towers, the awful depths of its mysterious canons, or to the beauties of vale and stream that everywhere abound from the Platte to the Colorado.

MU-AV CAÑON—WESTERN COLORADO.

But all of these subjects have been dwelt upon so often that even most Eastern readers have become more or less familiar with them.

For the convenience of the traveler, a collection of facts and information which may serve as a tourist's guide is presented here rather than in the closing portion of the book. Beginning with this chapter, routes of travel into and through Colorado are given, together with descriptions of towns, pleasure resorts, points of interest, and such other matter as is mostly likely to be called for. In this connection are tables of distances, elevations, and a variety of facts that will be found useful or instructive, if not especially interesting.

And by way of prefacing what is to follow, it may be well to say that, in going to Colorado, one does not necessarily bid farewell to civilization or to the comforts of ordinary life. There is as much culture, education, and refinement in Denver or many of the larger towns as in places of similar size at the East or West. There are as many well-stocked stores, as great a variety of goods of all descriptions, and as well-kept and comfortable hotels as anywhere else outside of the great cities. Everything one is likely to require can be purchased as cheaply or with but a trifling advance on New York prices. Owing to the scattered character of the population, and the difficulties attending their construction and operation, railway and stage fares are somewhat high, but this is so in all far Western regions. In some of the newer settlements up among the mountains time has not yet been given to secure all the accommodations desirable, nor do circumstances permit of low rates in all places—but this can hardly be expected. At the pleasure resorts are first-class hotels, and the charges compare favorably with those of like localities in other parts.

Those wishing to avoid to some extent the beaten track of the excursionist can enjoy a world of novelty by embarking on a "camping-out trip" through the mountains. And to do this but a very short distance need be traveled before one obtains all the solitude and necessary surroundings to enable him to "rough it" to his heart's content. To go on one of these camping-out tours in park or mountain glen, be it near or distant, all requisite equipments, tents, supplies, wagon teams, and saddle animals, can be obtained at reasonable figures at any of the prominent towns or cities.

All of the leading mining towns or health and pleasure resorts can be reached by railway or stage, and it is only the newer or smaller mining camps that still depend on the latter means of transportation, except in the case of remote localities. So, in going to Colorado, only about the same preparation is needed as in starting on a trip of a few weeks' duration to other sections. No laying in of stores or supplies is necessary, for everything that can be obtained in an ordinary Eastern town can be had there.

Schools and churches are as numerous and as liberally endowed as elsewhere, and the population will rank with that of any of the older commonwealths in all the requirements of life. The towns are well built, and most of them are being made attractive and beautiful as fast as circumstances will permit. Well-regulated railways extend to all thickly-settled parts of the plains, along the eastern base of the mountains, and several lines are being rapidly pushed up through the cañons and gorges of the Sierras. Some of these already connect the plains cities with their more elevated neighbors up among the gold and silver mines; beyond, first-class daily stage lines ply between all important points or mining districts.

Three great railways enter Colorado from the East, either one of which will land the traveler in Denver or some important objective point. These are the Atchison, Topeka & Santa Fe, the Kansas Pacific and the Union Pacific, or rather the Colorado Central, which diverges therefrom at Cheyenne. They are all supplied with Pullman palace cars and the usual comforts attending railway travel. Starting from the Missouri river, where connection is made with all leading Eastern lines, the great plains are gradually ascended until the summit of this inland plateau is reached, near the base of the mountains.

The cities of Denver and Pueblo are what may be termed the ports of entry for the country around about and beyond. While all points can be reached from either road, the more southern sections of the plains or mountains can be gained most advantageously by taking the Southern route. This extends up the Arkansas valley, with one line entering New Mexico and the others making connections with all important localities yet touched by rail facilities from the southern boundary up to Denver. At Pueblo the Denver & Rio Grande forks in four different directions, pointing towards the San Juan region and Leadville, and extending from El Moro on the south to Colorado Springs and Denver on the north. Some of the most desirable points to visit in the whole State—mines, mineral springs, and scenic attractions—can be reached by this route or its stage connections.

Denver is the natural halting-place for tourists and visitors, by reason of its extended connections with mining towns and pleasure resorts, its excellent hotel accommodations, and its size, prominence, and general attractions. It is the finest and most enterprising city of the New West. Few places can compare with it in beauty or in all that goes to make life desirable. While much will be found to interest the stranger, all parts of northern and central Colorado can be reached therefrom easily and quickly. Six railways centre here, radiating to all points of the compass. The great gold mines of Gilpin, or the productive silver mines of Clear Creek county, are all within a few hours' ride across the prairie and up the renowned mountain gorge and valley of Clear Creek. The Colorado Central railway conveys one there, or to the interesting towns of Golden and Boulder, whose smelting and reduction works are of great extent and capacity. Up the line of this same railway, nestling in its mountain retreat, is the famous watering-place and summer resort of Idaho Springs. In either direction are the great mining towns of Central, Georgetown, and Black Hawk, whose annual bullion product is counted by millions. All of these places have first-class hotels.

Southward, the Denver & Rio Grande road invites to those fashionable resorts, Colorado Springs and Manitou, the best patronized of all western watering-places. Near each and all of the localities above enumerated are points of rare beauty and attractiveness, well worth a visit to the Rocky mountains to look upon. Scenery, lovely and picturesque or grand and majestic, await inspection in all directions, and, to crown all, a climate of Italian mildness or Alpine purity.

To the southwest the Denver & South Park conveys the traveler to the weird beauties of Platte River Cañon, and up through the mountains to where the tide of humanity on its way to Leadville halts to take a fresh start, by stage or foot-path. North from this plains railway centre the Denver Pacific and the Boulder Valley take their respective courses to Cheyenne and Boulder.

After leaving the magnificent farming sections of eastern Kansas and Nebraska, the only available routes to the Rocky Mountains are up the courses of the streams which flow eastward to the Missouri or

Mississippi. Although lacking the moisture of more eastern localities, water is obtainable, agriculture practicable, and settlements are becoming numerous in the western uplands of the Arkansas and Platte valleys. While farming is successfully prosecuted with the assistance of irrigation in that comparatively rainless country, and stock growing is remarkably remunerative, the elevated tracts of country between these main watercourses are of little service.

The region known as the Great Plains rise to the westward from the Missouri river to the western basis of the Rocky Mountains, where they attain an elevation of a mile, more or less, above sea level. This rise is so gradual as to be imperceptible to the traveler, and yet it amounts to an average of nearly ten feet per mile. It is interesting to know how fast one is ascending in crossing the great inland plateau or among the mountains beyond, and no little diversion can be obtained from noting the variations of a pocket barometer. In the tables of elevations and distances on the great through lines and mountain roads given below, it will be seen that the upward tendency is slight until the "Rockies" themselves are reached, when it becomes much more rapid and manifest.

Distances between Eastern and Colorado cities vary with different routes. From New York to Denver the distance is 1,960 miles, more or less, by various railway systems. From Boston the distance is some 200 miles or more greater, and from Philadelphia 90 miles less. Different routes from Chicago run from 1,155 to 1,250 miles, and from St. Louis 916 miles and over. Pueblo is a little nearer from central and southern points, and about the same from Chicago and Boston. The railway jumping-off points at Central, Georgetown, and Cañon City are not far from 2,000 miles from New York, and Alamosa is over 2,100 miles distant.

The schedule railway time from Eastern points to Colorado is something as follows, in days of twenty-four hours and fractions thereof. To Denver, from New York, 3 days and 8 hours; Philadelphia, 3 days and 5 hours; Pittsburg, 2 days and 17 hours; Baltimore, 3 days and 3 hours; Saint Louis, 42 hours; Chicago, 50 hours; Kansas City, 32 hours. To Pueblo, 3 to 4 hours less; Cañon City, about the same time as to Denver.

ATCHISON, TOPEKA & SANTA FE RAILWAY.

The subjoined table contains nearly all the stations of the main lines of the Atchison, Topeka & Santa Fe railway, with their elevations in feet above the sea and distances in miles from Kansas City. Atchison, one of the eastern termini on the Missouri river, has an elevation above tide water of 803 feet.

Name of Station.	Miles from Kansas City.	Elevation.	Name of Station.	Miles from Kansas City.	Elevation.
Kansas City		763	Great Bend	286	1,854
Lawrence	41	845	Larned	308	2,011
Topeka	66	904	Kinsley	332	2,200
Carbondale	84	1,081	Dodge City	369	2,492
Burlingame	93	1,050	Lakin	440	3,013
Osage City	101	1,082	Colorado & Kansas State Line	482	3,129
Reading	112	1,072	Granada	497	3,296
Emporia	128	1,161	Las Animas	538	3,952
Cottonwood	148	1,183	*Arkansas Valley Line.*		
Florence	173	1,277			
Peabody	194	1,256	La Junta	571	4,137
Newton	201	1,433	Napiesta		4,395
Halstead	210	1,320	Pueblo	635	4,713
Burrton	220	1,410	*New Mexico Line.*		
Hutchinson	234	1,482			
Sterling	244	1,494	Trinidad	651	6,005
Raymond	265	1,679	Raton Pass	666	7,863
Ellinwood	276	1,738	Las Vegas	786	6,397

Kansas City to Santa Fe, 869 miles. Kansas City to Albuquque, 917 miles. Elevation of Santa Fe, 6,862 feet.

DENVER & RIO GRANDE RAILWAY.

Below are elevations of leading stations of this road, with their distances from Kansas City via the connecting A., T. & S. F. Railway. Elsewhere is a more complete table of the Denver & Rio Grande Stations.

Name of Station.	Miles from Kansas City.	Elevation.	Name of Station.	Miles from Kansas City.	Elevation.
North from Pueblo.			*Southwest from Pueblo.*		
South Pueblo	635	* {4,615 / 4,713}	Cuchara	684	5,893
			Walsenburg	691	6,134
Colorado Springs	680	5,985	La Veta	706	6,970
Monument	699	6,931	Veta Pass	720	9,339
Divide	703	7,186	Alamosa	765	7,492
Castle Rock	723	6,173			
Littleton	745	5,320	*South from Cuchara.*		
Denver	755	5,143			
West from Pueblo.			El Moro	721	5,825
Canon	675	5,287			

* Elevations taken by two different persons.

STAGE LINES FROM THE ABOVE RAILWAY SYSTEM.

In the San Juan Region, Lake City is 116 miles beyond Alamosa; altitude, 8,550. Silverton, 146 miles; altitude, 9,400. Summit gold mines, 49 miles; altitude, 11,500.

In Custer County, Silver Cliff is 30 miles from Cañon; altitude, 7,500. Rosita, 32 miles; altitude, 8,500.

Leadville, 126 miles from Cañon, altitude, 10,025 feet.

RAILWAY CONNECTIONS.

Continuing on to the mountains from Denver *via* the Colorado Central, an elevation of 8,300 feet is attained at Central, 40 miles from Denver; one of 7,531 feet at Idaho Springs, 37½ miles, and 8,452 feet at Georgetown, 53½ miles. Or, taking the Denver & South Park, an elevation of 10,139 feet is attained, the highest railroading in the United States, at the Kenosha Divide, about 75 miles from Denver.

KANSAS PACIFIC RAILWAY.

Names of leading stations, elevations, and distances from Kansas City. The elevation of Leavenworth is 783 feet.

Name of Station.	Miles from Kansas City.	Elevation.	Name of Station.	Miles from Kansas City.	Elevation.
Kansas City	....	763	Solomon	172	1,193
Armstrong	1	773	Salina	185	1,243
Edouardsville	13	801	Brookville	200	1,366
Lenape	22	799	Fort Harker	218	1,600
Lawrence	38	845	Ellsworth	223	1,556
Perryville	51	870	Bunker Hill	252	1,882
Medina	52	871	Victoria	279	....
Grantville	60	895	Hays	289	2,099
Topeka	67	904	Ellis	302	2,135
Rossville	83	951	Grinnell	364	2,922
St. Mary's	90	973	Sheridan	405	3,121
Bellevue	97	....	Wallace	420	3,319
Wamego	104	1,018	Monotony	440	3,792
St. George	110	1,018	Cheyenne Wells	462	4,295
Manhattan	118	1,042	First View	472	4,595
Ogden	129	1,078	Kit Carson	487	4,307
Fort Riley	135	1,090	Hugo	534	5,068
Junction City	138	1,100	Deer Trail	583	5,203
Detroit	157	1,153	Box Elder	617	5,430
Abilene	163	1,173	Denver	639	5,196

COLORADO CENTRAL RAILROAD—MOUNTAIN DIVISION.

Name of Station.	Miles from Denver.	Elevation.	Name of Station.	Miles from Denver.	Elevation.
Denver	....	5,197	Fall River	39.3	7,719
Golden	15.8	5,687	Mill City	43.1	7,930
Forks Clear Creek	29.0	6,893	Lawson	48.2	8,120
Black Hawk	35.8	7,875	Empire Station	49.5	8,286
Central	39.6	8,325	Georgetown	53.5	8,514
Idaho Springs	37.5	7,535			

DENVER & SOUTH PARK RAILROAD.

Name of Station.	Miles from Denver.	Elevation.	Name of Station.	Miles from Denver.	Elevation.
Denver	....	5,197	Fairville	58	8,175
Platte Cañon	20	5,487	Geneva	68	8,514
South Platte	29	6,037	Webster	70	9,120
Deer Creek	48	7,084	Kenosha Divide	....	10,129
Bailey's	54	7,880	Jefferson	80	9,754

The next important point to which this road will be constructed is Fairplay, with an elevation of 9,964 feet. Trout Creek Pass has an altitude of 9,620 feet.

UNION PACIFIC & COLORADO CENTRAL RAILROADS.

Below are leading stations, elevations, and distances from Omaha on Union Pacific to Cheyenne, and Colorado Central to Denver.

Name of Station.	Miles from Omaha.	Elevation.	Name of Station.	Miles from Omaha.	Elevation.
Omaha	....	1,003	Big Spring	361	3,360
Gilmore	10	1,013	Julesburg	377	3,535
Papillion	15	1,009	Sidney	414	4,108
Elkhorn	29	1,187	Pine Bluffs	473	5,061
Valley	35	1,157	Cheyenne	516	6,075
Tremont	47	1,220	*Colorado Central R. R.*		
North Bend	62	1,296	Colorado Junction	522	6,357
Schuyler	76	1,372	Fort Collins	564	4,815
Columbus	92	1,469	Loveland	576	....
Central City	132	....	Longmont	595	2,957
Grand Island	154	1,887	Boulder	605	5,278
Kearney Junction	195	2,143	Ralston	628	5,579
Stevenson	201	2,207	Golden	631	5,728
Plum Creek	231	2,406	Denver	652	5,196
Brady Island	268	2,683	*C. C. R. R.—Mountain Division.*		
McPherson	278	2,731	Central	40	8,300
North Platte	291	2,825	Georgetown	53½	8,452
O'Fallon's	308	3,012			

TABLES OF COLORADO ELEVATIONS, TOWNS AND CITIES, MINES, MOUNTAINS, PASSES, AND LAKES.

The reports of Professor Hayden and Lieutenant Wheeler give, among much other valuable information, the average elevations of different portions of Colorado's area. The greatest elevation of any one point is 14,464 feet, and there are about one hundred peaks of a greater elevation than 14,000 feet. The lowest part of the State is on the eastern or Kansas border, where it varies from 3,047 to 3,500 feet above the sea. There are valleys in the extreme southwest, on the tributaries of the San Juan, that are but little over 4,000 feet. Colorado contains 104,500 square miles. The mean height above the sea is 7,000 feet, being much greater than that of any other state or territory. The following table shows the approximate number of square miles of area between various elevations:

Elevations.	Square Miles.
Between 3,000 and 4,000 feet	9,000
" 4,000 " 5,000 "	21,800
" 5,000 " 6,000 "	15,000
" 6,000 " 7,000 "	10,000
" 7,000 " 8,000 "	11,000
" 8,000 " 9,000 "	14,000
" 9,000 " 10,000 "	10,000
" 10,000 " 11,000 "	6,800
" 11,000 " 12,000 "	5,000
" 12,000 " 13,000 "	1,400
Area above 13,000 feet	500

TOWNS AND CITIES.

Below are the elevations in feet above sea level of important towns and localities of Colorado:

Alamosa	7,492	Caribou	9,905
Alma	10,254	Central	8,300
Animas City	6,622	Colorado Springs	6,023
Baker Mine	11,956	Conejos	7,880
Bakerville	9,753	Del Norte	7,750
Black Hawk	7,875	Denver	5,197
Boulder	5,536	El Moro	5,886
Breckenridge	9,674	Empire	8,583
Cañon	5,287	Evans	4,745

Fairplay	9,964	Longmont	4,957
Fall River	7,719	Los Pinos	9,065
Fort Collins	4,815	Manitou	6,297
Fort Garland	7,945	Marshall	5,578
Fort Lupton	5,027	Montezuma (9,652)	10,295
Fort Lyon	3,725	Nederland	8,263
Frisco (about)	9,500	Nevadaville	8,800
Georgetown	8,514	Oro	10,704
Gold Hill	8,463	Ouray	7,640
Golden	5,687	Pagosa Springs	7,108
Granite	8,883	Present Help Mine, on Mt.	
Greeley	4,779	Lincoln	14,000
Grenada	3,434	Platteville	4,690
Gunnison	7,743	Pueblo, North	4,713
Hamilton	9,743	Pueblo, South	4,676
Hermesillo	4,723	Quartz Hill (about)	9,300
Hot Sulphur Springs	7,725	Rollinsville	8,323
Howardville	9,527	Rosita	8,500
Idaho Springs	7,512	Saguache	7,723
Jamestown	7,123	Saints John	10,807
Jefferson	9,862	Salt Works in South Park	8,917
Kit Carson	4,307	Silverton	9,400
Kokomo (about)	10,200	Stevens Mine	11,943
La Junta	4,137	Terrible Mine	9,243
Lake City	8,550	Trinidad	6,032
Las Animas	3,952	Uncompahgre Agency	6,400
Leadville (R. R.)	10,025	White River Agency	6,491
Leadville (Hayden)	10,247		

ELEVATIONS OF THE ROCKY MOUNTAINS.

Below are elevations of most of the prominent peaks of Colorado, with others of less elevations, but noticeable from mines or from being near towns or railways. There are a large number of peaks, especially in the San Juan mountains, yet unnamed, whose elevations exceed 14,000 feet, and some two hundred that run from that height down to 13,000 feet. It is impossible to give in this statement all of the higher peaks elsewhere, or of the multitude that exceed 12,000 feet. As there are several spurs or connecting ranges of mountains, the name of the range appears with the name of peak and elevation.

Central Colorado—Front Range.

Mount Evans	14,330	Mount Rosalie	14,340
Pike's Peak	14,147	Chief Mountain	11,833

Northern Colorado—Main Range.

Arapahoe Peak	13,520	James' Peak	13,283
Gray's Peak	14,341	Long's Peak	14,271
Irwin's Peak	14,336	Bald Mountain (Gilpin Co.)	10,322
Mount Guyot	13,565		

Central Colorado—Park Range.

Buckskin Mountain	14,296	Quandary Peak	14,269
Mount Cameron	14,000	Sheep Mountain	12,589
Horseshoe Mountain	13,988	Silverheels	13,897
Mount Lincoln	14,297		

Central Colorado—Sawatch or Main Range.

Mount Antero	14,245	La Plata	14,311
Mount Elbert	14,351	Massive Mountain†	14,298
Grizzley	13,956	Mount Princeton	14,196
Mount Harvard*	14,375	Shavano	14,239
Holy Cross Mountain	14,176	Mount Yale	14,187

* By Hayden. Wheeler makes it 14.151; and another, 14,388.
† Another measurement gives 14,368.

Southern Colorado—Sangre de Christo Range.

Baldy Peak	14,176	Hunt's Peak	14,056
Blanca Peak*	14,464	Spanish Peaks { W.	13,620
Culebra	14,069	{ E.	12,720

* Highest in Colorado, and highest but one in United States.

Southern Colorado, San Juan Region—Main Range and Spurs.

Mount Æolus	14,054	Simpson's Peak	14,055
Blaine's Peak	13,905	Mount Sneffels	14,158
Engineer Mountain	13,076	Stewart's Peak	14,032
Handie's Peak	14,149	Uncompahgre Peak*	14,235
Pyramid	14,146	Wetterhorn	14,069
Pridgeon's	14,054	Mount Wilson†	14,280
San Luis Peak	14,100		

* Wheeler makes this 14,408 feet.   † Wheeler, 14,300.

Western Colorado—Elk Range.

Capitol Mountain	13,997	Snow Mass	13,970
Castle Peak	14,115	Teocalli	13,113
Maroon	14,003		

ELEVATIONS OF LAKES.

Chicago Lakes	11,500	San Cristoval	9,000
Grand	8,153	San Luis	7,592
Green	10,000	San Miguel	9,720
Mary, or Santa Maria	9,324	Twin Lakes	9,357
Osborn's	8,821		

MOUNTAIN PASSES IN COLORADO.

The following gives the names and elevations of the more famous passes over the Rocky mountains and spurs:

Arkansas (about)...........	11,100	Hoosier......	11,500
Argentine.................	13,100	Lake Fork...............	12,540
Berthoud.................	11,349	Loveland	11,500
Boulder..................	11,670	Marshall..................	10,852
Cochetopa	10,032	Poncho...................	8,945
Cunningham..............	12,090	Raton	7,863
Georgia....................	11,811	Tarryall...................	12,176
Gore.....................	9,590	Trout Creek..............	9,346
Hamilton	12,370	Tennessee*	10,418
Hayden..................	10,780	Veta.....................	9,339

* Now estimated at 10,700.

The river cañons, or deeply cut ravines that are found in all of the more elevated portions of Colorado, constitute a peculiar and striking feature of the great Rocky Mountain system. In the countless ages of the past the waters of the streams have worn channels deep down into the hearts of the mountains, leaving the perpendicular granite or sandstone standing on either side for hundreds, and in some localities for thousands of feet. Nowhere are the grand and beautiful in Nature more effectually illustrated than in these mountain cañons. The glories of Boulder, Clear Creek, Cheyenne, and Platte cañons, and the Grand cañon of the Arkansas, all on the eastern slope of the Continental Divide, have already been noted. The walls of the Colorado, Gunnison, and Uncompahgre rivers, in the western part of the State, are still more massive and wonderful. In many sections they rise without a break or an incline to heights of thousands of feet, and along the Colorado continue in that way with hardly an outlet of any kind for hundreds of miles. The Grand cañon of the Gunnison is one of the world's wonders. Its walls on either side of the stream, and bordering it for miles, are usually not far from 300 feet in width, and are composed of stratified rock. In places these perpendicular sides, rising from the water for distances of from one to three thousand feet, terminate in level summits surmounted by a second wall of prodigious height, thus forming a cañon within a cañon. Through the chasm between these giant formations and huge bastions and turrets one above another, dashes the river, its surface white with foam.   The heights of these perpendicular cañon walls, and their elevations with that of the river above sea level at several points, are as follows: Level of the Gunnison at mouth of Mountain creek above sea level, 7,200 feet; of top of wall or plateau on north side, 8,800 feet; height of wall, 1,600 feet; height of wall at point below on east side, 1,900 feet; or west side, 1,800 feet; height of wall in gneiss rock, 900 feet. Some distance below, the cañon wall rises directly from the river, 3,000 feet, of which the 1,800 feet nearest the water is gneiss rock; total elevation of top of wall or plateau above the sea, 9,800 feet.

CHAPTER III.

ROUTES OF TRAVEL—POINTS OF INTEREST AND HOW TO REACH THEM
—RAILWAY AND STAGE LINES—FARES, DISTANCES, AND ELEVA-
TIONS—DENVER, PUEBLO, COLORADO SPRINGS, BOULDER, CEN-
TRAL, GEORGETOWN, LEADVILLE, GOLDEN, CAÑON, AND THE SAN
JUAN.

For the benefit of the traveler, tourist, and emigrant this chapter
will give a detailed account of the manner in which important points
of Colorado can be reached.   Persons taking either one of the three
through lines from the Missouri river, can be landed in Denver.
The Atchison, Topeka & Santa Fe railway connects with that place
by means of the Denver & Rio Grande north and south line.   The
western terminus of the Kansas Pacific is in that city, and the Union
Pacific connects at Cheyenne with the Colorado Central.   The great
gold and silver mining districts of Gilpin and Clear Creek counties
are reached by the mountain division of the Colorado Central, which
leaves the plains or Denver and Cheyenne division at Golden.   Leadville and Fairplay are approached for a distance of eighty miles
from Denver by the Denver & South Park road.   Much of the
Leadville travel goes in from Pueblo and Cañon via the Arkansas
Valley and Denver & Rio Grande.   Silver Cliff and Rosita have the
same rail communication but a different route for stage travel.   The
regular route to the San Juan and Del Norte, Silverton, Lake City,
and Ouray is via Pueblo and the Denver & Rio Grande road to
Alamosa in San Luis Park, thence by stage to the various points to
be reached.   The Atchison, Topeka & Santa Fe lines are in the same
latitude, and naturally secure the east and west travel for the San
Juan mines.   The Denver & Rio Grande is the only road that approaches these mines.   A branch line of 192 miles is being built to
Animas City, south of Silverton and Rico.   The A., T. & S. F. main
line leaves the Arkansas Valley at La Junta and passes southwesterly
through Trinidad and the Raton Mountains into New Mexico.   Las
Vegas, Santa Fe and Albuqueque have already been reached.   The
route is down the Rio Grande.   The Arkansas Valley division of

this same road passes westward up the river from La Junta to Pueblo. Here the Denver & Rio Grande line takes the inland travel, including scores of passengers daily, bound for Leadville via Cañon and the southern overland stage.

There are three classes of accommodations for this western travel, viz., first class, second class, and emigrant. Emigrant fare includes the ordinary passenger coaches in use, and all classes ride together on the mountain railways and stage lines. Each full ticket is allowed one hundred pounds of baggage, and each half ticket fifty pounds on the railways, while the allowance on the mountain stage lines is usually fifty pounds. The railways charge at the rate of from ten to fifteen per cent. of first-class fare on every hundred pounds of

SHOOTING BUFFALO.

extra baggage, while the stages charge express rates on the same. This can be avoided by shipping extra baggage by freight. First-class meals on the railways are usually seventy-five cents on express trains, and from fifty to seventy-five cents on all others. Sleeping-car or stop-over accommodations are not usually allowed on second or third class tickets, and baggage must be checked to destination.

Denver and Pueblo may be regarded as the starting-points for various parts of the mountains, although the former is considered the main base of operations for a trip in almost any direction. Eastern emigrants will find the time required to reach Leadville from Cañon pretty near the same as from Denver on the northern system. The railway construction now going on will alter distances and time considerably before the summer is over, both for northern and southern routes to Leadville. Colorado Springs is on the D. & R. G. line. All the northern points among the mountain mines, such as Georgetown, Central, and Idaho, must be reached via the Colorado Central from Denver, or, as with Boulder, from Denver and Cheyenne. By a glance at the map of Colorado the reader will gain a still better idea of the situation and of the routes of the different railway systems. By this it will be seen that the Colorado Central railway, with its forks and branches, is the main artery of communication between Denver and the Union Pacific and Kansas Pacific, and for most of the farming and coal districts and the mountain mining sections of northern Colorado. The Denver & Rio Grande acts in pretty much the same capacity for central and southern Colorado, and has the A., T. & S. F. for its outlet and feeder. This road extends through farming, pastoral, and coal lands, in a north and south direction, east of the base of the mountains, forking at Pueblo for Cañon, and at Cucharas for El Moro, while the main line continues southwesterly over the mountains to Alamosa —the latter place being 250 miles from Denver, while El Moro is 206 miles. The Denver & South Park is building up through the Platte and South Park country, and like the other two lines, is bound for Leadville. Since the last section of new road was completed, it has drawn heavily on the business of that locality. How to reach important towns, cities, and resorts will be the next matter considered.

Leadville is in the mountains, and quite a long distance inland from the plains. Through tickets can be obtained for that place from all leading railway centres in the East or West—including first class, second class, and emigrant. The last rates fixed from the Missouri river are $41 for first-class tickets, $38.50 for second class, and $34 for emigrant. Leadville can be reached by rail and stage by any one of three routes.

From Denver and Pueblo to Cañon by rail, thence by stage to Leadville; distance from Denver, 160 miles by rail, and 126 miles by stage; fare $17, and $3.50 for hotels at Cañon and on the road; time, about two days of day travel. Through passengers from the East, via the A., T. & S. F., arrive at Cañon at night, and then have the same two days of stage travel up the Arkansas Valley. This, of course, is their natural route.

The Denver & South Park railway and stage lines is largely patronized. This railway is building rapidly, with a proportionate decrease of staging. Fare, $17, which will be reduced with reduction of staging in the summer. Time, nearly two days. Meals and lodging at Fairplay and elsewhere, $4. The stage line charges ten cents per pound for all baggage in excess of forty pounds to the passenger.

The Colorado Central extends from Denver to Georgetown, 54 miles, connecting with stage to Leadville, 56 miles. Total distance, 110 miles; fare, $10.

All of the above roads are building towards Leadville. The A., T. & S. F. will have the grading of their roadbed completed to Leadville by the time they succeed in blasting a way through the Grand Cañon near the lower end of the route. It is asserted that this road will be running railway trains into Leadville in August or September. The other two roads are also building in the same direction as rapidly as possible, so that the amount of staging will soon be greatly reduced. Fairplay and the Park and Summit county mines are reached by the Denver & South Park railway and by stages from the end of track. Where no stages are in operation saddle animals can be obtained. In these counties are noted silver mines, and gold-bearing placers and gulches.

A., T. & S. F. AND D. & R. G. RAILROADS AND CONNECTING STAGE LINES.

The famous summer resort of Colorado Springs is situated on the line of the Denver & Rio Grande, 75 miles south of Denver and 45 miles north of Pueblo, and has no other rail communication. Parties coming west over the Atchison, Topeka & Santa Fe line can stop off there on their way to Denver, and it is but three and a half hours' ride from the latter place. Five miles from Colorado Springs is Manitou, famed for its mineral waters and as a great summer resort for health and pleasure seekers. Near by is some of the most beautiful mountain scenery in the country, and over all towers the majestic summit of Pike's Peak, where is located a United States signal service station.

Trinidad and El Moro, with their coal mines, coke manufactories, and excellent farming and pastoral country, can be reached from the East via the main line of the A., T. & S. F., without coming to

Pueblo. Passengers can also go to El Moro from Denver or Pueblo by the D. & R. G. road, whose southerly terminus is there. The first-named railway passes through both towns and beyond into New Mexico.

The Denver & Rio Grande railway is the only one approaching or entering what is termed the San Juan region. From Pueblo this

OVER THE SANGRE DE CHRISTO MOUNTAINS VIA THE D. & R. G. RAILWAY.

division of the road runs southwesterly up the Cucharas valley and by the Walsenburg coal mines to the Sangre de Christo range, which it crosses at Veta Pass. Its course is then westward through the great San Luis Park to Alamosa on the Rio Grande, 250 miles south-southwest of Denver. This is the jumping-off place for the southwest, and serves as the distributing point for a wide scope of country. Almost all merchandise and supplies going into the mountains to the west are freighted from this place, and all ore and bullion from the mines, and wool, hides, pelts, and other material from the farms and stock ranges are here started eastward by rail.

The Southern Overland Mail and Express of Barlow & Sanderson, bound for Del Norte, Wagon Wheel Gap, and Lake City, and to connect with Silverton lines, starts westward from Alamosa on the arrival of the train from Denver and Pueblo. Railway fare from Denver, $23, and from Pueblo, $13. Stage fare from Alamosa to Del Norte, $4; to Wagon Wheel Gap, $8.65; Antelope Springs, $11.65; Lake City, $19—distance, 116 miles. Connection is made with another conveyance at Antelope Springs or Junction, 35½ miles southeast of Lake City, for Silverton and neighboring towns. The trip to Ouray is usually made on horseback from either of these places. During the warmer months a conveyance plies between Lake City and Ouray, distance 80 miles by this route. Distance by trail over the range 30 miles. The Summit, or Little Annie gold mining district is 25 miles south of Del Norte, and off of the main line noted above; fare, $5. At Wagon Wheel Gap 30 miles west of Del Norte, are hot sulphur mineral springs of a very valuable character, which are beginning to attract people from abroad. South from Alamosa another line of Barlow & Sanderson's coaches leaves daily for Conejos and for Santa Fe, N. M., and way stations.

If the fare continues as it was not long ago, it is as follows from Denver, and $10 less from Pueblo: Denver to Alamosa, $23; to Del Norte, $27; Lake City, $42; Silverton, $55. Stage tickets are procured at the end of track. Meals at stage stations are 75 cents. Twenty-six hours' staging between Alamosa and Lake City.

One branch of the Denver & Rio Grande railroad extends up the Arkansas valley from Pueblo to Cañon, a distance of 40 miles. Here passengers for Leadville take Barlow & Sanderson's stages, as mentioned before. Passengers for Silver Cliff leave Cañon by way of Megrue & Smith's stage line.

All of the stage lines extending from the Denver & Rio Grande railway, except one, belong to Barlow & Sanderson's Southern Overland Mail and Express. These convey passengers to Leadville, the San Juan country, and New Mexico. Fifty pounds of baggage are allowed to each passenger, but all over that amount is charged express rates. These stage routes are as follows—distance from Cañon in miles and rates of fare given with names of stations:

Leadville Line.—Stations, distance from Cañon in miles, and fare: Copper Gulch, 14 miles, $1.75; Texas Creek, 28 miles, $3.50; Pleasant Valley, 39 miles, $4.90; South Arkansas or Cleora, 60 miles, $7.50; Centreville, 78 miles, $9.75; Lenhardy, 98 miles, $12.25; Granite, 108 miles, $13.50; Leadville, 126 miles, $14. Time from Cañon to Leadville, 26 hours, going day and night.

On arrival of the stage at Cleora, a conveyance starts southwesterly for Saguache and Ouray.

Saguache and Ouray.—Barlow & Sanderson run a regular buckboard or open wagon line from Saguache, in San Luis Park, westward over the mountains to Ouray. Connection is made at Saguache with the same company's conveyance that leaves Cleora on the arrival of the Leadville stage at night. Ninety miles east of Ouray, twenty-one miles east of Lake City, and seventy-one miles west of Saguache is Indian Creek, where the roads from those points intersect. New stage line from Cleora to Ouray, 130 miles.

Alamosa and San Juan Line.—Stations, distances in miles, and fare from Alamosa westward: Station No. 1, 10½ miles, $2.10; Venables, 21½ miles, $4.30; Del Norte, 34½ miles, $4; Bunker Hill, 46 miles, $9.20; Riverside, 57½ miles, $11.50; Rio Grande, 69 miles, $13.80; Junction, 80½ miles, $16.10; Clear Creek, 91½ miles, $18.30; Powder Horn, 103½ miles, $20.70; Lake City, 116 miles, $19. What is called through fare is charged to Del Norte; Wagon Wheel Gap, 64½ miles, $8.65; Antelope Springs, 84½ miles, $11.65, and Lake City, $19; which accounts for less than local rates.

Silverton, Howardsville, and Animas Forks and vicinity are reached in the summer and fall months by conveyance connecting with the above stages at Antelope. This is Brewster's line. Distance from Alamosa to Silverton, 142½ miles; from Antelope, 58 miles. Southern Overland stages connect Lake City and Ouray. The distance from Silverton to Ouray by trail is 21 miles. There is a trail to Ouray via Hensen creek, and over the mountains via Poughkeepsie Fork ; distance 28 miles or more.

Lake City to Ouray.—Conveyance plies between these points, following water courses, via Indian creek and Cevolla, distance 80 miles.

Alamosa and Santa Fe Line.—Distance from Alamosa to Santa Fe, 141 miles, fare $28 ; Alamosa to Conejos, 30 miles, fare $6. West from Conejos are the famous Pagosa Springs, so valuable that the United States government retains possession of them, and has set apart the locality as a reservation. Distance from Conejos 70 miles, and from Alamosa 100 miles.

A railway may some day be constructed from Alamosa westward, via Conejos, Pagosa Springs, and Animas river to Silverton, the metropolis of the mines of San Juan county. A good wagon road is already in operation that is open winter and summer. This has no high and difficult mountains to pass, and is much used by Silverton and La Plata freighters. The distances from Alamosa by this road are 30 miles to Conejos, 100 to Pagosa Springs, 180 to Animas City and 223 to Silverton.

Cañon to Silver Cliff and Rosita.—Megrue & Smith run a daily stage line between Cañon and Silver Cliff, connecting with another line to Rosita, 14 miles from Cañon, and 18 miles from Rosita. Fare to either point, $4 ; round trip, $7. A hack also plies between those two towns ; fare, $1 ; distance, 7 miles ; from Cañon to Silver Cliff, 30 miles ; to Rosita, 32 miles. These are prominent mining towns, and are so beautifully located, with fine valley and mountain scenery, as to be well worthy of a visit from the tourist.

COLORADO CENTRAL R. R.

The Colorado Central is the only railway leading up through the mountains to the great gold district of Gilpin county, with its flourishing towns, Central, Black Hawk, and Nevadaville, and to the productive silver belt of Clear Creek county, in which Georgetown, Idaho Springs, Lawson, Fall River, Freeland, Silver Plume, and Brownville are located. The Colorado Central extends from Denver to Golden (the headquarters of the road and the seat of smelting works and various manufactories, where the mountain division branches off to the westward), and then continues northward through coal and farming districts to Cheyenne; distance to Golden, 16 miles; fare, 80cts.; distance to Cheyenne, 138 miles; fare, $5.00. Twenty-nine miles from Denver and 13 above Golden, North and South Clear Creeks unite, and here the railway forks, one branch taking up one cañon to Central, 13 miles, and the other up another through

CLEAR CREEK CAÑON, C. C. R. R.

Idaho and on to Georgetown, 25 miles. Any of these points are less than three hours' ride from Denver; fare to Central, $3.10; to Idaho Springs, $2.90; Georgetown, $4.30. Outside of the picturesque scenery en route, these cities are of rare interest, on account of their famous and productive mines and numerous quartz mills and reduction works. They were the main source of Colorado's bullion product up to the time of very recent developments at Leadville, and are steadily increasing their yield. Black Hawk and Nevadaville adjoin Central, and are located in the same district. The Smith stage line makes tri-weekly trips to Caribou, leaving on Tuesdays, Thursdays, and Saturdays, and returning on alternate days. Surrounding and lying between Idaho Springs and Georgetown are many prosperous mining camps; also, such attractive resorts as Chicago Lakes, the highest body of water in North America; Green and Clear Lakes, Gray's and Irwin's peaks, Argentine pass, and other points of interest, all of which can be visited either by carriage or on horseback by a few hours' drive or ride. Livery charges in these towns are usually $3.00 per day for saddle horses and $10.00 per day, or less, for two-horse carriages. At Denver and Boulder livery charges are one-third less. Idaho Springs is famous for its mineral waters and as a fashionable summer resort. Here are fine hotels and bath-houses, hot and cold soda springs, fine drives, mines, and mills, and other attractions.

Boulder is located on the plains, at the gateway of that portion of the mountains where numerous mining camps are producing largely. It can be reached from Denver or Cheyenne by the Colorado Central railway; distance from Denver, 49 miles; fare, $3.75. W. & L. Smith's stage line leaves tri-weekly—on Mondays, Wednesdays, and Saturdays—for the silver districts of Caribou and Nederland; fare to the former point, $3.50. From Boulder to Cheyenne are numerous flourishing towns, such as Longmont, Loveland, and Fort Collins; fare and distance noted in table.

The Colorado Central railway runs morning and evening trains into and out of the mountains and to Boulder and Longmont and way stations, and a morning train to Cheyenne to connect with the Union Pacific. Omnibuses ply between hotels and other points and the railway stations at Denver, Boulder, Cheyenne, Golden, Central, Black Hawk, and Georgetown. The fare on these is usually fifty cents.

The towns on the plains division are: Denver, population, 27,000; elevation, 5,196 feet. Golden, population, 3,000; elevation, 5,687 feet. Boulder, 3,500; elevation, 5,536. Longmont, 600 inhabitants and 4,957 elevation. Loveland, population, 250; and Fort Collins, 800 inhabitants. Cheyenne is 6,075 feet above the sea, and has nearly 5,000 people. In the mountains are Black Hawk, with 2,000 people and an elevation of 7,775; Central, with 3,500 people and an elevation of 8,300. With Nevadaville they form a city of 6,500 people. Fares on the Colorado Central were reduced from one-fourth to one-third on the first of June. Fares from Denver to Golden, 80 cents; to Black Hawk, $2.85; to Central, $3.10; to Idaho Springs, $2.90; to Georgetown, $4.30; to Boulder, $1.75. Summer excursion rates much lower.

STAGE LINES.

Stages connect at Boulder for the mining camps of Caribou, Nederland, Four-Mile, and hacks with Gold Hill, Ballarat, Jamestown. In the summer months stages connect with the railway at Loveland, to and from the beautiful summer resort of Estes Park, distant a few hours' drive, where a first-class hotel is located. On certain days conveyances ply between Fort Collins and Greeley. Fare from Denver to Golden is 80 cents; to Boulder, $1.75; Cheyenne, $5.

Stages make regular trips from Georgetown, via Empire and Berthoud Pass, to Hot Sulphur Springs in Middle Park. This is a delightful trip and is made in either direction in a single day.

TO LEADVILLE, TEN MILE, GUNNISON AND SAN JUAN—NEW RAILROAD.

Barlow and Sanderson's Southern Overland stages ply between the D. & R. G. and the D. & S. P. Railway termini and Gunnison City, and other important camps of the Gunnison region. Buena Vista is in the upper Arkansas Valley, on the D. & S. P. road, 135 miles southwest of Denver, and 35 miles south of Leadville. West of it 32 miles, the railroad company is tunneling the great Sawatch range. From Cleora, near Poncho Pass and Monarch mining district, stages connect the Arkansas Valley railroad with Gunnison.

KANSAS PACIFIC RAILWAY.

The Kansas Pacific railway stations within the limits of Colorado and their distances from Denver are as follows : Denver; Schuyler, 10; Box Elder, 22; Kiowa, 31; Byers, 44; Deer Trail, 56; Agate, 67; Cedar Point, 77; River Bend, 83; Lake, 92; Hugo, 105; Mirage, 115; Aroya, 128; Wild Horse, 140; Kit Carson, 152; First View, 167; Cheyenne Wells, 177; Arapahoe, 187; Monotony, 202; Eagle Trail, 210. The distance to Kansas City is 639 miles.

DENVER & BOULDER VALLEY R. R.

The Denver & Boulder Valley railroad, extending from Denver to the Erie coal mines, thence to Boulder, uses the Denver Pacific

WINDSOR HOTEL, DENVER.

from Denver to Hughes, 20 miles; distance from Denver to the Erie coal mines, 34 miles; to Boulder, 47.

DENVER PACIFIC R. R.

Denver Pacific Railroad.—The Denver Pacific extends from Denver to Cheyenne, 106 miles, fare $7, with Greeley and Evans on the route. The stations and distances from Denver are Denver Junction, 2 miles; Henderson's Island, 14; Hughes, 20; Fort Lupton, 27; Johnson, 33; Platteville, 35; Evans, 48; Greeley, 52 (fare, $3.75); Pierce, 67; Carr, 86; Summit, 96; Cheyenne, 106.

The Golden Boulder & Caribou Company has 5½ miles of road in operation between Boulder and Marshall, where the Marshall coal mines are situated.

DENVER & RIO GRANDE MAIN LINE.

Dist. in Miles.	Name.	Elevation.	Fare.	Dist. in Miles.	Name.	Elevation.	Fare.
..	Denver............	5,143		105	Pinon..............	4,986	
2	Machine Shops....	5,189		117	North Pueblo......	4,657	
8	Petersburg........	5,270		120	South Pueblo......	4,615	
10	Littleton..........	5,320		129	San Carlos........	4,986	
17	Acequia..	5,479		133	Greenhorn........	5,045	
24	Plum	5,782		140	Salt Creek........	5,411	
29	Mill No. 2....	5,985		146	Graneros	5,750	
32	Castle Rock.......	6,173		176	Huerfano.....	5,600	
35	Douglas........ ...	6,273		169	Cuchara	5,893	
38	Glade..............	6,406		176	Walsenburg	6,124	
43	Larkspur..........	6,590		183	Wahatoya	6,512	
47	Greenland...	6,875		191	La Veta...........	6,970	
52	Divide............	7,186		199	Ojo	8,129	
56	Monument........	6,931		202	Mule Shoe........	8,724	
58	Borst's............	6,759		205	Veta Pass....	9,339	
62	Husted's..........	6,557		207	Sangre de Christo..	9,009	
67	Edgerton	6,303		212	Placer....	8,352	
75	Colorado Springs..	5,931		220	Fort Garland......	7,882	
84	Widefield........	5,660		238	Baldy.............	7,494	
88	Fountain	5,510		250	Alamosa	7,492	
94	Little Buttes.......	5,318					

CAÑON OR ARKANSAS VALLEY BRANCH D. & R. G. R. R.

Distances from Denver.	Names.	Elevation.	Distances from Denver.	Names.	Elevation.
120	South Pueblo.......	....	143	Beaver Creek.......	4,947
124	Goodnight	4,677	152	Labrun	5,130
129	Meadows...........	4,749	153	Coal Junction	5,145
134	Swallow...........	4,808	155	Coal Banks........	5,330
140	Carlisle Springs.....	4,905	160	Cañon City.........	5,287

Fare from Denver to Cañon, $14 ; from Pueblo, $4. Stages westward and south from Cañon, as noted above.

El Moro Branch.—This leaves main line at Cucharas and continues to El Moro, the coal mining and coke manufacturing headquarters. Stations : Cucharas, distance in miles from Denver, 169. Santa Clara, 180 ; elevation, 6,147. Apishapa, distance, 189 ; elevation, 6,106. Chicosa, distance, 198 ; elevation, 6,104. El Moro, distance, 206 ; elevation, 5,825. Fare, $18.60 from Denver and $8.60 from Pueblo to El Moro.

BUFFALO HUNTING ON THE PLAINS.

CHAPTER IV.

THE CITIES OF THE PLAINS—DENVER, COLORADO SPRINGS, MANITOU, AND SOUTH PUEBLO—FACTS AND FIGURES CONCERNING THE GREAT SUMMER RESORTS OF COLORADO—PIKE'S PEAK AND VICINITY—THE TWIN LAKES AND OTHER POINTS.

The beautiful and attractive city of Denver is doubly welcome to the traveler after the long journey across the plains, and the fascination attending first sight is increased rather than diminished on closer inspection. There is a dash and animation to the place, along with a finish and elegance that suggests prosperity, wealth, and Eastern stability, as well as the progressive and aggressive frontier. It is the healthy vigor of the thriving trade centre, the prodigality of the mining metropolis combined with the life and display of the great thoroughfare and pleasure resort that give the Queen City of the plains and mountains this doubly attractive appearance.

It is generally conceded that Denver is the best built city between Saint Louis and San Francisco, and there is no denying the fact that her growth at the present time is more rapid and her prospects more brilliant than any other place excepting that new-born wonder, Leadville. The city is situated at the junction of Cherry creek with the Platte river, and is mainly built on ground sloping slightly towards the mountains which rise so grandly along the entire western horizon. The line of vision takes in the "snowy range" and its outlying foot hills for a distance of one hundred and fifty miles, forming a landscape the eye can never grow weary of. The streets are broad, solid, and cleanly, and are lined in all directions with massive blocks, or elegant residences and pretty cottages in the midst of running waters, handsome shade trees, green lawns, and pleasant groves. Stately school and church edifices and fine parks and tree-lined boulevards are distinctive features of this young western emporium.

Great changes have been wrought within the past twenty years in this locality. When the pioneer gold hunters were just beginning to put in an appearance, a barren plain alone was visible where now are handsome avenues, bubbling fountains, and thronged and busy

LARIMER STREET, DENVER.

marts of trade. In place of the wilderness is a flourishing city of nearly thirty thousand people, with street-cars, gas and water works, telephonic, telegraphic, and railway facilities, an effective fire department, theatres, first-class newspapers and hotels, and all the seeming requirements of a great metropolis. Denver is a fast city, with appendages corresponding to the inclinations of her citizens and temporary residents.

Being the grand port of entry to the mountain mining regions and to the health and pleasure resorts, and the State capital, she is the temporary abiding place of multitudes of strangers and immigrants as well as Coloradans. The floating population is always large, especially in the summer months, and no other city of double its population does half the hotel business. In an almost equal degree is the mercantile and jobbing trade remarkable, for this is the supply point for almost a thousand miles of territory and of the most progressive mining regions in the world. Consequently Denver is the receiving and distributing point for an immense industry and population, while the half-dozen railways centering there are of no little service in carrying on the work.

It is estimated that the actual valuation of Denver real estate and personal property is not far from $25,000,000. Denver's business record in 1879 was one of which she may well be proud. The sales of merchandise approached $23,000,000 in value, the real estate transactions by 1,801 warranty deeds footed up $2,777,394, and the amount of deposits at the close of the year in the three leading banks was $3,306,749, or nearly double the deposits of a year previous. The city's rapid growth can be appreciated from the fact that several hundred buildings were erected, at an outlay of nearly $2,000,000. Among these, the Windsor Hotel, the finest between Saint Louis and San Francisco, and costing $325,000, the Tabor block, costing $225,000, and other costly business and hotel edifices and private residences aided greatly to beautify the city. The receipts of the Denver post office were $54,856.90 in 1878, and $82,005.43 in 1879 ; the expenses of last year were $20,076.91. The value of money orders issued in 1878 was $197,451, and in 1879, $325,379.25. The hotel arrivals exceeded 120,000. Men of wealth from the east, as well as those who have made fortunes in the mines, are selecting this attractive city as a place of residence. It is the great focal railroad point of the Rocky

Mountain region, and rapid transit or quick connection is afforded to and with all important points. Leaving Denver for the present, we will proceed to those most attractive of all Colorado resorts, Colorado Springs and Manitou.

The towns of Colorado Springs and Manitou—and one of these places cannot be mentioned without suggesting the other— have a greater number of wonders and attractions easily accessible and within a short distance than any other single locality. These and their own beautiful scenery and medicinal waters are the causes of their large summer population. Days of unmixed pleasure await those lovers of the beautiful in nature who have a few days to devote to the cañons, grottoes, mountains, and curiosities of this section. First of all there is that giant sentinel, Pike's Peak, towering over plain and foot hill, the view from whose summit is indescribably grand. Although this attains the enormous altitude of 14,147 feet, by following the trail it can be ascended on horseback. On the barren rocky mountain top is a government signal-service station. To witness sunrise from this elevated locality is an experience long to be remembered, and should certainly be set down on the pro- gramme of the tourist. The Garden of the Gods, so named from the grotesque and gigantic rocks of red and white sandstone thrown into all manner of fantastic shapes and worn by the elements, consti- tutes one of the State's greatest natural wonders. These rocks are scattered in picturesque confusion from the enormous portal of the enclosure to the lofty crags that rise on either hand. Some of these giant pillars and cathedral-shaped towers are hundreds of feet in height, and altogether form a scene at once weird and en- chanting. Ute Pass is a romantic spot amid almost perpendicular walls of rock, and rich in glens, grottoes, streams and waterfalls. Once solitary and unfrequented except by the tourist, it has recently been the thoroughfare of much of the Leadville trade and traffic. Long wagon trains are constantly ascending and descending this mountain defile on their way to and from the carbonate metropolis. Cheyenne and Williams cañons, with their sparkling brooklets, foaming streams, beautiful waterfalls, and general massiveness and sublimity of scenery are equally important objective points. Some distance to the northward is the famous Monument Park, and not far from Manitou is the lovely dell of Glen Eyrie. But it is impos-

sible to note at length all the points of interest or beauty which
abound on every hand. They are plentiful, from the plains to the
hunting and fishing grounds of South Park and of the great range
beyond. There is almost no limit to their extent and attractiveness.

GARDEN OF THE GODS.

On the western rim of the basin of the upper Arkansas are those
gems of the Sierras, the Twin Lakes. These beautiful bodies of
water are almost mountain locked, being located among the eastern
slopes of the great Sawatch Range. Around them are the Twin
Peaks, Lake Mountain, La Plata, and Mount Elbert. Leadville is

eighteen miles distant and Granite three miles. Always a favorite resort these lakes are doubly so since the influx of population among the carbonate fields. A good hotel has been erected and sailboats are at the disposal of guests. The pleasure-seeker can here enjoy the highest yachting in the world, while trout are abundant and game of all kinds plentiful. The lower lake is three and a half miles long by two and a half wide, and the upper one is somewhat smaller. The altitude is 9,357 feet.

COLORADO SPRINGS.—The City of Colorado Springs is beautifully situated on the Denver & Rio Grande Railway, seventy-five miles south of Denver, near the foot of Pike's Peak, and at the mouth of Ute Pass, through which an excellent wagon road runs to Fairplay, Leadville, Alma, Oro City, and other places in South Park and on the headwaters of the Arkansas river. Its present population (May 1, 1880,) is 5,000, and it is growing with great rapidity. The town site was purchased in 1871, and the first stake driven on the first day of August of that year. Since then the growth of the town has been rapid and its prosperity uninterrupted.

During the year 1878 there was about $1,500,000 worth of merchandise sold, of which nearly $500,000 was in groceries and produce. It is the centre of a large lumber trade. Upon the ranges in the immediate vicinity of the town are over 200,000 head of sheep and 30,000 head of cattle and horses.

Owing to its magnificent climate and its proximity to the celebrated soda and iron springs at Manitou, five miles distant, Colorado Springs has become one of the most popular resorts in the United States for seekers after pleasure and health. During the year 1878, over 13,000 visitors were registered at its hotels, while nearly as many more were quartered in private boarding-houses. The winters in this locality are usually mild, with but little snow, no rain, and the air is dry and exhilarating. In the summer the nights are always cool and pleasant. The livery establishments are numerous and their charges moderate. There are eight churches, representing all the principal religious denominations, a magnificent public school, attended by nearly five hundred pupils, several private schools, and a flourishing college, with well-endowed professorships. The streets of the town are level, never either dusty or muddy, and are lined with shade trees to the number of over 7,000. Within a few miles of Colorado Springs are to be found many of the finest pieces of scenery

COLORADO SPRINGS.

in the Rocky Mountain region. Cheyenne Cañon, Manitou, The Garden of the Gods, Glen Eyrie, Monument Park, Ute Pass are all within an hour's drive, and the summit of Pike's Peak can be reached with ease, on horseback, in a few hours' ride. The city has recently supplied itself with abundance of the purest water from Ruxton's creek, which is conducted in pipes through every street in the town.

MANITOU.—This delightful resort for health and pleasure seekers is located at the renowned soda and iron springs, eight in number, in a nook in the mountains, at the very foot of Pike's Peak, and about five miles west of Colorado Springs. The road from the latter place to South Park and Leadville passes immediately through it. Here are five hotels, three of which are quite large, capable of accommodating a thousand guests. In the summer season this resort is thronged with fashionable tourists from all parts of the United States and Europe. Owing to its thorough protection from the winds, it is a favorite winter resort for invalids. A number of beautiful villas have been erected here. Its present population is about 400. All the scenery tributary to Colorado Springs is equally accessible from Manitou. The town is well supplied with pure mountain water, in pipes, under heavy pressure. During the season of 1878, which was unusually short, 5,651 visitors registered at the several hotels.

SOUTH PUEBLO.—This thriving town is situated on the south side of the Arkansas river, immediately opposite Pueblo. It was laid out in 1872 by the Central Colorado Improvement Company, and now has a population of about 1,500. The business portion of the town is located on the first bottom of the Arkansas river, while the residence portion occupies the mesa or elevated table-land adjoining. The view from this part of the town is one of the finest in the country. To the west and southwest rise in full view some of the loftiest peaks of the Rocky Mountains, while to the eastward the eye takes in the almost illimitable sweep of rolling prairie, through which, as far as the view extends, flows the Arkansas river, on its way to the Father of Waters.

The climate of South Pueblo is peculiarly adapted to such invalids as require warm and dry winters, and there are but few days in the year when such persons cannot safely remain in the open air from morning until night. The winter temperature is many degrees higher than in any other locality in Colorado.

This is one of the principal railroad centres of the State. The Denver & Rio Grande railway, extending from Denver to the great coal mines of El Moro, and thence, via La Veta, to the gold and silver mines of the southwest, passes through it from north to south, with a branch running west to Cañon City, while the Atchison, Topeka & Santa Fe, coming in from the east, up the Arkansas river, gives a direct broad gauge communication with the Mississippi Valley. Large smelting works have been located here, and its cheap coal and fine water power, combined with its railroad communication with all parts of the State, will certainly make it an important manufacturing centre in the near future.

It is well supplied with water for irrigating purposes from a large lake near the town, the latter being connected by means of an aqueduct with the St. Charles river. Ten thousand shade trees have been planted on each side of the streets in the residence part of the town.

South Pueblo is located in the midst of one of the best stock ranges on the continent. To the southeast stretches a vast section of rolling plains that cannot be irrigated, covered with the richest grasses, which afford pasturage for countless herds of cattle, sheep, and horses, requiring no other food and shelter throughout the year than such as they can find on their ranges. Northeasterly another vast and excellent section for grazing rolls on to the Great Divide.

PUEBLO.—This city adjoins South Pueblo on the north, and is a point of considerable importance. This is the county seat of Pueblo county. The court-house and public school building are fine structures, the first costing $50,000 and the other $30,000. There are many large stores, several banks, and two daily newspapers. The place was founded in the winter of 1859–60, and soon absorbed the earlier settlement of Fontaine. Its growth was slow up to the advent of the railways, but business is now steadily improving and enlarging. With South Pueblo, this constitutes much the largest city in Southern Colorado.

CHAPTER V.

The Colorado Central railway has been a very essential co-oper-
ator in developing and advancing the wealth and industries of
Northern Colorado. It affords transportation and traveling facilities for some of the best mining and farming sections. The counties of Gilpin, Clear Creek, Boulder, Larimer, Jefferson, and Arapahoe are all traversed to a greater or less extent by this road. Until
Leadville came to the front, the two first-named districts supplied
two-thirds of the State's gold and silver export. The other counties
are equally conspicuous for their wheat and farming products, live
stock, or coal and other mines. Rapid transit, accessibility, and
cheaper freight and supplies are advantages of this railway system,
resulting in additional and enlarged mining, farming, and business
operations. A few years ago a tedious and somewhat disagreeable
mountain stage trip was necessary to reach the mines of Central or
Georgetown, and all machinery and supplies were freighted over
steep and difficult roads, and seemingly impassable hills and defiles.
Now the traveler is whirled along the enchanting cañon of Clear
Creek in luxurious railway cars, and ore and merchandise reach their
destinations speedily and cheaply by way of this iron trail of the
" Rockies."

This mountain division of the road is a marvel of engineering skill
and American enterprise, and much of it was constructed under more
than ordinary difficulties. There was lack of money, opposition from
rival schemes, and a belief that the project of building and operating a road up this wild and rugged cañon was impracticable. The
country had men, however, whose sagacity and public spirit led them

to conceive, and eventually to carry forward the undertaking to the present satisfactory condition. W. A. H. Loveland and Henry M. Teller, both prominently identified with building up the Territory and State, were the leading original promoters, and eventually secured the construction of the road from Denver to Golden, and thence northward to Boulder and westward to Black Hawk. It was an auspicious event when the wild cañons of the "Rockies" first echoed to the scream of the locomotive, and the mines of Gilpin were afforded rail communication with the world. This was in 1873, and nearly three years after the first track-laying began from Denver westward.

At the present time, the Colorado Central Company has 186 miles of railway in operation, of which 138 miles are of the standard broad gauge, and located on the plains or near the outlets of the foot hills, and 48 miles are of the narrow gauge of three feet, and extend up among the mountains and mining districts. The former passes through the most extensive, and what is considered the best farming section of the State. The mountain division presents rare attractions to the sight-seer, and is reached after crossing the fertile and cultivated country between Denver and Golden. Far above the latter point are the headwaters of Clear Creek and the mountain-walled cities of Georgetown, Idaho Springs, Central and Black Hawk. That section of the railway extending around the lofty and precipitous hills overhanging the former place is the most interesting and impressive portion of even this remarkable road, but may yet be surpassed by localities on the Leadville extension. In and near these places, gold and silver ores are mined and milled and the bullion forwarded to its distant place of coinage. At intervals is scenery as grand, majestic, and beautiful as the world can offer. The distance from Golden to Central is twenty miles, and the average ascent per mile of track is considerably over one hundred feet. There are places where grades of one hundred and fifty and even two hundred and more feet are encountered, but these are only for short intervals. Central is about 2,600 feet higher than Golden, and about 500 feet higher than Black Hawk.

The towns along the narrow gauge divisions of the road are Central, Black Hawk, Idaho Springs, Lawson, Mill City, and Georgetown. Adjacent to the line of the road are Nevadaville, Freeland, Silver Plume, and Brownville. On the plains or broad gauge are

Boulder, Longmont, Loveland, and Fort Collins, with Golden at the junction, and Denver and Cheyenne at either terminus. At Golden and Louisville, on the line of this road, are some of the most productive coal mines of the State.

In 1879, the railways leading east, north, and west from Denver, passed under the control of the Union Pacific Railroad Company. This consolidation includes the road described above, now known as the Union Pacific Railway Colorado Division, the Kansas Pacific, the Kansas Pacific Cheyenne Division (formerly Denver Pacific) the Boulder Valley, and the short line known as the Golden, Boulder, and Caribou railroad. This mammoth combination, with headquarters at Omaha, is superintended by S. H. H. Clark, with Thomas L. Kimball as general passenger and ticket agent. Here are over two thousand miles of railway—and connecting roads to the eastward and in Utah and Idaho make a total of four or five thousand miles controlled by Jay Gould, Sidney Dillon and associates. The latter is President of the Union Pacific and pooled lines.

The Colorado Division of the Union Pacific is superintended by A. A. Egbert, with headquarters at Denver. W. N. Babcock is general passenger agent, and located at the same place, and W. A. H. Loveland is president. In former times H. M. Teller, C. C. Welch, J. C. Hummel, O. H. Henry, C. A. Abbott, Foster Nichols, and E. V. Berthoud were officially connected with the road for long periods, and the latter still is. Extensions have been projected to cross the snowy range into the valleys of the Snake, Blue, Grand, Ten Mile, and Eagle rivers, with Leadville and other mining districts as objective points. Nott's stage lines connect Georgetown with Leadville, 63 miles distant, and with Breckinridge, Ten Mile, and other places. During the past winter, stage travel was mainly conducted on runners, affording a sleigh ride over the " Rockies "—the main divide being crossed twice. The Denver & South Park railway leading towards Leadville, and the Gunnison region makes connection with Union Pacific and Kansas Pacific trains at Denver.

The Union Pacific and its western extension, the Central Pacific, leading from Omaha to San Francisco, a distance of 1,927 miles, form the only line leading to Utah, Nevada, and California at present. Work was begun at Omaha on the great overland ocean to ocean route late in 1865. The grand enterprise was completed on the 10th day of May, 1869, when the tracklayers from the east and wes

met on the northern border of Great Salt Lake.   Since then, crossing
the continent has been a matter of a few days only, instead of many
months by wagon train, or of several weeks by the overland stage,
and more than a million square miles of territory have been afforded
communication with the Mississippi Valley, and the Atlantic and
Pacific seaboards.

Attractive resorts can be reached from points on all of the narrow
gauge railways, and by stages connecting therewith. By the Denver
and South Park, one can visit the beautiful South Park with its
excellent hunting and fishing and mineral springs, and adjacent
mines of silver and gold.   Still further into the mountains the same
road enters the valley of the Arkansas, and approaches quite near to
the famous Cottonwood and other springs, the massive Sawatch
range, the beautiful Twin lakes, and the wonderful city of Leadville,
with its world-renowned carbonate mines. No summer excursion
could be made that would afford more pleasure, satisfaction and
instruction than one taking in the above-mentioned points. The trip
might be extended to the Gunnison country by the Southern Overland stage or by private teams and pack animals, or northward to
the Eagle country by the Wall and Witter or other stage lines. Good
hunting and fishing can be found anywhere away from towns and
main lines of travel.

Manitou, the Saratoga of the West, is near the line of the Denver
and Rio Grande railway. In the vicinity of Canon city, on the line
of the latter road, are many attractive localities, more or less known
to fame and well worthy the attention of the tourist. The city
possesses a remarkably favorable climate for health-seekers, together
with some of the best iron and soda springs in the country. Among
the mountains, that rise to the west and south, are the Grand cañon
of the Arkansas, Grape Creek, Oil Creek, Temple and Oak Creek
cañons, and many other wonders of nature. Marble Cave, Talbott,
and Curiosity Hills and Temple Cañon excite the wonder and
admiration of all who visit them. The latter forms a subterranean
chamber of great size and beauty. The coal lands near cañon are
of great extent, and are said to contain the finest variety of lignite
coal in the world. The great coal mine at Labran, nine miles from
Cañon, is well developed and has produced largely. Other coal
lands not far away are being mined for extensive production.
Special trains are required to ship away the product of the mines.

Cañon City, with its iron and soda springs, attractive location and surroundings, and unusually favorable climate, is fast becoming a general resort for tourists, invalids and pleasure seekers. It has been the point where Leadville and Silver Cliff merchandise and supplies changed from the railway to wagon trains.

TABOR BLOCK, DENVER.

The coal measures near Cañon are of great extent and value. This is the finest coal for fuel purposes in Colorado, and is sold in all sections of the State at much higher figures than any other variety. Several concerns are engaged in developing these coal lands, more noticeably the Colorado Coal and Iron Company and the A. T. & S. F. Railroad Company. The former, once known as the D. & R. G. coal banks, are reached by a branch from the Denver & Rio Grande road, which has its own track to the mines. The supply is beyond all human calculation, for the valley of the Arkansas is one vast coal bed for mile upon mile.

The Grand Cañon of the Arkansas is at last penetrated by a railway. The Atchison, Topeka & Santa Fe Company completed several miles of track from Cañon City up through the Royal Gorge early in May, and the first passenger excursion train passed up and down on the 7th day of that month. Far down in the depths, beside the foaming waters of the river, steam cars will soon make their daily trips to the mountain metropolis of Leadville. No sunshine ever enters long sections of this massive defile, and but a narrow strip of the heavens is visible from the train. Many prefer the old way of seeing the cañon from above. This trip is made by carriage or on horseback.

The drive from the hotel to the Grand Cañon covers thirteen miles over a stretch of country which is almost bewildering in its wealth of startling features. It is possible to ride almost to the very edge of the tremendous cleft through which the foaming Arkansas roars with intense fury. And when one stands upon the brink of that vast precipice and gazes down thousands of feet, he is overcome by awe at the magnitude of Nature's handiwork. So far beneath as to be almost lost from sight, the river winds its way like a tiny thread of the purest white. Indeed, it is almost impossible to realize that what appears to be but an insignificant rivulet is in reality the mighty Arkansas.

Near at hand is the Royal Gorge—the greatest and most impressive chasm on the "Eastern Slope." It is in many ways different from the cañon, and excites the greatest enthusiasm among the lovers of grand scenery. At the first point of observation the walls, though frightfully steep, are nevertheless sloping to more or less extent; here at the Royal Gorge there are sheer precipices, as perpendicular as the tallest house, as straight as if built by line. So narrow is the gorge that one would think the throwing of a stone from side to side the easiest of accomplishments, yet no living man has ever done it, or succeeded in throwing any object so that it would fall into the water below. Many tourists are content with the appalling view from the main walls, but others more venturesome work their way six hundred to a thousand feet down the ragged edges of a mountain that has parted and actually slid into the chasm.

Few dare to look over the edge of the precipice more than once,

SPANISH PEAKS AND THE PLAINS FROM VETA PASS.

and one glance suffices for a comprehension of the meaning of the word depth never before even dreamed of, and never afterward forgotten. The gorge is 2,008 feet sheer depth. The opposite wall towers hundreds of feet above the one on which the tourist stands, and if possible to imagine anything more terrifying than the position on this side, that upon the other would be, were its brink safe to approach. Overhanging crags, black and blasted at their summits or bristling with stark and gnarled pines, reach up into profoundly dizzy heights, while lower down monstrous rocks threaten to topple and carry to destruction any fool-hardy climber who would venture upon them. Among all the thousands who have visited the Grand Cañon and the Royal Gorge harm has befallen none, for despite the seeming horror of the situation, the appalling depth and rugged paths, the fascination of the danger gives birth to the greatest caution. The cañon, except in the dead of winter, is approachable only from the top, the walls below being so precipitous and the river such a torrent as to defy all access. While the original railway surveys could be made only when the stream was frozen over, the Atchison, Topeka & Santa Fe Company is succeeding in blasting a road bed from the rocky walls for its Leadville extension.

There are, in addition to all these easily accessible places of interest, many points in the vicinity which may easily be taken in. Rosita, Poncha Springs, and other places may be visited, the trip occupying from two to four days. These journeys are inexpensive in the extreme, and the tourist may either camp out or put up at the various ranches which are found from time to time on all the roads leading out of Cañon City. The streams abound in magnificent specimens of trout, and among the woods and crags of the mountains the most enthusiastic hunter can find game in plenty.

A very pleasant journey, which will cover pretty much all the Southern portion of Colorado, may be made as follows, starting from Pueblo:

Cross the Sangre de Cristo range, over Veta Pass, on the Denver & Rio Grande Railway; thence by stage to Del Norte; thence up the valley of the Rio Grande through Wagon Wheel Gap to Antelope Park; thence to Silverton, the seat of the great silver district of the San Juan; thence into the Uncompahgre Valley and Park, making the circuit to Ouray; thence to Lake City; thence via the Los Pinos Agency, crossing the Continental Divide to Saguache; thence down the San Luis Valley over Poncho Pass to South Arkansas; thence to Chalk Creek, Twin Lakes, California Gulch, and the Mount of the Holy Cross, returning via South Park to Fairplay, thence through Ute Pass to Manitou and Colorado Springs. This the main line to be followed; numberless side jaunts are permitted, and

SCENE AT VETA PASS, D. & R. G. R. R.

nearly if not quite the entire tour can be made by stage. The most agreeable manner of making the tour is, however, the commingling of stage, wagon, horseback, and jaunts on foot, as in this way one is entirely independent of time schedules, gauging his rambles only so as to make connection with stage at such points as it is most desirable. It is not unfrequently the case that horses, mules, and equipment complete are purchased before starting, and at the completion of the trip sold readily for such prices as render the expense very small. Others charter conveyances for indefinite periods, and pay at a specified reduced rate per day. In short, one may make his own choice of preliminaries, and thus fix the cost according to the means at command.

TWIN LAKES—THE HIGHEST YACHTING IN THE WORLD,

Wagon Wheel Gap is becoming famous for its hot springs, and various other attractive features. It is an exceedingly romantic locality, and the road which leads to it follows along the bank of the river through scenery of the wildest description. The Gap is a sharp cut through walls of solid rock. In this cut the river flows, and there is just room for the stage road beside the stream.

From Wagon-Wheel Gap the road leads west up the Rio Grande, the valley narrow and rocky of surface to Antelope Park, twenty miles, where it widens out in broad opens, profusely and richly clothed with grass. Here the stage road leaves the river as it turns to the right, and passing over a series of picturesque, pine-covered hills, runs into the shadows of a long range of mountains presenting stupendous cliff faces of exceeding ruggedness.   They rise vertically to dizzy heights, and are relieved by innumerable columns and strange rock figures that stand out from the wall or crown the summit.   In the early summer, while the snow is still melting on the towering peaks, innumerable streams of water pour down over these cliff-faces, forming beautiful cascades hundreds of feet in depth.   Midway of this tremendous and magnificent rock scenery, and immediately on the left of the road, is Lake Santa Maria, two miles in length, but quite narrow, and without visible outlet.   It is dotted with little rocky islands, and from the farther shore rises a long, sloping, half-wooded mountain ridge.   The water is perfectly clear, perfectly smooth, and all indentations in the rocks, every streak of brown upon the majestic mountain sides, every tuft of evergreen that has gained footing, every tree from base to timber line, the peaks, and everything animate or inanimate, are pictured in the cool shadows with undeviating fidelity.

A few miles from Lake Santa Maria, or Mirror Lake, as it is often termed, is Clear Creek, a fine, large stream wonderfully beautiful in cascades.   Here the road turns to the northward to surmount the snowy range, and thence onward the slopes are easy and gentle, the country more park like, and we soon reach a point where Clear Creek plunges down hundreds of feet in one tumultuous leap.   Half a dozen miles farther is the pass over the summit of the Rocky range, the approach to which is not steep or abrupt on either side.   The first waters we come upon that flow toward the Pacific are the head streams of the Powderhorn, which unite with the Cebolla, a prominent branch of the Gunnison.   The streams are skirted by narrow, open valleys, but the road soon climbs up a timbered ridge—a mountain spur which diverges to the north—and for nearly twenty miles it winds through the dusky shadows of a dense forest, coming out at last at the summit of Slumgullion Gulch, a precipitous, rocky, and stumpy descent, with the Lake fork of the Gunnison at its mouth, and four miles beyond the largest commercial centre of the San Juan country—Lake City.   The site is decidedly romantic, surrounded as is the city by stupendous mountains, now bare and bald, and then finely zoned with prodigious forest growth.   The altitude of Lake City is 8,550 feet, and from a mere cluster of cabins in 1875 it has

grown into a thriving, busy centre of from 1,500 to 2,000 population,
its mills and reduction works comprising the most extensive system
of mining machinery in all the San Juan country. It has churches of
almost every denomination, three or four hotels, good schools, several
banks, five saw-mills, free reading-room and library, two excellent
and energetic newspapers, and other evidences too numerous to
mention of substantial and lasting prosperity. Hotel rates run from
$2 to $3 per day, and from $10 to $12 per week. Returning to Del
Norte it is sometimes pleasant to leave the San Juan country by way
of the stage route to Cañon City, and to take the cars at that point
for Pueblo, Colorado Springs, and the northern resorts.

U. S. SIGNAL STATION—SUMMIT OF PIKE'S PEAK

CHAPTER VI.

INTO THE MOUNTAINS—RAILWAYS AND STAGE LINES IN THE "ROCKIES"
—THE BEAUTIES AND ATTRACTIONS OF A ROUND TRIP AMONG THE
PARKS, CAÑONS AND MINING CAMPS—GEORGETOWN, IDAHO, CEN-
TRAL, BLACK HAWK, MIDDLE PARK, AND THE SNOWY RANGE—
HOW TO REACH POINTS OF INTEREST AND WHAT IT COSTS.

For many years the stage-driver and freighter have been steadily
receding from an immense scope of country in which their services
were once indispensable.   The ever-encroaching extensions of the
railways and the sharp competition of lower prices are ever and anon
crowding them to the newer fields which the prospector and pioneer
are continually proving worthy of occupation.   The same history is
being repeated in central and southern Colorado that the northern
settlements have seen enacted; and here, as there, the lips that
welcome the advance of the steam motor tender a heartfelt good-
bye and God-speed to the friends of other days.   Outside of local
farming or mining residents, once famous locations like Guy Hill
and Virginia Cañon live only in the recollections of other days.
They are now off the lines of travel and the locomotive wakens the
echoes where once sped the driver with his "six-in-hand."   Let
due honor be accorded these gallant knights of the ribbons, who
have conducted themselves with equal credit whether in scenes of
peril and danger or in the routine every day duties of the road.
Although crowded from their former scenes of usefulness, they
are yet the autocrats of travel over an empire of park and mountain
as matchless for grandeur and beauty as it is boundless in extent.
Here the tourist can still be treated to an exhilarating drive from
mountain top to cañon depth, or whirled at break-neck speed around
the brink of yawning chasms until his love of excitement is fully
gratified.   Indian bullets no longer greet the driver and his load of
human freight, as before the days of plains railways and Pullman
sleepers, but there is enough of the sensational about one of these
mountain excursions to satisfy the ordinary traveler.

In the multitude of inviting localities that await the inspection of the pleasure-seeker, all or half of which it is impossible to visit in a few weeks' time, or in a single season, it is a difficult matter to make a choice of routes, or to lay out a plan of travel and live up to it. But this region of picturesque novelties and ever-changing beauty is so vast in extent that one can hardly go amiss in making any one of the plains cities a base of operations, and any part of the mountains

BEAVER BROOK, C. C. R. R.

an objective point.   The lover of the beautiful will find a world of enjoyment, whether viewing the handiwork of the Great Architect from lofty peak, wooded dell, or sunless cañon.   In the variety that is offered one can go from forest of luxuriant splendor to mountains of unutterable barrenness and magnitude, from still lake to roaring cataract, from verdure and cultivation to galleries of nature's strangest fantasies, without the slightest hint of what the next transition may be. On any one of the most traveled routes, or near any of the pleasure resorts or railway termini, it is but a short remove from the bustling activity of the mining camp or business centre to the solitude and desolation of the mountain top with all its impressiveness. In recalling the attractions of a summer's excursion among the "Rockies," it must be confessed that each picture has a hundred phases rivaling some other in beauty and interest, and that every exquisitely perfect feature in mountain, lake, or river scenery is somewhere garnered here. So whether we explore the wonders of the Royal Gorge, scale the "snowy range," or view the rugged walls and towers of Clear Creek, the Platte or Boulder, there is enough in each or all to repay many long miles of travel. All of these places can be reached within four days from New York, and in less time from Chicago or St. Louis.

No one coming to Colorado should fail to visit the mountains. Without that the entire excursion would be like the play of Hamlet with Hamlet left out. This can be done from any one of several towns, but best of all from Denver. The railway towns of Boulder, Golden, Colorado Springs, and Cañon are located at or near the entrances to beautiful mountain gorges, rich with scenery of wooded dell, castled wall, and dashing waterfall.

At present the most entertaining trip that can be made, and the quickest and cheapest, is that by way of the Colorado Central railway from Denver to the mining cities of Central, Black Hawk, Idaho, and Georgetown. In this the tourist gets the greatest variety for the least expenditure of money that any single excursion affords that actually enters the mountains any distance. While this cañon may not compare with the Royal Gorge in massive grandeur, the tourist can derive infinite pleasure from the many and varied sights that continually offer themselves *en route* and at adjacent points on either hand. There is no finer prospect than that offered from Gray's lofty summit, no more beautiful lakes than those near Georgetown, and nowhere in Colorado are mines so deep or mills so numerous as on the headwaters of Clear creek. There are excellent hotels at all of the towns named, and one of the most noted pleasure resorts, with fine drives and livery turnouts, can be found on this line at Idaho Springs.

The railway time between these points and Denver is but a few hours, and the round trip can be made in a single day. The time between the arrival and departure of trains is too short, however, to permit of seeing the many interesting and instructive features of such an excursion, and at least one or two days should be devoted to each locality. The expense of the round trip should not exceed thirty dollars, although the outlay can be increased or diminished

CLEAR CREEK CAÑON, C. C. R. R.

according to time and number and variety of places visited. A few days enables one to take in some of the grandest scenery on the continent, and to learn much of the mountains and of mining and mining life.

Picturesque Clear Creek Cañon has been portrayed too often to require a detailed description here, and must be seen to be appreciated.

A twenty-mile ride up the curves and windings of this rocky defile brings one first to the creek mines and then to the stamp mills of Black Hawk. The business point of Central, by the wagon road, along which portions of these cities are built, is but little over a mile distant, but the difference of nearly five hundred feet in elevation is too much for any railway grade. Consequently, Gregory Gulch could not be followed, but a detour is made along the mountains until the requisite elevation is gained for a nearly straight shoot for the destination. Central is twenty-six hundred feet higher than Golden and over three thousand feet above Denver. Still further up among the hills is Nevadaville.

The first sight of these cities of the hills is one not soon forgotten. There is a novelty to the scene that attracts in spite of the general barrenness of the landscape—the forest having long since been consumed in furnaces or mines. Thus it is that the numberless prospect holes, dump piles, shafts, cuts, and tunnels that scar the earth's surface are all the more plainly visible. Streets and houses are wedged in narrow ravines and gulches, and again crowded up their steep inclines. The towns centre where streams and gulches unite; for there a little more room can be obtained than elsewhere, and room is an important item here. A main thoroughfare, over three miles in length, winds through these granite hills and busy, bustling towns. Down this numerous quartz teams make their way from mine to mill, loaded with precious ore. Far up the giddy slopes on either side hang cottages and mine buildings, seemingly ready to topple one on another. Where business centres are stately blocks of brick and granite, handsome banks, hotels, and warehouses, whose tops hardly reach to the levels of the streets behind. Beside the turbid streams are huge quartz mills, whose ponderous iron stamps never cease to thunder and rattle. These are the bullion producers and the receptacle of the gold-bearing rock that is constantly being blasted and hoisted from the shafts, levels, and tunnels of the honeycombed hill sides. Here one can be inducted into the mysteries of "wet crushing and raw amalgamation"—of extracting the precious metals from the ore.

It is a strange sight to the new comer, these cities built at the tops of the shafts or mouths of the tunnels which lead to nature's treasure vaults below and on either hand. Down in the depths, hundreds of feet from the light of day, are other cities, less habit-

FROM BLACK HAWK TO CENTRAL, COLORADO CENTRAL RAILWAY.

able, but equally active. Here, by the dim candle light, scores and hundreds of miners wield the drill, pick, and shovel, delving for the hidden wealth of centuries. Thus do they help to swell the millions that steadily find their way into the channels of commerce. A visit to these underground workings is a notable event to the tourist or stranger.

A trip on the Black Hawk and Central extension of this narrow-gauge railway is full of interest, and sensational in the extreme. The grade is even steeper than in the cañon below, and averages something like one hundred and thirty-five feet to the mile. But, as the train keeps on ascending, one is brought more into the sunlight than there, and the prospect becomes far more extensive and exciting. At one place streets are crossed above the level of the house tops, and at another, after circling the mountain sides for two miles, the train makes its appearance hugging the mountain side hundreds of feet above, and almost directly over the town. One can almost look down into the fiery chimneys of the great smelters, while streets rise above, and seemingly bottomless shafts and excavations yawn beneath in this thrilling ride among the gold mines.

At Central one can step into the banks and look upon the glittering gold retorts fresh from the mills, and ready for export. These big lumps of the yellow metal, varying in value from one hundred to fifteen or sixteen thousand dollars each, and in weight from a few ounces up to a thousand, are continually arriving, as one mill after another makes its "clean up," and consequently bank shipments are made almost daily. "Specimens" of gold and silver-bearing ore, of many colors and varieties, and often strikingly beautiful, are collectable at the mines and purchasable elsewhere. Many residents of these places have been diligent in gathering mineral collections which they would not part with at almost any figure. Magnificent views of the surrounding country can be obtained from James' Peak or Bellevue Mountain.

Taking the same railway, with its zigzags, curves, and windings, back again to the forks of the creeks, twelve miles below Central, the down train is exchanged for that bound up the main branch of Clear Creek for Idaho Springs and Georgetown; or if the delightful experience of a mountain drive is preferred, the short cut of six miles to Idaho by way of the Divide and down the famous Virginia cañon can be chosen. This was once the old stage route, but the railway around the line of the creek supplanted that some time ago. Seated in a carriage behind a first-class livery team, the prospect is well worthy of attention. All along the route are lode and gulch mines, and far away the great range glistens with its mantle of snow and disappears from sight as the rapid run down the cañon begins. Nearly a thousand feet to the mile is the descent made on this steep and rugged slope.

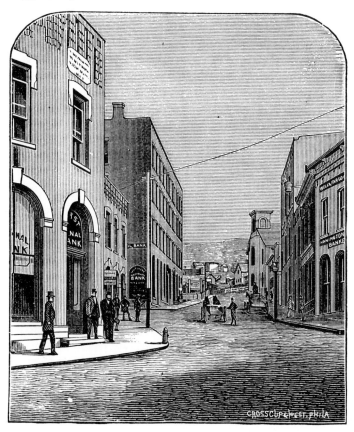

VIEW IN CENTRAL.

If a township several miles square, surrounding and including Idaho Springs, could be transplanted, with all of its wealth of mountains and dark cañons, whispering pines, bubbling springs, leaping, splashing waterfalls, and heavenly atmosphere, to some central location in the East, it would secure such a population and fashionable assemblage as no seaside resort can boast of. Idaho stands unsurpassed in natural attractions for those seeking health, pleasure, or novelty. The hotels are spacious and good, the hot soda springs highly beneficial, and the bathing facilities first-class. In the overhanging hills are gold and silver mines, and along the bars and creeks gravel and pay dirt are still washed for gold, as in the earlier days of the country. There are mills for crushing or concentrating ore from the lode veins, and streets of neatly-built cottages, with a mingling of more pretentious structures. The contracted cañon up which the railroad makes its way here widens into a beautiful sunny valley, with green sloping hillsides. All the way to Georgetown numerous mines dot the mountains, with here and there a thriving mining camp. A few miles distant are those noted resorts, Chief Mountain and Chicago Lakes, the latter comprising the highest body of still water in North America.

Beyond Idaho Springs the silver region proper is entered, and quartz mills are succeeded by concentrating and reduction works and ore-buying and sampling establishments.

Inviting as may be the appearance and surroundings of Idaho Springs, those of Georgetown are still more so. Under the shadows of grand old mountains, the "Silver Queen" reigns prosperous, productive, and progressive. All around are silver veins, whose annual output has been gradually creeping up into the millions. Close at hand are the mills for the extraction of the precious metal, and yet other mills where ores are purchased and shipped to distant smelters. The success that has attended mining makes itself manifest in the character and appearance of this fair city. Few western places can boast of as good a class of private residences, of as well-built streets or better patronized marts of trade. As at Central, and most other Colorado towns, the finest and most noticeable building that arrests the attention of the stranger is one devoted to educational purposes.

With Georgetown as a base of operations some of the most charming resorts that the country affords can be reached in rides or drives of a few hours. There are mines and tunnels along the steep mountains almost without number, and well worth the climb necessary to reach them. A few miles away are the famous Gray and Irwin Peaks, domes of the continent, rising respectively to heights of 14,341 and 14.336 feet above sea level. From their summits, reached

THE DOME OF THE CONTINENT—GRAY AND IRWIN'S PEAKS.

by well-worn trails and bridle-paths, views of surpassing grandeur are afforded. Far to the eastward extend the great plains, as level and boundless as the ocean. In all other directions countless peaks and mountain ranges rear their billowy heads like storm-tossed sea waves, while far below the western slopes are the green valleys of the Snake, Blue and Grand and of Middle Park. The range of vision embraces objects one hundred and fifty miles distant in any direction.

DEVIL'S GATE, GEORGETOWN.

Within two miles of town are Green and Clear lakes, the most beautiful of their kind that even Colorado has to offer. Here one can enjoy boating and fishing at an elevation of ten thousand feet above the sea. The Devil's Gate and Bridal Veil Fall are but a few minutes' walk from the Barton House, and are objects of rare interest.

In the neighboring mountains are tunnels driven into the mountains for distances of from a quarter to nearly half a mile, and other mining enterprises whose deeper workings are hundreds of feet below the starting point. Besides mines of great extent and richness, the tourist can view the silver mills, where the product is crushed, roasted, amalgamated, and converted into bright silver bullion.

From this same Colorado Central, a ramble up Boulder Cañon can be made in a single day from Boulder City. This will prove a rare

IN THE PARK.

treat, for it is the most beautiful of all of the northern cañons. If the trip can be lengthened to that extent, Boulder county should be included in the Georgetown and Central excursion. The mountain sections must there be visited by stage or other conveyance, and these are at the traveler's disposal at either end of the route. Pleasant summer retreats are afforded at Rollinsville and Fall River, both of which are unsurpassed for general attractiveness, and for hunting and fishing facilities.

An excursion to that delightful resort, Middle Park, should be by all means set down on the programme, if time and circumstances permit of it. This can be reached from Georgetown or Empire in a single day, by the regular stages of those localities. While stage and hotel accommodations are excellent, and such modes of travel simple and expeditious, many prefer to adopt the old Colorado style of summering in the wilderness by organizing "camping outfits" and to "rough it" in a more primitive and perhaps enjoyable manner. The saddle and pack animals, wagons, or materials and supplies for such an expedition, can be obtained at reasonable figures at Denver or the mountain cities of Central and Georgetown. Roads lead from either of the last-named places over mountain passes to the same destination.

It is difficult to convey a just idea of the world of beauty presented in this summer paradise of Middle Park. The broad expanse of mountain scenery unfolded from the passes of the Sierras or the valleys of the Park, and the rolling prairies and river bottoms, with their luxuriant carpeting of grasses and flowers diversified with groves of pine and aspen, form a picture at once lovely and enchanting. Here is everything that goes to make a mountain ramble enjoyable— cool, invigorating atmosphere, bright skies, unlimited hunting and fishing preserves, health-giving mineral waters, clear lakes, translucent streams and sparkling waterfalls; such are the attractions in store for the visitor. Once over the great Divide, whose lowest passage-way is more than two miles above the sea, and one can revel in the unrestricted freedom of mountain life in one of Nature's most favored localities. The mineral waters of Hot Sulphur Springs relieve all sorts of maladies, and are fast securing the invalid's attention. Distance and the intervening range alone have prevented as great a rush of visitors as at the railway watering-places. The groves and grassy slopes along and between the Frazer, Grand, Blue, and Troublesome abound in different varieties of the feathered species, and in deer, antelope, and elk. All of these and more dangerous game inhabit the timbered slopes of the surrounding mountains, while the streams referred to are alive with speckled beauties of the finny tribe. This variety and quantity is certainly sufficient to satisfy the most exacting disciple of the rod and gun, and the rewards that await his efforts are correspondingly liberal and satisfactory. To the pent-up denizens of the great cities nothing can furnish more rare enjoyment than a summer's jaunt among these far away solitudes of forest and stream beyond the "snowy range."

Less remote and difficult of access, but equally beautiful, is the lesser inland valley of Estes Park, reached by a few hours' staging from the Colorado Central railway towns of Loveland and Longmont. This lovely and fashionable resort is close to the eastern base of that giant sentinel of the great range, Long's Peak, whose summit is 14,271 feet above sea level. This park has a first-class hotel and is frequented by large numbers of visitors every summer.

EMMA LAKE, ESTES PARK.

CHAPTER VII.

THE GREAT KANSAS, COLORADO, AND NEW MEXICO THROUGH LINE-
DESCRIPTION OF THE ATCHISON, TOPEKA & SANTA FE RAILWAY—
ITS ROUTES, PROGRESS, AND OBJECTIVE POINTS—THE DENVER &
RIO GRANDE RAILROAD.

The construction of the Atchison, Topeka & Santa Fe railway
over the prairies of Kansas and into the mountains and plateaus of
Colorado and New Mexico is transforming an ocean of wilderness
into a region of thrift and plenty. It affords a great through line
of travel to or towards localities famous for their wealth and
productiveness. It conveys multitudes of people to the new
El Dorado of Leadville, to the health and pleasure resorts of
Colorado, and yet other hundreds into the silver-ribbed mountains
of the San Juan. The shrill notes of its locomotives waken the
echoes among the hills of New Mexico and rouse the indolent
descendants of the Spaniard and Aztec from their lethargic sleep.

The silver and gold veins of Southern Colorado and the traffic of
the Mexicos shaped the course of this railway, whose location and
objective points would be better understood if "Kansas, Colorado
& New Mexico" was the title instead of that adopted. But its
mission will not be complete with the construction of lines already
contracted for. An outlet to and for the Pacific coast and its commerce is wanted, and the mines of Arizona are a strong incentive to
further progress. Consequently, the road is to be pushed
westward from Santa Fe to unite with the on-coming Southern
Pacific or to secure through roads to California and Mexico of its
own.

Already the Atchison, Topeka & Santa Fe, and its north,
south, and west branches and leased lines, built and building, afford
cheap and rapid transit and transportation to an ever-increasing area
of immense proportions. What is termed the main line has already
crossed the Raton mountains into New Mexico and has reached and
passed Santa Fe and Albuqueque. The Arkansas Valley division extends to Pueblo, with Denver and Leadville connections. One road is

expected to reach the latter point early in the fall, if not sooner. The first-named line secures the traffic of New Mexico and the great southwest, and the latter will have all that one road can handle in the travel and transportation of the carbonate camps and the San Juan silver mines of the lower western slope. The corporation possesses ample means for carrying forward any and all of its construction projects, while its management evinces a degreee of enterprise commensurate with the magnitude of its operations. At the present time it is operating about 1,400 miles of railroad, which every week sees extending, and which will soon be increased to from 1,550 to 1,700. Connection is made at the eastern termini, Kansas City and Atchison, with the great routes leading through Missouri to Chicago, New York, St. Louis, and all leading eastern cities. It is the only direct route to New Mexico and San Juan, and is within twenty-six hours of Leadville by connecting stages.

After the two sections of the main line starting at the Missouri river unite at Topeka (the headquarters of the company), the road strikes off southwesterly to the fertile valley of the Arkansas, and follows up that stream on an ascending grade of not far from ten feet per mile to La Junta, Colorado. Here one division continues on up this valley to Pueblo, and the other passes southwesterly into New Mexico. Kansas has recently become the leading wheat-growing State in the Union, and ranks high in the production of other grains and of corn. This road passes through the entire length of this granary of the West, with its lands of unsurpassed fertility. The country is filling up with farmers all along the line of this road, a large portion of the settlers purchasing lands of this company at merely nominal figures. In Colorado the road intersects a splendid stock region, where cattle and sheep are raised at so trifling an outlay as to leave a wonderful margin of profit to those following the avocation. It crosses the great buffalo ranges of the plains, and for hundreds of miles follows the old Santa Fe trail, the natural highway of traffic adopted by the pioneers and Mexican traders of the last generation. Its travel and traffic is immense, especially into and for Colorado. Pullman palace cars are run on all through trains, and there is no better managed or equipped road in the country. The general officials of the company are

Thomas Nickerson, president; W. B. Strong, vice-president and general manager; George O. Manchester, assistant general manager; E. Wilder, secretary and treasurer; W. F. White, general passenger agent, and J. F. Goddard, general freight agent.

In 1878 the Atchison, Topeka & Santa Fe Company resumed the extension of their main line, with the Mexicos and the distant Pacific coast as objective points. Near the close of that year the graders and track layers left Colorado behind them, and New Mexico for the first time was connected by bands of iron with the outside world. Soon after, the Raton Mountains were tunneled, and Las Vegas was reached, and speedily grew from a village to a city. On the ninth day of February, 1880, the long isolated New Mexican capital, Santa Fe, the oldest city of the American Union, felt the contact of a new and superior civilization through that great civilizer, the locomotive.

In April, 1880, the road was completed to Albuquerque, 917 miles southwesterly from Kansas City. Thence construction continues down the Rio Grande valley to El Paso on the borders of the Mexican State of Chihuahua. At some point north of El Paso the route of the main line strikes off southwesterly through parts of Arizona and Old Mexico, until the seaport of Guaymas on the Gulf of California is reached. This has been chosen as the Pacific coast terminus of the great road that is to serve as the highway for American and Mexican commerce as well as for that from beyond the seas.

Already this railway causes the mining and pastoral sections of New Mexico to begin to show signs of increased activity, while the long-famous silver mines of Sonora and Chihuahua will be especially benefited, and will benefit in return. The Mexican government's grant of the right of way to this American company will bring about results highly conducive to the prosperity of several states of both republics.

To the tourist and lover of history few places are so rich in tradition, mystery and points of interest as the city of Santa Fe. It had been an important town of the half civilized Pueblo and Navajo Indians long before the arrival of the first Spanish adventurers in 1541, and its adobe dwellings of that period were much of the same character as those of the present day. The Spaniards made it their headquarters for Northern Mexico. Three centuries later the

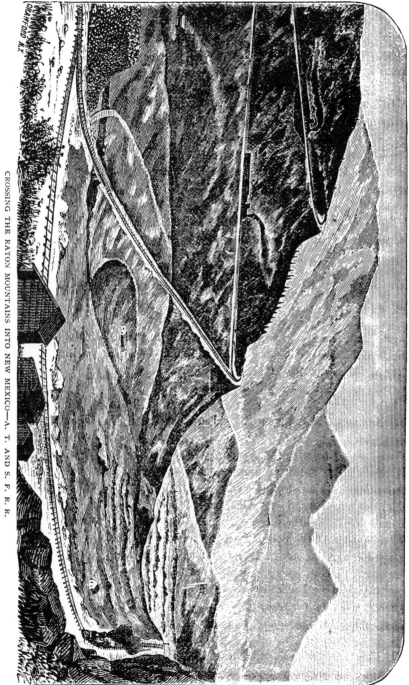

CROSSING THE RATON MOUNTAINS INTO NEW MEXICO—A. T. AND S. F. R. R.

Americans came into possession, but notwithstanding the change of rulers, Santa Fe has remained substantially a Mexican city, where Spanish is almost the only language spoken. Now that its quiet precincts have been invaded by the railway (a short branch from the main line), the process of Americanizing may be more rapid than heretofore. Some forty miles from Santa Fe are mines and mineral deposits whose value will soon be thoroughly tested. The town of Las Vegas possesses hot mineral springs of remarkable healing qualities which are making it a famous health resort. They are said to equal the Hot Springs of Arkansas, and have caused the erection of a fine hotel and baths.

Las Vegas is 786 miles from Kansas City ; Santa Fe, 869 miles ; Albuqueque, 917, and Guaymas over 1,500 ; elevations—Las Vegas, 6.397 feet, Santa Fe 6,862, Albuqueque 5,032. Fares from Kansas City to Santa Fe : first class, $40.95 ; second class, $28.25 ; to Albuqueque, $49.25 and $33.25. Pulman Sleepers on all through passenger trains.

The A. T. & S. F. Railway has been drawing much of its immense coal supply from the Trinidad coal mines, but having purchased some excellent coal measures near the superior Cañon City or Labran mines, will hereafter draw on that locality. A railway about 40 miles long was built there from Pueblo.

Serious obstacles have been encountered in railway building on this line as well as others. The Raton Mountains reach out from the great Sangre de Cristo range in a nearly easterly direction, and almost on a line with the boundary of Colorado and New Mexico. Fourteen miles south of Trinidad, Raton Cañon rises abruptly to Raton Pass, which slopes down to a similar cañon on the New Mexico side. A wagon road over this pass had long been the freighter's avenue for the southern trade, but this was entirely too heavy a grade for a railway. The company consequently decided to tunnel the range for the permanent line, and (that construction might not be impeded) to temporarily operate what is termed a " switchback " over the steep and difficult pass. By this means the summit was reached not by a direct line, but by reversing the direction several times, while elevation was steadily gained, as represented by the engraving on page 71. This temporary line had the enormous grade of 316.8 feet per mile, the heaviest ever operated by steam cars, and the sixty and eighty-ton engines used were the most powerful ever constructed. The tunnel is 2,011 feet long, 14.5 feet wide and 19 feet high, and was completed September 10, 1879, thus shortening the road several miles, and avoiding nearly 1,200 feet of grade.

Grand as was this achievement, one still more stupendous was accomplished by this same company in the Royal Gorge and Grand Cañon of the Arkansas river. After the first contest with and subsequent lease from the D. & R. G. company, the Atchison people began to construct a railway from Cañon City to Leadville. The work of building a railway through this cañon, which is further noticed in another chapter, was an undertaking long deemed impossible. Between the perpendicular walls of this magnificent cañon, which rise to elevations of from one to two thousand feet, dash the foaming waters of the Arkansas, with barely room for their occupation. As it was impossible to pass through the cañon at any time, except when the river was frozen over, the original surveys were made in winter. When construction finally began, a foothold was obtained at one section by lowering men, tools and supplies from the cliffs into the abyss below, whence the construction force worked and blasted its way out. Eleven miles of railway were in operation when another contest arose with the D. & R. G. company. For a long time each side maintained large forces of armed men in readiness for conflict, and then a receiver was appointed for the D. & R. G. road, and both contestants lost control of it. After months of litigation the courts awarded the cañon route, where but one road could be built, to the D. & R. G. company on the payment of cost of construction, and that company then began to build towards Leadville. It was a prize well worth fighting for, as the Leadville travel and traffic is of immense proportions.

The Atchison, Topeka and Santa Fe Railway is a favorite route between the East and Colorado. The D. & R. G. line connects it with Denver and the San Juan, Gunnison and Leadville. The compromise agreement permits its use of the Leadville line on reasonable terms, so that through freight as well as passengers suffer no impediment. The road across the plains is finely equipped and excellently managed. It extends through some of the finest towns and farming sections of the garden State of Kansas, where the company and adjoining lands are being rapidly purchased and settled on.

CHAPTER VIII.

THE DENVER AND RIO GRANDE RAILWAY—RECORD AND PROGRESS OF THE GREAT PIONEER NARROW GAUGE LINE—NEW ROADS AND EXTENSIONS.

The Denver & Rio Grande railway forms the great north and south connection between the different railway systems and farming, stock and mining sections of Colorado. Through it distant portions of the park and plains region are furnished with rapid transit and are afforded an opportunity to develop their resources. Extensive coal measures are supplied with a market, and some of the great gold and silver bearing belts are brought nearer to the great centres of trade and reduction. It was a grand conception, this idea of connecting with iron bands the outposts of the new and progressive American civilization with the land of the ancient Aztec and of the enervated descendants of his Spanish successors, yet great things have already been accomplished in the way of carrying out the original plans. General W. J. Palmer and associates, who projected this railway of the great inland plateau and mountain system of the continent, have been steadily extending the road from year to year as means and opportunity were afforded, until three hundred and twenty-seven miles of track are in operation and a point two hundred and fifty miles southwest of Denver has been attained. The first construction began at Denver not long after the advent of the Kansas Pacific, and seventy-five miles of track were laid south of that city in 1871. A town was then laid out, from which the beautiful city of Colorado Springs has resulted; and Manitou has been an outgrowth of this same railway enterprise. After a short stop, work was renewed, and Pueblo was reached in 1872. The next objective point was Cañon City, at the base of the mountains, where the Arkansas river debouches on the plains. The development of the excellent coal measures of that vicinity followed. A year or two later another move southward was made, and the northern base of the Raton Mountains was attained. Here were extensive coal fields, and the town of El Moro sprung into existence. Then came the work of crossing the great Sangre de Christo range, in order to reach the valley of the Rio Grande, and thus have a comparatively level water grade southward through New Mexico. Progress was sometimes slow and occasionally interrupted for lack of capital, but the eastern base of the range was reached in time, and then came the work that, in an engineering point of view, has rarely been equaled in the history of railway building. Onward and upward pressed the construction force until the grade was completed and the iron laid to the summit; and then began the descent of the western slope. Veta Pass is 9,339 feet above sea level, and this road was the first in the United States to attain such an elevation.

No other railway in the world makes an ascent at all comparable to this. In a distance of fourteen and three-tenths miles on the eastern slope, an elevation of 2,369 feet is gained, or an average of 169 feet per mile, the grade for two miles of that distance being 211 feet to the mile. On the upper seven miles of the western slope the average grade is 141 feet per mile, and three of these miles have an average grade of 211 feet per mile. The elevation of the summit of Veta Pass is very nearly one mile greater than that of Pueblo, and Blanca Peak rises yet another mile into cloud land.

With the advent of the railway on the eastern rim of San Luis Park, that magic town of the border, Garland, sprung into existence, only to be put on wheels and moved on to Alamosa as soon as the latter became the terminus. The bank of the Rio Grande was reached in the summer of 1878. In 1879, a contest arose with the A. T. & S. F. Company, for possession of the road, which passed into the hands of a receiver. Not long ago work began on several projected extensions; one from Alamosa west to Animas City, 192 miles, or to Silverton and Rico, 35 miles beyond, and one from Cañon to Leadville, 115 miles. These will give 756 miles of road.

The D. & R. G. Company has lately taken a new departure in building into several mountain mining districts. It is constructing 115 miles of road from Cañon to Leadville, 192 miles from Alamosa via Conejos to Animas City, 35 miles thence to Silverton, and 35 miles from Animas to Rico, and about 100 miles from Conejos to a point in New Mexico, 25 miles north of Santa Fe. This is as far south as the road can be built according to compromise with the A. T. & S. F. R.R. Here is a total of 477 miles in addition to the 337 miles of old track, making altogether 814 of narrow gauge for this railway, besides Arizona and Utah projected lines. The general officers of the company are W. J. Palmer, president, W. A. Bell, vice-president, Wm. Wagner, secretary, R. F. Weitbrec, treasurer, D. C. Dodge, gen. manager, and Walter Hinchman, general eastern agent, N. Y.

THE GRAND CAÑON.

CHAPTER IX.

THE DENVER, SOUTH PARK AND PACIFIC RAILWAY—THE GREAT SOUTH-
WESTERLY LINE TO THE GUNNISON AND SAN JUAN—TUNNELLING
THE SNOWY RANGE EN ROUTE TO THE UNEXPLORED REGIONS OF
THE WEST—ATTRACTIONS AND HEALTH AND PLEASURE RESORTS.

THE Denver, South Park and Pacific is considered more than any other railway a Denver enterprise. It was projected by and has been constructed under the auspices of some of the most prominent men of that city. It was backed by Denver money when the scheme looked difficult and doubtful, and it is gratifying to know that they who had courage to push it forward under adverse circumstances are now reaping the harvest their sagacity entitles them to. While the present extraordinary success is partly due to the unexpected productiveness of the carbonate region, yet it was the belief that rich mining developments would occur in the near future that caused the Denver and South Park managers to make this great forward movement to the south and west. Ex-Governor Evans, the president of the company, has been the leading spirit of the undertaking, and Walter Cheeseman, D. H. Moffat, Gen. B. M. Hughes and others, have been prominently identified with the road from the beginning

The design was to construct and operate a railway to the South Park and beyond, affording cheap and rapid transportation for many mining districts then beginning to show signs of future greatness. As the mountains became prospected and settled it was determined to push on over the Continental Divide, and westward on the Pacific Slope. These plans have been so far perfected that the road is now in operation for 135 miles southwest of Denver, to the point of junction with the D. & R. G. or Leadville route, and beyond this point to the great Sawatch or Pacific divide. The Gunnison and northern San Juan regions will soon secure both main and branch lines of this road.

Road building began in 1874 after Arapahoe county had voted bonds in aid of the enterprise. Sixteen miles of track were then laid between Denver and Morrison, or across the prairies to the base of the mountains. After unexpected delays, caused by the business and railway depressions of those days, a number of Denverites put their shoulders to the wheel and contributed money for the dif-

PLATTE CAÑON, D. & S. P. R. R.

ficult work of pushing the road up the rocky defile known as Platte cañon. The magnitude of this enterprise can be appreciated when the fact is stated that no local traffic of any importance could be expected until some ninety miles of road had been blasted through this river ravine or carried over and around steep hills and rugged mountains to the vicinity of the first great mining camp.

Nothing daunted, the plucky company began operations in 1877, and at the close of 1878 the cars were running to Hall Valley. Soon after the lofty Kenosha Divide was crossed at an elevation of 10,139 feet above the sea, the highest point then attained by any American railway and surpassed but by one or two in the world. The same road has since gone still higher, however, in tunnelling Alpine Pass in the Sawatch range. Beyond Kenosha Pass came the descent into South Park, whose valleys and plains were crossed before the close of autumn, 1879. The upper Arkansas valley was reached in February, 1880, and here the magic town of Buena Vista sprang into existence.

The intervening Mosquito or Park range of mountains prevented the direct advance of the road from the South Park to Leadville. Consequently it was necessary to skirt the eastern base of this range until a low pass or "break way" was reached. The route finally passed westward down into the Arkansas valley, and about 35 miles south of Leadville, and no nearer that place than was the road at Red Hill, some forty miles further north. Another and branch line has been projected from Red Hill to pass almost directly west to Leadville, tunnelling Mosquito range on the way. But the enormous work and heavy cost of the latter operation will require time. Previously chartered routes up the Arkansas prevent the D. & S. P. building from Buena Vista northward to Leadville, but they have the privilege of travel and traffic over the D & R. G. line.

The grand objective point is the new empire west of the snowy range, and construction forces are now working in the Sawatch mountains and the Gunnison country, and will soon move on San Juan. Last winter a force of men were set at work tunnelling the Sawatch range, at Alpine Pass, at an elevation of 11,000 feet above sea level. This tunnel is 1,600 feet long, and portions of it were driven when the surroundings were buried with snow to immense depths. It is 32 miles westerly from Buena Vista, 12 miles from Alpine and 10 from Pitkin on the western slope of the range.

When Buena Vista became the southwesterly terminus of the road, the Leadville travel took that course, making the town the transfer point for and from steam car and wagon transportation. Stages in large numbers were constantly in motion for Leadville and the end of track, or for the Gunnison country, and long lines of mule and ox freight trains vainly strove to keep up with the demands for

DOME ROCK, PLATTE CAÑON, D. & S. P. R. R.

merchandise, machinery, and supplies   Barlow & Sanderson alone have from eight to twelve coaches on the road, and other lines and private conveyances swell the daily passenger list to the centres of excitement to two or three hundred daily.   Gunnison city will continue the main western distributing point and place where branch roads lead north, west and south.

The amount of freight handled by this railway is very great,

THE SOUTH PARK AND THE SNOWY RANGE, D. & S. P. R. R.

and although repeated additions have been made to the rolling stock, the capacity of the road is taxed to the utmost. Passenger traffic is proportionately large. Day and night trains in either direction, but especially westward, are always crowded. Several elegant Pulman sleeping cars, manufactured expressly for this narrow-gauge line, are in constant use. Not long ago ten new locomotives were purchased, and freight and passenger cars were manufactured at the company shops or bought elsewhere, and yet such is the unprecedented growth of business that the demand on the carrying facilities is always fully up to or ahead of the supply. The entire equipments are first class, and the road forms an important portion of the three-feet narrow-gauge system of Colorado, and the most beneficial factor of Denver's inland commerce. Narrow-gauge roads are operated with much less wear and tear and expense than any others among these mountain ranges and defiles, where the grades are heavy and curves sudden and almost continuous. The energy with which construction has been and is being pushed forward, and the extremely successful operation of the Denver, South Park and Pacific, reflect credit on the management of President Evans, Superintendent Fisher, General Freight and Passenger Agent Hughes and associates. Few roads if any of equal length pay such handsome profits, and the enormous appreciation in the value of the original stock shows that the projectors' and investors' faith in the future of Denver and the supporting mining districts was not misplaced.

The Denver and South Park road penetrates a region rich in scenery, historic reminiscences, and gold and silver mines. Platte Cañon, the beautiful South Park, and magnificent mountain ranges on every hand, afford the lover of the beautiful such enjoyment as is rarely to be met with the wide world over. At various localities are health-giving mineral springs of great virtue, and attractive pleasure resorts invite the tourist and health seeker. Among these parks, valleys, and mountains, an army of pioneers pitched their tents and built towns and washed for gold twenty years ago. These placer mines are still worked, but the richer dirt was long ago exhausted.

Volumes could be written of the adventures, fortunes and misfortunes of the gold-hunters of the west. On the border of South Park, and near the line of the road, the famous Spanish Espinosa brothers committed their numerous robberies and murders, away back in 1864. Cold lead terminated the career of first one and then the other, but not until fifteen men had been killed from first to last. In the Park or Mosquito range are numberless silver mines, and a smaller number producing the yellow metal. Fairplay and Alma are the leading towns.   In the valley of the Arkansas are other placer mines flanked by rich silver lodes in the bordering mountains, from Monarch and Alpine to world-renowned Leadville.   This will

PLATTE VALLEY, FROM THE MOUNTAIN CURVE ABOVE WEBSTER.

ever be the main travelled route from Denver to Leadville and the Gunnison.   Connection is made with eastern trains at Denver.   The railway company is mining superior lignite coal veins at Como, in South Park.

Near Granite are the beautiful Twin Lakes, one of the most charming summer resorts of the country. Buena Vista is surrounded by many points of interests; west of it is the Sawatch mountain range, whose bald and barren summits rise like giant sentinels to the very skies. This is the highest average range in the United States, and snow never entirely disappears from it. Very many of its peaks are over 14,000 feet high. In full view of Buena Vista is Mount Princeton, the most beautiful of all its fellows, and south of it the Denver and South Park road ascends Chalk Creek and the grand divide, via the Alpine silver mines, to the tunnel already referred to. A few miles from this lively town, crowded with freight and freighters, speculators, and travellers, are the Cottonwood mineral springs, so beneficial for rheumatic and other diseases. The hotel and bath houses are well patronized by patients from far and near. In South Park are excellent hot sulphur springs. At Deansbury, near the mouth of Platte cañon, is a well kept hotel with other mineral springs, valuable for kidney and dyspeptic complaints. The country traversed by this road affords excellent hunting and fishing, so that the sportsman will here find as ample amusement as those of different tastes and habits. Antelope, deer, elk, birds of many varieties and delicious mountain trout abound in forest and stream, from the plains to distant Gunnison. The mineral wealth of the latter section is apparently as vast as it is various, and the veins of silver, gold, coal, iron, and galena are destined to cut an important figure when reached by the Denver and South Park Railway.

CHAPTER X.

TOWNS AND CITIES OF COLORADO ALPHABETICALLY ARRANGED—FACTS AND FIGURES FOR THE TOURIST.

ADELAIDE CITY.—This is in reality a suburb of Leadville, although not included within the corporate limits. The location is along the hillsides, and in a beautiful park two miles above the centre of the latter place. Near by is the Adelaide smelter; also, many mines. Some months ago the population was said to be several hundred, and increasing rapidly.

ALAMOSA.—Population, 500; elevation, 7,492. Southwestern terminus of the Denver & Rio Grande railway. Distances: Del Norte, 40 miles; Lake City, 116; Pueblo, 130; Denver, 250; Santa Fe, 145; and Kansas City, 764. Daily coaches to the San Juan mines and Santa Fe. Large amount of freighting done to and from this place. At Alamosa and the previous railway terminus of Garland, the following was received by wagon train and forwarded East by rail in the year 1878: gold bullion, $15,190; refined silver, $141,396; base bullion, silver and lead, 683⅔ tons, worth $114,150; ore, 121 tons, $30,333. Wool, pelts, and hides, over 500,000 pounds. Merchandise and machinery received from the East by rail and sold or sent west and south by wagon train, 2,250 tons. Sales of merchandise in Alamosa in first six months of the town, up to January 1, 1879, over $600,000. The town was laid out in June, 1878, and the railway reached there and established a station on the 27th of that month. The place contains several large forwarding houses, a school, religious societies, and two weekly newspapers. Alamosa is situated on the westerly bank of the Rio Grande, and almost in the centre of San Luis Park. Looking beyond the treeless plain, the surroundings are remarkably grand and beautiful. No such panoramic view is afforded from any town in Colorado, as regards extent of mountain scenery. The place is entirely encircled with ranges of diversified appearance and varying elevations, with that distance requisite for the finest scenic effect. To the east is the lofty Sangre de Christo range, with the massive

Sierra Blanca or White Mountains, not twenty-five miles away, and westward, at an equal distance, the mountains of the San Juan region, with the Summit range, come into view. San Luis Park has its greatest length in a northerly and southerly direction, and the two mountain systems referred to converge in the dim distance, with Poncho Pass as an outlet in one direction and the Rio Grande valley, in northern New Mexico, in the other. Hotel, Perry House.

ANIMAS FORKS.—This place is situated in one of the valuable and extensive silver mining districts of San Juan county. Distance from Silverton, 13 miles; population, 300.

ANTELOPE SPRINGS.—Located in Hinsdale county, about 60 miles west of Del Norte, and nearly 50 east of Silverton, and near the junction of the stage road between those points and that leading to Lake City. It is surrounded by a beautiful park and mountain ranges with the Rio Grande river flowing between.

ALPINE.—This is a promising camp and district on Chalk creek, in Chaffee county, some sixty miles south-southwest of Leadville. During the past summer over 200 people had collected there. Some rich and valuable silver veins are being mined.

BIJOU BASIN.—Small village in El Paso county, 25 miles northeast of Colorado Springs, and in a good farming and stock country.

BLACK HAWK.—This is a busy, bustling city of over 2,000 people, located in the rich gold and silver bearing district of Gilpin county, at the junctions of Gregory and Chase gulches with North Clear creek. The business of the place consists in mining, milling, and shipping ores. Most of the quartz mills of Gilpin county are located here, on account of the water supply. Black Hawk unites with Central in Gregory gulch, forming a continuous city, and is the first place arrived at in entering this great district by rail. The Colorado Central railway passes through and over the city, and on around the hills to Central. Distance from Denver, 36 miles; from Golden, 20; by rail to Georgetown, 32. The place contains many substantial brick blocks and business houses, several churches, a weekly newspaper and a graded school with five teachers, and not far from 280 pupils. Hotel, Teller House at Central.

BALLARAT.—A mining town in Boulder county, not far from Long's Peak and Jamestown. Here is the famous Smuggler mine. Fine summer resorts are afforded all through this section, and in Ward district, Jamestown, and Gold Hill.

BOULDER.—County seat of Boulder county, and a well-built city, beautifully located on the plains at the base of the mountains. Here Boulder creek leaves its rocky cañon to water the rich farm lands to the eastward, and several gulches open a roadway to distant mines. The situation is such that this is the natural gateway to the leading

THE FIFTEENTH OF AUGUST.

mining camps of Boulder county, while a market and trading point is here afforded for the adjacent productive farming districts. The town has been growing rapidly since the development of the Caribou silver mines and of the gold and telluride mines of Gold Hill, Ballarat, Sunshine, Magnolia, and other districts. Large stores and attractive private residences are seen on every hand. Boulder is a great summer resort, on account of its pleasant surroundings, equable climate, and general attractiveness. At all times of the year its hotels accommodate a very large number of guests, on account of the travel to and from the mines and other business points. Fine farms, superior stock, and excellent dairies can be seen all along the streams and intermediate country. There are two national banks, six churches, two weekly newspapers, and a graded school, with over 500 pupils and eight teachers. Here is the State University, with some eighty pupils in attendance. Boulder's location between the farms and mines has brought her two large flour mills, a foundry, Boyd's smelting works, one of the Boston and Colorado Company's ore buying and sampling mills, and other producing establishments. There is also an agricultural and industrial society that gives an annual exhibition of mining and farming products. The town is on the main line of the Colorado Central and is a terminus of the Denver & Boulder Valley railway. Another road (G. B. & C.) extends out to the productive Marshall coal banks, distant 5¼ miles. Stage for Caribou leaves on Mondays, Wednesdays, and Fridays. The sales of merchandise and other material in Boulder in 1878 exceeded $1,000,000. The population is not far from 4,000. Elevation 5,536. Distances: from Denver, 45½ miles; Golden, 28; Erie, 12; Caribou, 22; Nederland, 18; Gold Hill, 10; Sunshine, 6; Sugar Loaf, 10; Valmont, 4; Ward, 19. Hotels, Brainard, Sale and Boulder.

BRECKINRIDGE.—County seat of Summit and business centre of the placer and creek gold diggings on the headwaters of the Blue river. Population during the summer season, 250. There is a prospect of a large increase this year, owing to new mineral discoveries. Elevation 9,674. This place is on the Pacific slope of the main range, and is 95 miles from Denver, 24 from Fairplay, 32 from Leadville, 7 from mouth of Ten Mile or Frisco, 20 from Montezuma, and 40 from Georgetown. Passengers from Denver to this place leave the South Park stages at Hamilton.

CAÑON CITY.—This is the present terminus of the Arkansas division of the Denver & Rio Grande and of the A., T. & S. F. railways, and is the county seat of Fremont county. It is located at the point where the Arkansas river leaves the mountains and on an arm of the plains that extends a short distance into the foot hills. There is an excellent farming country from this point down to Pueblo. Fine crops of wheat, corn, and other grains and vegetables are raised, and this is the only locality in Colorado where great success has yet been attained in raising fruit. The apple and peach orchards at and near Cañon are quite productive. Back from the river are fine stock ranges. Just above town are several mineral springs, hot and cold. Cañon has peculiar advantages as a health resort, and is fast becoming a place of refuge for invalids. Some of the most inviting points for the sight-seer that Colorado affords can be reached in a few hours drive from this place. The royal gorge of the Arkansas, the grandest of all the cañons on the eastern slope, can be inspected from above by following a wagon road for thirteen miles, and the tourist will soon have the thrilling pleasure of making the trip along the creek bed by rail. The perpendicular walls of this cañon are nearly 2,000 feet in height. Still nearer town, is the romantic locality known as Temple cañon, and not far distant are the singularly beautiful cañons of Grape, Oil, and Oak creeks. Stages leave this city for Leadville every morning, and stages for Silver Cliff and Rosita arrive and depart daily. Long trains of wagons, loaded with ore and bullion, are almost continually arriving from Leadville, and in lesser numbers from Silver Cliff and vicinity, and return laden with merchandise and supplies. All of this business and the grading forces of the Atchison, Topeka & Santa Fe railway in the neighboring cañon have tended to make matters lively in this growing city during the past year. The travel through the place is immense, and every hotel is crowded to its utmost capacity. Cañon is a well-built place of some 1,200 inhabitants, with bank, newspaper, public schools, and several churches. It is noticeable for the neat and attractive character of its private residences. Here is the State penitentiary, an imposing structure of granite quarried from the neighboring hills. The elevation of the railroad station above sea level is 5,287 feet. A 'bus line plies between the railway and the business centre and hotels. Cañon is 40 miles from Pueblo, 126 from Leadville, 160 from Denver, 32 from Rosita, and 30 from Silver Cliff. Leading hotel, McClure.

CARBONATEVILLE.—This is a new town in the Ten Mile district, near McNulty gulch, and 17 miles from Leadville. Last reports gave it several stores and a bank.

CARIBOU.—The leading mining town of Boulder county and of

the Grand Island silver district. It is located in a well timbered region, close up to the "snowy range," at an elevation of 9,995 feet above sea level. Population, 350. Distance from Boulder, 22 miles; Nederland, 4; Black Hawk, 19; Central, 20, and Denver, 56. Stages arrive and depart on alternate days for Boulder and Central, so that the traveler can lay over two nights and a day, and make a circuit between those points. Here are the Caribou, Native Silver, No Name, Boulder County, and other rich mines.

CENTRAL.—The centre of business for the great gold mines that underlie the hills and gulches of Gilpin county, of which it is the county seat. Adjoining, and just below, is the city of Black Hawk, and above is the town of Nevadaville. The three places have a combined population of 6,500, and contain the deepest and many of the most productive mines in Colorado. More gold has been shipped from here than from all the State beside, and the locality has played a very important part in the history of Colorado. Central has six churches, a daily newspaper, three banks, an elegant opera house, and a graded school of nearly 400 scholars, with a well-selected library of nearly 2,000 volumes. Beside this, the Catholic academy affords instruction to a large number of children. The Teller House is the finest and largest hotel in the State outside of Denver, and compares with the hostelries of that place. Distance from Denver, 40 miles; Golden, 26; New York, 2,000; Georgetown by rail, 36; by wagon road, 18 and 20 by different roads. Further particulars of Central will be found elsewhere.

COLORADO SPRINGS.—County seat of El Paso, located on plateau just east of Pike's Peak, and 75 miles from Denver, and 45 from Pueblo. See chapter on "Cities of the Plains." Hotels, Colorado Springs and Crawford, and the National.

COLORADO CITY.—Small village between Colorado Springs and Manitou, and two miles from the former. Population, 100. Daily mail, express and hacks from railway. In the early times was for a very short period designated as the capital of the territory.

DEL NORTE.—The capital of Rio Grande county, located on the river of the same name, at the eastern gateway of the San Juan Mountains and mining region. It grew to be a place of importance in 1873-4 on the early opening of the Summit Mountain gold mines and the silver mines further west. Here is an elegant school building, a bank, weekly newspaper, and many large stores and ware-

WATER BASIN IN GYPSUM CAÑON.

houses. The location is remarkably fine, the climate pleasant, and the town is substantial and prosperous. Across San Luis Park, which is here forty miles wide, the Sierra Blanca and connecting range presents a grand and majestic appearance. The population of Del Norte is nearly 1,500. Elevation, 7,750. Stages arrive from and depart for Alamosa and the mountains every day. Distance to Alamosa or the railway, 34½ miles; Lake City, 81½; Denver, 284½; Pueblo, 164½; Kansas City, 800; Santa Fe, 180. Hotel, Cuenin House.

EL MORO.—This is the terminus of the El Moro division of the Denver & Rio Grande railway, and the seat of the coke manufactories. It is situated five miles from Trinidad and not far north of the New Mexican boundary. The town attained its importance as the most southerly Colorado railway terminus, and as the supply point for the New Mexican trade. It has lost much of this advantage since the Atchison, Topeka & Santa Fe came in from the east and built southward toward Las Vegas and Santa Fe. Yet the coal mines and interests of the Southern Colorado Coal and Mining Company, local business, and the coke ovens will always make it a place of some importance. Heavy coke shipments are made to distant points. The coal of this section makes the best coke in the west, and the business has grown until 75 ovens are now engaged in the work. At El Moro, the immense mercantile and forwarding and commission houses of Otero, Sellars & Co., Browne & Manzanares, and of Bartels Brothers once handled millions of dollars' worth of goods annually and carried stocks of immense value. Some of this traffic is now carried on at more southerly points. Long trains of wagons, loaded with the products of New Mexico and Arizona, were constantly arriving, and after disembarking their goods would load up their requisite cargoes and depart on their long journeys to the points from whence they came. The north and east bound freights consisted of wool, pelts, hides, and tallow from the pastoral districts, and copper and silver bullion from the southern mines, while the south and west bound freights embraced general merchandise, dry goods, and machinery. El Moro has a population of from 300 to 400. Its elevation is 5,825 feet. Distance from Pueblo, 86 miles; Denver, 206.

EMPIRE.—A mining town in Clear Creek county, four miles from Georgetown. The Middle Park stage line passes through this place.

A few miles west is Berthoud Pass, leading over the "snowy range." The town is one mile above its railway station. Valuable gold placers and lode veins are worked in the vicinity, and from one to three quartz mills are always at work. Distance from Denver, 48 miles; Idaho, 11. Population, 250; elevation, 8,583.

ERIE.—This town has been built up by the coal measures among which it is located. Several mines are worked, and have usually been quite productive. The Denver & Boulder Valley railroad passes through the place. Population, 200. Distance from Denver, 34 miles; Boulder, 12. Location, in the southwestern part of Weld county.

EVANS.—This was first settled by a colony organization of Saint Louis and vicinity, and is located in the Platte valley, in Weld county. Around it is a productive farming section and good stock ranges, and a large flour mill does a heavy business. Population, 700; elevation, 4,745. Distance from Denver, 48 miles; Greeley, 4, and Cheyenne, 58. The Denver Pacific railway passes through this place. A weekly paper is published there.

FAIRPLAY.—This is located on the banks of the South Platte river in the South Park, and is the county seat of Park county. The place has been of more or less importance for nearly twenty years, and took a fresh growth after the Park Range silver discoveries of 1871–2. The Denver travel to Leadville passes through here by stages and other conveyances, and the hotels are always crowded. The Bergh House averaged forty arrivals per day last year, and at present it must greatly exceed that number. A large placer mine is operated at Fairplay by Chinese labor. Seven miles west is Alma, and just beyond are the silver mines of Lincoln, Bross, Buckskin, and other mountains. Population, 500; elevation, 9,964. Distance from Denver by stage and rail, 100 miles; Leadville, 40 by Weston Pass, and 21 by Mosquito Pass; Alma, 6; Montgomery, 12; Breckinridge, 23. Two lines of stages pass here.

FORT COLLINS.—This is a flourishing town on the Cache la Poudre river and Colorado Central railway, and is the county seat of Larimer. The State Agricultural College is located here, for which substantial buildings were recently erected. There are two newspapers, and schools and churches; semi-weekly stages to Greeley and La Porte; excellent farming and stock country. Population,

1,000. Distances: Cheyenne, 45 miles; La Porte, 4; Denver, 65. Elevation, 4,815.

GOLDEN.—County seat of Jefferson, and headquarters of Colorado Central railway. Here are located the shops, car works, and repair shops of the railway company. Also three sets of smelting works (two of them recently completed) and reduction works. These are now in operation. There are two pottery manufactories, fire-brick works, four large coal mines, two flour mills, and a paper mill. Splendid water power is afforded from Clear creek, which leaves the mountains here. A large amount of ground is irrigated from this stream, and a good farming district is the result. This is the junction of the broad and narrow gauge divisions of the Colorado Central, and freight for and from the mountains breaks bulk here. The State School of Mines is located at Golden. The public schools are attended by nearly 350 pupils, and there are seven churches. The Court-house is the best in the State. Distances: Denver, 16 miles; Cheyenne, 122 miles; Boulder, 29½; Central, 23½; Georgetown, 27½; Beaver Brook, 7. Population, 3,000; elevation, 5,690. On account of its manufacturing interests Golden is sometimes called the Lowell of Colorado. Years ago it was temporarily the capital of the territory.

GOLD HILL.—This is a small mining town on the hill of the same name in Boulder county. Near by are several prominent mines. Owing to the fine view and airy location, this makes a pleasant summer resort. Population, 200. Distance from Boulder, 10 miles. Tri-weekly stage to that city.

GREELEY.—This is situated between the Cache la Poudre and South Platte rivers, and near their points of union, and is the county seat of Weld county. It was laid out by a colony organization and settled in 1870. Since then the growth has been steady and uniform. The town charter provides that no property or land can be leased or sold for liquor selling purposes, and, like Colorado Springs, Greeley is called a temperance town. The public school building is one of the finest in the State. There are several churches, two weekly papers, two banks, two flour mills, and some well-stocked stores. Large amounts of wheat and other grains and vegetables are raised here, and vast herds of cattle roam over the plain and the valley of the Platte clear down to the Nebraska line. Tri-weekly stages to Fort Collins and La Porte. Distance to Denver by Denver

Pacific railroad, 52 miles; Evans, 4 miles, and Cheyenne, 54 miles. Population, 2,500; elevation, 4,779 feet. The town is well laid out and watered from irrigating ditches, and the streets are lined with shade trees.

GEORGETOWN.—This is the county seat of Clear Creek county and the present southwestern terminus of the Colorado Central. Its appearance and surroundings are superior to those of any other mountain town. Around it are lofty mountains, ribbed with silver veins, which rise abruptly to heights of from twelve hundred to twenty-five hundred feet above the almost level valley in which the town is built. Here are silver reduction works, ore concentrating mills, and sampling and ore buying establishments, all of which do a large business. The mining operations of the district are very extensive, resulting in an annual export of silver bullion and ore to the value of over two millions per annum. The town has grown rapidly in the last ten years and now claims a population of 5,000. The town possesses an excellent system of water works, an effective fire department, five churches, an opera house and a graded school with some 360 scholars. There are two weekly newspapers, two banks, several hotels, and many business houses, some of which do a large trade. Three miles above are Silver Plume and Brownville. Elevation of Georgetown, 8,452 feet. Distance from Denver, 53½ miles; from Idaho, 14 miles; Central, 18 and 20 miles; Black Hawk, by rail, 36 miles; Leadville, by Loveland Pass and Ten Mile, 56 miles; stages to Middle Park—46 miles; Silver Plume, 2 miles; and to Leadville, 56 miles. There are many resorts near Georgetown that are unsurpassed in beauty and general attractions. Among them are Gray and Irwin's Peaks, among the very highest in the range, and from which magnificent views are obtained. Green lake is considered the most beautiful body of water in the State, and is supplied with boats and well filled with trout and salmon. There are good hotels and fine livery turnouts in Georgetown, with pleasant rides and drives above and below town.

GUNNISON—This is the county seat of Gunnison county and destined to be an important railroad and business point. It is beautifully located in a park at the junction of Gunnison and Tomichi rivers, and on the D. & S. P. railroad route.

GRANITE.—County seat of Chaffee county and formerly of Lake.

Population, 100. Distances: Twin Lakes, 3 miles; Leadville, 18 miles; Alpine, 42 miles; Cottonwood Hot Springs, 20 miles; Cañon, 108 miles.

HOT SULPHUR SRPINGS.—Small town in the beautiful section known as Middle Park, and close beside the valuable mineral springs of the same name. This is getting to be more and more a great summer resort, and has been frequented, by Colorado pleasure and camping-out parties for many years. There is a good hotel and a line of stages running over Berthoud Pass to Georgetown and Empire. Distance from Georgetown 46 miles; time of stages, one day. Middle Park has no superior for wild game and trout fishing, and the sportsman or angler will find it well worth his while to pass a week there, or in the same belt of country west of the range. Here are Grand lake and the head waters of Grand river.

IDAHO SPRINGS.—This is one of the most beautiful places in the country, and the only mountain town that has yet become a famous health and pleasure resort. This is mainly due to its hot soda springs and delightful surroundings. There are large and commodious hotels, extensive bath-houses, and fine livery turnouts here, and every summer sees a large influx of visitors from the East. Among the points well worth the attention of the tourist are Chief and Bellevue mountains, and Chicago lakes, said to be the highest body of fresh water in North America. The mineral springs of Idaho are highly beneficial to invalids. There are fine drives up and down the nearly level valley of South Clear Creek. Livery charges are from $2.50 to $3 per day for saddle-horses, and $10 for double team with carriage. The larger hotels charge $4 per day, with lower figures for permanent rates. Accommodations first-class. Good hunting and fishing in all directions. On the neighboring hills many lode mines are worked, and a quartz mill and two concentrating mills are employed along the creek. Here are also placer, creek, and bar mines that yield largely in gold. The air is cool and bracing in the summer months, and usually mild and pleasant in winter, and there are many features and sights about the place that recommend it to the tourist. Distance from Denver, 39 miles; fare, $4. Distance to Georgetown, 14 miles; Central, 6 miles; Golden, 22½. Population, 500; elevation, 7,512.

JAMESTOWN.—A small mining camp with valuable lodes and

mines. It is situated in Boulder county, up among the mountains, twelve miles from Boulder. Near by are valuable mineral springs. Population, 100.

KOKOMO.—New town in the Ten Mile District, Summit county. Claims a population of fifteen hundred, and 2,000 was the latest figure estimated. This is a beautiful section of country, and is proving to be rich in mines. Distance from Leadville, 20 miles; from Georgetown, 36.

KIT CARSON.—A small town on the Kansas Pacific, and once famous as the end of track on that road. Distance from Kansas City, 487; from Denver, 152.

LAKE CITY.—This is the county seat of Hinsdale, and its main town. For some time it has been the most populous place in the San Juan country, although Silverton is gaining somewhat at present. This place grew rapidly in 1876-7, following the development of many silver veins. The Crooke Concentrating and Smelting Works, and those of the Ocean Wave Company are located here, and handle large amounts of ore in the summer and fall months. There is also a chlorination and lixiviation mill. Lake City contains a population of 1,500, with the usual newspaper, bank, and collection of business houses. The situation is wild and romantic, beside the Lake Fork of the Gunnison and Hensen creek, and surrounded by lofty mountains. Elevation, 8,550 feet. Distance to Alamosa, 116 miles, and daily stages thereto. Stages to Silverton, 32 miles, and to Ouray, 80 miles, in the warmer months. Ouray can be reached on horseback by a ride over the mountains of thirty miles. Denver is distant 366 miles by Alamosa and 335 miles by Saguache and Cañon.

LEADVILLE.—The capital of Lake county and the metropolis of the carbonate region. The wonderful growth and history of this magic city will be detailed in a later place in this volume. The town is situated on an almost level plain beside California gulch, and four miles from its junction with the Arkansas, but is gradually building up the gulches and hills among the mines. There are a multitude of stores, large and small, with saloons, hotels, restaurants, and like institutions at every hand. The town is building with marvelous rapidity, as is evidenced by fourteen or fifteen saw-mills in active operation. There are two great ore buying and shipping firms, with sampling mills, who do an immense business, and others about to begin work. There are also two large smelters in town, and more above and below, beside many new concerns building. The number of furnaces will soon be very large. The population of the town and suburbs is estimated at from 10,000 to 15,000, and each day sees the number increased by at least 100. Leadville is 10,025 feet above sea level, by the recent railway surveys. By others, 10,200 or more is given. Distance from Denver by stage line to Fairplay and Webster and D. & S. P. railway, 140 miles. By Mosquito Pass soon to be opened for summer travel, 120 or 121. Distance from Cañon, 126 miles; Granite, 18; Ten Mile, 18; Cottonwood Springs, 38; Alpine or Chalk Creek, 70; Chalk Bluff, 10. Stages leave daily for the ends of track at Cañon and Webster, and for Ten Mile. Fare to Webster, $12; to Denver, $17; fare to Cañon, $14; to Ten Mile, $4 to $5. Line of coaches to Georgetown is soon to be opened. Hotels, Clarendon, Tontine, and Grand.

LONGMONT.—This is the second town in population in Boulder county, and is situated on the Saint Vrain river, in the midst of a splendid farming district. On the arrival of the Chicago colony at this place the old village of Burlington was united with Longmont. The Colorado Central railway passes through the town, and stages arrive and depart for Estes Park during the summer months. Distance from latter place, 32 miles; from Greeley, 30; Erie, 10; Denver, 58. Two trains daily to and from Denver. Population, 1,000. Elevation, 4,957.

LAWSON.—Mining town at Red Elephant mountain, Clear Creek county, six miles below Georgetown and eight above Idaho Springs. Located on the line of the Colorado Central railway. Population, 400.

LA VETA.—Station on the D. & R. G. railway at foot of Veta Pass, on the eastern slope of the mountains. Not far away are the Spanish Peaks, where silver veins have been opened. Population, 200; elevation, 6,970.

LOVELAND.—A new town on the Colorado Central, in a fine farming section known as the Big and Little Thompson country. Population, 150. Distances: Denver, 76 miles; Boulder, 27; Longmont, 17; Fort Collins, 14; Cheyenne, 62. Stages to Estes Park, 28 miles distant.

MALTA.—This place is between three and four miles below Leadville, and near the junction of California gulch with the upper

Arkansas. A set of smelting works is in operation there. Population, 300.

MONUMENT.—In El Paso county, on the line of the D. & R. G. railway. A weekly newspaper is published here. Fine stock country and some farming. Population, 200. Distance to Colorado Springs, 20 miles; to Denver, 55.

NEDERLAND.—This place is located on Middle Boulder creek, in Boulder county, four miles below Caribou, and eighteen above Boulder. Here is located the great Caribou silver mill and a gold quartz mill, several hotels and stores, and a saw-mill. Stages from Central, Caribou, and Boulder pass through the town. Population, 200. Distance from Central, 16 miles; Black Hawk, 15.

NEVADAVILLE.—This is a flourishing mining town in the mountains, just above and adjoining Central. It is located in Nevada gulch, between Quartz and Gunnell hills. The mines on either side of it have been extremely productive and have been worked more or less ever since the country was first opened. There are several quartz mills here; also churches, and a public school with 150 pupils. Population, nearly 1,000.

OURAY.—Few towns in the world are so beautifully located as Ouray, the county seat of the county of the same name. Grand and majestic scenery, health-giving mineral waters, and some of the best silver mines in the State are some of the attractions. The town is located on the banks of the Uncompahgre river, just above a series of fertile parks. It is situated far down on the western slope, with massive mountains all around it. The perpendicular walls of the stream rise to hundreds, and even thousands of feet. The place has been mainly built up within two years. Population, 700; elevation, 7,640. Distances: by trail to Silverton, 25 miles; Lake City, 30; stage to Lake City, 80; to Saguache, 115; Cañon, 215; Denver, via Saguache and Alamosa, 429; via Cañon, 335.

PLATTEVILLE. — Station on Denver Pacific railway, thirty-five miles north of Denver and seventeen south of Greeley. Good coal and farming lands.

ROSITA.—The county seat of Custer county. Beauty of location and surroundings should make this a popular summer resort. The town is built in a lovely valley among the Wet mountains, near the valley of the same name and in full view of the great Sangre de Christo range just beyond. A little above the town are valuable silver veins and productive mines, and below are reduction works. The mineral belt continues northward for miles, embracing some of the best mining properties in the country. Stages arrive and depart daily, except Sundays, for Cañon and the railway, thirty-two miles away, and every day for Silver Cliff, distant six miles. Population, 1,200; Elevation, 8,500. Distances: Denver, 192; Pueblo, 72. Hotels, Melvin and Grand View.

SAGUACHE.—County seat of Saguache county. It is located in the northwestern part of San Luis Park, and is the business centre for a fine farming and stock growing district; has a weekly newspaper. Stages to Cañon, Del Norte, Lake City, and Ouray. Population, 400; elevation, 7,723. Distances: Del Norte, 33 miles; Los Pinos Indian Agency, 40; Lake City, 96; Ouray, 115; Cañon, 100; Denver, 220.

SILVERTON.—This is a growing and prosperous mining town and the county seat of San Juan county. In the lofty mountains that overhang the beautiful park in which the town is built are numberless mineral veins, some of great size and many extremely rich in silver. Here are Greene & Co.'s smelting works, which have been running successfully for several summers. A stage line connects with Barlow & Sanderson's Lake City and Alamosa line, at Alden's Junction, forty-nine miles east. In the winter months there are no stages, on account of the snow, but the mail goes in on horseback or with a pack animal. Snow falls to an immense depth during the winter months, and avalanches occasionally sweep travelers on this trail down the mountain sides. In the summer months a conveyance runs to Lake City. A weekly newspaper is published at Silverton. Population, 1,000; elevation, 9,400. Distances: Alamosa, 131; Denver, 381; Ouray, 25; Lake City, 30; Howardsville, 4; Parrott City, 50.

SILVER CLIFF.—Wonderful discoveries of chlorodized deposits at and near Round Mountain, in Wet Mountain Valley in 1878, caused a town to spring into existence with wonderful rapidity. It was called Silver Cliff after the name given a locality where the first mining location was made. This town kept on growing in 1879–'80, a sampling mill was erected, capitalists began to come in, silver reducing mills of the Nevada Washoe process, and new to Colorado, were built, and several smelting works were put up not far away. With the summer of 1880, the amount of ore and bullion exported was very large, three daily newspapers, churches, schools, and two banks had been established, and the city claimed 3,500 people. Daily stages to Rosita, 7 miles, Canon and the railway 30, and Pueblo 40 miles; elevation 7,500 feet; railway projected. Several stamp and pan mills produce silver bullion and others are building.

SILVER PLUME.—This is a lively mining camp, two miles above Georgetown, at the base of Sherman and Republican mountains, and near the Dives, Pelican, Pay Rock, Baxter, Frostburg, Silver Plume, and many other mines. Daily mails and conveyances run to Georgetown at intervals during the day and evening. Here are the Silver Plume Concentrating Works. Population, 600, and with Brownsville not far from twice that number.

SUNSHINE.—This place is located in the telluride belt of Boulder county, and but six miles from the base of the mountains in Boulder valley. Less mining is carried on there now than formerly, but some of the mines have been very productive. Population, 250; elevation, about 6,600. Distance from Boulder, 6 miles; Gold Hill, 4.

TRINIDAD.—This growing and prosperous town is situated in the valley of the Las Animas or Purgatoire, among the low hills that intervene between the plains and the Ratoñ mountains. This valley, while of no great width as far as farming purposes are concerned, extends from the New Mexican border over one hundred and fifty miles to the Arkansas river. It is quite fertile, and produces excellent crops of wheat, corn, oats, barley, and vegetables. Last year it yielded, with some tributary valleys, something like 250,000 bushels of wheat. Las Animas county, of which Trinidad is the county seat, is one of the leading stock districts of the State. Sheep are raised in large numbers all over these valleys and uplands. The main wealth of the locality surrounding the town lies in the coal measures, which are of immense extent, but iron and other materials bid fair to make an important showing hereafter. Some half a dozen coal mines are being worked on an extensive scale, and others are being developed. The production of coal is several hundreds of tons daily, and could be doubled from present workings alone. Two companies are engaged in converting this coal into coke. One of these, near El Moro, operates on a very large scale. This is the best coking coal in the West. Trinidad has long enjoyed a heavy trade with New Mexico, and has largely acted as a supply depot therefor.

Since the completion of the Atchison, Topeka & Santa Fe railway to that place, last fall, its growth has been very rapid. Large numbers of substantial stores, warehouses, and dwellings have been erected, and the population is increasing rapidly. The leading hotel is being doubled in size, and another of large dimensions is nearly completed. Trinidad has resources at hand and a country to supply that will insure a steady growth. There are two daily and weekly newspapers, five churches, a catholic seminary, a private school, well attended, and a public school with some 300 pupils. There are three flour mills, planing and bucket shops, and several saw-mills here and in the adjacent country. About two-thirds of the population is American or European, and one-third Mexican. The proportions are reversed in the county. The population of Trinidad is over 3,000; elevation, 6,032. Distance north of boundary line of Colorado and New Mexico, 14 miles; to head of Ratoñ Pass, by Atchison, Topeka & Santa Fe railway, 15; to La Junta, 80; Kansas City, 651; Pueblo, 91; El Moro, 5; Denver, 211. Elevation of Ratoñ Pass, the gateway to New Mexico for this part of Colorado, 7,863. Hotel, United States.

WALSENBURG.—County seat of Huerfano. Has an extensive and productive coal mine; employs about 35 men. Population of the settlement, 250. The D. &. R. G. railway has a station here. Distance from Pueblo, 49 miles; Denver, 169.

WEST LAS ANIMAS.—County seat of Bent county and the business point for the most prominent cattle section of the State. Elevation, 3,750. Distance from Pueblo, 86 miles; Kansas City, 548; Fort Lyon, 4 miles. Population, 600.

GOTHIC CITY—A new and prosperous town of the Elk Mountain section of Gunnison county.

HILLERTON—A promising town on Taylor river, with numerous mineral veins near by.

IRWIN OR RUBY CITY—This bids fair to be a place of great importance. It is located in what appears to be the richest district of the Elk Mountain section.

PITKIN—A lively town located near rich mines, above Quartz Creek, just west of the Sawatch range and the Alpine Pass and rail-road tunnel. This place is on the route of the D. & S. P. railroad.

VIRGINIA CITY—Located in the Taylor river mining district, two miles from Hillerton, of which it is a rival for future greatness.

CHAPTER XI

SOMETHING ABOUT THE CLIMATE OF COLORADO—ITS BENEFICIAL EFFECTS ON PULMONARY AND OTHER DISEASES—THE MINERAL WATERS—THEIR EXTENT, VARIETY, AND STERLING QUALITIES— FACTS AND FIGURES REGARDING THE ABOVE POINTS.

So beneficial have been found the climatic influences of Colorado that her fame as a sanitarium is becoming world-wide, and the influx of health-seekers is annually becoming greater. The dryness and lightness of the air and its invigorating character, together with the almost constant prevalence of sunshine, impart new energy to the well, and a fresh lease of life for those whose constitutions are impaired. Here on this elevated plateau, far removed from the chilling winds and damp atmosphere of either ocean, all the conditions of life to the new comer are fresh and inspiring.

This region possesses influences that arrest the tendency to pulmonary diseases. Consumptives who do not put off their coming too long have been cured effectively, while others have had their days prolonged by months or years. Many eastern people have taken up a permanent abode in Colorado, because their health would not permit of their living elsewhere. Others have found the results of a sojourn so salutary that they return to stay. A variety of diseases, chronic or otherwise, find a speedy or partial cure in the pure air or in the health-giving mineral waters.

Investigation and long experience by the highest medical authority have summed the advantages of this climate somewhat as follows : To a person in the enjoyment of fair health, the sensations attending a first entrance into this elevated region are always pleasant. The dryness of the atmosphere, together with the electricity therein contained, combined with, perhaps, other peculiarities of climate, excites the nervous system to a peculiar degree of tension. The physical functions, which may have for some time been accomplished in a sluggish, inefficient manner, at once assume a vigor of action to which the system is a stranger. The appetite is keen, the digestion is vigorous, and the sleep sound. The result of these innovations is that all lurking ailments are swept away at once, and whatever there is in each individual to enjoy is called into the fullest action. He revels in what might be called intoxication of good health. An unclouded mind partakes of the elasticity of a healthy body, and a newly-aroused desire for activity is manifested, as well as an increased capacity to accomplish. This, in the beginning, is experienced to a greater or less degree by all who visit this section, and the pleasure attendant upon such a beginning will forever render the Rocky mountains a resort of unequaled attraction for the tourist.

But besides merely pleasure-seeking travelers who come westward every year, there are thousands of invalids, suffering from a wide range of chronic diseases, who come on a pilgrimage in search of health. In many cases the relief obtained is surprisingly rapid. The asthmatic forgets in the quiet of undisturbed slumber his nightly suffocation; the victim of chronic bronchitis discovers a new lease of life, and after the lapse of a very brief period he finds it hard to realize that he has been so recently afflicted with a cough so distressing, so violent, or so dangerous. The sufferer from malaria, in that most obnoxious form called fever and ague, is glad to have found a land where fever and ague never come.

While the climate is thus referred to in such seemingly flattering terms, the idea is not intended to be conveyed that there is no bad weather in Colorado. There are almost all kinds of climate, according to elevation and locality, from a warm temperate to that of the borders of the frigid zone, the latter being largely experienced on the lofty peaks of the main range of mountains. Under such circumstances, weather, good, bad, and indifferent must be expected. Still the belt of country skirting the eastern base of the mountains as well as a few other sections, enjoys an amount of sunshine and of delightful weather with a freedom from storms such as is but rarely encountered elsewhere, and in no section between Colorado and the seaboard. The temperature of a large portion of the foothills country, including such places as Central, Black Hawk, Idaho Springs, and Georgetown, is remarkably even for the entire year, there being less cold weather in winter and warm weather in summer than in any locality of less elevation. A record of three years at Denver shows the following temperature and rainfall: Highest range of thermometer for January of three years, 60°, 67°, and 58°; lowest, 5° above, 6° above, and 20° below zero;

mean, 29°, 34°, and 22.7° February, highest, 64°, 66°, and 64°; lowest, 1° and 13° above and 9° below; mean, 33°, 38°, and 34°. March, highest, 67°, 67°, and 78°; lowest, 8° below, and 10° and 4° above; mean, 32.7°, 46°, and 39°. April, highest, 80°, 80°, and 83°; lowest, 16°, 25°, and 25°; mean, 48°, 50.1°, and 49°. May, highest, 86°, 86°, and 89°; lowest, 40°, 42°, and 35°; mean, 56°, 65°, and 61°. June, highest, 94°, 97°, and 97°; lowest, 48°, 56°, and 49°; mean, 68.2°, 65.2°, and 69°. July, highest, 98°, 97°, and 93°; lowest, 53°, 58°, and 54°; mean, 74.2°, 78°, and 71°. August, highest, 97°, 95°, and 94°; lowest, 45°, 58°, and 52°;

BUTTES OF THE CROSS—WESTERN COLORADO.

mean, 64.8°, 75.2°, and 72°. September, highest, 89°, 86°, and 90°; lowest, 40°, 45°, and 35°; mean, 60°, 66.5°, and 62°. October, highest, 83°, 85°, and 88°; lowest, 27°, 24°, and 19°; mean, 47.8°, 53.5°, and 53.6°. November, highest, 68°, 70° and 69°; lowest, 20°, 0°, and 5° below; mean, 41.8°, 36°, and 36°. December, highest, 60°, 55°, and 60°; lowest, 18° below, 2 below, and 8° below; mean, 23°, 31.3°, and 28°. Rain-fall, 12.65 inches for first year, 12.35 for second, and 18.77 for third.

The United States signal station at Denver made the following

showing of climatology for the year 1878. Number of clear days
during the year, 163; fair or partly clear days, 137; cloudy days on
which no rain or snow fell, 13; stormy weather, 52 days. Total
amount of precipitation, rain or melted snow, 15.51 inches. This
amount accumulated from the rain or snow-fall which occurred on
127 days—the rain principally in the form of showers. With the
exception of a short interval, the remainder of any day on which
these occurred was bright and clear. The rain-fall of April was but
.05 inches, while that of May was 2.90 inches. The mean barometer
for the year was 29.973 inches. The greatest pressure occurred September 10, sustaining 30.447 inches, and the least April 8, when it
was 29.299. The temperature has ranged from 12 degrees below zero
to 100 above, while the mean annual temperature was 49.52. The
prevalent rains were from the south, giving a total movement of 5,043
miles.

The United States signal office at Colorado Springs gave the mean
temperature for one year at that place as follows: January, 27°;
February, 29°; March, 42°; April, 40.61°; May, 52.84°; June, 67°;
July, 69°; August, 67.31°; September, 58.65°; October, 45°; November, 40.76°; December, 26°. The year 1878 is not given, as it was not
up to the average.

As the weather of April, 1879, is still somewhat fresh in the memory of all, Denver's record is given in order that Eastern people may
see how far it excelled anything experienced along the seaboard or
in the Mississippi Valley. The number of perfectly clear days in
that month was 10; of fair days, 14; of cloudy days, 5; and the
number on which rain fell (including slight showers on some of the
days classed as fair), was 12. The mean humidity was 51.2; the pre-
prevailing wind, " south;" monthly velocity of wind, 5,855; maximum temperature, 76 degrees; minimum temperature, 28 degrees;
amount of precipitation, 2.62 inches; mean thermometer, at 5:43 A. M.,
40.2 degrees; 2:43 P. M., 58.6; at 9:08 P. M., 50.2; mean thermometer, 50.4; mean barometer, 29.940. The least daily range of temperature, was 6 degrees; mean of maximum temperature, 62.3; of
minimum temperature, 38.2; mean daily range of temperature,
24.1. Dates of frosts, April 2d, 3d, 7th, 14th, 17th, and 25th. It
will be seen that changeable, disagreeable, cold, and stormy weather,
such as prevailed during most of the month at the East, was rarely
felt in the capital of Colorado.

"Infinite" is the term used by an old Coloradan to describe in brief the climate of this region. Infinite it certainly is in variety, purity, and sunshine. But the variety comes from difference in altitude, rather than in latitude. The Italian or Virginian warmth of the plains, and the frigidity of "timber line," or of the mountain tops, are experienced on the same parallel and within fifty miles one of another. It is but a short remove from a northern to a southern temperature, and from either to the eternal snows of the Sierras. Owing to the dry, bracing qualities of the atmosphere, heat or cold are not felt as severely or readily as where there is greater moisture and humidity.

The quantity of the snow-fall is not great, except on the great mountain ranges and higher elevations. It never entirely disappears from altitudes of from 12,000 to 14,400 feet. Elsewhere the sun's rays are too powerful to admit of snow laying on the ground a great while unless in case of unusually cold weather, and sleighing is of rare occurrence in many mountain towns.

The mineral springs of Colorado are an important feature and have come to be regarded as a specific for diseases of many kinds. They are more numerous than in any other State, and are found bubbling out of ravine, hill-side, and glen, from Pueblo and Manitou to Utah. Taking all varieties—hot and cold, sulphur, soda, iron, and so on, and the collection is too numerous to mention in detail. Some of them are said to have no superiors in curative qualities. The Pagosa stands at the head of American mineral waters, and the hot sulphur springs of Wagon-Wheel Gap, Middle Park, and other points, are said to be equally beneficial. Still better known to the general tourist are the soda and iron springs, hot and cold, of Manitou, Idaho, and Cañon.

Members of the Colorado State Board of Health have investigated and made excellent reports on the mineral springs of this region. Statements of analyses are given hereafter. Near Ouray, over the mountains, in the far southwestern part of the State, are nine springs, six hot, two cold, and one sulphur, all easy of access and undoubtedly capable of greatly benefiting chronic forms of gastric trouble. The hot springs vary in temperature from 120° to 138°. Two of them give off carbonic acid gas in small quantities. Another is impregnated with sulphur. The carbonates abound, with that of lime in excess. Bath-houses have been fitted up. Near by

BASIN OF THE GREAT PAGOSA SPRING.

is a hot sulphur spring, strong and clear, with carbonic and sulphureted hydrogen gases; temperature 134°. Cañon Creek Springs in the same district embrace a warm chalybeate spring, another hot spring containing bitter salts, beside a hot soda and other springs. Ouray is beautifully located on the Uncompahgre, in the midst of some of the grandest scenery on the continent. There are other mineral waters, including hot sulphur of a lower temperature than a similar spring nearer town. Nine miles below Ouray, in the fertile Uncompahgre Park, are the famous Ouray Springs of the Ute Indians, which they hold in great veneration. Near here is the government Indian agency.

Iron Lake, near the mountain pass between Silverton and the San Miguel country, and twelve miles from the former place, is a great natural curiosity. It is circular in form and only seventy-five feet in diameter and impregnated with iron. The waters taken internally cause a fine appetizing and tonic effect.

That beautiful garden spot, beginning thirty miles south of Silverton, and known as the Animas Valley, is a most inviting locality for invalids. Here are several springs. The waters of three of them are of a red-brown color, containing carbonate of lime, magnesia, and iron; temperature 90°; taste similar to the Iron Chief of Manitou. Another flows a large stream and is of great value to those of debilitated constitutions. This spring is violently agitated, and the escaping carbonic acid gas issues with such force as to resemble escaping steam from an engine, and can be heard for quite a distance. There are also soda springs further down, near the banks of the Animas river.

The great Pagosa ranks first among mineral springs of this part of the West, if not of the whole country. So important are they considered that the United States government has set them and the adjacent grounds apart as a reservation. They are situated east from Animas, and west from Alamosa, and on the south side of San Juan river, about twenty-five miles from its headwaters. The deposit surrounding the larger spring consists mainly of carbonate of lime, and the principal outlet is underground, traceable by the steam rising through seams in the deposit. The altitude is 7,084, and the location is most advantageous for climate and surroundings. The river bottom is very productive; there are good grazing lands and the streams abound in trout, as do the hills and mountains in wild game. This will be a great resort in the near future.

The Parnassus Springs, near the foot hills of the Greenhorn range, and twelve miles from Pueblo, are found to be quite beneficial to invalids who frequent them. The Carlisle Springs, twenty miles from Pueblo, near the Cañon road, are also favorably regarded.

The springs at Wagon Wheel Gap are among the best in the State, and are visited quite extensively by the people of the San Juan region, as well as by strangers. In Chaffee county are several hot springs, whose waters are already beginning to be utilized. The hot spring in Puncha Pass is highly spoken of, and so are those of Cottonwood.

The Cottonwood hot springs, twelve in number, are situated at Mahonville, at the mouth of Cottonwood cañon, some distance south of Granite and near Yale and Princeton mountains. Patients from Leadville and elsewhere have obtained an entire or partial cure of rheumatism and other diseases. Bath-houses, a hotel, and other accommodations have been erected or secured, so that invalids can be properly cared for. The tests of several years show that these waters are highly beneficial for catarrh, rheumatism, dyspepsia, scrofulous affections, and for persons who have been "leaded" while at work at smelting furnaces.

The Hot Sulphur Springs of Middle Park have long been justly famous for their medicinal and healing virtues, and are beginning to be extensively visited now that stage lines are in operation to Georgetown. The surroundings are beautiful, and the fishing and hunting of Grand county cannot be surpassed. The Steamboat Springs in Routt county are also remarkable.

On the following page, in tabulated form, are statements of various analyses made of most of the prominent springs.

So far but two localities possessing valuable mineral waters have drawn large numbers of people from abroad. These are Manitou and Idaho Springs. The reason is mainly due to their proximity to railways, lines of travel, and centres of population, and to improvements made, liberal advertising effected, and excellent hotel accommodations. Other places can be made just as attractive, and possess equal merits, but their remoteness from railways and large towns has acted as a drawback so far. Time will see a great change in this particular as the country becomes settled up, and as health and pleasure seekers become better acquainted with what it has to offer for their advantage and amusement. This season large numbers of visitors may be expected at the Cottonwood, Middle Park, Wagon Wheel Gap, and Cañon City springs.

ANALYSES OF COLORADO MINERAL SPRINGS—CONSTITUENT PARTS IN ONE GALLON OF WATER.

Name of Spring.	Pagosa.	Parnassus.	Carlisle.	Hot Sulphur.	Hot Springs.*	Hot Springs.‡	Tonic Iron.	Navajoe.	Shoshone.	Iron Ute.	Hot Springs.	Little Ute.	Hot Springs.§
Temperature	150° F.	72° F.	60° F.	121° F.	148° F.	140° F.	50° F.	50°.2 F.	48°.5 F.	44°.3 F.	102° F.	51° F.	110° F.
Location	San Juan.	Pueblo.	Pueblo.	Middle Park.	W. W. Gap.	Arkansas.	Estes Park.	Manitou.	Manitou.	Manitou.	Canon City.	Canon City.	Idaho.
Carbonate of Soda	2.74	69.10	8.99	76.43	....	....	....	72.74	51.81	34.62	73.20	76.40	30.80
Carbonate of Lithia	.42	1.04	....	....	†	....	....	.14	Trace.	Trace.	Trace.	Trace.	9.52
Carbonate of Lime	34.42	31.82	22.40	18.86	18.09	2.40	2.08	75.49	63.30	34.44	33.50	22.50	2.88
Carbonate of Magnesia	2.83	13.09	11.39	11.26	2.98	.50	1.53	18.47	....	8.50	12.80	14.00	....
Carbonate of Iron	....	1.30	.30	....	....	Iron Oxide, .13	4.86	....	....	3.37	....	Trace.	4.12
Sulphate of Potassa	4.16	10.76	.70	....	6.13	....	.72	9.46	2.99	4.09	79.30	12.10	29.39
Sulphate of Soda	129.32	2.32	20.00	....	....	....	....	10.74	21.63	18.01	....	....	3.44
Sulphate of Lime	17.06	60.75	11.26	96.62	6.84	.35	.95	23.21	24.57	18.43	18.20	118.00	4.16
Chloride of Sodium	....	....	Trace.	....	....	.21	....	....	....	....	....	....	Sil. Soda, 4.08
Silica	3.33	4.63	Trace.	.54	.62	1.40	.58	.86	Trace.	1.56	....	....	....
Organic Matter	Trace.	Trace.	Trace.	Not determined.	Hydro. Sul., 7.00	1.16	1.31	....	....	....	....	....	....
Total Solids	194.27	194.81	75.04	228.87	41.65	6.24	12.04	211.12	164.30	123.03	217.00	243.00	107.11
Gases	Carb. Acid. Hydro. Sul.	....	....	Hydro. Sul.	Hydro. Sul.	....	....	Carb. Acid.	Carb. Acid.	Carb. Acid.	....	....	....

Hydro. Sul. 19.2 grains, 100 cub. in.

* Chloride of Potassium, 19.08; Sulphide of Sodium, 5.68; Alumina, .39.

† Lithia could have been estimated, had there been sufficient water.

‡ Iodine, .05.

§ Sulphate Magnesia, 18.72.

THE GRAND CAÑON OF THE ARKANSAS.

This cañon, and the first railway excursion therein, was thus described in the Denver Tribune:—The most stupendous achievement of railway engineering over Nature's efforts to obstruct the pathway of commerce, was triumphantly achieved on the seventh of May, 1879, by the Atchison, Topeka & Santa Fe Railway Company, which on that day made the passage of the Grand Cañon of the Arkansas, with a train of cars carrying an excursion party of ladies and gentlemen, numbering over two hundred persons. This rock-bound river pathway became known to the Spanish missionaries as early as the year 1642. From that time it was not known that any animal life had ever passed through it successfully until the winter of 1870. The approach to the Cañon is gradual. The distant hills draw nearer, and the valley of the Arkansas becomes narrower and narrower, until the river is shut in closely on both sides by high mountains, sloping gently away and covered with verdure. Then the slope of the mountains becomes more perpendicular, and the hills become higher, until suddenly the river is completely shut in by mountains with mighty tops. The roar and rattle of the train grows louder and echoes up and down. The train is fairly in the Cañon. It moves slowly. The mountain walls are of a dizzy height, and so close together that, looking ahead, they appear simply to form a crevice, a huge, awful, crooked crevice, through which the miserable little train is timidly crawling. The curves of the Cañon are superb. They constitute the finishing touch to its grandeur, and fill the mind with a fuller appreciation of this great miracle of nature. But the Royal Gorge! Imagine two almost perfectly perpendicular walls rising to a height of 2,000 feet, those walls presenting jagged and irregular masses of rock that on the railroad side hang over the train all creviced and ready to fall in thousands of tons. The road-bed is cut out of the solid rock, and masses of this hang over it stretching out a hundred feet. One cannot look up to the top of this wall on account of these projecting, irregular bluffs, but the height to the top, even as measured by the eye, disturbs the faculties and brings on vertigo. The cooped-up Arkansas rushes madly by, a narrow thread, made still more so by the rocks thrown into it. There is not room to step from the train without pitching into the river. Not a word is

uttered.   The engineer whistles occasionally and timid folks look for
the rocks to fall.   It is really a strain on the mind to take it in; and
this can be only feebly done on a single trip.   Two thousand feet
above you are the tops of the mountain walls.   You are imprisoned

BUENA VISTA GROTTO, NEAR MANITOU.

in a crack, thirty feet wide, and are partially under one mountain
wall.   You can see on the opposite side the gradations of the
verdure, rich below, impoverished above.   And the curves become
more awful as you look ahead or back.

There was no sun in the Gorge, but it slanted down the opposite

mountain wall as the party returned through the Cañon, increasing
the surpassing beauty of the scene. The Cañon is eleven miles in
length and the Gorge a mile and a half. The tourists had seen it all
—seen the greatest natural wonder of the West, and the first train of

MANITOU.

passengers had passed through the Gorge. In cutting the road-bed
in the Cañon the workmen would begin high up on the mountain
wall and blast down to the level of the road. In this way masses
of rock a hundred yards wide have been split from the mountain.
In that narrow crevice it was difficult to dispose of this material.

Some was used for the road-bed, and the rest of necessity was thrown into the Arkansas. This made the already too much shut-in stream still more contracted. The bed of the road is some twelve feet above the river, perhaps more. There is no danger apprehended from the masses of rock overhanging the track. Every inch of this wall, the contractors say, has been examined and tested. Immediately at the entrance of the Royal Gorge is the grandest of its many scenes. The rock-bound sides of the cañon recede from each other with a gradual departure to the height of a thousand feet, when they commence curving inward until the summits of the two sides have approached each other within thirty-five feet, at an altitude of nearly two thousand feet.

Early in April, 1880, this grand cañon railway, together with the entire Arkansas river route to Leadville, in accordance with a decree of the courts, was on the payment of all construction costs delivered over to the Denver & Rio Grande Railway Company. The latter at once began to push the long delayed work of railway building to Leadville, with the expectation of reaching it in three months.

This volume gives the best possible account of routes of travel and of the mining, farming, and stock growing industries, that circumstances permit of, but the State is growing too fast to admit of any publication fully keeping pace with it. New mineral discoveries are constantly being made, new towns are springing up as if by magic, and stage lines and railways are being established where they were unthought of a few months or years before. The author has done his best to keep up with the march of events, and here rests his case with the reader.

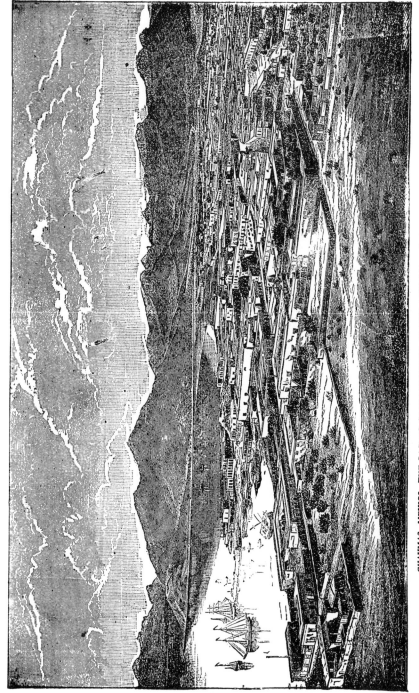

GUAYMAS, MEXICO, THE PACIFIC COAST TERMINUS OF THE ATCHISON, TOPEKA AND SANTA FE R. R.

PART SECOND.

CHAPTER I.

EARLY HISTORY OF COLORADO—AMERICAN ACQUISITION OF AN IN-
LAND EMPIRE — GOVERNMENT EXPLORING EXPEDITIONS — THE
FIRST DISCOVERIES AND THE MARCH TO THE LAND OF GOLD—
ANNALS OF THE FIFTY-NINERS.

France once claimed a large part of the vast region between the
Mississippi river and the Pacific ocean.   In the same indefinite manner Spain asserted ownership northward of the Gulf of Mexico and
westward to the Pacific.   In the year 1540, the Spanish viceroy of
Mexico sent Coronado and a force of troops and followers to explore the country toward the north for gold.   The march was
unsuccessful, and, consequently, this portion of the country, that has
since added so largely to the world's store of the precious metals,
was left for centuries in the undisputed possession of the buffalo
and of the red man.

Soon after the United States purchased from France the immense
territory known as Louisiana the government took steps to ascertain
the value and resources of its newly acquired inland empire.   In
1805, Lieut. Pike and twenty-three soldiers crossed the plains and
partly explored the mountains and headwaters of what has since
become Colorado.   He and his command were captured near or on
the Rio Grande by the Spanish military forces stationed there, and
were afterwards released.   The next expedition was that of Colonel
S.H. Long, in 1819.   The two most prominent peaks of the Colorado
mountain range, as seen from the plains, take their names from these
men.   In 1832 came Captain Bonneville of the American Fur Company.   Fremont's expeditions of 1842 and of 1844 were the most
effective and serviceable of any sent out under the auspices of the
government.

In 1846 the Mexican war began, and the comparatively unsettled and unknown regions forming the northern half of our neighboring republic were taken possession of by the American forces under Doniphan, Fremont, and Stockton. Since then this valuable territory has been found to be enormously rich in the precious metals, and states and territories have been organized therefrom. California, Nevada, Utah, Arizona, New Mexico, and most of Colorado, yielding a gold and silver product greater than all the world beside, are the results of this acquisition. The California gold discoveries of thirty years ago caused such a tide of immigration westward as the world has seldom witnessed. The main overland route was just to the north of the wilderness of plain and mountain that, through its golden treasure, caused a similar excitement ten years later.

Before and after the Mexican war, fur traders visited the Rocky mountains, and some of them built small forts on the Arkansas and Platte rivers. During this same period an active trade was carried on by means of caravans between the western limits of American civilization and Santa Fé, the outpost and trade centre of northern Mexico. The town of Independence, in western Missouri, was the usual point from which the long wagon trains, or "fleets of prairie schooners," set out on their annual voyages toward the setting sun. Many were the battles these daring train men fought with hostile savages, and several expeditions were captured and destroyed. Yet this traffic was so remunerative that men were willing to brave any danger to engage in it.

Up to the close of the war of 1846-8, the Republic of Mexico claimed all of what is now Colorado south of the Arkansas river, and west of the mountains south of the forty-first parallel, and its authority was recognized from the time of Lieut. Pike's capture, in 1806, up to the conquests of Doniphan and Fremont. A few years before the war the Mexican government had donated a princely grant of land south of the Arkansas river to Colonels Vijil and Saint Vrain. This was known as the Las Animas land grant, the full extent of which has not yet been recognized by the United States government, although some other land grants of the old Mexican times have been.

Before or about the time of the Mexican war, Colonel Bent established a trading post or fort on the Arkansas river. This served as a place of refuge and defense from the Indians in after years. Previous to the Colorado gold discoveries, Colonel Craig convoyed government and other supplies through Southern Colorado and into

New Mexico, stopping south of Trinidad to build a wagon-road over the Raton mountains. Some years later he became possessed of a part of the Las Animas grant, and in the State movement of 1865, was the democratic candidate for governor, as against William Gilpin, republican. A few Mexicans had settled near the New Mexican border, on the Las Animas river, prior to 1858.

In 1854 Lafayette Head, recently lieutenant-governor of Colorado, came northward from Taos, New Mexico, with some fifty Mexicans, or rather New Mexicans. They formed the settlement of Conejos, where a Jesuit Mission or school was soon after established. The Apache and Ute Indians attacked and besieged the place in 1855. Other New Mexicans afterwards moved into this same Rio Grande valley of Southern Colorado, and engaged in sheep raising and farming. Major Head built the first flour mill in the southern part of the territory, in 1864. All of the settlements of the Rio Grande and Las Animas were widely separated from one another, as well as from the gold regions of the northern districts. The Mexican populations have ever been devoted Catholics, and but few of them can speak or write the English language. From them comes the Spanish nomenclature of Southern Colorado.

Outside of traders, train men, explorers, Pacific coast emigrants and Mexicans, and the Mormons of Utah, no white men had ventured far west of the Missouri prior to the Green-Russell party of Georgia, in 1858. The advent of these men in Missouri and Kansas caused others to move on to the Pike's Peak country. Prospecting was carried on with moderate success on the tributaries of the Platte river, east of the base of the mountains. The reports carried back to the States by the Russell party spread like wildfire, and thousands prepared to visit the new Eldorado in the following spring. This was the year after the great financial crash of 1857, when so many time-honored houses went down in the storm, and men were ready for almost any venture that promised to better their fortunes. The opportunity was afforded by the gold discoveries of what was termed the Pike's Peak gold region.

The pioneers of the fall of 1858 founded the towns of Auraria, Denver, Boulder, Fountain City, and one or two minor settlements. The ambitious character of these early settlers, some two hundred in number, is shown in their choice of one of their comrades to proceed to Washington to procure a territorial form of government, and of another to represent them in the Kansas territorial legislature. While the mission of the first was unavailing, that of the second resulted in the establishment of a country called Arapahoe, embracing all of western Kansas. That territory then extended to the crest of the snowy range.

With the spring and summer of 1859 came a stampede westward to the land of promise such as has never been equaled except in the case of California. Over the broad expanse of six hundred miles of plain passed an almost continuous stream of humanity. The talismanic legend, "gold," had created a fever and enthusiasm that no distance nor hardship could repress, no danger or difficulty dispel. And so all routes over this ocean of dust and solitude were lined with caravans, and with pilgrims weary and footsore, but ever hopeful of the land and future before them That many were doomed to disappointment is told in the unwritten history of this as of all other mining excitements.

The roving, adventurous spirits that formed the vanguard in the settlement of Colorado came largely from the better and more enterprising classes of the East, West, and South. There was a smattering of good, bad, and indifferent characters, all equally desirous of bettering their fortunes, which, in many cases, could not have been worse. Probably over fifty thousand men aided in this eventful year to enlarge "that western trail of immigration which bursts into states and mpires as it moves." The wide-awake speculator, the broken-down merchant, the farmer, mechanic, gambler, or the wanderer from foreign lands, the cultured and the illiterate, all combined to swell the human tide that was setting in so strongly for the new land of gold out toward the setting sun. While many were admirably adapted to settle and reclaim a wilderness, large numbers soon became discouraged, and returned whence they came. But this could not arrest the progress of the oncoming multitude that followed. Probably nineteen-twentieths of these gold-seekers were as ignorant and inexperienced as regards mining as they well could be, and had but a faint idea of the work to be done or the experience to be undergone in this wild rush for wealth.

In the spring of 1859 the pioneers began to explore the rugged foot hills and mountains that extended on beyond the western border of the plains. Placer and creek mining was at the same

THE COURSE OF EMPIRE.

time prosecuted on all of the streams below the points where they left the hill country. Although gold had been found on South Boulder and on South Clear creek and tributaries a little earlier in the season, the grand discovery that gave the first undoubted assurance of value was that of John H. Gregory. This was made on the present site of Central and Black Hawk. When the news reached Denver and the valley that gold in plentiful quantities existed not forty miles away, there was a general stampede up the various creeks and cañons leading into the mountains. Gregory's discovery proved to be the outcropping of a great gold-bearing vein. The lode and district took their names from him. The Gregory has yielded more money than any other Colorado fissure. Thousands of men were soon encamped on Clear creek, Gregory gulch, and tributary streams, and rich surface deposits and vertical mineral veins were found in great numbers on every hand. Mining districts were organized, and subsequently subdivided, with local laws of their own framing and adoption. This was necessary, as these settlements were outside of the jurisdiction of any state or territory; and had the case been different, special laws for the pre-emption and government of an exclusively mining country would have been necessary. Between these mountain mining camps and the remainder of the inhabited world was a wilderness of plain on one hand and one of mountain and desert on the other—each as broad and boundless as an ocean.

Before the end of May the valleys of the streams that course through the mountains of the country that has since become Clear Creek, Gilpin, and Boulder counties were alive with men. Trees were felled, cabins erected, and sluice boxes constructed for washing the gold from the gravel and "pay dirt." Hand rockers were also used and arastras were subsequently operated. For this surface mining a plentiful supply of water was required.

Most of the more important early discoveries were made by men who had mined in Georgia or in California; many men who had never seen a mine before coming here were afterwards equally fortunate. In the districts of Gilpin county the miners' laws allowed the discoverer of a lode or vein two hundred feet thereon, while any other person could possess one hundred feet in length on the vein and no more. This course was adopted in most other sections. Such limited amounts of territory operated well as long as work was confined to no great depths below the surface. It divided wealth among a large number of people and kept money circulating freely. As greater depths were reached, the results were less and less satisfactory. When it finally became necessary to use steam machinery it was found that this subdivision of territory was a great drawback to the advancement of the country. Years were required in Gilpin county and vicinity to reach the time when the requisite consolidations of these small properties could be made that permitted profitable deep mining. For placer or gulch mining one hundred feet of ground up or down a stream were allowed, each claim being allowed a width of fifty feet. The results here were similar to those of lode mining as regards extensive operations.

As the summer of 1859 advanced the number of people in the above mentioned localities was too great for the opportunities offered, and prospecting parties began to move out in search of other fields. In July one of these passed southward over Mount Rosalia, and for the first time the South Park, radiant and beautiful in its summer garb, greeted the eyes of the gold hunters. Their discoveries on what they called Tarryall creek drew thousands in that direction, and the bustling and prosperous camps of Hamilton and Tarryall became great and famous. One hundred and fifty feet in length along the stream was the allowance to a claim there. This so disgusted the later arrivals, who were unable to secure their share, that they moved over to the Platte and established a camp, which they named Fairplay, where the ground was allotted so as to permit of a division among a larger number of claimants. Jefferson City, near Georgia Pass, was also a lively town, and one camp after another was established as the presence of golden sands or pay-gravel became manifest.

Early in 1859, W. A. H. Loveland and others founded the town of Golden. In Clear Creek county, Idaho was the leading town of the bar and creek mines. In Gilpin there was a cluster of towns adjoining or near one another. These included Black Hawk, Mountain City, Central, Missouri City, and Nevada. Further north there were lively times on the Boulder creeks and along the Saint Vrain and Left Hand creeks and tributaries. Gold Run yielded a hundred thousand dollars that summer. Late in the season gold was discovered on the headwaters of the Blue, over in Summit county. This is on the Pacific slope of the Continental Divide. A few small

CROSSING THE PLAINS IN THE OLDEN TIME.

CROSSING THE PLAINS TO-DAY.

and primitive stamp-mills were brought into the Gregory and Gold Hill diggings late in 1859.

As has been said before the gold hunters of " fifty-nine " were composed largely of the very best material the States could furnish. Men of enterprise and energy, these prospectors and explorers belonged to a class distinct in themselves, whose mission was to create what has been termed the mountain and plains empire. How well they and those that came after have accomplished the work the Centennial State attests. With these pioneers came those accompaniments of civilization, the printing press and free schools. The Rocky Mountain News issued its first number as early as April 23, 1859. Other newspapers in Denver and in the mountains had a varied career in these earlier years, but the only ones that still survive are the News of Denver and the Register of Central. Many of the journals of later date have also done good service and reflect credit on the State and her people.

In the spring of 1859 the Pike's Peak Express Company established a stage line between the Missouri River and the Rocky Mountains. The distance of seven hundred miles or more was soon after made in six days and nights, schedule time. This became the property of Ben Holiday in 1862, and afterwards of Wells, Fargo & Co. The main portion of the immigration was effected by means of wagon trains, and ox and mule teams.

This mode of transportation, occupying weeks or months, was in striking contrast to the rapid locomotion of the present plains travel, wherein the iron horse and palace-car play so important a part. The traveler of to-day can hardly appreciate the difficulties encountered at every step by those who " pioneer " the way for future generations and " rough it " in new and distant mining countries.

There were movements in 1859 looking toward the establishment of a territorial and state government. A state constitution was submitted to the people and rejected by a vote of 2,007 against to 649 for. In October, B. D. Williams was chosen to visit Washington to endeavor to secure the organization of a territory to be called Jefferson. County officers were chosen by those acknowledging the authority of the territory of Kansas, and a convention was elected and assembled for a state organization. State and county officers were finally chosen, but nothing eventually came of this provisional government.

CHAPTER II.

EARLY COLORADO HISTORY—THE PIONEERS OF 1860–63 AND THEIR MOVEMENTS, DISCOVERIES, AND OPERATIONS—GULCH AND PLACER MINING—PRODUCTIVE CHARACTER OF SURFACE DIGGINGS AND GOLD VEINS—THE MINING CAMPS OF THE FRONTIER.

In the spring and summer of 1860 mining was continued with redoubled vigor on streams and gold-bearing lodes from the Saint Vrain to the Arkansas. New comers from the East were plentiful, and many new sections were explored, with occasional rich discoveries. This season bands of prospectors crossed the Park range and the main crest of the Rocky mountains and began mining in earnest on the headwaters of the Blue and the Arkansas. California gulch was washed for gold and began to yield its millions, and in Summit county, Georgia, Humbug, Galena, and French gulches and Gold Run astonished the country with their wealth. Other exploring parties crossed the Sawatch range, and one venturesome band, led by Colonel Baker, made an unprofitable trip through the San Juan mountains and was ordered away by the Indians of that locality.

In Boulder several districts became very productive, noticeably that of Gold Hill. Mining was exceedingly lively in the Gregory and Russell gulch diggings of what is now Gilpin county, especially after the introduction of a reliable water supply by means of the consolidated ditch. Thousands of men were engaged in gulch and lode mining. Sixty quartz mills, mostly of small dimensions, were brought in and set at work. Thirty arastras were also employed, and did good service as long as soft surface dirt was obtainable. Mining affairs were lively on South Clear creek and tributaries, and over in the South Park the gold yield was large and general prosperity prevailed.

In the spring of 1860 the owners of the Pike's Peak stage line established what was known as the Pony Express. This served as a daily fast-mail line between the cities of the Atlantic and Pacific coasts, and was of great value to the business men of those sections previous to the construction of the overland telegraph lines. The scheme was a marvel of American enterprise. Previous to that time over three weeks were required to convey mails by steamer from New York to San Francisco. This Pony Express made the distance

THE PONY EXPRESS.

between the railway terminus on the Missouri river and the Pacific in eight or nine days. Brave men and first-class stock were required, for Indians and highwaymen were often encountered, and the relay stations were sometimes burned and the stock run off. Almost the entire distance of nearly two thousand miles to be traversed was one vast solitude. No delays were permitted, and the mail-bags were kept on the move during the whole time of these long and lonely trips. Horses were changed at every station and riders at intervals of from fifty to seventy miles. The rapid time made caused the government to send the mails overland, and the overland stage and railway, established one after the other, were the results. The construction of the telegraph line to the Pacific in 1862 caused the discontinuance of the Pony Express.

In the summers of 1860-61, there were busy, bustling mining camps on the headwaters of the South Platte, and portions of the South Park were alive with prospectors and miners. These flourished while the placers and gulches were producing largely. As they gave out or failed to pay, the men who had located there abandoned them or moved on to newer diggings of this or other territories. In 1862, rich gold lodes were mined in Buckskin district, and the town of Laurette had a newspaper, theatre, nine quartz mills and, like other camps, numberless saloons, an occasional variety show, and all the gambling-houses that were necessary to make the fortune-hunter contented and happy. In four short summers the population and glory of Tarryall, Montgomery, Laurette, and other camps had departed, and few old timers remained to tell the story of the dead cities of the Park.

Beginning with the summer of 1860, and continuing for several seasons, California and Georgia gulches were enormously profitable. It is reported that many an oyster can of gold dust and nuggets was filled there in a single day. Diggings near Montgomery yielded an average of a pound of gold per day to the man, and Spring gulch, at Central City, produced largely.

Denver grew rapidly in 1860. It was the point of arrival and departure for nearly all who came or left the country, although Cañon City was of some importance in this way for the southern routes from the East to the mines. Brick buildings were erected and large business houses were established at the future metropolis. Among the latter were three banks, one of which is said to have charged from ten to twenty-five per cent. interest on loans per month. Clark, Gruber & Co. added a coining and assay department to their banking-house. The government purchased their establishment in 1862, since when it has been used as a United States assay and refining office. The rates of freight across the plains in those days were from ten to twenty cents per pound. This was less than in 1864–5, but from five to ten times present charges. Some hard characters found their way to Denver and the mines at this time, and several murders were committed by them, which induced the citizens to organize a temporary vigilance committee and do a little shooting and hanging on their own account. This had a beneficial effect. The surviving roughs left the country and order prevailed from that time forward. Auraria and Denver were finally united under one municipal government.

In the stirring mining camps and ambitious cities of the gold diggings frontier mining life could be studied in all its phases. There were many men of many lands in the rude habitations that lined the hillsides and gulches. Their histories would read like romances. One could never tire of listening to the annals of the "fifty-niners," and volumes could be filled with narrative and story of their deeds and adventures. These towns of log cabins, tents, and unpretentious frames had much the appearance of a military encampment. Saloons were numerous, theatrical troupes made regular trips from one point to another, religious services were often held in the open air beneath the mountain pines, and bands of music invited the miner to show or gambling-house at almost all hours of the day or night. Paper money was rarely seen, and gold dust was the universal medium of exchange. This was usually carried in buckskin pouches, and the price of an article purchased was weighed in dust on gold scales used in all business houses. Gold as it came from the gulches was usually valued at about eighteen dollars per ounce. The population of Colorado for many years was ever changing, fresh arrivals taking the place of those who returned to the East or moved on to other territories.

Placers and gulches are what are termed poor man's diggings, because little or no money is required to test their value or put them into producing condition. Every man knew what his claim was yielding when night came. As one writer puts it, "The expressions of satisfaction or disappointment in those early Colorado mining times, when the sluice-boxes were cleaned, would challenge the greed of the miser and the disgust of the spendthrift." Many streams were worked to great disadvantage. Some ground, which should have been operated by long bed rock flumes or hydraulics, was divided among too many owners to secure such improvements, and the miners were in too much of a hurry to get rich and leave the country to think of combining for the slow but eventually sure work necessary for such enterprises. Consequently abandonment followed sooner or later, and no further work was done until consolidations permitted of mining on a wholesale scale.

The amount of gold obtained, however, in the four summers of 1860–63, inclusive, was very large. Good authorities indicate the yield to have been from the creeks, placers, and gulches alone, about as follows, and some give much higher estimates: Boulder county, $400,000; Gilpin, $2,500,000; Clear Creek, $1,700,000; Park, $1,500,000; Summit, $5,000,000; Lake, $4,000,000. This is exclusive of lode mines, which were worked at all seasons of the year, and were immensely productive in Gilpin and in a less degree in most other leading districts.

Congress organized the Territory of Colorado February 26, 1861, embracing the same area as the present State. The first territorial governor, William Gilpin, arrived in Denver, in May, 1861. A census taken at this time showed a population of 25,329, of whom 4,484 were females. H. P. Bennett was elected delegate to Congress in September, being the first Coloradan admitted to a seat in that body. The nine counties previously referred to elected full sets of officers and a legislature was chosen.

Soon after the breaking out of the war of the rebellion numbers of men left Colorado to take part in the great contest. The population had been drawn largely from all sections, but the number who went South at this time was small. The first regiment of Colorado infantry, afterwards changed to cavalry, did good service in repelling the Texan invasion of New Mexico in 1862. That same year another regiment was organized, whose ranks were afterwards reinforced by the fraction of a third regiment. This force won no little credit for itself at the time of Price's invasion of Missouri in 1864. Colorado also had a battery, and late in 1864 a three months' regiment was raised for protection against the Indians of the plains. This did good service in annihilating a large portion of the Cheyenne tribe at Sand creek.

In May, 1862, John Evans succeeded William Gilpin as governor, and S. H. Elbert became territorial secretary in place of L. L. Weld. In the September following H. P. Bennett, conservative,

was re-elected to Congress, receiving 3,655 votes to 2,312 for William
Gilpin, republican, and 2,754 for J. M. Francisco, democrat.

In 1862-3 large numbers of miners left the failing gulch and
placer diggings and what were then called the refractory lode veins.

OLD RANCHO AND TRADING POST ON THE BORDER.

Some went to the new camps of Idaho and Montana and others returned to the States. The gold product of these times was much
larger, however, than in preceding years. The gold-bearing lodes
of Gilpin were in many cases paying enormously and gulch mining
was still very remunerative. The mines at Empire had just been
developed and much gold was obtained by sluicing surface dirt as
well as by quartz milling. The gulches of Summit county were
generally very productive, and California gulch in Lake county was
turning out a round million each summer. Some of the Park county
placers had began to fail, but gold lodes were paying largely near
Buckskin, Laurette, and Montgomery. The same was true of many
localities in Boulder county.

The territory forming Gilpin county had been divided into many
districts and a multitude of veins and claims had been recorded and
worked more or less. Most of these veins were within a strip of
country extending from Black Hawk to the upper end of Nevada and
Russell gulches, embracing a length of but little over three miles.
Located there were the lively wide-awake towns of Mountain
City, Central, Missouri City, and Nevadaville, forming, with Black
Hawk, almost one continuous camp. Here were such lodes as the
Bobtail, Fisk, Gregory, Bates, Hunter, Kip and Buell, Winnebago,
Casto, Gregory Second, Gunnell, Kansas, Burroughs, Gardner, Mercer

County, Kent County, Flack, Forks, American Flag, California, Illinois, Missouri, Alps, Pewabic, and the Patch diggings on Quartz Hill. The lodes were mostly divided off into claims one hundred feet long. Discoverers of veins were allowed twice that amount of territory. Further north in this same county were the active mining camps of Wide Awake and of the Perigo and Gold Dirt section, beside districts of less importance.

Very few of the men who came to Colorado knew anything of mining or milling. They had pretty smooth sailing, however, when engaged in such simple work as placer or creek mining, or while the soft surface dirt or decomposed vein matter held out. When a depth of from sixty to one hundred feet was attained on the lodes great difficulty was experienced by most mill men in saving gold enough to permit of any profits. The soft quartz had been succeeded by ore from which the gold could not be so easily extracted, especially by the amateur mill men usually engaged in the business. In many veins the rich top material had been succeeded by poor rock, and in some places the veins pinched up to nothing. Many believed the quartz had disappeared for good, and sold their claims at almost any figures they could get. So in some localities there was a suspension of work or of production for the want of ore, and in others on account of inability to extract the gold. There were other claims, however, that had not been worked deep enough to get below the decomposed mineral, and at all times there were large numbers of paying mines.

CHAPTER III.

MINING INVESTMENTS IN COLORADO IN 1863-4—HOW MINES WERE
BOUGHT AND STOCKED AT THE EAST IN THE GREENBACK ERA
—EASTERN MINING COMPANY OPERATIONS AND THE CAUSES
OF THEIR FAILURE.

The continued receipts of gold dust and bullion finally created an
interest at the East in Colorado mines. The result was that capitalists began to regard gold-producing properties with favor. The
sale of the Casey mine on the Burroughs lode, in Gilpin county, and
the organization of the Ophir Mining Company in New York, in
October, 1863, were followed by similar transactions one after another.
During the following winter, and in the spring of 1864, there was a
wonderful excitement over mining investments and mining stocks.
Mines—good, bad, and indifferent—were bought up in rapid succession. The more productive claims on the Gregory, Bobtail, and
Gunnell lodes brought one thousand dollars per foot.

The war had inaugurated a speculative era, in which men acquired
wealth with a rapidity they had never before dreamed of being able
to do. Success in one class of operations caused them to embark in
others. The rapid fortunes made in operating mines, and the steady
output of gold, led men into this class of investments. So, in the
days of gold speculation and fluctuating values, a mining stock
board was organized in New York, and mines were purchased and
companies organized. These were often stocked at enormous figures
and swung on values much higher than they would bear. As time
passed on the excitement increased, and so anxious were people to
possess a mine or some mining stock that the quantity of properties
fell short of the demand. Agents were sent out to Colorado to hunt
up and purchase mining claims. It is evident they were not very
particular as to the value thereof so long as they could show evidence
of a record or transaction of some kind. Yet when a company came
to be formed these Eastern manipulators stocked what they paid the
miner but a few thousand dollars for at a hundred times the original
prices. It mattered little, however, just then, for all stocks would

sell, and no one seemed to stop to consider the value of what was behind them.

Nearly two hundred companies were organized in various Eastern cities on mining properties of Gilpin, Clear Creek, and Boulder counties. The capital stocks of many of these mounted way up in the millions, and some of them were held for a time at par. It was the age of greenbacks, and as these promises of the government were steadily depreciating it was feared they would eventually become nearly worthless. This was one inducement for investing in anything that promised to give gold instead. While the results would have been more or less satisfactory with proper management, they could not but be disastrous when the properties possessed no value. Although Wall street had a brilliant and for the most part an unscrupulous set of operators in mines in those days, and the public was in a venturesome mood, this condition of affairs could not last always. The bottom finally dropped out of the market, and from that time forward people were as much too cautious regarding mines as they had previously been too anxious to obtain anything that went by that name.

Meantime very many mining companies had taken steps to work their properties, or at least get rid of their working capital as speedily or foolishly as possible. The entire history of these company investments and operations, with a few exceptions, could hardly have been worse. In the first place, claims of from sixty to two hundred feet only were usually bought on one vein, and as much more on another or many others, instead of making the entire purchase on one vein or lode. Many of these had paid handsomely as long as work was carried on near the surface, but it is an impossibility to successfully work such small claims separately to depths of many hundreds of feet. It took years of depression and abandonment before the time arrived when these false steps could be remedied by consolidation. Poor management, foolish expenditures, or a failure to work the mines, with high prices of labor and supplies, were the other main causes of the failures of the companies. Of course there were some claims that contained nothing of value; but this was not the case with very many of them. This has been proved time and again by Colorado miners, who have leased idle properties of these companies and made fortunes therefrom in one, two, or three years. Instances can be mentioned where some of these lessees have bought mines with the money they have previously made in leasing them. It needed men to operate them who understood mining, just as any line of business needs men at the head who understand it. The man with a process caught a great many of these companies. The stamp mills had been the reliance of the lode miners, and although they lost much of the gold, this was due more to poor equipments, lack of care, and unskillful work than from any fault of that system. With the hope of saving a higher percentage of the gold, many companies took up with the process of some professor or inventor. These process mills required a vast amount of machinery, and cost from five to twenty times what a quartz mill would to-day. When completed some would not save the gold, and all were too expensive to work. They broke up nearly all the companies who meddled with them. The working capital was usually expended in building a mill of some kind, instead of on the claim to see if it had anything that called for a mill. Staffs of heavy-salaried and incompetent officials, dishonesty, and inattention to business, generally wound up these companies, or their money and property, when they were not squandered in the ways above-mentioned. To add to the misfortunes of the period, an Indian war broke out on the plains, and this caused freight charges to rise enormously. At this time the amount of machinery that was being transported to Colorado was enormous. It cost more to freight the inside works of a mill across the plains than a mill could be bought, and freighted, and put up for at the present time. As every company was erecting mills, works, and buildings at the same time, the cost of labor and supplies became very great, which the rebellion and Indian war aided to make still higher. The closing down of many companies and properties caused Colorado mining camps to wear a discouraging appearance in 1865–6.

Yet some of the lodes were so valuable that they continued to produce largely, and many companies operated them for years, with varying success. The condition of affairs was so different then from what it is now, that it was impossible to expect anything like the results of to-day. Since then successful smelting works for handling the richer ores, improved quartz milling, railways, bringing a reduction in cost of labor and supplies, and the knowledge which experience brings from many years of mining, have all come to aid the miner and render his labor profitable.

Careful investigation of the subject shows that not far from three and a half millions were paid Colorado men for mines in the first ten years of mining there. Probably as much more was expended for machinery, freights, and in working claims where no great returns were obtained. The remainder of the millions that were lost or invested in stock operations went to the eastern manipulators. It stopped in New York and at the East. As affairs were then managed, mining stocks proved what most railroad investments do to most stockholders—a losing venture all around. This need not be the case hereafter as regards Colorado mines. Purchasers or company managers should not be in too much of a hurry to build mills, but open the mine first and see if it can supply a mill with ore. They should entrust their mining and milling to experienced miners and mill men, instead of to worthless friends or relatives, and, in fact, conduct matters as they would in any legitimate business. The former are not likely to steal as much, if they were so disposed, as the latter would fool away. It requires as much ability and good judgment to operate a large mine as it does a manufactory or mercantile establishment. These facts are worth the attention of all men likely to be connected with mining operations.

In the spring of 1864 the plains Indians started out on the war-path, and for a time communication between Colorado and the States was almost stopped. Stages were often obliged to fight their way through or back to the nearest station, and were occasionally captured and their passengers massacred. Wagon trains encountered the same difficulties. Some of them containing supplies and mining machinery for the newly organized companies were abandoned on the plains. Scattering farm houses and numerous stage stations were burned, their inmates slaughtered, and the stock stolen. Troops were ordered west to protect the routes of travel, and a regiment of twelve hundred men was raised in Colorado. These, under command of Col. Chivington, attacked and nearly exterminated a band of hostile Cheyennes, which had a salutary effect on surviving Indians. The Cheyennes, Arapahoes, and other Indians continued their warfare on the whites in 1865, and renewed it at intervals down to 1870. Two railways had then been constructed across the plains, and the Indian fell back before the iron horse and other accompaniments of civilization. All of the plains tribes were removed to the Indian Territory in time. The Utes, of the mountains, have been friendly with the whites and hostile to most bands of their own race. By several treaties, dating from 1863 to 1878, they have ceded all of the mountain and park sections of Colorado to the

ATTACK ON OVERLAND STAGE.

whites, except a tract of country in the western part of the State. For these possessions they have received from the government various sums of money and annual allowances of cattle, supplies, and rations.

CHAPTER IV.

In the earlier years of Colorado mining, gold was the only metal
sought for. No one thought of prospecting for silver. Consequently, the main portion of Colorado's mineral wealth was never
dreamed of until more recent times. While many discoveries were
made for several years previous, no great silver yield was obtained
until 1870 and subsequently. The slow growth of this class of
mining was due to a lack of proper ore-reducing facilities and to
milling difficulties. Time has remedied these drawbacks, and all of
the older districts are now supplied with effective mills, smelters, or
amalgamating works. The first discovery of silver lodes in Colorado
was made in Summit county. They carried much lead but not a
large amount of silver, and, owing to their remote location, were
never worked extensively. Late in 1864, float ore was found on
McClellan mountain, near Georgetown, which proved to be rich in
silver. This caused considerable excitement and some lively prospecting in 1865. Valuable discoveries have been made every year
since, and flourishing towns and a large production has been the
result.

For some time gulch and placer mining had been on the decline,
and the miners had been leaving for the newly found diggings of
Montana and Idaho. The ground that had been easiest to get at or
handle had been largely worked out. This was not usually exhausted, for much of it has been worked over and over, with fair
returns, ever since. But more extensive and systematic operations
were required. Vast quantities of pay-dirt and gravel yet invite

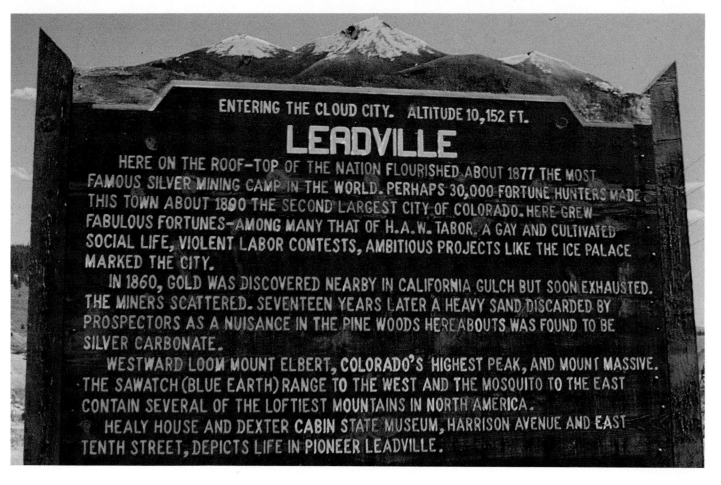

The Leadville story at the city limits, c. 1975

The Tabor Opera House and Main Street, c. 1975

Street scenes, Leadville, c. 1975

Healy House Museum, downtown church, Leadville, c. 1975

the attention of the miner and capitalist, and alluvial mining is once more on the increase.

In 1863, politicians began to agitate the State question. A convention assembled at Denver, July 11, 1864, and framed a constitution for the proposed State. Congress had previously passed an enabling act. The constitution was rejected by a vote of 5,006 to 4,219. In the following year another constitution, framed by a subsequent convention, presided over by W. A. H. Loveland, was adopted by a vote of 3,025 to 2,870. At the same time negro suffrage was defeated by a vote of 476 ayes to 4,192 nays.

On the 14th day of November, 1865, a legislature and state officers were elected. William Gilpin, a republican, was elected governor; G. A. Hinsdale, a democrat, lieutenant-governor, and George M. Chilcott, congressman. In 1864, John Evans and Henry M. Teller were named for senators, but the legislature of 1865–6 chose John Evans and Jerome B. Chaffee. Congress passed the necessary enabling act, but President Johnson vetoed it. A year after, the State movement received a quietus, when the necessary two-thirds vote to override the veto failed to be obtained in Congress.

A list of territorial and state officials from first to last will be found in the Appendix of this book. Also, the vote polled at most of the territorial and state elections.

In 1867, the process-mills having proved a miserable failure, the companies and miners generally returned to the quartz mills, as the only reliance for saving gold at that time. Many mills had been steadily in operation for years, but others resumed work in 1867–8. The result was that the output of gold from Gilpin county was very large up to 1870, and many mines would have paid handsomely, in spite of heavy expenses, had they been properly managed. As it was, the companies began to suspend work in 1869, and one after another of them shut down, until in 1873 but one or two were doing anything. As they left the field, however, the men who had been employed by them began to prospect or mine on their own hook. Some of them leased company properties and others left for the new silver camps of Georgetown and Caribou, and later, for Park county.

In the first decade of Colorado mining, the two leading cities were Denver, the territorial capital, and the mining camp composed of Central, Black Hawk, and Nevadaville. Each had two daily newspapers, and three banks, and churches, schools, and other evidences of civilization, such as any live town is expected to possess. Few places of much larger dimensions could boast of as enterprising populations or of as many citizens of superior abilities, accomplishments, or whole-souled qualities. There were miners, merchants, operators, and gold hunters, who had seen life in all its phases. Some of them were then on the high road to wealth; others had already lost or won several fortunes. The legal profession was also ably represented, as it has always been, and a class of politicians were coming into prominence, that, with business men, mining, milling, and railway operators, have since largely shaped the destinies of the State. It may almost be said, with one exception, that the little city of Central has furnished Colorado's entire representation in Congress for years. Mr. Chaffee was first sent to Congress as a citizen of that place, and Messrs. Teller and Belford reside there, as did Mr. Hill up to about the time of his election to the Senate. Gilpin county justly claims to be the mother of Colorado mining towns and camps. Her miners went forth to help develop new districts all over the mountains, and have exerted a very prominent influence in the direction of affairs wherever they have settled. Notwithstanding the thousands lost to the "old reliable bullion centre" by emigration, she contains more permanent residents now than ever before. As the old citizens move away new ones come to take their places in increased numbers. This is the history of all prominent lode mining districts in the Rocky mountains.

Denver organized a board of trade in 1867. That fall the Union Pacific reached Cheyenne, just beyond the northern border, bringing Denver within one hundred and ten miles of rail communication. This was a great advantage over being six times as far away, but the following year saw the beginning of work on the Denver Pacific. This was to connect the metropolis of the territory with the Pacific line at Cheyenne. The work was consummated in the summer of 1870. In August of that year the Kansas Pacific reached Denver, making two through lines to the East. The same season the Colorado Central railway was constructed from Denver to Golden, located at one of the main gateways of the mountains. The prosperity and greatness of Denver **was then** assured, and she grew rapidly from that time forward. Colorado was well represented at the World's Exposition at Paris in 1867.

Alexander Cummings succeeded John Evans as governor of Colorado in 1865, and was himself superseded in 1867 by A. C. Hunt. In 1869, Gen. Edward McCook became governor. He was followed by Samuel H. Elbert in 1873, but was again appointed in the following year. Then came the last territorial governor, John H. Routt, who was also state governor. In 1864, A. A. Bradford was elected delegate to Congress; then came George M. Chilcott, and then Bradford again. Jerome B. Chaffee was elected for the same position in 1870, and again in 1872. In 1874, Colorado chose a democratic delegate to Congress for the first time, when Thomas M. Patterson received 2,369 majority over H. P. H. Bromwell. This was mainly due to dissensions in the republican party.

The amount of creek and gulch mining grew steadily less as years passed on and the most easily accessible pockets and pay streaks were worked out. Yet most of the headwaters of the Blue and Arkansas and of Clear and Boulder creeks were still profitable to a limited number of miners, and have been so to this day. Recent operations of a more extensive character are at last bringing them into prominence again. From 1865 to 1870, more or less lode mining was carried on in nearly all of the gold-bearing districts then discovered. Many of them gave out temporarily, and have since been idle to this day. Others have had work resumed upon them within the past few years. Numerous lodes, especially in Clear Creek county, which had been worked for gold in former times and abandoned as unprofitable, were at length found to carry their main value in silver. As silver had not been looked for, the best part of their product had been lost. After silver mining became general, they were worked quite successfully.

So intent were the first settlers in the pursuit of gold that little attention was paid to farming or stock growing for many years. A few parties pursued those avocations successfully, however, for good prices could be obtained in the mining camps. Thousands of dollars were sometimes cleared in a season on a single mountain ranch. It was at first believed that the country was worthless for agricultural purposes. During the first winter at Denver no hay was obtainable, and the owners of cattle used in freighting turned them out on the prairie, as they supposed, to die. In the spring the animals were all found in good condition near the Platte river, and some thirty miles below Denver. This settled the stock question. After some reverses from dry weather, it was found that irrigation by means of ditches was necessary to assure successful farming. In 1867–69 these industries had become so extensive that agricultural and industrial societies and fairs were inaugurated at Denver and Boulder. In 1870, several colonies were founded in localities

INDIAN ENCAMPMENT ON WHITE RIVER.

adapted to farming, and peopled by immigrants from the States. The one at Greeley grew and prospered, and has since attained a population of nearly or quite three thousand. The colonies of Longmont and Evans have also grown steadily. The German immigrants of West Mountain Valley were less fortunate, and the organization finally broke up.

In 1871 the Denver and Rio Grande Railway was built from Denver southward seventy-five miles, and the town and colony of Colorado Springs was established at the terminus. Soon after the watering-place of Manitou was founded, and has ever since been the most fashionable pleasure resort of the State. The railway was afterwards extended to Pueblo, Cañon, El Moro, and over the Sangre de Christo range into San Luis Park. In recent years extensive irrigating ditches have been constructed from and near all the principal streams in Colorado, and farming and stock growing have been extensive and profitable industries. Crops are usually abundant and cattle and sheep thrive remarkably.

It came to pass as time went on that Gilpin county was one of the few mining camps where operations were carried on extensively. In fact, it was far ahead of any other district in number of mines and mills, as well as population and product. Most of Colorado's gold export came from there from 1867 to 1870. But all was not smooth sailing by any means. Great difficulty was encountered in saving the golden contents of the ore as the mines grew deeper and deeper. It is asserted that previous to that period the per cent. of the assay saved in most quartz mills ranged from 15 to 40 per cent. only. All outside of that was swept down the streams and lost. Somewhat better work was done in 1868 and 1869.

This condition of affairs could not result otherwise than in disaster, especially as high prices of labor, supplies, and material, enormous plains and mountain freights, bad management and poor mining all combined to exhaust the average product of the mines. Therefore, the establishment and successful operation of the Boston and Colorado Smelting Works, at Black Hawk in 1867-8, by Professor Hill, came very opportunely, and helped to prevent much loss and misfortune that would otherwise have occurred. So many works and processes had failed, that all innovations on the stamp mill method were regarded with a skeptical eye. Yet when Professor Hill continued operations steadily year after year, affording a cash market for the assorted or richer parts of the ore, the immense advantage of these smelters began to be appreciated.

The main bulk of the ores was too poor to admit of treatment anywhere except by raw amalgamation in the quartz mills, but it was found of great benefit to select the richer mineral and sell to the smelter, on account of the very high per cent. saved. Together the stamp mills and smelting works went on adapting themselves and their methods to the country, each working out their special mission. By handling both grades of ore as it came from the ground they made otherwise impossible mining operations profitable. This smelting company went on enlarging their works until, as railroads were constructed, they became almost as important to many silver districts as they had been to Gilpin county. Other concerns were also erected elsewhere. Still the leading gold district was in a very depressed condition up to 1875.

The construction of the Colorado Central Railway up through the mountains to Black Hawk caused several parties to start in to re-open some of the deserted and water-filled company mines. By 1876 the advantages resulting from the operation of the railway became manifest. It was apparently the salvation of the district, for expenses soon fell to such figures that mines, either active or idle, could be handled to advantage. But the grand success that has been brought about in Gilpin county cannot be attributed entirely to the railway and the smelting works, although their assistance has been invaluable. During all the years of failure and disaster, varied with an occasional rich bonanza, the miners and mill men had been becoming familiar with the mineral veins of the country, and were learning how to mine and mill to advantage. The companies who had continued work so long stopped a little too soon. These Gilpin and Clear Creek miners, after some delay, took up the job where they left off, and have made a success of it. So the change in the character of operations, and their present great extent and general success may be attributed to the railway, the smelting works, improved mining and milling, and a class of men with the nerve and energy to wrest victory from disaster.

Up to 1872, several silver mills at Georgetown had been run more or less extensively, of which the Stewart works had turned out the most silver. That year, Hall, Martine and Marshall began to purchase and ship high grade silver ores to Germany. This gave the miners much more of a competing market than they had previously enjoyed, and was the forerunner of the present advantageous ore-buying and shipping facilities. Discovery after discovery had been made on the lofty mountains around Georgetown, and notwithstanding the heavy cost of transportation and of treatment, the yield of ore and of silver increased wonderfully from 1870 forward. In 1872-3, some enormously rich mines were developed, and the product of the district for 1874 exceeded for the first time that of the sister county of Gilpin. Meantime several eastern reduction works had established agencies there for the purchase and shipment of ores.

In 1868 the Printer Boy and other rich gold discoveries in California Gulch turned attention to Lake county once more, although some inviting pockets of quartz near Granite had paid largely in previous years. About this time a company of Boston capitalists inaugurated heavy mining and smelting operations in Summit county, west of the snowy range. Other companies also worked silver mines there, but unsuccessfully.

The discovery of the Caribou silver lode in Boulder county, late in 1869, caused the founding of a town and flourishing mining camp there in 1870. Many veins were discovered, and the district became quite prominent and productive, and is still so. In 1871 came the excitement over the silver bearing deposits of the Mosquito range in Park county. These drew miners and prospectors from all quarters to the slopes and summits of Lincoln and Bross mountains. Owing to the lateness of the season when the more important developments began, and the severity of the winter, the full tide of prospectors did not set in until the spring and summer of 1872. Fairplay again revived and Alma and one or two other towns were soon after founded. So extensive were the deposits found to be that the smelting works at Black Hawk started a branch establishment at Alma. Park county has since been as famous for its silver product as it was for that of gold when the placers were all worked.

Owing to the bad manner in which gold mines had been operated, the cessation of work became a necessity in many quarters. The veins had usually been stripped of whatever of value remained in sight, and then work was abandoned. There was no thought of looking out for continuous development of ore reserves ahead, or of permanent operations of a lifetime character. In these later years this is not often the case, but it took time to bring about the change. The building of the Colorado Central from Golden up Clear Creek cañon to Black Hawk was the turning-point in mining affairs and general prosperity. That permitted of lower and quicker transportation, of cheaper goods and supplies, and of a general reduction of expenses. It made it possible to work mines profitably that were losing concerns before. Several properties resumed work in that and the following year, but so much time was required to put them in order or develop them into pay that no notable advance was made up to 1876. That year the bullion product was a long way in excess of any former period, and each season witnesses an improvement. In 1874 much of the business portion of Central was destroyed by fire, entailing a loss of over half a million. It has since been rebuilt.

In 1872-3 the mountainous country in southwestern Colorado, to which the term of the San Juan region has been applied, began to attract attention. This was of immense extent, and mostly composed of vast chains and spurs of mountains extending far above timber line. Exploring parties had ventured into this section a dozen years before, but no permanent settlements were made beyond the San Luis valley. The discoveries were such that the mountains were alive with prospectors in the summers of 1874-5, and quartz mills and smelters began to be erected. The Summit mountain gold mines attracted much attention, and so did the great silver belts, among which grew up the towns of Silverton, Lake City, and, later, Ouray.

Silver-bearing veins came to notice in what was then Fremont county in 1872-3. In the following years they were quite productive. Still more important discoveries have been made during the past two seasons, showing a remarkable amount of wealth where least expected.

For more than a decade subsequent to the early gold discoveries settlers had been moving into the southern part of Colorado from New Mexico. They were mostly of mixed Spanish and Indian blood, but a portion were descendants of Spaniards only. They engaged in pastoral pursuits, raising large herds of sheep. The amount of their farming was limited and of a primitive character. For years these Mexicans, as they are called, constituted almost the entire population of the southern counties. They have always secured a number of members in the territorial and state legislatures, and, as few of them speak or write the English language, interpreters have always been required. Owing to the rapid increase of American and foreign population, their political influence has been steadily waning.

CHAPTER V.

COLORADO'S POPULATION AND PROGRESS—ANOTHER AND SUCCESSFUL
ATTEMPT AT STATEHOOD—COLORADO'S ADMISSION INTO THE
UNION—THE FIRST STATE ELECTION—RAILROAD BUILDING AND
GENERAL ADVANCEMENT—NEW AND RICH MINING DISCOVERIES
AND MORE SMELTERS—WANTED A MINT OF COINAGE AT DENVER
—CLOSE OF THE HISTORICAL NARRATIVE.

Probably one hundred thousand people had resided in Colorado for longer or shorter periods up to the year 1870. Yet so many left the territory from first to last that the population did not exceed from twenty-five to thirty-five thousand at any one time up to 1868. The census of 1870 showed the number of inhabitants, exclusive of the Indians, to be 39,864. From that time immigration set in steadily from the East, and the railways aided largely to bring this about. Rapid transit by rail was very different from making the long trip across the plains in coaches or in ox or mule trains. It was believed that the population had doubled in four years after the advent of the railway. The generous production of the mines, the harvests of the farmer, and the increase of the stockman had their effect, and eastern people began to move in this direction.

No attempt had been made to secure a state government for over six years up to that time, but in the winter of 1874–5 the subject was again agitated. The movement was successful this time in receiving the sanction of both Congress and the President. It was provided that in case a constitution was framed and adopted by the people that Colorado should not become a State before July 4, 1876. A convention was in session in the winter of 1875–6, of which Joseph C. Wilson was president, and the constitution framed was adopted July 1st by a vote of 15,430 to 4,053. On the third day of October state officers were chosen. There were 27,461 votes polled for governor, and the republican ticket was elected by majorities ranging from 491 to 1,728, Routt's majority over Hughes being 838.

James B. Belford, republican, became congressman for the short term ending March 4, 1877, and Thomas M. Patterson, democrat, for the two years succeeding. The first State legislature, consisting of 49 representatives and 26 senators, assembled at Denver in November, 1876, when the state government was inaugurated. Jerome B. Chaffee and Henry M. Teller, republicans, were elected United States senators. On drawing for terms, the former obtained that expiring March 4, 1879, and the latter that terminating in 1877. The legislature then elected Mr. Teller for the full term of six years from March 4, 1877. For full lists of officials and popular vote of elections see Appendix.

Great advances were made in wealth and prosperity in 1876. The older counties were progressing finely and the San Juan region was promising much for the future. An indication of the high opinion abroad of the State's capacity and resources was the construction of another through line of railway from the Missouri. The Atchison, Topeka & Santa Fe Company completed their road west to Pueblo this year, making Colorado's third outlet to the East. The last territorial legislature appropriated the sum of ten thousand dollars for the purpose of having Colorado properly represented at the World's Exposition at Philadelphia in 1876, and Governor Routt appointed Messrs. Decatur and Richmond commissioners.

The succeeding year was still more prosperous. The farmers, who had experienced two bad seasons, were then rewarded with bountiful harvests, which set them on their feet once more, or. gave them heavy surpluses. The mines made a larger gain than had been known since the early discoveries and developments. Increased railway and ore reducing facilities were being supplied in various quarters. The Colorado Central Railway was extended into Clear Creek county as far as Georgetown, and north from Longmont, connecting with the Union Pacific at Cheyenne. In the south, the Denver & Rio Grande road was pushed on over the Sangre de Christo mountains to Garland, and afterwards to Alamosa, on the Rio Grande. But rapid as had been the progress, and handsome as had been the gain of previous years—the year 1878 eclipsed them all. This is true regarding financial improvement, as well as increase of population and production. The yield of gold and silver showed a gain of nearly fifty per cent. over the best previous year. The old districts that had been the main reliance in former times, all surpassed their previous records, with one exception, while Lake county came to the front and distanced every one of them. The production of that section had been small for several years; but the new carbonate mines of Leadville paid handsomely in 1877. Last year, however, their output surprised almost everyone. Yet, it was but a fraction of what will be recorded hereafter. As during the two preceding years, Colorado maintained her place as one of the few States extensively engaged in railway building. The Atchison, Topeka & Santa Fe railway was extended southward over the Raton mountains into New Mexico, and a heavy force of men were kept at work blasting a way through the Grand cañon of the Arkansas for the Leadville extension. This was the season of the railroad war for the possession of that route, in which the above-named company and the Denver & Rio Grande were engaged. The Denver & South Park road, which had been built as far as Morrison, in 1874, had its line completed from Denver up Platte cañon to the mouth of Hall Valley, at the close of 1878, or soon after. Central was also afforded rail communication this year.

The second biennial State election occurred October 1, 1878, with three tickets in the field. The republican nominees were elected by pluralities ranging from 1,923 to 2,890. The greenback nominee for governor received a total vote of 2,783. The republican candidate for governor was Frederick W. Pitkin, and the democratic W. A. H. Loveland. For Congress, Thomas M. Patterson was the democratic nominee and James B. Belford, the republican. The total vote polled in Colorado was from 28,876 to 28,900. See Appendix. The second legislature assembled January 1, 1879, and the State government was inaugurated January 14th. After an exciting contest, Prof. N. P. Hill received the republican caucus nomination, and was elected United States Senator to succeed Mr. Chaffee, for the term of six years, from March 4, 1879.

While the mines of Leadville were attracting attention far and wide, and causing a stampede for the land of carbonates all over the country, several valuable districts were developed in other quarters. Not far away great deposits of argentiferous galena were found in Summit county, and during the same fall of 1878 the unexpected discoveries of Silver Cliff drew large numbers of people and started a promising mining camp. The magic cities of these several localities are growing rapidly, and are evidently the forerunners of more to come among the mountains and valleys of western Colorado. There is seemingly no end to the mineral wealth of these mountains, and each season witnesses the disclosure of some new district rich in gold or silver. The immense extent and value of Leadville's mines and traffic is attested by the continual blockade of transportation facilities, and by the fact that three different lines of railway are all building in that direction. It is further shown in the growing ore production and the recent and projected addition of a score of smelting furnaces. The capacities of other districts are likewise being duly appreciated. Several extensive smelting establishments have just been completed at Golden, which is so situated as to be a natural receptacle for ores shipped for treatment from Gilpin and Clear Creek counties. The Boston and Colorado Company have erected the finest works in America at Argo, two miles from Denver. It is evident that Colorado will hereafter reduce her own ores and turn out her own bullion to a far greater extent than heretofore.

What Colorado and the entire mineral region between the plains of Colorado and Nevada require is a mint of coinage. The government should establish this at Denver. No other point can compare with it in natural and general advantages for that purpose. It is located midway between British America and Mexico, and is the most central point for Colorado, and for all the gold and silver bearing territories not adjacent to the Pacific coast. It is the metropolis of a mining region whose production equals nearly all others, excepting California and Nevada. It is evident that Colorado will soon surpass even those favored localities. A yield of from sixteen to twenty millions this year, and as much more from neighboring territories, whose bullion would be tributary to such an institution, calls loudly for coinage facilities. A product of ninety millions since 1859 is one this State may well be proud of, especially when it appears that work in earnest has but just begun. Montana has commenced shipping ores to Argo, recognizing that as a better market than the East or her own local works. The extensive smelters of Argo, Golden, Pueblo, and Leadville, and the mills of Gilpin and Clear Creek, are doing a combined business of immense proportions. Denver is the centre of a system of railways radiating in all directions. Supplies are as cheap there and expenses as low as in any other place that could be selected. Therefore, the government may as well do a portion of its coinage there as at any other point, while the producing miner will be vastly benefited if relieved from the heavy expense of bullion shipments to the East.

The United States geological and geographical surveys, conducted under the supervision of Prof. F. V. Hayden, by authority of the national government, have been an important factor in making known the nature and character of the immense region beyond the Missouri river. These have been carried on with the assistance of competent and experienced officials, army officers, civilians, and experts ever since 1869, and a very considerable amount of time and attention has been devoted to Colorado by members and divisions of the survey. The labors and reports of Messrs. Hayden and Wheeler have been of great value to the state and country.

The year 1879 brought an accession of many thousands to the population of Colorado, and the present time is witnessing an incoming tide of immigration rarely equalled in Western history. It has been predicted that the State will have gained fifty thousand additional settlers before the year closes. The mining product of 1879 showed the enormous increase of about eighty per cent. over 1878, which was, by far, the best preceding year. Denver and Leadville added largely to their population, the latter doubling in size. In the summer and fall of 1879, a large portion of Gunnison county was explored, and, although but slightly prospected, many valuable mining districts were discovered. Gunnison and Summit are now the great theatres of the prospecting excitement.

In the fall of 1879, the Ute Indians, who, for many years, had been comparatively friendly to the whites (although committing an occasional murder) became hostile, murdered Indian Agent Meeker, and perpetrated other outrages, after which they attacked an advancing force of soldiers who were on the way to White River Agency. The pursuit of the savages was prevented by orders from the Interior Department at Washington, and negotiations were begun which resulted first in the release of the female captives of the Agency, and finally in a treaty for the cession of much of the Indian country to the whites. This treaty provided, that for the payment of certain moneys and annuities, the Indians would retire to new reservations provided for them in and near New Mexico, on the lower Grand river in Colorado, and on the Uintah reservation of Utah. The result is, a vast tract of country has been opened to white immigration. This includes a small amount of agricultural lands along the rivers, some grazing country, and an extensive mountainous region that is believed to be rich in minerals.

The most important era in Colorado history is the recent discovery, development and extraordinary production of Leadville carbonate deposits, through which an unprecedented interest in mining has been awakened, leading to countless Eastern investments and mining organizations for all parts of the State. Noteworthy events of the time have been Colorado's rapid exploration and development, the advent of leading Pacific coast miners, whose millions have secured many of the best mines, the organization of New York mining boards, the transfer of the mining headquarters of America to New York, the westward movement of Eastern capital and labor, and the attention the press bestows on mining matters; in short, "a mining boom of enormous proportions" has been inaugurated, with Colorado the investor's and fortune-hunter's favorite by long odds.

The year 1880 witnessed a renewal of railway building, which the rivalry of two corporations had partially suspended. Railways are now going forward to Leadville and to Silverton by the Denver & Rio Grande Company, while the Denver & South Park, which has been steadily building southwesterly into the mountains, will serve as the great avenue of trade for the South Park, the Gunnison, and northern San Juan regions. Colorado's present rapid growth and prosperity is unprecedented. The wonderful production of the mines and the heavy investments of Eastern and California capital, with the vast influx of visitors and settlers, all go to enrich and bene-fit her people. After years of patient endeavor and discouraging obstacles, the people of Colorado have the satisfaction of knowing that theirs (above all others) is the favored land, and that it leads the world in the production of the precious metals.

In closing this brief narrative of Colorado's settlement, rapid growth and general progress, it is perhaps needless to speak of the prevailing prosperity or of the inviting opportunities for capital or labor. The situation is beginning to be comprehended to a greater or less extent at the East as well as West. Much information, sta-tistical and descriptive, can be gained by carefully perusing this volume. A trip to Colorado would be far more effective, and the only way to obtain a true appreciation of her wealth, enterprise, and general attractions. The reader can then see for himself how new regions are explored, the wilderness settled up, and towns and cities built; how energetic and skillful miners go down into the depths for precious ores that the mill-men or smelters subsequently turn into bullion.

PART THIRD.

CHAPTER I.

COLORADO—PAST AND PRESENT PROGRESS AND FUTURE PROSPECTS—
GREAT MINERAL WEALTH OF THE ROCKY MOUNTAINS—MINING,
FARMING, AND STOCK GROWING—STATE AND COUNTY STATISTICS,
ASSESSED VALUATION, EDUCATIONAL FACILITIES, AND FACTS RE-
LATING THERETO—RAILWAYS AND RAILWAY BUILDING.

The remarkable advance recently made by Colorado in the development of mineral resources and the consequent accession of population and increase in production and wealth, have been among the most
noteworthy events in the history of the West. While every industry
of the State seemed to receive a fresh impulse some three years ago, it
was not until within the past twelve months that this progress was so
marked as to excite general notice. What have aided to fix the attention of the whole country and turn the tide of humanity Colorado-
ward more than all things beside are the wonderfully productive
bonanzas of Leadville, and while they seemingly form the principal
magnetic attraction, all parts of this matchless region will be correspondingly benefited. Nor should the intrinsic worth of other sections be overlooked in the prominence accorded the carbonate fields,
for all through these Colorado mountains an extent and variety of
mineral wealth is embedded and is now being explored such as has
seldom, if ever, been found elsewhere. The consequence is that
capital and labor are both moving in the direction of the legendary
star of empire, and gold and silver mining is attracting the world's
attention to a greater extent than for many years. Month after month
witnesses an increase in the volume of immigration as each successive disclosure is followed by others still more marvelous. So we

see people from all parts of the country, and even from Europe, coming to swell the population of this most thrifty of states, while yet other multitudes are contemplating a similar movement.

With the ever-occurring discoveries of new mineral veins and belts a steady and often rapid increase in the yield of bullion is recorded in the older districts. So, while the field of operations is continually enlarging by fresh accessions, mines that have been pouring out their hidden treasures for years are being opened for greater things in the hereafter. Rapid as has been the exploration of this wilderness of mountains of late, the present season is likely to eclipse all previous periods in that respect. There seems to be no limit to the wealth awaiting the advent of the miner, and as each new discovery is reported the fact becomes only the more evident that but little of the State has been half prospected, and the remainder almost entirely unexplored.

The extraordinary developments that have been and are being made are convincing men from abroad, in common with the most enthusiastic mountaineers, that Colorado's store of the precious metals exceeds that of any other State. At the same time it is generally conceded that a better field for investment is offered here than elsewhere, and that the State has a future before it of the most promising character. The supplies of gold, silver, and coal, although but little encroached on up to the present time, are seemingly inexhaustible, and lead and copper aid to a considerable degree to swell the value of veins carrying the first mentioned metals. Iron is also found in large quantities and may yet prove the source of an important industry, while the deposits of salt, lime, gypsum, fire-clay and other materials are all proving serviceable.

Colorado's agricultural and pastoral resources are quite extensive, and if the mining and city population becomes too great for home supplies, the bountiful fields of the neighboring State of Kansas are a never-failing resource. As it is, a ready cash market in the mines and business marts is afforded to both farmer and stock grower. While the extent of arable land is limited, compared with the State's total area, it embraces many thousand square miles, and additional tracts are being made available every year by artificial irrigation. The stock growing industry has been increasing in importance until the annual exportation of cattle, sheep, and wool makes a handsome showing. This industry has been remarkably and uniformly profitable, both on the plains and in the parks. For the past two years Colorado has raised as much wheat and five times as much beef as is needed for home consumption. Splendid farming and pastoral lands in western Colorado will in time be peopled by an industrious population.

The climate, mineral waters, and scenic attractions of Colorado, which may almost be considered as resources in themselves, have been sufficiently referred to in the first part of this volume. They alone will bring people and money to this section; for many men of wealth are making this State their place of residence on account of its superior attractions and inducements in those respects.

The mines of Colorado have produced, from 1859 up to date, something like eighty-two millions, in round numbers, of which ten and a half millions were the result of last year's operations. The indications are now good for a yield of nearly twenty millions, and perhaps twenty-five millions, in 1879. The possibilities are so great that it is impossible to predict with accuracy. The farming products amount to several millions per annum, and the pastoral districts make an equally creditable return.

The State auditor gives the assessed valuation of real estate and personal property, according to the returns of 1878, at $43,072,648.26. The enormous growth of Leadville, Denver, and some other localities, and the State's gain in population and property since then indicate an assessed valuation at least one-half larger for the present year. As it was, the actual value of the property assessed last year, together with that which escaped assessment, must have approached $65,000,-000. The mines, which are the chief source of wealth, are not assessed nor taxed at all—nor can they be, according to the provisions of the State Constitution, for nearly eight years to come. Were these counted in the general valuation, the total would possibly run up to hundreds of millions. The assessed valuation of 1878 was divided among various classes of property, of which the principal are given below.

Land and improvements	$9,755,038 17	Horses	$1,914,339 50
Railways	5,013,685 83	Mules, etc.	244,050 00
Merchandise	2,599,660 00	Cattle	4,928,147 50
Capital and manufacturers	205,099 00	Sheep	1,026,482 25
		Money and credits	2,130,650 07
Town and city lots	11,035,620 75	Household property	902,062 00
		Bank & other shares	730,396 00

The counties, thirty-one in number, wsth their county seats, area, estimated population in 1879, assessed valuation in 1878, and vote at the last State election is given in the table below. The area of the newer and a few of the older counties is estimated. Lake county which contains Leadville, and from which Chaffee county was set off last winter, probably has a valuation of over $4,000,000 at the present time, or nearly seven times that given for last year. Denver and its county of Arapahoe have also greatly enhanced the total valuation of property, and so have many other towns and counties.

COUNTY.	COUNTY SEAT.	VALUATION, 1878.	AREA, Sq're Miles.	POPULATION. 1879.
Arapahoe	Denver	$11,076,761 00	4,800	31,000
Bent	Las Animas	2,279,376 00	9,126	3,000
Boulder	Boulder	3,097,320 00	792	12,000
Chaffee	Granite	....	1,240	500
Clear Creek	Georgetown	1,932,991 31	437	3,000
Conejos	Conejos	244,346 00	2,558	6,000
Costilla	San Luis	319,571 90	1,685	4,000
Custer	Rosita	500,654 00	1,100	5,000
Douglas	Castle Rock	951,713 00	833	3,000
Elbert	Kiowa	1,202,052 52	6,030	2,500
El Paso	Colorado Springs	3,076,335 00	2,628	9,000
Fremont	Cañon	946,363 00	1,268	4,500
Gilpin	Central	1,827,997 00	158	7,500
Grand	Hot Sulphur Springs	63,866 75	4,278	500
Gunnison	Gunnison	62,014 00	11,000	1,500
Hinsdale	Lake City	564,396 50	1,528	4,000
Huerfano	Walsenburg	796,038 38	1,584	5,000
Jefferson	Golden	1,988,529 00	792	7,500
Lake	Leadville	603,858 92	400	15,000
La Plata	Parrott City	254,447 00	4,095	1,500
Larimer	Fort Collins	1,502,330 00	1,825	5,000
Las Animas	Trinidad	1,455,230 00	9,072	12,000
Ouray	Ouray	220,622 95	2,333	3,000
Park	Fairplay	796,239 00	2,222	3,000
Pueblo	Pueblo	3,069,639 00	2,412	9,000
Rio Grande	Del Norte	501,874 00	1,332	3,500
Routt	Hayden	74,661 00	5,000	300
Saguache	Saguache	637,607 00	3,312	3,000
San Juan	Silverton	255,378 00	726	3,000
Summit	Breckenridge	169,360 00	8,289	6,000
Weld	Greeley	2,583,827 00	10,494	7,500
	Total	$43,055,419 22	.....	190,300

At the present rate of increase of population and wealth, the true figures of many parts of the State would far exceed those given above. New towns and mining camps are springing into existence every month, and some of the farming districts and business centres are growing rapidly. The immigration for April must have been over ten thousand, and for May, fifteen thousand. The A., T. & S. F. Railway alone brought in 936 people in the last week of May, and there are two other through routes from the East. Before the end of summer the State may have a population of a quarter of a million, and a valuation of one hundred millions, exclusive of mines. With mines included, the valuation would be at least three times that sum.

The following-named plains counties are largely engaged in farming and stock growing: Arapahoe, Weld, Larimer, Jefferson, Douglas, El Paso, Fremont, and Las Animas. Those devoted mainly to stock growing are, Elbert, Bent, Pueblo, and Huerfano. Boulder county is about equally divided between the plains and mountains, the former embracing a fine farming district and the latter rich in minerals. There are considerable farming and stock growing carried on in the mountain county of Custer, and in Saguache, Rio Grande, and La Plata counties in the San Luis Park and San Juan regions. Costilla and Conejos counties are mainly engaged in pastoral pursuits. Of the mountain mining counties considerable stock is raised in Park, Lake, and Grand, and more soon will be in Gunnison, Routt, Summit, and Ouray counties. While farming is pursued to some extent all through the mountains, it is proportionately small as compared with mining in Gilpin, Clear Creek, Summit, Lake, Hinsdale, San Juan, and Ouray.

The growth of Colorado towns and cities is shown by the following, the census returns of 1870, for towns then in existence being compared with estimates of population in 1875 and 1880:

	1870.	1875.	1880.
Denver	4,579	17,000	33,000
Leadville	None	None	25,000
Central, Black Hawk and Nevadaville	4,401	5,000	6,500
Pueblo and South Pueblo	666	4,500	5,500
Colorado Springs	None	2,500	5,000
Georgetown	802	4,000	4,000
Boulder	343	2,800	3,700
Trinidad	562	2,000	3,500
Golden	587	2,000	3,000
Silver Cliff	None	None	3,500
Greeley	480	2,000	2,750
Lake City	None	300	1,200
Canon	229	800	1,200

	1870.	1875.	1880.
Del Norte.........................	None	1,000	1,000
Rosita............................	None	1,200	1,200
Kokomo...........................	None	None	1,000
Silverton.........................	None	300	600
Brownville and Silver Plume........	150	700	1,000
Gunnison.........................	None	None	1,000
Buena Vista.......................	None	None	1,000
Fort Collins......................	None	None	1,000

Leadville has grown from nothing to its present size in two years. Denver will expend over a million dollars in new buildings this year. Two mammoth hotels and ten or twelve hundred buildings and residences are in course of construction there.

No better evidence of Colorado's present and prospective capacities and importance can be asked for than in the continuous railway construction that is going on within its borders. Although railway building has almost ceased in nearly every quarter since the financial disasters of 1873, this is one of the few states where it is still vigorously prosecuted. During the past three years the mileage has been nearly doubled, and is still being increased. Various enterprises are projected, some of new roads and others of extensions of old ones that are likely to add considerably to the rail facilities before the year is out.

At the beginning of 1879 there were 1,218.6 miles of railway in operation within the limits of the State, or 174 miles more than a year previous. Of that amount 758.16 miles were of the standard broad gauge, and 460.44 miles of narrow gauge. Of this railroad mileage the Atchison, Topeka & Santa Fe has 259 miles, the Denver & Rio Grande 327, the Kansas Pacific 195, the Colorado Central 177, the Denver & South Park 75, the Boulder Valley 26, the G. B. & C. 5½, Denver Pacific 99 and Union Pacific 9. Early in 1880, the D. & S. P. railway had completed 60 additional miles, and is still building, and the D. & R. G. is pushing several extensions.

The assessment of 1879 places the total taxable value of railway property in Colorado at $7,687,457. This heavy increase over the previous year is in accordance with the plan adopted for an advance of general assessments of all classes of property in the State. The consequence will be a much larger showing for the State's valuation than that noted in the first part of this chapter. It is evident that some 250 miles or more of railway will be constructed in Colorado during the ensuing year.

Colorado has ever been a liberal supporter of the press. No other section or community of anything like the same number of inhabitants contains as many newspapers. There are fourteen dailies with weekly editions, and forty-four weeklies—a pretty large list for a

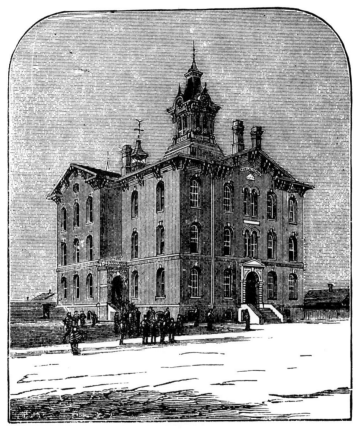

DENVER HIGH SCHOOL.

population of less than two hundred thousand. The superior character of a very large portion of these speaks well for the State and its people. There are four well conducted dailies in Denver, and another recently established, three in Leadville, one in Central, one in Colorado Springs, two in Pueblo, and two in Trinidad. The News and Tribune of Denver are the largest, handsomest, and best dailies between Saint Louis and San Francisco. The first was founded in 1859, and the latter in 1867. There are many weekly as well as daily papers in the various towns and cities that are a credit to their owners and of substantial benefit to the localities where they are published. A full list of Colorado newspapers will be found in the Appendix.

Colorado has a public school system in no way behind that of any of the older States. It is modeled after the best established organizations elsewhere, with such improvements as have been deemed necessary. The plans and labors of its early originator and champion, Prof. H. M. Hale, have been effectually followed and continued by his successor, the present Superintendent of Public Instruction, Joseph C. Shattuck. The public school law of 1876—since slightly amended—provides for teachers of the very best classes, and for other regulations and requirements of the most systematic character.

GREELEY PUBLIC SCHOOL

Owing to the transitory nature of the population, public schools did not receive the attention prior to 1870 which they have since been favored with. Still they were liberally endowed in the few large towns, and some excellent private academies had been established. In 1871 there were 160 public schools in the Territory, and 7,742 persons between the ages of six and twenty-one years, 4,357 of whom were enrolled. There were then 80 school buildings, worth $82,574, and $44,148.95 were paid for teachers. The progress which has since been made can be seen by a glance at the last report of the Superintendent of Public Instruction.

In 1878 Colorado had 26,473 persons between the ages of six and twenty-one years, of whom 16,641 were enrolled in the public schools, beside a larger number attending private schools and academies. There were 249 school edifices valued at $474,771, the number of teachers employed was 567, and the total expenditures for the year were $243,850.37. The figures for the present year will be much larger. It must be remembered that much of the population of Colorado is widely scattered, so that means cannot be afforded everywhere for securing free school advantages. But in every town, village, or settled farming or mining district schools are in operation, and every city or town of importance has one or more graded schools, with handsome and costly buildings for the accommodation thereof— for nowhere is money expended with such proportionate liberality on schools or churches as in Colorado. Some of the leading counties made the following showing as regards public schools in 1878 :

COUNTY.	No. Pupils Enrolled.	Av. Daily Attendance.	No. of Teachers.	Av. Cost per Month per Pupil.	Value of Buildings, etc.	Expenditures for Year.
Arapahoe.......	3,464	2,160	80	$2 28	$190,085	$77,100
Boulder.	1,957	1,129	78	1 89	41,495	21,593
Clear Creek.....	945	493	17	2 07	29,450	6,968
El Paso.........	1,056	556	31	3 00	43,500	8,909
Gilpin	954	566	19	2 76	34,150	14,287
Jefferson	961	541	39	2 68	26,195	11,997
Las Animas.....	917	545	27	4 41	......	3,336
Pueblo..........	758	526	35	3 27	33,280	6,430
Weld	1,118	683	50	3 34	44,132	16,677

The average daily attendance would be larger but for the numerous private schools, academies, and seminaries, the scattered population in many sections, and the yet imperfect school facilities in some of the Mexican districts. Several of the leading towns of the State are now erecting school buildings that will cost from twenty to thirty thousand dollars each, which will add greatly to the total value of school property.

By territorial legislative enactments, provision was made for a School of Mines at Golden, in 1870 ; for a Deaf Mute Institute at Colorado Springs at a subsequent date ; and for a State University at Boulder, and an Agricultural College at Fort Collins in 1874–6. All of these were aided with appropriations for buildings and for maintenance. The first two of these State institutions have been in

STATE UNIVERSITY, BOULDER.

successful operation for several years. In September, 1877, the State University began its educational work in the elegant buildings prepared for it at Boulder, and has since been most successfully conducted. The building for the State Agricultural College at Fort Collins is now ready for occupation. There are private and sectarian schools, colleges and seminaries in nearly all of the larger towns.

In subsequent chapters the farming and pastoral interests will be touched upon, and some facts and figures given relating thereto ; after which considerable space will be devoted to mining—the great industry of the State. Facts, figures and detailed statements will be given concerning mining and milling and the mineral resources of counties and districts.

CHAPTER II.

FARMING ON THE PLAINS AND IN THE MOUNTAINS — WHAT IS DONE BY ARTIFICIAL IRRIGATION—THE FINEST CROPS IN THE WORLD — FACTS AND FIGURES REGARDING THE YIELD OF CEREALS, VEGETABLES, ETC. — SUPERIORITY OF COLORADO WHEAT, BEEF, AND DAIRY PRODUCTS—LARGE PROFITS IN FARMING.

In the rush for gold in the earlier years of Colorado mining but little attention was paid to agriculture. That was considered too slow a method for accumulating wealth. Recent years have shown that it is not so slow as was supposed. A few of the pioneers, and less fortunate gold hunters, who were not disposed to leave the country, began to cultivate the soil. They were incited to do this from the occasionally high price of provisions, and in view of the fact, since everything consumed came from the States, that a scarcity might some time bring with it high prices to the farmer. It was not long until the lands bordering the streams on the plains and the valleys of the mountains were found to be extremely fertile.

The lack of a sufficient and regular rainfall acted as a drawback, until the true situation and resources of the region were understood. The disappointments attending early agricultural efforts led to experiments in artificial irrigation, so successfully conducted among the Mormon farmers of Utah. Then ditches began to be constructed from the rivers out onto the arid plains. The natural fall of the streams was from seven to one hundred feet per mile. These ditches, by the slight fall of two or four feet per mile, could, in the course of a few miles, be extended far out on to the sloping uplands bordering the stream. From these larger ditches water gates led into smaller or branch ditches, used as required. Thus regular and continuous supplies of water were obtained during all of the warmer months; for when most needed the streams were the fullest of water from the gradual melting of the snows on the mountains. The results of irrigation were so favorable, and the mines afforded such a high-priced ready cash market, that farming was more and more successfully prosecuted with each succeeding year.

While the amount of cultivated land was small during the first decade of the territory, farming had become an important industry in 1867–9 along the streams in Boulder, Larimer, Jefferson, and Arapahoe counties. The scattering farms or ranches of those days produced abundant crops, and each year saw the river bottoms slowly settling up with an industrious and thrifty population. In 1870 a more rapid movement began in the way of peopling the country, and in making what had been termed a desert bloom, blossom, and reward the husbandman. Several colony organizations were perfected in the States to the eastward, and hundreds of families were transported to the various localities selected for the purpose. Near the junction of the Cache la Poudre and the South Platte river the colony of Greeley was founded. That of Evans was established four miles further south, and that of Longmont on the Saint Vrain. These organizations were co-operative as far as the sale of lands, the construction of irrigating canals, and carrying on general improvements were concerned. Outside of that, the lands were owned and cultivated by colony members who had purchased them. Other colonies were also established, among them that of Colorado Springs in 1871.

In recent years, settlers have been locating on farming lands all along the valleys of the streams in great numbers, and the advance which this industry has made has been both rapid and gratifying. Farms large and small extend through all available localities, and the latest and most improved machinery and implements of husbandry are in use. Irrigating canals and ditches of great extent and value are constructed every year, and each season sees thousands of acres of land reclaimed and made valuable. The steady increase of population in the mining regions and trade centres more than keeps pace with that of the farming districts, thus insuring a ready demand for whatever may be offered. Severe losses were sustained in several seasons from grasshoppers, but not since 1876. The farmers have paid much attention to these pests and to their habits and movements, and are confident that the crops can hereafter be protected from serious damage.

The last two seasons were so favorable for farming that some very extensive land reclaiming enterprises have been carried through, and others of great magnitude are projected. New canals and irrigating ditches have been constructed from a score of streams, and the tillable belts of land are steadily growing wider. Some of these canals are six, ten, and even fifteen feet in width, several feet in depth, and carry a great volume of water for many leagues out on to the uplands. Reservoirs or lakes are prepared here and there, in order that the water supply may the better be economized, and in the general conduct of affairs the best interests of the farm, the dairy, and of stock are considered. Long experience, intelligent management, and adaptation to circumstances and locality are causes of the great success of the husbandman in this State. As new ditches are constructed, and additional areas supplied with water, these lands are purchased or pre-empted and settled on—and so the amount of tillable land is steadily growing larger. Still further gains and advances will be made this year with the completion of several irrigating canals.

The cost of constructing the main canals is usually borne by a neighborhood of farmers, and sometimes these enterprises are carried forward and operated by associated individuals, under a company organization. Although this system of irrigation necessitates a trifling expenditure for water rental, or the employment of a small amount of labor, it is believed that the flowing streams give back as much fertilizing material as is lost by cultivation, while the increased production of this method of farming more than makes up for all outlays incurred.

It is a well-established fact that heavier and more reliable crops can be obtained by the aid of artificial irrigation, taking one year after another, than where the uncertain natural rainfall is depended on. This is shown in Colorado as well as in other regions. The prosperous, well-to-do farmers along the South Platte, the Cache la Poudre, Saint Vrain, Boulder, Ralston, and Clear creeks, the Fountaine, Cucharas, and the Arkansas and Las Animas rivers are all illustrative of the truth of this statement. Rich, waving fields of grain now greet the eye where once were barren, uninhabitable wastes, and vegetables of such prodigious size and in such immense quantities are raised as would astonish those unaccustomed to the results of Colorado soil. Farming has often been enormously remunerative, and few that have followed it steadily have failed to accumulate money or property. Many men have well stocked farms of great extent and value, the results of a few years' industry and effort.

Colorado has from thirteen to fifteen thousand square miles of land that can be made available for agriculture, of which something like one-fifth is now under cultivation. The State Auditor's report of May, 1878, returned not far from 2,000,000 acres of land as taxable, with an assessed valuation, with improvements, of $9,755,038.17. This did not by any means include all lands under cultivation, as the assessors of many counties where considerable farming is carried on appear to have failed to make any return, while many localities are not represented by figures that come up to the true condition of affairs. Probably an accurate statement would make the number of acres of land under the above head over 2,500,000, and the valuation $15,000,000. Before the close of the present season these figures will be greatly enlarged. A single irrigating canal, that is to be still further extended, was so far completed in April, 1879, that the water was running therein for a distance of thirty-four miles. This already irrigates that length of territory for a width of from two to three miles—making over eighty-five square miles, or fifty-five thousand acres of hitherto untillable land available for cultivation. Many other enterprises of similar character are going forward.

The State Auditor's report of 1878 allotted the acreage of the farms of various counties, together with assessed valuation of land and improvements thereon, as appears beneath. These figures are far below the present facts in the case—and assessed valuations are of course lower than the actual value.

COUNTY.	Acres of Land.	Value with Improvements	COUNTY.	Acres of Land.	Value with Improvements
Arapahoe	119,528	$1,006,147	Huerfano	15,077	$72,520
Bent	63,159	117,516	Jefferson	128,252	801,298
Boulder	117,688	1,223,715	Larimer	55,532	419,540
Custer	16,818	143,269	Las Animas	229,210	403,011
Douglas	135,277	366,578	Park	47,046	237,165
Elbert	35,583	80,253	Pueblo	219,718	550,728
El Paso	223,757	773,290	Saguache	136,826	216,118
Fremont	64,924	281,288	Weld	140,307	709,920
Gilpin	11,005	....			

While this statement does not make a very extensive showing, it must be remembered that it is under the actual condition of affairs,

and that each season sees large additions thereto. It is given here
in order that an idea may be obtained of the proportionate agricultural importance of different districts. Owing to the way in which
stock and town property is sometimes apparently included, it is
difficult to ascertain their relative standing in all cases. While a
portion of the stock owned in the State might very appropriately
come in under the head of farming, it will be considered under the
head of stock growing, since no means are at the disposal of the
author to obtain the figures on farm-houses, and on cattle and other
animals, as distinguished from those raised especially for marketable
purposes.

The annual farm products of Colorado are steadily increasing in
quantity and value. Correct data of a detailed character have been
difficult to gain, and reports from various sources are often conflicting. The farmers are not always willing to have the full extent of
the wheat crop known, lest prices fall to a lower figure than
might otherwise be obtained. Consequently, it is sometimes difficult
to get correct estimates. Millers and speculators always figure out
a much larger crop than the farmers are willing to acknowledge.
The former are the buyers, and work for low prices, while the latter
are the sellers, and of course want as much money for their products
as it is possible to get.

The farming product of 1877 was far ahead of that of any
preceding year. The season was a remarkably favorable one, and the
acreage of land sown or planted was much greater than ever before.
The result was that a large portion of the farmers, who had previously suffered losses from grasshoppers and from other causes,
came out with a handsome cash balance in their favor, as did those
who had newly embarked in the business. The good fortune attending the season of 1877 caused an increase of tilled land in 1878
of at least twenty-five per cent. In some sections the acreage in
wheat was one-third greater, and in other fifty or sixty per cent.
The harvest was not as bountiful, however, as in the preceding year.
While the aggregate may have been somewhat greater for the entire
State, the return of grain and some other crops per acre was considerably less.   In the northern counties this was partly due to
frequent rains just before harvest time, causing wheat to "rust."
In southern Colorado no such misfortune was reported.

The average yield of wheat per acre has been from twenty to

twenty-five bushels. Possibly twenty-two bushels comes nearer the truth, taking one year with another. This includes the entire State and all localities, and is above that of 1878. There are many farms and belts of land that yield thirty, forty, and occasionally fifty bushels to the acre. This, of course, is far above average returns of the State. Colorado flour is the finest in the world. Quantities of it are shipped to Illinois and other States. Oats, rye, barley and other cereals do as well proportionately as wheat. Potatoes return all the way from one hundred to five hundred, and rarely seven

FARMING ON THE BOULDER.

hundred and eight hundred bushels to the acre. The average runs from one to two hundred. Vegetables of nearly all descriptions grow to prodigious size both on mountain and plain. The comparatively inexpensive system of irrigation constantly replenishes the soil. The water is let into the ditches and onto the land in June, when the streams are full of mineral and vegetable matter borne down from the mountains. The water goes down into the ground and leaves the mineral and vegetable substances on the surface, adding to the soil.   The ground continues productive **after** years of cultivation, because the irrigation brings in new material. Corn does not thrive as well in the northern counties as small grains, owing to the chilly night atmosphere, yet the yield is considerable and steadily getting larger.   South of the "Divide" it does much better and large crops are raised—sometimes seventy-five or eighty bushels to the acre.   Large quantities of hay are cut and cured in the parks and in most of the larger plains and mountain valleys. The good prices prevailing in the mining camps make this an important article to the farmer and stock owner.

For a long time fruit culture in Colorado was deemed impracticable.   The experiments and experiences of the past few years show that fruit of various kinds can be raised successfully, and in some of the southern counties profitably and extensively.   There are thrifty orchards of apple and peach trees at and near Cañon City. North of the Divide much more difficulty has been experienced; but apple trees are made to grow and bear fruit when protected from the winds by other trees.   Several very fair crops of apples have been obtained in Jefferson, Boulder, Larimer and other counties.

The dairy has become an interest of no little importance within the past few years.   Owing to the nutritious character of Colorado grasses, the milk, butter, and cheese are of unrivaled excellence. Large quantities of these articles are sold in the numerous towns and camps.   Several cheese manufactories have recently been established in El Paso, Boulder, and Larimer counties.   There and in Arapahoe and Jefferson, more than elsewhere, are remarkably large numbers of superior cattle, many of them of the best blooded stock, and valued at very high figures.   Some of the finest cows and bulls of Eastern localities have been purchased and imported by these enterprising farmers of the far-away Colorado border.   There are finely-stocked dairy farms in other sections beside the counties enumerated, including Douglas, Fremont, Lake, and Saguache, but those named first take the lead.   At the state and county fairs the displays of Durham, Alderney, Hereford, Shorthorns, Jersey, and Swiss cattle, and of stock crossed therewith, are very fine.

There is a remarkably large amount of money invested in horse flesh in Colorado, and the average quality of stock is very high in some quarters. The liveries and private stables (especially the latter) **of** such cities as Denver, Leadville and Colorado Springs are of a **very** high order. On the farms are large numbers of horses, some of them splendid draft, work, or saddle animals. Good blood is as manifest there as among the fast trotters of the towns.

Colorado can make no such showing in amount of farming products as the Mississippi valley states, where farming is the main industry; but in the yield per acre, or in quality of wheat and beef cattle, and extent of stock farms, she far surpasses them. With little care or trouble these Colorado uplands and river bottoms turn out nearly or quite double what an equal area gives in Illinois or Iowa, and far more than is known in Minnesota or Kansas. While no accurate data of the annual farm production is at hand, the figures given below for the years 1878 and '79, are not far out of the way, being estimates based on statements of farmers and millers:

COUNTY.	Acres in Wheat.	Yield per Acre.	Number of Bushels.	Acres in Wheat.	Yield per Acre	Number of Bushels.
Larimer	7,500	20	150,000	10,225	21	217,000
Boulder	14,500	19	275,500	15,000	24	360,000
Weld	10,000	16½	165,000	13,500	20	270,000
Jefferson	6,818	22	150,000	8,000	23	184,500
Arapahoe	3,000	20	60,000	3,200	22	70,500
Elsewhere	500	15	7,500	1,875	20	37,600
Total North of Divide	42,318	19.1	808,000	51,800	22	1,139,600
Fremont	3,000	24	72,000	3,000	13	39,000
Las Animas	5,000	20	100,000	5,000	20	100,000
Saguache and Conejos	2,000	20	40,000	2,000	20	40,000
Huerfano	500	20	10,000	650	20	13,000
Elsewhere	2,000	16	32,000	2,000	20	32,000
Total South of Divide	12,500	20.3	254,000	12,650	17.8	224,000
Total of State	54,818	19.3	1,062,000	64,450	21.1	1,363,600

The value of wheat in the winter of 1878–'9 was about one dollar per bushel, and a year later it was about twenty per cent. higher. This would give the crop of 1878 a value of $1,062,000, and that of 1879 a value of $1,636,320. On the following page is another estimate of the crops of Colorado for 1878. The figures given above may be more than the average selling price, or

than the market rates of last fall and winter.   A rough estimate of
the more important streams figures up as follows: Poudre and Big
and Little Thompson, 200,000 bushels; Saint Vrain, etc., 160,000;
Boulder creeks, 100,000; South Platte, 200,000; Clear and Ralston
creeks, 100,000; Bear, Plum, and Cherry creeks, 60,000; Arkansas
river, 120,000; Purgatoire, Apishapa, etc., 230,000; Saguache,
Rio Grande, etc., 50,000.

Over 300,000 bushels of corn were raised, of which 75,000 bushels
grew in Las Animas county and nearly or quite as much more in
Fremont.   At seventy cents per bushel, the value was $200,000.
There were about 250,000 bushels of oats raised, worth $125,000;
nearly 150,000 bushels of barley, worth $80,000; and 50,000 bushels
of rye, worth, say $30,000.   The potato crop ranged from 400,000 to
500,000 bushels, worth $350,000.   There were probably 50,000 tons
of hay cut and cured in the valleys of the plains, parks and mountains.   This varied greatly in price, being far more valuable in the
mining camps than on the plains.   The total value may be placed
at $800,000.   Garden produce probably counted up $250,000, and
the dairy product of milk, butter, cheese, with eggs, etc., $350,000
more.   The total agricultural productions of Colorado for 1878,
exclusive of stock, may be summed up, as follows:

Wheat	1,310,000 bush.	$1,310,000
Corn	300,000 "	210,000
Oats	250,000 "	125,000
Barley	150,000 "	80,000
Rye	50,000 "	30,000
Potatoes	450,000 "	350,000
Hay	50,000 tons	800,000
Garden produce		250,000
Butter, cheese and eggs, milk—dairy product		350,000
Total		$3,515,000

Wages of farm hands usually range from $15 to $20 per month,
with board, for the entire year or season, or about the same as female
domestic servants receive.   Laborers hired especially for harvesting
receive from two to three dollars per day and board.   There is quite
a difference in the prices received for farming products, according to

locality. No country has a better market, and one beauty of this is that it is right at home. Hay is usually from $20 to $30 per ton in the mountain mining camps, and about half that sum on the farms of the plains and parks. By the cental, or hundred pounds, potatoes ranged during the past year or two from $1.50 to $1.75; corn from $1.50 to $1.75; wheat, $1 to $1.70, or from seventy cents to one dollar per bushel; flour, $2.20 to $3 per hundred; oats, $1.75 to $2.50.

Before the railways reached Colorado there were occasional scarcities of articles of food. A single potato crop of a mountain farm near Central cleared for its owner $17,000 one year when potatoes did not do well on the plains. Many years ago receipts were often very large, from the sale of crops on such large ranches or estates as those of Col. Craig and others. A leading farmer, near Denver, who, from his penchant for potato culture, has been called the Potato King, usually raises from 40,000 to 60,000 bushels annually from 200 to 300 acres of land, and has received for his crops all the way from $40,000 to $70,000. He plants those varieties that are found to do best, and, as in most parts of the State, many grow to prodigious size. The highest reported yields of any extensive potato crops run from 500 to 800 bushels per acre. These are exceptional cases; but two and three hundred bushels to the acre are common returns.

Magnificent crops of the finest quality of wheat ever grown are usually harvested in the fertile and beautiful valleys of the Boulder creeks, and of Ralston, Saint Vrain, Poudre, Clear, Bear, and Saguache creeks, and in parts of the Las Animas, and Arkansas and Platte valleys. The profits of a farm in those localities are often many thousands of dollars annually. Some farmers have hundreds of acres in wheat, and harvest from 5,000 to 15,000 bushels per annum. From three to six times as much land is usually sown in wheat as in oats or corn. The most approved sowing, planting, and harvesting machinery are used, and steam threshing machines are moved from one place to another, as their services are required. These machines handle from 40,000 to 90,000 bushels each in the more populous districts. In July, 1877, over $75,000 worth of farming machinery was sold in Boulder county alone.

Greeley colony has over 35,000 acres of land under ditch, most of it in a high state of cultivation. Some fifty or sixty square miles of territory were made available for agriculture by the recent completion of a section of twenty miles of the Larimer and Weld Canal. The total length will be fifty-four miles, and a tract of country thirty-six miles long, and from three to ten miles wide, will be irrigated. The canal starts from the Cache-la-Poudre river, at the Colorado Central Railway crossing, and continues eastward until the Denver Pacific is crossed. A part of this land was pre-empted, and some is being sold at from $3 to $10 per acre.

Western Colorado is beginning to be settled up by miners and farmers. For many years the great Sierra Madre acted as a barrier to immigration and advancement; but population is moving in that direction at last. Beside the wonderful mining discoveries of that region, the farming and pastoral resources are considerable. There are fine parks and numberless valleys enclosing the streams. These are extremely fertile, and will prove very serviceable and valuable now that a demand has arisen for their products. The Gunnison river alone has from 50,000 to 100,000 acres of farming land available for irrigation that is lower than San Luis Park, and which yielded 20,000 tons of hay last season.

For a long time it was believed that fruit could not be raised in Colorado. It has been found, however, that with care and culture, good crops of apples can be secured, while small fruits give better and more bountiful returns than in the east. The strawberry crops of the Greeley and other sections are quite extensive and profitable, and many small patches of ground return handsome livings to the owners. Other small fruits are grown. Apples are successfully raised in Boulder and other northern counties, and still more extensively near Cañon City in southern Colorado. At the latter place are productive peach orchards, and peach and pear trees have been planted elsewhere. At Trinidad fruits and vines grow finely.

Corn of the Egyptian variety has lately been introduced in Colorado and returns wonderful crops.

CHAPTER III.

STOCK GROWING—THE NATURAL ADVANTAGES AND LARGE PROFITS
RESULTING THEREFROM IN COLORADO—THE BEGINNING OF A
GREAT INDUSTRY—RAISING CATTLE, SHEEP AND HORSES ON
THE GREAT PLAINS AND IN THE PARKS AND MOUNTAINS—
STATISTICS RELATING THERETO.

Colorado is one of the best grazing regions of the world. Her
pastoral lands are of immense extent, and so profitable has been the
avocation of stock growing that this industry has begun to assume
immense proportions. The exports of beef cattle are exceeded only
by those of Texas, while her sheep and wool products, which interest is not yet as fully developed, are fast approaching the extent of
those of California and New Mexico.

The plains of Colorado will not feed as many cattle, sheep or
horses to the square mile as lands in many of the older States, but
the almost limitless area, combined with its winter as well as summer
supporting qualities, render it particularly advantageous. It is only
in case of severe storms that cattle on these plains require hay, grain,
or feed, and no stock men supply it even then unless it be one of the
few engaged in raising stall-fed animals. Yet the quality of Colorado beef is far above that of Texas or most other extensive stock-
growing countries. This is due to the superior character of the
grasses, of which the "gamma" and "buffalo" are the most common species. The former grows ten inches high, and has a single,
round stock with oblong heads. The other grows closer to the
ground, being but about three inches high, and is very curly.
There is still another kind called bunch grass, which keeps green at
the roots all winter. Colorado grass starts about the first of May,
and continues to grow until about the middle of July or August,
when the dry season commences. It then dries up and cures as it
stands on the ground, and having no frosts to cut it, it retains its
strength, and stock keep fat on it all winter.

Strangers passing through the country in the fall and winter
wonder what the stock find to eat, for it looks to them like a

barren waste. Yet the results of letting the cattle run at will are highly satisfactory and extremely remunerative. Unlike the eastern grass, which turns to ashes or decay after the frosts come, these upland species are as fine in January as hay in the mow. The dryness of the climate helps them to survive the winters. A heavy fall of snow usually evaporates in a day or two, and rains are so short and infrequent that the moisture is readily absorbed.

In case of storms, stock can find shelter under the bluffs and in the many small valleys and ravines, while the clusters of pines, piñons, and cottonwoods almost serve the purpose of barns and stables. There have been winters when a single storm of great severity has occurred, followed by the snow crusting over. At such times the loss of cattle was quite extensive, and of sheep much larger. The storm of December, 1878, was an instance, and led many men to take steps for the better protection of stock. Winter feeding will probably be followed in many localities in time of storms and heavy snow-falls. The increase of cattle, allowing for all losses, is placed at eighty and even as high as eighty-five per centum on the whole number of cows. Others have estimated it as low as seventy-five. The value of four-year old steers ranges from $23 to $30. Cows are not rated quite as high. With the aid of corn or grain crops, about double the above prices can be obtained.

The shipment of cattle to Chicago, Kansas City, and elsewhere began some years ago, and later that of dressed beef in refrigerator cars became quite an item. In 1877 some 80,000 cattle were forwarded by rail, and some 88,000 in 1878 and in the ensuing winter. The rapid influx of population created an increased home demand, which it is said called for 20,000 head last year. The cattle exported or consumed were steers, mainly four-year olds. The increase of cows is, of course, large, as these are retained for breeding purposes. The sales of 108,000 head, at an average of $25, gives $2,700,000. Add to this the increase of female calves and the total of receipts and addition to stock represents something like $3,500,000 for the year.

Of the Eastern cattle exports 24,500 went by way of the Union Pacific, 19,800 by the Atchison, Topeka & Santa Fe, and 18,700 by the Kansas Pacific. The main shipping points are Julesburg and Cheyenne on the first named road, Grenada, Las Animas, Pueblo, and Rocky Ford on the second, and Deer Trail, Hugo Denver, and Wallace on the third.

The cattle men of Colorado usually started in the business by securing a quantity of Texas cows—"long horns," as they are called—and a suitable number of bulls, of American or foreign breeds. Some of the finest bulls in the world have been brought to Colorado. Most of them are of the Durham, Hereford, Jersey, Canadian, and other fine species. Their average value runs from $100 to $150, but some are worth several times those figures. Until recently Durham bulls were generally brought to Colorado in preference to others, but now the white-faced Herefords are the favorites, and are being introduced extensively. It is claimed that they are more hardy than Durhams or short-horns. By crossing these with Texas cows the increase is very much superior to the latter, and a second cross with the half-breeds still further improves the stock. So the pastoral ranges of Colorado have at last come to support large numbers of first-class cattle, as well as thousands of the less valuable Texans. Colorado beef is pronounced the best that finds its way to the Eastern market that is not stall-fed. Cattle lose flesh in the winter, and consequently poorer beef gets into the home market in February and March than at other seasons. Stock on the dairy farms and in the agricultural sections is sheltered, fed, and cared for to a greater extent than those on the regular stock ranges.

Notwithstanding the fact that cattle and sheep are able to obtain their own subsistence for the entire year, the avocation of stock-growing is attended with no little care and labor. During the winter the cattle roam at will over the plains, and different herds mingle together, and perhaps wander for long distances from their original ranges. With spring comes what is called the "round ups," when all the cattle of large tracts of country are driven together in one vast herd, and with their increase separated and driven to their former ranges by their owners.

These "round ups" are important occasions with cattle men, and usually occupy their time from late in April to July or August, when branding time begins, and continues until the beef shipments of autumn and early winter. The cattle often scatter over the plains into adjoining counties, fifty or one hundred miles away from their starting-place. To complete the "round up" the ground has to be gone over two or three times, although most of the stock is secured

THE ROUND UP.

the first trip.   There is a law, as well as rules and regulations, for the guidance of stock-growers.   These district off the country and designate the points of assemblage.

On or near the 25th day of April, when the time comes for the "round ups" to begin, the stock men in each of the sixteen districts assemble together with their herders at their respective places of rendezvous and begin to drive the cattle from the creeks and branches to the main stream or river.   Gradually the scattered herds are gathered together.   After many days and weeks from twenty to two hundred thousand head are massed together in a comparatively small space of territory.   Then comes the separating and driving away of the stock of various owners, each of whom can distinguish his property by the brands placed thereon in the previous season.

After the country has been scoured over until the last of the wanderers are driven in and assigned to their owners, the latter return to their respective stock ranges, when the work of branding follows.   Every cattle man has a peculiar brand, separate and distinct from that of his neighbor, in order that he may know his property wherever he finds it.   By the time fall arrives cattle are fat and in prime order for market, and shipments begin and are continued until the surplus steers are disposed of.   Large numbers of yearling steers are driven in from Texas, and kept on these prairie ranges until they are four years old, when from $40 to $45 are sometimes received for them.

A State board of cattle inspection commissioners was provided for by the last Legislature.   Early in 1872, the Colorado Cattle Growers' Association had been fully organized.   Since then it has held its annual sessions at Denver or in some other prominent town, and has been of no little service to the industry which it aims to advance, regulate, and represent.   A cattle association for southern Colorado was organized in 1877.   The first purely blooded live stock farm in Colorado was that established by Captain J. S. Maynard, in Weld county, in 1870, with a start of thirty-six thorough-bred short-horns. The same year, Childs and Ring brought a short-horn herd into El Paso county.   Stock and animals of similar character had arrived in Saguache county in 1868, and in Huerfano, Park, and Lake in 1869. The growth of the cattle interest can be appreciated from the fact that but 145,916 were assessed for taxation in 1871, while 483,278 was the number in 1878.   There are probably nearly 900,000 head in the State at the present time. It has been claimed that assessment returns of live stock for many sections have been far too low to give any just idea of the extent of this industry. Consequently the numbers and value of cattle and sheep of leading stock counties for 1879 are given as estimated by prominent dealers and owners :

NAME OF COUNTY.	Number of Cattle.	Value.	Number of Sheep.	Value.
Bent	125,000	$2,000,000	90,000	$190,000
Weld	95.000	1,500,000	65,000	145,000
Elbert	90,000	1,500,000	100,000	225,000
Arapahoe	60,000	1,000,000	87,000	190,000
El Paso	33,000	550,000	230,000	500,000
Las Animas	40,000	600,000	210,000	420,000
Pueblo	36,000	600,000	100,000	210,000
Larimer	27,000	450,000	70,000	160,000
Douglas	40,000	650,000	40 000	85,000
Huerfano	24,000	380,000	180,000	360,000
Saguache	25,000	400,000	25,000	55,000
Conejos	10,000	150,000	120,000	230,000
La Plata	50,000	900,000	30,000	65,000
Other Sections	200,000	3,100,000	570,000	1,385,000
Total	855,000	$13,680,000	2,002,000	$4,220,000

Ten years ago Colorado had less than twenty thousand head of sheep. To-day there are something like two millions or more. The State has millions of acres of land that can never be irrigated, and consequently can only be used for grazing. The sheep industry is young yet, but is fast approaching cattle-growing in importance, and will soon be followed to a far greater extent. Colorado possesses many advantages for sheep-growing over Eastern or even Pacific coast States. Sheep live the year round on the open prairie. While numbers of them have died off from exposure to snow-storms of unusual severity, such disasters are of so rare occurrence that little attention has been paid thereto. Yet shelter of some kind is desirable from these storms, as well as a reserve of ten or fifteen tons of hay to every thousand sheep. The herders take the sheep out on the prairie at sunrise and remain with them until dark, when they are driven into corrals or fenced enclosures for the night. One man herds from two thousand to twenty-five hundred head in one band. If the range is fresh they will do well in bands of that size, but a somewhat smaller number will thrive better. Mexican sheep can be run in larger bands than the graded ones. Sheep are usually through lambing about the tenth or fifteenth of June, when shearing commences. Shearing is generally done by the head—five cents for Mexican sheep, and six cents for one-half and three-quarter bloods. The Mexican sheep shear from two and a half to three pounds per head, half-breeds from four to five pounds, and three-quarter bloods from five to eight pounds. The shearers go from place to place in bands of from six to fifteen men at the above prices. All they have to do is to catch their sheep, shear it, lay the fleece on the folding and tying table, when a man takes it, folds and ties it, throws it to the sacker, who sacks and marks the sack, and it is ready for shipment. Most of the wool is sent East to commission houses, that sort and grade it before selling. A good shearer will shear from seventy-five to one hundred Mexican sheep and from thirty to forty grades. It will be seen that the cost for help is wonderfully small.

Good authorities estimate the number of sheep in Colorado at nearly or quite 2,000,000. The increase is very rapid. Allowing a value of $2 per head in the Mexican counties, and of $2.25 elsewhere, and the total value would be from $4,000,000 to $4,500,000. It is claimed that last year's wool clip was 5,000,000 pounds, which at 17 cents per pound would be $850,000. Add to this the increase of lambs, valued at $700,000, and something like $300,000 for sheep consumed or marketed, and the total products or receipts from the sheep industry would be $1,850,000 for 1878. For 1879 this should be much greater; possibly 700,000 pounds of wool, worth $1,200,000, nearly 800,000 lambs worth $1,200,000, and $300,000 for sheep marketed or consumed. This gives a total of $2,700,000 as the receipts and increased value for one year. This is a remarkable showing for a business that employs but a very few thousand men, and a large portion of them merely herders at low wages. The distance from an Eastern market has so far acted as a drawback for the shipment of sheep or mutton, except into the mining camps and large towns.

Thus far, the business of sheep-raising in Colorado has been very profitable. A flock of 1,800 ewes, costing $4,500, were placed on a ranch in Southern Colorado. In eight years 1,600 sheep were killed for mutton, and consumed on the ranch, and 7,740 were sold for $29,680. There are 14,800 head on hand, worth, at $3 per head, $44,400. The wool clips paid for shepherds and all current expenses.

These figures may be too high, but many men can be mentioned who have grown wealthy within eight or ten years, from an investment of from four to eight thousand dollars in this stock. They have realized more than the original capital from sales of wool and sheep, besides having from 10,000 to 20,000 head on hand. Heavy losses are sustained occasionally from severe snow storms. The dog *is* a valuable auxiliary in the care of sheep. The "Scotch Collie" surpasses all others for his natural aptitude for this work.

Many of the sheep men have two ranges for their herds—one for summer and the other for winter. The herder usually collects the sheep at night on a side hill, and sleeps by them. They lie quietly unless disturbed by wolves, who are the most troublesome in stormy weather. Shepherd dogs are very useful in the protection and herding of sheep, and are born and raised, and die with them. Lambs are weaned about the first of October. Sheep will travel about three miles out onto the range and back to water or the herding grounds each day. Those coming to Colorado to engage in the sheep business should go onto a sheep ranch, and stay there long enough to understand all about the methods of conducting the business. In selecting or taking up land for sheep-growing, plenty of range or room, with hay land and a water supply are requisites for successful operations. Good sheep should be purchased, to begin with, as they are the cheapest in the long run, and close attention must be given to the business in order to make money and build up a fortune.

While large numbers of the sheep of Colorado are of the American breeds, hosts of them are of the Mexican species. Still larger numbers are of mixed blood, obtained by crossing the long-legged, gaunt, coarse, light-wool Mexicans with Merino rams. The Cotswold has not been crossed so successfully with the full-blood Mexican, but makes fine stock when crossed with the three-quarter Merino. This brings size to the sheep, weight to the fleece, and length of staple. Since Colorado has been found to be the sheep-growing State of the West, large herds have been driven into her borders from other sections. California has been a heavy contributor, on account of the small expenses and large profits attending sheep raising here as compared with the Pacific slope. Thirty thousand sheep were driven in from that State but a few months ago.

CHAPTER IV.

SOMETHING FURTHER ABOUT FARMING AND STOCK GROWING—AGRI-
CULTURAL AND PASTORAL LANDS OF COLORADO—SOME EXTEN-
SIVE STOCK FARMS—THE ANNUAL REVENUE FROM FARMING AND
STOCK GROWING.

The foregoing chapters on farming and stock-growing will enable the reader to make a very fair estimate of the extent of these partially developed but rapidly growing interests. The values represented and the results obtained can be briefly summarized. The value of farms, cultivated lands, improvements, and property, exclusive of live stock, may be set down at $12,000,000. The vast tracts of land utilized as stock ranges are not included in that estimate. The value of horses and mules on farms and stock ranges may be set down at $1,000,000, and of dairies and domestic cattle, $1,000,000. In the regular stock-growing interests the value of cattle may be placed at $12,680,000; of sheep, $4,300,000; and of horses, $1,100,000; other property in stock interest, $500,000. Here is a total capital representation of $14,000,000 in the agricultural interests, and of $18,580,000 in stock, exclusive of that included with the farm valuations. Nearly all of those sums were the growth and accumulation of a few years from small investments of money or muscle. The value of horses and mules outside of the farming and stock sections, something like $3,000,000, is not included in the above figures.

The receipts, gains and profits of the farming industry for 1878 was not far from $4,000,000, including increase of dairy and other stock. Those of stock-growing were about $6,200,000. Of this $2,700,000 came from sales of beef cattle, and $800,000 on growth and increase of herds, and $300,000 for sheep consumed or marketed, $1,200,000 for increase of herds, and $1,200,000 for wool sold. This $6,200,000 represents the returns and gains of some 40,000 people, men, women and children, living on farms and stock ranges. The figures for 1879 will be much larger.

The agricultural, pastoral, and mineral sections of Colorado can be outlined somewhat as follows: The eastern third of Colorado, made up of the great plains, may be classed as pastoral land, outside of that bordering the streams, which is available for both farming and stock growing; elevation from 3,500 to 6,000 feet, excepting the timbered divide south of Denver, which is somewhat higher. The pineries of the latter have furnished a vast amount of lumber, but the plains away from the streams are barren of timber. Central and western Colorado is made up of mountains more or less covered with timber.

To the northward are the fine farming and grazing counties of Weld and Larimer, and south of them Arapahoe and Boulder. The last, beside gold and silver mines, has vast measures of excellent lignite coal that are already producing largely and which extend into Weld and south into Jefferson county—the same belt leading southward to New Mexico. Coal also appears here and there in the parks and valleys of the mountains of central and western Colorado. All through the northern part of the mountain sections are fertile valleys and grazing lands. Many of the former are too elevated for crops, excepting oats, rye, potatoes, and other hardy vegetables. There are countless farms or ranches all through the mountains, some of them of considerable extent and of great fertility. In the little mining county of Gilpin, the annual farm and dairy products must exceed seventy-five or eighty thousand dollars. The Rollins farm at Rollinsville alone has a strip of meadow and valley land amounting to three or four square miles in extent, which produces heavy crops of hay, vegetables and of the hardier grains. There are similar farms all through the hill country of Boulder, Jefferson, and Park counties. On some of these the hay crop returns thousands of dollars per annum.

Western Colorado will be settled up within the next few years to come both for pastoral and agricultural purposes according to elevation and character of land. There is a large area that can be made available in the counties of Routt, Grand, Summit and Gunnison.

That part of Colorado extending from the Middle Park and the vicinity of James Peak and Central southward through Clear Creek, Summit, Park, and Lake to Chaffee county and the vicinity of Trout Creek, Granite, and the Twin Lakes, comprises some immense ranges of mountains, with valleys and parks intervening. The latter are, in some cases, well adapted to grazing, but are mostly too elevated for agricultural purposes. The principal valleys are South Park, with an altitude in the western part of from 9,500 to 10,000 feet above the sea; the Upper Arkansas valley, 9,000 to 10,600 feet: the lower section of the latter near Chalk Creek, Cottonwood, and the South Arkansas, which is from 1,500 to 2,500 feet lower, and produces fair crops; the Blue River basin, 8,700 to 10,600; Ten-Mile Creek, 9,500 to 11,000; the Blue River Valley, 7,800 to 8,700. The timber found on the inclosing mountains is spruce and pine, valuable for lumber, while cottonwood is found along the streams. Mining is the great business of this section, and but few supplies can be raised outside of Chaffee county, except in the way of beef. Large herds of splendid cattle are kept in the parks. The mountains include the great Snowy range proper, or Continental Divide, with its spurs, such as the Front and Park ranges. West of the Arkansas

ON THE A. T. & S. F. R. R.

the main Divide is called the Sawatch range. This is the highest average mountain range in North America. From the western slope of this flows the Gunnison and its tributaries, whose valleys improve, in an agricultural point of view, as the descent toward the western ocean continues. Luxuriant grasses are found there, and large crops of hay were cut last season. In the park, near Gunnison City, an irrigating ditch is being constructed that will water six thousand acres of land. Early in May grass was four or five inches high on this slope.

Further down the mountain valley of the Arkansas, and within the limits of the new county of Chaffee, is a fine stock section, and a very fair farming district. Wheat and other grains are raised there as well as vegetables. The elevation runs from 7,300 to 8,800 feet, with mountains on either side. Still further down is Pleasant Valley; elevation, 7,000 feet. In the valley of the Platte, in the lower part of the South Park, stock growing is quite successful; elevation, 8,500 to 8,800.

Wet Mountain Valley in Custer county has fine farming and grazing land, and is pretty well occupied with ranchmen and stock owners. This is just east of the Sangre de Cristo range and adjoins the Sierra Mojada or Wet Mountains. In and near it are the mining camps of Silver Cliff and Rosita. The elevation is from 6,700 to 8,300 feet.

The San Luis valley or park is over one hundred miles long, and from forty to fifty miles wide near the centre, but gradually closes up toward either end. From the east the grand old Sangre de Cristo range rises far above the spruce and pine forests that line its lower sides, and to the west are the foot hills and spurs of the San Juan Mountains. San Luis Valley slopes slightly towards the centre, where the streams that enter it from the mountains sink and disappear in the great swamp known as San Luis Lake. What is remarkable about this strange locality is, that the streams, after coursing through the park for some distance, gradually grow smaller and smaller, and divide or disappear, as if drank up by the earth, until the waters are entirely absorbed in the great sink. Little irrigation is required in the northern part of this park, and in some portions none at all. The northern half of this great valley, together with some of the mountain sections, comprises the county of Saguache. A stream of the same name comes down from the hills to the westward, and in the fine farming and stock district watered thereby, is the well-to-do village of Saguache. The amount of farming around it has been steadily growing, until the crops comprise some 50,000 bushels of oats, 20,000 of wheat, 50,000 bushels of potatoes, 15,000 tons of hay, beside vegetables in great numbers. The yield of wheat is reported at from 25 to 40 bushels per acre, of oats at twice as much, and of potatoes 200 to 400 bushels. From 60 to 100 square miles of land can be and in time will be cultivated on the Saguache side of the park. Elevation above the sea, 7,500 feet. Further south are other streams and farming districts, and then comes the Rio Grande itself. In time this can be made one of the leading farming sections of the State, for this river can furnish an immense amount of water for irrigating purposes. Portions of this park are thickly covered with grass, and support many cattle, and other parts are almost barren, and can sustain but little animal life. The southern half of San Luis Valley is mainly peopled by Mexicans and their descendants, with a sprinkling of Americans and Europeans. Alamosa, however, is an American town. Conejos and Costilla counties were gradually settled from New Mexico in two decades following 1854. Sheep growing is extensively prosecuted, and there is some farming done, and a fair quantity of wheat and other grains are raised. Most of San Luis Valley is from 7,000 to 8,000 feet above sea level. There are flour mills at Saguache and Conejos.

There are fine farms and stock ranges in the Animas valley south of Silverton and the San Juan silver mines, and near the New Mexican border. This stream flows southward into the San Juan river, and is nearly parallel with the La Plata and Mancos. This is in southwestern Colorado, and should not be confounded with the Rio Las Animas or Purgatoire of the Trinidad section, and which flows northeasterly to the Arkansas. The quantity of cattle, horses, etc., and of cultivated land in the Animas valley is already large, and settlers are coming in steadily. The elevation is from 6,000 to 7,000 feet.

The cost of irrigation varies with different localities. In some sections it is as low as three and five cents per acre and in others as high as ten. Ditch companies have charged from one to three dollars per inch for water. Ditch agents and superintendents are hired by the companies or owners to attend to water-leases, repairs, and collections.

Among the irrigating canals is what is known as the Big Greeley Ditch on the north side of the Cache la Poudre river. This is 36 miles long, with 3 to 3½ feet depth of water, and is 25 feet wide on the bottom at its head, diminishing to 15 feet at Greeley. Its fall is from 2½ to 3½ feet per mile. Total cost $66,000. The ditch south of the same stream is 11 miles long and 12 feet wide at the bottom, with 2½ feet depth of water. The Big Evans ditch on the south side of the South Platte river has a length, with its branches, of forty-five miles. The main trunk is ten feet wide on the bottom, with from 1½ to 2 feet depth of water. Grade five feet and four inches to the mile. There are many others, large and small, all over the farming sections, with grades all the way from two to ten feet per mile.

The men longest in the cattle business in Colorado are the best off financially, showing that the accumulation of wealth in this industry is only a matter of time. When John W. Iliff died, in 1878, he owned more cattle than any other man in the State—the accumulations of many years in the business. His herds numbered something like 30,000 or 40,000 cattle, valued at over half a million; thousands of calves were branded, and from 5,000 to 7,000 steers or oxen shipped East every season. His ranch or cattle range was 156 miles long, extending from Greeley eastward to Julesburg, and from the Platte river south to Lodge Pole creek. Of this immense range, Mr. Iliff had purchased some 20,000 acres. At the chief rendezvous, forty miles from Julesburg, were houses, sheds, corrals, chutes, and facilities for handling and branding stock. There are sections of inclosed land on this territory, some twenty houses, and mowing machines, wagons, and farming tools, beside nearly two hundred head of horses. From thirty to forty herders are employed. Eighty Durham and Hereford bulls are located on the Patterson ranch alone. N. R. Davis, of the same county of Weld, rebranded over 6,000 cows or heifers last season, and sold 1,500 head of fat steers.

It is impossible to mention all of the leading stock men of the State. There are large numbers who own from five to ten thousand head of cattle, others who own still larger numbers of sheep, and others still whose wealth is divided among both cattle and sheep, with here and there large herds of horses. In El Paso county alone there are thirteen men, each of whom have flocks of from five to ten thousand sheep, and one firm has nearly or quite fifteen thousand. Some of the heaviest sheep growers are in Las Animas, Conejos, and Huerfano counties. Single stock farms in northern and central Colorado have from two to three thousand head of fine horses.

The wool shipments from points in Colorado, in 1878, amounted to about 4,000,000 pounds, of which about one half came from New Mexico, via wagon trains to the southern railway termini. These shipments embraced 1,250,000 pounds at El Moro, 500,000 at Alamosa and Garland, 600,000 at Colorado Springs, 200,000 at Fort Collins, 200,000 at Greeley and Cheyenne, 500,000 at West Las Animas, 100,000 at Pueblo, 100,000 at Cañon, 100,000 at Walsenburg, and 450,000 at other places.

Estimates of the wheat crop of different years have varied greatly. The "Colorado Farmer" placed the wheat crop of northern Colorado at 450,000 bushels in 1876, at 750,000 bushels in 1877, and at 900,000 in 1878. Wilbur, after personal inspection, footed up the acreage of wheat in the Boulder and Saint Vrain valleys, in 1877, at 13,399. The "Greeley Tribune" estimated the acreage of wheat, in 1877, at 32,500 in northern Colorado, with a yield of 731,250 bushels, and 17,500 acres in southern Colorado, with a yield of 393,750, allowing for an average yield of 22½ bushels per acre.

Flour mills, some of which turn out fine brands of flour, are at work in Pueblo, Lake, Larimer, Boulder, Jefferson, Arapahoe, Fremont, Saguache, Conejos, and other counties. Las Animas, Jefferson, Arapahoe, Larimer, and Weld have three mills each. Boulder county has six mills, two of which are at Boulder, two at Longmont, one a little further down the Saint Vrain, and one at Saint Louis. These six mills convert over 300,000 bushels of wheat into about 120,000 one hundred pound sacks of flour. Boulder county crops were below the average in 1878, and above it in 1879. The average yield of wheat to the acre was 23¼ bushels in 1877, about 19 in 1878, and 24 in 1879. Many farms yielded from 25 to 40 bushels per acre in 1879, and the wheat was of superior body and quality. Other crops were excellent. Boulder county has some 4,000 horses, worth $250,000, 250 mules, worth $30,000, 10,000 cattle, worth $170,000, and some 2,500 sheep, valued at $8,500. There is much superior dairy stock, and many head of blooded horses and cattle.

The lands of the Rio Grande, Las Animas, and other valleys raise bountiful crops. Forty bushels of wheat to the acre are often obtained, and sometimes more, by both American and Mexican farmers. Much land of great fertility will soon be brought under cultivation on the western slope of the "Rockies," on the tributaries of the Grand, Gunnison and San Juan.

The amount of land in Colorado that is capable of being irrigated so as to produce crops, is given by Professor Hayden at 7,519 square miles, or nearly 5,000,000 acres. Behind and near this are vast tracts of country suitable for grazing purposes. The number of square miles of irrigable land in the various sections is as follows:

In the valley of South Platte and tributaries, 1,849 square miles; Arkansas and tributaries, 2,976; Rio Grande and tributaries, in San

Luis Park, 874; Grand river, Gunnison and tributaries, 1,327; White river, 174; Yampah and tributaries, Egeria Park, etc., 319. Only a portion of the Platte Valley is under actual cultivation, and but a small fraction of the Arkansas and Rio Grande. The other streams are not yet entered upon for agricultural purposes. All these valleys are very fertile.

Mr. Stanger, of the Colorado Farmer, gives the following estimates of Colorado farming products in 1879 : 45,000 acres of ground yielded 1,000,000 bushels of wheat, 15,000 acres gave 450,000 bushels of oats, 12,000 acres gave 400,000 bushels of corn, 3,500 acres 110,000 bushels of barley, 3,000 acres 75,000 bushels of rye, 6,000 acres 600,000 bushels of potatoes; there were some 15,000 acres in vegetables, 1,500 acres in alfalfa and red clover, or about 100,000 acres altogether cultivated by irrigation. About 50,000 acres yielded 60,000 tons of hay, worth $960,000.

Other estimates are higher than this. The total value of farming and dairy products in 1879, including the hay crop, probably approached 5,000,000. This includes mountain ranches as well as the plains sections. Stanger's estimate is $4,100,000.

W. E. Pabor divides the wheat crop of Colorado for 1879, among the various river valleys, creeks, and sections, as follows :

Locality.	Bushels.	Locality.	Bushels.
Poudre Valley	320,000	South and Middle Boulder	58,000
Big Thompson	57,500	South Platte Valley	120,000
Little Thompson	11,000	Ralston, Clear Creek, Bear	160,000
St. Vrain Valley	240,000	Valleys south of the Divide	150,000
Left Hand	35,350		
		Total	$1,151,850

The Colorado Farmer estimates that there are over 1,000,000 head of cattle in Colorado at the present time, worth $12,000,000, with a net return of over $3,000,000 for the investment for the year 1879. The same year over 3,000,000 pounds of wool were exported, and the number and average grade of sheep is rapidly increasing.

Huerfano County makes a very fair showing in farming, stock growing, and coal mining. Fred. Walsen, its leading business man, makes the following estimates for 1879 : wheat crop 13,000 bushels; corn, 6,000; oats, 10,000; wool, 600,000 pounds, worth about 20 cents per pound. There are over 50,000 cattle, averaging $15 each.

RESIDENCE OF COLONEL WILLIAM CRAIG, HERMOSILLO.

In the extreme southwestern part of Colorado, and near the Utah and New Mexico boundaries and the Arizona corner, are a succession of fertile valleys, as remarkable for their agricultural as for their stock-growing capacity. These valleys are watered by streams issuing from the great San Juan Mountains, and flowing southward into the San Juan River or into one another. Mountains and hills intervene, and several streams are walled up at intervals with huge cañons, but withal there are numerous tracts of valuable land which lay so low that wheat, and other grains and vegetables are raised successfully; across a portion of these valleys and divides is an immense coal belt of superior character. It is believed that this section will, in time, be the smelting depot for much of the San Juan silver region, and that a railway will be built in from Alamosa, Pagosa, and the east. As it is, a good market is afforded the farming and stock products of this county of La Plata. Animas City is the leading town.

Last season the lands already occupied by settlers in these valleys numbered 20,640 acres of farming land, outside of stock ranges in bordering hills. This was before the strip of land known as the Indian reservation, and since ceded, to the United States, was open to settlement. As it was, there were forty-five farms, with 7,200 acres in the twelve-mile valley of the Animas, twenty-one farms, with 3,360 acres of tillable and hay-land along the Rio Florida, and forty-three farm locations and 6,880 acres of land on the Los Pinos. The more westerly streams have not been settled up so thickly. In the La Plata valley only five ranches or farms were occupied, with an acreage of 800 acres; in the valley of the Mancos were seventeen farms, with 2,720 acres. On the northwest slope the Rio Dolores has nineteen farm locations, with 3,040 acres. There are also large stock ranches. The late Indian reservation is being settled up rapidly. Some 40,000 head of cattle are owned in this section, and one farmer on the Animas has seven or eight thousand sheep.

A Mormon settlement, mainly composed of proselytes from Europe, was started in Conejos county early in 1879. The colony has 3,000 acres of land, on which the town of Manassa is being built. The location is seven miles north by east of the village of Conejos, and the number of inhabitants is 156, with more on the way. Polygamy is not practiced there, nor will it be.

MISCELLANEOUS.

Colorado Post-offices in Operation April 1st, 1880.

"ch" indicates county seat.

Arapahoe County.
Bennett.
Brighton.
Byers.
Cherry Creek.
Deer Trail.
Denver (ch.)
Island Station.
Littleton.
Watkins.

Bent County.
Catlin.
Cheyenne Wells.
Fort Lyon.
Granada.
Higbee.
Kit Carson.
La Junta.
Las Animas (ch).
Rocky Ford.
Sanborn.
West Las Animas.

Boulder County.
Altona.
Balarat.
Boulder (ch.)
Canfield.
Caribou.
Crisman.
Jamestowr.
Gold Hill.
Longmont.
Louisville.
Magnolia.
Marshall.
Nederland.
Ni Wot.
Orodelfan.
Pella.
Salina.
Sugar Loaf.
Sunshine.
Valmont.
Ward District.

Chaffee County.
Alpine.
Arboursville.
Buena Vista.
Centreville.
Chaffee.
Chalk Creek.
Cleora.
Cottonwood Springs.
Divide.
Granite (ch.)
Helena.
Hortense.
Maysville.
Mears.
Poncho Springs.
Riverside.

Clear Creek..
Brookvale.
Empire City.
Freeland.
Georgetown (ch.)
Idaho Springs.
Lawson. .
Red Elephant.
Silver Plume.
Spanish Bar.

Conejos.
Alamosa.
Cockrell.
Conejos (ch.)
Lajara.
Manassa.
Pagosa Spring
Piedra.

Costilla.
Fort Garland.
Russell.
San Luis (ch.)

Custer.
Blumenau.
Clinton.

Dora.
Rosita (ch.)
Silver Cliff.
Silver Park.
Ula.
Quirida.

Douglas.
Acequia.
Castle Rock (ch.)
Douglas.
Franktown.
Greenland.
Larkspur.
Pine Grove.
Deane.
Rock Ridge.
Sedalia.
Spring Valley.

Elbert.
Arroyo.
Elbert.
Gomer's Mills.
Hugo.
Kiowa (ch.)
Kuhn's Crossing.
River Bend.
Running Creek.

El Paso.
Bijou Basin.
Colorado City.
Colorado Springs (ch.)
Easton.
Edgerton.
El Paso.
Florissant.
Fountain.
Gwillimville.
Husted.
Manitou.
Monument.
O. Z.
Suffolk.
Summit Park.

Sun View.
Table Rock.
Turkey Creek.
Weissport

Fremont County.
Cañon City.
Coal Creek.
Currant Creek.
Florence.
Galena.
Glendale.
Greenwood.
Hayden Creek.
Pleasant Valley.
Texas Creek.
Yorkville.
Hillsdale.

Gilpin County.
Bald Mountain.
Black Hawk.
Central City.
Rollinsville.
Russell Gulch.

Grand County.
Fraser.
Grand Lake.
Hermitage.
Hot Sulphur Springs.
Troublesome.
Twelve Mile.

Gunnison County.
Barnum.
Crested Butte.
Crookeville.
Gothic.
Gunnison.
Irwin.
Los Pinos.
Hillerton.
Pitkin.
Powderhorn
Tin Cup.
Tumichi.
White Earth.

Hinsdale County.
Antelope Springs.
Belford.

Burrows Park.
Capitol City.
Lake City.
Rose's Cabin.
San Juan.
Sherman.
Tellurium.
Timber Hill.

Huerfano County.
Apache.
Badito.
Cucharas.
Dickson.
Gardner.
Huerfano Cañon.
La Veta.
Saint Mary's.
Santa Clara.
Walsenburg.

Jefferson County.
Arvada.
Beaver Brook.
Bordenville.
Brownville.
Buffalo Creek.
Cresswell.
Crosson.
Enterprise.
Evergreen.
Forks Creek.
Golden.
Hutchinson.
Morrison.
Mount Vernon.
Resort.

Lake.
Howland.
Leadville (ch.)
Malta.
Oro City.
Soda Springs.
Tabor.
Twin Lakes.

La Plata.
Animas City.
Dolores.
Florida.
Hermosa.

Mancas.
Parrott (ch.)
Pine River.
Rockwood.

Larimer.
Berthoud.
Bristol.
Buckhorn.
Elkhorn.
Estes Park.
Fort Collins (ch.)
La Porte.
Livermore.
Loveland..
Pinewood.
Tyner.
Virginia Dale.
Wheatland
Moraine.

Las Animas.
Apishapa.
Barela.
Bent Cañon.
El Moro.
Grinnell.
Linwood.
Pulaski.
Raton.
Starkville.
Stonewall.
Trinidad (ch.)

Ouray.
Alder Creek.
Mount Sneffels.
Ophir.
Ouray (ch.)
Placerville.
Portland.
Rico.
San Miguel.
Windham.

Park.
Alma.
Bailey.
Buffalo Springs.
Como.
Dudley.
Fairplay (ch.)

Fairville.
Grant.
Hall Valley.
Hamilton.
Hartsell.
Jefferson.
Kestor.
Park.
Platte Station.
Rocky.
Webster.
Mountaindale.

Pueblo.
Beulah.
Booneville.
Greenhorn.
Jackson.
Juniata.
Muddy Creek.
Nepista.
Osage Avenue.
Pueblo (ch).
Saint Charles.
South Pueblo.
Table Mountain.
Taylorville.
Undercliffe.

Rio Grande.
Cornwall.
Del Norte (ch).
South Fork.

Summit.
Wagon Wheel Gap.

Routt.
Hahn's Peak.
Hayden (ch).
Steamboat Springs.
Windsor.

Saguache.
Cochetopa.
Cotton Creek.
Rito Alto.
Rock Cliff.
Saguache (ch).
Sangre de Cristo.
San Isabel.
Villa Grove.
Carnero.

San Juan.
Animas Forks.
Eureka.
Grassy Hill.
Highland Mary.
Howardsville.
Mineral Point.
Niegoldstown.
Silverton (ch).
Poughkeepsie.

Summit.
Breckenridge (ch).
Carbonateville.
Decatur
Dillon.
Frisco.
Haywood.
Kokomo.
Lincoln City.
Montezuma.
Preston.
Saints John.
Ten Mile.
White River.
Chihuahua.
Red Cliff

Weld.
Buffalo.
Erie.
Evans.
Fort Lupton.
Greeley (ch).
Hillsborough.
Morgan
New Liberty.
Platte Valley.
Platteville.
Sarinda.
South Platte.
Sterling.
Weldon Valley.

COLORADO NEWSPAPERS.

Before the opening of summer, 1880, Colorado had 58 newspapers with more expected. Of these 19 were dailies with weekly editions and 39 were weeklies. The counties, locations, and names are given below—papers both daily and weekly marked dw, all others weekly. The Denver and Leadville dailies rival those of any localities except the great cities, and some of them will bear comparison with even those.

Arapahoe Coun'y, Denver.—Rocky Mt'n News, d w; Denver Tribune, d w; Denver Times, d w; Denver Republican, d w; R. M. Herald, Inter Ocean, Colorado Post, Colorado Journal, Mining Review, Financial Era.

Bent, West Las Animas.—Las Animas Leader.

Boulder County, Boulder.—News and Courier, Boulder Banner, Boulder County Herald, d w; *Longmont,* Longmont Press, Longmont Ledger.

Chaffee County, Buena Vista.—Chaffee County Times.

Clear Creek County, Georgetown.—Colorado Miner, Georgetown Courier, *Idaho Springs,* The Iris.

Custer County, Silver Cliff.—Prospect, d w; Miner, d w; Republican, d w.

Douglas County, Castle Rock.—Douglas County News.

El Paso County, Colorado Springs.—Gazette, d w; Colorado Springs Mountaineer, d w; Monument, Monument Mentor.

Fremont County, Cañon.—Fremont County Record.

Gunnison County, Gunnison.—Hillerton Occident.

Gilpin County, Central.—Register-Call, d w; *Black Hawk,* Black Hawk Journal.

Jefferson County, Golden.—Golden Transcript, Golden Globe.

Lake County, Leadville.—Leadville Democrat, d w; Leadville Herald, d w; Leadville Chronicle, d w; The Times, d w.

Larimer County, Fort Collins.—Fort Collins Express, Fort Collins Courier.

Las Animas, Trinidad.—Trinidad News, d w; Trinidad Enterprise, d w.

Park County, Fairplay.—Fairplay Flume.

Pueblo County, Pueblo.—Colorado Chieftain, d w; Pueblo Democrat, d w.

Saguache County, Saguache.—The Chronicle.

The San Juan Region, Alamosa.—Alamosa, The News; Del Norte, The Prospector; Lake City, Silver World; Silverton, La Plata Miner; Animas City, The South West; Ouray, Solid Muldoon, Ouray Times; Rico, Dolores News.

Summit County, Kokomo.—Summit County Times, *Breckenridge,* Summit County Tribune.

Weld County, Greeley.—Greeley Tribune, Greeley Sun; *Evans,* Evans Journal.

face on the situation, and now Colorado, in addition to the old continuous veins, can boast of huge ore bodies and enormous deposits that will compare with those of any country in size and value. In fact, the world, to-day, cannot show anything superior to the Colorado developments that have followed the temporary decline of the Comstock.

The growing importance of the mining industry, its immense production, the rapid accumulation of fortunes, and the well-known prosperity of some mining regions, have created so widespread an interest in gold and silver mines that any information relating thereto is beginning to be eagerly sought after. There has ever been a fascination and romance attending the search of the precious metals, and time intensifies rather than diminishes the feeling. Under the magic influence of gold and silver discoveries a spirit of enterprise has been engendered that has brought about the accomplishment of results as unexpected as they are grand and wonderful. The wilderness is peopled, states are founded, and almost an empire established where the presence of civilized man was unknown but a few short years ago.

Gold mining comes under two heads—lode and placer, and silver mining is included in the first of these. Lode-mining is much the most important interest of the two in Colorado, since the quantity of the precious metals contained in quartz and ore is many times that of the gold of alluvial deposits. When a gold district is discovered, the first work is usually done in the placers and gulches, where the work is more simple, and the gold readily obtained. Less money is required than in lode-mining, where quartz mills or a market for ores are demanded. Silver lodes usually require still further time for development and for the procurement of the necessary reduction works.

There are an immense number of metalliferous lodes or veins already discovered in Colorado, and every month witnesses additional discoveries. A large majority of these are silver bearing, accompanied with copper or lead. The main value of some is in the gold they contain, and others carry all of these metals and iron, as well as other materials. What is sometimes termed a fissure vein, and is considered to be identical with a lode, is a body of gold or silver bearing quartz or ore filling a crack or crevice of the foundation rock with which a country or district is underlaid. These veins vary in

width from several inches to many feet.　Some have been proved to
have a length of thousands of feet, and others of several miles horizontally.　They extend downward into the earth for unknown distances.
The ore bodies contract or close up at intervals, but no well-defined

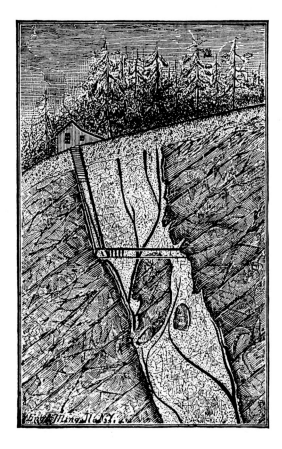

A LODE OR VEIN.

veins are believed to have given out entirely.　Some of them have a
perpendicular direction, and others are nearly flat or incline heavily.
Most of the argentiferous mineral bodies of the Park or Mosquito
Range appear in the form of egg-shaped or irregular deposits instead
of veins.　Some of the Leadville carbonates are claimed to be in the
shape of deposits and others are evidently in the form of veins.

Alluvial deposits consist of sand, gravel, and dirt, produced by the disintegration of the silicious, granitic, and other igneous and metamorphic rocks, and transported by the agency of water from the mountains above or around them. These are handled by one of the methods known as placer, gulch, creek, or bar mining, but to all of which the term placer is loosely applied. Gold is disseminated through the gravel or pay-dirt and lodges in considerable quantities on the rocky beds of streams. It is washed therefrom by water and secured in pans, flumes and sluice boxes, quicksilver being used to retain it where swift running water is used. No roasting, smelting, or milling is required, as where the gold is firmly embedded in the vein matter of lodes.

In operations of great magnitude large sums of money are often expended in bringing the requisite water supply to the desired placer diggings. When no water supply exists close at hand, one must be obtained from a distance, in order to work over these surface deposits. This often compels the building of miles of ditches and flumes. Powerful hydraulics are also used for the purpose of driving water with great force into the hill-sides, and tearing them down more rapidly than could otherwise be done. These placers and gulches call for appliances of varying extent and capacity, from those just referred to down to the ordinary sluice-box, the pick and shovel and the still more primitive hand-rocker and pan. Creek mining is carried on along the stream, and on their bed rocks far beneath the gravel and boulders immediately underlying the water.

In gulch mines, a flume composed of sluice-boxes is laid in the ravine or gulch, extending up to the bank or head of the excavations. Hose, hydraulics, or falling water from a flume above are used at this point to wash the bank or hill-sides down into the sluice-boxes. The latter are from one to four feet high and wide, and of uncertain length, and overlap one another. On their bottoms are fastened strips of board for riffles, or round blocks sawed from trunks of trees, and of a thickness of two or three inches. These, with quicksilver placed therein, aid in catching the gold dust and nuggets which the swift running waters sweep along with the dirt, gravel, and boulders. The gold being heavier than the other materials, sooner or later sinks to the bottom before it reaches the end of the sluices. It is always the intention to run the flume on the firm "bed-rock" as it is called, which underlies the gravel of the hills and

GULCH MINING—SLUICING FOR GOLD.

streams. Some of these flumes are run for hundreds and even thousands of feet before bed-rock can be reached, on account of the nearly level character of the ground worked. In other places the fall is so great that bed-rock, even if twenty-five or fifty feet deep, can be reached in a short distance and still retain the requisite incline to the sluice-boxes. Once a day, or as often or seldom as desired, the water is turned off and the gold taken from the sluice-boxes. This is called a " clean up."

In bar and creek diggings sluice-boxes are used, and the stream is turned from its natural channel, the boulders or heavier stones removed and shafts or pits are sunk until the permanent granite or bedrock of the country is reached. The gold in such localities is usually found extending up and down the course of the stream in a narrow streak or strip of ground. Drifts are excavated along this pay streak, and the gravel, dirt, and rock overlying the same are raised to the surface or packed in the drift as an adjoining and parallel one is opened. These drifts are run from six to seven feet high and wide, and are supported by heavy timbers, which keep the gravelly, rocky bed of the stream, often from fifteen to fifty feet thick, from caving in. If no " pay streak " is found on sinking the shaft, it is prospected for by running drifts as already noted. The water which continually leaks into the mine from above is removed by pumps, sometimes of great capacity.

In recent years, placer operations of great extent have been inaugurated in Summit, Park, Lake, Routt, and Ouray counties, and there are some extensive mines of this character in Clear Creek and Gilpin. These are supplied with hydraulics, great flumes, and other facilities for handling vast amounts of dirt and gravel. The rapidity with which the ground is worked permits of large profits where they would not be possible under the old systems so long in use.

Lode mining is very differently conducted from placer operations. After the decomposed surface material has been passed, gold is not so easily extracted as from pay-dirt and gravel, and silver ores are usually much more difficult to handle. Hard as are most ores, the enclosing rock is still harder, and the miner's difficulties do not end with blasting, breaking, and raising the ore to the surface; for then comes the reduction of the ore, and this calls for costly machinery, and for skill and experience in conducting the same,

Church and main street scenes, Leadville, c. 1975

Courthouse and Museum, Leadville, c. 1975

and in operating the milling or smelting process in order to secure the desired results.

The requisite entrances into the domains of mother earth, for the purpose of breaking and securing the ore, are made by digging and

LODE MINING NEAR THE SURFACE—SHAFT AND LEVEL.

blasting out perpendicular shafts and horizontal levels or excavations on the vein. To do this, hand or machine drilling and blasting powder and high explosives are brought into play. As work progresses solid timbers are required to brace the sides of the mine. These timbers, logs, or stulls extend from wall to wall, and keep them from falling in. For fifty or one hundred feet below the surface man power and the windlass are sufficient for hoisting the ore, waste rock, and water. After that horse power is required, which is used with a " whip " or pulley, or more generally by a whim or large drum of timber, around which the rope winds and unwinds as the bucket ascends or descends. This usually answers all purposes down to a depth of two hundred feet or more, when the steam-engine and accompanying hoisting is used. Sometimes the whim is dispensed with, steam following man power and the windlass. When greater depth is gained and the mine is enlarged there is more ore to handle and the water becomes more troublesome. More powerful hoisting works are then required, and huge pumps are a necessity.

As levels are extended and the vein material is broken down, iron tracks are laid, and the ore is conveyed in cars from various parts of the mine to the shaft, where it is placed in buckets and hoisted to the surface. From there it is assorted and taken to the mill or smelter. There are a number of requisites in lode mining, the development and working of mineral veins, and in the treatment of ore after it has left the mine, both in stamp mills and reduction works, that will be more fully explained hereafter. The entire business requires no little ability, care, and skill to insure success, even if the mine is a good one. The operations are much more difficult and intricate than in gulch mining, where the miner can clean up his gold every night instead of waiting for the results of the somewhat tedious processes of shipping, milling, and smelting.

In past ages the gold has found its way from lodes on the hillsides down into the streams or outlying ground, where it has been gradually working its way through the loose gravel onto the hard bed-rock, and that is where the richest streaks are found. The gold is usually as fine as powder, but is often found in coarser particles and in nuggets or lumps of various sizes. It is not free from impurities and consequently does not come up to the value of artificially refined gold, which is worth very near $20.67 per ounce. Placer or gulch gold in Colorado is worth from $17 to $18.50 per ounce. Large nuggets of gold have been found in Summit and Gilpin counties. One was found below Black Hawk, some years ago, that, with its attached rock, was much larger than a hen's egg and sold for $240.

City hall and old steam locomotive, Leadville, c. 1975

Remnants of yesterday, Leadville, c. 1975

Although nuggets or particles of gold are often seen in the quartz, the precious metal is usually disseminated through it so as to be

invisible to the naked eye. Beneath the surface the ore is so hard as to require the aid of ponderous stamps, driven by water or machine power, to crush it to the requisite fineness for washing or raw amalgamation or for roasting and smelting. Even then the stamps do not always pulverize it fine enough to admit of successful raw amalgamation.

IN THE MINE.

The most brilliant example of the superior profits attending mining for the precious metals as compared with those obtained in other avocations is afforded in the record of the two bonanza mines of the Comstock lode. Those mines cleared more money in four years than any two firms or companies in other lines of business have done in a generation of time since the world began. The most noticeable accumulations of wealth in mercantile and manufacturing pursuits cannot compare, in point of time and amount, with the larger fortunes acquired, at various times, in North and South American mining history.

As many names and terms are used in mining regions that are unknown or unfamiliar elsewhere, the following collection of definitions are given; likewise something concerning values, weights, and measurements. All of these should be carefully read and referred to when words used are unintelligible.

WEIGHTS AND VALUES.

A ton of gold or silver contains 29,166.66 ounces.

A ton of gold is worth $602,875.

A ton of silver, at the standard rate of $1.29,29, would be worth are slightly dearer. The figures of 1864–5 represent coin values as well as those of 1879. The greenback values paid at the former period were vastly higher. The left hand column represents the charges when the eastern company operations were most numerous and extensive and when the failures and suspensions began.

	1864–5.	1879.
Miners.............................	$4 00 to $5 00	$2 00 to $2 50
Foreman...........................	5 00 to 7 00	3 00 to 3 50
Laborers..........................	3 50 to 5 00	2 00
Head masons......................	9 00 to 12 00	4 50
Other masons and helpers..........	5 00 to 7 00	3 50 to 4 00
Carpenters	5 00 to 6 00	3 50 to 3 75
Flour, per sack of 100 pounds......	12 00 to 19 00	2 25 to 2 50
Lumber, per M....................	40 00 to 46 00	23 00 to 25 00
Hay, per ton......................	50 00 to 70 00	23 00 to 25 00
Powder...........................	6 00 to 9 00	3 65
Fuse, per M......................	15 00 to 23 00	6 50
Candles, per box..................	10 00 to 15 00	6 25
Rope, per pound..................	30 to 45	15
Quicksilver.......................	1 10 to 1 60	48 to 50
Machine Oils	80 to 1 30	35 to 40
Sheet Copper, per pound	60 to 75	30 to 32
Iron, per pound..................	18 to 24	4½ to 5
Sheet Iron, per pound.............	17 to 24	4 to 5
Nails, per pound..................	16 to 22	5
Shovels, each.....................	1 80 to 2 35	1 10 to 1 40
Wood, per cord...................	8 00 to 12 00	5 50
Milling Ore, per cord.............	35 00 to 50 00	20 00 or less.

There were times when the prices of labor and some supplies varied greatly. Wood and timber is dearer in Central City than anywhere else in the mountains. In Gold Dirt, near Black Hawk, at Caribou, Ward, Leadville, Ten Mile, and all of the southern and western counties, wood usually sells at from $2.50 to $3.00 a cord. Lumber sells in the same localities at from $30 to $35 per thousand feet. Carpenters and mechanics at Leadville have been getting ten or fifteen per cent. more than the figures given in the table, and lumber has been higher there. This is due to the wonderfully rapid growth of the place.

There has never been a time or locality more favorable for individual or company investments and organizations than this year of

1879, among the mines of Colorado. With a reasonable amount of ready capital to open and push mining development, a harvest is very sure to follow that cannot be blighted by floods, frost, nor insects, nor increased or diminished in value, but one that is sure, substantial and enduring—the pure metal itself. This product in reality represents the basis of all prosperity and wealth.

The mineral resources of Colorado of every description have hitherto been imperfectly appreciated, because but slightly developed. Recent discoveries and the results of well-directed labor, aided by superior mechanical and scientific processes, are attracting the attention of sagacious capitalists in this and foreign countries. The present rate of progress, development, and discovery will place Colorado ahead of all other sections in the production of the precious metals before the close of another year.

Mining, with the help of moderate capital, is one of the most certain and profitable industries in which men of enterprise can engage. The more thoroughly and systematically mines are worked, and the greater the milling facilities for the reduction of ores, the more satisfactory will be the amount of bullion produced. Colorado is now amply supplied with milling, reducing, and smelting facilities in all but the very newly discovered districts. Gilpin, Clear Creek, Boulder, and Park counties and the San Juan region and Leadville have all the works required for the extraction of the precious metals produced at present, and these are located within their borders or in localities not far away. Summit and Gunnison counties have been and are still receiving similar establishments. Good prices are paid for ores, and milling charges are as small as in any other state or territory. This is vastly beneficial to the miner, and quite the reverse of the condition of affairs a few years ago.

For the most part mining has been conducted by men of limited means or no means at all when they started in. These mountaineer prospectors and miners have worked out their own salvation, and have made their state rich and famous almost by their own unaided labors, strong hands, and characteristic energy and enterprise. But little outside capital came in to help them during the fifteen years of the State's greatest progress. What has been secured is due to the splendid showings and remarkable returns previously made, and which would have been much greater had these western pioneers had the means to begin with to conduct operations, instead of waiting in nearly all cases to make it out of the ground.

Capitalists in the older states, where rates of interest are low and speculative enterprises uncertain and more hazardous than mining for gold and silver, can strike the path to certain fortune if they will organize companies controlling ample ready means to develop mines, intrusting the management to honest and efficient business men and practical miners. This done, and the better classes of property secured, and there would be no such thing as failure, but success would be inevitable.

The day of unsuccessful experiments and losing investments has gone by. Colorado has the mines, and at last her miners and mill men know how to work them and how to reduce the ores. Skilled labor is on the ground, and metallurgists and mineralogists thoroughly acquainted with their professions and the character of veins and deposits encountered. With their assistance and that of judicious investments, intelligent direction, and proper economy, the capitalist need fear no loss.

Careful investigation of the subject shows there has been immeasurably less loss from capital wisely invested in mines, and generally far greater profits than have been realized in any commercial or manufacturing pursuits, or in railway stocks or operations. With the largest mineral belt in the world, unsurpassed rail connections within and without, ample reducing works, a first-class ore market, cheap supplies, and countless veins of a very high average value, the Rocky Mountains certainly afford the true field for future investment, and rare opportunities for success.

For years after gold mining began in Colorado the laws adopted by the miners and ratified by the Territory and Congress provided that a lode should be 1,400 feet in length, and that the discoverer thereof should be entitled to one claim of 100 feet on the vein, and another of 100 feet as a bonus for discovery. Each additional locator could pre-empt but one hundred feet on that vein. It was also provided that this location carried with it twenty-five feet of surface ground on either side of the centre of the vein, if this did not invade neighboring claims previously entered. Afterwards the laws were changed for subsequent locations, so that a discoverer could have 1,400 feet in length on the vein, instead of 200. Later, there was a short period when the discoverer could obtain 3,000 feet. No great number of locations were made under that law, and at length the present law was adopted, allowing a discoverer to pre-empt 1,500 feet on a vein, extensions taken up in the same manner by the same or other parties. In 1874 the Colorado legislature enacted that all locations made thereafter in the Territory should carry with them 150 feet of surface ground on either side of the centre of the vein (if such claims did not enter on ground already located), except in the four counties of Boulder, Gilpin, Clear Creek, and Park, when seventy-five feet either side of the centre of the vein should be the rule. None of these laws interfere with lodes discovered prior to their adoption.

After a government title or United States patent has been issued for a lode the owner can hold it against all comers and claimants, whether he works it steadily or allows it to remain idle forever. It cannot be relocated, nor is there danger of losing ground or territory secured in this way through litigation or opposing claims. Some years ago these titles carried with them the land for twenty-five feet on each side of the centre of the lode and vertically downward.

The owner can follow his vein anywhere so that he does not go outside of his end lines. At the present time, seventy-five feet on each side of the centre of the vein is allowed in Boulder, Gilpin, Clear Creek, and Park counties, and outside of them 150 feet.

Colorado has six United States land offices, viz.: Denver, Central, Leadville, Peublo, Del Norte, and Lake City. Up to April 1 1879, the Central City office had issued 765 government patents or titles for lodes or mining claims. Of these patents Gilpin County obtained 274; Clear Creek, 334; Boulder, 135, and Summit, 22, besides a few issued direct from the General Land office. At the same time there were 372 mineral entries on the Central City office books, likely to be issued soon. Whole number of mineral applications, 1,480.

The average cost of procuring a government patent or title is $125 when the location embraces 1,500 feet by 150, and over $160 when 1,500 feet by 300 are included. The former class embrace 5.16 acres of land and the latter 10.33. The costs include $25 for the Surveyor General, $45 for the Surveyor's patent, $12.50 for certified copies and abstracts, $10 for filing, $18 for publishing, $15 for notary fees, and from $30 to $60 for land. The law contemplates that five hundred dollars' worth of work shall be done on a vein before application for a title can be made. This is in order that the owner may prove up and ascertain the course and dip of his vein. Several months are usually required to apply for and secure title papers.

In regard to relocating abandoned lodes, section 15 of the Mining Laws says: "The relocation of abandoned lode claims shall be by

GREEN LAKE, NEAR GEORGETOWN—ELEVATION 10,000 FEET.

sinking a new discovery shaft, and fixing new boundaries in the same manner as if it were the location of a new claim; or the relocator may sink the original discovery shaft ten feet deeper than it was at the time of abandonment, and erect new, or adopt the old boundaries, renewing the posts if removed or destroyed. In either case a new location-stake shall be erected.   In any case, whether the whole or part of an abandoned claim is taken, the location certificate may state that the whole or part of the new location is located as abandoned property."   The discoverer or re-locator has sixty days after disclosing the lode before sinking a ten-foot shaft; hence, he should employ that time in ascertaining the exact direction of the strike of his vein, if necessary.

Probably not less than one hundred thousand locations have been made from first to last in the various recorders' offices of Colorado of what purport to be lodes, ledges, claims, or deposits.   A large portion of these may not prove valuable enough to work.   Others are abandoned or left idle because paying mineral has not been found and others are unworked at present, owing to remoteness from reduction works, ore markets, or for lack of roads and inaccessi-bility.   But a few thousand lodes are steadily worked at this time, but the number of active properties is rapidly increasing.   Nearly all sections but Gilpin possess the fifteen hundred feet locations. There are over 15,000 in Clear Creek county, embracing fourteen, fifteen, and thirty hundred feet locations.   There are thousands of claims recorded in Park, Lake, and Summit counties, and a vast number in the San Juan region.

Where the number of lodes and mines is so great as in Colorado it is of course impossible to mention but a small portion even of those that are being worked.   The design of this book is not to give a complete list of locations or of mines, but to show in a general way what Colorado possesses, what her people have accomplished and what has been and can be done in the Rocky Mountain region in the way of mining, farming, and making money.   The figures and statistics of the state at large and of counties are very extensive and accurate.   A few mines in every large district will be described at length, and in some cases their production will be published.   There are other properties as valuable as some of these, that want of space, time, and opportunity to gather statistics of prevents the author from noticing at length.   The character of the latter class may be judged from what is said of the others.   Before the summer is over discoveries may be made as rich and extensive as any previ-ously reported.   This mining region is in a state of transition and grows and develops faster than the world is aware of.   A mine that is unknown to-day may become famous to-morrow or next year.

CHAPTER III.

METHODS OF EXTRACTING THE VALUABLE METALS FROM THE ORE—
THE STAMP MILL, COPPER MATTE, LEAD SMELTING, AND OTHER
PROCESSES—DETAILED ACCOUNT OF OPERATIONS—DESCRIPTION
OF VARIOUS WORKS, INCLUDING THOSE AT ARGO AND GOLDEN.

Several methods or processes for the extraction of the valuable
metals from the ore or rock are in use in Colorado. Some ores are
found to be best adapted to one kind of treatment, and others require
a very different style of reduction. There is the stamp-mill raw amalgamation process, for low grade gold ores; then comes a number of
smelting and reduction processes, for rich and for medium grade
ores; copper matte smelting, adapted to all except ores very rich
in lead; smelting with lead riches, and the blast smelter, which is devoted to silver-lead bearing ores handle a large part of the values
of the mining product. There are mills devoted to chlorodizing-
roasting and amalgamation; others to chlorination and leaching,
and chlorination and lixiviation has been more or less in use.
Recently Silver Cliff silver ores are treated by raw amalgamation.

The system of wet crushing and raw amalgamation, by means of
stamp or quartz mills, is used on the great mass of what are termed
free gold ores. A considerable portion of the gold is lost, and most
of the silver and copper, but owing to the fact that no roasting or
smelting is required, this method, by its cheapness, is the only one
adapted to the low grade ores, of which most gold-bearing veins are
composed. Nearly nineteen-twentieths of the gold-bearing ores of
Gilpin county are handled by this process, and about twelve twenti-
eths of the entire gold product is obtained therefrom. The richer
mineral is sold to the smelters. The same process is in use in Boulder, Clear Creek, and Park counties, and the San Juan region. The
cost of treatment, where steam power is used, is from two to three
dollars per ton, or from fourteen to twenty dollars per cord. The
smaller figures represent the expense where the operator handles his
own ore, under the most favorable circumstances. When water

power can be used, the outlay is still less. Custom mills charge from $2.25 to $3.00 per ton, or from $18 to $20 per cord, varying with the season, mill power used, and character of ore.

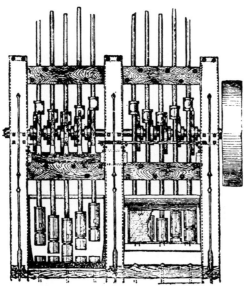

TEN STAMP QUARTZ MILL.

The stamp mill process is very imperfect, but has been vastly improved during the past fifteen years, as far as operations in Colorado are concerned. At one time only from fifteen to forty per cent. of the gold contained in the ore was saved, while from fifty to seventy per cent., and occasionally more, are saved at the present time. One mill claims a saving of over eighty-five per cent.. including returns of buddled tailings. Blankets and pans help to increase the returns.

The mill proper consists of a solid frame work, heavy iron stamps and attachments, propelled by steam or water power by means of a horizontal shaft and connections. Mortars, inclined tables, and other accessories go to make up the contents of the establishment. The framework is upright, as are also the iron stamps, which are made to rise and fall by means of cams or arms extending from the revolving shaft above. The stamps rise from twelve to eighteen inches and drop on the ore in iron mortars or troughs beneath from twenty-seven to thirty-five times per minute. These mortars are several feet long, and from twelve to fourteen inches high, and nine or ten deep, and rest on solid wooden foundations. They are placed between the upright wooden posts of the frame; the stamps, usually five in number, that rise and fall thereon form what is termed a battery. The mortars are the receptacles for the ore, which is shoveled or fed into them as fast as it can be advantageously crushed by the stamps, at the same time that a constant stream of water flows

in the same direction. Some mills have but a single battery of five stamps; others have ten or twenty, and there are some that have fifty and seventy-five.

On the side of the mortars where the ore feedng is done, the framework is boarded up some distance, and on the other side are sheet iron screens, through which the pulverized ore and water is forced on to the sloping copper plated inclines or tables below. Quicksilver is fed into the batteries and onto the tables when the mill man deems it necessary. This retains most of the gold on the tables while the pulp or slimes from the batteries are being carried onward by the water to the buddling tanks or stream beyond. The stamps are stopped, the water turned off, and the mortars and the plates of the tables are cleaned once a day, or once in several days, and the amalgam, or gold and quicksilver combination, is taken to the retort-room. Here it is skimmed and cleaned and pressed in a cloth so as to get rid of as much of the quicksilver as possible; the remainder is retorted and the crude bullion sold at the banks at from fourteen to eighteen dollars per ounce, or shipped in other ways. Gold from different mines varies in fineness and value, the quantity of silver accompanying it having much to do with this. The average fineness of Gilpin county bullion or retort gold is 787 parts pure gold, 198 parts pure silver, and 15 parts copper. The bullion obtained is from one-fourth to one-half of the amalgam, but rarely the latter. The quicksilver, after being condensed, is saved for future use.

After the pulverized ore leaves the batteries it is usually washed over two sets of inclined tables—the lower ones being covered with blankets. Some mills use pans, modeled after the principle of an arastra. The pulp or slimes, on leaving the mill proper, are generally worked over or concentrated by washing or buddling, when the concentrates are sold to the smelters. This often adds a dollar or two per ton to the total receipts from the ore. Formerly, no effort was made to save anything beyond the tables. About one ton of these tailings can be saved and sold to every ten tons of ore crushed.

The stamps used in these mills weigh from five hundred to seven hundred pounds, are generally ten or twelve feet high, and consist of a stem, head, shoe, and a collar, by means of which the cam raises them. The stem is made of wrought iron, and is from two to three inches in diameter, while the shoes attached to the lower part of the stem, and which come in contact with the ore, are thicker, and are made of steel or hardened iron. These stamps crush the ore to a pulp or powder, and much of the gold contained therein falls to the bottom of the mortars, and is taken up by the quicksilver placed there. Other portions of the gold are caught on the tables, blankets, and in the pans. The stamp-mill affords the only method of treating the low grade ores, of which the veins are mainly composed. Something like 140,000 tons are crushed in the Gilpin county mills every year. The smelting works are the destination of the high grade mineral, from which they save nearly all of the gold, silver, and copper.

The first quartz mills were brought into Colorado late in 1859. They were primitive affairs, with wooden, unplated tables, and had only from three to six stamps each. Up to this time the surface dirt and soft outcroppings of the veins had been shoveled into and washed in sluices, while other material was treated in arastras. Copper plates on tables and cyanide were not used at first, and few of the mill men knew anything about treating ores. It took a decade to bring quartz milling into even passable shape in Colorado, and nearly another to get it up to its present partly satisfactory condition.

This detailed account of the quartz mill is given because it is the basis of some other processes, and enters into their construction more or less. All ores must be pulverized before the silver and gold is extracted, and this is done either by stamps or by crushers and rolls. One or the other is found in all reducing, smelting, sampling and concentrating works.

Smelting with lead riches, is carried on at the works of the Golden and Valley companies at Golden, Hunt & Company's at Orodelfan, and at some points in the San Juan section. The lead comes out in bars, and the silver and gold in other bars. No copper is saved.

Chlorodizing-roasting and amalgamation is carried on at the Caribou mill at Nederland, and the Farwell reduction works at Georgetown, and has been used elsewhere. The ores are first broken in Dodge crushers and Cornish rolls, dried, sampled, and assayed, and then crushed dry by stamps, after which they are roasted in revolving iron cylinders, and then amalgamated in pans. Separation then takes place in the melting-room, and bars containing from $1,500 to $1,800 each, and of a fineness of from 800 to 900, are melted ready for shipment.

The pulverized ores are placed in the cylinders in charges of 3,500 pounds more or less, and the cylinders are then revolved at the rate of one revolution in two minutes. After four hours, from six to eight pounds of salt are introduced for every one hundred pounds of ore. Caribou ores require only from eight to eleven hours of roasting, and Georgetown ores from ten to twenty, according to lode. From 2,000 to 2,500 pounds of the roasted ore goes into each amalgamating-pan or leaching-tub at one time. In the pans, mullers do the grinding, and after one or two hours from 350 to 400 pounds of quicksilver are added, when the grinding continues from eight to twelve hours longer. The pulp is then thinned by water, and the specific gravity of the quicksilver and of the silver it has attracted causes it to seek the bottom of the pans, when it is drawn off, the pulp or dirt discharged, the amalgam still adhering removed, and the pans made ready for another charge. Retorting and melting into bars closes the proceedings

Chlorodizing-roasting and leaching is carried on at Georgetown and elsewhere. Works of this description have been operated at Rosita. The same kind of crushers, stamps, and roasting cylinders or furnaces are used as in the process just described, and the work is the same until the ore has been roasted. It is then placed in large agitating tubs, partially filled with a concentrated solution of hot water and salt kept in motion. This liquor dissolves the chloride of silver, and with the silver in solution is siphoned off and conducted into and through a series of tanks containing upright copper plates setting at intervals one behind and below another. The silver precipitates itself on these copper plates, when the brine or liquor is pumped back again into the agitating tubs for use.

The blast smelting furnace is used on ores carrying a high per cent of lead. When no roasting is required, as on carbonate ores, the process is rapid and somewhat simple. Skilled labor, attention, and experience are required, however, or disastrous results are likely to ensue. These furnaces are constructed of sheet iron and are usually circular in shape and of much greater height than diameter horizontally. Some are of square or oblong shape. They are built so that ore, coke, charcoal, and slag or iron are fed from an upper floor into the body of the furnace, while the lead and

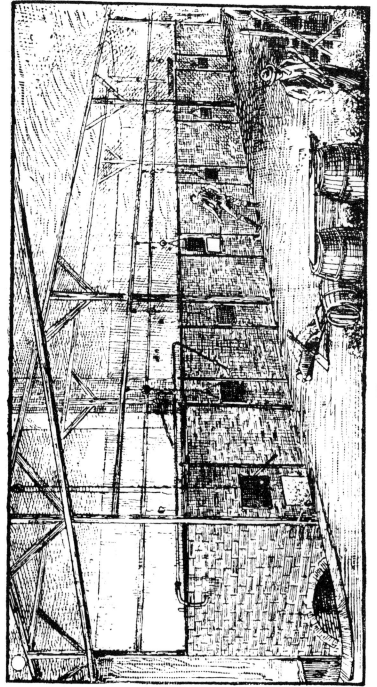

REVERBERATORY FURNACES FOR ROASTING ORE.

silver bullion and the slag make their way from separate outlets at the base of the furnace and in the story below. The hot liquid, composed of lead and silver or other metal, is ladled out into the molds made for the purpose, and cools into bars called base bullion. The interiors of these iron furnaces are lined with brick made of fire-clay.

A reverberatory furnace is constructed of brick. The various compartments, hearths, or chambers, in which the fires are kept up and the pulverized ores roasted, are lined with fire-brick. These furnaces are often forty or sixty feet or more in length, and are divided into connecting hearths. The ore, while being roasted, is moved along from one hearth on to another, by means of long iron shovels, reaching into the furnace. These furnaces are used in the large smelting works, except at Leadville.

No Colorado silver ores have been found in large quantities that can be treated by the cheap raw amalgamation process outside of the recent discoveries at Silver Cliff in Custer county. The same is true of ores nearly equally rich in both gold and silver. By that process the free milling gold ores are handled in custom mills at a charge of $2.25 and $3.25 per ton. All other classes of ore have been treated, by some one of the processes mentioned above, outside of that just named, and are purchased on the basis of a charge of from $25 to $40 per ton, and an allowance for loss in treatment. Cheaper reduction is effected at Caribou and a few places where the mines have mills of their own, and the Leadville carbonates can be smelted at lower rates now or in the hereafter.

As silver ores rich enough for such outlays cannot be found as plentifully as ten dollar gold ores, it will be seen that the drifts, shafts and excavations of a silver mine, although equally expensive, give up less available ore in a given breadth or distance than those of a gold mine. Consequently it must cost more to mine a ton of silver ore of the requisite richness than one of gold, since better ore must be had for silver reduction than for gold. The surpassing richness of much of the former ore is what sets things even, and often proves wonderfully profitable for a time. In Gilpin it costs from $2 to $5 to get out a ton of gold ore. In Clear Creek it costs from $12 to $40 for a ton of silver ore.

Years ago it cost one hundred dollars a ton to simply mill silver ore in Georgetown. A little later that sum would pay for mining,

TUBS OR VATS FOR LEACHING ROASTED ORE.

milling, and hauling.   At present, these items cost from $50 to $60 per ton, and less where the ore bodies are large.   The same work costs more in some districts and less in others.   In the San Juan region there are many miners that pay more for shipping their ore to a market—which, in the absence of roads, is mainly done on the backs of pack-animals—than they do for mining or smelting it. Twenty-five dollars a ton for transportation is not an unusual figure there.   Mines in northern and central Colorado, along the line of, or in close proximity to railways, avoid heavy shipping charges.

The raw amalgamation process for silver ores is somewhat on the same basis as that for free milling gold ores, with pans in place of tables, and can be prosecuted only where the silver has already been chlorodized in the rock by the hand of nature.   In the volcanic formation at Silver Cliff such has been the case, and consequently the above cheap and rapid method is going into use in that district. The process includes dry crushing by the ordinary stamps.   The pulverized ore then goes into large pans, where water and quicksilver are applied.   Here the pulp is kept agitated a requisite time, as in pan amalgamation described in Caribou and Georgetown mills.   When thoroughly amalgamated, the charge is drawn and the amalgam retorted and the silver melted into bars of a fineness of about 900. This system is called by some western men the Washoe process, because used so extensively in that Nevada silver district.   In order to save the charge of thirty or forty dollars per ton that must be paid for smelting or roasting, as with other ores and processes, the owners of the Racine Bay and Silver Cliff mines have been treating ores by this cheaper method at the Pennsylvania works at Rosita.   Those works include crushers, dry stamps, revolving roasting cylinders, and pans and tubs.   For treating Silver Cliff ores, the roasting part of the process is omitted, for nature has already chlorodized them. The result is it costs only from $3 to $5 per ton to handle these ores. A large stamp and pan mill is to be erected at Silver Cliff, and then this method of treatment will handle nearly or quite as much ore as any other, except that of the similar gold quartz mills.

Concentration is a method of separating the valuable portions of low grade ores from the gangue, in order that the miner will have the expense of smelting a smaller number of tons while securing nearly the same total value.   There are two systems of concentration, known as dry and wet.   Each embrace a great deal of machinery. There are crushers, rolls, stamps, screens, jigs, hoppers, tables, elevators, etc., in one or both processes. The Krom, or dry process, is represented in the Clear Creek Company mill at Georgetown and elsewhere, and the Collom and other methods at Black Hawk, Silver Plume, Idaho Springs, and Spanish Bar. The machines known as frue vanners are used in Boulder county, in Salina, Ballarat, Nederland, and Gold Hill district. By the above named mills the crude or low grade ore is dressed and separated, so as to leave only marketable and paying mineral in place of rock too poor to sell to the smelter.

In seven years up to the summer of 1878 the adjoining counties of. Clear creek and Gilpin gave a combined product of over $23,200,000 out of Colorado's total yield of $35,000,000 for that period. Gilpin gave about $12,200,000, nearly all in gold, and Clear Creek $11,000,-000, nearly all in silver. They will turn out together nearly or quite $5,000,000 this year. Clear Creek cañon is their natural outlet, and the mouth of this cañon and beyond has become the smelting depot for their richer ores. Golden and Argo are two of the great ore-reducing centres of the West.

The confidence of capitalists in these gold and silver mines is evinced by the great smelting enterprises carried on at the above mentioned points. Some of these smelting works have just been established; others have been enlarged. During the year three new ore-reducing concerns have been started at Golden. These, together with the works that have long been operating there, extend along the Colorado Central railway and the banks of Clear creek, and the name " Smelter's Row " has been applied to the locality.

The Valley Smelting Works of Golden were erected in the spring of 1879 by Gregory Board & Co., and have been in constant and successful operation since that time. They have recently been incorporated under the laws of Colorado into the Moore Mining and Smelting Company, which owns. and works the Murray mine, near Lawson, Clear Creek County. The advantages of cheap reduction for the product of this mine are thus afforded in addition to profits derived from the purchase and treatment of ores from elsewhere.

These works were planned and constructed by the superintendent Professor Gregory Board, formerly of the London School of Mines, a skillful metallurgist of long experience in treating all varieties of Colorado ores. They were designed and arranged to allow every

Golden Sm. Co. Works.

Malachite Works.

French Smelting Works.

Valley Smelting Works.

SMELTERS ROW—GOLDEN.

facility and the greatest economy in smelting, with all the latest improvements in furnaces and machinery. The location is favorable for securing cheap fuel and labor, and lime rock and fluxing material. Direct rail communication is afforded to all mining camps entered by railway. Under Professor Board the method of reducing all varieties of ores by lead smelting has been demonstrated a financial success, and this field of treatment has been recognized and acted upon by other operators. This process, one of the oldest, as well as one of the most direct and simple, has here been wise'y adapted to the ores encountered—and no little skill is required in the proper mixing or fluxing of the minerals, the smelting in blast furnaces for the reduction of the metals, and the collection of the gold and silver by means of lead in the mixture. The copper is separated in the form of matte.

The plant consists of a substantially erected main building with roof and sides of corrugated iron, two six-ton calcining furnaces, one fifteen-ton reverbatory furnace, two twenty-ton water jacket blast furnaces, two cupel furnaces, a complete set of tanks for the separation of copper from copper matte, a thirty-five-horse-power engine, a forty-five-horse-power boiler two Blake crushers and rolls for crushing, and all appliances for sampling. Attached to the office headquarters is a completely equipped laboratory for assaying and analysis. Twenty tons of ore can be handled daily, but under the arrangement of the plant, the works can be enlarged to any capacity the company's interests require. From the beginning of active operations in June, 1879, to March, 1880, these works treated 2,220 tons of ore, producing 1,650 ounces of gold, 110,300 ounces of silver, 275 tons of lead and 50 tons of copper matte, having a total value of over $200,000. These are better results than most establishments can show for the first year's operations. The matte is separated at the works. The company has sampling works for the purchase and shipment of ores at Black Hawk and Idaho, and agents at Georgetown, Alma and Leadville. Ores are received from all important mining districts of the State. With a tried superintendent and trained assistants and workmen, there can be no doubt of steadily increasing business and prosperity.

The French Smelting Works were erected by French capitalists and metallurgists in 1878–9, but a variety of causes delayed their operations. They are of the same character as those at Argo, but are less

SMELTING WORKS OF THE MOORE M. & S. COMPANY, GOLDEN.

extensive. Their capacity is some 20 tons of ore daily. The Golden Malachite Company. erected works in 1878, and for a time engaged in the manufacture of acids from ores of Gilpin County.

The first smelting at Golden was done in the year 1872. After a while the works suspended operations, and subsequently what has been known as the Golden Smelting Company came into possession. Considerable bullion was turned out in 1876-'7, when work was prosecuted pretty steadily. In the latter part of 1878 the capacity was increased to 18 tons of ore daily. That year the product is reported at over $300,000. The yield of 1879 and the total returns of ores that were treated from each county were as follows :

COUNTY.	TONS OF ORE.	GOLD.	SILVER.	LEAD.	TOTAL.
Boulder.............	310	$4,774 77	$57,274 00	....	$62,048 77
Gilpin...............	*1,521	57,359 25	39,589 68	$1,640 00	84,963 25
Clear Creek..........	792	6,387 03	59,610 25	17,672 00	83,669 28
Summit............ ..	76	....	3,134 25	2,879 00	6,013 25
Park.................	118	....	11,010 72	1,400 00	12,410 72
Lake................	192	475 91	37.847 25	3,664 00	41,986 66
Total............	3,009	$68,996 96	$238,4'6 15	$27,255 00	$306,011 58

* Partly mill tailings.

The firm of Netter, Matthews & Co., with headquarters at Denver, does the largest ore shipping business in Colorado. Their operations represent a value of over a million and a half dollars per annum. Immense shipments are made to the Omaha smelting works. The Silver Cliff branch of this house, known as Dillingham & Co., has a fine sampling mill, which handles from 500 to 1,000 tons of ore monthly—largely from the Bassick, Humboldt and other mines. The Georgetown sampling mill of the company does probably the largest business in that section. The great buildings in the upper part of Golden, formerly the Trenton Smelting Works, are now used by Netter, Matthews & Co. for roasting tailings from the Gilpin county stamp mills, and for sampling ores.

The smelting works at Argo are the successors of the Boston and Colorado Company's long established operations in the mountains. Professor N. P. Hill was the founder and has ever been the managing director of that company's smelting establishments. He began work at Black Hawk, in January, 1868, with one calciner and one smelting furnace. All around him were wrecks of preceding attempts at ore reduction, but, while encountering many difficulties in the earlier years, there has never been an interruption of work, general progress or success.

As the ore-supplying mining districts became more numerous and extensive, the furnaces and working forces were increased, and in time a corps of assistants had been secured such as is seldom met with, and whom it would almost be an impossibility to replace. The rare business and executive qualifications of the general manager have been ably seconded by those whom he has called to responsible positions, while the State has shown its appreciation of services rendered its main industry by awarding him a seat in the United States Senate.

This copper matte method of smelting, old and tried in other lands, has required many adaptations to the numerous and varied ores it has had to deal with, and as now conducted at this establishment can be termed the Colorado more appropriately than the Swansea process. When Professor Richard Pearce took charge of the metallurgical department, away back in 1873, the production of the first absolutely pure silver bullion in the West began. Before that the valuable metals had been sent from Black Hawk across the ocean to Swansea, in the form of copper matte, where they were purchased, separated, and refined. Since 1875 the gold has also been parted and refined in Colorado, and by a method of Mr. Pearce's own invention.

In 1873 branch works were started at Alma, among the Park county silver mines, and in 1876 an ore buying agency was established at Boulder. In 1877-8 the capacity of the Black Hawk works was over fifty tons of ore daily, instead of ten or twelve, as at the beginning. The working force had increased to a hundred men, the annual production of bullion from a coin value of $193,490 in 1868 to one of over two millions, and the average stock of ores on hand represented a value of three quarters of a million. Ores were coming in steadily from almost all parts of the State, and began to arrive from Montana, even, a thousand miles away. But the question of fuel was becoming a serious one, a more central and generally accessible locality was desirable, and as it was necessary to again enlarge the works it was deemed best to build entirely anew, and near the coal measures and the railway centre of the plains.

A location was selected two miles from Denver, to which the very appropriate name of Argo was applied, after the good ship in which a hero of Grecian mythology is reputed to have set sail in search of the golden fleece. The new works were so far completed in December, 1878, that several furnaces were fired up, and soon after all business, except roasting ores on hand, and sampling, purchasing and shipping, was discontinued at the old place at Black Hawk.

The works at Argo were constructed after the most approved plans which long experience and the necessities and advantages of the situation could suggest. The result is the finest and most extensive gold and silver reducing establishment in the world. This will be enlarged hereafter, but already possesses a nominal capacity for treating 120 tons of ore, or a practical capacity of 100 tons daily from one year's end to another, with the following enormous plant: 30 great kilns for roasting and desulphurizing the ore, and requiring wood for fuel; 10 ore calciners or roasting furnaces; 8 ore smelting furnaces; 8 calcining furnaces in the refining department; and five melting furnaces; together with engines and other necessary machinery. Two hundred men are employed, more than a quarter of a million in bullion is turned out monthly, and one hundred tons of Cañon and El Moro coal are consumed daily, beside a small quantity of wood. The stock of ores carried on hand exceeds $1,000,000 in value. Ore and coal trains pass over side tracks from the adjacent Colorado Central railway into the yard and receptacles prepared for them.

In the great ore building, 450 feet long by 120 wide, are scales for weighing loaded and empty cars, steam engines for propelling the ore-crushing and sampling machinery, and ten calciners—each roasting 9,600 pounds of ore every twenty-four hours. Adjoining are thirty roasting kilns, and a smoke-stack 100 feet high, that carries off the sulphurous fumes of both calciners and kilns. The products of all the different furnace buildings are conveyed from one to another in cars over connecting railways.

THE BOSTON AND COLORADO SMELTING WORKS AT ARGO.

In another building nearly 300 feet long and directly opposite
are eight furnaces that smelt 100 tons of roasted ores into five of
matte every twenty-four hours, while the refuse remains in
what is called slag. After the slag has been skimmed off of the
matte, the latter is transferred to another massive building, pulverized by crushers and rollers and roasted in the calciners of the refining department—eight
in number. A line of
vats is the next recep-
tacle, into which contin-
uous streams of hot
water are conveyed by
pipes. This hot water
holds the silver in solu-
tion, and in a series of
tanks below, the silver is
precipitated or retained
on lines of standing cop-
per plates from which it
is removed every week.
The bright, pure flaky
metal is secured in im-
mense crucibles, and is
shoveled into buckets
and conveyed to the
melting furnaces, five in
number. There it is
melted into solid bars
of an average weight of
about 1,700 ounces,

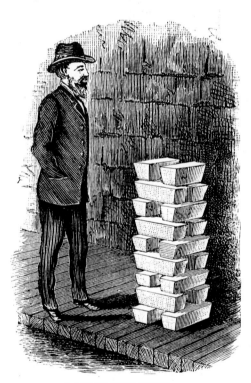

A TON OF PURE SILVER.

valued at $1,900 more or less. The copper and gold are saved
separately from the silver, the copper being secured on scrap iron.
The gold bricks vary in value from $15,000 to $27,000 each. Centrally located is the handsome structure used as the headquarters and
offices of managers Hill and Wolcott.

All of the buildings are of cut stone, covered with roofs of corrugated iron, and outside of the works are buildings for the employees
and their families. This village has three hundred people, with a
school and church,

The production of the works for four years in the various metals, and by counties, was as follows:

1875.				
COUNTIES.	Gold.	Silver.	Copper.	Total.
Gilpin	$357,000	$94,000	$51,000	$502,000
Clear Creek	4,000	438,000	......	442,000
Park	41,000	618,000	19,000	678,000
Boulder	113,900	74,000	......	187,000
Fremont	......	126,000	.....	126,000
Gold and Silver, San Juan and elsewhere	.....	......	.....	12,000
Totals	$515,000	$1,350,000	$70,000	$1,947,000

1876.				
Gilpin	$594,000	$132,000	$78,000	$804,500
Clear Creek	5,400	529,000	.....	534,400
Park	39,000	458,000	14,000	511,000
Boulder	86,000	49,000	......	135,000
Fremont	......	102,000	......	102,000
Other Sources	......	......	......	11,000
Totals	$724,400	$1,270,000	$92,500	$2,097,000

1877.				
Gilpin	$591,500	$137,500	$86,000	$815,000
Clear Creek	6,500	707,000	3,000	716,500
Park	38,000	221,500	8,000	268,000
Boulder	169,000	90,500	......	259,500
Custer	14,500	76,500	.. ..	91,000
Other Sources	.....	....	... ..	4,000
Totals	$819,500	$1,233,000	$97,500	$2,154,000

1878.				
Gilpin	$608,500	$181,000	$79,000	$868,500
Clear Creek	4,500	559,500	2,000	566,000
Boulder	178,000	73,000	......	251,000
Park	16,500	114,000	4,000	134,500
Custer	83,000	52,500	......	135,500
Montana Territory	.....	254,000	36,000	290,000
Other Sources	3,500	10,000	......	13,500
Totals	$894,000	$1,244,000	$121,000	$2,259,000

Product of 1879.				
LOCALITY RECEIVED FROM	Gold.	Silver.	Copper.	Total.
Gilpin	$591,000	$263,000	$103,000	$957,000
Clear Creek	53,000	368,000	9,000	430,000
Boulder	189,000	66,000	1,000	256,000
Park	4,500	314,000	....	318,500
Custer	6,000	11,000		17,000
Montana Territory	....	297,000	136,000	433,000
Other Sources	4,000	34,000	....	38,000
Totals	$847,500	$1,353,000	$249,000	$2,449,500

The company bullion product by years up to 1880, was as follows: coin value in recent years; greenback value before.

1868	$270,886	1874	$1,638,877
1869	489,875	1875	1,947,000
1870	652,329	1876	2,097,000
1871	848,571	1877	2,154,000
1872	999,954	1878	2,259,000
1873	1,210,670	1879	2,449,500

Total $17,017,662

This company now has sampling and ore buying mills at Boulder, Black Hawk, Lawson, Georgetown and Alma, but does all of its Colorado smelting at Argo. In the fall of 1879, smelting works were set in operation at Butte City, Montana Territory, where the ores are smelted and the copper matte sent to Argo for separation.

Gilpin county gives the largest product of any one district, but the newly purchased sampling mills at Lawson and Georgetown and the large products of the Freeland and Hukill mines, similar to Gilpin ores, will cause a heavy gain for Clear Creek county. Freeland ore has supplanted Gilpin stamp mill tailings in smelting.

The Argo works have received the following additions since the enumeration was made on page 240: 5 calcining furnaces, 3 melting furnaces, each of 12 tons daily capacity, a house for crushing metal, coal houses, new broad and narrow gauge railway tracks, and an extension to the great ore store-house, making it over 550 feet long.

Mather and Geist's works at Pueblo were established in 1878. They have roasting furnaces and three blast smelting furnaces, and their ore supply comes mainly from Leadville, Silver Cliff and San Juan. The Mallett reduction works at Canon run at intervals.

CHAPTER IV.

COLORADO'S MINING PRODUCT FROM THE EARLY DAYS TO THE PRESENT TIME—A MASS OF STATISTICS—THE YIELD OF GOLD, SILVER, LEAD, AND COPPER—OVER A HUNDRED MILLIONS—THE WORLD'S GREATEST PRODUCER IN 1880—$25,000,000 PER ANNUM—TONS OF GOLD AND SILVER.

No definite record was kept of Colorado's mining product prior to 1868, and the estimates of miners and bullion shippers alone remain to base a statement of the yield of the earlier years on. Neither the mints nor express companies handled anywhere near all of the gold produced in those days. A published statement of Colorado's output has appeared in print once or twice in recent times, but it is wide of the mark. The amounts given for the early placer mining times are too small, and those for the nine years up to 1872 are too large.

The excess from 1863 to 1869 was evidently as much as six millions, and for the three years succeeding the latter date at least three millions. The figures given for the latter period were like those furnished by Colorado men to Professor R. W. Raymond for his annual reports. The yields for both periods were originally computed on a currency basis, when gold ranged from $1.30 to $2.50, and after the lapse of years were rated as coin values. The express agents of Wells, Fargo & Co. always furnished their figures on a currency basis, and so did all Colorado bankers, smelters, mill men and miners, unless the words "coin value" were given. The figures in this book represent coin values unless otherwise stated.

The placers and gulches of Lake, Summit, Park, and Gilpin counties yielded largely for several summers, beginning with that of 1860, and when they were on the decline, the lode mines, mainly in Gilpin county, came to the front. These were doing well in 1862, and still better in 1863-4. Lodes and placers gave a varying yield, however, from 1860 to 1865. Besides the above named counties, both classes of mining were prosecuted in Clear Creek and Boulder. The product of the territory dropped to low figures in 1866, and there was no heavy increase from that time until the silver mines began to be extensively worked in 1870. What gain there was should be credited to the revival of lode mining in Gilpin county in 1868–9, and in a less degree to the then new discoveries in Lake.

The custom of counting the yield of mill gold in ounces may have been caused or strengthened by the continual variations between the values of the gold and greenback dollar. Such variations are shown in the price of silver, whose valuation per ounce should be $1.29, instead of $1.10, or $1.13. The reduction in the price of silver bullion has been a source of much loss to silver miners. The silver product of Colorado in 1878 would have had a valuation nearly one million larger, had silver been held at the same rates as prevailed prior to 1876. As has been stated elsewhere, all figures given in this book represent coin values unless otherwise stated. The reduction of numberless items and tables from currency to coin was a job of enormous proportions, but has been perfected.

The reader can rest assured that outside of the estimates for the earlier years, the figures of the Colorado gold and silver yield are in the aggregate correct and reliable. The tables of the production of the entire State, and of most of the counties for several years past, are the only accurate ones ever published, having been revised from the author's widely copied newspaper reports and statements. The best attainable information indicates the following yield of Colorado mines down to 1870—all gold, excepting about $330,000 in silver, and perhaps $40,000 in copper.

YEAR.	COIN VALUE.	YEAR.	COIN VALUE.
1859............	$500,000	1865............	$2,525,000
1860............	3,250,000	1866............	1,575,000
1861............	3,250,000	1867............	1,750,000
1862............	3,400,000	1868............	2,000,706
1863............	3,400,000	1869............	2,482,375
1864............	3,350,000		

The following tabulated statement shows Colorado's production of the four valuable metals and the total yield prior to 1879:

COLORADO'S MINING PRODUCT PRIOR TO 1880.

(*Coin Value.*)

YEAR.	GOLD.	SILVER.	COPPER.	LEAD.	TOTALS.
Previous to 1870	$27,213,081 00	$330,000 00	$40,000 00	....	$27,583,081 00
1870	2,000,000 00	650,000 00	20,000 00	....	2,670,000 00
1871	2,000,000 00	1,029,046 34	30,000 00	....	3,059,046 34
1872	1,725,000 00	2,015,000 00	45,000 00	$5,000 00	3,790,000 00
1873	1,750,000 00	2,185,000 00	65,000 00	28,000 00	4,028,000 00
1874	2,002,487 00	3,096,023 00	90,197 00	73,676 00	5,262,383 00
1875	2,161,475 02	3,122,912 00	90,000 00	60,000 00	5,434,387 02
1876	2,726,315 82	3,315,592 00	70,000 00	80,000 00	6,191,907 82
1877	3,148,707 56	3,726,379 33	93,796 64	247,400 00	7,216,283 53
1878	3,240,384 36	6,041,807 81	89,000 00	636,924 73	10,008,116 00
1879	2,920,326 43	12,068,930 27	131,000 00	1,893,947 59	17,014,204 29
Totals	$50,887,777 19	$37,380,690 75	$763,993 64	$3,024,947 32	$92,257,409 90

Nearly 84¾ tons of pure gold, 1,145 tons of pure silver, 1,819 tons of copper, and 47,810 tons of lead.

Coin or gold values of Colorado's mining products are given for all periods instead of the greenback values in which the yield of the territories was originally computed, because coin values being uniform permit of the proper comparison of one year with another. Greenback values may have varied from those of coin sixty per cent. one year and ten another. Happily there has been but one valuation in recent years—that of solid gold and silver. The figures for Colorado's yield prior to 1868 are based on estimates of express shippers, miners and others, as no exact data was published in those days.

From the foregoing it will be seen that in a little over four years up to 1864 the yield of gold was $13,800,000. This was the lively period of placer and gulch mining, and of lode mining by individual miners.

From 1864 to 1870, inclusive, a period of seven years, the yield was $16,121,435. This was when companies organized at the east did most of the mining. During the year 1864 the Colorado miners were selling out and quitting work, and the companies were beginning to produce. About $1,000,000 in silver, and $80,000 in copper came out before 1871, mainly in 1869-70. From that time silver mining made rapid strides, and from the beginning of 1872 its product has surpassed that of gold mining.

In eight years, 1871 to 1879, inclusive, Colorado yielded $45,006,-124.57—nearly all the result of individual work by Colorado miners. Eighteen hundred and seventy-eight gave $10,008,116.90 of that amount.

The yield of 1879 was $17,014,204.29—nearly one fifth of the total of over twenty years. Colorado is now producing over $2,000,000 a month. The preceding table shows the former steady gain and the recent enormous increase of the bullion yield.

The product of lode mining in gold, silver, etc., the yield of gold-bearing lodes alone, and the total yield of the placers up to 1880 was about as given below:

All lodes, silver and gold........................$72,057,409.90
Gold lodes, gold only.............................. 30,687,777.19
Placers, gold..................................... 20,200,000.00

Probably $13,000,000 of this placer product was obtained before 1865. The decrease of the gold yield of Colorado in 1879 was due to a lack of water among the placers.

COLORADO   MINING   PRODUCT   BY   COUNTIES—
1870-'71-'72-'73.

NAMES.	1870.	1871.	1872.	1873.
Gilpin	$1,552,000 00	$1,400,000 00	$1,389,289 00	$1,340,502 00
Clear Creek...	481,354 08	869,046 34	1,503,291 00	1,204,761 00
Lake..............	125,000 00	100,000 00	133,000 00	230,000 00
Park.............	60,000 00	100,000 00	250,000 00	459,000 00
Boulder...........	130,000 00	250,000 00	346,540 00	390,000 00
Summit...........	150,000 00	66,000 00	125,000 00	106,600 00
Other Products	171,645 92	274,000 00	50,000 00	297,737 00
Total of Colorado..	$2,670,645 92	$3,059,046 34	$3,790,000 00	$4,028,000 00

COLORADO MINING PRODUCT BY COUNTIES, 1874-'75-'76.

COUNTIES.	1874.	1875.	1876.
Clear Creek.......................	$2,203,947,00	$1,780,054 31	$1,982,548 28
Gilpin...........................	1,531,863 00	1,520,677 13	2,105,544 78
Park......	596,392 00	716,258 62	550,044 84
Boulder........	539,870 00	605,000 00	547,085 20
Lake	223,503 00	104,258 62	90,900 00
Summit.........................	126,108 00	122,413 78	350,000 00
Fremont..........................	....	294,827 58	251,121 06
The San Juan Region.............	.. ..	90,517 24	244,663 66
Other sources and unaccounted for	40,620 00	200,380 55	70,000 00
Totals..............	$5,362,383 00	$5,434,387 02	$6,191,907 82

COLORADO MINING PRODUCT FOR 1877.

COUNTY.	Tons of ore treated or exported	GOLD.	SILVER.	LEAD.	COPPER.	TOTALS.
Gilpin	147,000	$1,963,485 07	$161,255 38	$1,000 00	$82,296 64	$2,208,037 09
Clear Creek	19,503	96,500 00	1,984,077 91	123,000 00	3,000 00	2,206,577 91
Park	4,040	108,000 00	489,959 32	10,000 00	8,500 00	616,459 32
Boulder	10,000	356,722 49	234,602 86	2,000 00	....	593,325 35
Lake	3,700	55,000 00	23,930 00	76,400 00	....	555,330 30
Custer	2,000	196,000 00	155,081 34	....	....	354,081 34
Summit	500	150,000 00	40,000 00	....	....	190,000 00
The San Juan Region	9,500	105,000 00	237,472 52	35,000 00	....	377,472 52
Other sources	......	118,000 00	....	....	....	118,000 00
Totals	200,258	$3,148,707 56	$3,726,379 33	$247,400 00	$93,796 64	$7,216,283 53

The coal product was about 160,000 tons, worth $600,000.

COLORADO MINING PRODUCT FOR 1878.

COUNTIES.	Tons of ore treated or exported.	GOLD.	SILVER.	LEAD.	COPPER.	TOTALS.
Lake................	21,746	$117,946 00	$2,591,054 71	$443,924 73	....	$3,152,925 44
Clear Creek........	22,000	134,000 00	2,025,105 85	98,000 00	$4,000 00	2,261,105 85
Gilpin.............	147,000	1,974,964 36	225,936 75	1,000 00	79,000 00	2,280,901 11
Boulder...........	11,500	445,500 00	233,623 50	....	....	679,123 50
Park..............	4,500	78,200 00	338,498 00	4,000 00	6,000 00	426,698 00
Custer...........	4,000	185,000 00	167,500 00	....	....	352,500 00
Summit...........	1,500	165,774 00	125,000 00	30,000 00	....	320,774 00
The San Juan Region...	10,000	39,000 00	335,089 00	60,000 00	....	434,089 00
Elsewhere.........	....	100,000 00	....	....	....	100,000 00
Totals........	222,246	$3,240,384 36	$6,041,807 81	$636,924 73	$89,000 00	$10,008,116 90

The coal product of 1878 was 200,630 tons, worth about $800,000.

In 1878, the mines of Colorado turned out a little over $5\frac{3}{4}$ tons of pure gold, $183\frac{1}{2}$ tons of pure silver, 222 tons of copper, and 9,989 tons of lead.

COLORADO'S MINING PRODUCT FOR 1879.

COUNTIES.	Tons of ore exported or treated.	GOLD.	SILVER.	LEAD.	COPPER.	TOTALS.
Lake (Leadville)	111,124	$46,376 37	$8,455,655 68	$1,687,489 32	......	$10,189,521 37*
Gilpin (Central)	150,000	2,144,245 00	365,193 68	3,312 00	$113,000 00	2,625,750 00
Clear Creek Georgetown	21,000	175,000 00	1,695,000 00	80,000 00	17,000 00	1,967,000 00
Boulder	11,000	313,280 00	373,079 00	......	1,000 00	687,359 00
Park	4,500	49,500 00	380,010 72	2,400 00	......	481,910 72
Custer (Silver Cliff)	2,700	75,000 00	262,000 00	30,000 00	......	367,000 00
Summit	2,000	50,000 00	212,500 00	47,200 00	......	309,700 00
Chaffee	600	20,000 00	59,000 00	......	......	79,000 00
Gunnison	100	......	25,000 00	......	......	25,000 00
San Juan Region	3,500	21,925 06	241,491 19	43,546 27	......	306,972 52
Elsewhere	...	25,000 00	......	......	......	25,000 00
Totals	306,524	$2,920,326 43	$12,068,930 27	$1,893,947 59	$131,000 00	$17,014,204 29

* Exclusive of ore containing over $920,000 received and paid for at smelters.

Colorado mines turned out in 1879 nearly 5 tons of pure gold, 368 tons of pure silver, 23,674 tons of lead, and 312 tons of copper.

The gain in production over 1878, the best preceding year, was $7,006,087.39, or over 70 per cent.

The coal product of 1879 was about 260,000 tons, worth $960,000.

CHAPTER V.

THE MINES OF BOULDER COUNTY—THE GOLD, SILVER, TELLURIDE, AND COAL BELTS—REVIEW OF THE MOUNTAIN MINING DISTRICTS —BRIEF NARRATIVE OF OPERATIONS—THE YIELD OF THE PRECIOUS METALS FROM 1859 TO 1879—DETAILED STATEMENTS OF PRODUCTION—MINES, MILLS, AND SMELTERS.

Boulder county embraces a combination of mountain, valley, and plain that reverts in the highest measure to the advantage of its people. Its mineral deposits are of great extent and variety, and its agricultural sections are extremely fertile, and in a high state of cultivation. Flourishing towns and beautiful farms dot its surface, and mines and mills are profitably operated all over the mountain sections, from the sunny plains at Boulder back to the snow-barren summits of the snowy range. On the plains are extensive coal measures, which will be referred to more in detail in another place. The farming sections have already been described. The mines and the mining industry will be the subject matter of the few succeeding pages.

The mineral deposits of Boulder are very extensive, and embrace a wonderful variety. First there are alluvial deposits in creeks and gulches, but these are of limited extent and mainly worked out. The gold and silver lode veins, and the coal measures are the main source of wealth. The former are located on the mountains and the latter on the plains.

The lode veins of Boulder county may be classed under three heads—silver, gold, and telluride ; the latter carrying both metals. They are generally of the kind referred to as "true fissures," very many of them having well-defined walls and seemingly unending depth. They commonly occur either in gneiss or granite rock, or between the two. There are exceptions, however, both regarding formation, regularity, and continuity. There is a multitude of them, good, bad, and indifferent.   Some thousands of locations have been recorded, and the number worked with a profit is large.

The alluvial gold deposits of the gulches were operated by the pioneers, and more or less every summer since. Some are abandoned, however. Some large gold-bearing lodes were discovered in 1859–60, and for several years quartz mills were turning out a great deal of bullion. After considerable depth was attained, more difficulty was experienced in reducing the ores and extracting the gold than is usual with free gold ores of other counties. This caused companies or individual owners to stop work. Process mills also brought disaster in certain localities. Long before the discovery of silver at Caribou, mining affairs were at a low ebb, although work was never entirely suspended in Ward district.

The productive character of the silver mines at Caribou turned attention once more to the entire section, and prospecters, and miners who had not found anything valuable near the Boulder creeks, began to move out over the hills to the northward. While looking for gold and silver bearing veins, they often encountered mineral of a strange and peculiar appearance, which was passed over as worthless. After a while Professor J. Alden Smith and others began to test this mineral, and found it to be of the telluride species, carrying gold in remarkably large quantities.

Tellurium is a metal that has been discovered in very few places, and Colorado miners were as little acquainted therewith as they had been with silver a few years before. Its existence in Colorado was first known in 1873, in the Red Cloud mine on Gold Hill. Ores from this vein could not be made to produce well in the stamp mills, although assays demonstrated the presence of gold in large quantities.

After their true character was ascertained, the owners commenced shipping ore to the smelters, large returns were obtained and men began to flock in to the district and to prospect for tellurides. Many discoveries were made in the succeeding two or three years, and the production and rich pay streaks of the Cold Spring, Red Cloud, American, Slide, Keystone, Magnolia, John Jay, Melvina and other veins created more excitement than did the Columbia, Horsfal and Hoosier gold lodes a dozen years before, or the Caribou silver finds of more recent times.

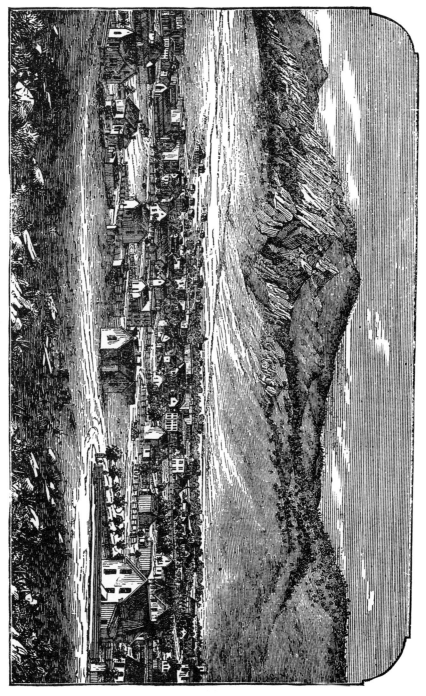

BOULDER.

These mines built up the towns of Sunshine, Salina, Providence, Ballarat and Magnolia, and caused a return of population to Gold Hill and James Creek. While many of these discoveries are no longer worked, some valuable gold veins have been found and operations have been resumed on some of the long idle mines that paid so well in the early days. Between the gold, silver, and telluride belts the mining portion of Boulder county is enabled to show a steady development and a gain in production.

Several mines of Boulder county yielded large amounts of gold from 1859 to 1865, inclusive. The Columbia lode, in Ward district, paid largely for a time, especially those parts since known as the Ni Wot and Baxter properties. The Horsfal mine on Gold Hill was also very productive, as was the Hoosier and some others. The yield of gold for the entire county, up to 1870, may be safely set down at $950,000. The gold yield had been decreasing for some time when the Caribou silver mines began to be developed. In four years, 1870–4 inclusive, before the telluride mines began to be generally worked, Caribou district had probably yielded nearly $700,000 in silver, and all other districts $270,000 in gold. From that time the gold product was much larger. The total yield of Boulder county up to January 1, 1879, was not far from what appears in the following table:

Prior to 1870........	$950,000	1874............	$536,582 00
1870...............	130,000	1875.............	605,000 00
1871...............	250,000	1876.............	547,085 20
1872...............	346,540	1877.............	593,325 35
1873...............	390,000	1878.............	679,123 50

1879, $687,359.

Total for twenty-one years, $5,715,025.05; total gold, $3,396,211; silver, $2,317,079. For detailed statement of 1879, see page 260.

The product of 1875 embraced $266,000 in silver from Caribou district, probably about $70,000 from the few gold lodes and from the gulches, and $269,000 from the telluride veins, whose product was mainly gold. The total product may be set down as $305,000 in gold, and $300,000 in silver.

In 1876 the silver product of Caribou was only about $80,000, and of the county possibly $120,000, leaving $427,085.20 as the gold product, mainly from telluride camps.

The mining product of the county for the years 1877 and 1878 was as follows:

1877.		1878.	
Gold	$356,722 49	Gold	$454,123 50
Silver	234,602 86	Silver	223,000 00
Lead	2,000 00	Lead	2,000 00
Total	$593,325 35	Total	$679,123 50

Last year Boyd and other smelters purchased about $25,000 worth of Lake and Clear Creek county ores and Gilpin stamp mill tailings for fluxing purposes. That amount is deducted from the export and output of Boulder, which was actually $704,123.50.

The yield of 1877 passed through the following mills, smelters, and avenues:

	Tons of Ore.	Value.
Silver bullion—New Jersey, at Caribou	600	$100,000
Gold bullion—Gulch and stamp mill gold	3,000	60,000
Gold and silver bullion at Boyd's smelting works, Boulder	1,800	150,000
Ores smelted at B. and C. works at Black Hawk.	1,800	248,325
Ores smelted at Golden smelting works	200	20,000
Ores shipped to West Denver works	75	5,000
Other shippers and consumers, and crude ore concentrated	50	10,000
Total tons and value	8,125	$593,325

The concentrating mills reduced the bulk of some 3,500 tons of low grade ore down to one-third of that amount, and then sold to the smelters, as appears in the above figures.

The gold and silver mining product of 1878 passed through various channels, in amounts as follows:

Gold and silver bullion from Boyd, Hunt, etc	$120,000 00
Silver bullion from Caribou	130,000 00
Silver bullion from Washington Avenue mill	15,000 00
Gold dust and mill retort	65,000 00
Gold taken out of county outside of banks and express,	25,000 00
Ore sent to Boston and Colorado Works at Black Hawk,	251,000 00
Ore sent to Golden Smelting Co	48,123 50
Ore sent to Omaha, St. Louis, and elsewhere	50,000 00

Deduct from above $25,000 due ore of other counties.

The ore product of 1878 was not far from 11,500 tons, of which all but 1,500 were handled in the county. About 1,000 of the first amount were concentrated into less than two or three hundred tons, and then mainly shipped, so that they eventually appear in the second or export figures. The quartz mills treated about 4,000 tons of ore, yielding an average of about $15 per ton. The silver ores exceeded 2,500 tons, and were mostly treated at the Caribou mill, with an average of $66 per ton. Others went to Boulder, Black Hawk, and Golden, and smelted from $80 to $200 per ton, and occasionally $200 to $600 and more. The telluride mines are supposed to have yielded nearly 3,500 tons. Most assorted ores gave from $100 to $400. Crude ores, before concentrating, contained only from $15 to $50. The tellurides went to Boulder, Golden, Black Hawk, and Argo. The last two places represent the Boston & Colorado Smelting Company, whose purchases yielded $74,782 in gold and $42,608 in silver in 1876, about $160,952 in gold and $86,190 in silver in 1877, and $178,000 in gold and $73,000 in silver in 1878.

The mines that appear to take the lead at present are the Caribou, Native Silver, Seven-Thirty and some others at Caribou, the Melvina Slide, and Smuggler in the telluride belt, and the Golden Age gold mine. The Cold Spring, Keystone, Mountain Lion, Last Chance, and some other telluride mines are reported to be producing largely again. Some of the gold lodes of Ward district, such as the Columbia, Celestial, Utica, Stoughton, and others, are beginning to pay once more. There is more than usual activity in Caribou, Ward, Gold Hill, and Central districts. The last embraces the Left Hand, James Creek, and Ballarat sections. Magnolia is also reviving. There has been a steady improvement nearly all over the county for the past twelve months.

Many quartz mills, smelting and reduction works, have been in operation in Boulder county since mining began. The varied and novel character of some of the ores, and the refractory nature of others, offered a fruitful field for experiments, and for the trial of various processes, resulting in failure and loss. The old stamp mill methods, melting with lead riches and cupeling, and chlorodizing and amalgamating are the processes by which the ores are handled at present. The frue vanner concentrating tables had a big run two years ago, and some twenty or more were in use, but most of them are now idle or discarded.   Other concentrating mills are at work.   The smelting and reduction works of Boulder county that are at work are stated below.

NAME.	LOCATION.	Character or Process.	Reducing Capacity in Tons.	PLANT.
Caribou Cons. Company...	Nederland.	Stamping, chlorodizing roasting and amalgamating......	15	15 stamps, 4 cylinders, and 10 pans, etc.
J. H. Boyd.....	Boulder....	Smelting with lead and cupeling...........	8 to 12	Crushers, 10 stamps, reverberatory and smelting furnaces, and cupel furnace.
Hunt, Barber & Co......	Orodelfan .	Smelting with lead and cupeling............	4 to 8	Crushers, reverberatory, water jacket and blast furnaces, and cupel furnace.
Pomeroy.......	Ward......	Stamping, roasting and amalgamation, and concentration..	5 to 8	Stamps, 2 cylinders, 3 pans and concentrating tables.
Atchison Co....	Salina.....	Concentration, smelting, and amalgamation.	4 to 6	Stamps, furnaces, etc.
Washington Avenue	Sugar Loaf District..	Conc., chlor., roasting, and leaching with copper ; dry concentration..	8 to 10	10 stamps, cylinders, leaching tubs and vats, and concentrating machinery.

The raw amalgamation stamp mills, for treating the low grade gold ores and quartz, have a total crushing capacity of 130 tons daily, but only about half of them are usually at work.   They are as follows :

NAME.	LOCATION.	CHARACTER.	CALIBRE.
Baxter.............	Ward District.......	Raw amal..........	20 Stamps.
Ni Wot.............	" "	" "	50 "
Humboldt..........	" "	" "	10 "
Pomeroy...........	" "	" "	15 "
Brainard..........	Central "	" "	10 "
Golden Age........	" "	" "	25 "
Corning Tunnel.....	" "	" "	15 "
Hetzer.............	Nederland District..	" "	15 "
First National......	" " ..	" "	25 "

The "eye" house, and another relic, Leadville, c. 1975

"This Ol' House", Leadville, c. 1975

Total, 9 mills and 185 stamps. There is also a small quartz mill in Sugar Loaf district.

The concentrating mills (mainly for telluride ores) now at work are the Melvina or Everitt mill at Salina, and the Black Cloud mill, near that point and Gold Hill. The Van Fleet mill at the Smuggler mine is also run occasionally. Pomeroy has concentrating tables in his mill at Ward, and the Washington Avenue mill operates the dry concentration process.

Boyd, and Hunt Barber & Co. treat gold, silver, and telluride ores. Their bullion is mixed gold and silver, in which the former largely predominates. The Boston & Colorado Smelting Company have a sampling mill and ore-buying agency at Boulder. This handles large quantities of ore, shipping to Argo.

The Native Silver Company's mill at Caribou will soon be at work again with stamps, roasting cylinders and leaching vats and tubs.

A ten ton smelter was built in 1879 for the Ni Wot and Nelson mines in Ward district.

The works and mills named on the preceding page were more or less idle in 1879–80—some doing but little. The cause of over three months' stoppage of the Caribou mill was due to the burning of the mine's buildings and hoisting works, since replaced. Most quartz mills ran less than half the time, and some not at all.

BOULDER COUNTY MINING PRODUCT FOR 1879.

SHIPPED BY OR TO	Gold.	Silver.	Copper.
First National Bank, dust..............	$11,100 00	....	....
" " mixed bullion....	46,725 00	$25,728 00	....
State National Bank, dust; silver bars.	5,000 00	8,500 00	....
" " retort...........	32,000 00	....	....
Valley Smelting Works, ore...........	1,880 23	563 00	....
Golden " ore...........	4,774 77	57,274 02	....
Boston & Colorado Smelting Works, ore	189,000 00	66,000 00	$1,000 00
Caribou Mill, silver bullion...........	....	210,513 98	....
Other Sources........................	22,800 00	5,000 00	....
Totals.................	$313,280 00	$373,079 00	$1,000 00

Total product................. $687,359.

The Caribou mine showed by far the largest gain and gave nearly one-third of the county's product. The Native Silver and Seven-Thirty gained, and, among the telluride camps the Slide and new Prussian. Some noted telluride mines lost, and some were idle.

CHAPTER VI.

BOULDER COUNTY MINES—THE SILVER BELT ON THE HEADWATERS OF THE BOULDERS—STORY OF A GREAT SILVER MINE—THE CARIBOU, ITS RECORD, YIELD, AND PRESENT CONDITION—HARD MONEY, AND PLENTY OF IT—THE NATIVE SILVER, SEVEN-THIRTY, NO NAME, IDAHO AND OTHER LODES OF THE CARIBOU DISTRICT.

Up to 1870 the forest-clad hills up towards timber-line and the headwaters of the Boulder creeks had seldom been visited. While hunting for deer, Samuel Conger had located a gold lode there away back in 1864, but never did much work on it. Years after he saw some Nevada silver ore, and was struck with its similarity to rock he had stumbled over in his lonely hunting excursions among the pines near Arapahoe Peak. He induced some Gilpin county men to accompany him on a prospecting trip, and the result was the discovery of silver. Conger struck the outcroppings of a vein which he called the Poor Man, and William Martin and George Lytle found a lode just above, which they named the Caribou. This was on the last day of summer, 1869.

An assay of the "blossom rock," made at Central, caused them to return with pick and shovel, and blaze a trail to their new camp. Supplies were furnished by three ranchmen named Mishler, McCammon, and Pickel, who were partners in the discoveries. The others carried these winter supplies in on their backs, and over the deep snows. Conger traded his interest in the Caribou in such a way as to become the sole owner of the Poor Man. Before winter came on, one load of ore was sold for good figures to the smelters.

Martin and Lytle built a cabin on the spot where the town of Caribou now stands, and kept at work on the mine whenever the weather would permit. The locality was close to the snowy range, and ten thousand feet above sea-level, and storms and snows were of frequent occurrence. When summer came the owners constructed a wagon-road, and began to break ore and team it to Prof. Hill, at Black Hawk, twenty miles distant.

Memories of yesterday, Leadville, c. 1975

The Tabor Mansion, Leadville, c. 1975

Reports of the value and quantity of the ore soon became noised abroad, and a stampede ensued for the new district. Many lodes were found that season, some of which paid handsomely, and a town sprang up in the adjacent valley, which, after the big vein, was called Caribou. Among other mines that sold ore in 1870, were the Idaho, Boulder County, Trojan, No Name, Sherman, Spencer, Sovereign People, Poor Man, and Seven-Thirty. The entire tract of country was called Grand Island Mining District.

In the fall of 1870, A. D. Breed, of Cincinnati, purchased the western half of the Caribou lode for $50,000, and constructed a road to and began the erection of a mill at what is now called Nederland. Up to January, 1871, the main shaft had reached a depth of 200 feet, and $70,000 was said to have been obtained from sales of ore. Breed completed his great silver mill late in 1871, and by October 1, 1872, had mined 3,650¾ tons of ore. The discoverers also made money on the eastern half of the lode.

In the spring of 1873 the Mining Company Nederland was formed in Holland, and purchased the Caribou mine and mill property at the nominal figure of $3,000,000, although the actual cash payment was but a little more than half that sum. The Holland organization encountered trouble from the start. It is said that Breed stripped the mine of much of its rich ore after the examination and before the property was turned over. Some of the Company agents were of no benefit, and contentions, mismanagement, and debts caused a cessation of work at the close of 1875, and the disposal of the mine at sheriff's sale, to Jerome B. Chaffee, in October of the succeeding year. During 1873-'4-'5, the mine had yielded largely, and if properly conducted would have paid handsomely. From the date of discovery to the time when the company closed down, the yield was not far from $750,000, of which sum $130,000 came from 1,800 tons of ore in 1874, and $210,703 from 3,819 tons of ore in 1875. Tribute workers are said to have taken out about $25,000 during the spring and summer of 1876. The mine was then 470 feet deep, and over 3,250 square fathoms of ground had been broken or excavated.

Since Mr. Chaffee and associates acquired the property, they have recovered the mine from the bad condition in which it had been left, and have steadily pursued the policy of development until the ore reserves are of immense extent. Although the work is almost entirely confined to sinking and drifting, the product and profits are now rarely equaled. Eben Smith, who has operated important mines nearly all over the State, has been the superintendent since the purchase in 1876. The results are a mine and mill in splendid condition and working order, and the beginning of the payment of regular dividends, with no probability of stoppage.

While the mine was being brought into producing condition and ore reserves were being gained the yield was not large. The ore sales to October 1, 1877, were $26,449.80, and for the succeeding year, $83,507.31. The probable smelter's yield of both years was over $150,000. The mill was started up in February, 1878, and ten stamps and three roasting cylinders were employed until March, 1879. Since then the mill's full capacity has been in use (on half the old force of mill hands), excepting for a little over three months succeeding the burning of the mine buildings and hoisting works. Milling was resumed late in December, 1879. Silver bullion valued at $210,513.98 was produced in less than nine months of actual mining and milling in 1879. Of this $118,513.98 came out after the company's organization, May 1, 1879. The yield of the last two months of 1878 was $30,224, and the present yield averages over $25,000 a month. The mine had yielded $1,168,000 up to 1880. The silver is not refined at the mill, and when shipped away is worth about one dollar an ounce. The mine and mill shipments for the three months ending April 1, 1880, aggregated between $75,000 and $80,000 worth of bullion.

The superintendent is confident of being able to continue for years to mine fifteen tons of ore per day, or over four hundred per month —the full capacity of the mill—without exhausting or even reducing the reserves, and to pay from ten to fifteen thousand dollars in dividends every month. The average yield of Caribou ore at the mill, just as it came from the mine, has been $66 per ton. Assorted lots of from one to seven tons each, sold at the Boston & Colorado smelting works, gave from 235 to 666 ounces per ton. Thirty-nine tons sold at near the same dates averaged over 300 ounces. Pieces of ore are found every day that will assay among the thousands.

The Caribou pay vein varies in width from two to eight feet. It is remarkable for its great size and comparative uniformity of value one month with another. It pitches toward the north, and is the

The old railroad depot, and home sweet home—Leadville, c. 1975

Dead and done for, Leadville, c. 1975

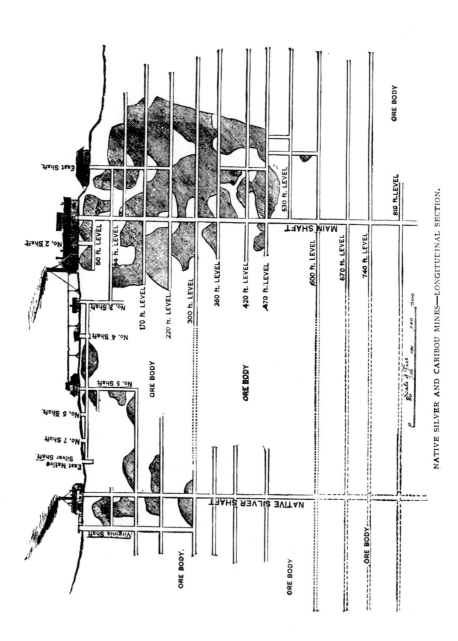

NATIVE SILVER AND CARIBOU MINES—LONGITUDINAL SECTION.

great mother vein of the hill.   The course and direction of this and neighboring veins are such that the Caribou will be found to absorb several of them before much greater depth is attained.   In fact several have already merged into this great ore channel, as branches of a tree connect with the parent trunk.   Other feeders and blind lodes have been discovered, by means of cross cuts driven north and south, all pitching in the same direction.   The result of the union of two or more veins is to increase the quantity and quality of the ore. Late developments go to show that the Caribou vein is richer at great depths than near the surface.   The best ore ever mined there was raised within the past few months in solid blocks, ten or twelve inches long and wide.

About sixty men are employed in the mine.   Most of them are engaged on contract or on tribute work ; others receive $2.50 per day for their labor.   The cost of drifting or running levels by hand-drilling varies from $12 to $18 per foot, according to hardness of ground and size of vein, and eight dollars is the lowest price ever paid for drifting.   Where machine drills are used, the cost is thirty three per cent. less.   The main shaft is sunk with the aid of the latter at $40 per foot; with hand-drills the cost was $60.   This shaft is five feet wide by fourteen long inside of timbers ; has a double hoisting copartment or bucket-ways, and will be 810 feet deep as soon as the present "lift" is sunk.   A duplex Wood patent air-compressor, capable of running four machine drills, that strike from 500 to 700 blows per minute, is used.   In rock of the unusual hardness of that of Caribou Hill the amount of time and money saved by this system of rock-drilling is strikingly apparent. It is claimed that twice as much ground can be broken in a given time by using these machine drills as by hand-drilling.

As sinking and drifting are five times as costly in this mine as stoping is, expenses will be vastly reduced when breaking down the ore reserves.   Mining costs but $9.15 per ton, according to past experience.   Ore is hauled to the mill at a contract price of $2 per ton.   Milling expenses, including all outlays for labor, fuel, salt, chemicals, etc., as per monthly statements, are only $8 per ton. This makes a total cost of $19.15, or say $20 per ton.   It takes a big vein and favorable ore to admit of such small figures.   The average yield of the fifteen tons of ore mined and milled daily has been $66.   Allowing a return of $60, and the per cent. of profits on

Deathhouse for Baby Doe; The Tabor Matchless, Leadville, c. 1975

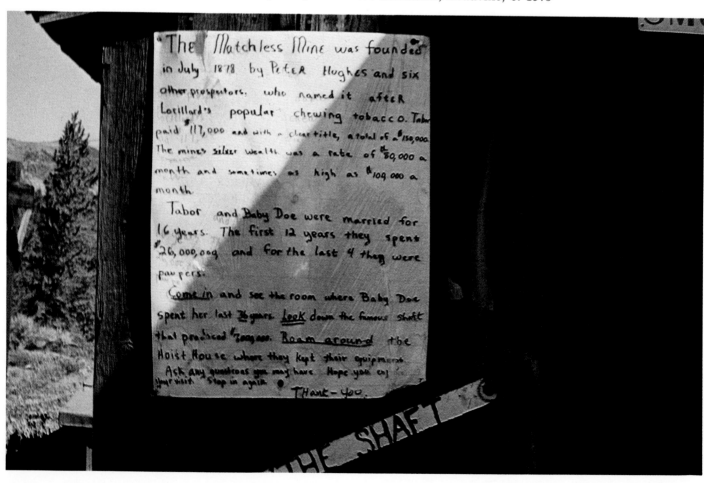

The Tabor Matchless shaft, Leadville, c. 1975

the gross yield is over sixty per cent., or at the rate of $15,000 per month. Some extremely rich ore has been uncovered, and it is said the mine never looked better.

The developments of the Caribou comprise eight shafts, one hundred feet apart, with a total of 2,500 feet, and thirteen levels connecting the main shafts, of a combined length of nearly 6,000 feet. A tunnel intersects the lode 300 feet below the surface. The main shaft will be continued on from a depth of 810 feet to one of 900 with a level 880 feet deep. This will make a gain in depth of 430 feet since the fall of 1876. A shaft was recently sunk between shafts 6 and 7, which entered the Seven Thirty level 300 feet east of its main shaft.

In September, 1879, a terrible forest fire swept over this section, destroying several mine buildings and a portion of the town of Caribou. The great building over the Caribou main shaft, together with costly hoisting and pumping machinery, was destroyed. The work of rebuilding was begun at once, and in three months a finer structure and newer and better mine equipments stood on the site of the old ones. The new building is 150 feet long, covered with an iron roof and supplied internally with hoisting machinery, pumps, engines and boilers of the most effective character. Tramways for ore transportation extend overhead, and the entire plant has no superior in the State. There are also buildings over several other shafts along the lode.

The Caribou silver mill is located at Nederland, four miles from the mine, on account of abundant water and fuel facilities. The main building is 165 feet long by 100 wide, and is terraced in five floors for automatic handling of the ore. In the upper end of the mill is the ore room, where are located a Blake crusher of forty tons daily capacity, and three automatic feeders of twenty tons daily capacity. Adjoining and on the next lower floor is the stamp room, with fifteen stamps, weighing seven hundred and fifty pounds each, for pulverizing the ore by dry crushing. Then comes the cylinder room, where four Bruckner cylinders are kept slowly revolving while the ore within them is being roasted and chlorodized. On the next lower terrace is the pan room, where the roasted ore is placed in pans with water and quicksilver, and kept in motion until amalgamated. There are ten of these amalgamating pans and four settlers for the same. In the melting room, to which the amalgamated silver

CARIBOU MILL, AT NEDERLAND.

is taken for retorting and melting into bars, are two retorts and a double melting furnace, ten amalgamating pans, and four settlers for the same. In apartments near the furnaces are a hundred horse power engine, and two boilers of one hundred and fifty horse power. In the building there are also elevators, ore hoppers, dry kiln, cooling floor, water and steam pipes and connections. Close by is a finely equipped assay office, a weighing house, office and residence building, stable and other buildings. This mill can handle fifteen tons of Caribou ore every twenty-four hours. The process used is referred to elsewhere. Outside of the mine itself, the mine buildings, machinery, mill and lands are worth $150,000, and originally cost over $200,000.

The Caribou Consolidated Mining Company was organized in 1879, with a capital of $1,000,000, in 100,000 shares of $10 each. Its property consists of 1,400 feet on the Caribou lode, patented ground, situated on the northern slope of Caribou Hill. The officers of the company are ex-Governor A. G. Curtin, of Pennsylvania, president; John T. Graham, secretary, and treasurer; Eben Smith, superintendent; and A. G. Curtin, James B. Metcalf, H. H. Hollister, P. W. Holmes, and Eben Smith, trustees.

The Native Silver lode is considered the western extension of the Caribou. The ore shipments are of unusually high grade and large in quantity. In developing this lode Adin Alexander is said to have taken out nearly $25,000. He sold it to ex-Governor Curtin, J. T. Graham, Senator Cattell, Secretary Robeson, and others of Pennsylvania and New Jersey, who organized the Mining Company of New Jersey thereon. A silver mill was then erected at Caribou, and in 1877, not far from $140,000 was obtained for the silver product of the ore mined and milled. The process was chlorodizing-roasting and leaching with copper. After John T. Graham's retirement from the management in March of that year, eastern men unacquainted with the business, conducted affairs unsuccessfully and work ceased. This was not from lack of ore or from any fault of the mine. In the summer of 1878, Graham started up the mine and mill again, and the former has been paying good profits ever since. The mill has been idle since that year, but will be set at work again without delay. The mine has been in charge of an excellent miner, Joseph Irwin, who worked it on tribute up to the time when the Native

Silver Company became fairly organized and purchased the property. In 1879 the receipts for ore sold were about $45,000, carrying an actual value of some $55,000. The total yield of the mine to April, 1880, must have approached $300,000. Large amounts of ore have been sold that carried from 125 to 800 ounces per ton. The average of four months' work in the company mill gave 460 ounces of silver per ton for assorted ore, and 57 ounces for low grade. While some of the vein matter has gone lower, many shipments have been made of richer material. Blocks of ore have been mined that went as high as $1,000 per ton. Very rich native silver specimens are encountered. At one period for which figures are shown the ore averaged 188 ounces per ton, and the lessees paid 20 per centum royalty. Recently the mine has been paying a profit of several thousand dollars monthly from sinking and drifting. The main shaft is approaching a depth of 600 feet, and levels are going forward through rich paying ground. The reserves are now sufficient to insure dividends for a long time to come. Besides the main shaft 429 feet west of the line of the Caribou property are other entries in the vein, one shaft being 285 feet deep. Cross cuts at a depth of 460 feet will soon intersect two parallel veins of the company.

The company mill is located at the head of Caribou village, not far from the mine, and is supplied with water by means of an underground boxed ditch a mile and a half long. About ten tons of ore can be reduced daily. The plant embraces a Blake crusher, ten stamps, a roasting cylinder, and reverberatory furnace, soon to give place to another " Bruckner," four supply tanks, five agitators or vats, five settlers, twenty-two precipitation tanks, two copper liquor pumps and steam machinery, samplers, conveyors, elevators, etc. The ore is dried, crushed, sampled, pulverized, roasted and leached. The silver is finally melted into bars over 900 fine, and valued at over $1,000 each, and sent east.

The Native Silver Mining Company has a capital stock of one million in five-dollar shares. The officers are Edward Jordan, president, John T. Graham, treasurer, J. W. Schuckers, secretary, and Ex-Governor A. G. Curtin, U. S. Senator J. B. Gordon, Gen. Thomas Ewing, F. W. Foote, of John J. Cisco & Co., P. W. Holmes, and J. T. Graham. The mine is said to be capable of paying as largely as the Caribou.

The Poor Man lode is just below the Caribou, approaching it to the westward at an acute angle.   The workings are intersected by the Caribou tunnel, and the mine approaches a depth of 300 feet, with numerous levels.   The vein has been from one to two feet wide in much of its course, with ore yielding from one to three hundred dollars per ton.   In 1874–5 one hundred and fifty-two tons of ore sold for $21,504, with a profit of $12,000.

The Sherman has a very rich vein, often from six to twelve inches wide.   This lode was purchased by the same men who bought the No Name in 1874.   There were 300 tons of ore sold in 1876, that averaged $270 per ton.

The No Name has a northeasterly and southwesterly direction, and the ore obtained from the mine has come from a point at and below the point of intersection or union with the Caribou.   The shaft is 528 feet deep.   The original owners, Donald, Shaw, and associates, sold over $50,000 worth of ore in a little over three years, and then disposed of the property to L. M. Bates of New York, for $55,000.   Afterwards William Fullerton, A. G. Dun, and M. A. Smith, of the same locality, became owners and still retain possession.   The yield in 1874–6, inclusive, is said to have exceeded $60,000.   Since then the property has been worked on lease, and the yield is supposed to have been somewhere between forty and fifty thousand dollars.   These parties built a chlorination and lixiviation mill on North Boulder creek, in 1875, and operated portions of two years on ores from the No Name and Sherman mines.   The No Name has yielded some enormously rich ore, some of it showing native silver in large quantities.   The two mines may have produced, from first to last, nearly $250,000.   Joseph Irwin, who has for years been conducting some of the leading mining operations of the district, and who has been operating the Native Silver mine, has worked the No Name on lease.   The ore was often extremely rich at and below the intersection of the veins.

The Idaho yielded $9,000 within a few weeks after its discovery in 1870, and showed a remarkably rich pocket of ore.   It had too many proprietors, and interests in it have changed hands until three of the discoverers of the Caribou have come to be the main owners.   Mishler, McCammon, and Martin put up a large shaft house with steam hoisting machinery a few years ago, but have not worked the property much of the time.   The pay seems to run in pockets, and the mine is troubled with a great deal of water.

Extending through and on either slope of the main range near Arapahoe Peak is the Fourth of July lode. This is of great size, but the mineral is very much scattered; developments, shafts and approaching tunnels. The Boulder County, below Caribou, is a large, strong vein, which has produced some valuable ore. The company has a 15-stamp quartz mill at Nederland, containing concentrators.

The Seven Thirty is one of the best mines in the district. It extends westward from the Caribou claims, and is nearly parallel with the Native Silver. The vein is often large and yields some very rich silver ore. In former years the original owners took out from fifteen to twenty thousand dollars. In January, 1878, Gilbert Lehmer purchased this property, 3,000 linear feet patented, and having put up steam hoisting machinery, proceeded to systematically develop it. Less than twelve months gave a production of $35,000. When greater depth was gained a Knowles pump was set to work. The year 1879 gave a return of $45,000. The ore body has varied from the thickness of a knife blade to eight feet, yielding from $50 to $900 per ton. About 30 men mine nearly 40 tons of ore monthly, besides low-grade material. The shaft is several hundred feet deep, and the levels—1,000 feet—extend in either direction therefrom. One level east is 300 feet long.

The Santa La Saria or Blue Bird mine, near North Boulder Creek, and operated by W. G. Case, has produced extremely rich ore. Shafts, lodes and tunnels show a nearly vertical vein, instead of a flat one, as at first. A fifty-thousand-dollar mill like the Caribou is being erected.

CHAPTER VII.

BOULDER COUNTY MINES—GOLD HILL, CENTRAL, MAGNOLIA, SUGAR
LOAF, AND WARD MINING DISTRICTS—THE TELLURIDE BELT—
GOLD, SILVER, AND TELLURIUM VEINS—SOME ACCOUNT OF PROM-
INENT MINES— THE MELVINA, SMUGGLER, SLIDE, COLD SPRING,
COLUMBIA, GOLDEN AGE, KEYSTONE, AND OTHERS.

The telluride belt is about twenty miles long and several miles in width, extending from the Smuggler on the north almost to South Boulder creek on the south. Within this belt are numberless telluride veins, and some regular gold and silver lodes. Telluride ores have been found in very small seams or pockets in one lode, and in bodies or veins in another, but when large the ore is generally of low grade with occasional rich mineral. Some have continuous veins of high grade ore, and have yielded a great deal of money and profit. Most of them are mainly made up of ore too poor to smelt and too refractory to treat in the cheap stamp mills. Concentration answers as a remedy or great benefit on some lodes and will not answer on others. Smelting is the only mode of extracting the gold and silver. The telluride mines of the entire belt have yielded something like a million dollars since work first began on them in 1873, '4, '5, '6. The ore sold has generally been very rich.

Tellurium is a metal of no intrinsic value in itself, but owing to its combination with the precious metals, veins carrying it are often extremely profitable. It gives the mineral in which it shows itself so different an appearance from other gold and silver ore as to be readily distinguishable. American miners had never encountered it before discovering it in Colorado, as it is found in but few places in the world, and Boulder county prospectors had been passing over these veins and their blossom rock for years without dreaming of their value.

The crevices of telluride veins are often of good size, but the amount of mineral that pays for mining and smelting is generally small compared with gold or silver veins. As much of very rich mineral can be found in these classes of lodes as in the tellurides, while the available ore of lower grades is vastly greater. Some of the leading telluride mines show continuous veins several inches wide of extremely rich ore, sometimes widening out to pockets, and bordered by poorer material that is often concentrated into marketable ore, but nearly all of them require as large a force to assort, separate, and "hand dress" the product as they do underground miners. The rich part of the veins are more likely to be from half an inch to four inches wide than of larger size. The Melvina and Smuggler are two of the lodes that are larger and better than the average. The Cold Spring, Slide, American, Last Chance, John Jay, Red Cloud, Keystone, Victoria, and others have also shown fair sized veins and pockets. There are a large number of lodes that have yielded by close assorting a few hundred pounds of ore that were worth from less than a dollar up to several dollars per pound, but the trouble is to get a ton of such material at one time from any one mine. Still, it has been done occasionally from some of those named. The combinations of tellurium are many, of which the more important are sylvanite, carrying nearly twice as much gold as silver; petzite, over twice as much silver as gold; calavarite, or telluride of gold; altaite, or telluride of lead; and tetradymite, or telluride of bismuth. The native or pure metal is rarely found. The value of the gold in the above greatly exceeds the value of the silver. Lodes of this character often carry several feet of low grade ore that cannot be made available.

Gold Hill mining district contains a multitude of lodes and some gulch diggings, and has turned out a great deal of money since 1859. Gold Hill rises far above the surrounding country, and is bordered by Left Hand Creek and Gold Run. On this hill are the Horsfal, Columbus, Red Cloud, Cold Spring, Victoria, Cash, Saint Joe, and Slide veins. The district has probably produced half a million altogether.

The Cold Spring is a telluride lode of great value, close by the Red Cloud, and is bordered by a large porphyry dike, in a gneissic formation. Its yield in 1874–6, inclusive, was $50,000. It has not been worked steadily but is developed by a shaft over 400 feet deep, and by several levels. The ore reserves contain several times the value of the mine's past product. The mine is paying and has a fine set of steam hoisting machinery. The vein varies from a few inches to two feet. The assorted ore runs up in the hundreds, and one ton brought several thousands of dollars. It is one of the most valuable of the telluride veins. The owner is Truman Whitcomb.

In 1873–4 the Red Cloud yielded in much the same manner as the Cold Spring has done, but gave out at a depth of several hundred feet. The Columbus has been worked at times by a large force of men, and so has the Cash and Saint Joe. The Victoria has been opened extensively, has extensive buildings, and has been paying profits.

The Horsfal is a free gold vein, which is said to have yielded nearly a quarter of a million in the first few years of mining in Colorado. When a depth of over two hundred feet was attained difficulty arose among the owners, and the ore became more difficult to reduce, and the mine shut down. It was idle for many years up to late in 1878, when work was resumed and development commenced again. The results are said to be so satisfactory that the mine is likely to be worked steadily from this time forward.

The Black Cloud mine has been extensively developed, and is owned by a company of the same name. It carries gold and silver, gray copper, zinc-blende, sulphurets and copper and iron pyrites. A mill was erected last year for handling the ore at Summerville, one mile from Salina. Its concentrating capacity is given at twenty-five tons in twenty-four hours. The lode is worked through a tunnel intersecting the vein one hundred feet deep, below which a shaft is sunk on the vein one hundred feet further. The location of the mine is on a high hill on the opposite side of Gold Run from the Hoosier mine.

The Slide lode on the northern slope of Gold Hill is one of the best of the telluride veins. Its present reserve of ore is said to approach $400,000 in value, and to surpass that of any mine in this part of the county. It was discovered in July, 1875, by J. G. Pell, who sold it to W. A. Campbell and Colonel Seymour. It is now the property of the American Consolidated Company, owning the American mine, reorganized under new managers. The value of the ore, carrying tellurides, iron and copper pyrites, etc., is mainly in gold with some silver. Some wonderfully rich pockets and specimens of tellurides have been found in many other lodes, but the Slide evidently excels them all in this respect. Several hundred pounds of ore are now in possession of the company that contains as many thousands of dollars. The first two years of work returned, besides low-grade material, $28,927—an average of $350 a ton. Owing to company complications and other causes, the mine was not worked steadily until late in 1879, but the yield was considerable. The output of that year was about $42,000, including some ore on hand. In the last three months of the year, 2,197 cubic feet of ground were excavated, with an average return of $9.50 per foot. In this work of sinking and drifting only, there were 60 tons of ore sold, containing $16,930.57, besides 90 tons mined, containing $3,960. The Corning Tunnel intersects the ore vein 536 feet below the surface. Many levels are going forward; also a shaft down to the tunnel. Steam hoisting machinery is employed. George Teal is superintendent. The yield has exceeded $5,000 per month for some time, over two-thirds being profit—this from sinking and drifting, while the ore reserves are left intact. Less than half a ton of ore lately sold for $2,245.

The discovery of the Sunshine lode in 1874 was followed by the opening of the American, Grand View, Osceola, Sheridan, and others, and the building of the town of Sunshine. The American took the lead and became quite famous. It was purchased by Hiram Hitchcock, of New York, and superintended by Professor J. Alden Smith. This remarkable vein carried rich streaks of sylvanite, petzite, calaverite, ruby silver and free gold, and yielded thousands of dollars monthly from ore running in the hundreds. Small lots brought from $1,000 to $5,000, and there were also low grades. Since 1877 work and production have not been regular.

The Melvina mine is located on Melvina Hill, between Gold Run and Four Mile Creek and Salina. It was discovered by Henry Meyring, who dug a prospect hole and located the lode. In July, 1875, Henry Neikirk received an interest for developing it. It was then not known to be valuable. His first month's operations resulted in uncovering a telluride vein of surpassing value, when over $8,000 were received for ore sold to the smelters. The pay vein was soft material, and sometimes gave several dollars in gold per pound. The mine kept on producing steadily, and the world has seldom seen such proportionately large profits. In February, 1876, ore was sold that brought $15,800, and the expenses were only $800. Only eight men were at work, most of them being owners in the mine. In the monthly shipments the ore has usually been assorted in three lots, and there would usually be a few hundred pounds that yielded at the rate of from two to nine dollars per pound, or from $4,000 to $18,000 per ton. In the first fifteen months of work the mine had yielded $84,600 from the labor of eight men, including the proprietors. In that time 151 tons had been sold and the average value was over $560 per ton. While a pretty continuous vein of ore was maintained, the best material came in or was found at depths of 50 feet, 200 feet and the present lower workings, where the width was from six to eight inches. In four months, ending May 1, 1877, there were 60½ tons of ore sold for $31,830, of which $24,200 was profit. Up to March the actual yield had been about $100,000 and the profits $65,000. These extremely rich lots of ore were largely obtained by assorting from the entire crevice matter, although there had been parts of the mine where a solid streak six or eight inches wide had been composed entirely of the high grades. Gradually large amounts of ore had accumulated at the mine that would not pay for smelting. As a mill had been established at Salina for concentrating tellurides —that is separating the mineral from the gangue or waste rock—some of the Melvina dump pile was tested. The result was one ton of dressed concentrates containing $270, and another ton containing $430, instead of ten or twelve times as much crude ore, with only fifteen or thirty dollars' worth of gold in each ton. This led to the leasing of the Everitt concentrating mill, which has lately been purchased by the Melvina owners. Both concentrates and high grade mineral is sold to the Boston & Colorado Smelting Company. Up to May 1st, 1878, the receipts for ore sold exceeded $130,000, and the supposed ultimate yield $155,000. The receipts for the year 1878 were $90,000, indicating a yield of $100,000, and the profits must have been 75 per cent. of the receipts. Last winter twelve men were at work, breaking and raising about 235 or 250 tons of ore monthly. Most of this was low grade, and ten or twelve tons of it were dressed down into one at the mill. In different portions of the mine the high grade pay vein has varied in width from five to ten inches, and the accompanying low grade from fifteen to twenty-five, and from thirty to forty. The total ore receipts of the Melvina for the four years of work ending July, 1879, would probably foot up $230,000, and the actual smelters yield $280,000. The lean ground encounted at times in sinking has given away to good ore, and the mine is especially rich at depths of 420 and 470 feet.

The richness of much of the ore is as remarkable as the large total yield and small working force and outlays required. Henry Neikirk, Henry Meyring, Melvin Bailey, and Marion Kessler have all made fortunes out of this richest of the telluride veins.

The Winona is an extension of the Slide, and the Dexter is on the same vein, further down the northern slope of Gold Hill. The Eugene is on the same vein as the Horsfal, which is now selling large quantities of smelting ore. These three lodes and the Yellow Jacket belong to the Winona Gold Mining Company, and are all producing profitable ore. Steam hoisting works are employed on both the Winona and Eugene where sinking and drifting are carried on, and continuous veins and large pockets of rich ore have been opened. Gold Hill is the theatre of great activity at present, and work is progressing on a large number of veins outside of the Slide, Prussian, Horsfal, Victoria, Little Pittsburg, and others already mentioned.

The Baron lode was discovered in 1875, but it is only lately that its true value has been developed. The crevice between walls is five feet wide, containing four veins of mineral or tellurium, each from one to three inches wide. Four men were at work in May, and received $1,500 for ore sold in drifting eleven feet. Twelve tons of the low grade ore, averaging $30 per ton, concentrates down into one ton of marketable mineral, with a loss of only thirty per cent. Most of the high grade ore sold brings $400 more or less, but small lots contain from $5 to $8 per pound. The owners are C. C. Eddy, Sr., C. C. Eddy, Jr., F. R. Eddy, and A. R. West.

The Great Eastern lode is about two hundred feet southwest of the Melvina, and is opened by a shaft 175 feet deep. It has paid well.

Central mining district extends along Left Hand and James Creeks, and adjoins and separates Gold Hill and Ward. It contains both free gold and telluride lodes. Near Jamestown the John Jay, Last Chance, and Longfellow are prominent telluride veins. The Summit lode shows a very large crevice. The Mountain Chief is on the divide between the two creeks. At and near Springdale are some productive telluride lodes, such as the Big Blossom, Grand Central, J. Alden Smith, Louis, B. F. Smith, Rip Van Dam, Hecla, Ellen, King William, and Gladiator. These have sometimes been enormously rich. The Bondholder is a profitable free gold lode The Golden Age and Standard free gold mines are in this district.

and further north is the famous Smuggler. At Springdale are seltzer springs, similar to those of Germany, and a fine hotel. The country is well timbered.

The Last Chance has produced a great deal of rich telluride ore. One lot of three tons was sold not long ago that brought $980 per ton. Last year two tons sold for $1,267, two and three-fourths tons for $2,337, two tons for $951.15, and four and a quarter tons for $1,749.61. One lot carried $530 in gold and $22 in silver. The John Jay was discovered late in 1875, and has yielded many thousands of dollars. An Illinois company that bought property at Jamestown, last fall, has sold ore that yielded $200 per ton.

The Golden Age is one of the best mines in the county, and the most successfully operated of those having free gold milling ores. It has been steadily developed for thirty months or more, and has paid good profits from the surface down to the present depth of between 230 and 300 feet. A fifteen stamp mill was erected early in 1877, and this was since enlarged. Since January, 1878, twenty-five stamps have been crushing some fifteen tons of quartz daily. The product for last year was 2,200 tons of quartz, yielding over $40,000. Since then the mine has been opened in better shape, and the yield has been proportionately larger. During the month of April twelve men were at work at the mine, and about sixty cords, or over 400 tons of quartz were mined and milled, with a yield of $6,900. There were 390 ounces of gold, worth not far from $17.75 per ounce. Much the larger half of the yield must have been profit. The mill contains, besides stamps and tables, two iron Bartola pans. There are said to be several thousand cords of ore in sight. The vein matter is a pure white quartz, containing a very light trace of anything beside gold, and streaks and nuggets of the yellow metal are constantly met with. The mine has produced more handsome free gold specimens than any other in this part of the State. The yield is usually from an ounce to an ounce and a half of gold per ton. It is reported that both mine and mill were sold in May to Messrs. Pike, Parmly & Shedd, of Chicago, for $194,000. Hiram P. Walker, the late owner, purchased the mine of the discoverer, "Indian Jack," some thirty months ago.

The Smuggler is one of the few very productive telluride lodes. It not only yields quantities of very rich ore but also carries a large, strong vein, with occasional pockets of great size and varying richness. If worked systematically, so as to keep ground and ore reserves opened in advance of immediate necessities, it would make a much better record than it has done, and be a source of greater profit to the owners. For a long time it has been worked on temporary leases and tribute work, which, in the end, cannot fail to result in injury to the mine and its owners.

In April, 1876, Charles Mullen, a veteran prospector, wandered up into the hills near Long's Peak, and on a gulch near the south fork of the St. Vrain, discovered what he called the Smuggler lode. The quantity of mineral and the enormous assays convinced him that he had "struck it rich" enough to insure a fortune. General Lessig and W. A. Christian were also partners in the discovery. A great deal of ore was mined and sold that summer, which yielded all the way from one hundred up to one thousand dollars per ton. Mullen sold out his interest to Kennedy, Eaton, Freeman, and Flowers, of Greeley, and went to the Centennial.

Afterwards Freeman and Flowers sold, and Christian disposed of one-half of his interest to a son of the late Dean Richmond, of New York. The entire property comprises the Smuggler, Wamego, Careless Boy, Sweetheart, and two other veins, and their government patents cover the entire hill. The first is the main source of production.

There seems to have always been a great deal of trouble about the mine's management. Perhaps it had too many owners. One of them estimates the yield of gold and silver up to December, 1877, at $186,000. The receipts in 1878 were $81,400, indicating the actual yield of the ore at the smelters to have been $95,000. The receipts for January last were $4,600. The total yield in less than thirty-three months after discovery is given at $286,000.

In January, 1877, a small lot of ore was sold that assayed 285 ounces in gold and 214 in silver. At the same time second-class ore yielded 13 ounces of gold and 15 of silver, and third-class 3¼ ounces of gold and 6 ounces of silver. Forty men were at work. In April of the same year nineteen tons of ore were sold to Boyd, at Boulder, for $7,600, and low grade ore made the total yield $2,000 more. The expenses were $4,600. Fifty-two men were at work, and numerous shafts and levels were being driven.

In time a large amount of ore of poor quality had accumulated, and four frue vanner machines were put up at the mine for concentrating purposes. In January, 1878, Boyd paid $7,000 for ore, much of which contained over $400 per ton. In March the main shaft was 130 feet deep, and the vein had been opened for a length of 440 feet, and was intersected by the Careless Boy tunnel, 270 feet long.

In the summer of 1878 six parties were leasing on different portions of the property, some of them paying from 25 to 50 per cent. royalty on gross receipts. They and their employees numbered forty men altogether. Their receipts for ore taken out in thirty-five actual working days of July and August footed up $20,492.34, indicating an actual yield of $24,000. Here was an average return of $14 and over to the man for every working day. J. P. Maxwell received $8,654.34 for one lot of ore, and $5,127.35 for another lot of 3,026 pounds. Some lean ores that were concentrated by the frue vanner machines sold for $578.16. The ore sales for August were $8,900, and for six weeks ending October 15 about $17,500. These were the exceptionally good months. The yield was much less at other times. It is said that the royalty for the year exceeded $40,000. For some time the main shaft has been sunk on fifty per cent. royalty, the ore-body being unusually good at that point.

The crevice sometimes opens out into a pocket several feet wide, and a width of two feet is not unusual. This includes rich and lean ore and gangue rock. The telluride ore itself has been from three to eighteen inches wide for long distances, but is not all high grade. Last winter about twenty-five tons of ore were sold per month, that yielded from three to four hundred dollars per ton. The poor grades of ore are very plentiful, but it is claimed that two or three hundred tons can be dressed down into marketable mineral monthly. There is a rich, but very crooked streak of tellurides outside of and nearly parallel with the main vein.

Three tunnels intersect and drain the upper part of the vein. Below that the main shaft extends 240 feet, with several levels. Fifty feet below the tunnel the vein has been opened several hundred feet each way, and much further nearer the surface. There is more silver in the southern part of the vein than elsewhere. Some lots of ore sold from the mine yielded $2,400 in gold to $100 in silver, while others gave the same amount of silver and but two or three hundred dollars in gold. The Smuggler is the largest of the telluride veins, and the Melvina, Slide and Prussian are the only ones returning better grade ore in large quantities.

Among the mines of Sugar Loaf district those of George Williamson are prominent. What is often called the "Gray Copper" lode is known far and wide. The Yellow Pine is said to be one of the best mines in the county. Mill runs of 200 ounces of silver per ton of ore are common occurrences. In one place the vein is said to be over four feet wide. So rich and plentiful is the ore that lessees sink and drift (without stoping) on 40 per cent. royalty of returns. An extension of this, operated by Thomas Owens, has yielded mineral carrying forty per cent. of copper. The Maine lode carries a gold and silver-bearing lead vein 18 inches wide. The Washington Avenue, Lindley, Ogallalah, Vucleus and Logan are noted veins.

The Prussian is a new mine on Gold Hill, below the Slide, but already rivals the best lodes of the telluride section. It was opened by three farmers, named Zweck, Gifford, and Bissell. Eight miners took out 27½ tons that sold for $12,277.28 in a single month, an average of about $450 a ton. The prices paid for several lots of ore were as follows: 670 pounds brought $1,221.02; 2,160 pounds sold for $1,180.89; 3,361 pounds $1,940.42; 868 pounds $1,319.72; 365 pounds $904.63, or at the rate of $4,959.90; and 9½ tons sold at the rate of $246.18 per ton. Every month shows handsome profits. The Little Pittsburgh is an extension of the Prussian, and is exceedingly profitable.

Magnolia district is situated among the mountains near Boulder creek, and from six to ten miles above Boulder City. It was opened in 1875-6, and afterwards experienced dull times, but now shows considerable activity. Within a year such valuable telluride veins as the Keystone and Mountain Lion and the Sac and Fox have resumed work and production, and are said to be paying handsomely. These are operated by steam-hoisting works, one engine for the first two and one for the last two mines.

The Keystone and Mountain Lion are on the same vein, and the hoisting is done for both by machinery over the 230 foot shaft of the former. The Mountain Lion lower workings are still deeper below the surface of the sloping hillside. The pay vein is from half an inch to six inches wide. About five tons of ore are sold monthly, at $350 and upwards per ton. Twelve men clear over $10 daily on this Mountain Lion mine, after paying the owners twenty-five per cent. of the receipts. The total yield has been $40,000. That of the Keystone has been much larger. Twelve men are also at work there. Rich sylvanite is found, and the marketable ore runs from $100 to $1,500. Both mines have long levels and ore in fair quantities.

Ward district is situated high up towards the snowy range, and not far from Long's Peak, and has been very productive in gold. No telluride lodes are reported in this section. The total yield is believed to have been over half a million dollars, mainly from the Columbia lode. The Stoughton, Celestial, Utica, Ute, Humboldt, and others have also been quite productive. Mining has been carried on there ever since 1860, and most of the gold was obtained in the first six or eight years. Affairs went on very successfully until the surface quartz was exhausted. The ores at great depths appear to be much more refractory than in Gilpin county. Being of low grade, the average vein matter will not pay for smelting, and as the stamp mills do not seem to succeed, operations have failed of success on some of the leading properties. Considerable quantities of ore are mined that are so valuable that it pays to mine and smelt them. Concentration is said to help matters, and a process of that kind is in operation in connection with a quartz mill. There appears to be a revival of work with several mines and stamp mills.

The Columbia is the great vein of this district, and is often found to be of tremendous size. It has been located and opened for a long distance, and is divided among many owners. The best developed and heretofore the most productive portions are known as the Ni Wot and the Ward Mining Company or Baxter properties. The entire lode has probably yielded $350,000, coin value.

The Ni Wot mine, on the Columbia lode, was purchased by an Eastern company some fifteen years ago. A large fifty-stamp mill and other buildings and hoisting works were erected, at a cost of $150,000, in the days of high freights and prices. This mill was burned and replaced in 1866 by one of equal capacity, costing $55,000. Most of the product of this mine came out within a few years of that date, but for some cause the company was not financially successful. In after years W. A. Davidson, the company superintendent, became the owner of the property. This embraces 1,500 feet on the vein, covered by government title and shaft houses, steam hoisting machinery, barns, office buildings, boarding houses, and a fine fifty-stamp mill; also chlorination works. Work has been stopped and resumed several times. Large bodies of paying ore are reported at a depth of 480 feet and above, and continuous production is looked for. A part or all of the quartz mill stamps will be steadily operated. Superintendent Benson has a large force of men employed. Since first opened the mine has yielded ore valued at from $8 to $250 per ton, and the crevice has sometimes ranged from 12 to 20 feet in width. What is often called the Baxter property forms a very important part of the lode, but is less productive than the Ni Wot. Yet it has shown from six inches to twelve feet of crevice and valuable quartz. A few years ago Superintendent E. K. Baxter sunk to a depth of 500 feet. Near by claim No. 8 yielded $15,000.

The Chicago and Colorado Company is driving three tunnels by the aid of machine drills and compressed air. Colonel Brainard has a mile and a half of pipe and many men employed.

The Nelson is a smaller but richer vein than the Columbia. It is operated by Delvan Peck, who has recently been systematically developing it, and who has erected a ten-ton smelter for handling its ore. The low grade quartz is treated at the Ni Wot mill. The higher grades, rich in gold and copper, have smelted from $100 to $125 per ton. The pay vein is often over two feet wide. Steam hoisting machinery is employed. Nelson Place, the residence of Mr. Peck, has had its natural attractions greatly improved by its owner. He is working one vein yielding 30 per cent. copper.

The Humboldt is a large, well-defined, gold-bearing quartz lode, with a pay vein of from one to two feet in width. It has been proved up and located for a length of 7,500 feet, and embraces four different properties. The main shaft has attained a depth of considerably over 200 feet, and a large force of miners is employed there, and in connecting levels. There is a large shaft-house with steam hoisting works, also a mill with three Pomeroy concussion tables, ten stamps and steam-engine. The Celestial mine is producing ore that yields in the stamp mills from $100 to $150 per cord. Six and a half tons of smelting ore lately sold for $594, and a ton of concentrated tailings for $43.

The Pomeroy mill at Ward has lately received some additions, and now contains ten stamps, two Bruckner roasting cylinders, three amalgamating pans, and two concentrating tables, all supplied with steam power by two engines.

CHAPTER VIII.

GILPIN COUNTY MINES—THEIR LOCATION, HISTORY, AND PRODUC-
TION—THE SPLENDID RECORD OF TWENTY YEARS—$30,000,000
IN GOLD—RESUMPTION OF WORK AND DEEP MINING—FACTS
AND FIGURES REGARDING GOLD MINING—THE GOLD PRODUCT
BY YEARS—THE QUARTZ MILLS AND WHAT THEY ARE DOING—
SOMETHING ABOUT STAMPS.

Gilpin county extends from the junction of North and South
Clear creeks westward to the Snowy range. Boulder county borders
it on the north, Jefferson on the east, Clear Creek on the south, and
Grand on the west. Its territory is made up of rugged hills, divided by deep valleys and ravines. It was once heavily timbered,
but those portions in and near the towns, mines, and mills are so no
longer. The population is mainly embraced in the three contiguous
towns of Black Hawk, Central, and Nevadaville, which extend in
the order named up North Clear Creek, Gregory Gulch, and tributary
streams. Outside of these are scattered mining camps and farms,
and around them a great deal of land that has never been of any
value except for the timber that grew upon it.

Rising abruptly from the dividing ravines and city streets are a
number of lofty hills, among which the mines are located. From
Black Hawk westward to Nevadaville are Bates, Bobtail, Gregory,
Mammoth, Central City, Casto, Gunnell and Quartz hills, which, with
their intervening gulches, are intersected by numberless metalliferous
veins or lodes, the sources of the golden millions of the past and
present. From these lodes, that are traced along the surface for
distances of from a few hundred feet to one or two miles, gold was
washed by the rains and floods of former ages into the recently
profitably mined creeks and gulches. The lodes are divided among
many owners, each of whom has more or less extensive underground
workings that go to make up a mine.

The main rock or formation of Gilpin county is a gneissic one,
but granite occupies most of the territory where the mineral veins

are found. Some veins lie between granite and gneiss. Hornblende occurs in dikes, and there are occasional patches of porphyry. There are two main systems of lodes in the gold belt, those having an east and west direction, which are much the most numerous, and those extending almost northeast and southwest. Of the former class are the Bobtail, Kansas, Gardner, California, and of the latter the Gregory, Bates, Leavitt or Buell, and Fisk. Some veins are nearly or quite perpendicular, and others incline ten, twenty, and even forty degrees therefrom. Some dip to the northward for several hundred feet, and then change their course to the opposite direction. The veins termed gold-bearing are composed of copper-iron pyrites, or sulphurets of iron and copper, carrying gold, and a less value in silver. The gangue includes quartz, feldspar, crystals, and other matter. Many veins contain galena, and some of them in large quantities. The vein matter is usually decomposed near the surface, and down to a depth of seventy or eighty feet. This is called surface quartz. The gold contained therein is more freely extracted and more frequently visible than in the vein material of greater depths. Many silver veins north of Black Hawk have a south of east strike. This is also the case with many of the gold lodes. Copper is present to a greater or less extent in nearly all Gilpin county lodes. Two or three per cent. of some ores are copper, and more rarely five, ten, and fifteen per cent. Gray copper and ruby silver are found in the richer ores of the new silver district, and a great deal of lead in those between Black Hawk and Clear Creek county.

The main portion of the gold-bearing veins are located in an area less than four miles long, by one wide, and in the midst of this is the almost continuous city known under the names of Black Hawk, Central, and Nevadaville; but many valuable gold lodes and all of the silver district is situated outside of this. This gold belt continues northerly into, and nearly through, Boulder county, and southwesterly into Clear Creek as far as and beyond the Freeland mine, on Trail Creek. Of the precious metals contained in the ore, the proportion of gold is larger as compared with silver, in the veins near Gold Dirt and Black Hawk, and smaller in those on Quartz Hill and toward and beyond South Clear Creek. Thus, on the western end of Quartz Hill lodes contain more silver than they do one mile further east. There are exceptions to this, however. This is shown in assays, in smelting

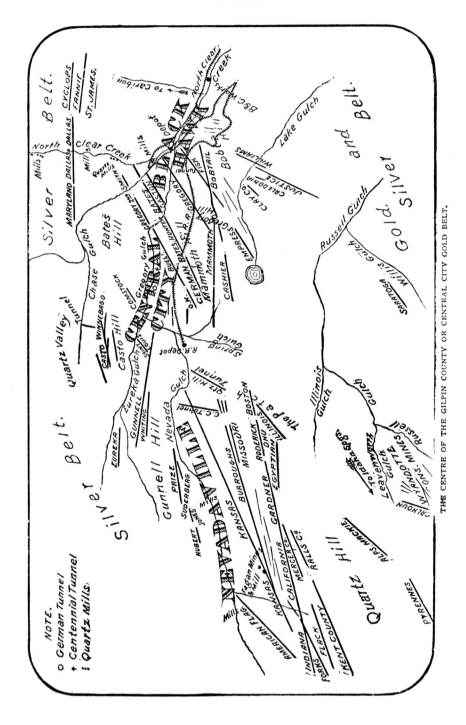

THE CENTRE OF THE GILPIN COUNTY OR CENTRAL CITY GOLD BELT.

returns, and in the difference in value per ounce of stamp mill retort. Near Idaho Springs and Trail Run, lodes on the same belt carry nearly as much silver as gold, and some have increased their silver yield as depth was gained.

It has been ascertained that the retort gold as it comes from the mills runs pretty much as follows in fineness: Bates, .746 in gold, .241 silver; Bobtail, .849 to .866½ gold, .128 to .140 silver; Briggs, .803½ to .816 gold, .172 to .180 silver; Buell, .800 to .860 gold, and .120 to .140 silver; Burroughs, .820 to .833½ gold, .158 to .166 silver; Illinois, .781½ gold, and .211 silver; and Kansas and Kent county about the same. The value of Bates gold retort is $14.30; of Bobtail, $17 to $18; Briggs, $16.30 to $17.00; Buell, $16.70 to $18; Burroughs, $16.50 to $16.90; Illinois, $15.90; Kansas, $15 to $16; Kent County, $14.50 to $15; Gold Dirt, Ophir, and Perigo, $17.50 to $18; Dallas, $14 to $14.50. Continued tests show that the average of all the Gilpin county gold mill retort, or bullion handled, contains about 787 parts gold, 198 silver, and 15 copper.

What is termed the new silver belt of Gilpin county extends to the north and northwest of Black-Hawk, across North Clear Creek and other hills, from York Gulch, Chase Gulch and Wide Awake to the Dory Hill. The first silver discoveries of that locality were made late in May, and in June and July, 1878. Prospecting has continued since, and hundreds of lodes have been located—some of them of proved value. One or two already appear to rank with first-class silver veins of the Georgetown and San Juan districts. Silver lodes were worked with profit in Silver Gulch, near the smelting works of Black Hawk, from nine to eleven years ago, and more recently in Willis Gulch and Virginia Mountain.

Mining in Gilpin county fairly began in the summer of 1860, with the completion of the Consolidated Ditch and the introduction of many stamp mills. Before that, work had been done by sluicing, rocking, and panning, and by means of arastras. In a year or two the more productive gulches had been worked over, the decomposed vein matter in the leading lodes had been exhausted, and the mill men were at a loss to know how to get gold in paying quantities from the solid ore, or "iron" as it was termed. At one time nearly all of these mills were idle, but afterwards the ore was handled with less difficulty. In 1862–3 many rich "strikes" were made on claims that had shown nothing but barren rock after the surface pockets were exhausted. The Gregory, Bobtail, Bates, Kansas, Burroughs, Gunnell, Gold Dirt, and Perigo were paying enormously for much of the time up to 1863, when the eastern companies began operations. The gold product continued to be large until 1866, when many companies had discarded the old stamps, and were spending their money in putting up and testing process mills. On returning to stamp mill crushing in 1867-8, business revived.

At this time the district possessed a population such as has rarely been gathered together in so small a compass, and remarkable for enterprise, intelligence, and sterling qualities. Operations were carried on by numerous companies, whether they paid expenses or not, and leasers and owners of mines were making money at intervals all over the hills. There was eastern money as well as western gold to help matters. A large number of mills and stamps were in operation in 1868, and, in the summer of 1869, nearly 700 stamps were operated, but not continuously. In November, 1869, when several water mills had closed down, there were still 29 mills and 624 stamps at work. Outside of the companies, the California and U. P. R. lodes, worked by Gilpin miners, were paying largely.

The companies on the Gregory, Bobtail, Bates, Hunter, Burroughs, and other lodes were suspending operations in 1869-70-71, and their employees began to lease some of the same company properties, and to start up other mines new and old that had been idle. Quartz Hill and Nevadaville were the more active localities in 1870-71, when nearly all the mines or claims on the Kansas, Burroughs, California, Gardner, Flack, Prize, Suderberg, Jones, Roderick Dhu, Illinois, and some other lodes were in full blast. From 1871 to 1875 the Buell mine was the leading producer of the lower part of the county.

In these years large numbers of miners left for the new silver districts of Georgetown, Caribou, and of Park county, which some of their own number had been discovering. Gilpin county has furnished explorers, settlers, and colonists for every new mining camp that has been started, thereby earning the title of "the mother of Colorado mining camps." Those who remained at Central and Nevadaville finally exhausted the pockets and ore bodies of many leased mines, and left them to fill with water, and in bad condition for succeeding operations, as they were poorly timbered, and many of them "in cap."

The entire district had a dull appearance in 1873-4, but the previous record and known value of the lodes caused several Central men to resume work on their own or leased properties. The success which rewarded their nerve and enterprise caused others to do likewise. Time and money were required to remove water and sink or drift into new ore bodies, but a few years brought about a great increase in production and prosperity. When many of these reopened mines got fairly to producing, in 1876, the county's gold yield was larger than at any former period. Since then every month sees great improvement and progress. These results are largely due to the enterprise of such Colorado men as Briggs, Fagan, Sullivan, Buell, Fullerton, Kimber, Mackay, Young, Standley, Thatcher, Holman, and others, whose faith in the mines has been proved to have been well founded.

Many old properties are now worked under one management. Some lessees have made enough money to buy the mines of the owners, the companies, or their successors, and others have retired in one, two, or three years, with a fortune. These were the mines that the companies could not make pay. If these company stocks had been made assessable, as in California and Nevada, the mines would probably have been worked steadily, and eventually have paid a profit—where the agents were good for anything. Non-assessable stocks permit of the dog-in-the-manger policy—for some stockholders will not advance money when it is needed for exploration, development, or machinery—while sure to come in for their share of the dividends if any money is made. All that is left for those stockholders who are anxious to have work progress, is to pay for it, and take all the chances on loss and only a part of those on gain, or else let the mine lie idle. The latter has been the course generally adopted.

In Nevada, men who will not pay their assessments are sold out, to give room for those who will. Had this not been the case the great bonanzas of the Comstock (whose yield and profits for five years were the grandest in the history of mining) would never have been found. The best way for these old companies to do (that are not working their properties) is to sell out for any price, for their claims are usually too small to work successfully by themselves. The only other sensible move would be to buy up adjoining claims, and so procure territory enough to pay for deep mining. It should be remembered that it takes just as much machinery and steam-power to work 100 or 200 feet of the vein to a depth of 1,000 feet as it would to work 1,000 feet of territory to the same depth. The only old companies that have operated since their formation, in 1864, with hardly an interruption, are the Consolidated Bobtail and New York & Colorado ; and the reason is largely due to the fact that they had more than the usual quota of contiguous property on one vein, and have subsequently increased it by purchase. As to the stocks in the old defunct companies, they may be considered utterly worthless. Any mining company organized in 1864–5 in Gilpin county which is not now at work is never likely to make any money. Stockholders should consider their stock worthless.

The permanent and healthy character of the revival in mining in this district is shown by the large number of mines supplied with steam-hoisting works. Steam machinery indicates deep mining, extensive operations, probably extensive production, and, at all events, a high estimation of the value of the property. No heavy mining work can be carried on without steam-power. There are now forty-four different mines in the district operated in this way. Some of them have engines of from forty to one hundred horse-power each. One engine answers for a long stretch of territory, and for what was once several separate properties. Out of these forty-four mines, the Consolidated Bobtail, the Briggs-Gregory, and the N. Y. & C. Gregory, the Gunnell, and Monmouth-Kansas are each supplied with one, or several hoisting engines of great capacity, beside additional ones for the great pumps with which they are supplied. In place of three or four active steam-hoisting works on Quartz Hill, as in most previous years, there are now twenty — most of them put up during the past twenty months on mines that had been idle for years.

For twenty years Gilpin county has been the leading gold district of Colorado. In that time it has probably turned out more bullion than any other one gold mining locality in America. So uninterrupted has been this outflow of the precious metals that the county has justly earned the title so often applied to it, of the " Old Reliable." This production has been going on ever since the arrival of the pioneers in Gregory Gulch, in 1859, and is much larger now than at any former period. There are more valuable lodes in the immediate vicinity of Central, Black Hawk, and Nevadaville, than in any section of equal size in the known world, and there are more mill stamps in operation than anywhere else. Various causes have prevented all of the profitable or valuable mines from being operated at any one time, but the closing of one was usually followed by the reopening or discovery of another. No suspensions are reported of late, but more than a score of mines have lately resumed specie payments, and more are to follow. Parts of or all of every valuable lode (with a few exceptions) are now in active operation, and the time is not distant when every mine on these lodes will be worked separately or with consolidated properties. The unfailing character of so many hundred veins, and their combined and continuous production, long ago caused this, the smallest of Colorado's counties, to be considered the richest district of the State.

Below is a statement of Gilpin county's mining product prior to 1879. The figures for the years previous to 1868, are estimates. From that time they are reliable and are very accurate for the past four years. Any productions or shipments made in or through Gilpin from mines of other counties does not appear in these figures. For several years prior to 1879, the actual bullion and ore shipments exceeded $3,500,000 per annum, but large portions came from outside ores treated at Black Hawk.

YEAR.	COIN VALUE.	YEAR.	COIN VALUE.
1859	$250,000	1869	$1,680,000
1860	900,000	1870	1,552,000
1861	750,000	1871	1,400,000
1862	1,200,000	1872	1,389,289
1863	1,600,000	1873	1,340,502
1864	1,800,000	1874	1,531,863
1865	1,500,000	1875	1,533,909
1866	750,000	1876	2,105,544
1867	1,000,000	1877	2,208,037
1868	1,305,000	1878	2,280,871

Product of 1879; ore and mill tailings, 155,000 tons; value, $2,625,750
The total yield up to 1880 was, $30,702,765; currency value, $37,500,000

Of this amount very near $29,115,000 were gold, $1,075,000 silver, $593,000 copper, and a small value in lead. It is estimated that more gold has been lost in milling, washed down the creeks and gulches, than the amount saved as given above. The actual number of mill stamps running steadily in Gilpin County is less than 800 (the figures given on page 296) as two or three mills have not always their full complement running.

The county's product in 1868–9 was as follows, coin value:

SOURCES.	1868.	1869.
Mill and Gulch Gold..........................	$1,175,000	$1,380,000
Boston and Colorado Smelting Works......	193,000	367,400
Other bullion...........	50,000	50,000
	$1,410,000	$1,797,400
Deduct for Clear Creek....................	105,000	117,000
Total for Gilpin....................	$1,305,000	$1,680,400

The production and sources of reduction and export for 1872–3–4, was as follows:

SOURCES.	1872.	1873.	1874.
Stamp Mills....................	$959,439 00	$710,996 00	$1,044,575 89
Boston and Colorado Smelting Works	419,850 00	510,635 00	483,928 57
Other sources, exports and works....	10,000 00	118,871 00	3,358 54
Total value......	$1,389,289 00	$1,340,502 00	$1,531,803 00
Tons of ore handled................	100,000	90,000	115,000

The average number of stamps at work in 1872 was not far from 430; of 1873, probably 400; of 1874, over 470. There were several mills that did not keep steadily at work.

The county's product in 1877–8 came through the following sources:

SOURCES.	1877. TONS ORE.	1877. VALUE.	1878. TONS ORE.	1878. VALUE.
Stamp Mills..............	140,000	$1,289,142 33	140,000	$1,283,569 36
Placers..	......	45,000 00	......	35,000 00
Boston and Colorado Smelting Works......	5,000	779,894 76	5,500	868,500 00
Golden Smelter..........	1,200	80,000 00	1,500	83,801 75
Mill tailings to Boulder, etc.	......	14,000 00	......	10,000 00
Totals..............	146,200	$2,208,037 09	147,000	$2,280,871 11

The tonnage of mill tailings is not counted above, but the value is. It amounted to from 7,500 to 9,000 tons each year.

The yield in the various metals for four years was as follows:

	1875.	1876.	1877.	1878.
Gold...........	$1,390,253 90	$1,878,818 34	$1,963,485 67	$1,974,934 36
Silver..........	97,409 00	151,569 50	161,255 38	225,936 75
Copper........	44,155 80	70,672 64	82,296 64	79,000 00
Lead..	2,100 30	4,484 30	1,000 00	1,000 00
Total.......	$1,533,909 00	$2,105,544 78	$2,208,037 09	$2,280,871 11

The express shipments of mill and placer gold, which are substantially the same thing as the shipments of the three Central banks, have always been considered as an indicator, from month to month, of what the mines of Gilpin county are doing. The amount is almost entirely the product of ores crushed in the stamp mills. From $25,000 to $40,000 only come from the gulches and creeks of Gilpin, and smaller amounts from the same sources and from lode mines in Clear Creek county. The express shipments of 1876 were larger than those of 1878, but the heavy increase of productions by the smelting works and in gold taken away by private parties brought the county's total product for the latter year ahead of any previous time. The bank and express shipments of 1875,'6,'8 were as follows:

	1875.	1876.	1878.
January	$86,149 56	$104,984 15	$102,154 00
February	62,817 50	111,411 00	91,494 00
March	75,526 76	124,305 37	102,544 00
April	78,219 80	102,902 49	98,800 00
May	73,359 92	107,194 89	103,194 00
June	95,403 25	105,734 50	100,484 80
July	92,272 80	100,184 03	98,476 56
August	102,615 21	118,081 52	120,900 00
September	96,340 81	145,870 91	99,502 00
October	94,450 86	93,894 47	124,592 00
November	96,818 01	99,592 54	107,536 00
December	114,223 67	107,084 65	125,892 00
Total	$1,068,198 15	$1,321,240 52	$1,275,569 36

Gilpin county ores are treated either by the stamp mill or by the smelting process. Most of them contain too little value to stand any other treatment than that of stamp milling.

One smelting process saves very nearly all of the gold, silver, and copper, and another nearly all of the gold, silver, and lead. Since the last reduction in smelting charges, gold ores are bought at a price, allowing for a charge of twenty-five dollars per ton, and ten per cent. deduction from the assay for waste, etc. On ores containing one hundred and twenty dollars in gold, thirty dollars in silver, and ten in copper or lead, the miner would receive $110 for his ton of ore. The same ore treated by amalgamation in stamp mills, would return but $70 or $80, allowing for a saving of sixty or seventy per cent. of the gold and very little of the silver or copper. But most of the ore mined contains but fifteen or twenty dollars of all the metals per ton, and the stamp mills that handle it for two or three dollars per ton comprise the only means of profitably extracting the gold. The ore of a mine is now divided into separate lots, a few tons of very rich mineral being sent to the smelter, to ten, twenty, or thirty times as much crushed in the stamp mill. By this means as much money is made in gold mining as on smaller but richer silver lodes.

The stamp mills crushed about 21,000 cords, or 108,000 tons of ore in 1875, of an average yield of $9.70. The average yield of 1876 was a little over $10, and that of 1878 was $9.12. This decrease was not due to growing poverty of ore but to closer assorting, and sending a larger proportion of the rich ores to the smelters. From seventeen to nineteen quartz mills were at work in 1878 with from 550 to 630 stamps. The average number of stamps at work in 1876 was 560, and in 1878 it was about 590; yield nearly $1,300,000.

Over a hundred small quartz mills of five, ten, and fifteen stamps each, arrived in Gilpin county in the earlier years of mining. Only a portion of them were ever at work at one time, and on one occasion nearly all were idle. Some were worn out long ago, others were sold to the foundries for old iron, a few were moved to other districts, and many went to make additions to the more pretentious mills of later days.

Gilpin county quartz or stamp mills, as now conducted, may save sixty or seventy per cent. of the gold contents of ordinary ores, and very little of the silver or copper, or say half of the ore's total value in the three metals. Better work is done on some quartz and poorer on others. Thorough tests in several mills, where only one kind of ore is treated and that low grade, show a saving of from seventy-five to eighty-seven per cent of the gold. A mill stamp, as run in Colorado, will crush three-fourths of a ton of ore every twenty-four hours, and ten stamps will crush one cord or seven or eight tons in the same time.

Several mills have recently resumed work, and others have been enlarged. One new mill has been completed and another is being constructed, beside a concentrating establishment. Early in May,

1879, nineteen mills and 624 stamps were at work, in June, 662 stamps, in July, 735, in the winter and early spring of 1879–'80, from 520 to 580, and early in May, 1880, twenty mills and 800 stamps; names, capacity and locations given below.

No.	NAMES.	No. of Stamps.	LOCATION.	TOWN.
1	Randolph...................	50	North Clear Creek.	Black Hawk.
2	New York..................	75	" "	"
3	Kelty.....................	38	" "	"
4	Richman (California).......	50	" "	"
5	Cons. Bobtail..............	125	" "	"
6	Hidden Treasure...........	20	" "	"
7	Briggs....................	50	Gregory Gulch....	"
8	New York and Colorado....	40	" "	"
9	Wain and Reynolds........	25	North Clear Creek.	"
10	Kimber...................	35	" "	"
11	Bostwick...	25	" "	"
12	Fullerton (Lower)..........	40	" "	"
13	Fullerton (Upper)..........	33	" "	"
14	Wheeler..................	25	" "	"
15	Lewis and Aulsebrook......	25	Nevada Gulch.....	Nevadaville.
16	Monmouth-Kansas....	52	" "	"
17 18	} Mackay Mills..............	37	" "	"
19	Waterman.................	20	Eureka Gulch.....	
20	Cashier...................	35	North Clear Creek.	Black Hawk.
	Total.....	800		

In addition to the above, the Arrighi mill of 10 stamps, and the Winnebago, of 15 stamps, are likely to be running at any time. All of the stamps of the Kelty mill and of the new Cashier mill are not generally in use. Among the idle but serviceable mills are the Buell, of 60 stamps, the Illinois, of 22, the Becker, of 20, and the Hendrie mill, of 15. The 14-stamp Rollins mill may have 50 or 100 stamps added this season. It is expected that two mills, one of 40, and the other of 16 stamps, will be erected in Russell this summer. The New York mill, of 75, and the Cashier mill of 35 stamps, were built in 1879; the Tucker, 32-stamp mill, was burned. Twenty stamps were added to the lower Fullerton mill, and recently 50 stamps to the Bobtail. The total number of available quartz-mill stamps in Gilpin County is 936, besides those in two concentrating mills. From 100 to 150 may be added this year.

GILPIN COUNTY'S PRODUCT FOR 1879.

The sources of reduction and export and the value in the various metals were as given below. Total, $2,625,750.

SOURCES, ETC.	GOLD.	SILVER.	COPPER.	LEAD.	TOTAL.
Stamp mills................	$1,254,239	*$20,000	....	......	$1,274,239
Gulches and creeks........	20,000	....	....	......	20,000
B. & C. Smelting Works...	591,000	263,000	$103,000	......	957,000
Valley Smelting Works....	36,647	27,604	10,000	$1,672	75,923
Golden Smelting Works ..	57,359	39,589	....	1,640	98,588
Mill tailings................	130,000	35,000	10,000	......	175,000
Other sources and exports..	25,000	....	....	......	25,000
Totals................	$2,114,245	$335,193	$123,000	$3,312	$2,625,750

* Silver in the gold retort.

The unusual gain of $344,878.89 over 1878 was partially attributable to the unprecedented quantities of mill tailings sent abroad. Netter & Matthews estimate the contents of the tailings purchased by them at $150,000. The value of those sent to the Golden and Argo smelters is not included in the above item of "mill tailings." It will be noticed that while the stamp-mill product has varied but little from 1877–8, that the yield from the richer smelting ores is far greater than ever before. This is mainly due to closer assorting, caused by cheaper smelting. The stamp mills handled about 140,000 tons of ore in 1879, and the smelting works 7,000 or 8,000, besides as large a tonnage of mill tailings.

The removal of ore leaves extensive cavities. There are mines where this worked-out ground extends (for the few feet in width between the walls of the veins) hundreds of feet vertically and horizontally. There are seven or eight shafts on the Kansas lode over 300 feet deep, two of them about 600, and one 1,000 feet deep. The Burroughs and California-Gardner are opened in a similar manner, and so are the Gunnell, Gregory, and Bobtail.

About fifteen hundred men have usually been employed in and about the mines, mills, and works of Gilpin county, and the result of their labors is a product of over two and a quarter million dollars in bullion per annum. This, if equally divided, would give $1,520 to each person directly engaged in obtaining it; or allowing an expenditure of half a million for machinery, mining and milling supplies, and other outlays, and there would still be $1,166 to each employee, or nearly $300 for each man, woman, and child in the district. As the operations in many mines for a year or two have been mainly of a preparatory character prior to the heavy production now setting in, the results hereafter are likely to be twenty per cent. better than those given above. The three banks of Central have very nearly three quarters of a million of deposits from the miners of the district, which is a very large sum when the fact is considered that so much is continually expended in opening mines, in expensive buildings, and machinery, and in permanent town improvements, beside moneys sent out of the State to friends and relatives. Every year there are nearly or quite one hundred and thirty or forty thousand dollars sent away in the shape of money orders through the post office of Central, and nearly or quite as much at Black Hawk and Nevadaville. All of these facts indicate how profitable and enduring the mines of these mountains are. No eastern town or county can show average returns to the whole population any where nearly as large as are known in all leading Colorado mining camps.

CHAPTER IX.

THE GREGORY AND BOBTAIL LODES AND THEIR PRODUCTIVE MINES—
MILLIONS OF GOLD AND TONS OF BULLION—THE MILLS, HOISTING
WORKS, AND PUMPS OF THE BIG MINES—FIGURES OF COST AND
CURRENT EXPENSES AND ANNUAL AND TOTAL YIELD—HOW FOR-
TUNES WERE MADE.

The Gregory lode stands pre-eminent as the first found and the
most productive of Colorado mineral veins. While not yielding as
much at present as some of the later discoveries, its total output
from first to last still surpasses that of any American lodes excepting the Comstock and two or three others on the Pacific slope. Its
surface outcroppings were first panned and tested for gold by the
pioneer prospector John H. Gregory on the 6th day of May, 1859.
This discovery proved the existence of gold in these mountains in
paying quantities, and at once brought in an army of gold hunters.
The surface dirt was exceedingly rich, and large amounts of gold
were sluiced therefrom. The vein has always produced larger or
smaller quantities of gold whenever worked in the more central portions. It has been located and claimed for nearly a mile, including
extensions, but the productive and developed portion is embraced
in 2,440 contiguous feet of ground. This extends from the summit
of Gregory Hill northeasterly across Gregory Gulch into Bates Hill,
and embraces what are now known as the Narragansett, Consolidated Gregory, Briggs, and New York & Colorado properties.

The Gregory vein material has maintained a width and continuity far above the average, and has, consequently, yielded
immensely. The width between walls has usually been several feet,
and sometimes ten or twelve and even twenty. The distribution of
the ore is variable, occurring in seams of from a few inches to two
or more feet, with intervening bands of poor rock, and sometimes
for short distances it has pinched out or given place to vein matter
of barren quartz and feldspar. There have been huge bodies of ore,
extending for hundreds of feet in length and depth, and very broad

in places. The walls are not regular, being sometimes smooth and
well defined and again rugged and uneven.   The inclosing rock is
granitic gneiss, showing much mica in some places and little in
others.   The retort gold from the Gregory is of higher value than
the average of the county, indicating that the proportion of silver is
small.   Seams and pockets of ore of surpassing richness have
occasionally been found in both upper and lower workings, and a
large amount of nugget and wire gold.   On the northeastern slope
of Gregory Hill is a parallel and branch vein of the Gregory, called
the Foot and Simmons, which is evidently the same as that known
further east by the name of Briggs.   This is separated from the
Gregory by a granite wall from a few feet to seventy in width.

The lode, like others in the early times, was staked off in claims
one hundred feet long.   Gregory, the discoverer, secured two of
these, which he soon sold to E. W. Henderson and A. Gridley for
$21,000.   The purchasers cleared $18,000 from the first summer's
work, and other men were making money above and below.   After
a time the surface dirt was exhausted and the owners were discon-
certed at the appearance of the solid iron pyrites or barren cap rock.
All difficulties were to some extent sooner or later overcome, and
some portions of the lode would return to "pay" as others grew
poor and unproductive.   Claims or parts of claims changed hands
several times between 1859 and 1863.   James E. Lyon, Pullman, of
palace car fame, Wilkes Defrees, Joseph E. Bates, E. W. Henderson,
John Bruce, Benjamin Smith, D. S. Parmelee, J. S. and C. H. Briggs,
and Lee, Judd & Lee were among those who owned and operated
properties there prior to the sales to Eastern men and companies.
The last named firm tried to sell their claims for $6,000 in 1862, when
they were not paying expenses.   They could not find a purchaser and
so kept at work.   They soon after struck a rich ore body that widened
to twenty feet.   It yielded over three hundred thousand dollars, two
hundred thousand of which was profit, up to April, 1864.   Then
they put the property into the Black Hawk Mining Company, organized in New York.   The five hundred feet adjoining and extending
up the hill were bought in June, 1864, for the Consolidated Gregory
Company at the rate of one thousand dollars a foot.   Other claims
sold at lower rates.   The Narragansett Company was organized on
the adjoining four hundred feet southwesterly.   The Briggs Company
was organized on the claims immediately west of Gregory Gulch and

the Smith & Parmelee and the New York & Colorado on those northeast of it.

The following will show how productive and profitable were the Briggs and Black Hawk claims at one time, notwithstanding it was in the era of high prices and heavy expenses. In 1867 the Black Hawk company obtained 12,193¾ ounces of gold, worth in currency $279,647.76, from about 12,000 tons of ore, showing an average yield of $23.30 per ton, with an outlay of $194,425.63, or at a total average expense of $11.43 per ton, or over double the cost at the present time. Gold was at $1.37. The pump then broke down and the water prevented further mining operations until a new and powerful pump was placed in the shaft. During the year ending July 1, 1869, when the company closed business, the yield was $154,135.76, the outlay $92,381.78, and the profit $61,753.98. In four years and six months previous to 1869 the Black Hawk three hundred feet produced $1,358,149. In four years and eleven months the Briggs two hundred and forty feet yielded 534,615. During these years gold ranged from $1.33 to $1.50 in currency. The expenses in the Black Hawk property in 1867, in coin value, were $8.17 for mining, $2.48 for milling, and $1.05 for teaming; this makes a total of $11.50, or $10.45 without teaming. In 1869 the cost was $11; it is now $4.50.

The Briggs Mine comprises the two hundred and forty feet known as the Briggs claims, and the three hundred feet formerly owned by the Black Hawk Company, and includes the diverging but nearly parallel Gregory and Briggs veins. Over the Briggs claims and shafts is a fine brick mill building, containing powerful hoisting works, pumps, and fifty stamps, with double issue batteries throughout, one-half furnished with automatic ore feeders. Here is the main shaft, 925 feet deep, driven a portion of the way forty feet long and ten wide. From this shaft levels are being driven at intervals through the entire 1,040 feet, including the 500 feet of leased ground, called the Consolidated Gregory. The amount of ore in reserve between these levels ready to be broken down is immense. Very little stoping has been done in the lower 450 feet of the Briggs property, and in the lower 600 feet or more of the Consolidated Gregory.

There is ore enough to keep fifty or seventy-five stamps at work for five years without sinking the shaft deeper. The machinery and appli-

Gregory Lode.

BLACK HAWK.

Bobtail Mill.

ances are first-class, and embrace many improvements not yet introduced in many mines.   Among the pumps is one which was put in by the old Black Hawk Company that is fifteen inches in diameter.   The mine usually makes 140 gallons of water per minute.   There are several shafts between five and six hundred feet deep.   Both the Briggs and Gregory veins are worked, and are connected here and there by cross-cuts.

The Briggs brothers conduct operations at a less cost per ton of ore mined than any other firm or miner in the State.   The yield of the mine for the last year or two has ranged from $11,000 to $16,000 monthly, and the profits are said to average over $6,000 per month for the entire year.   When the expenses reach $9,000 per month about $5,500 go for labor, $2,300 for supplies, $1,000 for coal, $300 for powder, and $175 for candles.   The working force, including both mine and mill, approaches one hundred men.   A few men work on tribute—that is, pay a certain royalty or percentage on ore taken out from a piece of ground worked by them.   Expenses are very low, the average cost, per ton, of mining being $1.90, of hoisting forty cents, and of milling $1.70, or $4.00 altogether.   The hoisting and pumping machinery of the Briggs mine is of the most efficient character, and embraces great engines and boilers of one hundred horse power or less, one of which furnishes power for the fifty-stamp mill.

The mines on the Gregory lode yielded $225,934 in 1875, and $222,405 in 1876.   The monthly bullion shipments of the Briggs portion of the lode have since increased.   Its yield was about $134,000 in each of the years 1875–6, and $150,000 in 1877.

It is reported that the Briggs mine yielded $31,500 in the months of May and June, 1878 combined, with $18,000 profit, and that the yield of August and September together was $34,500.   The sales of smelting ore ran from $6,000 to $8,000 per month nearly all of the year, and as the mill ore generally paid expenses, those figures may be supposed to represent the clear profit of the mine.   Last year rich pockets and fine gold specimens were found.   Three lots sold at one time returned as follows: 100 pounds yielded $32 per pound, or at the rate of $64,000; a few hundred pounds sold at the rate of $4,000 and $1,200 respectively.   Other small lots gave at the rate of $7,669 per ton, $1,541 and $408; 156 pounds yielded $1,496 and $2,350 worth of gold was panned out of only 92 pounds of ore.

Such returns help along the profits, but the thousands of tons of mill ore yielding less than $8 a ton with a profit of $3.50 per ton and the hundreds of tons of ore that the smelter buys for $100 or so per ton are the reliances of the mine. As the mill is directly over the mine, and no hauling is required, nearly or quite all of the crevice matter is fed into the stamps. This and close sorting for the smelter are causes of the low grade of the mill ore. Of the two veins the Gregory averages the larger.

The New York & Colorado company own some 1,200 feet on the two veins northeast of the Briggs mine. This company absorbed the Smith & Parmelee company and took in its property. Eight hundred feet of the veins are developed by long levels extending from a shaft that is nearly 800 feet deep and gradually getting deeper. Over this shaft is a building containing a forty-stamp mill and fine hoisting works, propelled by an eighty-horse power engine, which also furnishes power for the Cornish pump. The yield of this mine was $76,310.75 in 1875, with a small margin of profit, and matters have continued in about the same way ever since. The ore is generally of low grade, but there is a great deal of it. The company's workings extend from Gregory Gulch under Bates Hill. These lower levels can be carried forward as far to the northeast as the veins extend.

The following is something like a correct statement of the yield of the entire Gregory lode from its discovery up to July 1, 1879, coin value. The currency value would approach $10,000,000. Some estimates go still higher.

Estimated yield by old owners up to June, 1864, coin	$3,500,000
Black Hawk, 1864–69	936,654
Briggs mine, 1864–69	368,700
Briggs mine, including Black Hawk, 1869–79	600,000
Consolidated Gregory, from 1864–79	500,000
Smith & Parmelee, 1864–69	375,000
New York & Colorado, which now includes Smith & Parmelee, from 1869–79	450,000
Narragansett, 1864–79	100,000
Total	$6,830,354

The Briggs mine, which includes the old Black Hawk mine, and the adjoining Consolidated Gregory, now worked by the Briggs firm, embrace the 1,040 feet in the central part of the lode. From the best data at hand it would seem that the yield of this 1,040 feet from discovery to July, 1879, was not far from $4,205,000, coin value, or $5,500,000, reckoning the currency values in which the gold was sold. This property is now said to have as much ore above the line of the deepest workings as has already been mined and milled by the upper excavations.

The Narragansett Company of New York own 400 feet of the Gregory lode, adjoining the Consolidated Gregory property on the southwest, and their buildings, on claims 11 and 12, are on or near the crest of Gregory Hill. This mine has been operated only at intervals and has never yielded as well as those described above. Last fall some practical miners obtained a two years' lease and have since been sinking and drifting with fair results. The deep shaft is down over 530 feet.

The Bobtail is one of the great lodes of Colorado, ranking next to the Gregory in past production. Its ore has been of a higher grade than that of its great neighbor, but until recently a smaller amount of ground had been worked, owing to unproductiveness near the surface. This is why the aggregate yield has been less than that of the Gregory. Yet the total foots up over $4,500,000. Much production was prevented by the closing down of the company claims with which the lode was too much subdivided.

The intersection of the vein by tunnel, the consolidation of different properties, and the reopening of them by deeper shafts and levels, has enabled the Consolidated Bobtail Company to work to great advantage and profit. From 1875 to the time when the Little Pittsburg mine began to produce so heavily, the Bobtail was the most productive of Colorado mines. It still continues to increase its product, and now that it has paid off the purchase price of numerous claims, and of a seventy-five stamp mill, beside rebuilding the latter and furnishing the mine with new shafts and splendid machinery, it will undoubtedly pay dividends much more frequently than heretofore.

The ground along the line of the Bobtail was very rich in surface material or "float," and was pre-empted in many separate claims under the name of Field or Bobtail soon after the Gregory discovery. The surface dirt was taken to the creek and sluiced for the gold it contained. Much of it was hauled there by a solitary ox, whose caudal appendage had been abbreviated. From this historic animal the lode took its name.

Some of the claims changed hands for trifling considerations prior to the spring of 1860. The vein or lode itself was not found until then, many believing the pay dirt previously obtained to be merely a wash deposit. One claim was given away that, long after, sold for $60,000. The vein proved enormously rich, and when it gave out in one place it opened out in another. In 1861–2–3 there seemed to be no cessation to the golden shower that some of the lucky owners encountered. This carried the workings down to depths of from 60 to 250 feet. Hundreds of dollars per cord were common returns at the stamp mills, where the amalgam gathered so fast on the tables that two "clean-ups" were made daily. Among the men who figured prominently in the Bobtail in those days were Joseph W. Holman, D. G. Wilson, B. O. Russell, L. D. Crandall, J. F. Fields, W. H. Hurlbut, the Cotton brothers, and John Sensenderfer. Hill and Armstrong and Hale and Patterson purchased interests in 1862, and made fortunes. Jerome B. Chaffee made his first great strike there. He and Eben Smith leased Sensenderfer's claim, which was "in cap." Early in 1864 they had cleared from that and from the working, purchase, and sale of another claim, over $100,000. Sensenderfer and other claim owners are said to have netted from one to two hundred thousand each in a few years' time.

In 1864 eastern companies purchased most of the best developed parts of the lode, in very small claims, excepting the Bobtail Gold Company. It survived and prospered when the others failed at depths of four or five hundred feet, because it had as many feet of territory on the lode as all of them combined. In the two years ending September 1, 1868, the Sensenderfer one hundred and twenty-eight feet, produced $197,155, which was mined and milled at a cost of $77,935, leaving a net profit of $119,220, or of over 60 per cent. Ten dividends of $10,000 each were paid previous to November, 1867. At that time mining, milling, and other expenses footed up an average expense of $13.50 per ton, coin value, as against $6 at the present time. The Bobtail, Field, and other claims also paid largely.

In 1872, when most of these mines were idle, the shaft-houses were burned, and the shaft timber work rendered useless and unsafe. The Bobtail tunnel was afterwards driven to intersect the lode and afford drainage and an outlet for the product of the mine. The Fisk lode was penetrated 574 feet, and the Bobtail 1,110 feet from the mouth of the tunnel. This was in 1873. Superintendent A. N. Rogers, who had had charge of affairs from 1864, then induced the company to reopen the mine on a large scale, and to purchase the adjoining company properties and the great Black Hawk Mill. This required time and expense, but the present yield, the thousands of cords of broken ore on hand, and the immense ore reserves in sight show the wisdom of these movements in place of suspending work or operating on a small scale. The Bobtail Company owned 433⅓ feet on the vein originally, and after many years bought the Sensenderfer, 128 feet, separated therefrom by the Black Hawk Company's 72 feet, the Brastow, 66⅔ feet, the Teller, 100 feet, and the Sterling, 66⅔ feet. In the course of several years these were all purchased, making 900 feet of territory, less 33⅓ feet owned by J. F. Field, beside the Branch lode and other claims.

A large excavation in the solid rock at the head of the tunnel, and 471 feet below the surface of the hill, contains huge engines and boilers for propelling the hoisting machinery and great pumps. A brick and iron smoke-stack extends up an old shaft to daylight. A splendid perpendicular shaft has been sunk some 400 feet below the tunnel level, 8 feet by 16 in the clear, divided in four compartments, one for sinking, one for pump and ladder way, and two for cage-ways, up and down which ascend the great iron cars loaded with quartz, men, or supplies. The cars, each loaded with two tons of ore, are run from the iron tracks of the various levels of the mine directly into these cages. They are then hoisted to the tunnel level and run out on another track to the ore building and daylight. Here the ore is dumped onto a floor below the track by the two halves of the car parting at the bottom. The hoisting machinery for the cage is as substantial as wood and iron can make it. The two drums are seven feet in diameter. Upon these are wound the flat steel wire ropes, of English manufacture, three inches in width and half an inch in thickness, with breaking strain of fifty tons, which are attached to the cages. These drums are driven by spur-gear, twelve feet in diameter and twelve-inch face. The engine driving this makes direct connection, and has reversible link motion.

This mine drains other lodes and makes more water than several of its neighbors combined. It compares in this respect with some of the Comstock mines. Drainage is one of the big items of expense, costing in 1879 alone, $36,659.84. Powerful Worthington pumps have been purchased and set at work at an outlay of $10,000, which discharge from the mine 500 gallons of water per minute, or 720,000 gallons every twenty-four hours.

The main working shaft of the Bobtail is driven perpendicularly from the tunnel level, and off of the vein. Several hundred feet below, cross-cuts from 70 to 90 feet long are required to reach the vein. As the lode has once changed its dip, it may do so again, and be found at greater depths on the line of the shaft. The lower workings are over 900 feet below the surface.

The company lately sold its twenty stamp mill and added fifty stamps to its seventy-five stamper. This mill is a model of its kind, and no other in the state, and few out of it are as large. Early in May the entire 125 stamps were at work crushing nearly 100 tons of ore daily. With the additional capacity, the mine's output should approach $400,000 per annum, and now that mining and milling and pumping demands have been complied with, a large margin will be afforded for dividends. The mill, ore buildings, shops, compressors, machine drills, hoisting and pumping machinery are known as permanent improvements, will last for years, and, must have cost with adjoining mining claims purchased, over $275,000—all paid for by the mine in five years, besides $147,781.90 in dividends. This sum of $147,781.90 has been paid in four dividends,—on November 1, 1877, November 11, 1878, in September, 1879, and March 30, 1880. The company will be able to pay two dividends per annum hereafter, each amounting to 15 cents a share, or $34,098.90, and more if the mine improves. There are over 2,000 tons of quartz broken in the mine ready for the mill, and vast reserves of unbroken ore at depths of from 250 to 425 feet below the tunnel level.

The company employs over 200 miners, mill men, teamsters, and shop men. This includes those working on contract who generally make about $2.25 per day, or about the same as those receive who work for wages. The pay-roll foots up nearly or quite $13,000 every month for labor, exclusive of superintendent and assistants. Five steam engines, combining 200-horse power, are employed at the mills, including one used for the air compressor of the machine drills. There are five engines, combining about 225-horse power, in the mine. Two machine drills have generally been operated in the underground workings.

The receipts and expenditures of this company are given for 1876, not that they make as good a showing as those of later years, but because they are the only ones in the writer's possession. The receipts for that year were $232,206.70 for bullion from ore milled and $44,147.47 from ore sold smelters. Tributors paid a royalty of $1,253.25, and rents and interest on loans gave $629.37; total receipts, $278,236.79. Net profits of the year $46,976.80. The figures on expenses and profits for 1877–8 are not at hand, but are believed to make a better showing for the company than the above. To enable the reader to see what outlays are required in a great mine, the following statement is given:

The expenses for the year 1876 included $156,555.87 for mining, $51,154.21 for milling, $14,358.46 for drainage and superintendence; taxes and other expenses, $9,181.45. Of the mining expenses, mining contracts took $51,386.95; day labor, $49,052.98; candles, powder and fuse, $13,165.71; fuel, $4,853.77; timber and lumber, $3,165.94; and hardware, foundry work, and machinery, $12,591. In the mills fuel cost $9,878.09; hauling ore, $8,734.51; and chemicals and oil, $1,052.29. Something like seven-tenths of a ton of coal is burned for every cord, or seven and a half tons of ore milled, and the coal consumption at the mine and mill together probably exceeds three thousand tons per annum.

The Consolidated Bobtail Gold Mining Company has a capital stock of $1,136,630, in 227,326 five dollar shares. The trustees and officers are George A. Hoyt, president; John Stanton, Jr., secretary and treasurer; and E. C. Litchfield, Jerome B. Chaffee, L. H. Brigham, E. H. Litchfield, John Ewen, R. J. Hubbard, and Walton Ferguson.

Below is a four years' statement furnished by the company. It shows the amount of ore milled and smelted, of mill tailings dressed and sold, the average yield per ton and cord in ounces of gold and in dollars; also the cost of milling per ton and of mining per foot, fathom, and ton. Its completeness should insure for it attention. Few companies or miners keep so close or accurate a knowledge of just what they, their mine, ore and mills are doing, and in this the management deserves commendation.

CONS. BOBTAIL MINE—QUANTITIES, YIELD, AND VALUE.

	1875.	1876.	1877.	1878.
Cords of Ore milled	1,913½	3,225	3,511	3,276½
" " by Tributors......	93½	70½	50	83
Tons of Smelting Ore sold by Company	574	395¼	350	402
" " " Tributors	111½	30¼	25	102
Tons of Dressed Tailings sold........	545	981¼	1.149½	1,500
" " per cord Ore.	0.3	0.3	0.32	0.45
Ounces Gold yield per cord Ore	3.62	3.71	3.788	3.98
Currency value per cord Ore...........	$71 60	$71 85	$68 97	$70 26
Currency value of same, including } Tailings........................ }	74 22	74 68	72 31	73 75
Value of Tailings per cord Ore........	2 62	2 83	3 33	3 49
" " sold, per ton........	8 73	9 33	10 18	7 63
" Smelting Ore sold, per ton....	83 60	88 53	109 64	118 10

The quantity of ore milled in the different years has been governed almost entirely by the number of stamps operated.

COMPARATIVE COST OF WORK.

	1875.	1876.	1877.	1878.
Drifting, per foot	$12 15	$10 18	$9 89	$9 45
Stoping, per fathom..................	26 50	24 33	23 07	22 48
Sinking, per foot (excepting No. 4 } Winze—see below)............. }	.....	10 76	12 88	12 85
* Passing dirt and filling buckets, per } cord............................. }	3 67	3 10	2 00	2 17
† Hoisting, per cord....................	.....	1 60	1 53	1 93
‡ Loading and Transportation (con- } tract with Tunnel Co.), per cord. }	6 00	6 00	6 00	6 00
Assorting Ore, per cord..............	1 80	1 60	1 80	1 70
Hauling to mill, per cord.............	3 20	2 10	2 12	2 26
Milling expense, per cord	13 76	12 86	11 88	11 87
Dressing Tailings, per cord	.....	90	96	1 43

* Refers to new ground being opened.   † Does not include hoisting from winzes,
‡ Actual cost of loading, $1.00 per cord.

The increased saving of tailings adds correspondingly to cost per cord for dressing.

Mine openings during the year, 318 feet sinking winzes, 1,595.7 feet drifting and cross-cuts, 1,865.52 fathoms stoping, No. 4 winze was carried down double size to accommodate pumps. Average cost, $17.00 per foot.

Careful and oft repeated tests and assays in 1878, show that the quartz mills of the Consolidated Bobtail Company made the remarkable savings of 75.8 per cent. of the gold contained in the ore with the stamps and tables, and 87.96 per cent. of the gold and 6 per cent. of the silver, including both the product of the batteries and tables and of the buddled tailings. A higher per cent. of the gold contents of ores can be saved when they are of low or average grade like the Bobtail than when they are very rich. As will be seen by the tabulated statement the cost of milling, $11.87 per cord, would make the expense only $1.70 per ton allowing for seven tons in a cord and only $1.58 allowing for seven and a half tons.

The Bobtail Tunnel Company is distinct from the Cons. Bobtail, but embraces some of the same members. Its tunnel is the outlet of the mine. Ore transportation brought it $22,079 in 1879. It helps drainage and ventilation.

In 1879, the Cons. Bobtail Company, mined and milled 3,365 cords of ore, returning $231,074.35. It sold 434.09 tons of smelting ore for $51,786.70; 1,753,849 tons of tailings for $12,943.85; and received from tributors (who milled 62 cords of ore, and sold 110 tons), $1,868.74. The actual return to the tributors was $11,736.03, which should be counted to get the mine's true receipts, viz: $310,562.17. The expenses were $248,471.25, besides $13,340 for addition to mill, pump connections, etc. The mine or mining cost $155,496.50. drainage, $36,659.84; milling, $47,287.82; and salaries, taxes, etc.' $9,027.09. Average yield of mill ore per cord, including tailings, $72.76, or about $10 a ton.

The entire Bobtail lode yielded in five years up to 1880, $1,888,837.23, which added to the lode's estimated previous yield of $3,250,000, gives a total to 1880 of $5,138,837.25. In the following five years' statement the difference between smelters' prices and the ore's probable yield is added to get the mine's full product.

NAME OF MINE.	1875.	1876.	1877.	1878.
Cons. Bobtail, Receipts of—				
Ore Milled, including Tribute full ore yield.........	$142,899 61	$232,206 70	$245,627 00	$236,191 58
Tailings sold............	4,777 85	9,155 06	11,701 91	11,445 00
Ore sold smelter...........	57,307 80	37,625 15	41,115 00	59,522 40
Total of Cons. Bobtail Company...........	$205.985 26	$278,986 91	$298,443 91	$307,158 98
Estimated yield of ore and tailings over prices paid for them............	35,000 00	35,000 00	40,000 00	45,000 00
East Bobtail...............	1,900 00	2,000 00	14,000 00	72,000 00
Lake Claim, etc............	12,800 00	20,000 00	10,000 00	
Total actual yield of entire Bobtail lode.....	$255,685 26	$335,986 91	$362,443 91	$424,158 98

Yield of Bobtail Lode in 1879.

Cons. Bobtail receipts, and tributors full product...........$310,562 17
East Bobtail receipts.. 107,000 00

West Bobtail, est.... $25,000 00
Est. yield of ore and tailings over receipts............. 60,000 00

Total yield of lode................$502,562 17

Among the expenses of the Cons. Bobtail in 1879, are transportation through the tunnel, cost, $22,079, mining contracts, $46,585.59, day labor including mechanics, etc., $47,855.80, powder, candles, etc., $14,065.22, fuel, $14,080.99, timber and lumber, $3,164.80, hardware and foundry work, $5,570.39.

The East Bobtail is the name applied to the mine on this vein adjoining the consolidated company property on the east. Little work was done there until recent years, because no ore could be found near the surface. A shaft was finally sunk and the vein discovered over 400 feet down. Below that a fine ore body has continued to the bottom of the shaft, 850 feet deep, and beneath and east of present workings. The mill ore is often very rich, and the amount of smelting ore is remarkable, averaging a foot wide in several localities.

The entire vein averages over 2½ feet, but has opened in places to five, eight, and ten feet. The mine has shown a remarkably large profit in proportion to the total yield. In 1879 from 15 to 20 tons of ore were milled daily, yielding from $50 to $150 a cord, or from $7 to over $20 a ton, and about one ton of smelting ore was sold daily at prices varying from $60 to over $180 per ton. In 1877 the receipts were $12,237.75, and a few thousands came out previously. In 1878 the product is figured at $72,000 with 40 per cent. profit. In the first eleven months of 1879 the mining receipts were as follows:

Milling ore, 4,474 oz. gold retort...................... $74,156 94
Smelting ore, 340 tons and 1,284 pounds, sold for........ 26,634 07
Product of December, about........................... 6,208 99

Total receipts for the year.................... $107,000 00
Est. difference between receipts and smelters' yield...... 8,000 00

Total actual yield for 1879.................... $115,000 00

The profits were not far from $40,000, and would have been larger under one management with quartz mill attached instead of under divided owners and lessees. The lower workings of this and the Consolidated Bobtail indicate great depth to the ore body. The shaft located near the line of the latter property is covered by a substantial shaft-house containing first class steam machinery.

West of the Consolidated mine, are the Lake and Whipple claims, which with others may be called the West Bobtail. The Whipple property lies at the point where the Fisk crosses the Bobtail. Each vein has been employing about 15 mill stamps. These claims were idle for years previous to 1878, when Messrs. Potter, Pearce, and Wolcott leased them. The ore is of very good grade.

Beyond the East Bobtail is the Denmark, 1,425 feet, whose surface ore is said to have been rich. Not long ago J. W. Holman started up work on this with the requisite hoisting machinery. It is expected that extensive exploration will make this a valuable and productive property. The Colorado Central Railway crosses the patented ground of this claim.

The New York and Colorado Company, whose mine is noticed on page 304, is reported to have paid a dividend in July, 1879, of 20 cents a share on its 50,000 shares. The ore supply is said to be plentiful in the 800 level and below.

CHAPTER X.

GILPIN COUNTY MINES—THE GUNNELL, CASHIER, BUELL, BATES,
   PRIZE, SUDERBERG, GERMAN, JONES, O. K., EMPRESS, AND
   OTHERS—A GOLDEN RECORD—RICH STRIKES, LARGE PROFITS,
   AND GOOD MINING.

The Gunnell ranks third among Gilpin county lodes in the production of gold. Its total yield is estimated at nearly two
millions and a half. It was discovered by Harry Gunnell, in 1859,
and paid enormously on the surface. The dirt on some claims of the
eastern portion has been known to yield one hundred dollars in gold
dust to the pan. Among the original pre-emptors were Harry
Gunnell, J. F. Bailey, D. McLeod, C. Cooper, D. J. Sanders, A. P.
Wright, Chase, Sewry, Morey, Getz, and Bashore, and later W. H.
Doe, John Ralfe, John Scudder, John Hense, James White, Alexander and Coleman were owners of portions.

Early in 1864 the profitable claims on the lode were sold in New
York, and companies were organized. The production was then
very large. The Central Gold Mining Company paid John Armor,
W. H. Russell, and John Scudder $80,000 for two hundred feet, and
the Gunnell Gold Company bought four hundred and eighty feet of
Warren Hussey, A. P. Wright, and W. H. Dodge for $300,000. The
owners of the last, including W. H. Doe, made $30,000 from the
gold product obtained by a postponement of the sale for one month.
It is said that the entire lode had yielded half a million (coin and
currency values) up to that time. The Coleman, University and other
claims yielded a great deal of money when worked during the succeeding fourteen years. John Scudder now owns or controls much
of that part of the lode

General Fitz John Porter was the first agent of the Gunnell Gold
Company, and after him came John J. Fitzpatrick. In three years
they took out gold of the currency value of $591,000, or about
$400,000 coin. The heavy expenses of that period and mismanage-
ment caused the company to shut down when the shaft was five

hundred feet deep. Afterwards, New York men who had lent money to the company on its bonds, came into possession of the property. In 1872-3 the mine was leased, cleared of water, and made to produce $53,718 before work suspended.

In January, 1874, J. V. Kimber, William Fullerton, Richard Mackay, E. Clinton, and associates leased the mine, and at heavy expense placed it in working condition. Little ore having been found in sinking to a depth of 700 feet, a level was driven westward, which came into one of the finest bodies of ore ever opened in the county. The receipts for ore sold and milled in 1874-5 were $170,854.42, and $162,722 for 1876. In twenty-five months, up to February, 1876, the yield had been about $313,000. The profits of 1876 were reported at $66,151.69. In September of that year the shaft house and hoisting works were burned, and soon after the lessees bought the property of the bondholders for $50,000, being money they had cleared from the mine. A solid stone building was erected, and first class hoisting machinery and pumps were set at work. They afterwards purchased eight hundred feet of the western part of the lode of James C. Fagan. This was known as the Grand Army property. In 1877 the receipts were about $180,000, and the actual yield of the entire lode over $210,000. The mill gold was shipped every month in a single retort, worth from $14,000 to $16,000. The value per ounce is about $16. Work ceased in June, 1878, owing to litigation over the two hundred feet of ground, between the Gunnell Gold and Grand Army. This property was purchased early in 1879. A part of the Marine lode at the western end of the Grand Army was also bought.

The owners soon after began to free the mine from water, and to put up hoisting works on the Grand Army shaft. There are levels a quarter of a mile long in the mine, and the vein of several feet in width holds good in the lower westerly and central workings. The shafts are to be deepened, probably to 1,000 feet, and the usual number of 68 mill stamps will soon be at work again. An iron column one thousand feet long was received in May, and as much as is needed has been put in the seven hundred feet pump shaft. The property has been one of the best paying in the district.

The time may soon come when the eastern half of the Gunnell will be worked in the same systematic manner that prevails on the 1,180 feet of Fullerton and associates. The entire lode yielded over $650,000 in four years preceding the summer of 1878.

Tabor Matchless "Diggin's", Shaft, Leadville, c. 1975

Tabor Matchless Shaft; Ruins Leadville, c. 1975

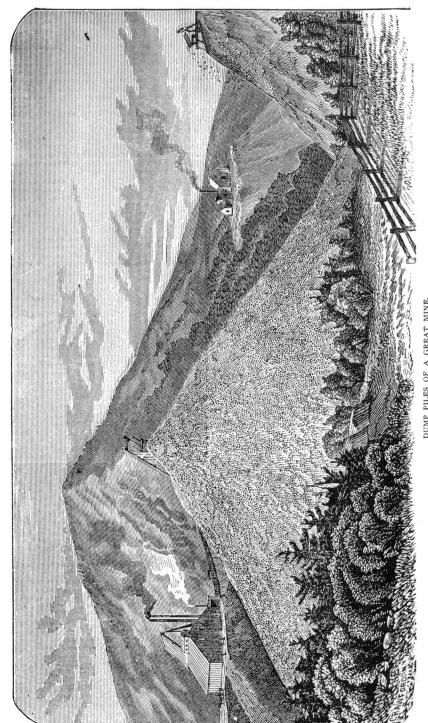

DUMP PILES OF A GREAT MINE.

The Cashier mine is situated on Mammoth Hill, one fourth of a mile distant from the railway depot at Central City, its easterly boundary terminating in Packard's Gulch. It was originally located and owned by Joseph W. Holman, by whom the preliminary developments were made, and became the property of the present company in March, 1878. Since then the opening of the mine has rapidly progressed under the direction of Mr. Holman as Superintendent.

The system of development adopted is the result of the best practical workings of the district. This contemplates a production of ore consistent with the location of the mine among the noted properties on the same vein, and in the near vicinity, which will undoubtedly place it foremost among the bullion producers of Gilpin county.

The contour of the ground is exceedingly favorable to economic workings, admitting of tunneling on the vein. A tunnel has been begun in Packard Gulch, and driven forward about 200 feet. This will reach the main shaft, near the centre of the property, 310 feet below the surface, and through it, when completed, the mine will be worked.

The principal part of the development has been made within the past year, and embraces a main shaft, down to a depth of 245 feet, west of present shaft workings, and two others further west, the first of which is down 50 feet and the other 119 feet. The last two are designed for winzes for future level explorations west. East of the main shaft, a surface winze connects the east adit at a depth of 60 feet and a depth of 120 feet below the rim of the main shaft. The adit has been driven west to a point where it connects and intersects the east 100-foot level from the main shaft. This adit, 446 feet in length, will be used for a tramway for all backstoping above a depth of 100 feet from the surface. To facilitate this and carry out the plans inaugurated, cars have been procured, an iron railway track has been put in, and the ore is backstoped and trammed through the adit to the surface. The present amount of levels that have been driven east and west from the deep shaft is as follows: 50-foot east level, 26 feet; 50-foot west level, 60 feet; 100-foot west level, 134 feet; east level (forming a portion of adit driven from the east), 446. The crevice in the bottom of the main shaft measures $5\frac{1}{2}$ feet between walls, and is saved for milling and smelting purposes. The ore thus far treated under stamps has yielded from $3\frac{1}{2}$ to 6

Graveyard of men's hopes, Leadville, c. 1975

Ghost houses, empty homes, Leadville, c. 1975

ounces gold per cord. There is a large amount of low and medium grade ore in the dumps and mine workings. Better vein matter has lately been found. Several feeders and spurs intersect the main vein. The Lake or Dickerson mill site below the old smelting works has been purchased, and a new 35-stamp mill built thereon. This made a trial run in December and resumed work in April with Colonel Peter French as superintendent. It is well built, with fine steam machinery; run in the summer by water power. The company owns 1,500 feet on the Cashier, and the two parallel veins known as North and South Cashier. Sinking will go on to a depth of 500 feet.

Among lodes worked near Black Hawk, are the Wain, Maryland, Dallas, Margaret Glennan, Centennial, Linden Castle, Running, Arctic and Jennie Blanche. The latter has lately yielded smelting ore, rich in silver and gold. The Running lode carries much lead.

In Russell and Lake districts the following properties of more or less prominence are worked; Wyandotte, West Leavenworth, Gold Cloud, Pewabic, Kingston, Hazeltine, Aduddel, Gilpin County Williams, Updegraph-Williams, Cashier, Powers, Empress, Silver Dollar, Helmer, S. P. Chase, Saratoga, Becky Sharp, Fairfield, Topeka, Golden Eagle, War Dance, Rose and Plume, Richardson, and the Decatur company and other Willis gulch mines,—the first ten or eleven have steam hoisting works, and others soon will have. The once productive Pewabic, Leavenworth and Wyandotte are again in good pay. All of these lodes were idle not long ago.

The Empress mine is situated on Mammoth Hill, Gregory mining district, and is about one fourth of a mile distant from the Colorado Central railway depot at Central, and near the Cashier mine. This is evidently on the Fisk vein, which further east has been so productive in gold. Surveys and developments lead directly from one to the other, with the Treasury location intervening. The Empress property embraces 1,500 feet in length by 150 in breadth, and under former workings had been developed by shafts sunk to depths of two hundred and ten, sixty, and twenty-five feet, and 150 feet of levels, and the ore yielded from $4\frac{1}{2}$ to 9 ounces under stamps. It was acquired in March, 1879, by the Empress Mining Company, and since then the work of development on an extensive and systematic plan has been pushed forward as rapidly as possible, with a view to a large and continuous production as soon as requisite shafts and levels are opened. The Empress Mining Company of Colorado was organized on a capital of five hundred thousand dollars, in shares of a par value of two dollars, full paid and unassessable. The company headquarters are at 52 Broadway, New York. James Howell, mayor of Brooklyn, is president, and Junius Schenck secretary and treasurer. The ore has been milling five ounces of gold per cord, and two shafts are being sunk as fast as possible. The last mineral found assays $400.

The Emperor mine is situated on Mammoth Hill, between the Bobtail and Fisk veins, and opposite the Cashier, supposed extension the former, and the Treasury and Empress of the latter. It was located by Joseph W. Holman, of Central City, and consists of 1,500 feet on the vein by 150 feet in width. The vein is supposed to be the same as the "Minnie" and "Cotton." None other than the preliminary development have as yet been made on this property. The surface dirt has yielded under stamps the average of the surrounding properties.

The Washington mine, at Central City, Colorado, is situated on Gregory Hill. The property consists of 1,100 feet on the vein by 150 feet in width. The topographical features of the ground admit of tunneling on the vein from Packard's Gulch, striking some 300 feet below the surface a short distance in. The developments consist of several shafts, varying in depth from 10 to 60 feet, and an adit from the gulch driven 60 feet in, and are preliminary to the adoption of a large and systematic plan of operations in the near future. The dirt recently taken out yielded 11½ ounces gold to the cord under stamps, and the vein in all the different workings shows the characteristic features of the prominent adjoining and surrounding mines for the depth attained.

The Buell mining property embraces five thousand linear feet of veins, about half of which are covered by government patents. The Leavitt and its eastern extension, the Vasa, from which the U. P. R. pocket was mined, and the Kip are the main veins. There are many shafts, and an immense amount of underground work, mainly in the Leavitt, which has been the leading producer. The whole property is said to have yielded $800,000 currency, or $650,000 coin.

The Leavitt was reopened in 1871, at a point beneath Gregory street and gulch, Central City. At a depth of 50 feet an ore body of soft gangue rock was entered, ten feet wide, of an average value of $10 a ton. Subsequent work continued in ore, the vein widening and

Tortured landscapes, Leadville, c. 1975

Dreams in ruins, Leadville, c. 1975

closing, but never giving out for long distances. At a depth of 130 feet a rich body of black, decomposed sulphurets was entered, having a width of four feet. Thousands of dollars were obtained at the Black Hawk smelting works for single lots of this ore—there being many tons in each shipment. Several tons were sent across the ocean to Swansea, and brought $300 per ton. The gangue rock, lying beside this in the vein, was worth $80 a cord. In one place there were over four feet of ore, carrying 15 per cent. of copper. The ore body was generally four to ten feet wide, but at a depth of 400 feet widened to 16 feet, averaging $10 under the stamps. Great pockets and seams of smelting ore were found. Unbroken masses of ore, weighing over one thousand pounds each and assaying $200, were occasionally raised. The showing was a remarkable one. From 40 to 100 stamps were employed in crushing the ore, varying in number as the product of one season or year increased or diminished. A great stone mill, with sixty stamps, and costing $100,000, was erected, and ore and shaft house adjoining. A splendid shaft was sunk 500 feet and over, with double compartments for cages and first-class hoisting machinery. The ore was cheaply mined, but expenses were greater in 1871–3–5 than now, and so a profit of only $150,000 was made, where a much larger figure could now be secured. In the last eight months of 1872 there were 7,917 tons of ore mined, that returned $105,185, currency value. The cost was $83,443, or $10.43 per ton, and the profits $21,742. Eleven months of 1873 returned 14,850 tons of ore, and $143,706.86 currency, with a profit of $46,878.86. The total expenses were then reduced to $6.52 per ton. This mine and mill should now be operated at a cost of less than $5 per ton, but has not been extensively worked of late, owing to the low grade of the ore-body in the bottom of the shaft, now 580 feet deep.

The O. K. is the southwesterly extension of the Leavitt or main Buell vein. Work was begun in 1875 by J. W. Hanna, the present superintendent of the O. K. Mining Company. Not long ago the main shaft had attained a depth of 325 feet, through an ore-body averaging 42 inches wide for its entire length. At the same time five levels were driven as follows: At a depth of 50 feet, 50 feet in length west; depth, 115 feet, 185 feet in length west; depth, 225 feet, 175 feet in length west; depth, 285 feet, 95 feet in length west; depth, 225 feet, 110 feet in length east. The levels are all connected by winzes from the top, affording excellent ventilation. Since these figures were given, the O. K. Winnebago Company, with J. W. Davis as superintendent, has extensively developed both lodes after which the company is named, and the showing is said to be better than a year ago. The O. K. shaft has been enlarged and supplied with cageways and cages, and arrangements have been perfected for heavy operations. The ore formerly milled from 3 to 6 ounces, the latter with the aid of concentration. Much valuable smelting ore, very rich in copper, has been produced. The Winnebago has yielded ore of various grades. The stamps of the Winnebago mill have been removed, and the new concentrator is not used. The company's capital stock is $500,000 in ten-dollar shares. The O. K. ore has been concentrated to advantage, but does not mill as freely as most gold ores.

The Golden Flint mine has lately been operated by Hendric, Macfarlane, Cameron and other Central City men. It is located at the head of Gamble Gulch and between the new silver district north of Black Hawk and Gold Dirt. It once yielded very rich ore. It has lately been supplied with steam hoisting works, and has a fifteen-stamp mill.

The Gregory Second is considered the extension of the Buell on the northeast, and the Smith, in Chase Gulch, as the extension of the Gregory Second. The latter has been opened to depths of four and five hundred feet, and has yielded largely, and the Smith to a less amount.

The Bates is one of the main veins, and, although worked only at intervals, has yielded considerably over half a million. It was discovered by John H. Gregory, May 19, 1859, and was the second lode found in the mountains. Its surface dirt was extremely rich, and so was much of the vein. In 1863-4 ten Eastern companies were formed on different parts of the Bates. In those years the Baxter and Union company claims were among the most productive in the mountains, but other properties were very profitable. But little work has been done, however, since 1869-70, except by parties leasing on the Loker company mine on the Chase Gulch slope. The Union was idle mainly on account of a lawsuit concerning a money loan. It yielded $205,000 currency value in sixteen consecutive months of 1866-7, and the ore has never given out.

The same vein east of the gulch and on Mammoth Hill is called

All for what? Leadville, c. 1975

The ravaged earth, Leadville, c. 1975

the Bates-Hunter. Southwest of Gregory street this is owned by several Central miners and has paid largely in places. A movement is on foot to consolidate this and the Bates lode in one great combination and mine them extensively. Six hundred feet of the Bates have already been secured, with $100,000 to sink a shaft 1,000 feet deep, run levels, and build a stamp-mill.

Still further southwest the German lode gave a yield of 3,900 tons of ore and $146,250 in two years. The Susquehanna company claim is worked to a depth of 310 feet by lessees, and the Kline claim to about the same extent.

The Fisk lode has yielded a large amount of money—some say as much as a half million. Two different firms are working several claims each, to depths of over 600 feet, and another property is nearly as deep. All are said to be making money. The vein is small, but rich, and the ground hard. In 1873-4 one of these properties gave nearly $60,000. The average yield of mill ore was nearly $20, and the expenses nearly $12. The smelting ore was of high grade. Further east the same vein is called the Sleepy Hollow, owned by M. Rasin, and developed to a depth of 265 feet within the past two years. This property embraces a length of 1,500 feet. Considerable smelting ore is sold, carrying more or less gray copper.

The Prize and Suderberg lodes are located on the upper portion of Gunnell Hill and close to Nevadaville. They approach each other from the west, and the claims where they unite were the scene of a great deal of trouble when the ore bodies of 1870-71 were paying so largely. The courts finally enjoined the Prize company, and after a time the Suderberg men exhausted much of the ground. In two or three years the yield exceeded a quarter of a million coin value. This was one of the richest large bodies of ore ever found in Gilpin county. The amount of high grade smelting ore sold was very great. There was over five feet of milling ore that yielded from six to twelve ounces of gold per cord. The Prize also yielded a large amount before work ceased. Afterwards Richard Mackay took out $75,000 from the Suderberg. These mines are now idle, but may not be much longer. The eastern part of the Prize, called the Commonwealth property, yielded some $371,000 during the same period.

The Jones is situated on a line and nearly west of the Suderberg. The vein is not as large as some, but is of very high grade. The McGonnigal and Phillips properties have maintained a pretty regular vein from the surface down 400 feet, and there is ore below the bottom of the shaft and lower level. At one time fifty feet only of the Phillips claim netted over $4,000 in a few months' time and it is said that both properties are doing as well now. The ore has milled all the way from nine to thirty-one ounces. From nine to eighteen ounces per cord have been the returns of the past year. Many tors of smelting ore are sold monthly at from $60 to $90 per ton. The crevice matter is three feet wide, with one foot of rich solid mineral.

The Hubert is located near the Jones, and is thought to be on the same vein as the Suderberg. It has been worked to a depth of 400 feet, and was paying a profit at last accounts. Quite a large amount of ore has been taken from this mine. The vein has usually been of good size and carries some high grade ore and considerable galena.

The Eureka is a large vein, is located on the hill of the same name. It has been worked to a depth of over 400 feet and is supplied with good buildings and machinery. Its owner, Alexander Taylor, mined large amounts of ore from it in previous years. The crevice has sometimes been ten or twelve feet wide. Among mines on Gunnell Hill are the Saint Louis, Pleasant View, Ashtabula, Whiting, and Butler, and on Casto Hill the Winnebago, Casto, Cincinnati, Comstock, Ellery, and Furnald. The Maryland yielded $30,000 in one summer.

Russell district shows unusual life and activity. The names of most lodes now worked appear on page 318. The once productive Pewabic has been supplied with steam hoisting works, cleared of water, and brought into paying condition. Likewise, the Kingston, West Leavenworth, Wyandotte and others. White men and Chinamen do much gulch mining every summer and fall in Russell and Lake districts through the aid of the Consolidated Ditch. A 40-stamp mill will replace a 33-stamper lately burned, and a 10-stamper has been erected. The Williams, described on page 349, was deepened to 600 feet in 1879–'80. Sinking 185 feet and drifting yielded $16,000, or $2,000 over expenses. The Hazeltine was lately started up for its eastern owners by Henry Paul, with engine and pump. Its levels and 200 feet shaft yield many tons monthly of ore, worth from $60 to $150 per ton in silver. First class ore has gone as high as $600 and $800. Over the county line are the Virginia Cañon gold mines, such as the Champion, Specie Payment and Trio.

CHAPTER XI.

Quartz Hill is one of the grandest depositories of wealth that the world possesses. Here is a network of mineral veins, spurs, and feeders, and a number of great lodes, such as are rarely seen in any country. Millions in gold have been taken from this hill and there are millions in it yet. The two longest and most reliable of the great fissures are the Kansas and that known in different portions under the names of Indiana, Hidden Treasure, California, Gardner, etc. These two veins are nearly parallel, but approach one another on the west. The Burroughs is another nearly east and west vein, which approaches and unites with the Kansas from the east. Above the California is the lode known under the names of Mercer County and Flack, another called the Kent County, and still further south the Alps-Mackie and Pyrennes. South of the Burroughs is the Missouri, and beyond that are the Kinney and the Roderick Dhu and Borton veins (considered as the extensions of the Gardner), and the Illinois and other lodes. Taking a more northerly course is the great Forks lode. This is on the western part of the hill, along with the Mount Desert, American Flag, and others. Further east are the Camp Grove, Sullivan, Ute, Columbia, Lewis, Corydon, Fortune, Fourth of July, and others too numerous to mention. The total yield of the hill from first to last has probably exceeded ten millions coin value, and the future annual production is likely to reach a million and a quarter or a million and a half. The Kansas and the California-Gardner, if worked extensively for a mile in length, as they are likely to be, should yield that amount them-

selves, and the half dozen other leading veins of the hill ought to produce an equal sum.

Ever since the days of the pioneer miners the Kansas has been known as one of the main veins of the county. Few have been as continuous, reliable, or productive, and but three in the State have exceeded it in the yield of the yellow metal. It has been developed for a greater distance than any other in the county. Its eastern and western tracings are nearly a mile and three-quarters apart and near either end of Quartz Hill. In one of its shafts mining is carried on to a greater depth than anywhere else in Colorado, and possibly anywhere east of Nevada and Idaho.

Many individuals and companies own portions of this lode. Too much division has been the cause of the irregular manner in which it has been operated. Notwithstanding intervals when first one claim and then another were unworked, some two millions in gold have been obtained altogether and the indications are good for an increased annual yield hereafter. This is rendered certain by the increased amount of territory mined, many claims having been re-opened during the past six months. After the stoppage of work by eastern companies the more centrally located claims were worked under lease, and the lessees retired with money on hand.

Since then the railway has entered the district, and opportunities for profit have grown better as expenses grew less. The success attending the resumption of work on the Fagan or western part of the lode, where several properties have been united in one, has at last caused the twelve hundred feet embraced in several mines further east to be worked again—and all with evident profit. The former has been one of the few great producers of the country ever since the close of 1873.

One mine after another had been closing down, as their lessees had stripped them of ore, and at the time James C. Fagan took hold of what had been the Kansas Colorado Company property, many had begun to despair of the district's future. Not so with the lessee and subsequent purchaser of this mine. He believed the gold was there and that a moderate outlay of money and muscle would bring it to the surface. The removal of the water from the mine and the deepening of the shaft one hundred feet proved his opinion to be correct. An outlay of twenty thousand dollars accomplished this and brought the property into paying condition, and subsequent developments have kept it there.   This and the entire western portion of the lode that has since been purchased have been worked in the most advantageous manner possible, under the personal supervision of one of the best mine managers in the state.   A splendid record has been made and large dividends disbursed, notwithstanding the fact that much of the profit has been required for additional property and for permanent improvements necessary on greatly enlarged operations.

Beginning with three hundred feet in length on the vein, the owners have extended operations vertically and horizontally until a depth of one thousand feet has been attained, and a large portion of a length of two thousand feet has been developed or partially explored.   Ore reserves of great extent have always been kept ahead of present requirements ever since the mine was fairly opened five years ago.   Since then about $550,000 worth of gold bullion has been obtained from the thousands of cords of ore milled or smelted, and the mine never looked better than it now does in the lower workings.   Had all needed milling, hoisting and pumping apparatus been at hand to begin with, and had production been forced to the utmost, the yield could have been much larger.   Such was not the condition of affairs, however, and consequently matters necessarily progressed slowly to begin with, and at intervals subsequently.   Yet the profits have been sufficient to procure all of the above requirements, to repay the heavy outlay of putting an idle and water-filled mine in order, to construct a great shaft, discover vast ore chambers, and to erect buildings and increase the mill's capacity fivefold, as well as to purchase the original property and many times as many feet of adjoining claims.   All of this called for an expenditure of over $120,000, and yet the profits to the operators, in excess thereof, have approached $100,000, making over $200,000 of net receipts above ordinary or current expenses.   With the present development and showing, all of the above figures may be more than doubled, with no further outlay for permanent improvements, except, perhaps, an addition to the mill's stamping capacity.

Levels from the Monmouth shaft extend along the vein far to the westward, and thus afford an outlet for that portion of the property.   Iron tracks are laid in these levels, over which cars convey the ore to the hoisting place.   As ground is worked out the rails are removed to newly opened drifts below.   On the surface are substantial buildings containing powerful engines and boilers that afford power for the hoisting machinery and great Cornish pump. This pump elevates the water to the surface in four alternate lifts of two hundred and fifty feet each. Its connecting rod alone weighs many tons, and far down in the depths is the huge walking-beam attached thereto. The hoisting and drainage machinery will answer every purpose for five hundred feet below present workings.

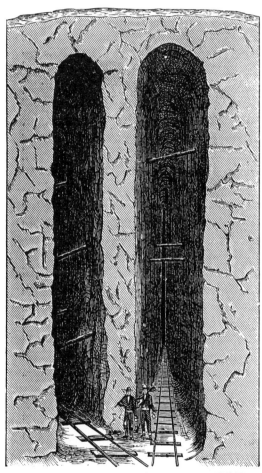

DOWN IN THE DEPTHS. JUNCTION OF THE KANSAS AND BURROUGHS.

The mine itself is substantially timbered throughout, and is in first-class condition. Levels have been driven from the great shaft at intervals as far east as the property extends, and westward for varying distances. Most of the vein has been worked out to a depth of five hundred and fifty feet below the surface, and for several hundred feet east and west of the shaft, excepting some low grade material. The level 650 feet below the surface has been driven west of the shaft over 1,300 feet, and from this a cross cut enters a rich side vein. The 720 level has been driven west nearly 950 feet. The western portion of both of these passes through the same rich ore body that paid so well around the shaft and nearer the surface two or three years ago, and which pitches downward as it extends westward, but the valuable ore has been nearly all worked out. From the 720 level to a depth of about 940 feet, poor ground generally prevailed in the Monmouth. While the mine was never destitute of paying ore, it did not do as well in 1878-9 as previously. In November, 1879, sinking was resumed in favorable ground which 50 feet deeper contained good ore.

In the spring of 1880 a new organization, called the Kansas Con solidated Mining Company, succeeded the Monmouth Company and came into possession of the Monmouth and Fagan properties. These embrace 2,200 feet on the Kansas vein west of the east line of the Monmouth claim, 330 feet on the Camp Grove, and 800 feet on the Irish Flag, together with the mine buildings, hoisting works, pumps and a quartz mill of 52 stamps. The company has a capital stock of $600,000 in 200,000 three-dollar shares, and is mostly composed of previous owners, or interested parties.

The new company are sinking the shaft, which will soon be 1,200 or 1,300 feet in depth, and are driving levels at depths of 945 feet, 1,045 and 1,105 feet on a fine vein of quartz and iron. The mill ore returns about $10 a ton, and the selected ore sells to smelters at $100, more or less. For several years a greater depth has been maintained in this shaft than in any other in Colorado, or east of Nevada and Idaho. Over 40 tons of ore are dumped into the great quartz mill daily by the aid of a railway leading from the adjacent shaft building. This mill building was built for a process that was never used. Its original 12 stamps have been increased until with the present addition that is being made, 60 stamps will be in motion. The mine should hereafter pay handsomely.

Among Quartz Hill mines lately reopened and supplied with steam hoisting machinery, are the Nimrod, on the same vein as the Pyrennes, the Ralls County, probable extension of the Kent County, and the Roderick Dhu. Sullivan and Wheeler's Forks mine has reached a depth of 700 feet. The East Flack, Monitor, Egyptian, and all the mines noted above are said to be paying. Just below Quartz hill is the Newfoundland mine of the old Montezuma Company, which a lessee has lately started up with steam hoisting works. The rich ores now coming from depths of 1,100 feet in the Kansas and California mines, are evidences of the valuable and lasting character of Gilpin county gold lodes.

The Kansas for 450 feet belongs to the First National Comppany. Sullivan and Wheeler made money in leasing this ground in 1869–71. It was afterwards worked in the Fagan combination, and is still producing. The shaft is about 600 feet deep. East of this the University Company property has a shaft 590 feet deep. This and adjoining claims, making 659 feet, has lately been re-opened and worked by Newell & Co. It has turned out $200,000, currency value, altogether, mostly when worked by George Easter-brook, in 1871–72. A number of claims further east are combined and worked together, and beyond them is the Pease claim. Both of these resumed work not long ago, and both are paying. The mines are over 300 feet deep, and sinking and drifting continues. A thousand feet further east is what has been known as the English Kansas, because operated by an English company that bought it in 1871. It had just previously enriched three lessees in eight months' time. Further down the hill the Olga Kansas is worked, near where the Central City tunnel intersects it.

The California-Gardner-Indiana vein is one of the most produc-tive in Gilpin county. It has been traced for a distance of over one mile, and has yielded altogether something near $2,150,000. These figures include the production of the Roderick Dhu and Borton, which seem to be an eastern extension of the Gardner. The Cali-fornia embraces that part of the vein between the Gardner and the Indiana, and is about midway between the nearly parallel Kansas lode and the summit of Quartz Hill. The Hidden Treasure mine is made up of claims on the California and Indiana. The latter is the westernmost part of the vein as far as opened.

The Hidden Treasure mine is remarkable for its large yield and profit and the size and value of its ore-body. The seven claims included in this property were formerly divided among many owners, and were worked years ago with varying success. The last attempt previous to 1878 to work the central claims was made in 1872, when ore in paying quantities was not found, and work ceased. The leading owner had no money to expend in further explorations, and the property remained idle until January, 1878, when he induced some miners to take a lease with him on adjoining claims, and thus work six hundred feet of ground together. The result was that the shaft was sunk but a few feet before a vein of rich ore was entered, and this grew large with depth until it proved to be one of the best ore-bodies ever opened in the district. The men who abandoned the mine six years before had stopped sinking just a few days too soon.

The mine began to pay in May, and two or three months later was attracting universal attention. The ore body has been from thirty inches to seven feet wide in the central portion of the under-ground workings, and there has generally been two feet of very rich ore. The returns in the stamp mills are from five to seven ounces per cord after smelting ore had been selected. There were months when from 100 to 130 tons of mineral sold at an average price of nearly $80 a ton. Last summer and fall the ore came from the vicinity of the 500 and 550 levels. Since then the mine has reached a depth of over 800 feet, with over 3,000 feet of levels, and the 700 level west is looking as well as any portion of the mine has done. The average number of men employed at the mine has been from forty to forty-five, and of stamps, sixty, showing a yield of a ton daily to every man employed.

The receipts from the Hidden Treasure up to February 1, 1879, almost entirely taken out in nine months, were $167,000, of which $67,000 came from sales of smelting ore. The profits were $90,000. The actual yield at the smelters' and mills in 1878 was probably $185,000. In twenty-one months, to 1880, the receipts exceeded $320,000—over half profit. A. M. Jones, S. V. Newell, and John Johnson own 700 feet on the vein, having bought T. Whitcomb's 200 feet on the Indiana. The mill will soon have 50 stamps.

The California, as at present owned and located, embraces 1,033 feet, beside claims forming a part of the Hidden Treasure. For years after its discovery it was worked at intervals by various owners of claims. Among them were Joseph Standley and W. J. Stalker. As they had found a rich pocket at the surface, they felt sure, even after the vein disappeared, that they would find it again below. Consequently, they continued to sink the shaft. For a year or two the result was most discouraging, for the granite walls hung to-gether most obstinately for two hundred and twenty feet. A ray of hope came at last, with the appearance of ore, and before many months money was as plentiful with the persevering owners as it had previously been scarce.

The California was the "big paying mine" in 1869, '70, '71. In three and a half years the currency receipts for ore sold and milled were $521,000, and April, 1870, gave $30,000. Within a year after the ore body was entered, Stalker paid Standley $75,000 for his half interest in this 350 feet of ground and purchased other contesting claims beside. From depths of from 300 to over 500 feet below the surface the ore was unusually rich. In 1872 the richer pay ore was pretty well exhausted, and the yield was small from that time forward. Stalker died and the mine was idle for several years after 1874.

Late in 1877, Standley, who had been engaged in the banking business, and in other pursuits away from Central, resolved to start up the mine. He acquired 1,033 feet on the vein at low figures, all of the claims then being idle, and prepared to mine on an extensive and systematic scale. He had plenty of money to operate with, the result of the former harvest, and so labored under no disadvantage in that direction. Quite an important item was the fact that he had more feet on the vein to get returns from than before, in case it turned out well.

But there was no ore in sight and the future yield was somewhat problematical. Standley went ahead, nevertheless, as if he knew it was there. He picked a first-class foreman and went up the hill to a shaft 370 feet deep, and several hundred feet east of the old bonanza. A solid stone building of ample dimensions was put up and steam hoisting machinery of the most effective and improved pattern was procured and set at work. The search was almost as long a one in depth as it had been ten years before, but Standley was better prepared for it than then. After sinking for a time in barren rock, levels were run and a good vein developed.

Over thirty thousand dollars were expended before the gold began to come out of the ground, and then sinking and drifting were continued without using up the ore reserves, in order to have deposits in this underground mineral bank as plentiful and substantial as in the owner's establishment elsewhere. The work of drifting and sinking gave ore enough in the summer of 1878 to keep first twenty, and finally thirty stamps at work. Early in 1879 the quantity of mineral increased so that the fifty-stamp Richman mill was leased. All this time the vein was exceedingly rich and the shaft going down, down at a rate seldom seen in Colorado mining.

The California cleared more money than any mine north of Leadville in 1879. The yield, including some smelting ore on hand, was $160,000; the profits were $102,000. It is still

THE MONMOUTH-KANSAS GOLD MILL.

said to be making more money even than any of its prosperous rivals. The present production and condition of the property, and the immense amount of ore that has been developed and uncovered, show that the owner knew how to mine and went at it in the right way. The shaft is now 940 feet deep, and the deepest worked in Colorado, except that of its neighbor just below, the Kansas. The ore body varies from fourteen inches to nine feet in width, and mills from $60 to $90 a cord, and sometimes $125 or $150. This is after smelting ore has been selected. This sells at from $70 to $75, and occasionally at $100 to $160 a ton. There are hundreds of tons of this mineral stored in the shaft house. The vein has been opened by levels at depths of five, six, seven, eight, and nine hundred feet, for hundreds of feet from the shaft. The three hundred level also shows ore. The shaft has been carried down seven feet wide by sixteen long, and is twelve feet inside of end timbers. It has cost $30 a foot to sink and timber it. The mill retort gold from this ore is worth from $14.30 to $15.40. Thirty men were engaged in breaking ore some time ago and a larger force now. The ground has been worked out but little below the 500 level. The daily yield of mill ore is about fifty tons. The mine yields from $14,000 to $15,000 monthly, and cleared $50,000 in six months to July 1, 1879.

The Gardner is that part of the lode extending from the California eastward to the Roderick Dhu and Kinney, and embraces 1,154 feet in length, Of this S. B. Hawley owns the western 354 feet. The Hawley-Gardner 200 feet comes next, and then the 300 feet of the Clark-Gardner Mining Company, including the Utley claim. East of this is the Philadelphia and Colorado Company's 300 feet. These claims are said to have given an aggregate yield of half a million dollars. The two company properties have been the richest, but all have paid at one time or another, and none have been worked steadily.

The Clark-Gardner mine is owned by a company in Rome, New York, and has shown some of the best ore bodies in the district, but was not worked to the greatest advantage until recently. An effort was made to strip the mine of ore a year or two ago, and over $17,000 was taken out in two months, when the company stopped the operation. Ten years ago, when this company suspended work, twelve ounce ore had been found in the bottom of the shaft 405 feet deep. When the present superintendent, J. W. Brown, started up the mine, it was not in condition to lead to dividends without expenditures for sinking and drifting. It had been pretty well worked out down to depth of 320 feet for some distance each side of the shaft, and the best ore below had been removed. It is reported to have paid expenses, however, for twenty-five or thirty employees. The usual yield has been a cord and a half, or eleven tons a day, with mill returns varying from an ounce and a half a cord up to ten, or from $22 to $160. The crevice is from thirty to forty inches wide, but sometimes much larger. The last reports say the ore mills seven ounces. The mine is being systematically opened, and is economically managed. It costs only $15 a foot for sinking the shaft four feet by nine, $3 a foot for drifting, and $8 a fathom for stoping, contractors furnishing their own powder, candles, and fuse. Not long ago the shaft was 440 feet deep, and there were prospects of finding an ore body like that worked out above, or like that of the California. What is needed for success is the consolidation of the entire lode into one mine, worked by one shaft and set of machinery.

The Roderick Dhu has yielded a great deal of money when worked by companies and by lessees. Five hundred feet owned by John Scudder has at times shown an immense crevice, is 550 feet deep with long levels and excavations. The Borton is east of the Roderick Dhu and both are considered parts of the Gardner vein. Several hundred thousand dollars are said to have been taken out altogether from these two mines. The Kinney, leading out of the Gardner northeasterly, is said to have been paying a few men $1,000 per month.

The Burroughs extends from the western part of the Kansas lode eastward, making an acute angle with the latter, and is nearly parallel and about four hundred feet north of the California-Gardner. Ben Burroughs discovered it in May, 1859. Its history has been a chequered one, varying from "rich strikes" to suspension of work with change of owners and lessees. There are many separate properties, embracing altogether 2,509 feet, most of which are now worked. The richest portion is included in the 462 feet owned by the Ophir Company. Here Pat Casey made his "big raise" in 1862–3, and here a party of Cornish miners made fortunes in 1874–5. Casey was an uneducated Irishman—energetic, lively, and generous. After the claims he had bought on time of the Burroughs brothers "capped on him" and he had exhausted his funds and credit he discovered one of the richest bonanzas of the mountains by the accidental caving of a part of the mine. Wealth then rolled in on him in a steady stream, a large force of miners was employed, and Pat Casey's wild rollicking "night hands" are remembered to this day by old timers. This was the first property sold in New York in 1863. It brought $90,000. Casey afterwards got rid of his fortune and is now in the Black Hills. The Ophir Company took out an immense amount of money, but it did not make much difference to eastern organizations in those days how much a mine yielded—they were no better off for it. In 1868-9 when there was a large sum of money due the men employed, they worked the mine awhile and soon took out their back pay. The mine was full of water for years until six of these miners leased it in 1873. In twenty months they took out $160,000 and returned to Cornwall with $100,000 of that amount. The mine was then 714 feet deep. It was soon leased by other parties, but owing to the vein dividing they lost money and abandoned it at a depth of 1,000 feet. The Gilpin and La Crosse company claims have been worked steadily for some time by lessees. The vein splits in the latter about 350 feet below the surface, but is producing something at a depth of over 400 feet. The Burroughs vein has produced altogether nearly $1,250,000 coin.

The Flack is another famous lode, parallel with the California and Indiana, and probably terminating in the Mercer County. There have been times when rich ore was mined in plentiful quantities. Like the Forks, it has been idle most of the time for years. Long ago one of the shafts reached a depth of 580 feet. Several hundred thousand dollars are said to have come out of the vein. The Mercer County also paid well once. Work was resumed on it eighteen months ago, and the shaft deepened to 550 feet. The two main properties or sets of claims on the Flack have been worked for a year or two. Last winter steam hoisting works were erected over each of them, and sinking and drifting is now successfully prosecuted. The shafts are 640 and 350 feet deep.

The Forks lode, on the western portion of Quartz Hill, was at one time one of the most productive mines in the county, and could be made so again if reopened and worked as other prominent veins have been. It has a course north of east, and intersects the Flack and California. It pitches southward quite strongly, which would bring it into the Kansas at depths of from 700 to 1,000 feet. There is evidently a bonanza along the line of junction. The Forks produced heavily in the first decade of its history, and was famous for the mammoth size of its vein, as well as for its profitable character. The deepest shaft is down 700 feet. Last fall work was resumed on the Wheeler claims. A new building with steam hoisting works was put up, and the shaft carried down to a depth of 700 feet, with rich mill and smelting ore all the way. It is said that over four hundred thousand dollars' worth of gold have been taken from the Forks lode. The vein carries considerable silver and lead.

The Alps-Mackie mine is situated on two contiguous locations on the lode of that name. There is also another vein that pitches in an opposite direction from that first mentioned and crosses it over three hundred feet below the surface. These and other lodes, with buildings and strong hoisting works for two shafts, belong to the Cleveland Gold Company, organized on the property in 1875–6, on the basis of a capital stock of $250,000. Previous to that time George R. Mitchell held the property for debts due from the Alps and Grenada Companies. The latter expended their working capital in a large mill and other improvements. The mine had paid handsomely at intervals, and the ore was often very rich. Within two months after the discovery in 1863, the receipts for ore milled was $17,591 from the Mackie claims alone. The profits were $9,399.87. There were 20¾ cords that gave an average yield of $552.68 per cord, and 17¾ an average of $345. The Alps claims yielded $54,537.14 in four months, with the wonderful average of $818 a cord, or over $100 a ton. The profits of both properties in these lots of ore in four months were $52,253, of which $42,853 came from the Alps.

The ore bodies yielded large amounts in subsequent years, but it seems the mistake of following the crossing vein led the company into unprofitable ground. The property had been unworked most of the time from 1870 to 1876.

In eighteen months of 1866–7–8, the yield was $78,415, and $10,654 soon after came from assorted waste materials of the stulls. After 1869 lots of smelting ore were sold at good prices. The following shows the product of the Alps-Mackie mine up to 1875, currency :

Mackie product from July, 1863, to October, 1863.... $31,449 15

     "   from October, 1863, to February, 1864.   41 792 18

Alps product from July, 1863, to December, 1863.... $54,537 14
    "   from December, 1863, to February, 1864.   37,911 16
Alps and Mackie product from July, 1866, to January,
     1867..   78,415 41
Alps and Mackie product from March, 1868, to July,
     1868..   10,654 74
Alps and Mackie product from September, 1868, to
     September, 1869................................   20,040 64
Alps and Mackie product from September, 1869, to
     March, 1870...................................   11,035 90
Estimated product of the mine not included in the
     above...   75,000 00

         Making the total product.................... $360,836 32

The Cleveland Company has been developing the mine for some time, and has deepened the shafts and extended the levels east and west until at last another rich ore-body has been opened up. One of the shafts is now down over 567 feet. The last reports were extremely favorable, the ore milling twenty dollars a ton after smelting ore had been selected. The latter sells at high figures, and is similar to some of the rich quartz that brought up the milling average to such high figures before the days of smelting works. Some extraordinary lumps of ore are found. Very high assays were lately obtained. Ore is being mined in the 450 ft., 500 and 560 levels. The latter has recently opened out a vein three feet wide, that yields about $23 per ton after the richer ore averaging $200 has been selected therefrom. Two steam pumps are used in the mine.

The Jessie mine is worked to a depth of two hundred feet with steam-power, and the R. D. Kenney, Gauntlet, Dutchman, Barnes, and National are said to be paying. The Missouri is profitably worked on two claims, and has yielded over $100,000.

The Illinois and Confidence lodes extend along the northeastern slope of Quartz Hill, and is developed at that part bordering on what was called the Patch Diggings, near the Roderick Dhu and Borton properties. About three hundred feet in length of the Illinois, partly worked to a depth of two hundred and sixty feet, has yielded not far from $300,000, currency value. A company made a great deal of money there in 1867–8, and large mill and mine buildings, with fine machinery, were put up at a cost of $100,000. In 1869 B. S. Buell, one of the original owners, and others, came into possession of the property and worked it at intervals afterwards. The mine has paid profits in many different years. The cost of mining, milling, and hoisting, $5.00 to $7.00 per ton. In 1868, 1,500 tons milled $15.88 per ton, and forty tons sold for $112 per ton. Occasionally the vein widens, showing ore-bodies ten feet thick. The immense buildings over the mine and the two shafts contain a twenty-two stamp mill, shops, store-rooms, and offices necessary for an establishment of the largest kind, and a splendid set of hoisting works.

The Kent County is one of the leading veins of Quartz Hill, and is said to have produced several hundred thousand dollars. Richard Mackay, who has been one of the district's most skillful and prominent miners among such lodes as the Gunnell and Suderberg, owns the western 3,256 feet of the Kent County. This embraces most of the valuable portion of it. Since 1876 he has opened this mine in a very extensive manner to a depth of over 700 feet, with long levels at intervals of one hundred feet down to that depth. The vein is generally large and profitable, the ore-body varying from four to seven feet wide. Thirty-seven stamps have been almost entirely supplied from this mine for three years, and the yield of salable smelting ore has been as high as sixty tons monthly. The mill ore has generally yielded from four to seven ounces to the cord, and the smelting ore sells at from $50 to $100 a ton. The main shaft is covered by a large mill building, supplied with one of the best set of steam-hoisting works in the county. The production of the mine is not generally known, but many months of past years have given from four to five thousand dollars' worth of mill gold, and in one month the mine produced $11,000. Mr. Mackay is building a fine fifty-stamp mill for this mine.

The American Flag lode extends in a northeasterly direction through a part of the western section of Quartz Hill down into Nevada Gulch. It is a large vein and is said to have yielded over three hundred thousand dollars. It was worked only at intervals in the first decade of mining in the district, and has been idle for its entire length since 1872. The last work done was on the Clayton property in that and the preceding year, when the profits are believed to have been large. Previous to 1869 the American Flag

Company had worked two or three shafts on some five hundred feet of the property, to depths of from three to five hundred feet. The caving in of some of the underground workings had placed the mine in bad condition, requiring a considerable outlay of capital to resume work effectively.

Men were found, however, in the immediate neighborhood, who were willing to take hold of the property. The recent record of one mine after another that had been developed into producing condition were inducement sufficient for the resumption of work on the American Flag. In June, 1879, and association of Central and Nevada miners, bankers, and business and mill men, leased 550 feet of the company property, and since putting up the requisite machinery, have been clearing the mine of water preparatory to continuous work. This furnishes another instance of the confidence which Colorado men have in these mines. They show their faith in the country by putting their own money into its mines and fissures, even if large expenditures are required for preliminay work and exploration. If eastern company owners lack the nerve to work their own properties, these men that live around the mines are willing to invest their accumulations, their money and muscle on temporary leases only (where the permanent improvements they make must revert to the owners), confident that they will encounter no exception to the rule that a vein that paid well on the surface can be depended on for continuous production below. At the present rate, at which old mines are being reopened, there will soon be no idle ground in the county—and there are hundreds of veins studded with claims and shafts in this same gold belt, whose courses can be traced from any hill side.

The American Flag Company property embraces 550 feet on the American Flag and Bennett lodes, which are said to have yielded gold to the currency value of $300;000. The lease referred to in the last paragraph is of five years' duration—the company to receive twenty per cent. of the gross earnings of the mine, less $3\frac{1}{4}$ ounces of gold per cord of the milling ore. The capital stock of this company is 60,000 ten-dollar shares.

The Colorado men who are working the American Flag under lease have organized under the name of the Budweiser Company, of which E. Goldman is president, who is also interested in the Goldman-Kansas, Irene, Harkaway and other mines.

CHAPTER XII.

GILPIN COUNTY MINES—NEW MINING ENTERPRISES ON OLD AND WELL-TRIED MINES—WYANDOTTE AND GOLD DIRT—HOW FORTUNES WERE MADE IN THE LONG AGO—RICH POCKETS AND LARGE VEINS—THE NEW SILVER DISTRICT—RICH ORE AND GOOD LODES—THE VALUABLE DISCOVERIES OF 1878.

Among the productive localities of this gold region is Leavenworth Hill. It contains a perfect net-work of mineral veins, most of which converge toward the centre of its eastern slope, as if some mammoth deposit had been forced toward the surface in fragments. Old miners say there were no better diggings than those of the surface outcroppings of this locality. Much of the surface of the hill has been dug over, and the vein material gophered out without system for short distances downward. Thousands of cords of ore have been milled, with a reputed yield of something like a round million. The companies took out much gold, but the original owners more.

There has been no time since the first discoveries when all the claims were idle, for men have been making money there every season. The properties were too much subdivided, however, to permit of profitable deep mining, and until recently many owners held their property at too high figures to permit of buying and consolidating to advantage. Within the past two years some of these men have united and combined their claims with others purchased and relocated, and the result is the Wyandotte Consolidated Gold and Silver Mining Company, organized with a capital stock of six hundred thousand dollars, in shares of a par value of three dollars, for the purpose of developing the dozen valuable lodes of the hill. Among these are the Wyandotte, Elmer, Leavenworth, and East Leavenworth, Gold Ring, Calhoun, and others, and the total number of feet of veins covered by government titles is 12,270 feet.

A shaft is being sunk at a point where several of these lodes converge or unite, with the design of driving cross cuts in the underground workings so as to intersect and develop them. This shaft is

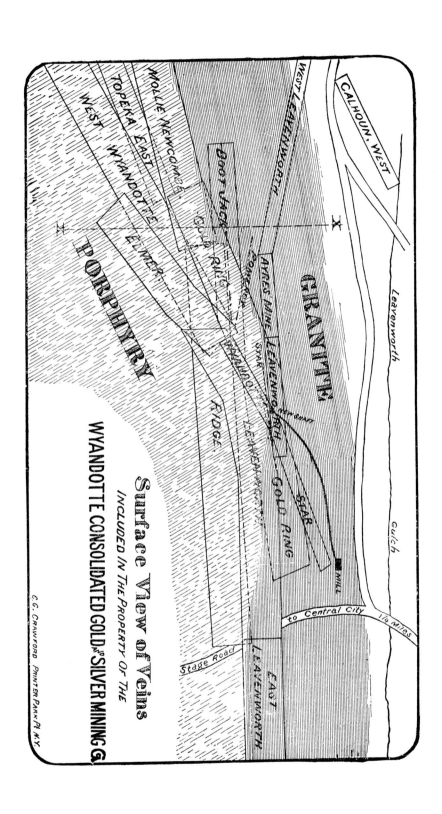

Surface View of Veins
INCLUDED IN THE PROPERTY OF THE
WYANDOTTE CONSOLIDATED GOLD AND SILVER MINING Co.

C.G. CRAWFORD PRINTER PARK PL N.Y.

now over 200 feet deep, and the crevice matter penetrated has shown a steady improvement as depth was gained. The last reports say there is five feet of crevice, and much ore worth $90 a ton. It costs $14 a foot to sink the shaft 5 feet by 9.

The figures of the past yield of the property of this company are not obtainable, owing to repeated changes of ownership of the many claims and of the mills where the ore was treated. It is known that one company took out three hundred thousand dollars from a space 230 feet long and an average depth of 90 feet on the Leavenworth vein, after the discoverers had previously made snug fortunes there. Individual troubles caused another company to suspend work when they had ore in the bottom of the Wyandotte shaft that sold for $300 a ton. The numerous crevice and shaft excavations and remains of dump piles are silent yet telling monuments of past productiveness. For years mill men, when short of ore, were accustomed to team away the refuse from the shafts that had been thrown away as worthless. Professor Pearce, when operating smelting works fourteen miles distant, obtained ore from this place at a cost of ten dollars per ton for freight alone. Very valuable pitch blende ore has been mined in the Leavenworth, beside quartz worth several dollars a pound.

For long distances bodies of ore from two to four feet wide have been developed in the two Leavenworth properties, and the great Wyandotte or Harsh vein has carried from four to ten feet of pay material within well defined walls. The presence of porphyry is considered a good indication of the mineral character of this group. Another year will undoubtedly see Leavenworth Hill take a high rank among gold-producing localities, for the work of development is going steadily forward with a uniform improvement in character of ore encountered.

Northward from Central and Black Hawk the Gilpin county gold belt makes itself especially prominent at Gold Dirt. There are veins in that locality that rival in size and value of contents those mentioned in preceding chapters. The yield of the Gold Dirt and Perigo lodes in the earlier years of Colorado mining was something marvelous. There were also many other mines in that section that paid for working.

Mining began there in 1860, and two or three years later one of the liveliest camps in the territory was fairly established. Gamble

Gulch was lined with arastras, quartz mills, sluice boxes, cabins, stores and saloons, and almost everybody had money who operated claims in that vicinity. The best days of the settlement were from 1862 to 1864, when some five hundred votes were polled in that precinct at the annual elections.

Some of the quartz gave up the precious metal so plentifully that little care was taken in milling or saving it, and the dumps and mill tailings were long after found to be quite valuable. Sluices and stamp mill coppers were lined and coated with gold, and dust enough could be panned from the surface dirt to satisfy the most avaricious prospector. Some idea of how loosely it was scattered about may be formed from the fact that when the camp began to break up, a miner obtained over a thousand dollars' worth of gold by cleaning up the fireplace and dirt floor of a deserted cabin where retorting had been done occasionally.

In 1864 a committee of Gold Dirt citizens, appointed for the purpose, approximated the yield of the Gold Dirt lode for the two preceding years at $930,000, in the varying currency values at which it had been sold. J. Q. A. Rollins had obtained $250,000 from a claim only 33⅓ feet long on the vein, and Hollister & Company $200,000 from an adjoining claim of equal size. Such a production from so little territory in so short a time has seldom if ever been equaled in Colorado. Fairbanks & Keene, on another claim, obtained $70,000; then came Grill, Hulbert & Co., with $150,000; Elliott & Fowler, $65,000; the Mulligan Brothers, $15,000; the Gold Dirt Company, $120,000; and Hall, Evans & DePeyster, $60,000. The banking house of Clark, Gruber & Co., of Denver, paid $150,000 for gold from the Hollister claim alone.

These claims were mostly sold to Eastern companies in 1864. The Hope Mining Company, owning on the present Ophir location, including the two small but rich claims noted above, made money until it embarked in a process mill operation. It took $125,000 to build this great mill, and then cost more to operate the imperfect concern than there was gold in the ore handled. Because no profit could be obtained in operating this mill the company concluded that the vein was worthless, and stopped work after having sunk through a large vein all the way in the lower sixty feet of the main shaft. A depth of 500 feet had then been attained, and men who worked there say the ore was of more than ordinary value.

The Perigo was worked by a score of different owners through as many shafts, and is said to have yielded altogether not far from $400,000. This yield, like that of the Gold Dirt, from mines worked without system or concerted action, indicates what could be done under happier auspices. Poor milling caused more gold to be lost than was saved. The superintendents of companies on these lodes came from entirely different pursuits at the East, and knew nothing of mining and cared less. Finally one mine after another shut down and the miners departed for more inviting fields. The yield of ore ranged from $150 to $600 a cord, and $300 were common returns at the Rollins mill.

It was the old story of abandoned and lost mines—lost by debts and taxes, or more frequently by relocation under the late congressional abandonment act. The camp fell to decay, and ruined mine and mill buildings were all that was left of the once flourishing but since deserted village of Gold Dirt. As the place was off of the traveled road it was seldom visited, and gradually became almost forgotten. The mines were there, however, and a few of the " old " timers believed they could be made profitable.

J. Q. A. Rollins owned some isolated claims on these lodes. He preferred to let them remain idle until he could secure adjoining properties, and thus be surer of successful mining. Owners of the latter paid no attention to the annual assessment work required by the congressional act of 1875. Rollins was aware of this, and relocated many of the idle mines and purchased others. In time he came to be the owner by government title of the lodes and timber and placer lands of the entire locality, and is now preparing to carry into effect his long-cherished plans of mining on a scale commensurate with the size and magnitude of the property.

The Gold Dirt vein west of Gamble Gulch is called the Savage, on which a tunnel has been started that will eventually attain a depth of 1,000 feet on the vein. East of the gulch is the Crown Point location, on the same lode, on which a tunnel is being driven that will be 400 feet deep after it enters the more easterly Ophir location. The most of the vein's past production has come from the Ophir and Virginia. The latter has but 300 feet of the lode, but has yielded not far from $400,000. A tunnel driven in the Perigo would eventually attain a depth on the vein below surface outcroppings of nearly 2,000 feet.

The Rollins property embraces 20,000 feet of lodes, whose surface locations include nearly all that part of the district that has been very productive. On the Gold Dirt lode are four locations— the Ophir, 1,500 feet; Virginia, 300; Crown Point, 1,500; and Savage, 1,500; or 4,800 altogether. On the Perigo lode, 3,200 feet are included, and 1,500 on each of the once productive Colorado (Maurer), the Comstock, New York, Surprise, and some other veins. Beside the lode veins covered by government patents are over 400 acres of patented placer lands along South Boulder Creek, Gamble Gulch and tributary streams—and the largest amount of mountain farming land in any one locality in this part of the State.

The Rollins steam quartz mill is located at Rollinsville, on a down grade from the mines. It is terrace built, 100 feet long by 65 feet wide, and has one of the finest water-powers in the State, the water being conducted along the upper side of the building in a flume or raceway. Here are twelve stamps and room for fifty more, and an eighty horse-power-engine.

There is no property in the State that offers greater inducements for the resumption of work than the Gold Dirt, and although it will take money to drain, open and outfit it, but a short time need be required to get it back again. With persistent development under economical management the same favorable results may be expected that are met with in the reconstructed mines around Central and Nevadaville.

The valley of the South Boulder is one of the most beautiful in the mountains, and affords a most charming summer resort, with its spacious hotel, green sloping meadows, streams and lakes, and adjacent hunting and fishing resorts. A wagon road leads over the snowy range to Middle Park, thirty miles distant. This farm, or series of farms, yields seven or eight thousand bushels of potatoes every season, hundreds of tons of hay, while rye and oats grow seven feet high.

Not long ago the Rollins Gold Mining Company was organized under the laws of the State of New York, with a capital stock of $5,000,000, in 200,000 shares of $25 par value each. The company officials are, J. Q. A. Rollins, president and general manager; A. J. Severance, vice-president; Elisha Cole, secretary and treasurer, with the same, and Horatio Reed, Richard B. Kimball, Matthew Taylor, S. L. Warner, D. C. Ferris, George Gillum, Isaac Freese,

Ezra White, C. F. Collins, and R. Sherwood as trustees.   Early in
1880, Mr. Rollins began the work of reopening the mines.   Fine
hoisting machinery was placed on the Perigo.   Five tunnels were
started on the most prominent lodes and immense quantities of sup-

ROLLINSVILLE.

plies were brought into camp.   Many men are employed, and Gold
Dirt is renewing its former activity.   The quartz mill will soon be
trebled in size.   It is evident that these mines will be so profitable
as to render Rollins stock one of the most desirable in the market.
    The Williams lode in Lake District was profitably worked by

simply sinking and drifting. The ores carried both gold and silver in paying quantities, with a generous amount of copper. The richer mineral was sold to the smelter at from $60 to $150 per ton, more or less, and larger quantities of ore were treated in stamp mills, where little more than the gold was saved. The yield there was from $60 to $85 per ton for a long period. Up to the time when a depth of 315 feet had been attained, but little stoping had been done. In two years $42,000 had been received for ore treated, and experts say there was a still larger value in reserve in the mine above the lower workings. This refers to 550 continuous feet, sold in April, 1879, to R. F. Weitbrec and K. G. Cooper, of Denver, for $42,000, and which is now worked by the Gilpin County Mining Company, of their organization. Since then a shaft house, 30 by 50 feet, has been contructed, with engine, boiler, and hoisting rig, and the mine will be deepened and developed rapidly. Beside this property disposed of by L. & E. Drake, the more westerly part of the Williams vein is worked to a depth of 250 feet. Up to April last there had been removed from the Gilpin Company claims 522 fathoms of ground, with an average per fathom of $80.46, viz.: smelting ore per fathom, $53.64; mill ore per fathom, $26.82. This vein carries liberal quantities of gold, silver, and copper. A rich vein has been found in the Updegraph and Packard claims.

The Dallas lode crosses North Clear Creek a short distance above Black Hawk, and has been worked by shafts and excavations in the mountains on either side. The part in Silver Mountain and east of the creek carries more silver and lead than the western half of the lode. It has been traced up to the locality where the rich Cyclops and Fannie group of silver mines has been opened. The main production of the lode has come from the part in Dallas Mountain which is west of the creek. For two years the mine opened there has been very profitable. Various causes prevented vigorous development, but several shafts have been sunk and levels driven down to a depth of 120 feet. The vein has usually been from four to seven feet wide, with very little waste rock and considerable smelting ore, rich in gold, silver, and lead. One or two cords of ore have been milled daily for a long time, which gave returns of from four to eight ounces of gold, or of from $60 to $120 a cord. The record of four days' work taken from the receipts of the owners made the following: Besides $100 for smelting ore, three cords of ore yielded at the rate of $96.18 per cord; two cords at $106.50, and one cord and a quarter, $107.30; total, six cords and a quarter, $635.66; an average of about $100, or seven ounces per cord. It costs from $15 to 16 per fathom in these levels to mine or break down the ore and raise it to the surface—the latter being done by horse power, and a contrivance called a "whip." On a vein of this unusual width a fathom of ground, when broken down, will make about two cords, or sixteen tons of ore, showing a cost for mining and hoisting of $8 per cord, or $1 per ton. The expense of hauling a cord of ore to a mill, and of crushing it and extracting the gold, is $24. This shows a total outlay for mining, milling, etc., of $32 for a return of from $70 to $115. It cost only $200 to obtain the $635.66 from the six and one-quarter cords of ore noted above.

The mine has so far paid all expenses of development, besides leaving a considerable amount of surplus or working capital in the company's treasury. The shaft is being deepened and the levels extended as rapidly as possible, and when double their present length, they will, with the aid of the stoping ground, be able to pay big dividends to the owners. In the mean time, two cords of ore yielding $200 daily from the labor of seven miners, is a very good thing for any firm to have—and those were the returns at last accounts.

There are a number of tunnels in Gilpin county that are being driven to intersect lodes and to work the same. Some of these have been pushed forward steadily by the labor and money of business men and miners for many years. The Bobtail tunnel at the Bobtail lode has already been noticed. There are several that have not been extended for some time, and others, such as the Centennial, Black Hawk, German, Quartz Hill, and Central City are pushed forward more or less energetically. The La Crosse tunnel, owned by the company of the same name, passes into Quartz Hill something like 1,000 feet, 150 of which was driven last year. It is only from 180 to 200 feet below the surface above, and consequently can be of no great benefit in working mines.

The Central City tunnel was started by D. G. Wilson, who organized a company on the enterprise. It enters Quartz Hill just above the Quartz Hill tunnel and the limits of Central, and is headed in the direction of such main lodes as the Burroughs, Missouri, Illinois, and Roderick Dhu, which it will intersect some five hundred feet beneath the surface of the ground. Steam drills and an air-compressor are used, and are thought to do cheaper and better execution than hand drills. The eastern portion of the Kansas lode has been intersected, and the Fortune and Corydon, Lewis and Columbia are some distance ahead. The tunnel had penetrated the hill about five hundred and fifty feet at last accounts. The enterprise is a promising one, as old lodes can be explored and several blind lodes may be discovered. For drainage purposes this tunnel should be of great service.

The German tunnel is a home enterprise of Central business men, which has been driven nearly seven hundred feet into Mammoth Hill. There are many valuable lodes crossing the territory ahead of it, which will be intersected hundreds of feet in depth. Several veins have already been reached. The outlook is good for dividends when the Mammoth and other lodes have been opened.

The Centennial tunnel is in Mammoth Hill, is about four hundred feet long, and has crossed several blind lodes that have yielded large amounts of ore. The enterprise has paid well at times. The breast of the tunnel must be near the Tierney lode.

The Saratoga is a large vein, worked at the depth of one hundred and twenty feet by an intersecting tunnel, with levels extending therefrom. The soft iron-stained dirt and quartz is easily mined, and the mill gold is of unusually high value. The Silver Dollar mine is extensively opened by shafts and levels, and is reported as quite profitable. Its main value is in silver. The Powers is very rich in copper, carrying from ten to forty-five per cent. The vein carries enargite or sulphide of copper and arsenic.

In the silver belt of the southern part of the county is one very large vein, which extends from Willis Gulch clear over Clifton or Virginia Mountain, a distance of over a mile. It carries considerable galena, sometimes forty to sixty per cent, and a fair amount of silver. The developments of some portions are extensive, and the yield pretty large. This vein is known under the names of Aduddel, Serle, Clifton, and Rara Avis. Nearly all parts of it have been worked extensively. The Aduddel has been yielding paying ore for several years, and almost from the time of discovery. It carries considerable galena, and is a large, strong vein. Not far distant are the War Dance, and Rose and Plume. Last winter, while sinking a shaft on the former thirty-five feet, and driving a level fifty feet, two men obtained ore that sold for $2,674, and yielded $4,300. The vein carries from $50 to $90 in silver to the ton, and from $5 to $12 in gold. Later, from three to ten tons of ore were mined and sold per week. Henry Paul has valuable silver mines in this same section, where he has been lode and placer mining for years, and at the same time raising crops of grain and vegetables nearly 9,500 feet above sea-level.

THE BLACK HAWK SILVER DISTRICT.

This includes Silver Hill and the sections at and near Hughesville, Wide-Awake district, Bald Mountain, and the Harper Ranch. The first discoveries were made on Silver Hill, near the close of May, and in June, 1878, by Professor S. W. Tyler, assayer and engineer, and E. A. Lynn, an old time prospector. During the summer and fall, while lodes were being opened all around them, they worked their mines and continued to make an occasional discovery. They located the Cyclops and Fanny at the beginning. The Saint James was also one of the earliest veins recorded.

In August, the Hard Money at Hughes' ranch, a mile and a half from the Cyclops, was discovered; likewise the Boss lode on the Harper Ranch. All of the above have since produced regularly, and have paid well, at the same time that they have attracted many prospectors and miners to their districts, resulting in new discoveries. There are now over one hundred men at work and some five hundred locations have been made. Among these veins the galena ores seem to be the most valuable, but some ruby silver and gray copper are found. The best ore yields from 400 to over 1,000 ounces of silver per ton. Most of the silver discoveries are among the hills and mountains to the east and north of North Clear Creek. South and west of that stream is the great gold belt.

The Cyclops was discovered May 29, 1878, and is owned under the affix of numbers one and two, by Tyler and Lynn. The first ore was sold July first. Ten shafts have been opened to depths of from 20 to 100 feet. Six of these, at intervals of 100 feet, have yielded ore, and three of them are now paying handsomely. The ore vein varies in width from a few inches up to three feet, and generally carries from 100 to 900 ounces of silver per ton. Some of it shows streaks of ruby silver mineral of unusual size and value. Up to May 31, 1879, the Cyclops had yielded over 20,000 ounces of silver. Good profits have been divided, beside developing the property into its present productive condition.

The Cyclops has, beside rich vein matter, gangue of quartz and feldspar, or quartz, hornstone and calcspar, the latter with true silver minerals. The minerals or ores proper, are galena, zinc blende, and iron pyrites, and considerable proportions of ruby and brittle silver, occurring in solid streaks from one to eight inches thick, or scattered throughout a foot or more of quartz, in the latter class making up the second-rate ores.

The Fanny is just below the Cyclops, and is owned by Tyler, Lynn, Gray, and Pease. Its workings are confined to a shaft 100 feet deep and a 50 foot adit entering the same at a depth of 30 feet. The width of the vein is shown by the development to be from two to six feet, with a pay streak of from two inches to three feet in thickness, generally clinging to the north wall. The sixty foot level east shows for twenty feet in the floor an average of eighteen inches of pay, of which from two inches to one foot is solid mineral —galena—milling over 300 ounces of silver per ton, and the balance mixed ore—quartz, with mineral, sulphurets of silver and native silver—milling from 40 to 200 ounces. Total ground removed in shaft, levels, and stopes, 52 fathoms; portion bearing ore, 45 fathoms. The gross value of silver produced has been, in round numbers, $17,000; net return for same, in round numbers, $13,000. The net profit on same over all expenses has been 50 per cent., or $8,500. For every fathom of ground removed in the whole mine the average has been: Gross product, $230; net return, $173; net profit, $26.50. Per fathom of ore ground proper: Gross product, $266; net return, $200; net profit, $100.

The character of the ores of some of the best and richest of these silver veins is exemplified in returns of the Fanny lode. In the latter part of May, 1879, S. W. Tyler sold 9 tons and 358 pounds of ore for $1,832.93, and in the first week of June 4¾ tons for $1,212.65. Average receipts per ton, $218; average yield per ton, over $260. The four richest lots gave 608 ounces, 605 ounces, 490 ounces, and 470 ounces of silver per ton. The three poorest lots gave 71 ounces, 87 ounces, and 88 ounces per ton. Total receipts for sales of less than four weeks, $3,045.58. Expenses less than $1,000.

The Silent Friend, Humboldt, Mary Graham, and Joe Reynolds, on this same Silver Hill, are promising veins, but have not been opened extensively. The Mary Graham has a good vein of paying ore which is producing well.

Between Silver Hill and the Hard Money lode are many locations, of which the Toronto, Wellington, New York, and Emerald are the principal ones. The two first named have turned out much ore, yielding from 80 to 300 ounces per ton. The Wellington main shaft is 50 feet deep. This lode is of the unusual size of nine feet, and what are considered average samples of the crevice assay from 20 to 50 ounces of silver. Tons of assorted mineral have been sold, carrying from 200 to 1,000 ounces per ton.

The Hard Money is owned by Hunderman and Locke. Its size, great value, and profits, are making it famous. Its product, mainly obtained after October, and from then to July, is said to have been over $40,000. One report makes it 50,000 ounces of silver; another 55,000; the deepest shaft is 128 feet. The Philadelphia is nearly parallel with the Hard Money. The Rough and Ready appears to be nearly on a line with the Hard Money and Boss lodes; time may prove all three to be parts of one continuous vein. The Bonanza, a more recent discovery, bids fair to be a first-class vein. Many locations were made and some good lodes found all through this section too late in the year to permit of prospecting or continuous work. This summer will enable their value to be tested. The Boss lode, owned by Sayer & Owens, pays handsomely; steam hoisting works have lately been put up. Smith E. Stevens is driving the Silver Flag tunnel from North Clear Creek towards the silver belt and veins of the mountains above and beyond. Many veins will be crossed at great depth. The Queen Emma is a valuable lode.

The Rough and Ready lode has probably shown the richest ore in the district; specimens have assayed from 14,000 to 21,000 ounces, and small mill runs which yielded at the rate of several thousand dollars a ton. The Forrester and Fremont lodes on Bald Mountain have shown rich ore. There are more than fifty of these silver-bearing lodes discovered within a year that are yielding more or less money. The district will add considerably to Gilpin county's bullion product, and bids fair to rival most other Colorado silver camps in importance. The number and value of veins discovered in so short a time is remarkable.

CHAPTER XIII.

CLEAR CREEK COUNTY—MINES OF SILVER AND GOLD—DETAILS AND STATISTICS OF THE GREAT SILVER DISTRICT—THE COUNTY'S YIELD OF THE PRECIOUS METALS NEARLY $20,000,000—ANNUAL STATEMENTS OF THE PRODUCT—GEORGETOWN, SILVER PLUME, IDAHO SPRINGS, AND THEIR COUNTLESS MINERAL VEINS.

Clear Creek county includes the region drained by South Clear Creek, and embraces the best known and best developed silver district of Colorado. It is bounded by Gilpin county on the north, Jefferson on the east, Park on the south, and Summit and Grand on the west. South Clear Creek and its branches sweep down the cañons in and below the Snowy Range, forming long narrow valleys, wherein the population mainly finds its abiding place. The steep and rugged mountains that flank these valleys and ravines are ribbed with veins of silver, often of immense value. Here and there are newly built villages, thriving mining camps, or solitary cabins to indicate the presence of the miner or prospector. The entire section, up to elevations of 11,000 or 11,200 feet, is more or less thickly covered with pine and other forest species.

South Clear Creek is formed by the union, four miles below Georgetown, of the Empire and Georgetown forks. All around are lofty mountains, and between rises a steep and rugged spur of the range, which, beginning at the junction of the forks and running south and west, is known under the names of Douglas, Colfax, Democrat, Republican, Sherman, and Brown mountains. Opposite Republican are Griffith and Saxon mountains. Two beautiful streams, fresh from the springs and snows of Gray's Peaks and Argentine and Geneva passes, unite at Georgetown to form the fork referred to above. Between these extends a spur of the snowy range. One portion is called McClellan mountain, and that overlooking Georgetown is known as Leavenworth. Close by Gray's Peak is Kelso mountain. These elevations embrace the silver-bearing localities around Georgetown. North of the Empire fork of the creek are Silver and other mountains, noted for their gold veins and alluvial deposits. Further down South Clear Creek is the famous silver locality of Red Elephant mountain, and opposite that of

GEORGETOWN.

Columbian mountain. Other lodes and veins, generally carrying gold, silver, and copper, are found at intervals from Mill City to Gilpin county, and from upper Trail Creek to Idaho Springs, while the streams are productive of gold. A large portion of the silver lodes near Georgetown, and for miles above and below, carry black sulphurets and gray copper. Ruby and native silver and silver glance are met with. The same belt contains many veins of the heavy galena, zinc blende order. From eight to ten per cent. of lead is a common occurrence, but from thirty to sixty per cent. is not unusual.

Georgetown is built at the head of a level valley, with mountains rising above it, covered with pine and ribbed with silver. Above Georgetown, and at the feet of Republican, Sherman, and Leavenworth mountains, are the adjoining towns of Silver Plume and Brownville. These and the still newer village of Lawson are the main settlements of this part of this great silver belt.

Gold was discovered on Chicago Creek, Spanish Bar, and above and below the present site of Idaho Springs in 1859. The Empire gold lodes and placers produced largely in 1862-4. The first silver discovery was made late in 1864, on McClellan mountain, and prospecting became lively all around Georgetown in 1865-6. The territory then possessed no means of treating silver ores, as the only successful mills at that day were the gold stampers. A few attempts were made to reduce the ores, and in 1866-8 chlorodizing-roasting, and amalgamation mills were erected, and a few smelters of small capacity. Then came the Brownville smelter, that turned out great silver buttons worth from ten to fifteen thousand dollars each. Joseph Watson, C. A. Martine, and Garrett, Hucpeden, J. O. Stewart, Schirmer & Bruckner, and Frank Dibbin, were engaged in ore reduction, and later Palmer & Nichols and the Stewart Reducing Company. After 1865 gold-mining declined around Empire and Idaho, but the silver mines began to produce largely in 1869, '70, '71. Among those especially prominent in the earlier years of silver-mining were the Equator, Terrible, Brown, Coin, Compass and Square, Anglo Saxon, Astor, Belmont, and International. For years many lodes near Georgetown, Idaho, and Spanish Bar were worked for gold whose value lay mainly in silver. Garrett, Martine & Co. made Colorado's first silver brick and first practically tested the Bruckner roasting cylinder.

The great increase of the county's yield in 1872, was due to developments or discoveries of rich ore in the Pelican, Dives, Maine, Phœnix, Colorado Central, Saco, O. K., Hukill, Terrible, and other mines. In 1874 the Dives and Pelican, and mines on Leavenworth, Republican, Democrat, and Sherman mountains caused the heavy gain. The Dunderberg and Boulder Nest aided greatly in 1878, and the suspension of shipments, while development work was going on and machinery and mills were procured by newly organized companies, caused the falling off of 1879. A very large number of the county's 20,000 or more mining locations are now worked.

CLEAR CREEK COUNTY'S TOTAL PRODUCT.

The county's yield of the valuable metals prior to January, 1880, was as follows :

Silver.........	$15,761,907 99	Lead...........	$431,000 00
Gold...........	3,015,661 05	Copper.........	37,000 00
	Total......................$19,245,569 04		

The yield of Clear Creek County from 1859 to 1880 was as given below. After 1867, mostly silver, with some gold, etc.

1859 to 1868, gold,	$2,000,000 00	1873............	$1,259,761 06
1866-7, silver ...	40,500 00	1874............	2,203,947 97
1868...........	141,820 35	1875............	1,928,161 74
1869...........	400,354 00	1876............	1,982,548 31
1870...........	481,354 08	1877............	2,206,577 91
1871...........	869,046 34	1878............	2,261,105 85
1872...........	1,503,391 43	1879............	1,967,000 00
	Total......................$19,245,569 04		

MINING PRODUCT OF 1879.

Silver.............	$1,695,000	Lead...............	$80,000
Gold.............	175,000	Copper.............	17,000
	Total........................$1,967,000		

Value of ore shipped out of county, $1,437,000 ; value of silver bullion produced in the county (C. C. and Farwell mills) $425,000 ; quartz mill and placer gold, $105,000. About 10,400 tons of smelting ore or concentrates were reduced or shipped, and over 3,500 tons of gold ores were stamp milled. Some 7,000 tons of low grades were concentrated. Original tonnage of crude ore, 20,900.

The yield of 1878 on page 354 is $250,000 too large; no allowance was made for the same ores handled by two mills or firms.

	1871.	1872.	1873.	1874.
Silver Bullion..........	$396,011 24	$235,187 43	$345,263 46	$555,268 49
Gold Bullion..........	20,000 00	30,000 00	34,000 00	42,500 00
Ore shipments to Colorado Works....... }	....	406,648 00	438,746 16	520,968 60
Ore shipped out of Colorado* .... }	453,035 10	831,556 00	441,751 44	1,085,210 88
Totals..........	$869,046 34	$1,503,391 43	$1,259,761 06	$2,203,947 97

	1875.	1876.	1877.	1878.
Silver Bullion..........	$534,372 28	$473,414 00	$388,189 74	$389,871 70
Gold Bullion..........	70,000 00	85,161 00	70,000 00	115,000 00
Ore Shipped to Colorado Works....... }	408,621 46	650,000 00	822,645 92	810,403 00
Ore shipped out of Colorado......... }	915,168 00	663,973 31	925,742 24	1,195,831 15
Total..........	$1,928,161 74	$1,982,548 31	$2,206,577 91	$2,511,105 85

PRODUCT OF THE DIFFERENT METALS, 1876, '7, '8.

	1876.	1877.	1878.
Silver....................	$1,837,387 31	$1,984,077 91	$2,275,105 85
Gold....	95,161 00	96,500 00	†134,000 00
Lead....................	50,000 00	123,000 00	98,000 00
Copper..................	....	3,000 00	4,000 00
Totals..	$1,982,548 31	$2,206,577 91	$2,511,105 85

* A large portion was shipped to Germany for treatment.
† Includes gold in lodes carrying both gold and silver.

The following statistics for 1876 appeared in the report of the author, published in the New York Engineering and Mining Journal:

Sources and Shippers.	Ore.	Ore.	Silver.	Coin Value.
	Tons.	lbs.	oz.	
SILVER BULLION—				
From Judd & Crosby, Pelican, Clear Creek and Stewart Mills....................	3,500	....	401,198.9	$473,414 00
SILVER ORE SHIPPED—				
Church Brothers & Co.........	2,073	775	381,573.8	450,257 03
G. W. Hall & Co...............	1,218	....	294,813	347,879 34
Matthews & Co.....	671	167	113,333.8	133,733 88
L. F. Olmsted....	634	310	88,781.7	121,948 63
W. Bement....................	451	463	60,276	....
Silver ores from Idaho, etc......	250	....	21,190	25,000 00
Other silver and lead ores, etc...	1,278	...	87.875	145,629 09
CONCENTRATED ORES—				
Clear Creek Company—crude ore dressed......	4,000	....	108,150.9	127,618 04
GOLD—				
Gold from lode veins...........	2,000	....	....	40,000 00
Gold, placer and bar...........	....	....	....	45,161 00
Total..................	16,075	1,715	1,557,193.1	$1,982,548 31

About 11,000 tons of ore were concentrated altogether. Deducting 2,500 tons of concentrated ore, credited above to mills and ore buyers, the amount of ore mined in the county will appear as 9,575 tons of high grade, and 11,000 tons of low grade ore (afterwards concentrated), or 20,575 tons altogether.

The smelting works at Black Hawk received ores to the value of $534,400, and those at Golden and Denver smaller amounts. Some 1,676 tons went to St. Louis, Pittsburg, and Wyandotte, Mich.

Rich discoveries were made just at the close of the year on Red Elephant and Leavenworth Mountains. The Free America and S. J. Tilden were prominent among these. The Dives and Pelican mines were the largest producers, and then came the Stevens, Baxter, Pay Rock, Colorado Central, Marshall Tunnel lodes, Chelsea Beach, Polar Star, Magnet, and Burleigh and Lebanon Tunnel mines. The Hamill and Chaffee mines, on Brown and Sherman Mountains, were this year consolidated with the Terrible of the English Company, with a capital stock of $1,500,000.

The product of 1877 came from or passed through the following channels:

	Tons of Ore.	Value.
SILVER BULLION—		
Pelican, Clear Creek, Judd & Crosby, and Stewart Mills.	3,200	$388,189 74
GOLD—		
Dust from Creek Mines.	....	30,000 00
Retort, etc., Idaho and Empire Mills.	3,200	60,000 00
ORE SHIPMENTS—		
Church.	$1,503\frac{262}{2000}$	325,467 56
Hall & Co.	783½	258,339 48
Mathews & Morris.	$1,035\frac{1039}{2000}$	204,755 07
Olmsted & Ballou.	1,881	222,938 86
McCann & Co.	200	43,062 20
C. C. Co., Silver Plume, to the East, and Boulder	1,200	157,000 00
Other ores to Black Hawk, Golden, etc., silver and gold, less Summit County.	3,300	416,825 00
Totals.	$16,303\frac{301}{2000}$	$2,206,577 91

An allowance for low grade ores before concentrating would bring up the total tonnage mined to 19,503.

The Stewart and Judd & Crosby mills did but little work.

The Clear Creek Company's mills sampled, concentrated, and reduced ores.   The Pelican Mill, after being repaired, ran ten months,
mainly as a custom mill, by Napheys & Ballou.   The Silver Plume
Mill turned out 694 tons of dressed ore for the market, and 400 tons
were shipped away.   The Boston and Colorado Works, at Black
Hawk, bought $645,500 worth of ore from Clear Creek county in
1877, all silver-producing, except $6,500 in gold and $3,000 in copper.   The Golden Smelting Company bought ore to the value of
 150,000, of which $20,000 was gold, $7,000 lead, and the balance
silver, all coming from about one thousand tons of ore.   General F.
J. Marshall shipped to Pittsburg, St. Louis, and Wyandotte, Michigan, via the Kansas Pacific Railway, 362 car loads, or 3,982 tons of
ore, valued at $800,000.   About $15,000 worth of bullion was obtained at the West Denver Dry Ore Reduction Works from the Polar
Star Mine.

The average value of the 11,903 tons of high grade silver ores
was $160.44 per ton; of high and low grades, $127.80, and of all
ores, including gold stamp mill quartz, $111.70.   Some lodes carry
a great deal of lead, from 30 to 65 per cent., and others carry a few
per cent. of copper.   Nearly or quite 5,000 tons of ore, too poor
for smelting, were dressed and separated so that the mineral was retained in one-third or one-fourth of that bulk, and thus rendered
profitable for reduction.   Nearly all of this work was done by the
Silver Plume wet concentrator and the Clear Creek Company's dry
dressing works.   Near the close of the year the Silver Queen Works,
at Georgetown, and Miles' Works, at Idaho, began to dress ores.

The year 1877 was noticeable for the development of several very
rich and valuable lodes.   The more important of these were the
Free America and Boulder Nest, on Red Elephant mountain, where
a lively mining camp was started, the S. J. Tilden and Kirtley,
on Leavenworth, and the Dunderberg on Sherman mountain.   The
Tilden gave the richest average ore of any mine in the district, and
the Boulder Nest showed the largest very valuable ore body during
the latter eight months of the year.   Just at the close of the year
the Dunderberg was opened.   Among older mines that were large
producers were the Pelican and Dives, the Pay Rock, Baxter, Terrible, Brown, Stevens, the Colorado Central group, the Hukill, and
Specie Payment.

YIELD OF 1878, SHOWING PRODUCERS AND SHIPPERS.

PRODUCERS AND SHIPPERS.	Tons of Ore Handled.	VALUE.	TOTALS.
SILVER BULLION—			
Pelican Mill........	1,241	$155,241 00	
Clear Creek Company Mill*	2,741	124,966 56	
Farwell Reduction Works.........	500	109,664 14	$389,871 70
GOLD BULLION—			
Dust of placers and retorts of lodes of Empire, Idaho, etc.....	4,000	115,000 00	115,000 00
ORE SHIPMENTS—			
Mathews, Morris & Co.............	1,646	430,555 07	
G. W. Hall & Co............. ..	1,000	276,594 47	
Olmsted & Ballou.................	1,493	191,111 86	
Silver Plume Conc. Mill of Franklin Ballou*.....................	1,788	116,481 22	
P. McCann.......................	900	238,995 00	
Clear Creek Company..............	3,934	493,604 25	
J. B. Church.....................	715	145,000 00	
Ores sent to Golden, Black Hawk, and elsewhere, not included in the above†................. .	2,042	113,892 28	2,006,234 15
Totals.................	22,000	$2,261,105 85	$2,261,105 85

* Mainly low grade ores before concentrating.

† This includes 1,400 tons or more of low grade ores concentrated at the Miles and Hukill Mills.

Of the ore shipments of 1878, $810,403.05 were the result of ores sent to and treated at works in Colorado outside of Georgetown, and $1,195,831.05 worth of ore went to various points East, mainly to Omaha, Saint Louis, and Pittsburg. Large amounts of ore are said to have been treated at the Omaha Smelting Works. Of ores treated in Colorado the Boston & Colorado Works obtained $566,000, the Golden Smelting Works $204,403, Boyd's Works about $10,000, and the Cañon Reduction Works $30,000. Of the gold bullion some $25,000 came out of the 25-stamp quartz mill at Idaho Springs, and about as much at the three stamp mills at Empire, only one of which was running steadily.

The 12,071 tons of silver ore, outside of the low grades concentrated, averaged $174.35 per ton. The average of all silver ores handled, high and low grades, including mixed gold and silver ores near Idaho, was $133.11. There were about 17,000 tons. The average of all ores, including the low grade stamp mill quartz, was about $112. The free gold milling ores yielded from $10 to $20 per ton. Over 5,000 tons were crushed.

The Dunderberg, on which mining began just at the close of 1877, yielded $255,000. The Boulder Nest, which began to yield about eight months earlier, produced over $200,000 in 1878. The Terrible, and other connecting mines are said to have turned out about $150,000, and the Pelican, Dives, Pay Rock and Baxter, each about $60,000. The Kirtley, discovered in October, 1877, gave a very large product, probably as much or more than any of the last four estimated. The Equator must have yielded between $75,000 and $100,000. The Free America was among the productive mines of the county. The Freeland shipped ore but a few weeks, and the Hukill product was not sent forward very extensively. Still their export was considerable. No figures have been given concerning the Stevens, but the return probably reached $80,000. The Colorado Central, S. J. Tilden, Frostburg, Brown, the Lebanon Tunnel mines and Specie Payment were quite productive.

The ruling Georgetown prices for ores last winter were about the same as those of Mathews, Morris & Co., which, rating silver at 1.18 per ounce, were as follows, per ounce of silver to each ton of ore:

30 oz.	6 cts.	80 oz.	60 cts.	180 oz.	79 cts.	350 oz.	89 cts.
35 "	19 "	90 "	64 "	190 "	80 "	400 "	90 "
40 "	27 "	100 "	67 "	200 "	81 "	450 "	91 "
45 "	36 "	110 "	69 "	210 "	82 "	500 "	92 "
50 "	42 "	120 "	71 "	220 "	83 "	550 "	93 "
55 "	46 "	130 "	73 "	230 "	84 "	600 "	94 "
60 "	50 "	140 "	75 "	240 "	85 "	700 "	95 "
65 "	53 "	150 "	76 "	260 "	86 "	800 "	96 "
70 "	56 "	160 "	77 "	280 "	87 "	900 "	97 "
75 "	58 "	170 "	78 "	300 "	88 "	1,000 and over 93 "	

Mathews, Morris & Co. crushed, sampled, bought, and shipped at the Rocky Mountain Mill, in Georgetown, 1,646 tons and 409 pounds of ore, containing 372,024.9 ounces of silver, 58.4 ounces of gold, and 123 tons 1,112.3 pounds of lead. The total value was $430,555.07. The average contents of ore handled was 8 per cent. of lead, and 234 ounces of silver, or $270.82 per ton.

F. M. Taylor's statement of the Clear Creek Company's business at Georgetown shows that 2,741 tons and 510 pounds of ore were concentrated and sampled and sent to the reduction works of the company and to other ore buyers of Georgetown, beside 3,934 tons and 901 pounds concentrated or shipped; total tonnage, 6,675 tons 1,411 pounds, for which $300,976.67 was paid, making an average of $45 per ton. The average assay was 82 ounces of silver, making a total of 547,407.8 ounces of silver, of a value of $618,570.81. This represents value of both shipments and mill bullion product. The latter alone amounted to $124,966.56. The company paid out for labor $42,013.88, and for fuel $9,647.86.

Olmsted & Ballou deal heavily in lead-bearing ores as well as others. They operate the Washington Mill in Georgetown, which is supplied with the usual sampling and crushing machinery. The Silver Flume Concentrating Mill handles the lower grade ores. The combined business of both mills for the year was $302,519.32.

G. W. Hall & Co. is the oldest ore-buying, sampling, and shipping firm in the county. In 1872 General F. J. Marshall and C. A. Martine began to purchase the richer ores of the miners and ship them across the ocean to Germany for treatment. This was the actual beginning of a high-priced competition ore market for the Georgetown mines. Recent sales to American works only.

In 1879, the B. & C. works of Argo bought McCann's Lawson and Georgetown sampling mills (see following table for 1878), and bought and changed the Pelican reduction works to a sampler for Georgetown. Montgomery's Idaho concentrator ships to Golden.

The new concentrating mills of 1879 were the Freeland, 100 tons daily, and the Stevens, at Lawson—and of 1880, the Dunderberg, wet process, all running. The Hukill concentrator was demolished.

In 1879 the county's silver bullion, $425,000, came entirely from the Clear Creek Company and Farwell reduction works.

The following mills ran all or parts of 1878. For subsequent changes and additions see the above ten lines.

NAME.	CHARACTER.	Daily Capacity in Tons.	PLANT.	TIME EMPLOYED.	Established.
Clear Creek Company, Georgetown..	Silver Red'g	12 to 15	10 stamps, 6 cylinders, leaching tubs.	Full year	1876
Farwell Red. Works, " "	"	6 to 8	10 stamps, 3 cylinders, amal. pans	Last six months	1872 1878
Pelican Mill, " "	"	10 to 12	10 stamps, 5 cylinders, amal. barrels	First five months	1867 1874
Clear Creek Company, "	Dry Concentration	45	Crushers, screens, jigs, etc.	Full year	1875
Colorado United M. Co.	Wet	..	" "	....	1877
Silver Plume (F. Ballou)	"	45	Crushers, screens, jigs, tables, etc	Full year	1875
Hukill Company (Spanish Bar)	"	24	Crushers, screens, jigs, tables, etc	Last 4 or 5 months	1878
Miles (Idaho)	"	15	Crushers, screens, jigs, tables, etc	Most of year	1877
Sunshine, at Idaho	Gold, raw amal	16	25 stamps with tables	Full year	1877
Pioneer (Empire)	"	12	16 stamps	Most of year	1878
Knickerbocker, Empire	"	15	20 stamps	Latter part of year	1865
Bay State, Empire	"	11	15 stamps	Few months	1865

The ore sampling, buying, and shipping firms and mills of Clear Creek county are as follows:

Rocky Mountain Mill, Mathews, Morris & Co., Georgetown. Established in 1876; rebuilt from fire in 1877. Capacity, 30 tons.

Washington Mill, Olmsted & Ballou, Georgetown. Mill rebuilt 1872. Capacity, 30 tons in ten hours.

G. W. Hall & Co., Georgetown. Buildings used for present purposes since 1871-2.

Clear Creek Company Mill, Georgetown. Established 1876. Capacity, 40 tons.

J. B. Church, Georgetown. Established 1874. Capacity, 30 tons.

P. McCann, Georgetown and Lawson. The first established in 1877, and the latter in 1878.

Silver Plume Mill, Ballou & Co., Silver Plume. Established in 1875.

Harry Montgomery, Idaho Springs. 1876, for Golden smelters.

Probably two thousand men are directly engaged in mining, milling, and hauling ore in Clear Creek county, or in prospecting. Allowing for an outlay of $300,000 for mining and milling supplies, and the yield of 1878 would have returned over $1,100 to each man at work had it been equally divided. At the same time, this same labor proved up and vastly increased the value of many properties. Outlays for buildings and machinery are not counted above, as they are permanent improvements. The mines of Clear Creek county have averaged a return of over three dollars per day per man employed for many years, and in those years the value of mining property, with new discoveries, has been increased $20,000,000. It can hardly be an exaggeration to say, that while the average bullion return for nine or ten years has averaged three or four dollars per day to the men engaged directly or indirectly in producing it, that in that period each man so engaged has each day advanced the value of mining property an equal amount. The same industry has furnished the means or inducements for the growth of well-built and prosperous towns, for permanent improvements of various descriptions, and for the support of a large population.

The following very appropriate review of past and prospective work appeared in a late number of the Georgetown Miner: "For a period of about sixteen years, that enterprising individual, the 'honest miner,' has prospected and dug for the precious metals in our county with that energy and tenacity which is a distinguishing characteristic of 'miner men,' and, to some extent, is born of the circumstances in which he is placed. He has lived hard and worked harder, and with an undaunted brow has often faced the bitterest and sternest realities of life. He has gazed down the misty avenues of probabilities until what to others appeared to be the vague outlines of chance were to him all but an absolute certainty of his hopes. He has acquired fortunes with a few weeks' or months' labor, and often, with a generosity bordering on recklessness, he has squandered it again in but little less time than it took to accumulate it. On the other hand, he has toiled incessantly for years without taking out a single 'red,' but his faith still continues unshaken and his perseverance unimpaired. He has accomplished labors compared with which the cleaning out of the Augean stables would be but an ante-breakfast chore. He has penetrated to the very foundations of the eternal hills, and the innermost recesses of 'earth's gigantic sentinels' have echoed with the sharp ring of his steel-impelling strokes and bellowed back the infernal roar of his fiery persuasions.   He has carved his way through sullen solitude in search of metalliferous wealth, and a liberal and enlightened civilization has followed close upon his heels.   If he has not discovered the secret of the transmutation of metals, he has unfolded their rock-bound hiding-places; while mechanical and chemical science have sprung to his aid and rendered him indispensable assistance in their extraction.   The brave and persistent miner has done all this and much more; not with the magic wand of an eastern fairy, but with a striking hammer, weighing from six to eight pounds, and other implements necessary to his vocation.

"Notwithstanding the fact that he has accomplished so much, however, reason, experience and observation assure him that he is upon the first round of his ladder.   In this case it is the topmost round, and however paradoxical it may appear, he must rise to wealth and position by sinking.   In his very natural and potent desire for gain he instinctively grasped at that which came first within his reach, and many were the rich surface 'pockets' that he legitimately and profitably rifled.   With this object in view he has burrowed in and through the mountains, until the latter are dotted with the results of his subterranean labors, but thus far he has rarely penetrated below the streams which flank the bases of the secondary ranges of mountains.   He recognized the fact that there was no necessity for descending lower while so much remained above.   Surface chimneys and pockets are not inexhaustible, however, and with their deflection deep mining is the next step in the exploration of true fissure veins. We would not insinuate that the surface deposits, or a tithe of them, are worked out, but there certainly is not as many of them as there were a dozen years ago, while the expense of downward development is much less now than it was at that time.   In the matter of deep mining—which is abundantly suggested by circumstances and by the records of the development of mining properties in all parts of the world—it must be admitted that the probability of realizing a snug fortune with a small outlay of money and muscle, is less likely to occur than in surface explorations, while it is equally true that the former presents a more certain and satisfactory field for investment."

CHAPTER XIV.

CLEAR CREEK COUNTY MINES—THE GOLD AND SILVER COPPER-IRON BELT—THE HUKILL MINE—ITS HISTORY AND PRESENT CONDITION AND PROSPECTS—THE FREELAND—HOW A GREAT MINE WAS DEVELOPED—THE FIRST COLORADO PURCHASE OF THE CALIFORNIANS—MINING ON THE NEVADA PLAN—GOLD AND SILVER VEINS OF VIRGINIA CAÑON, SEATON HILL, AND IDAHO—THE TROPIC MINE—CREEK AND BAR MINING.

Clear Creek county is in reality one large and continuous mining district, extending from Gilpin county and Floyd Hill southward and westward to the "snowy range." The mineral wealth of the northeastern portion is mainly embraced in the extension of the great copper-iron gold belt of Gilpin, which carries much more silver here than there. This belt enters the county from the head of Virginia Cañon, and in Bellevue and other mountains, and crosses South Clear Creek and Chicago and Trail Creeks in the vicinity of Idaho, Spanish Bar, and Fall River. Near Black Hawk, Willis Gulch, and on Clifton and Seaton Mountains are silver-bearing galena veins. The streams of this section are worked for gold.

The two great mines so far developed in this copper-iron belt, and in this part of the county, are the Freeland and Hukill, but there are scores of lodes in the same districts, and great activity is displayed in their development. An idea of the capacity and character of the two lodes mentioned can be had from the fact that after a critical examination of many Colorado mines the Freeland was the first one purchased by Californians, and the Hukill was the second in which they became interested. Moderate figures may have had something to do with this, but the size, continuity, and reliability of the veins and their large ore reserves were the original attractions.

The Hukill mine is situated in Spanish Bar mining district, two miles above Idaho Springs, and is crossed by South Clear Creek and the Colorado Central railway. Its outcroppings, surface workings, tunnels, and mine and mill buildings are plainly visible from the railway and stage-road, and are the most extensive for miles around. The location on the steep mountain slopes permitted of tunneling in on the vein at various elevations above the creek-bed, and this is the way the Hukill was opened until it was deemed best to further develop it by attaining greater depth. Recent explorations near and under the creek prove the Hukill and Whale mines, that were so long worked on opposite mountains, to be on one and the same vein. This is indicative of greater worth than if the veins were separate and distinct. The largest and richest body of solid ore ever found on either location is that recently discovered in and now being explored from the new Whale shaft.

John M. Dumont began to develop the Hukill lode in 1871. It paid handsomely from the start, and work was steadily continued until few mines could show as much value in sight, and none better internal development. Little ore was sold outside of that removed in drifting and shafting. This paid all expenses, and a satisfactory profit beside. At the end of five years the mine was sold for $200,-000. The excavation of 1,600 feet of adits, drifts, and shafts had returned, beside a large amount of low-grade ore, 1,700 tons, that sold for $195,200. The cost was $167,140, and the profit $20,060. The average yield was $114.82 per ton. There were thousands of tons left standing in the mine between the levels. Some of this was removed by a subsequent operator—probably $70,000. Then the Hukill Mining Company came into possession of the property.

Through the action of the two leading stockholders, very important additional property was secured in June, 1878, at no cost to the company itself. This property was the Whale mine, mill, and placer claim, purchased of John M. Dumont and E. S. Platt. The transaction increased the company ownership to 3,188 feet—1,900 on the Whale, and 1,288 on the Hukill previously obtained. Recent developments show that the Whale and Hukill locations are on one and the same vein, which underlies South Clear Creek and intersects the steep mountains on either side. Some time ago the lower shaft on the Hukill claim had reached a depth of 220 feet below the creek level, with good ore in the lower part and in the East level.

In 1879 the same Californians who had bought the Freeland, purchased a controlling interest in the Hukill company property. The manager of the former, F. F. Osbiston, formerly of the Comstock, and one of the most experienced of Pacific coast miners, was then appointed superintendent. Work has since been prosecuted on an enlarged plan, and with an unusual degree of system and energy.

A new and vertical shaft is being sunk on the Whale property, which will hereafter be the main outlet for the entire mine. This shaft is twelve feet square, and is supplied with cages for hoisting ore and water. It has the most convenient and approved steam hoisting machinery. A spacious building has been erected over the shaft, from which a railway for ore transportation leads across the creek to the Colorado Central railroad. As the vein dips strongly, levels are run thereto from the shaft. These have all intersected good bodies of ore, but the lower one makes a splendid showing of mineral. As the levels are driven from the line of the shaft under the mountain, ore reserves and stoping ground will be secured for hundreds of feet above the starting point.

The vein has gradually expanded to the lower workings, besides giving a larger proportion of rich ore than elsewhere. Much of the vein is composed of solid mineral, that brings good prices at the smelters without concentration. Quantities of it have been sold at an average of $200 per ton, carrying over $40 worth of copper and the remainder in silver and gold. There is also heavy lead ore in places running low in silver—also a large proportion of concentrating material. Small streaks and pockets have been found in both mines that have milled as much per ton as the higher grades of Georgetown ores, but the hundred-dollar ores, and about twice as much that concentrates from forty dollars up to one hundred, have been the main dependence. A body of mineral is now visible in the lower level from this shaft that appears to average about $2,000 per ton. From three to ten, and rarely twenty per cent. of the mine's product is copper. The inclosing walls of the lode are of mica schist and gneiss formation.

The Whale property included an immense brick building, nearly 300 feet long, in which a pan and then a smelting process had been used. In 1878 wet concentrating works were introduced. The site having been undermined, and rendered unsafe by underground placer workings, the concentrator were removed.

A large mill, similar to that of the Freeland mine, will soon be erected for ore dressing purposes. In the meantime, the low grades are sent to Lawson for concentration. The Hukill location alone yielded from the time work began in 1871, down to the summer of

1879, about $515,000, of which $250,000 came out in the last two years. The Whale produced considerable money long ago, but is now in far better shape than then. The Hukill property has over 5,000 feet of levels, adits, shafts, and winzes, the mining supplies are ample, and the machinery and equipments first class. The mine is in condition to pay handsome dividends for a long time to come, while each month sees additional paying ground opened. Of the officials of the Hukill Company, J. L. Brownell is president, and E. W. Willett secretary.

The Freeland is one of the great veins of the famous gold and silver belt and has few equals in the State or country in substantial worth and aggregate wealth. Its value, as previously demonstrated, has been vastly enhanced by the developments of the past few months. While the average yield of its ore is less per ton than in many silver lodes, the great width, uniform tendency, and seemingly limitless extent of the mineral body entitle it to a place in the front rank of the best of mines. But a trifle of all the ore so far penetrated has been removed or sold.

The vein is mainly composed of copper and iron pyrites, with occasional bodies of nearly pure galena, carrying 65 per cent. of lead and about 50 ounces of silver. Nearly 60 per cent. of the product is in gold, the remainder being credited to the silver and copper. From three to ten per cent. of the ore is composed of the latter metal. The ore is usually in the shape of a vein of copper-iron, rich enough to ship to market, flanked by poorer material and mixed mineral and gangue. The poorer grade requires concentration—from two and a half to three tons of crude ore being dressed down to one of salable mineral. About one-third of the ore brings good prices at the smelters without separation. Not taking into consideration the small per cent. of lead, the average value of shipping ores and concentrations is from $50 to $60 per ton. In the ground entered last year the ore-body was generally from one to two and a half feet wide. The two lower tunnels or adits have lately been passing through from three to five feet of ore, showing the vein to be of greater size at the furthest points from the surface. These widths are not in pockets, but continue for long distances, and at the tunnel breasts. There are also streaks of very rich ore that assay far above the average. The cheapness with which this great vein can be worked is remarkable, and combined with its great size renders it extremely

HUKILL MINE.

Wreckage of yesterday, Leadville, c. 1975

Kilroy was here, Leadville, c. 1975

profitable. Mineral of this character is especially desirable to smelters of the copper matte process, on account of its fluxing qualities in the treatment of baser ores.

The Freeland lode is on a branch of South Clear Creek, a little over two miles from the Colorado Central railway, and four miles from Idaho Springs. It was recently purchased by California parties, and is superintended by F. F. Osbiston, a well-known mining manager and expert of the great bonanza firm. The property is over a mile long.

The owners are developing the mine with all possible dispatch, and have been making permanent improvements on a scale commensurate with the general magnitude of their operations. An immense mill for concentrating ore was put up in a remarkably short space of time, and set in motion late in October, 1879. This mill, with its enormous amount of machinery, was completed under the supervision of a superior Comstock mechanic in three months, or in one-half the usual time of similar undertakings in these mountains. The full capacity of this mill is 115 tons of ore daily, but owing to lack of water only from 50 to 70 tons of ore were dressed daily during the past winter. Here the valuable mineral is separated from the gangue or waste rock, and sold to the smelter at good figures. Thus from two and a half to three tons, averaging from $19 to $22 per ton, is reduced to one ton, averaging from $56 to $59.50 per ton, and smelters' charges on the poorer material are avoided. The cost of concentrating the crude ore was only 70 cents per ton last winter, and less when 100 tons are milled daily. Twelve men are employed in both shifts when the mill runs the entire twenty-four hours. The usual ore shipments have been over 800 tons a month, mainly concentrates.

The Freeland mill building is 117 feet long by 62 feet in height, and is divided into three compartments. The ore comes direct from the mine through the Freeland tunnel into the ore room. Here it is screened and the coarser portions sent through Blake crushers and Cornish rolls. It is then elevated to the receiving screens and sized, all of the coarser particles being passed back to other rolls, which crush to the desired size. The crushed material continues on through a succession of cylindrical sizing screens to the last jig, and is then ready for shipment to the smelter. These jigs, of which there are a large number, are inclined wooden troughs, bottomed with

THE FREELAND MINE AND MILL.

A century of "progress"; bird's eye view, Leadville, c. 1975

Gone, but not forgotten, Leadville, c. 1975

wire screens, through which water is constantly forced upward, by the aid of a pump, thus lifting and keeping the ore and pulp in motion. By this means the heavier portions, containing the valuable metals, gradually work their way to the bottom, while the lighter, or non-mineral matter, is carried away by the flow of water. The former are called concentrates, and vary from the fineness of sand to the coarseness of wheat kernels. The jig room occupies much the larger part of the building. Steam-power is afforded by a hundred-horse-power engine, driven by twin boilers located in a room set apart therefor. The entire structure and its contents are of the most substantial character, and excellent results are obtained by the mill superintendent, J. M. Palmer.

A stamp mill is projected, for milling the low grade material to obtain what gold can be saved before concentrating. A tram railway will be constructed from the mine and concentrating mill down Trail Creek, to connect with the Colorado Central Railway.

Few mines are as closely tested as this, and few owners are as correctly informed of the true value of their ore product and reserves. Every fathom of ground is examined by practical miners and experts of the company, and their investigations and assays tell to a certainty the kind of ground the levels and stopes are penetrating. These examinations conclusively prove that there is ore enough above the Freeland tunnel to supply the mill 100 tons daily and pay large dividends for two years, while the tunnel floor shows the ore to extend downward indefinitely. There are also two thousand tons of ore already broken in the chutes in the mine, or outside, awaiting milling. Something over ten per cent. of the vein has been estimated by Messrs. Keyes, Palmer and Vivian to be high grade ore averaging more than $57 per ton. Present indications lead to the belief that the vein below the Freeland tunnel will be richer than that above, and that the proportion of high grades will be increased.

From the head of the Freeland tunnel, the "back" is over 700 feet vertical; that is there are 700 feet of vein to work out, before reaching the surface of the mountain, and this will increase as the tunnel progresses. The two lower tunnels have been steadily driven forward on a vein from one to four feet wide, and it is the purpose of the company to keep developments far ahead of the mill capacity. All of the tunnels or adits are now connected by winzes or shafts— one of 400 feet passing from the Platt down to the Freeland. These adits are 200 feet apart and of the following lengths in March, 1880; the upper or Platt, 950 feet; the Minnie, 1,600; Freeland, 1,575. A vertical shaft will soon be started westerly from the mouth of the Freeland tunnel, designed to cut the lode 1,000 feet below that level. The vein pitches or inclines something less than forty-five degrees, and will be reached at varying depths by cross-cuts, and then drifted on. At and near the breast of the Minnie level, the lode carries a vein of solid ore 18 inches wide, that averages $100 a ton without assorting, and in the stopes near by are from one to four feet of ore that yields from $50 to $100 per ton.

The remarkable uniformity and continuousness of this vein insures unlimited amounts of ore. The product is so desirable for its fluxing qualities that it brings the most favorable prices known at the Argo Smelting Works, where it has taken the place of quartz mill tailings. A ton of concentrates represents a total outlay for mining, reducing bulk by concentration, teaming, railway transportation and costs of smelting of about $30, leaving a profit of nearly as much more. On the richer ores not concentrated the cost is less than $26 a ton. Not far from fifteen thousand tons of concentrates and high grades can be marketed per annum, indicating a profit of hundreds of thousands of dollars. Although the mill was not running to anything like its full capacity, the mine probably yielded nearly $300,000 in a little over six months prior to May, 1880, when dividends began to be paid.

The purchasers of the Freeland were George D. Roberts, Harry Rosener and F. F. Osbiston. They organized the Freeland Mining Company, whose stock was mainly taken in a few days' time after the books were opened in New York. The capital stock of the company represents $5,000,000 in 200,000 shares of a par value of $25. The officers are: Ex-Governor R. C. McCormick, president; T. M. Lilienthal, vice-president; Edward W. Willett, secretary; Bank of Nevada, treasurer; and F. F. Osbiston, superintendent. The trustees are the president and vice-president and Senator J. P. Jones, Harry Rosener, and S. V. White.

This property presented a very different appearance and valuation a few years ago. The district and the score of mining claims had been abandoned long before, because the gold would not save satisfactorily in the stamp-mills, and silver was then unlooked for While working the Hukill, John M. Dumont was gradually pur-

Skyline sentinel, wealth's labor lost, Leadville, c. 1975

The sky above, the earth below, Leadville, c. 1975

chasing or relocating these claims, and after disposing of the latter began to develop the Freeland in connection with E. S. Platt and Sheldon Collins. The enterprise was at first considered somewhat problematical, but the proprietor's confidence and the expenditure of many thousands of dollars [in drifting, timbering, in roads, buildings, and permanent improvements, were certainly justified by the results that were gradually attained. The lode was so situated that the cheap and advantageous system of adit levels was adopted. In this way the further the mountain was penetrated the greater was the height of ore between a level and the surface. Rugged mountains barred the way to the outside world, and as it was no thoroughfare, little was known of the persistent work that was going on in this out-of-the-way place. During the year or two of operations the working force had increased to more than one hundred miners, and a pretty village had grown about the mine. Dumont had practically a little kingdom of his own in this isolated but picturesque valley, for there were no competing mining interests and no work save that of his own direction. Ore shipments began at last at the rate of fifty tons daily, the adits were from seven to ten hundred feet long on the vein and vast quantities of ore had been broken. But a concentrating mill was needed for the greater portion of the ores. At this juncture the Californians came along, examined the property, and paid a quarter of a million for it. They have since extended developments and increased the ore reserves so that with the necessary mill and improvements the mine is worth many times the price paid for it.

About one thousand feet west of, and running parallel to the Freeland, is the Lone Tree lode, one of the most strongly defined mineral veins of Clear Creek county, and one which bids fair to rival even the first named mine. This assertion is made on the record and merits of the lode itself, coupled with the significant fact that it is owned and will be developed by John M. Dumont, of Spanish Bar. This means that it will be opened up in an economical manner, regardless of all necessary expense, as was the Freeland during Dumont's ownership. The property was recently purchased by its present owner from James W. Craven. It consists of two patented claims, having a course north, 27 degrees east. These are the Lone Tree claim, 1,300 feet long, and the southern or Lone Tree Extension, of 1,500 feet. A placer claim less than 1,000

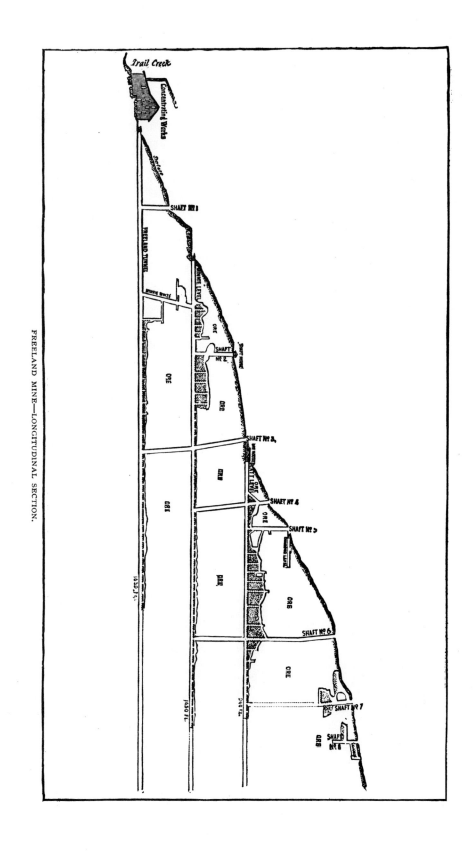

FREELAND MINE—LONGITUDINAL SECTION.

To sleep, perchance to dream, Leadville, c. 1975

Only God can make a tree, Leadville, c. 1975

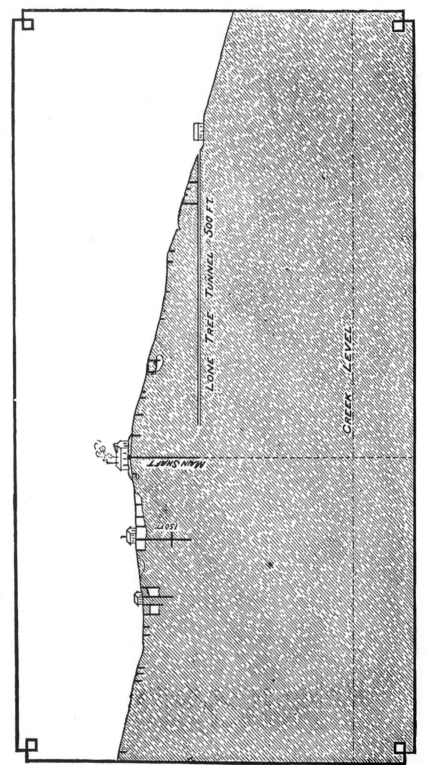

THE LONE TREE MINE, LONGITUDINAL SECTION.

feet distant takes in Trail Creek for half a mile, affording ample room for concentrating or other works that may be needed. The location of the Lone Tree is extremely favorable for development, both by shafts and by adits on the vein. Roads can be easily built around the mountain sides, and there are immense bodies of excellent pine timber on and adjacent to the claims.

The amount of development on the property has been slight, but work will be pushed forward rapidly from this time on. Years ago, when the lode was divided among many owners, a number of shafts were sunk to depths of from twenty-five to seventy-five feet, and a large amount of decomposed surface quartz extracted. Much of this paid well, and mill runs of $250 per cord are reported. No attempt was made, however, to develop the lode systematically, although the discovery shaft of the extension reached a depth of 150 feet, showing all the way down from two to five feet of auriferous quartz and oxidized minerals, running into fine grained iron pyrites.

About three hundred feet south of the northern end of the Lone Tree a tunnel was started. This has been driven southward on the vein nearly 500 feet, and shows a fine vein of ore, which is improving as length and depth are gained in the mountain. This further proves the decided mineral character of the lode. Nearer the centre of the property the width between walls is very great, and the pay vein and crevice of remarkable size. In that locality, a main shaft is being sunk to reach a depth of 1,000 feet. This, like the vein, is nearly perpendicular, and is covered by a substantial mine building. New and powerful hoisting machinery, including a sixty-horse-power engine and boilers are aiding to push the work. The creek level is about 400 feet lower than the Lone Tree Tunnel. A cross cut may be driven to intersect the lode when the latter will be drifted on in a southerly direction. This should leave much stoping ground and paying ore above. As soon as development warrants, it is the intention of the manager to arrange for such milling facilities as may be necessary to successfully reduce the Lone Tree ores.

The ore is similar to that of the Freeland and other lodes of the district—except that it seems to carry more gold—that is, gold-bearing pyrites carrying paying quantities of silver and copper. A large number of assays indicate that ore now in sight ranges in value from $40 to $200 per ton—and these figures seem to approach the old time mill records of decomposed quartz. The crevice is usually from five to eight feet wide, generally mineralized throughout. The vein pitches at an angle of ten degrees from the perpendicular, and preserves remarkable uniformity of course, width, pitch and general characteristics.

The Lone Tree is one of the strongest veins in the county, and its further development will undoubtedly prove it to be one of the most productive. Whatever method of opening the lode may be adopted, the public may rest assured that the work will be vigorously and wisely conducted by one having many years' experience among the mines of that section. Operations have commenced on the vein in solid earnest, and another year will witness important developments.

A company has been organized on this property, under the laws of New York, with a capital stock of one million dollars in two hundred thousand five-dollar shares. The officers of the Lone Tree Gold and Silver Mining Company are: J. L. Brownell, president; G. H. Seeley, vice-president; John M. Dumont, treasurer and manager of the mine; and H. L. Brownell, secretary. The trustees are: Samuel Wann, R. Weston, J. L. Brownell, G. H. Seeley and J. M. Dumont.

Columbia Mountain is directly opposite Red Elephant Mountain and the town of Lawson, and is separated therefrom by the valley of South Clear Creek. Within two years many valuable lodes have been discovered there, and with a few older locations have produced some rich ore. Among them are the Murray, Joe Reynolds, Dictator, Hugo, Moore and others.

The Murray mine was located long ago as the Live Yankee, and although having indications of worth, remained idle for years. Some time since, Colonel William Moore, who had closed out a successful business at the East, visited Colorado, and, like others, becoming enamored with the excitements of mining life, determined to locate permanently among the Rocky Mountains. On looking about for a favorable field of operations, he concluded that the older mining counties offered as safe and profitable opportunities for investment as Leadville or the Gunnison, and accordingly, in connection with F. E. Everett, the Golden banker, purchased the Murray lode. The Crown Point, Platts, and John D. Long lodes were also secured. Subsequently the Moore Mining and Smelting Company was organized, with Colonel Moore as president and general manager, and F.

THE MURRY MINE.

CRAWFORD N.Y.

(1) (2) Tunnels of Colo. U. M. C. and Terrible Shaft.

THE TERRIBLE-DUNDERBERG GROUP OF MINES.

(3) (4) East Terrible and Dunderberg.

E. Everett as secretary and treasurer. This company, in addition to its mines, own what was formerly called the Valley Smelting Works at Golden. Work began on the Murry late in 1879. The requisite buildings and hoisting works have been erected, two shafts sunk and several drifts run. One of the shafts will be pushed to a depth of 300 feet before sinking is discontinued, and both shafts will soon be connected by a level to be 180 feet long. All the workings show a continuous vein of ore which carries a pay streak of mineral from 8 to 12 inches wide. This consists of yellow pyrites of copper and galena near the surface, and changes into a gray copper vein of larger size and higher value below. The former carry from 4 to 15 per centum copper, and the galena runs from 15 to 30 per centum in lead. The vein yields from 50 to 150 ounces of silver per ton.

During the month of January, when ore began to be shipped, 60 tons were taken out from development work alone, bringing $3,500. As the mine is but 300 feet up the mountain side, and only an eighth of a mile from Lawson railroad station, it costs but fifty cents a ton to place ore upon the cars. The product is handled in bulk as it comes from the mine with very little sorting. Its favorable mountain side location, where depth is gained on the vein by both drifting and sinking, and the quantity and character of the ore render the property a very promising one, and the manager seems as likely to be as successful in mining and smelting as he has been in previous avocations. The other mines are also worked, and altogether the company had four shafts over 100 feet deep some time ago.

A number of lodes are being developed in Trail Creek and Spanish Bar districts. The May Flower, operated by a New York company, has employed a large force of men, and has a fine hoisting plant over the working shaft. As yet there has been no production of importance.

Around the head of Virginia cañon and midway between Central and Idado Springs, is a group of free milling gold lodes that are well worthy of attention. This group is a continuation of the Gilpin gold-bearing belt. Most of the mines are just over the line in Clear Creek County. As a rule, the veins are not large, but are rich in gold, with occasional bunches and pockets of ore that pay handsomely. There has been quite a mining revival here since the opening of the Specie Payment in 1876-7. Besides that lode are the

Champion, Trio, German, Sunshine, Rocket, Clarissa, Gold Cloud, and others. The Specie Payment kept from fifteen to twenty-five stamps employed for several years, and has probably yielded $80,000.

The Champion was discovered in 1878, by Edward Williams and others, and was soon after purchased by Thomas I. Richman and some Chicago men. The average mill returns are about $15 a ton, but have sometimes trebled those figures. The smelting ore sells for over $100 a ton. There are two shafts on the lode, and the lower workings are more than 200 feet below the surface. It has kept five stamps employed for two years. The Trio mine was purchased in 1878, by Frederick C. Hardy, of New York. It had previously yielded very rich ore—some of it containing several hundred dollars a cord. It has since been opened by a tunnel which will have a depth of 600 feet on the vein as it passes beneath the summit of Bellevue mountain. The German has yielded some $25,000 altogether, and carries a broad seam of valuable smelting ore besides mill dirt. Near Idaho are the Fairmont and Patton mines, said to be on the same vein. The former has been extensively developed.

A belt of silver lodes extends from Gilpin into Clear Creek county, a mile southeast of Virginia Cañon. None of the veins are very large, the Seaton, Victor and Tropic taking the lead in this respect. The ore is often from 8 to 20 inches thick, and sells at from $60 to $125 or more. At one time more money was coming out of the Seaton than in the remainder of that end of the county. The Queen, Santa Fe, Kangaroo, Metropolitan, Argo, Cincinnati and Telephone, have all made money for their owners.

The Tropic has more ore in its reserves than any mine on Seaton hill. The vein is remarkably continuous, as shown by levels down to a depth of nearly 300 feet. From four to fourteen inches of ore are visible in nearly all parts of the mine. There is some low grade material requiring concentration. The marketable ore carries from 90 to 150 ounces of silver, and from $2 to $12 in gold per ton. The character of the vein is galena, zinc blende, gray copper, and iron pyrites. So far but little ore has been stoped, and the mine has been opened so as to make the best show possible.

South Clear Creek and its branches, including Chicago Creek, have been mined for gold every summer since 1859, and have probably yielded three quarters of a million in gold dust. Creek mining has been carried on there throughout the year by means of shafts, drifts, and tunnels, and occasionally by partially diverting the channels of the streams. There is one tunnel over nine hundred feet long extending into the bank and hill-side adjoining the creek, and just above Idaho numerous shafts have been sunk and long drifts extended through auriferous gravel. There are a number of creek and bar mines above and below Idaho that clear several thousand dollars every season. Hydraulic pumps and other appliances are used.

Where Geneva and Hall valleys slope eastward, and Montezuma valley dips in the opposite direction, the bald and barren crest of the snowy range is ribbed with silver veins, and extensive mining enterprises are going forward. Some veins extend from the summit down either slope, and are, consequently, partly in Summit county and partly in Clear Creek or Park. Geneva district includes many of these, Hall Valley district others, and Montezuma district the remainder. The ores in this cluster are argentiferous galena, gray copper, iron pyrites, zinc blende, and bismide, and carry ruby, brittle, and native silver. The argentiferous bismuth ores are very rich in silver, but are not usually very plentiful. Most lodes of this section carry some gold. Here are the Revenue-Star, the Gilman, United States Treasury, Baltic, Celtic, and others. On Teller and Glacier mountains are the Radical, Chatauqua, Erie, Star of the West, and the mines of the Boston Mining Company.

These lodes are from 11,000 to 13,000 feet above sea level. Below them the mountain slopes are covered with magnificent forests of pine. During the winter season it is impossible to approach or leave some of the more elevated mines, except on snow-shoes, and a season's supplies are taken in before the snows of the later autumn settle down on peak and valley. Securely housed, in warm and comfortable quarters, the miners continue to tunnel, drift, and blast, regardless of storms without. Years ago, huge avalanches of snow rolled down the mountain sides and swept buildings and several Whale and Champion miners to destruction. Steps have since been taken to avoid similar disasters at those localities.

The Revenue Mineral Company has driven the Brittanic tunnel into the range over 1,025 feet, at an elevation of 11,900 feet above sea level. It has intersected fourteen lodes, of which the Celtic, Baltic, and Revenue are the best. The Leviathan tunnel has penetrated the same mountain over 800 feet, and has intersected the green and blue lodes, carrying silver, gold and bismuth.

CHAPTER XV.

CLEAR CREEK COUNTY MINES—RED ELEPHANT MOUNTAIN AND ITS
SILVER VEINS—THE FAMOUS WHITE, BOULDER NEST, AND FREE
AMERICA—COLUMBIAN MOUNTAIN—THE JOE REYNOLDS AND
OTHER VEINS—THE EMPIRE GOLD DISTRICT.

Red Elephant Mountain is six miles northeast of Georgetown and about eight miles from Idaho Springs. It rises abruptly on the north side of South Clear Creek Valley. Although the Young America silver lode was located there long ago, no conception of the hidden wealth of the mountain was entertained by the old-time Georgetown miners or travelers. A veteran prospector named D. E. Dulany lived in that locality, and the presence of rich float ore among the slide and granite led him to hunt for silver veins long after less persistent men would have abandoned all hopes of success. He was finally so fortunate as to strike a lode of extraordinary richness, which he called the Free America or Purchase. Reports of mill runs quickly brought in an army of prospectors from Georgetown and Central. Dulany soon sold to General J. I. Gilbert and W. H. Moore for $25,000, and the latter sold to Joseph Reynolds, of Chicago. Other discoveries were made, the town of Lawson was built, and the next summer the Colorado Central railway was extended from Floyd Hill to Georgetown, passing close by Red Elephant, and within a half mile of its mines. Since then the district has been a very prosperous one.

The Free America was paying handsomely in the following spring and summer. When the location was made there had not been work enough done to determine the course of the vein, and the consequence was that only a part of it was secured. The remainder fell to the Free America Extension on the east, and the Boulder Nest on the west. The White, an equally important discovery, unites with the Boulder Nest, or is the same vein.

The Free America has five levels from the main shaft, the lower one just started being 600 feet below the surface. There is a small vein of solid ore in the lower workings, and there were large pockets and ore-bodies at various places from the surface down. A cross cut driven on the second level for a distance of thirty-six feet encountered no walls. The latest work done showed an increase of ore, indicating as good a body near by as in the upper levels. The yield of the Free America is said to have been $100,000 in 1877, and the receipts for ore sales about $60,000 in 1878.

Few mines in the country can show as fine a record for production and profit as the Boulder Nest in the twenty months since work fairly began upon it. Dubois Tooker, Walter Clark and A. Fellows leased a portion of it for one year, and began work in May, 1877. They did not get their shaft down to ore until some months later. Up to January, 1878, and mainly in three months, the actual smelter's yield was $116,133, currency value, or nearly $110,000, coin. This came from 718½ tons of ore, averaging $137.50, and 391 tons that averaged 37½ ounces of silver per ton—the last sold at concentrating works.

In six months ending April 30, 1878, the Tooker leased ground yielded 2,192 tons of ore that sold for $125,151. The average amount received per ton for all ore, high and low grades, was $57.60. The expenses averaged about thirty per cent. of the receipts. The receipts for the month of December were $35,721, and for March $31,376, and the expenses of the latter month were $9,376. Up to May 1, 1878, the lessees cleared about $72,000. The owners' royalty was about $27,000.

The actual yield of silver of the Boulder Nest mine for the year 1878 must have exceeded $230,000, for the receipts from sales of ore were $157,000. The receipts from time of discovery to December 1, 1878, were $214,376.17. The mine may have yielded $400,000 worth of silver to date.

The entire mine averages about 250 ounces of silver per ton for first class, from 100 to 150 for second, and from 30 to 40 ounces for third class. The latter is the most plentiful. So far only the eastern part of the lode has paid.

The White lode enters the Boulder Nest location and lode from the southeast. It has a breadth between granite walls of from twenty-two to twenty-six feet, with varying seams and bodies of ore, but extensive enough wherever opened to insure a heavy production. Several shafts have been sunk and an adit driven, and what is

especially noticeable in the length of ore vein.   Litigation kept the
White idle for a time, but all parts of it eventually passed under one
management.   The ore sold in 1878–9 was valued at over $100,000,
and generally carried from $70 to $350 per ton.   Four men mined
11¼ tons in two weeks, which brought $3,869.   Two and a half
tons contained $2,670.   What is called the Cleary adit has been
driven over 800 feet, having followed the White ore vein for the last
250 feet to its junction with the Boulder Nest lode and workings 366
feet below the surface.   Above this adit to the surface, the ore body
is believed to be continuous, except where a small amount of stoping has been done.   The vein is often large, and carries some very
high grade ore.   A level started from a shaft near the eastern
end of the Cleary adit, and 80 feet deeper, will be driven 800 feet,
or until it reaches the Boulder Nest.

The main shafts of the Boulder Nest and Free America have
lately been deepened, disclosing valuable bodies of ore that are
now being drifted upon and broken down.   Levels are being run
at depths of 500 feet in the former and 550 feet in the latter, and
also at intervals above.   These mines and the White have a total
of more than 2,300 feet of shafting and 4,600 feet of drifts.

The White, Boulder Nest and Free America include four or five
locations, but only two distinct lodes.   Their ore and general
characteristics are much alike, and they dip to the northward.   The
enclosing rock is granite.   So far, the ore has come from against the
hanging wall of the Boulder Nest, but cross-cuts have disclosed a
pay vein on the foot wall.   This may yield as much as the other,
and in parts of the mine supposed to be worked out.   In seventeen
months to March 1, 1879, the yield of the Boulder Nest and Free
America is given at $508,980 currency; an average of 144½ tons
of ore, and $29,940 monthly.   Of this, the Free America gave
31¼ tons monthly, averaging 150 ounces of silver.   The proximity
of the Colorado Central Railroad, and of the Boston and Colorado
ore buying and sampling mill, are advantages not possessed by every
camp.   This ore is very desirable for the copper matte process.

These mines, comprising 5,550 feet of veins, are now the property
of the Red Elephant Mining Company recently organized in New
York with a capital stock of $5,000,000, in 500,000 shares of ten
dollars par value each.   The company comprises many prominent
business men of New York and other localities, with the following

list of officers: Harvey Durand, president; C. T. Liebold, vice-president; J. H. Weston, secretary; and Wm. G. Smith, treasurer. Now that new hoisting machinery has been placed on the mines, and rich bodies of ore of great extent have been discovered in all of the lower workings, there seems to be no reason why regular dividends should not follow for years to come. Few properties have as bright an outlook as this. Some time ago the company working force was increased to 160, and may be 200 when work on the reserves has fairly begun.

The Free America extension embraces 1,500 feet (patented) of the Free America lode immediately east of the Red Elephant Company property. In sinking a shaft 140 feet, and drifting 40 feet, over $28,000 was obtained—one day returning $1,000. Messrs. Weston, Fish and Gilbert are the owners, and are working the mine to a depth of 400 feet from the Free America shaft. A rich vein of ore 18 inches thick has been uncovered. Further east the great Comstock lode, owned by J. G. Gilbert and J. H. Weston, is yielding paying ore in a shaft and intersecting tunnel at depths of 200 and 300 feet.

Empire is located on the northern branch of South Clear Creek, about two miles above where the stream forks, and was built up by the gold diggings on Silver and Colorado Mountains in 1862–'3. Sluicing and stamp milling were extensively carried on in those days and a lively mining camp was the result. In time nearly the whole surface of Silver Mountain was washed over, dug up, and scarred with the operations of the gold hunters. Russell, Majors & Co., S. F. Nuckolls, Charles Martin, Judge H. C. Cowles, J. S. Jones, Dr. Carlton, and others were the leading placer and lode miners. At length much of the property was sold in New York, and companies were organized who operated with more or less success for several years. Up to that time the Great Equator, Silver Mountain, Tenth Legion and Rosecrans had been extremely rich and productive, and the Conqueror, Liebig, Humboldt, Livingston County, Pioneer and Atlantic were noted mines. The Empire placer was also rich and famous. Over a million dollars in gold were mined within a few years.

After years of depression Empire is again the theatre of extensive mining operations. For three years David Ball has made money from his Pioneer lode and sixteen-stamp mill. Placer claims are worked—one of them by hydraulics. The most important enterprise is that of the Silver Mountain groups of lodes, which are consolidated under one ownership, and include 14,400 linear feet of veins. The group on the western slope of Silver Mountain embraces the Great Republic, Colorado State, Grand View, Keystone Picket and Rainbow, and on the eastern slope are the Silver Mountain, S. R. Platt and Great Western.

The Silver Mountain lode has been the largest producer. Its ore occurs in chutes and chimneys found at pretty regular intervals. The first one of these chutes yielded W. H. Russell $66,000 in ninety days of 1863. At one place the ore was 12 feet wide. The Ball shaft chimney paid well, and the Andre shaft gave 200 cords of ore, milling $24,000, in a few months' time. This lode has well-defined walls, save where crossed by a porphyry dike, and often carries from one to two feet of solid pyrites and much wider bodies of mixed gangue, quartz and mineral.

There are several hundred feet of shafts and levels on the Silver Mountain lode, and recent examiners report a great deal of valuable ore in all sections. An engine is at work on one shaft, and sinking and drifting progresses steadily. This entire group of lodes will be worked from this shaft. Sample assays from all parts of the mine return from two to seven ounces of gold, and from four to ten ounces of silver per ton.

The Great Republic is the principal lode of the western group. Two adits are being driven on the lode. The upper one (160 feet above the lower) is 258 feet long—the last 115 feet on a vein of iron and copper pyrites from one to ten feet thick. Much of the ore assays from $20 to $40 in gold, from $5 to $10 in silver, and considerable copper. The Colorado State and Rainbow cross the Great Republic. The Grand View is opened on the surface for 1,000 feet.

The company intends to erect a concentrating mill for handling all but the richer ores. It is believed that 3½ tons of crude ore can be dressed down to one of saleable smelting concentrates. Allowing for the usual percentage of loss, ores containing $30 per ton would return concentrates carrying over $100. Placing the cost of mining at $2, of concentrating at $1 per ton of crude ore, and $3 for railway freight, and the total outlay, smelting included, would be less than $35 per ton, leaving over $60 profit on each ton of concentrates. With a yield of thousands of tons annually of ores of this class the advantages of concentration are apparent.

CHAPTER XVI.

CLEAR CREEK COUNTY MINES—THE GEORGETOWN SILVER DISTRICT—
REPUBLICAN AND DEMOCRAT MOUNTAINS—WHAT HAS BEEN DONE
THERE—THE PELICAN-DIVES SILVER BONANZA—A MONSTER LODE
AND A MINT OF MONEY—STORY OF A GREAT MINING CONTEST—
THE PAY-ROCK, BAXTER, SNOWDRIFT, SILVER PLUME, AND OTHER
MINES.

Between the two forks of South Clear Creek, and extending southward toward Georgetown and westward toward the Continental
Divide, is a spur of the latter. The northern portion of this is
known under the names of Douglas, Columbia, and Colfax mountains,
whose mineral developments are not extensive. Still further south
is Democrat Mountain, overlooking the lower part of Georgetown.
Here are several lodes and groups of veins, some of them noticeable
for the high percentage of silver they carry. Among the principal ones worked at present are the W. B. Astor, Fred. Rogers,
Junction, Lucky Hesperus, Little Emma, and Polar Star, the latter
on a small scale. It is claimed that the ores of some of these lodes
can be treated by raw amalgamation. The entire mountain must
have yielded nearly a million in silver.

The W. B. Astor lode is situated near the summit of Democrat
Mountain. It had been worked to a depth of nearly or quite three
hundred feet in 1868. Its production was quite large for a time, but
work was afterwards suspended. It is again operated extensively.
The total yield is said to have been between sixty and one hundred
thousand dollars. There is one tunnel, 860 feet long. The Matilda
Fletcher has yielded over ten thousand dollars. Little mining
was done on Democrat in the years 1870–72.

In 1874 W. H. Moore sold some properties of this mountain to
Nebraska men, and about that time such rich developments were
made that a great prospecting excitement ensued. The results were
some valuable discoveries, fortunes for a few and good revenues for
many. The main vein and point where the ore-body seemed to
centre was the Junction-Galie lode; but the Fred Rogers, uniting

with the same, was nearly as productive, and there were numbers of parallel and crossing veins, spurs, and feeders between the granite formation that were exceedingly renumerative. Black sulphuret ore was mined from all of these, yielding from five to twelve hundred ounces of silver per ton. The Little Emma doubled those figures. There was a nest of veins in the gangue rock where the granite walls were from forty to sixty feet apart. The Lucky Hesperus yielded a great deal of money, and is doing so still. The Rogers has yielded over $200,000, currency value, mainly since 1874, and the entire Junction group of veins something like $600,000. Water from the snows of this timbered region is very troublesome, and has stopped or impeded work, and caused considerable tunneling. At the main producing point these lodes have been worked to depths of from four to five hundred feet.

The Junction is one of the oldest locations on Democrat Mountain, having been discovered in 1867, and application made for patent in 1873. There are two surface locations patented; the Junction, 800 feet, and the Galie, 1,590 feet in length; the Junction patent being wholly west of the discovery, and the Galie, 90 feet west and 1,500 feet east of its discovery shaft. But little work was done on the property prior to 1874, when systematic developments were commenced. The developments consist of three main openings; lower adit, 1,000 feet long; upper adit, 700 feet long, and the whim shaft, 200 feet deep, that is connected with the upper adit at a point 530 feet from its mouth. The work at present going forward is at the upper adit, where three parties of lessees are at work, and driving the lower tunnel and cross-cutting for the south wall of the vein. A cross-cut has been driven 35 feet in crevice matter, which is enough to show the lode to be one of the mammoth fissure veins. So far the mine has only been worked for the solid ore veins, and no attention has been given to the large bodies of concentrating ore that are exposed at various points in the mine, which can be made valuable only by the aid of machinery to dress them, but with a concentrating mill conveniently located would be of considerable value. The dump at the upper adit is estimated to contain an average of thirty ounces per ton.

Further west are the Silver Cloud and Queen of the West. The latter paid largely at one time, and yielded $60,000 altogether, but is now idle. A tunnel, already several hundred feet long, is being driven for drainage and working purposes for the Silver Cloud; this lode yielded about $40,000, currency value, in 1876, '7, '8.

The Polar Star mine was for a long time one of the most productive lodes on Democrat mountain; its total product to date is reported at $160,000, currency value. The lode was discovered in 1872, and several thousand feet of shafts and tunnels have been driven. The owners state that 314 tons of ore had an average value of $213.22 per ton, and 200 tons an average of $173.75, and that the yield of 1874 was $25,766; that of 1876 was $23,263, and that of 1877 was $15,000. Only a small part of the property is worked at present.

Republican Mountain has probably produced more money than any other around Georgetown. It rises almost perpendicularly from the streets of that city, and likewise from those of Silver Plume, some two miles to the northwest, and extends from Democrat to Sherman mountains. Near its western extremity is the great Pelican-Dives group of lodes, whose aggregate production for seven or eight years mounts up into the millions. The principal lodes worked on this mountain at present are the Pelican, Dives, Dunkirk, Baxter, Pay Rock, Vulcan, Elm City, Silver Cloud, Edward Everett, Morning Star, Red Bird, Lebanon Tunnel Lode Number Five, and several veins intersected by the Diamond Tunnel, and owned by the tunnel company.

On this same mountain are other lodes that have been productive at times, such as the James Guthrie, Ben Hardin, Elijah Hise and White, located by John T. Harris in the days of the first silver excitement, and the Corry City, Loretta, South America, and Caledonia. Still more noted are the Snowdrift and Silver Plume, that yielded largely five and ten years ago.

The Pelican and Dives, until recently the most famous of Colorado silver mines, are located on the southern slope, and near the western end of Republican Mountain. The vein outcroppings are about seven hundred feet above, and in full view of Silver Plume, which dates its birth from the opening of these great ore deposits. The lodes were discovered in 1868, but for two years Streeter and McCunniff did not think the Pelican worth recording. The Dives produced little until 1871.

That same year the McCunniff brothers started to do a little work on the Pelican, with no expectation of finding anything very valuable. They were astonished at the size and richness of the vein that

steadily developed with their labor.   Nothing like it had previously
been encountered in the district, taking the great quantity of ore
into consideration, notwithstanding the fact that a Terrible, Equator, and Brown had been developed.   In a few short months up to
November, 1871, the coin value of the ore sold had amounted to

SILVER PLUME AND THE DIVES-PELICAN GROUP OF MINES.

$121,172.28.   The vein or series of veins were found to be of great
size, and no such thing as a wall on one side.

Then began the great war and almost endless litigation between the
Dives and Pelican.   As the yield of both mines grew larger and larger

the conflict became something like a battle of giants, in which the services of a small army of fighting men, leasers, and guards were secured, along with nearly all of the leading lawyers of the State, and some from the Pacific Slope. Suits and counter suits, injunctions and counter injunctions, followed each other in rapid succession, and much of the enormous revenues that came out of the mines went to the lawyers or were divided among supernumeraries and lessees. The latter, on account of the risks taken, mined only on very liberal terms for themselves. Some of them made fortunes; for the vein was from one to seventeen feet wide, and worth from $40 to $800 a ton.

In 1874 the richest spot of ground held by the Dives or Perdue Company was enjoined. Before that the Pelican men had been attaching the ore for a time, until the others evaded attachment by disposing of it on Sundays. This was done for several successive weeks, and on the last Sabbath before the injunction came it is claimed that 65,000 worth of ore went out of the Dives mine. The lessees of the richest piece of ground cleared $42,000 that week.

At last the upper part of the great bonanzas had been mainly worked out, the owners had become exhausted with the long and costly struggle, and the lawyers and outsiders having reaped most of the harvest that should have gone into the owners' pockets, the latter concluded to sign a truce, "take a breathing spell," and suspend hostilities for a time. But the yield from that time forward was much smaller than before. Jacob Sneider, of the Pelican, had been killed by a lessee of a part of the Dives. McMurdy, the head of the latter mine, died some time after. Some of the Pelican owners were unable to escape financial difficulties, and were finally sold out at sheriff's sale—W. A. Hamill, who then controlled the Dives, getting the property. These mines afford examples of the great changes occurring in mining countries. Away back in 1871, before the value of the Dives was known, Hamill sold that lode for $2,000 to John H. McMurdy, who borrowed $200 to make the first payment. The latter organized the Perdue Company on the west 500 feet. Hamill was without money in those days, and was vainly endeavoring to secure his interest in the Terrible, but the English company laughed at his claims. In 1874 he became manager of the then productive Dives. This enabled him to open his Silver Ore lode into the Terrible mine workings, to enjoin the latter from work, and finally to consolidate almost the entire side of Brown Mountain.

Afterwards Hamill sold the East Terrible for $100,000, bought in the Pelican, and once more secured the Dives.

The yield of the Pelican and Dives for six years up to 1878, previous and subsequent products not included, was as follows:

PELICAN MINE.

	Receipts.	Expenses.	Profits.
Jan. 1, 1872, to Jan. 1, 1877....	$902,905	$331,122	$571,783
1877.........................	114,471	34,098	80,373
Total..................$1,017,376		$365,220	$652,156

DIVES AND PERDUE CO.

	Receipts.	Expenses.	Profits.
Jan. 1, 1872, to Jan. 1, 1877....	$676,377	$185,600	$490,777
1877.........................	97,500	42,500	55,000
Total Dives.............. $773,877		$228,100	$545,777

Total Pelican and Dives yield......................$1,791,253

Add to this yield of both mines previous to 1872, and for the
    past year and a half, estimated at.................... $170,000

Total Receipts would be...........................$1,961,253

The probable excess of contents of ore over what was paid
    for it, should add $650,000 to the above, making total
    silver product in eight years............. ....$2,611,253
Additional product in 1879, probably..................... 100,000

Making total silver product of less than nine years.....$2,711,253

Of this sum the Pelican probably yielded $1,450,000, and the Dives the remainder. Their combined yield in 1874 is said to have exceeded $650,000 worth of silver, and nearly as much in 1875.

Early in 1880, General Francis J. Marshall, James M. Ormes and others organized the Pelican and Dives Mining Company in New York, which came into possession of these consolidated properties March 28th. Thus is inaugurated one of the grandest mining operations of the time. The capital stock has a par value of $5,000,000 in 500,000 ten-dollar shares. These are mainly taken by leading officials of the great telegraph, telephone and express companies, and other prominent individuals. The officers are Norvin Green, president, who holds the same office in the Western Union Telegraph,

Henry S. Russell and Theodore N. Vail, vice-presidents, George C. Wilde, secretary, and R. H. Rochester, treasurer. The trustees are Norvin Green, Henry S. Russell, General F. J. Marshall, J. H. Munson, Henry B. Plant, president of the Southern Express Company, I. C. Babcock, treasurer of Adams' Express, Assistant Postmaster General T. J. Brady, A. B. Chandler, president, and W. C. Humstone, general superintendent Atlantic and Pacific Telegraph, and D. I. Carson, Theodore N. Vail, and James M. Ormes of the Bell Telephone Companies ; Clarence Cary and J. F. Manning, counsel.

This mine, or its patented territory, contains an aggregation of several veins, within the walls of one great lode or fissure, and these veins have been explored by shafts, levels and tunnels, to the amount of several thousands of feet. The Diamond tunnel intersects the Dives at a depth of over 600 feet. The amount of ore exposed in the lower workings, some four or five hundred feet below the surface, is very large. Previous to the late sale, lessees were working in different localities, paying twenty per cent. royalty. One piece of ground yielded in one month, low grade ore, whose concentrates gave $11,000. Most localities produce ore worth from $80 to $600 a ton, as in former times, when the output was treated in both American and European works.

For a long period of time the Pelican yielded an average of 240 ounces of silver for all ore handled, and both properties, especially the Dives, yielded much ore, milling from 700 ounces down. A rich vein was lately found in the Dives. The new workings there and elsewhere are said to be from 30 inches to $7\frac{1}{2}$ feet wide. The indications are that rich ore will be found as plentifully as in former times; and as work can be pushed without interruption and to better advantage than before, the yield should be correspondingly larger. A depth of 1,000 feet will be attained as soon as possible.

The Pelican Company has $150,000 cash paid in for working capital, and is controlled by men of great enterprise and wealth, who operate it on a most extensive scale. Practical miners manage the property, and the best skilled labor and machinery is secured—all of which the company's ample means permit of. There will be three main working shafts to the mine, and concentrating works will be erected or purchased. With a mine already in pay, and developments progressing large products and profits seem assured.

The Dunkirk is considered the eastern extension of the Dives.

The shaft, finely equipped with hoisting machinery, is nearly, 500 feet deep. Charles H. Morris operated this property for a long period for the Herman Company. A good vein has been developed.

The Pay Rock is one of the leading mines in this mountain, having produced altogether some $450,000 up to 1880, or more than any other, excepting the Dives and Pelican. The lode was discovered in 1872, and has usually yielded about $60,000 per annum. The mine comprises the three regular veins of the Pay Rock lode (which diverge from one another with depth) and the Hopewell, —all parallel—and a cross vein called the Silver Point. These veins have been intersected by several tunnels driven at right angles into the mountain, one below another. A pump and steam hoister are used for workings below the lower tunnel. Levels extend east and west hundreds of feet on all of the veins. These show ore of nearly all grades. From $40 up to $800 a ton are common returns. The Pay Rock Company, of New York, came into possession of the mine in 1879. Before that, the property had generally been worked by numerous lessees, who often made much money.

The Baxter is a very rich and profitable lode, located below the Dives. Its lessees employ forty or fifty men, and turn out about $60,000 per annum. The ore generally yields from $200 to $300 per ton, but some goes as high as $1,000 and even $1,500. A part of the mine is worked through the Diamond Tunnel. Total yield to 1880, about $360,000. The Snowdrift and Silver Plume mines yielded largely in 1869–70–71. The Snowdrift yielded $96,316.80 currency value in 1870. The Elm City produces one-thousand-dollar ore.

The Diamond Tunnel enters Republican Mountain about a quarter of a mile, and intersects the Dives, Baxter, and other lodes.

The Lebanon Tunnel is owned by a company of the same name, and has been driven into Republican Mountain some nine hundred feet; the location is between Silver Plume and Georgetown, and the objective point the belt of lodes that includes the Hardin, Guthrie, White, and others. So far, eight lodes have been intersected, several of which are valuable, and one called Tunnel Lode Number Five has paid steadily for years. The Prentice and Hardin lodes, owned by the same company, have been worked from the surface. Opposite the mouth of the tunnel is a concentrating and sampling mill. The tunnel will cut some lodes from 1,000 to 2,000 feet deep. J. G. Pohle is general manager.

CHAPTER XVII.

CLEAR CREEK COUNTY MINES—SHERMAN, BROWN, McCLELLAN, AND LEAVENWORTH MOUNTAINS—THE DUNDERBERG-TERRIBLE GROUP OF MINES—MILLIONS IN SILVER—THE EQUATOR AND COLORADO CENTRAL GROUP—MINING IN CLOUD LAND—THE STEVENS AND BAKER—SOME LONG TUNNELS.

Sherman Mountain is immediately west of Republican. In reality this is all one continuous range, in whcih ravines of no great depth serve as boundaries. Cherokee Gulch lies between the mountains just mentioned, and further west Brown Gulch is the dividing line of Sherman and Brown Mountains. All of these elevations are very abrupt and rugged and contain many nearly perpendicular silver-bearing veins whose course is almost parallel with the creek and valley below.

But few localities contain as much mineral wealth as Sherman Mountain. Here are a large number of famous veins, of which the Dunderberg, East Terrible, Sub-Treasury, Backbone, Mendota, Cap Wells, Eagle Bird, Mammoth, Glasgow, Corry City, and a few others, are actively worked. Not long ago work was temporarily suspended on such noted and once-productive lodes as the Frostburg, Phœnix, Coldstream, Cashier, Silver Cloud, and Cascade. The Mammoth and Glasgow have been worked steadily for many years.

The Phœnix and Coldstream lode or lodes are situated on the eastern portion of Sherman Mountain, approaching and underlying Cherokee Gulch. They began to pay in 1871, and litigation and bitter contests, in which one or two men lost their lives, were carried on by the owners of the respective properties for several years. The total yield of both mines must have exceeded $300,000. Mill runs gave from one to sixteen hundred ounces of silver. The Coldstream was at first called the Maine. It yielded in the first eight months of work $64,100, at a cost of little over $14,000. The ore vein is argentiferous galena, containing more or less gray copper, ruby silver, iron and copper pyrites.

Twelve years ago the Burleigh Tunnel enterprise was inaugurated under the auspices of the inventor of the Burleigh drill. The design was to penetrate Sherman Mountain and furnish an ore and drainage outlet for lodes outcropping one or two thousand feet above, and to explore for blind lodes. Work fairly began in 1868, and has been prosecuted at intervals down to the present year. It is now the longest tunnel in the State, having been driven forward over 2,300 feet. Several veins have been intersected, including the Rider, I. Phillips, and New Era. The latter yielded ore in paying quantities that carried from 60 to 70 per cent. of lead and a low value in silver. Colonel Ivers Phillips, an old Massachusetts railroad man, is general manager of this tunnel enterprise.

The Dunderberg, East Terrible, Sub-Treasury, Silver Chain, Muldoon, and Elephant, embracing 7,900 feet of mineral veins, were recently purchased by the Dunderberg Mining Company, organized in New York, with a capital stock of a million and a half in ten dollar shares. The East Terrible is that part of the Terrible lode that was not sold to the English company in 1870. It extends from the main shaft in Brown Gulch, used by both properties, eastward in Sherman Mountain to where the Dunderberg begins. The latter is the same vein further east, the location including 3,000 feet. The Sub-Treasury, supposed to be on the same vein, is still further east. This has occasionally shown sixty ounce galena ore for a width of two feet. It is said that $300,000 has been paid for East Terrible ore. The first class averaged about $500 a ton, and the second class $150.

No work of any importance was done on the Dunderberg until 1877. In December of that year George Tyler and Mr. Antoine, lessees, struck a very rich body of mineral, similar to that of the Terrible. The mine was soon after the most productive and profitable in the mountains, and has paid largely up to the present time. It appears that in a little over four months, to April, 1878, there were sold 474¼ tons, bringing $112,528.97, at an average price of $237 per ton. Four hundred and fourteen fathoms were extracted, with a net yield of $297 per fathom, and the average yield of one foot of drift, six feet high, was $49.50.

Hayes, Tyler & Co. received $255,000 for ore sold in 1878, and the total receipts from the time this ore-body was discovered to March 1, 1879, a period of a little over fourteen months, were

$308,468 ; mining cost but 21 per cent. of returns, the largest profit of that time in northern Colorado. Development work, introducing new hoisting machinery, and building a thirty-ton wet concentrator occupied the year ending May, 1880. Superintendent J. Warren Brown has placed the mine in fine producing condition. The nine advancing levels (200 to 600 feet deep) all show ore. The lower level will strike the property's eastern end 1,600 feet below surface. Low grade ores, of which there are 1,500 tons on hand, are dressed and the concentrates sold with the richer mineral.

The Terrible-Dunderberg fissure pierces the granite nearly vertically, with a course east of north and west of south. It has a crevice of from four to six feet, carrying a vein from one to eight inches wide, that averages from two to five hundred ounces of silver per ton. This vein carries argentiferous galena, gray copper, and sulphides of silver, and the gangue that makes up the remainder of the crevice is porphyry and quartz. A vein of this character has been traced pretty continuously for a distance of two thousand feet in Brown and Sherman mountains.

Brown Mountain has been one of the leading producers in the county ever since silver mining became prominent. The more prominent lodes are the Terrible, Silver Ore, Brown, Chelsea Beach, and others belonging to the Colorado United Mining Company, together with the Duncan, Hercules-Roe-Seven-Thirty, Shiveley, Owasco, Brick Pomeroy, Atlantic, and some others, all actively worked.

Previous to September, 1870, the Terrible lode had yielded $270,000, coin value. The product of 1872 was $168,625 from sales of ore, and the actual yield of 1874 was $203,000. Up to the close of 1876 the Silver Ore is said to have yielded $140,000. The latter and the English company property must have yielded a round million from time of discovery up to the close of 1877. The yield of these and of the East Terrible to the present time is estimated at $1,500.-000. The Colorado United Mining Company have been turning out from one hundred to one hundred and fifty thousand dollars per annum from its Terrible and Hamill and Chaffee group of mines.

The underground workings of many of the company lodes are very extensive. Work is progressing in both the Silver Ore and Terrible shafts—the lower workings of the latter being 650 feet deep, and of the former 500, and 170 feet deeper than the Union Tunnel. This part of the property, called the West Terrible, gives employment to over one hundred men. Lessees and employees of the company elsewhere foot up as many more. The Union tunnel is 570 feet long to the Terrible lode, and the Silver Ore tunnel is 900 feet long.

At the foot of the mountain are the old Brown Reducing Works, no longer used for smelting, and the concentrating mill, where the low grade ores are rendered available. This mill concentrates about twenty tons of ore daily, that averages about $17 a ton. Twelve tons are concentrated down to one composed of one-third galena, milling at the rate of 250 ounces, and two-thirds zinc-blende, milling at the rate of 125 ounces of silver per ton.

The Hercules, Roe, and Seven Thirty lodes, all crossing or nearly parallel veins at a point in Brown Gulch, are owned by a Denver company. They have been traced for long distances into either mountain, and pierced with a cross-cut tunnel and many levels, winzes, and shafts. Work is being prosecuted steadily, and the owners report the property quite profitable. The total yield from the beginning approaches $230,000. There are no less than ten leasing parties in various parts of this great property, and a fair amount of ore is in sight. The receipts for ore sold in May, 1879, were $2,466, and the ore taken out of different places gave the following yields per ton: 318 ounces of silver, 283 ounces, 163 ounces, 175 ounces, and 600 in one place and 300 in two others.

The Shiveley lode has produced nearly or quite $60,000. It was purchased by the Equitable Mining Company not long ago. The Duncan, Atlantic, and Pacific are all rich veins. On Hanna Mountain the Silver Cloud and Specie are worked.

Kelso Mountain is close beside Irwin's Peak, and opposite the circling McClellan ridge, with a valley and fork of South Clear Creek intervening. Richard Irwin, John Baker, and Fletcher Kelso prospected here in the summer of 1865, after having left the swarm of silver hunters that had congregated on McClellan mountain. They were so fortunate as to find a great vein that paid largely, sold for big figures, nearly broke up a company, and afterwards made money for lessees. The lode took the name of Baker, the mountain on which it was located that of Kelso, and a neighboring peak that has but few equals in height in the country, was named after Irwin. Some other discoveries were made in this section. In recent years the Brooklyn, since known as the Diamond

Joe, has yielded a great deal of rich ore, and is said to be quite remunerative.

Eastward from the solitudes of Gray's Peak extends the long elevated ridge known as McClellan Mountain. The side sloping towards Argentine Pass and Creek is smooth and grass-clad, but that facing Irwin and Kelso is as rugged and perpendicular as it well can be. Amid these granite cliffs of McClellan, far above timber line and nearly 12,000 feet above sea level, is the famous Stevens Mine. The sight of this, perched as it is a thousand feet above the valley in a seemingly inaccessible position, causes the Gray's Peak tourist to wonder how it was ever discovered and how it is worked. Closer inspection shows a tramway fastened to the mountain side and leading to the cabins and tunnels that appear above. One would think the dauntless prospector who found this lode must have come over by way of the southern slope, descending from the summit, or else have discovered "float ore" and "blossom" at the base of the mountain, and thereafter "lit" upon the vein in some unaccountable manner.

The Stevens has been worked pretty steadily for nearly twelve years. Long ago a kind of aerial tramway and ropeway had been built for transportation. In 1877, a substantial tramway was constructed to replace one partially demolished. This is 1,050 feet long, and has a superstructure resting on trestle-work high enough to prevent snow accumulations from blockading the ascending and descending cars. Beside this is a hand-rail and in its bed-timbers are cleats, to enable the miners to ascend and descend. Among the savage rocks at the upper terminus is the mouth of the tunnel and an ore house, with apparatus for operating the "tram," and for miners' and storage quarters. From this cars descend with four or five tons of ore on a trip, and return laden with provisions, powder, steel, charcoal, timbers, and lumber. From the ore house down on the edge of the valley wagons convey the ore to Georgetown during the summer months, and sleds are used at other times to Bakerville.

The Belmont and International on McClellan Mountain turned out together $100,000 about 1870-1.

Leavenworth Mountain extends eastward and southward from McClellan for a distance of several miles, and breaks off suddenly at the head of the valley of Georgetown. This has been one of the richest and most productive localities around the "Silver Queen."

Here is a cluster of celebrated lodes that have added largely to the county's product, and most of them have made fortunes, or a good deal of ready money, for those connected with them. The Colorado Central, Equator, Kirtley, Ocean Wave, O. K., Argentine, Steamboat, Gilpin, Alpha, Gates, S. J. Tilden, Ni Wott, and some others, are all actively worked and all said to be paying. On the southern slope of this mountain is one of the most important groups of lodes in the State, and below is the village of Silver Dale.

Among the early operators here was General F. J. Marshall, who has ever been one of the leading miners and ore shippers of the district. He developed a number of lodes, such as the Compass and Square, Robinson, Reynolds, and others, and started the Marshall and other tunnels, designed to pierce the mountain through to its northerly slope and discover and work the many veins of this belt. The results have been so satisfactory that an immense amount of ore and silver have been produced. The operations of General Marshall and of the Marshall Tunnel Company have led to many important discoveries and to a yield of nearly half a million in bullion. A half dozen lodes are now worked in this combination. The underground excavations embrace over 7,000 feet of workings. The Marshall Tunnel is 1,300 feet long, and 9,382 feet above the sea, and the upper tunnels are from 350 feet to 500 feet long. A score of shafts, and cross-cuts have been driven and long levels extended therefrom, at a cost of $160,000, and nearly half as much more for the extraction of $160,000 worth of ore. This does not include the returns of several lodes worked by the same manager.

In 1872 many men were making money by collecting and selling the float ore in the "slide" of Leavenworth Mountain. This led to much prospecting and to W. P. Lynn's discovery of the famous vein called the Colorado Central. Weaver, Shepard and others secured a lease of this, and all made fortunes in a year or two. The ore sometimes milled up in the thousands, and portions of it were so rich in lead and silver that it would not pulverize under the stamps. Marshall, Martine & Hall paid these lessees $68,918.23 for ore in 1873 alone. Up to 1876 the vein had yielded receipts to the amount of $150,000, and had been opened to a depth of 200 feet.

About the close of 1876 some leasers, engaged in driving a crosscut from some of the interior tunnel properties, discovered one of the richest veins of ore ever developed. This was named the S. J.

Tilden, and yielded over $100,000 in 1877, the first year of production. Some of the ore brought from four to six thousand dollars a ton, and the average for a long time was about twelve hundred. The discoverers paid a royalty equal to one-third of the gross receipts.

The Colorado Central Consolidated Mining Company has lately been organized on the lodes and tunnels just described, of which the Colorado Central mine and the Marshall Tunnel are the most prominent features. This is one of the most important combinations ever perfected in the Rocky Mountains and is destined to cut an important figure in the future silver product of the State. Reliable authorities estimate an annual yield after a moderate amount of development has been done of half a million per annum. The contiguous locality of the veins, their unusual richness, and the facilities afforded by the tunnel as an ore outlet ought to render a very large proportion of that sum clear profit. The foundation of all sound mining properties is of course both quantity and quality of ore. This group of veins possesses both of these requisites. The average receipts of all ore shipped from the Colorado Central for one year was over $500 per ton, aggregating a yield of some $80,000. Before the advent of reduction works or railways at Georgetown the Compass and Square produced ore so rich that the average selling price was nearly fifty cents a pound, or nearly $1,000 a ton. This property is now included in Tunnel lode No. 5 and the Robeson. The O. K. has shown remarkably rich mineral in large quantities.

The Colorado Central is one of the great mother lodes of the State. Within its walls, which are over seventy feet apart, are four (and in one level five) distinct ore veins or pay-streaks, varying from a few inches to one foot in thickness. A chimney of ore extending from the surface down to and below the lower workings shows a larger quantity of ore standing in the reserves than has already been taken out. Yet, one of several ore buyers alone obtained $119,485.59 from Colorado Central ore. Recently this mine was making a better showing than any in that district. The yield in 1879 exceeded $100,000, most of which came out in the latter part of the year from patented Colorado Central ground, on which work had been suspended by reason of litigation until the courts awarded it to Gen. Marshall and associates. In two months 316¾ tons of ore yielded

75,926 ounces of silver, or $85,417. The average return per ton was over 269 ounces for one month and 209 for the other.

The ore of this lode consists principally of argentiferous galena, zinc-blende and gray copper. While the average value is high, the veins are often enriched by streaks and bunches of ruby ore, carrying silver at the rate of two or three thousand dollars a ton. This grade is sometimes found several inches thick.

The Colorado Central Cons. company is organized with a capital stock of $3,000,000 in 300,000 ten-dollar shares. The officers are Paul Lichtenstein, president; H. F. Verhuven, secretary and treasurer; Paul O. d'Esterhazy, assistant secretary; and Paul Lichtenstein, William H. Guion, Charles C. Dodge, H. R. Baltzer, D. C. Wilcox, James C. Parrish, C. F. Tag, George W. Hall and George Turnbull, are trustees.

The consolidation embraces the following: the Marshall, Robeson, Thompson, and O. K. tunnels, and the Colorado Central, or Tunnel Lode No. 5, the Robeson and the W. B. Astor, Bull Dog, Reynolds' tunnel lodes numbers two to ten inclusive, and the O. K., Tilden, Wash Lewis, Henry, and Excelsior lodes—in all 19,000 feet of lodes, secured by government titles, or patents applied for. All of these are valuable properties, and some of them have been known far and wide as prominent mines of the State. The design is to push the Marshall Tunnel, now 1,300 feet long, clear through Leavenworth Mountain. It will pass 1,060 feet below the summit, and will be 3,912 feet long when completed. Several known veins of the company will be intersected and others of great value will, undoubtedly, be discovered.

Work will be pushed in all directions from this time forward, and a concentrating mill will be erected below the mines where the fork of Clear Creek affords an ample water supply. When this tunnel and contemplated developments are perfected, it is believed the consolidated properties will be worth many millions.

The Kirtley has been one of the most prominent mines of the district since first opened. Some years ago several Georgetown men began to drive a tunnel into Leavenworth Mountain, with the hope of discovering mineral veins. In time the Gates lode helped to repay the outlay, but the enterprise did not become a remunerative one until the Kirtley was intersected in October, 1877. This has paid handsome profits from the start. The developments are the

Kirtley tunnel, driven 700 feet to cut the lode, over 200 feet of shafts and 2,000 feet of levels run, and some 200 feet of "upraises." The mine is finely timbered, and its levels and tunnels are supplied with the usual railway tracks. The lode is wide and regular, and the ore vein varies from an inch to two feet in thickness. From four to eight inches of solid ore of high grade are often encountered. The ore as assorted generally yields as follows : firstclass, $500 to $600 per ton; second class, $300 to $400 a ton ; third class, $150 to $160 per ton. Outside of the pay vein are lowgrade material and gangue. The mine had yielded up to April, 1880, about $250,000 worth of silver. The ore standing in the mine and exposed by the various workings, could not be exhausted in less than a year and a half or two years. S. C. Bennett is superintendent, and he and Kirtley, Martine and Roberts embrace all but one or two of the owners.

The Equator is a wonderfully large and rich vein, but has not been worked as steadily or extensively as its value warrants. This was the leading producer of Clear Creek county for a time in 1868. Up to 1869 the yield was $68,600. The ore sold at from one to five hundred dollars a ton. The main shaft was carried down some 400 feet, but for reasons best known to its Chicago and Colorado owners, mining was not continued for years after 1870 except by tributors. In 1878 work began on an extensive scale, and one of the best ore bodies ever mined in the country was developed. There was a seam of ruby silver ore several inches thick, that is said to have yielded from one to five thousand dollars per ton, while the main portion of the mineral ran in the hundreds. It is reported that the lessee of this ground took out $40,000 in one month.

Anglo Saxon and Griffith mountains rise abruptly from the south side of Georgetown Valley. Here are several high grade veins. The Anglo Saxon caused much excitement when first worked in 1867, on account of its extremely rich ore. Some yielded among the thousands, and there were pieces of nearly pure silver. It has paid well at times since then. The Saxon Extension, Pickwick and Summit, are yielding very rich mineral. The Magnet yielded $50,000 up to 1875, and the Sequel is quite profitable. A tunnel nearly 1,000 feet long is being driven to intersect the Comet lode 450 feet deep.

CHAPTER XVIII.

LEADVILLE—CALIFORNIA GULCH AND ITS EARLY HISTORY—DISCOVERY
OF CARBONATES—THE SILVER AND LEAD BONANZAS—THE
FOUNDING AND GROWTH OF THE MAGIC CITY—THE ERA OF
GOLD AND THE DAYS OF CARBONATES— LUCK IN LEADVILLE—
THE DAYS OF 'FORTY-NINE REPEATED IN 'SEVENTY-NINE.

Late in the spring of 1860 a band of Gilpin county gold hunters
crossed the Park range of mountains and entered a heavily timbered
ravine, which they called California Gulch. They panned the surface dirt for gold and found it rich beyond expectation. The
reports that spread abroad brought in a continuous stream of prospectors, and the locality was soon alive with men. The original
discoverers secured two hundred feet up and down the stream, and
those who came after were allowed one hundred feet, until the
gulch was pre-empted for 33,000 feet, or nearly its entire length.

There was almost a continuous street bordering the stream, and
skirting the bases of the hills, but there were two points that were
centres of trade and traffic. One of these was at the place where
the hills break away towards the present site of Leadville, and since
called Old Oro. A few of the log structures of 1860 are still
standing as landmarks of the olden times. The other business
point, the Oro of to-day, was two and a half miles further up
the gulch. The last has continued to be a place of more or less
importance up to the present time, partly on account of the subsequent discovery of the Printer Boy and other gold veins.

Parts of the gulch were fabulously rich, but the water supply
was limited. This was used over and over again by each successive
claim owner, and by the time it reached the lower part of the
district was of the consistency of liquid mud. The sluice-box,
"long tom," and "rocker" were all used, and although difficulty was experienced in handling the dirt, the returns have seldom
been equaled in any country. Some claims yielded over a thousand dollars a day, and one firm is said to have taken out one
hundred thousand dollars in sixty days.

tive men believed was produced, although some enterprising reporters of the present time are doubling up the original estimates every few months, and in a way that may soon result in a total greater than the entire production of Colorado.

The camp was "pretty dead," as the "old-timers" would say, in 1868, when the development of the Printer Boy lode began. This was so remunerative that quite an excitement sprang up, much prospecting was done, and several gold veins located. The Printer Boy was the only very profitable mine worked; this showed an immense body of soft quartz that was very rich in gold. It was not long until a twenty-five-stamp mill was erected, and the Philadelphia company that was operating this and the great mine ought to have made a great deal of money. Up to 1875 the yield had exceeded a quarter of a million from work carried on about half of the time during six years. Previous to these gold lode discoveries in California Gulch, some profitable mining of a similar character had been inaugurated some seventeen miles distant, and near Granite; this began in 1866, and continued for two or three years before the surface pockets were exhausted so as to cause a suspension of work.

In the years succeeding 1871 some attempts at ore treatment were made at Granite, and a few discoveries were made thirty miles north, near the headwaters of the Tennessee fork of the Arkansas. One of these, called the Homestake, was of great size, and was rich in lead but poor in silver. Its promising character, and the result of ore shipments to the Golden Smelting Works, with the known presence of silver-lead veins among the hills east of the Arkansas, led to the building of a smelter near the junction of California Gulch and the Arkansas river. The place was called Malta, and the Malta smelting works fired up and did some business in the fall of 1876, and then remained idle until partly built over a year and a half later.

In 1874, W. H. Stevens, a wealthy Michigan and Colorado miner, came over from Park county, in company with A. B. Wood, and began to construct a twelve-mile ditch for the California Gulch placer claims that they had purchased. The plan was to bring in a sufficient water supply to permit of hydraulic mining and the cheap handling of the unworked gravel banks that bordered the stream. The headwaters of the Arkansas were the source of supply, and several summers were required to complete this great enterprise of the organization known as the Oro Ditch and Fluming Company. The first full season's work was put in on the placers in the summer of 1878.

Experience proves that, although these Colorado mountains have been annually overrun by restless hordes of prospectors, who have brought to light some marvelous revelations, the mineral wealth that underlies them has been but indefinitely comprehended. California Gulch had been occupied for a decade and a half, and had been worked over until millions of gold had been extracted, and yet close by an apparently exhaustless treasury of the valuable metals had lain embedded, unknown and untouched, until within the past two or three years.

During all the time that gulch mining had been going on in California district, the miners had suffered much inconvenience by reason of the great weight of the boulders they were obliged to move over and over in the creek. None of them knew, or stopped to investigate, the character of this heavy dirt they were obliged to handle. Messrs. Stevens and Wood found it to be carbonate of lead, carrying silver, but did not make their discovery known until they were in a fair way to secure government titles to nine claims. These were taken up lengthways along what they considered the crest or apex of the lodes, and each comprised 1,500 feet by 300, or thereabouts. The territory crossed California Gulch and extended high up on the hills. The name of the principal locations commencing at the south were, the Dome, Rock, Stone, Lime, Bull's Eye, and Iron. The ore was first found in place in the Rock claim, where it was over ten feet thick. It was rich in lead, but carried only a small amount of silver. A Mr. Durham claimed to have discovered carbonates prior to this, in sinking a shaft on the Oro La Plata lode.

For several years Maurice Hayes was conducting an assay office at Oro, and he and his brother were mining and prospecting extensively. They made some of the earliest carbonate of lead locations in the district, and were firm believers in the ultimate development of good mines outside of those then opened. As to who were the original discoverers or first locaters of carbonates the writer does not pretend to decide.

The first strike that was considered exceptionally good was that made by the Gallagher brothers, on the same hill as the Iron, but

CHESTNUT STREET, LEADVILLE.

nearer Stray Horse Gulch. But even here they were well-nigh discouraged before carbonates rich and plentiful enough were found to insure a profit. This claim was called the Camp Bird, and in the same fall and winter (1876–7) the Adlaide, Pine, and Charleston were "staked."

For quite a time previous to 1877 A. R. Meyer had been purchasing ores in Park and Lake counties for the St. Louis Smelting and Refining Company with headquarters at Alma. In April of that year the prospective production of the Rock, Camp Bird, and other claims, led him to establish sampling works on the present site of Leadville. A month later the Saint Louis Smelting Company began to erect a smelter, and had a blast furnace in operation in October. To insure an ore supply a contract was made with Stevens and Wood to furnish one thousand tons of ore from the Rock mine. Before that had been entirely delivered such development had taken place, and so many discoveries had been made, that the only difficulty was in handling what was brought to both sampling and smelting works. The latter were called the Harrison Reduction Works, after the president of the company, Edwin F. Harrison.

Late in June, 1877, Charles Mater came up from Granite and started the first building on the original town site of Leadville, and opened out a stock of groceries. Several cabins were completed before Mater began to sell goods. In the meantime splendid mines were beginning to be developed in the neighboring hills, and settlers were slowly drifting in from the older camps of the State. H. A. W. Tabor, who had conducted a small store for many years up the gulch at Oro, brought a stock of goods to Leadville in this same summer of 1877.

About this time A. B. Wood sold his interest in the nine claims before mentioned to L. Z. Leiter, of the great Chicago dry goods firm of Field, Leiter & Co., for $40,000. The true value of the Iron lode was then unknown, and the low grade Rock mine was considered the best of the lot. The purchaser would hardly sell for a million to-day. In the fall of 1877, the former claim began to be worked extensively, and proved to be of immense value. The Camp Bird had been counted the best mine, but was then distanced by the Iron, which came to the front, and, more than any other property, gave the district its first great fame. It maintained the lead up to the time of the Fryer Hill developments in the latter half of 1878.

In the fall of 1877 several hundred men were in the district—most of them prospecting or sinking prospecting shafts, but the amount of mining done was considerable. The ore shipments were steadily increasing in volume, and a vast amount of low grade mineral was mined for which no market was afforded. It was becoming more and more evident that the mineral wealth of California district was of immense extent. Mines were being developed on every hand, notwithstanding the fact that it was necessary to team ore one hundred and twenty miles to the plains, and then send by rail nearly a thousand miles further to Saint Louis, or nearly as far to Omaha. Shipments to the latter place were made by Berdell & Witherell, who had established a sampling mill in the district late in 1877. To meet the growing demands of travel, Spottswood & McClellan extended their Denver and South Park stage lines to Leadville, and several ore transportation and freight lines were established between that point and the railway termini. The best paying mines at that time were the Iron, Camp Bird, Carbonate, and Long and Derry.

The population of Leadville increased steadily during that winter and spring, and a weekly newspaper, school, and two churches were established. In March, 1878, the first important transfer of mining property was made. Members of the St. Louis Smelting Company, having become aware of the value and quantity of ore in the Camp Bird claim, through purchases at their smelters, bought that and the adjoining Pine, Keystone, and Charleston claims for $225,000. Those who sold had been poor, hard-working men previous to the time when their mine began to produce so heavily.

The fame of the carbonate district had spread far and wide before the summer of 1878, and a tide of immigration was started that has since continued with ever-increasing momentum. Several discoveries already made were wonderfully rich and productive, but the developments that have given Leadville its grand pre-eminence over any other section in the world at the present time were those on Fryer Hill. Claims opened that same season were sufficiently explored in the ensuing fall to give pretty extensive indications of their immense extent and value. From that time the future of the district was assured and destiny beckoned in the direction of Leadville.

At first the town obtained its increase from older Colorado settlements, but more distant sections were drawn upon before the season was over. Each succeeding week saw the volume of immigration grow larger and larger, and every evening witnessed the arrival of new comers by stage, by freight teams, on horseback, and on foot. Friends or acquaintances who had not met for years found themselves together again in the new and fast-growing metropolis of the carbonate belt. There were gold-hunters who had left Colorado years agone for the newer territories; there were men who had been

THE BANK OF LEADVILLE.

rich and poor by turns, but were still as hopeful and ambitious as when life was new; there were men of every profession and calling; and every state and section were drawn upon to help swell the population of Leadville.

Many mines were already paying, and whenever mineral was struck in a new locality men were on hand ready to take it off of the finder's hands at liberal figures. New streets were built up in a single week and sleeping accommodations were ever at a premium.

This was Leadville before it grew to assume metropolitan proportions.

Visitors from abroad were at first distrustful of the camp's future, but would, ere long, catch the enthusiasm that pervaded the entire population, and be among the loudest to sound the praises and wonders of the magic city of Carbonateland. The district's growth was greatly accelerated, and its fame still further enhanced, by the wonderful developments and production of the Fryer Hill mines in the summer and fall of 1878. These ore deposits were so rich and plentiful and so easily mined that they surpassed anything previously discovered in the State, and, as far as mineral was concerned, in any other state or territory outside of the Comstock bonanzas. Meantime the Iron, Argentine, and other great mines, kept on producing as heavily as ever, and every month saw fresh additions to the many paying mines.

Winter came, but brought no cessation of the ever-augmenting caravan headed for the new land of promise. No matter how distant the land or locality, all roads seemed to lead to Leadville. Railways were started in that direction, roads were blocked with long lines of freight and immigrant teams, stage lines trebled their carrying capacity, and yet travel increased faster than accommodations could be afforded. A dozen saw-mills were turning out lumber night and day, and still could not half meet the demands made upon them for building purposes. Men who had made fortunes from working or selling their mines turned about and bought up prospects, or newly developed properties, at what would have seemed fabulous prices in former times. The streets and entire camp has been one whirl of excitement, and each successive month only added to the animation that pervaded all industries and every branch of trade. Men who had never before had a dollar ahead of actual necessities found themselves rolling in wealth, and the possessors of bank accounts far beyond what they had ever dared to dream of. The reports of prizes drawn by the few and of opportunities afforded the many were the magnetic influences that attracted less fortunate mortals from abroad. The snows and suffering attending a trip over mountain ranges had no terrors to those who had caught the "Leadville fever" and feared to lose their chances for a fortune by delay. One hundred a day was the average number of arrivals much of the time from January to June.

HARRISON AVENUE, LEADVILLE.

One of the most important features of Leadville's history has been the immense freighting business between the several railway termini and the carbonate camp. One of these mountain routes employed two thousand horses and mules. As many animals and a thousand men are engaged in hauling ore from the mines to the smelters.

Leadville continues its unprecedented growth, but during the past year has assumed the metropolitan airs which the enterprising character of its people and its superior commercial and mineral importance entitle it to possess. Newspapers, schools, churches, smelters, the telegraph, telephone, and other conveniences and necessities have been established, and mercantile houses, saloons, and hotels without number enjoy a lively business.

The result of all this increase of population and prodigious mining production and profit is to make Leadville the liveliest town the world can show to-day. The activity in building and in all branches of trade due to the above condition of things, and the vast amount of shaft prospecting, added to regular mining operations, all aid in giving work and opportunities to the new comers. The overplus of population that had accumulated before the disappearance of the spring snows is much less manifest at the present time, for with the summer, thousands moved out to explore the broad expanse of mountain that awaited the coming of the prospector.

The town is a marvel of activity, begotten of circumstances, surroundings, and great natural wealth and prosperity. Difficult as it is to make one's way along the main thoroughfares by day, it is still more so just before and after nightfall. Leadville by lamp-light fairly " booms " with excitement and life. The miners then drift into town in swarms ; a dozen bands are drumming up audiences for the theatres and variety shows, scores of saloons and numerous gambling-houses are in full blast, and the entire scene gives the town and place the appearance of one grand holiday. Many of the places referred to do a tremendous business, for those who make money easy generally spend it quickly, and life in such places tends to prodigality. Thus those who come on business or pleasure, or to stay, are all bent on seeing what there is to see, regardless of expense, and with as little delay as possible. Such a condition of affairs helps to distribute money among all classes and callings.

Nearly every business or professional man, clerk, saloon-keeper, mechanic, or mill employee in Leadville is engaged in mining or prospecting.   This is usually done by furnishing what is called a grub stake—consisting of supplies, the necessaries of life or wages to men who will sink a shaft, while the backer of the enterprise continues to follow his own calling.   In this way a large number of men are afforded employment, and many has been the paying mine or sale of property resulting therefrom.   Numerous instances

ON TO LEADVILLE—FREIGHT TRAIN ASCENDING UTE PASS.

can be related of men who came to the camp poor, and in a few months retired with a fortune. Others stay to win additional wealth, and have been almost universally successful, for money in this place, combined with experience and good judgment, has worked wonders.

Leadville began to be settled in the summer of 1877, and a year later possibly numbered 1,500 people. A census taken in January, 1879, showed 5,040 residents, besides half as many more outside of the city limits. At the beginning of summer in 1880 the population is variously estimated at from twenty-five to thirty-five thousand, besides other thousands scattered for miles in either direction among the mining and smelting camps. Notwithstanding the haste with which the place has been built, there are scores of pretentious frame structures and many substantial brick edifices. The Tabor Opera House is the finest in the State, and the Catholic Cathedral would be an ornament to any place. The city is illuminated with gas, is supplied with water-works, has police and fire departments, and several efficient military organizations. Chestnut street was formerly the great thoroughfare, but soon after William H. Bush and others began to purchase and build on Harrison avenue, trade drifted that way until it has become the main street of the city. Fortunes have been made in real estate, and lots have sold for hundreds and even thousands of dollars which but a month or two before brought but twenty-five or fifty. Corner lots on the best thoroughfares are valued at from four to ten thousand dollars. There are five banking institutions in Leadville; three were established in 1878, one in 1879, and one in 1880. Two of these have nearly two millions of deposits.

The trade report of Leadville for 1879 shows that the mercantile business of that year exceeded $20,000,000, and while a much higher sum was claimed as the total value of mining transfers, the actual purchase money paid must have equalled fifteen or twenty millions. These sales and purchases were largely made among Leadville men, for that city is the best mining market in the world. It is peopled with business men with the energy and nerve for large enterprises and that decision of character necessary in seizing upon great opportunities. The Post-office is a wonder in itself, and does a larger local business probably than any other between Saint Louis and San Francisco. Many thousand letters are received as well as forwarded every day. Tons of mail matter have arrived within twenty-four hours. In 1879 $569,070.58 were forwarded to the East or other offices through the money order department, and $120,910.92 were received through the same channel. Long files of men can be seen at all hours of the day at the general delivery windows.   Postmaster A. A. Smith's fourteen clerks have no time to spare during working hours, for no other city of anything like its size does a post-office business equal to that of Leadville.   Some idea of the hotel business of the place may be formed from the fact that the Clarendon alone reported $260,000 receipts during the first nine months.   Yet there are scores of places where public accommodations can be had.   There were a number of merchants whose sales ranged from $100,000 to over $500,000, and the amounts expended in new buildings, lumber, mining machinery, equipments and supplies, and smelters footed up many millions.

The press is an important feature of Leadville, and does most efficient service in informing the world concerning its greatest mining camp.   The sight of an eight-page daily almost as large as the great New York papers, in a city that has sprung up in the wilderness within two or three years, excites the wonder and admiration of eastern visitors.   Leadville has four first class daily newspapers, all enterprising and ably conducted and all publishing weekly editions. Besides this, are several weekly papers.   Not behind the world in other respects, this city has its swarms of news boys and street gamins of the genuine metropolitan pattern.   In the amusement line every species of entertainments are represented, from a first class theatre to variety shows and concert saloons by the dozen.   In the floating population attracted from the east and elsewhere are many rough characters whose deeds of violence have given the camp an unenviable reputation, but the police force has ever been competent to repress any extensive riotous demonstrations.

The predictions that this mining district will soon be exhausted or that the camp will be short-lived, are made only by those unacquainted with the true situation, or with the amount of mineral explored.   The ore deposits of many mines are so extensive that years will be required to exhaust them, while every month witnesses new discoveries.   The ease and rapidity with which large products are obtained are so much in favor of carbonates, for all prefer to make what money is to be made in the shortest time possible.   Over sixty productive mines are reported, some of them embracing several claims each.   These and hundreds of properties now being prospected should ensure work for many years and possibly a generation.   The product of the camp is steadily approaching two millions per month.

CHAPTER XIX.

LEADVILLE MINES—THE CARBONATE BELT, ITS FORMATION AND
CHARACTERISTICS— GOLD AND SILVER YIELD—RAPID INCREASE
IN THE BULLION AND ORE PRODUCT—SMELTING AND SAMPLING
WORKS—PROSPECTS AND POSSIBILITIES OF THE DISTRICT.

The Arkansas river flows in a southerly direction for some distance from its sources among the lofty Sierras. The valley that
incloses it is bordered by the great Continental Divide on the west,
whose peaks for a hundred miles average over 14,000 feet high, and
the almost equally elevated Mosquito or Park range on the east.
Both of these mountain systems unite near Mount Lincoln and the
head of the easterly fork of the Arkansas. Below the bald and
barren crest of the Mosquito range are what might be termed its
foot hills, sloping westward to the Arkansas valley. Among these
heavily timbered hills is the famous carbonate belt, and through it
California, Stray Horse, Evans, and Iowa gulches lead westward
down to the main stream. The Mosquito or Park range separates
the Arkansas valley from that great natural basin of the "Rockies"
called South Park. Leadville is on an inclined plain, sloping west
and at the base of the carbonate hills, 10,025 or 10,200 feet above
the sea.

The course of the carbonate zone or belt is north and south, and
the general dip of the ore is eastward and from twelve to twenty-
five degrees downward from the horizontal; but there are numerous faults and displacements, as with the overlying porphyritic
trachyte and underlying limestone. Above the porphyry may be
more or less " drift," and below is the limestone formation, quartzites, crystalline schists, and granite, tilting downward one below
the other, but occasionally pushed out of place.

The direction of the ore deposits is often changed from the
ordinary incline to the vertical, or to wave-like depressions and
elevations corresponding to those of the limestone. The depressions
contain most of the richer ore when it is in ordinary or thin layers.
The underground workings are often like so many irregular steps

and landings, making the construction of regular inclines for large productions an advantageous operation. On Fryer hill the ores lie more in the shape of deposits and pockets than in some other localities, and shafts are the outlets of the mines. Many claims on Iron and Carbonate hills are operated by inclines from the surface, through which ore is conveyed to daylight by means of railways.

The veins or deposits are overlaid with porphyry and underlaid with limestone, but in many places masses of porphyry or iron are found under one body of ore and over another, thus giving rise to the untenable theory of two or more veins, ore stratas or "contacts," one below another. The ore bodies that have been found at varying elevations or depths are undoubtedly displacements of one and the same strata. Pay material varies from a mere seam to many feet in thickness. In the Little Chief there are over 80 feet of ore in one place, and the Highland Chief, Chrysolite and Morning Star are remarkable for thickness of carbonate material. Discoveries are made by sinking shafts, and not by surface outcrops, as in most other districts. This method of operation is somewhat uncertain, being simply prospecting on an extensive scale. Carbonates were found in the Little Pittsburg claim at a depth of 26 feet, but shafts of some claims have been sunk from three to five hundred feet deep, before pay material was encountered. The limestone formation is often found in undulations like the waves of a disturbed sea, with the ore bodies thickest and richest in the depressions, or between the so-called limestone "waves."

The ore varies in value of silver contents from a few dollars up to thousands of dollars per ton. The quantities of the latter class are not large, and the average of ore shipped or smelted in the district has been not far from 90 ounces of silver, and from 15 to 30 per cent. lead. The present per cent. of lead is much smaller than formerly, as most of the discoveries of 1879–'80 have carried little of that metal. At times during the past winter the average of all ore smelted was but twelve per cent. lead, and at the present time it can hardly exceed fifteen. Some smelters have been obliged to suspend work, because they could not get lead-bearing ores. Much of the vein material is heavily impregnated with iron, thus aiding its fluxing value. Many mines on Carbonate, Iron, and Fryer hills yield ore carrying from thirty to sixty-five per cent. lead, and pure galena ores are met with. A few mines yield gold.

THE MEYER SAMPLING WORKS AND HARRISON SMELTER.

The yield of Leadville or California mining district, from the old-time era of placer mining down to 1880, was as follows:

PRODUCT OF LAKE COUNTY, 1860 TO 1880.

Gold, 14 years.		Gold, Silver and Lead.	
1860–1873, inclusive ...	$6,400,000	1876..............	$85,200 00
1874, gold and silver...	145,000	1877..............	555,330 00
1875, gold and silver...	113,000	1878..............	3,152,925 44
	1879.......................		$10,189,521.37.

Total product up to 1880, $20,640,976.81. Including ore on hand at works, December 31, 1880, the product of 1879 was $11,105,521.37, and previous to 1880, $21,560,976.81.

The product of 1877, principally obtained in the last five months of the year, was 3,700 tons of ore, $414,000 in silver, $76,400 in lead, and $55,000 in gold.

In 1878, the tonnage of ore was 21,746, giving 5,549½ tons of lead. The yield and form of shipment were as follows:

Value in different Metals.		Form of Shipment.	
Silver.............	$2,591,054 71	Bullion.............	$686,422 39
Lead..............	443,924 73	Ore shipped........	2,366,503 05
Gold..............	117,946 00	Gold dust..........	100,000 00
Total..........	$3,152,925 44	Total...........	$3,152,925 44

Before the close of summer in 1879, Leadville had become the world's leading bullion producer, has since maintained that proud pre-eminence, and is likely to do so for years to come. As the Comstock declined, Leadville advanced, showing a gain of seven or eight millions, and trebling the output of the previous year. The product of 1879 in the various metals was as follows:

Silver, $8,455,655.68. Lead, $1,687,489.32. Gold, $46,376.37.

Total export for 1879....................... $10,189,521 37
Add ore on hand at works, paid for.......... 920,000 00

Makes actual output of mines.............. $11,109,521 37

Silver rated at $1.12½ per ounce, and lead at $80 a ton.

The above $920,000 include the yield of 10,000 tons of ore on hand, whose estimated value was $800,000 in silver and $120,000 in lead. From the total export is deducted $90,000 in silver and $10,000 in lead for ores from Summit county, treated at Leadville, and whose product is credited elsewhere to Summit county.

PRODUCT OF LEADVILLE OR LAKE COUNTY IN 1879.

NAME OF SMELTER OR SHIPPER.	No. of Furnaces.	Daily Capacity.	Tons of Ore handled.	GOLD.	SILVER.	LEAD.	TOTAL PRODUCT.
Grant Smelter	8	160	25,000	....	$2,142,388 32	$355,124 36	$2,497,512 68
La Plata	4	130	19,822	....	1,498,000 94	263,040 00	1,761,040 94
Billings and Eiler	2	60	10,580	....	828,470 00	194,390 00	1,022,860 00
J. Dickson	2	60	10,796	....	639,247 00	107,780 00	747,027 00
J. B. Stein	1	25	1,121	....	38,954 30	10,240 00	62,794 28
Harrison	2	70	8,784	$13,760 00	854,905 50	153,491 28	1,022,156 78
Leadville	1	20	4,531	....	130,400 00	25,600 00	156,000 00
California	2	50	1,400	....	72,655 00	24,000 00	96,655 00
American	2	50	2,577	....	173,644 00	50,195 00	223,839 00
Ohio and Missouri	2	35	2,440	2,616 37	111,752 56	38,360 68	152,729 00
Cummings & Finn	3	90	3,500	....	259,227 00	64,960 00	323,024 00
Gage, Hegeman & Co.	1	25	3,200	....	225,305 81	44,000 00	269,305 81
Raymond, Sherman & Co	1	25	2,349	....	103,286 00	34,200 00	137,486 00
Elgin	1	35	5,470	....	189,800 00	61,200 00	251,000 00
Little Chief	1	35	2,827	....	172,963 75	40,620 00	213,588 75
Adlaide	..	..	300	....	8,900 00	26,000 00	34,900 00
A. R. Meyer & Co	..	..	1,974	....	441,722 63	87,166 63	528,888 63
Eddy & James	..	..	4,453	....	637,591 50	117,122 00	754,713 50
Gold placers	..	..	.....	30,000 00	....	....	30,000 00
Total exports	..	..	111,124	$46,376 37	$8,545,655 68	$1,697,489 32	$10,289,521 37
Deduct for Summit County ores	..	..	600	....	90,000 00	10,000 00	100,000 00
Leaves actual export of county	..	..	.....	....	$8,455,655 68	$1,687,489 32	$10,189,521 37
Add ore paid for and on hand at works	..	..	10,000	....	800,000 00	120,000 00	920,000 00
Total	..	..	.....	....	$9,255,655 68	$1,807,489 32	$11,109,521 37

The ores of Leadville district are treated by smelting without roasting, nature having obviated the necessity of the latter. The same method has long been in use in Missouri, Utah, and elsewhere. Ores are smelted in what are known as water-jacket furnaces constructed of iron, of circular or square shape, six feet more or less in diameter, and of much greater height. They are lined internally with fire clay and rest on a cement and clay foundation. The ore is shoveled into the furnaces along with the necessary proportions of coke, charcoal, and slag, from a floor over that where the bullion is discharged—the furnaces being uprights and extending upwards through the building, with outlets for fumes and smoke above. The proper mixture of ores and fuel are important points to success, and the more refractory the ores the greater the care needed to avoid chilling the furnace and other troubles. Weighing the ores is one means of determining their character, as the per cent. of lead can thus be approximated. The molten mass separates itself in the furnace according to its specific gravity—the lead with its silver contents settling into a lead well at the bottom and one side, from which it is dipped into iron moulds, where it cools into bars of about 100 pounds weight. The slag is drawn off and dumped outside of the smelter. A furnace turns out from 60 to 200 of these bars daily. A ton of bullion may carry $400 worth of silver—or more or less. Furnaces are run night and day from one month's end to another—to allow them to cool down would entail a heavy expense in drilling out the mass of iron and slag that would have to be removed—and in fact would stop business completely. Coke is shipped from El Moro, and some has come from Pennsylvania. Charcoal is supplied from the adjoining forests.

The Grant Smelter turns out more bullion and a larger valuation of product than any reducing establishment in America if not in the world. The export for the year 1880 may approach $4,000,000. It has nine furnaces and a capacity for smelting from 150 to 180 tons daily. From five to seven thousand tons of ore are purchased monthly, and the ore on hand has a value of several hundred thousand dollars. The works have grown gradually in size as one furnace after another was added, until the present mammoth proportions have been attained. The first furnace was fired up October 1, 1878, the second three months later and others previous to November, 1879. The ninth one began work in the first part of 1880. The output of 1879 was

FURNACE BUILDINGS OF THE GRANT SMELTER.

valued at $2,497,512.68, although but a portion of the furnaces had been procured in the first half of the year. With the beginning of 1880 Eddy and James and J. B. Grant formed a partnership whereby all became jointly interested in the smelter just described and the ore-sampling and shipping works of the former, forming the leading ore-purchasing, shipping, and reducing establishment of the world. The values handled at the sampling mill are likely to equal those at the smelter. Over 200 men are employed at the latter, and acres of ground are occupied with furnaces and other buildings, and by wood, charcoal, and ore yards. The bullion export has gone as high as $457,712 in a single month.

Eddy & James completed their ore-buying and sampling mill in July, 1878, to which additions have since been made. They have ever done an immense business. In 1878 they exported $730,081.70 worth of ore. In 1879 they purchased and shipped 2,300 tons of lead bullion, worth $1,173,000. They also shipped abroad or to home smelters 15,301 tons of ore, containing $2,183,845.28. They had paid over $100,000 for the ores remaining on hand at the close of the year.

A. R. Meyer put up the first ore-buying and sampling works at Leadville, and may have caused the building of the town on the location selected. This was early in the summer of 1877. This establishment has handled more ore than any other. It shipped $400,000 worth in 1877, and $1,162,559.39 in 1878, besides a large amount turned in to the Harrison smelter. In 1879 A. R. Meyer & Co. bought and sampled 24,131.66 tons of ore, containing $3,161,246. They also bought and shipped bullion to the value of $1,429,652.

The Harrison works were the first established in Leadville. They started with one furnace in October, 1877. Since the summer of 1878 two furnaces have been employed—largely on ores from the Argentine and Crescent mines. Berdell & Witherell began to smelt in the fall of 1878. Their establishment is now included in the La Plata Company's property and ranks next to Grant's in production.

In 1878 sampling works shipped the following values: A. R. Meyer & Co., $1,162,559.39; Eddy & James, $730,081.70; Berdell & Witherill, $448,861.96. The smelters' shipments were: Harrison, $271,860.69; Grant, $156,657.50; Berdell & Witherell, $139,129.00; Malta, $86,100; Adlaide $32,735.20. For products of 1879, see table, page 423.

CHAPTER XX.

The first noticeable mines of the carbonate belt were those of
Stevens and Wood, on either side of California Gulch, and the Camp
Bird, now the Argentine.   These discoveries on the southern and
northern ends of Iron Hill led to locations in the centre and on the
western slope.   Among them was the Iron claim, whose showing at
the close of 1877 was mainly instrumental in giving the district its
first great prominence.   Before its value was known L. Z. Leiter,
of Field, Leiter & Co., of Chicago, had purchased the entire Wood
interest in this and eight other claims.

The Iron, so called from the color of its ore, is considered the representative carbonate vein.   There are larger ore bodies, but none
more uniform, regular or continuous.   This mine, under the supervision of W. H. Stevens, was the first to be systematically opened
and developed, and was the most prominent property of the camp
up to the time of the Fryer Hill discoveries.   Some believe it will
outlast all rivals.   Although work has been seriously interrupted by
contests with adjoining claimants, the Iron has thousands of feet of
levels and inclines, and must have produced over half a million dollars
prior to the organization of the Iron Silver Company.   This occurred
early in 1880.   Roberts and others of California and New York then
came into possession, and W. S. Keyes, of the Chrysolite, became
general manager.   The Iron Silver Company not only owns the
Iron claim, but also the Bulls Eye, Lime, Stone, Rock, Dome and

other claims, all known under the name of the "Iron Silver Mine." The Rock claim and its neighbors show a large body of ore rich in lead, but not generally of very high grade in silver. The Iron is the most valuable part of the property, although the adjoining Bulls Eye is beginning to make an excellent showing, six feet of sand carbonates being reported. Around the entrance of the Iron mine quite a village has sprung up, including mine and ore buildings, boarding-houses and residences. The main inclines and workings of the mine are substantially timbered, and usually show a vein from three to four feet wide, but which varies from six inches to ten feet. The average of all grades may be 60 ounces of silver per ton, and of high grades alone, 130 ounces. Above rests the chalky porphyry, jointed in crystalline forms, and below is the solid, unbroken limestone foot-wall with a uniform general dip eastward in a series of undulations, slopes and steps. Here and there are batches of solid galena and of chlorides. The deeply tinged iron is often of low grade, but there are immense quantities of hard and soft carbonates. Two main inclines are being driven downward, into the hill, and will soon be 1,000 feet long.

The mine began to produce in August, 1877, and a yield of $150,-000, with $70,000 clear profits, is said to have been made by the ensuing June. Since then litigations and contests have greatly retarded work. It is claimed $200,000 was produced in 1878, and that in two years 800 tons of ore averaged 221 ounces of silver per ton, and 54 per cent. lead. A large product was also taken out by other parties from the Williams shaft. The yield of 1879 was probably greater than that of both preceding years. The ore reserves are of immense extent and value, and each month sees a large gain in amount of stoping ground.

In the fall of 1878, a man named Williams went up the hill beyond the Iron side lines and sunk a shaft until he reached the "contact," 200 feet below the surface. He then barricaded the Iron incline, and by force of arms held the interior workings against the Stevens and Leiter miners, at the same time hoisting and selling ore as fast as possible. During the ensuing winter it is said a force of old Georgetown miners, the heroes of many mining contests, were engaged to hire to the Williams party as guards. They turned the barricaded workings back into possession of Stevens. Before and afterwards the mine was heavily guarded, and internally resembled a magazine. The courts finally decided in favor of the Iron mine owners, permitting them to work and follow their vein wherever it led to.

The Iron Silver Mining Company has a capital stock of $10,000,000 in 500,000 shares of a par value of ten dollars. Its officers are George D. Roberts, president; S. V. White, vice-president; James D. Smith, treasurer; D. F. Verdenal, secretary; W. S. Keyes, general manager. Trustees—W. H. Stevens, George D. Roberts, R. C. McCormick, Jonas H. French, Luther R. Marsh, L. Z. Leiter, S. V. White, George B. Robinson, and Jas. D. Smith.

The Argentine mine is located on the northerly slope of Iron Hill, just above Stray Horse Gulch, and comprises the Camp Bird, Charleston, Keystone, Pine, and Young America. The Camp Bird claim was located by three brothers, Patrick, Charles, and John Gallagher. The surface ground had gradually washed away and left the carbonates outcropping. The Gallagher brothers did not have a very profitable time at first. One and then all of them were so discouraged with trying to get a living out of their lode that they were about to abandon it altogether when a final improvement in the ore was noticeable. In 1877, it began to pay handsomely, especially after the completion of the Harrison smelter. The brothers squandered their earnings, but finally the mine made money faster than they could spend it. Then they sold to members of the Saint Louis Smelting and Refining Company for $225,000 and one went to Paris and the others to different parts of America. All seemed bent on getting rid of their money as fast as possible. The mine had yielded nearly $150,000 up to that time, and some $80,000 had been paid for the ore. The mine had been badly gophered, and much time was required to put it in safe condition after the company purchased it. Since then the mine has generally produced from 5 to 15 tons of ore daily that yielded from $60 to $100 per ton. Besides new buildings, shafts, and levels, a tunnel, now over 1,100 feet long, will soon reach a shaft 300 feet deep, to be used as the main hoisting outlet. The total yield of the property is not known, but probably exceeds $300,000.

Between the Argentine and the Iron Silver is the Colorado Belle, and below the former is the Adelaide, owned by an eastern company. A smelter was once in operation there, but the ore was too poor in silver, and the furnace managers too unfortunate to make a profit.

From 50 to 70 per cent. of the ore was lead.   Not far away is the Agazziz and Double Decker, carrying gold, silver, and lead.

The Smuggler is not far from the Iron and Bull's Eye on the southern slope of the hill.   It has been worked extensively, and has produced considerable money.   The ore is not generally high grade, but there is a great deal of it.   The Cleora and Star of Hope are both producing.

The Garden City on Iron hill has eight feet of ore.   Near it are the Lone Tree, Globe and Josephine claims.   All of these are owned by Colonel William Moore of the Moore M. & S. Co., of Golden and Lawson.

On the hill south of Oro many locations have been made, and several fine gold-bearing veins are worked.   The hill-sides have been washed by sluices and hydraulics for gold, and this part of California Gulch has always been quite productive.   Of the gold veins, the Printer Boy, discovered by Charles Mullen in 1868, is the most valuable.   This paid largely in 1869, and at subsequent times.   A Philadelphia company purchased it and erected a twenty-five-stamp quartz mill at Oro.   About $60,000 were produced during the first year of actual work, and several hundred thousand alogether.   Among other mines are the Pilot, Tiger, Mike, Yellow Jacket, Miner's Hope, Maria, and Lower Printer Boy.   The Oro La Plata, near the Dome and Rock claims, is said to be paying very good profits.

Further south is Long and Derry Hill, located between Iowa and Empire Gulches, where are the Long and Derry, Doris, Himmala, Ready Cash, Florence, Belcher, and other carbonate mines.   They are near the edge of timber line, 11,000 feet above sea level and four miles southeast of Leadville.   Jacob Long and his brother came to California Gulch in 1860, and have been pretty much all over Colorado.   For sixteen long years they prospected and mined with unvarying ill fortune.   Of the typical prospecting class, they were often ragged and generally without money, but ever hopeful and persevering.   Late in 1876, in company with a Mr. Derry, they made the discovery of four carbonate locations, which are known as the Long and Derry mine.   It was a prize worth toiling years to secure ; but they could have had it years before if they had known anything about carbonates.   Little work was done until 1877, and shipments could not be made regularly at all seasons until a road to Leadville was constructed early in 1878.   Drifts and shafts to the extent of nearly 2,000 feet have been run in various directions and places. The amount of mineral in gross taken from the mine up to June, 1878, was 738 tons and 116 pounds, yielding 209 tons and 412 pounds of lead, and a total value 'of silver and lead of $98,840. From these figures it will be seen that the yield per ton has been very nearly $134. There has been no system or skill displayed in mining, and much dead work has been done. Up to 1879 over 1,000 tons of ore (besides a few small shipments milling over 500 and 1,000 ounces per ton) averaged over 95 ounces of silver and 30 per cent. lead. The main tunnel was then 524 feet long. The Florence has been shipping considerable quantities of valuable ore, and the Ready Cash is said to return its owners plenty of what its name indicates. The Belcher has rich chlorides and carbonates.

Carbonate Hill became famous before the close of summer in 1877, by reason of the discovery of rich ore on the Carbonate claim. It is situated west of Iron Hill, and between that and Leadville. It overlooks the city, and its westerly slope is rapidly being occupied by streets and residences as well as mines and mine buildings. The claims located in 1877 were along what was considered the apex of the vein, and were called the Shamrock, Carbonate, Yankee Doodle, Crescent, Catalpa, Evening Star, Morning Star, Waterloo and Henriette.

The Carbonate gave the highest average yield per ton in 1877, and for some months later, of any mine in the district. The owners were Nelson Hallock and Captain A. Cooper, who found their carbonates much more profitable than the saw-mill they were operating. In the first eleven months of work to July, 1878, the ore sales were $81,136.08 and the profits $70,723.53. Several tons of ore averaged 662 ounces of silver per ton, another lot sold at $462.50, and from 275 to 600 ounces were not unusual returns. The receipts up to October 10, 1878, were $108,614.90, and about $150,000 up to January, 1879. At that time New York and Colorado men purchased the property and organized the Leadville Mining Company thereon, with a capital stock of $2,000,000 in ten-dollar shares; the property has since been known as the Leadville mine. Afterwards the adjoining Shamrock mine was purchased, and a company formed thereon. The Leadville owns a portion of the stock, and the mines are reported as consolidated. Several inclines have been driven in on the vein of the Leadville, which is usually from one to five feet wide, and a large

THE LEADVILLE MINE.

amount of ore has been extracted in drifting and stoping. The Leadville company paid $150,000 in dividends in 1879.

Above the Leadville mine is the Little Giant, which has been a paying enterprise. In December, 1879, the dividends amounted to $9,318,81. In February and March, 1880, there were 174.6 tons of ore sold for $24,868, altogether yielding an average of 137 ounces of silver per ton, and 42 per cent. lead, making an actual yield of $35,931.36 for two months. At that time the shaft was 220 feet deep, and the incline therefrom 150 feet long. The hoisting was done by a whim. Below the Leadville is the Ætna claim, which has been worked extensively.

The Carbonate Hill mine, formerly known as the Yankee Doodle, is owned by a company of the same name, of which Charles R. Bissell, of other prominent Leadville enterprises, is president. In 1878–9, J. W. Plummer and associates worked this property, and after a time it began to pay handsomely. Monthly profits of from $3,000 to $5,000 were reported. The mine was then but little developed, and worked was not pushed for large production. After the present company purchased, the carbonate vein, which had barely been entered before, was explored much more energetically. Two steam engines and hoisting machinery were secured, the upper shaft was sunk into "pay," and operations on a larger scale are now going forward. The shafts are 110 feet and 275 feet deep respectively, and are both down in carbonates, carrying ninety ounces of silver per ton. This is the same vein or strata that continues through the Crescent and Morning Star, and is likely to be as productive with further development.

For a long time the Crescent ranked next to the Carbonate on this hill, and is still quite productive. In 1878, the sales of ore netted the Meyer M. & E. Company some $40,000. An incline over 500 feet long, with many diverging levels, comprise the later workings. The yield of 1879 is said to have exceeded $100,000. The Catalpa has been sold to a Boston company and stocked at large figures.

The Evening Star mine lies between the Catalpa and Morning Star. It has been paying handsomely since some time in 1879, having a part of the same ore body to work on that is found in its eastern neighbor. There are four working shafts, two of them over 300 feet deep. From one of these, drifts have been started in four

directions. Drifting is also progressing elsewhere. W. S. Ward is
general manager.

The Morning Star Consolidated is one of the four or five great
mines of Leadville. The ore already explored by levels and inclines
is valued at millions, and yet there is every indication of the vein
continuing onward and downward without cessation. The production, large as it is, could be made many times greater if the ore
reserves were stoped out instead of being steadily increased. The
hoisting capacity has been inadequate, but a new shaft and inclines
are remedying this. The various outlets of the property indicate
that most of the surface area is underlaid with carbonates, while the
vein can be followed onward into the hill indefinitely.

When John L. Routt was governor of Colorado and George C.
Corning was State treasurer, they, in company with Joseph W.
Watson, became owners of the location they called the Morning
Star. The earlier operations were not generally remunerative.
While pockets and occasional rich seams were encountered, no continuous ore body of great extent was reached near the surface, as on
several other claims. Nevertheless Superintendent Watson kept on
exploring and developing, doing his work so well that the same
main shaft and development have answered subsequent demands.
After a varied experience in Central gold mines and as the leading
operator in Georgetown's early silver days, followed by disastrous
ventures in Utah, he was not the man to be easily discouraged. So
when the Morning Star bonanza was eventually found, the more credit
was reflected on the persistence and judgment of the fortunate discoverer. Since the spring of 1879 drifts and cross-cuts have been
driven in such enormous bodies of paying carbonates that no other
mine on the hill can compare with it at the present time.

The fine shaft, sunk to a depth of 250 feet in the winter of 1878-9,
was the point from which successful explorations were conducted
and furnished the only ore outlet of the claim until the sinking of
the new shaft several hundred feet further up the hill. The incline,
driven as near as possible on the vein, dips from 10 to 15 degrees,
with numerous drifts and avenues leading to the north and south.
Paying material is opened up in all directions. The ore body has
ranged from six to twenty feet and over in thickness, and is so
rich in lead as to ensure the most favorable selling prices at the
smelter's. The average value of the ore was about $60 per ton, and

its uniform character was remarkable. But little stoping has been done, and the past yield has come almost entirely from drifting, there being over 2,000 feet of levels in this claim.

In 1878, before the main ore body was found, the ore sales were only $7,447.70. In the summer and fall of 1879, from 800 to 1,000 tons of ore were coming out monthly, and receipts for ore sold that year footed up $290,491.26 from 7,182½ tons of ore. In 1880 the January receipts were $70,600, February, $70,000, and March, about $75,000. Last year different parties sunk shafts on adjoining claims, and on ground owned by the company, and the same great ore body was penetrated, returning many thousands of dollars monthly. These claims were all finally purchased by the Morning Star and Waterloo owners. The actual silver-lead values from these and other claims in the consolidation to the summer of 1880 must approach a round million. Recently the mines have been yielding from 50 to 70 tons of ore daily, and this can easily be doubled when the company completes its new shaft, perfects its hoisting and development work and begins to stope from the reserves. The great ore body is already known to extend hundreds of feet in all directions from the central portion of the property and cannot well be exhausted in several years. Up to this time the mine has never been made to produce half of what it is capable of yielding without reducing the ore reserves. In April, 1880, the Morning Star Consolidated Mining Company, was organized, with a capital stock of $6,000,000. This is a remarkably low figure, especially for a concern started in New York, for there is ore enough in sight to sell for more than the market valuation of the stock, besides the vast probabilities of future exploration. The property embraces the Morning Star, Waterloo, Half-Way House, Forsaken, Buckeye Belle, Anchor and Carrolton claims—in all twenty-six acres of ground. Ore in large quantities is coming out of the shafts of several of these, and all are believed to be valuable. The officers of the company are ex-Governor John L. Routt, president; F. Taylor, vice-president; George S. Terry, secretary; and the same and Joseph W. Watson, Z. E. Elkin, S. V. White, B. la S. Buell and George S. Terry, trustees.

Well down on the western slope of Carbonate Hill and just on the outskirts of the thickly settled portion of Leadville is the Glass-Pendery mine, a combination of those richly paying claims and the Rough and Ready. The Pendery was named after one of its owners at the time "carbonates were struck," in the summer of 1879. It was generally considered that it was a waste of time and money to sink a shaft in that locality, as no one expected that the carbonate deposits dipped in such a direction. After ore was discovered, at the then unusual depth of nearly 200 feet, it was believed to be another strata or vein dipping downward under the surface, so as to underlie the contact already explored in the Leadville, Crescent, Morning Star, and other claims further up the hill. It is evidently, however, only a portion of the same great formation that rises and dips in all sorts of directions from Leadville to the Mosquito Range. The Pendery began to pay largely as soon as drifting began, for there was plenty of ore and much of it was high grade. Many shipments were made that yielded from $100 to $400 per ton. While the yield would vary at times, it was generally quite extensive and the present showing is exceedingly fine. Near the Pendery is the Glass, now consolidated therewith, and yielding over 20 tons daily from sinking and drifting. It began to pay soon after the former did, and appears to be just as valuable. The combined properties must have yielded a quarter of a million in the first nine or ten months after ore was found. The Glass claim alone has from 5 to 15 feet of ore exposed in much of its 1,500 feet of drifts and openings. T. Foley is one of the main stockholders.

The Niles-Augusta mine has been paying largely for many months. The Washburn is also considered very valuable. The Weldon claim extends down into the borders of Leadville. The Henriett shaft has been sunk to a depth of about 400 feet in search of the Carbonate Hill ore body. Among other claims are the Cyclops, Vanderbilt and Prospect—the latter with a 400-foot incline. The California and Colorado Tunnel has been driven many hundred feet into the southern side of Carbonate Hill, and sand carbonates are reported in plentiful quantities. Among the owners are W. A. H. Loveland and L. J. Smith.

The Small Hopes Mining Company own the Robert Emmet, Forest City, Amanda H., Result, and Ranchero. This property has yielded more or less steadily for two years. The Double Decker, not far away, carries a great deal of gold as well as silver. In this same Stray Horse section is the North Star consolidation. The Modoc mine, not far away, has a fine body of carbonates, which the owners were obliged to sink a shaft 430 feet to discover. The Boreel Company own the Gone Abroad mine.

Breece Hill became prominent for the first time during the summer of 1879, when the Breece Iron, Highland Chief, Colorado Prince, and other mines began to be brought into paying condition. Since then the Miner Boy, Little Prince, Black Prince, and other mines have been developed.

The Breece Iron mine is located on the westerly slope of the hill, and embraces four claims, or over forty acres of surface ground. The location is the oldest of that section, and was made by S. D. Breece. He soon learned that the ore did not carry a large amount of silver, but the smelters discovered that this iron ore, above all others yet handled, was the most desirable for fluxing purposes in smelting. As the smelting business increased, so did the demands on this iron deposit. At last C. R. Bissell and others saw that this was likely to prove as much of a bonanza as many of the high grade mineral claims, and accordingly purchased it for $76,000. This was early in the summer of 1879, and before much work had been done. A company was soon after organized, and operations began on a large scale.

So great was the demand for this iron that not many months passed until a hundred tons were mined and sold daily. The smelters paid from $7 to $8 per ton for it, although the average silver contents did not exceed that sum. It costs but a trifle to mine it, and the owners have the whole side of a hill to draw on. There seems to be no limit to its depth or extent. Thousands of tons have been carted away, and yet but a beginning has been made of exhausting the deposit.

At sight of this property, with its huge excavations, one is reminded of an immense stone quarry, rather than of a mine. Inclines have been driven, immense pits have been dug, and quite a large slice of the hill side has been removed—almost the entire mass going to the smelters. Numerous railway tracks run from the pits to the dumps, and a hundred tons of ore are shipped daily. The mineral carries but a few ounces in silver. Free gold has sometimes been found. An engine has been put up at the mine with Ingersol machine drill and compressor, with which the property is being prospected at great depth. This was the first steam or machine drill used in the district, and is so effective in blasting out the iron that mining expenses have been reduced one-half. A large prospecting shaft is being sunk in search of carbonates.

Tests and assays have proved the iron of the Breece property to possess the requisite qualities for the highly prized Bessemer pig iron. It is said to compare with the best foreign and domestic ores. It is remarkable for the entire absence of titanium, phosphorus, manganese, and lime, while the presence of a trifling amount of sulphur does not materially affect its value for Bessemer purposes. The very low percentage of silica renders it an indispensable flux for carbonates. The United States Assay Office in New York has given the following assay: Oxide of iron, 98.57 per cent.; silica, 0.60 per cent.; sulphur, 0.247 per cent.; loss, 0.583 per cent.; titanium, phosphorus, manganese, and lime, none. The Colorado Coal and Iron Company, organized for the manufacture of iron, iron rails, and steel, has contracted for 50 tons daily of this ore, to be shipped by rail to South Pueblo, the location of the works. The Colorado Coal and Iron Company is composed of Denver and Rio Grande railway men.

The Colorado Prince is a gold-bearing mine near the Highland Chief, which came into prominence last year. The pay material is said to be of great extent, and much of it showing free gold. Superintendent S. G. Patrick reports 2,000 tons of ore on the dump. The shafts and the levels from the 80 and 155-foot stations are said to be in good ore. A stamp mill similar to the Gilpin county gold quartz mills has been erected to handle the product. Near by is the Black Prince of similar characteristics and formation. The Little Prince is shipping ore, some of which mills 250 ounces of silver per ton.

The Cumberland, adjoining the Nettie Morgan, has a shaft 500 feet deep, driven in search of carbonates. These are said to have been found at last, with some free gold material a short distance above.

Over fifty claims are worked within a radius of three-quarters of a mile from the head of Big Evans gulch. Among these valuable properties are the Ashtabula, Lulu, Nevada, Adriatic, Ajax, Fairview, Dauntless, and North American.

West of Leadville and the Arkansas river is Frying Pan Gulch, around which are some valuable mines. The T. L. Welsh is producing rich ore in quantity, and the Defiance, General Shields, Gertrude, Tiger, Sunshine, Keystone and others, are prominent.

The Andy Johnson has fine buildings, and steam hoisting machinery and the largest pump in the camp. At a depth of 200 feet, contact material 35 feet thick was opened with some chlorides. Some distance easterly are the Great Hope, Independence and De Bosco group.

The Highland Chief property consists of four claims which were developed into pay in 1879. The contest which arose over the various locations was finally settled by a consolidation. The immense size of the mineralized body has attracted attention far and wide. While it is of low grade, the ease with which it is mined has caused good profits on large amounts of ore sold. The carbonates carry but little lead, but have yielded from 20 to 125 ounces of silver per ton. The immense iron deposit, opened by a tunnel and by shafts and drifts, is from 20 to 80 feet thick. In this are large bodies of carbonates. A company has been organized, with a capital stock of $2,000,000, most of which sold in New York at high figures. Colonel C. A. Manners and T. Foley are leading stockholders.

The Lowland Chief property, consisting of four claims, adjoins the Highland Chief, and the same mineral body is found in both. There are six shafts altogether, varying in depth from 65 to over 200 feet. F. B. Beaudry is superintendent. A company has been organized in New York by ex-Senator Dorsey and others, and it is said the property was turned in at a nominal figure of $445,000.

The Great Hope, below the Little Prince, shows galena carrying silver and gold-bearing quartz showing much fine gold. Steam hoisting works are used. Assays show as high as from $300 to $480 in gold and over 100 ounces of silver per ton.

The Nettie Morgan is south of the Little Prince. The Highland Chief ore body is found to extend there. The carbonates are rich in silver and carry from 40 to 60 per cent. lead.

The Miner Boy is near the Highland Chief, and adjoins the Colorado Prince. The shafts, levels and tunnels have opened immense bodies of mineral, comprising carbonates as well as iron and gold-bearing pyrites. In the 150 and 200-feet levels leading from one shaft are seams of ore similar to that of Gilpin county gold-bearing veins. These have yielded as high as from $250 to $300 per ton in gold, with some silver and a little copper. Overlying this and higher up the hill are carbonates. In another shaft are carbonates 20 feet thick, carrying 40 per cent. of lead and over 60 ounces of silver. In one part of the claim the mineralized body is 50 feet thick.

The Miner Boy was located early in 1879, when the snow was deep on the ground in that locality. A shaft was sunk, and when carbonates were found at a depth of 100 feet, the discoverers sold out for $75,000. Large figures were subsequently paid for other interests. During the summer the discovery of gold-bearing ore in the neighboring Colorado Prince caused the sinking of shafts to get the same vein. This was found at a much greater depth than on the other property, but the returns were as good if not better. Recent reports say that ore has been raised from the shafts carrying from $500 to $1,000 per ton, while assays of selected ore go much higher. The principal value is gold, although there is some silver. The claim is a full one, and the shafts are covered with substantial buildings. The owners, J. G. Bedford, H. C. Clay, A. A. McLeod, J. W. Hamilton and others, have organized a company on the property.

The Little Johnny has been opened by shafts and several levels showing a vein of ore worth about $80 a ton. There is a copper-bearing streak two or three feet thick. The Uncle Sam yields from $30 to $170 per ton. It carries silver and gold. Its developments are shafts, levels, and a tunnel. A very large body of iron pyrites carrying gold has been found. The Independence has sent ore to the smelter that brought from $100 to $149 a ton. These claims border on Little Evans gulch, where South Evans comes in. It is reported that the Little Johnny and Shoo Fly lodes have been sold for $63,333. The James B. claim on Little Evans has four feet of ore, averaging 76 ounces of silver, 13 per cent. of copper and some gold and lead.

Sloping down from a spur of the Mosquito range, not far from Bald Mountain and Breece hill, is a ridge called Little Ella hill. The Little Ella is one of the leading mines of the locality, and below it are the Little Rische, Trade Dollar, Silent Friend, Jesse C., Patrick Sarsfield, Chief Warrior, Virginius, Cleveland, Last Chance, Carrie and Port Hudson, the latter near the junction of Big and South Evans. The Little Ella mine ships ore regularly and is considered very valuable. The Iszard claim shows mineral of various kinds.

The Alps mine is located between Bross and Bald mountains, near the South Fork of South Evans, and almost on the slope of the Mosquito range. Alps claims numbers one and two and the Helvetia and Columbus locations, each 1,500 feet long by 300 wide, are in-

WINTER SCENE AT THE ALPS MINE.

cluded in this property. The **Alps** and the Long and Derry appear to be the upper and most easterly ore bodies of great importance in the district. An immense mass of mineral outcrops on these claims, and has been entered for short distances by shafts, open cuts and tunnels.

The appearance and characteristics of the vein are much the same as those of the Iron and some other prominent Leadville mines— carbonates of lead carrying silver, and heavily stained with iron and manganese. This seems to be one of the best contact veins yet discovered. While but little developed, it is evident that it will cut an important figure in the carbonate camp in the hereafter. As far as ascertained the gray carbonate ore which is found in such quantities has carried from 15 to 450 ounces of silver per ton, and from 60 to 70 per cent. lead. These statements are corroborated by some of the best miners and engineers of Leadville, who have made personal examinations of the property.

Mr. F. Prentice, the present head of this mining enterprise, visited Leadville in the fall of 1879 on business connected with the purchase of the Big Pittsburg. While there he was induced to examine the Alps, then rapidly coming into notoriety. His thirty years' experience in mines and quick perception of good points enabled him to appreciate its great value at once, and the result was its purchase and the organization of the Alps Consolidated Mining Company. The capital stock is held in large blocks by leading New York and Leadville business men, such as George I. Seney, president of the Metropolitan National Bank, W. H. Lee, Isaac H. Bailey, F. Prentice, W. S. Williams, and others. F. Prentice is president of the company, Berkley T. Wood, treasurer, and Howell Smith, secretary. A road has been constructed connecting the mine with the main Leadville road, and the necessary supplies and machinery for the mine have been procured. A large force of miners is engaged in sinking shafts and driving levels. A heavy output is expected, for experts report that thousands of tons of mineral can be had for the mere cost of shovelling.

Adjoining the Alps on the east and north are the Tenderfoot, Alps No. 3, and Mary claims, belonging to the Tenderfoot Consolidated Mining Company. In the two first-named of these claims is the apex or outcrop of the vein, the same as shown on the Alps, with the same general characteristics and indications. The Tenderfoot mine is situated nearly opposite the Highland Chief, and has over 17 feet of carbonates. This should be assurance of large products and dividends.

That portion of Lake County known as Upper Tennessee Park has been attracting considerable attention of late from prospectors, miners, and purchasers, who believe it destined to be one of the richest galena producing localities in the district. A smelter has already been located in the Park and active work commenced. Stevens, of the Iron Silver mine, Farwell, of the Little Chief, and F. Prentice & Co., of New York, have purchased a large number of valuable lodes, which they are developing.

Of those who have made fortunes from Leadville mines some have gone abroad, many have embarked in other mining operations, and a number have purchased or erected handsome business blocks or private residences in Denver and their own city. H. A. W. Tabor was elected lieutenant governor of Colorado in 1878, and then resigned the offices of postmaster, mayor and county treasurer. Jerome B. Chaffee was United States Senator when he invested in the Little Pittsburg, and his banking and mining partner, D. H. Moffat, was the treasurer of three railroads. These three men are supposed to have realized together over three millions from their mining operations. But Tabor has made other millions from the Chrysolite, and from various mines, ventures and investments. T. Foley is another millionaire of many mines, and had made money in California before reaching Leadville. George Fryer, the first locator on Fryer hill, has made several fortunes since 1878, and knows how to enjoy them. Dr. C. R. Bissell, who returned from the Little Pittsburg with several hundred thousands, is operating other leading mines from New York headquarters. A part of the Robert E. Lee owners were well to do before they secured the mine; all of them have plenty of money now. Joseph W. Watson, ex-Governor Routt and George C. Corning are mainly devoted to the interests of their one great mine, the Morning Star. W. H. Stevens, the first discoverer of carbonates, was always a man of wealth who has mined in Colorado for twenty years; but the Iron-Silver added greatly to his fortune. Rische, like Tabor, has invested liberally in mines, real estate, residences and fine horses. A. R. Meyer, J. B. Grant and Eddy and James have amassed wealth from ore buying, mining and smelting, and do the largest business in those lines in the world.

CHAPTER XXI.

LEADVILLE MINES — THE BONANZAS OF FRYER HILL—THE GREAT
TREASURE VAULT OF THE TIMES, AND HOW IT WAS DEVELOPED—
THE CHRYSOLITE, LITTLE CHIEF, AND ROBERT E. LEE—MILLIONS
OF SILVER—THE LITTLE PITTSBURG, AMIE, DUNKIN AND CLIMAX—
CHLORIDES AND CARBONATES—HOW FORTUNES WERE MADE.

While the mining camp of Leadville was excited over the Iron, Camp Bird and Carbonate mines, George H. Fryer went over to an unprospected locality and sunk a shaft on a hill north of Stray Horse Gulch. He found carbonates on the 4th day of April, 1878, and called his claim the New Discovery. At first the ore was not rich in quality, but was good enough when found in such quantities to insure very fair profits. This was the beginning of a mine that has since yielded millions.

A month later other prospectors were at work. Among them were August Rische and George T. Hook, who had left shoemaking for the more exciting avocation of carbonate hunting. They had no money with which to obtain supplies or tools, and H. A. W. Tabor, one of Leadville's merchants, supplied their needs for a one-third interest in whatever they might discover. It cost about seventeen dollars to outfit the party. They sunk their shaft but 26 feet before "striking mineral," the first wagon load of which sold for over two hundred dollars. As drifting progressed, ore became more plentiful, and in July they were mining 75 tons weekly. Hook hailed from Pittsburg, and as there was already one claim in camp named after that city, this mine was called the Little Pittsburg. The Union and Winnemuck claims were among the first located in this neighborhood. Afterwards shafts were sunk on claims recorded as the Little Chief, Carboniferous and Chrysolite, as well as other properties. These were paying handsomely before snow fell. The locality was called Fryer Hill, in honor of the first discoverer, and by that name it will ever be famous as the richest silver depository the world could show in 1879–80, and probably for many years after. Iron and Carbonate hills had made the district famous, but it was reserved for Fryer Hill to cause that fever of excitement which turned the entire nation's attention to Leadville.

The commencement of what has since grown into the mammoth Chrysolite mine began with the opening of the Carboniferous and Chrysolite claims. The former adjoined the Little Chief and the same rich ore body was reached at a depth of 100 feet and over. Before the close of 1878 a drift had been run 80 feet long through a rich ore body averaging 22 feet in thickness. Further down the northern slope of the hill a rich strike was made in a small triangular piece of ground, 35 feet by 60, that had been left out when the Vulture, Eva and other claims were surveyed. The Triangle, as it was called, yielded from its diminutive territory $58,000 before exhausted. This discovery led to the sinking of shafts all around it and to splendid discoveries in the Vulture and Little Eva. The longer these claims were worked the larger the production became. Meantime properties were changing hands all over Fryer Hill, many shafts were being sunk, and horse power was giving place to steam for hoisting purposes. It is said that one avaricious prospector, who despaired of discovering carbonates on his claim, " salted " it with rich ore and sold it for $2,000. After boasting of this achievement he was chagrined to learn that the purchasers had discovered a bonanza by sinking his shaft a little deeper.

When the Little Pittsburg harvest was fairly rolling in, late in 1878, H. A. W. Tabor and associates bought up all the properties near the Chrysolite that could be had at reasonable figures. There was no outcrop on the surface of the ground to indicate what was beneath, and considerable " nerve " was required at that period to pay ten, twenty, or fifty thousand dollars for unproductive land. The developments that followed, however, showed that Tabor's judgment was correct, and led to subsequent purchases on less favorable probabilities all over the district by numberless miners and speculators. Marshall Field, of Chicago, who was interested here with Tabor, eventually made as much money as his partner Leiter did on the Iron or his mercantile rival Farwell did on the Little Chief. In the summer and fall of 1879 the output of the Tabor, Field and Borden, or Chrysolite mines had grown to enormous proportions. The Vulture alone yielded prior to October 17, 3,100 tons and 1,235 pounds of ore, selling for $287,645.54, and the other claims gave $777,213.16.

Chrysolite.   Little Chief.   Amie.   Little Pittsburg.

FRYER HILL.

In October, 1879, the great California operator, George D. Roberts, and others, purchased these properties for \$2,778,000, and organized the Chrysolite Silver Mining Company thereon. W. S. Keyes, who had been one of the prominent mining superintendents of the Nevada Comstock, took charge of the property as general manager. He was at the head of all the great mining operations of the same firm in and near Leadville—and these embrace such giant concerns as the Iron Silver, and Little Chief, as well as the Chrysolite—all but the last purchased subsequent to the beginning of the year. Under his control, including miners, mechanics, teamsters, etc., are nearly one thousand men. His lieutenants were selected from among tried and experienced Comstock miners, one of the few lodes of the world so large as to require the same kind of timbering as at Leadville. His development of these mines has been as rapid and systematic as it is fruitful of big results. The Iron Silver and Chrysolite have lately become the largest producers of the time, and surpass anything before achieved east of Nevada, while the Little Chief is but a little way behind them. It would seem that five millions have been put in sight during the time that a million and a half has been taken out.

The Chrysolite mine embraces 66.57 acres of surface area and all that can be found beneath. In it are included the Chrysolite, Carboniferous, Little Eva, Kit Carson, All Right, Fairview, Pandora, Colorado Chief, Vulture, Muldoon, and Eaton claims. Up to the time of sale the original owners had run drifts here and there in different localities, aggregating 3,282 feet. In the first seven months of the new management, the amount of such openings were more than doubled, and were driven to such purpose as to connect all the main workings with one new central shaft, the present grand outlet of the mine. Levels were driven into new and previously unexplored ground, and the ore reserves were quadrupled in extent, at the same time that the mine's producing capacity was increased immensely. Some time ago the most conservative estimates placed the ore reserves at over 100,000 tons, valued at \$7,000,000. Explorations goes on much faster than does stoping, and consequently there is a steady gain in quantity of ore blocked out or drifted on. The underground workings present a labyrinth of drifts, cross cuts, and inclines, but the main avenues are those recently driven from the new shaft to the limits of the property east, south, and west, and now going north-

DOWN IN THE BONANZA MINES—UNDERGROUND WORKINGS.

ward.   There will soon be two miles of such excavations.   Among the permanent improvements made, the new Roberts shaft and its great building and splendid hoisting machinery are the chief.   These have no equals in the camp unless it be the new Daly shaft on the adjoining Little Chief mine.   The shaft house comprises spacious shaft, timber, machine, and blacksmith rooms, with tracks leading to extensive ore buildings and bins.   The hoisting machinery, driven by a sixty-horse-power engine and boilers, is capable of raising hundreds of tons of ore daily.   The entire equipments are as perfect as can be made.   The shaft has three compartments, one for pump and ladder way, and two for the iron cages used for hoisting ore.   There are three landings or stations, 115, 165, and 215 feet below the surface, and levels leading therefrom to intersect workings of various depth opened when the ore bodies dipped downward or raised towards the surface.   No great amount of barren ground has been encountered, while the extension of the bonanza northward into what was considered doubtful ground has been proved by the newer levels.   The ore body is from ten to forty feet thick—and occasionally more and less.   Its general dip is to the east, and its roll or pitch northerly and southerly.   It comprises sand and hard carbonates with some galena seams of chlorides.   In different periods the average receipts for all ore sold have varied from $61 to $83.50, and the value per superficial foot exceeded $30.   But a fraction of the entire property's area has yet been explored.   A few tons of chlorides lately came from the Vulture that contained from one to ten thousand dollars per ton.

The amount of ore produced by the Chrysolite previous to April 1, 1880, and the receipts therefor were as given below.   That sold by the original owners nearly all came out in eleven months' time.

	Tons of Ore delivered.	Tons of Ore paid for.	Receipts.
Tabor & Co., prior to Oct. 17, 1879................	unkn'n	12,806	$1,064,85 70
Chrysolite Co., from Oct. 17, 1879, to April 1, 1880.	20,373	19,340	1,193,528 93
Total for first 18 months of mine....	......	32,146	$2,258,387 68
Add $25 per ton for average smelters' charges for 18 months...................................	......	......	803,650 00
Gives probable actual value of silver and lead....	......	......	$3,062,037 68

In less than five and a half months, while the company was putting the Chrysolite mine in shape for future production, five dividends, amounting to $1,000,000, were paid, and another one of $100,000 in April. With shares at $20, an investor would get his money back in two years, and there appears to be sufficient value in the mine's reserves to pay for the entire capital stock, when having a market value of $4,000,000.

The officers of the Chrysolite Company are Daniel S. Appleton, president; Henry A. V. Post, vice-president; L. M. Lawson, treasurer; Drake De Kay, secretary; and the first three and John P. Jones, William Borden, H. A. W. Tabor, Arthur Sewall, W. S. Nichols, E. B. Dorsey, C. A. Whittier, and Ulysses S. Grant, Jr., trustees. The capital stock is $10,000,000, in 200,000 fifty-dollar shares.

The Little Chief is another of the great mines of Leadville. Here the carbonate deposits of the district seem to attain their greatest thickness, at the same time that they maintain an unusually high value. The claim extends north and south over Fryer hill, cutting the Little Pittsburg property in halves and lying between Little Pittsburg claim proper and the Chrysolite. It was located by four hard-working men, Peter Finerty, Richard and Patrick Dillon, and John Taylor. Soon after Tabor and his partners began to take out ore in quantity, these men "struck" carbonates, and in a few months they had more money than they knew what to do with. They received about $100,000 for ore sold, and in December, 1878, sold for $300,000. J. V. Farwell, the great dry goods merchant of Chicago, was already interested in reduction works in Colorado, and since his great rival, L. Z. Leiter, had been so fortunate in his iron mine investment, he concluded that he would try his luck in the carbonate camp. Accordingly he and other Chicago men paid the above-mentioned sum for the Little Chief. Finerty has since made other fortunes in mines and enterprises of various kinds, and his old partners have been having a good time on what they received—one of them having little left. The Chicago purchasers put up a thirty-five-ton smelter on the claim, sunk several new shafts, and erected a number of mine buildings supplied with steam hoisting machinery. The product of the mine for 1879 reached the enormous amount of 17,496 tons of ore, returning $1,487,000; 4,329 tons of ore were taken out in the first six months, and 13,167 in the last half of the year. The smelter was at work 120 days, but was shut down during the winter by the Little Chief Company. The mine was brought into first class producing condition in February, 1880. The actual value of the product in 1878, and before the sale to Farwell & Co., was $158,000. The total ore product and receipts to April 1, 1880, have been as follows :

Product of 1878	1,200 tons	$158,000 00
" 1879	17,496 "	1,487,000 00
" first three months of 1880	6,540 "	273,685 98
Total	25,236	$1,918,685 98

Add $22 per ton for difference between smelter's price and actual yield, gives a grand total for 21 months of.......................... $2,473,857 98

Beginning with March, monthly dividends of $100,000 are paid, or 12 per cent. per annum on the capital stock. At the beginning of 1880 George D. Roberts and associates purchased the mine and organized the Little Chief Mining Company, under the laws of New York, with a capital stock of $10,000,000 in 200,000 shares of a par value of $50 each. The officers are Gen. Adelbert Ames, president; George D. Roberts, vice-president; Dumont Clark, treasurer; D. F. Verdenal, secretary; George Daly, general manager. The trustees are Jonas H. French, A. P. K. Safford, Jesse Spaulding, A. D. Breed, Albert Ames, John R. Hall, R. C. McCormick, Henry Havemeyer, G. A. Bruce, L. R. Marsh, E. H. Potter, A. D. Davis, S. Elliott, and George D. Roberts.

On taking charge of the Little Chief, George Daly at once began to retimber it—and this was sadly needed in many places. His experience in the great mines of the Pacific slope had fitted him for all such difficult emergencies as this, and in a very short space of time he had executed the job in a masterly manner, thus placing the property in splendid working condition. Probably no mine off the Comstock, with the exception of the Chrysolite, is as substantially timbered as this, and no other has deposits whose removal calls for such solid underground work. As the ore is taken out the ground above is kept from caving in by "square sets," composed of massive timbers two feet more or less in diameter. The upright posts are from seven to ten feet high, and these are capped by similar timbers from four to five feet wide. Thus one set is built above another until the top of the cavity once occupied by ore is reached. It must be remembered that these carbonate deposits in this hill are horizontal or nearly so. Their enormous extent can then be appreciated from the fact that these sets stand one above another in tiers from three to eight and ten deep, the ore body being 80 feet thick in one portion of the claim—and this good paying ore. A long period of time gave the average price of over $70 per ton for all ore sold. Some of the ore is much richer, however, and the glistening chlorides and sand carbonates often mill way up into the hundreds. Since this company got fairly at work the daily output has averaged over 100 tons of ore daily, and the quantity of reserves to draw from is enormous. Nearly 200 men are employed, and the product may yet be doubled. In April, 1880, all of the workings of the Little Chief, both old and new, could be covered by a surface area 275 feet wide by 600 feet in length. Of this not over half had been developed by the levels, drifts, and cross-cuts. But a small portion had been stoped. The north end of the claim had not had the slightest amount of work done upon it, and the Daily shaft, situated further in that direction by many feet than any of the older workings, had just come into the extension north of the great ore body. This is a new three-compartment shaft—the main working outlet of the mine to which avenues lead from all underground workings. It was sunk at the rapid rate of five feet per day, which is exceedingly good progress when its great size and fine equipments are taken into consideration. It is supplied with cages and all the latest improvements, with machinery capable of hoisting one thousand tons of ore daily. At a depth of 100 feet carbonates of the same valuable character as in the old shafts were entered ; so there is seemingly no limit to the ore body. In the first eleven days of May the Little Chief shipped 1,274 tons of ore.

The Little Pittsburg claim began to produce carbonates in May, 1878, and in July it and the New Discovery claim were each turning out 75 tons of ore per week. A shaft was started on a claim, called the Winnemuck, before Rische and Hook came on the hill. They found ore at a depth of only twenty-six feet, and in locating the Little Pittsburg took in the then barren Winnemuck shaft. Before that time Dr. C. R. Bissell, A. H. Foss, George W. Trimble, and A. V. Hunter had purchased most of the Winnemuck, and subsequently owned all of it.   They did not "strike mineral" until the shaft was 150 feet deep, and then they had from ten to thirty feet of it. Tabor and Rische claimed it, and so matters stood near the end of September, when Bissell and partners went over to the other side of the Little Pittsburg and bought out Borden's half interest in the New Discovery for $40,000.   They had cleared that in a few weeks' work in the Winnemuck.   This purchase was a serious flank movement, as the older title of the New Discovery might eventually take in the Little Pittsburg, if the ore strata was decided to be a regular vein.   Before the Winnemuck men could secure Fryer's interest, Senator Jerome B. Chaffee bought it for $50,000. About that time Tabor and Rische bought the one-third interest of their partner Hook in the Little Pittsburg for $98,000, and soon had their money back out of the mine.   Before Chaffee left camp they took the New Discovery off his hands for $125,000, and then had no more fears about titles.

The mines kept on improving faster than ever, and Chaffee and Moffatt becoming enthusiastic over them purchased Rische's entire interest for $262,500.   On the 18th day of November, 1878, the owners of the New Discovery, Little Pittsburg, Dives and Winnemuck united their properties by forming the Little Pittsburg Consolidated Company.   The Little Pittsburg had previously returned the handsome total of $375,000 and the Winnemuck $153,000. The latter came out in forty-nine days, clearing the owners $112,000. J. C. Wilson became Superintendent of the consolidated mines, and during the following winter sunk new shafts, erected buildings and introduced steam hoisting machinery in the camp.

Developments showed that the main portion of the ore body was in the New Discovery, and the claim that had previously remained in the background came to the front with an enormous bonanza. There were from 5 to 25 feet of high grade ores and low grade iron. The enormous size of the deposit called for a different style of timbering than had been used in Colorado before, and the Comstock square-set system was adopted.   A set comprises four upright logs or timbers of great size capped and underlaid by six shorter but similar ones.   Where the ore was twenty-five feet thick, three sets of these, one above another, were required to support the roof of the mine's excavations.

It is stated that the average contents of the ore sold for five months of 1878–9 were $111\frac{40}{100}$ ounces of silver per ton, and $22\frac{47}{100}$ per cent. of lead. This surpassed anything discovered in the district up to that time. The average selling price of the ore was $62.12, freighters', smelters', and shippers' charges then being from $70 to $75.

It is reported that the Company's first $539,269 of receipts were obtained at a cost of only $93,665 for mining and timbering, and $14,693 for building and machinery. In the spring of 1879, the Little Pittsburg Consolidated Mining Company was incorporated in New York, with a capital stock of $20,000,000 in 200,000 one-hundred-dollar shares. In June of that year Professor R. W. Raymond examined the mine and estimated that the ground opened would yield ore that would bring about $2,000,000 at the smelters. Subsequent operations have proved this to have been a pretty close estimate.

The production of the mines from time of discovery in the spring of 1878, to April 1, 1880, amounted to the enormous sums of $2,697,534.91 for receipts of ore sold, and $4,246,239.81 actual yield—nearly all obtained in a year and a half. The yield is given below, first under the original owners, then under the consolidation, and lastly under the company organized in New York.

FROM DISCOVERY TO NOVEMBER 18, 1878.	TONS OF ORE PAID FOR.	RECEIPTS TO OWNERS FOR ORE SOLD.	SMELTERS' YIELD OF ORE SOLD, ESTIMATED.
Little Pittsburg	4,000	$375,000 00	$600,000 00
New Discovery	1,000	60,000 00	100,000 00
Winnemuck	2,000	153,000 00	200,000 00
Total	7,000	588,000 00	$900,000 00

	TONNAGE OF ORE PAID FOR.	RECEIPTS TO OWNERS.	ACTUAL YIELD OF ORE SOLD OR ASSAY.
From November, 18, 1878, to May 5, 1879	8,376	$519,321 10	$1,078,586 00
From May 5, 1879, to April 1, 1880	29,248	1,590,213 81	2,267,653 81
Total yield since discovery in 1878.	44,624	$2,697,534 91	$4,246,239 81

A recent statement of the company shows that in a little less than eleven months ending April 1, 1880, the receipts for ore sold were $1,590,213.81, the profits $1,201,578.47, the amount of dividends disbursed $1,050,000, and the cash on hand $55,403.32. Of the outlays, $388,635.34 were for mining expenses, etc., $60,453.40 in payment for the Union claim and south end of New Discovery and $35,721.25 for buildings, machinery, etc. Most of the ore came out of the northern 300 feet square of the New Discovery claim.

In the spring of 1880 it was found that several large blocks of mineral standing in the mine that had been counted on as valuable reserves were mostly so poor in silver as to fail to pay expenses. At the same time advancing drifts in various directions showed a discontinuance of the bonanza. The company consequently gave notice of the suspension of the payment of dividends. This needlessly caused distrust and almost a panic in New York, as far as mining stocks went, a heavy decline setting in and continuing for a long time. The company discharged most of their mining force, but continued exploration and the hoisting and shipment of considerable quantities of ore. H. A. Kirkham succeeded George C. Lyman as secretary, and John T. Herrick became superintendent of the mines. At the annual meeting Senator W. H. Barnum, of Connecticut, succeeded ex-Senator Jerome B. Chaffee as president, and D. S. Draper succeeded D. H. Moffat as vice-president. Late explorations in the mine indicate the existence of valuable bodies of ore in the Dives and New Discovery claims.

The Amie is located on the summit of Fryer Hill, with the Little Pittsburg on the west, and the Climax on the east. The claim is 1,500 feet long by 270 wide. Although several shafts were sunk, it did not pay until the summer of 1879, when A. P. Hereford and G. K. Hartenstein sold to Senator P. B. Plumb, of Kansas, S. B. Elkins and others. The Amie Consolidated Mining Company was then organized with a capital stock of $5,000,000 in ten-dollar shares. The main ore body was 140 feet below the surface when first entered. From September, 1879, to March, 1880, $255,000 in dividends were paid. Up to the close of April, 1880, there were 5,786 tons and 1,578 pounds of ore sold and paid for, returning $461,229.91 to the company, and about 216 tons sold were still unpaid for. From July to January the receipts were $315,199.62 and the receipts of three preceding months were $146,030.29. The ore sold in January brought the high prices of from $153 to $268.74 per ton. So far the ore has been found in the porphyry, the limestone not having been reached, which leaves a chance for other ore bodies below those already mined. The hoisting machinery is new and first class. The depth from the surface to the ore bodies has ranged from 120 to 220 feet.

The Climax is owned by the La Plata Mining and Smelting Company, stocked at $2,000,000, and which has paid several dividends. The mine has several shafts and has produced considerable money, but the company's heavier revenues must come from smelting. The Climax is turning out some very rich ore. Lately one lot of twenty-three tons is said to have averaged 1,170 ounces of silver per ton.

The Dunkin mine is east of the Climax and near the Robert E. Lee and Matchless. It has paid good profits much of the time since the summer of 1879. The ore bodies, found from 75 to 110 feet below the surface, have ranged from one to twenty-seven feet in thickness. From August 20 to November, about 1,000 tons of ore were sold, yielding from 58 to 274 ounces per ton, and from ten to sixty per cent. of lead. The returns were about $35,000. The mine was then sold for $300,000, to ex-Governor Rice and John B. Alley, of Massachusetts, and Senator James G. Blaine, and a company organized with a capital stock of $5,000,000.

The Matchless was purchased some time ago by H. A. W. Tabor, for $117,000. There are other claims worked by the aid of steam hoisting machinery, such as the Virginius, Denver City, and Big Pittsburg consolidation, but none of them have produced much yet. Still their proximity to the Lee, Amie and Dunkin lead to the belief that they may cut an important figure hereafter.

Rising eastward from the Lee mine and southward from Evans' Gulch, is Yankee Hill. Here are the Scooper, Chieftain, Del Monte, Superior, Hard Cash and other valuable properties. During the past year this locality has grown greatly in favor and important discoveries have been made.

The Scooper has yielded some extremely rich ore, along with grades of moderate value. Its earlier owners, Peter Klinefelter and George Washburn, began work in 1877 and continued it whenever their limited finances would permit. Four shafts were sunk in immense bodies of iron without success, and then a splendid seam of chlorides was found by drifting from a point half way down in one of the shafts. Two mill runs of several tons each yielded over $800 and $2,000 per ton respectively. Other lots gave several hundred dollars per ton. Two hundred tons of carbonates are said to have sold at an average of $60 per ton. Assays have been obtained showing an enormous amount of silver and a little gold, with from 10 to 60 per cent. of lead. The mine was purchased by J. W. Bonta for $125,000 and stocked in Philadelphia not many months ago, under the name of the Iowa Gulch Mining Company, which owns other claims elsewhere.

The Chieftain adjoins the Scooper and is likely to contain some of the same classes of high-grade ores. As it is the yield has already been considerable. Inclines and shafts show a large body of paying ore. This mine was purchased in 1879, by J. W. Bonta, and a company organized thereon. The Del Monte adjoins both the Chieftain and Scooper and is being developed so as to enter the same ore strata. It is likely to prove as valuable as its neighbors. It belongs to the Del Monte Company, organized on this and other claims, with a capital stock of five millions.

The Robert E. Lee mine stands unrivalled as a producer of rich silver ores in large quantities. It has undoubtedly produced a greater amount of unusually valuable mineral than any other mine in the country, and there is a far larger tonnage of similar character uncovered in the mine than has ever come out of it. The property comprises about five acres of ground, only a small part of which is opened by levels and cross cuts. Outside of seams of gray sand containing quantities of chlorides and horn silver, and bunches of mineral coated with pure chlorides, is an immense body of carbonates, milling in the hundreds. There are also large amounts of low grade material, containing from twenty to forty dollars a ton.

This property, which is now valued at millions, was bought of the original owners in 1879 for some $7,000. It is said that one of the locators had previously sold for fifty dollars. Nothing of great value was discovered on that part of Fryer Hill for a long time. Mineral was found in the Lee in February, 1879, but for a long time much trouble was experienced from water and later from litigation. Other parties claimed the property, and the contest prevented active operations. The contesting parties were finally bought out, and negotiations for the purchase of the property for over two hundred thousand dollars having fallen through, mining began in earnest on the 2d day of August.   Ore was found at a depth of 150 feet, which soon proved to carry hundreds and in some places thousands of dollars to the ton.   Rich as had been the bonanzas of many Leadville mines, this surpasses them all as far as high grade ores are concerned.   The mine is as superior in this respect as was its namesake in deeds· of arms.   The deposit is many feet thick, so that quantity as well as quality is assured.

The yield for the first three months of production ending November 1, 1879, rolled up the extraordinary product of $495,000. In October, $125,000 was taken out in ten days, $100,000 of which came from various lots of ore which were sold on the following remarkable assays: 520 ounces of silver per ton; 708, 767, 882, 1,098, 1,412, 1,516, 2,825, 2,878, 3,014, 5,405, and 10,306.   The larger portion of the ore shipped from the mine, however, carries from 150 to $250 a ton.

The ore mined in the month of January, 1880, sold for the enormous sum of $301,494.79. Eddy, James & Co., gave a single check of $130,775.86 for 344 tons of ore from that month's product.   Some of the lots of ore contained the following weights and number of ounces of silver per ton—to get value in dollars add about one-seventh to number of ounces—3,341 pounds of ore contained at the rate of 11,535 ounces of silver per ton; 2,576 pounds, 4,767 ounces; 5,208 pounds, 4,670 ounces; 13,059 pounds, 1,290 ounces; 14,852 pounds, 1,215 ounces; 10,484 pounds, 1,088 ounces; 14,199 pounds, 729 ounces; 14,852 pounds, 576 ounces; 15,364 pounds, 568 ounces; and 20,561 pounds, 530 ounces.

On the 13th day of January, an effort was made to see how much could be taken out of the mine within twenty-four hours. The result was 95 tons of ore, valued at $118,500, showing an average value of over $1,200 a ton.   Two tons of these chlorides and carbonates carried 11,839 ounces of silver ·per ton, four tons averaged 4,993 ounces and eight tons 1,234 ounces.   The general daily product was from seven to ten thousand dollars at that time. The Lee has given the largest yield for a single month and a single day of any mine in the country outside of Nevada.

The mine had yielded a round million up to February, 1880, a period of only six months after active work fairly began.   Probably nine-tenths of that sum was clear profit.   The owners of this magnificent property during that time were J. F. Sigafus, B. F.

Crowell, Irving Howbert and Joseph F. Humphrey, of Colorado Springs, and W. H. Rodebush, J. Y. Marshall and Homer Pennock, of Leadville.

In the spring of 1880 the company erected a lixiviation mill at the mine for treating the low grade ores that carried but little lead. The ore passes from the ore bins to the drying floors, then through chutes to leaching vats containing liquid solution of hyposulphate of soda. Thence the liquid passes to settling vats, the precipitate is finally drawn off, concentrated by roasting and the roasted product shipped to eastern refining works.

The Hibernia claim joins the Robert E. Lee on the south. Recent developments show that the same ore body extends from one into the other. The ore produced is of exceedingly high grade. One lot of 22 tons averaged 392 ounces of silver per ton. Ten tons of ore were coming out daily at last accounts. The Hibernia Consolidated Mining Company, capitalized at $7,500,000, has been organized in New York on the Hibernia, Surprise and May Queen claims. The leading stockholders are prominent Leadville and New York men, such as Edward Eddy, W. H. James, J. B. Grant, H. A. W. Tabor, George R. Fisher, W. H. Bush and J. H. Talbott. They are confident that the mine will rival the Lee. It may do so yet.

The names of all of Leadville's reduction works or smelters are not given in the tabulated statement of the bullion product. Some have been erected since the beginning of the year and others have been enlarged by the addition of more furnaces. Among the latter are the Grant, Elgin, Cummings & Finn, and Ohio and Missouri. The Davis smelter, lately erected, is different from the others in using no blast, but depending on its smoke-stack for draft. It has been found that large quantities of Leadville ores containing but little lead can be handled advantageously by the leaching process. A new mill is being erected for this method, to contain fifty stamps and many pans. P. McCann is manager. Messrs. Foley, Eddy, James, Grant, Tabor and Foss are interested. A similar mill is operated at the Lee mine. In the first three months of 1880, Leadville's bullion and ore export was not far from $3,700,000 in value, or about double what it was in the corresponding months of 1879. Every month now shows an increase. It is fair to infer that the district is producing at the rate of from sixteen to twenty millions per annum. Leadville had 6,000 voters registered and cast 4,043 votes at the city election of April, 1880.

EDDY & JAMES' SAMPLING WORKS, LEADVILLE.

CHAPTER XXII.

CUSTER COUNTY MINES—SILVER CLIFF AND ROSITA—CHLORIDES AND
MIXED GOLD AND SILVER ORES—BASSICK'S WONDERFUL FIND—
A HILL FULL OF MINERAL—A CLIFF OF SILVER ORES—THE
RACINE BOY BONANZA—THE PLATA VERDE, JOHN BULL, DOMINGO,
AND IRON MOUNTAIN—THE WORK OF VOLCANIC AGENCIES—THE
POCAHONTAS-HUMBOLDT TRUE FISSURE.

Custer county extends from the Sangre de Cristo Mountains easterly
to the borders of the plains and the foot hills of Fremont county.
It was set off from the latter by act of the legislature in 1876.
Within its limits are the Wet Mountains and the valley of the same
name. The mineral wealth of the district has recently been found
to be far more varied, novel, and extensive than was supposed, and
the pastoral and farming resources are by no means insignificant.
On the north and east is Fremont county, and on the east and south
is Huerfano, both excellent farm and stock regions, and both possessing coal measures of great extent and superior quality.

The three pioneer prospectors and miners were Irwin, Robinson,
and Pringle, who discovered the Senator lode in the fall of 1872.
They named the settlement Rosita—the Spanish for "a little rose."
It has since grown to be a pretty town of twelve hundred people,
and the centre of a valuable mining district. The location is a
beautiful one, surrounded as it is by dome-shaped hills, smooth and
grass-clad on the sides facing Wet Mountain valley and the great
Sangre de Cristo range and covered with pines on the reverse.

In 1874 the Pocahontas-Humboldt and other lodes began to produce and have since yielded not far from $600,000 in silver. In
1877 the wonderful Maine or Bassick mine began to turn out its gold
and silver ore, and a year later the Silver Cliff excitement sprung
up. This arose from the discovery of a veritable bonanza in the
way of chloride silver ores, called the Racine Boy, and of other
lodes of great importance. The year 1879 opened very favorably
for the district.

Custer county yielded $1,659,529.98 prior to 1880, mostly silver.

1874 and previously...	$40,000.00	1877..................	$354,081.34
1875..................	294.827.58	1878..................	352,500.50
1876..................	351,121.06	1879..................	367,000.00

Total.............................$1,659,529.98.

The Humboldt lode was discovered in April, 1874. The following month the Pocahontas and Southeast Leviathan and Leavenworth were located to the northwest of it, and the Virginia on the southeast. Subsequent explorations proved these to be all on one vein of great length and uniformity, and rich in silver. The enclosing formation is trachytic, bordering on the granite of the hills and ridges to the northward. The lode extends across the head of the valley in which Rosita is built. The Pocahontas and Humboldt did not produce largely until 1875-6. During the last year and a half poor ground has been encountered, and the old owners of the former suspended work. The Pocahontas, Powhattan and Pawnee lodes were recently purchased by California men of the Silver Cliff Company, who will develop and operate them extensively. The Pocahontas and Humboldt each have 1,385 feet on the vein, the Virginia 1,500, and the Leviathan, Leavenworth and others foot up over 3,500 feet additional, or a mile and a half on one vein.

Up to the end of 1877 the Pocahontas mine yielded 2,543 tons of ore, containing $279,353.02, and selling for $167,523.33. Of this 564½ tons averaged 36.8 ounces of silver per ton, and 1,979 averaged 98.7 ounces, or $127.61. It cost $190,375 for buildings, machinery, and to mine, hoist, and open up ground; but a large portion of this was for the first two items, which are good for years to come. The cost of sinking the shaft is given at $20 per foot of depth; of driving levels, $5 to $5.50; adits, $7. When George C. Munson operated the mine in 1878 he drove a level 112 feet, at $5.50 per foot.

The Humboldt became the property of the Humboldt Silver Mining Company in October, 1875, 1,900 feet of the vein being included. The vein of paying ore has varied from four inches to four feet in width. The main shaft is 540 feet deep. Three levels have been driven at intervals of 100 feet westward to the Pocahontas ground and eastward nearly or quite the same distance. A cross-cut, starting 400 feet down the shaft, was driven nearly 200 feet at right angles from the vein to explore ground, into which ore-feeders were found to branch off in sinking the shaft. This cross-cut passes through a kind of conglomerate cement, with occasional ore seams, and has cost six dollars per foot of advance. The cost of sinking the main shaft five feet by twelve was from eight to thirty dollars per foot. It costs to break rock in the levels, four feet by seven, from four to six dollars per foot. Stoping costs two dollars for every foot of advance six feet high and two feet wide. The hoisting machinery is of the best description, and includes a fifty horse-power engine. The explored ground has been mostly exhausted for a depth of 300 feet. A. Thornton is general superintendent.

The Virginia has been owned by a company of the same name since April, 1876. Its main shaft is 355 feet deep and there are 700 feet of levels and 465 square fathoms of stoping. The hoisting and pumping machinery is first-class. The Leviathan has a shaft 171 feet deep and several short levels.

The Humboldt and Virginia companies built the Pennsylvania reduction works in 1876. They contain 10 stamps for crushing, 2 revolving cylinders for roasting, 6 amalgamating pans, 2 agitators and vats for leaching with copper. Five men are required by day and four by night. Daily capacity 9 to 10 tons of Humboldt ore.

R. Neilson Clark, M. E., who has operated the Virginia and other mines, compiled a pamphlet on the Pocahontas-Humboldt vein, from which the following statement of the workings and yield of the four mines to 1878 is taken, with product of that year added. The values are currency, with gold ranging from 115 to 100.

	Shafting.	Drifting.	Adits and Tunnels.	Stoped.	Shipped.	Currency Value.	Mill Returns.	Average per Sq. Fathom.	Average per Ton.
	Feet.	Feet.	Feet.	Sq. Fath.	Tons.				
Southeast Leviathan	171	190	....	....	50	$4,300 00	$2,100 00	....	$86
Pocahontas	690	1,946	460	2,300	2,559	323,477 51	171,247 91	$138	124
Humboldt..	1,490	2,200	....	3,100	2,105	275,604 15	132,145 06	73	107
Virginia....	510	700	140	465	179	18,547 85	9,821 20	40	103
	2,861	5,036	600	5,865	4,893	$621.929 51	$315,314 17	....	...

The vein, with an average trend of north 50° west, conforms to the part of the range in which it occurs. Its hanging wall is remarkably regular and smooth; the foot-wall is less regular, and often swells from the hanging wall. Many insist that the vein is at least twenty-five feet thick; they assume that a parallel streak occurring on the foot-wall side is part of the vein, and that all the rock between is fissure matter. I question the correctness of this view, for in most places both walls of this one pay streak are identical in all respects, except perhaps smoothness and hardness. The gangue is a soft clay, easily mined as a gouge, occurring usually towards the foot-wall; it is undoubtedly decomposed trachyte, usually showing the characteristic color, etc., of that portion of the wall against which it lies. The pay-streak usually lies against the hanging wall, often separated from it by a clay selvage. It is always accompanied with heavy spar (remarkably free from rhomb-spar), and galena is also found. Generically the ore is a barytic-tetrahedrite; copper and iron pyrites are common, together with stephanite and the like. The more valuable specimens are the antimonial compounds of silver. The vein pitches strongly to the southeast."

The Leavenworth is the westernmost portion of the same vein, and has much the same characteristics as the Pocahontas. The main shaft, 140 feet deep, and levels extending therefrom, yielded 150 tons of ore, that brought $10,000 in fifteen months ending March, 1879. The mine was opening up finely at last accounts. There are several cross veins. One of these yields ore similar to the main vein—or from two to three hundred dollars per ton. The owners are Paul Gerkie & Co. The Pioneer and Chieftain cross the Leavenworth.

A number of tunnels have been driven into the hills of Rosita district. The Custer County Tunnel Company has pushed one of these into Robinson Hill over 300 feet. W. A. Offenbacher, Charles Baker, and other Custer county men, are the officers and stockholders of the enterprise. Pockets and bodies of ore yielding from 300 to 400 ounces of silver per ton have often been found on the surface of this hill, which led to the opinion that a great ore-body existed somewhere in the vicinity. Last May a valuable vein was intersected by this tunnel. There is said to be three feet of 40-ounce ore, but parts of the vein yield from $100 to $400 a ton.

The Michigan Tunnel Company have driven a prospecting tunnel

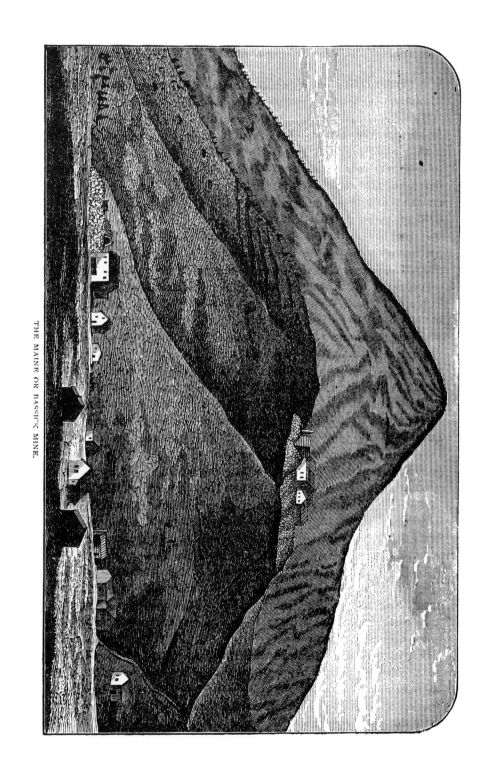

THE MAINE OR BASSICK MINE.

into Tyndall Hill, adjoining the Bassick Hill, some 400 feet. The Minnesota tunnel has penetrated Robinson Hill over 300 feet.

The Benjamin Franklin lode was discovered on a hill near the Bassick in July, 1877, and is owned by Thurman, Prescott, Maxwell & Co., who purchased it early in 1878. In less than a year they sold seventy tons of ore for $9,940. A level is being driven at a depth of 200 feet in the main shaft which is a little deeper. The crevice is large and the ore is found in pockets of from a few hundred pounds to ten or fifteen tons. The ore of the first sixty feet was carbonates, below that galena and zinc-blende, and copper pyrites and gray copper have lately been plentiful, with black sulphurets and some very rich ore. Mill returns from 80 to 175 ounces.

Among veins that have paid are the Chieftain, Lucille, Victoria, Polonia, Hector, Tecumseh, Triumph, Twenty-six, Plymouth and others. Forty tons of ore from the Victoria, sold in a portion of 1878, yielded 1,680 ounces of silver. Richard Irwin operates the Golden Eagle gold lode in Hardscrabble district.

Among those who settled at Rosita while the Pocahontas and Humboldt mines were at the height of their production was Mr. E. C. Bassick. He had been pretty much all over the world and had once made a fortune in the Australian gold mines, but had subsequently lost it. In the summer of 1877 he was engaged in tunneling Tyndall Hill, something over two miles north of Rosita. In passing to and from his work he had often noticed float or blossom rock of a peculiar appearance scattered along a neighboring hillside. He finally had some of this assayed, and the result caused him to take some of the surface material to the reduction-works. This brought thirty dollars, and as the ground proved more profitable than that of the tunnel, he continued to sink in his new prospect hole, which he called the Maine, after his native state. He soon after sent a lot of eight or ten tons of ore to the mill, and, to his astonishment, received over $12,000 therefor. This unexpected good fortune was all the more acceptable to one who had experienced many and long-continued reverses.

From that time forward the immense value of the discovery seemed assured, and subsequent developments have made its wealth more and more apparent. Month after month saw an increase in production, and the owner was raised from poverty to affluence in a very short space of time.

The character and appearance of the mineral and formation were so different from anything previously known in Colorado that prospectors had overlooked or passed by this hill as worthless. It remained for Mr. Bassick to unlock the treasure-vault that has few equals anywhere. From the time of the first sale of ore he kept steadily at the work of development. Near the surface a nest of boulders coated and mixed with chlorodized mineral was encountered, supposed to be a huge mineralized chimney nearly perpendicular in direction. Decomposed material was found to extend downward about one hundred and fifty feet with a yield of from one hundred to over one thousand dollars per ton, and the same boulder formation. Below, the crevice is less decomposed and oxidized. The great quantity and superior quality of the ore enabled the owner to reap a very respectable fortune

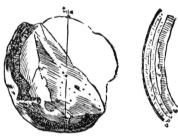

BOULDER AND SHELL.

monthly. A rich ore-body was drifted on at a depth of sixty feet, which was followed southward seventy feet, where sinking was again resorted to. Finally, the old shaft was driven downward on an incline so as to connect with the other, and then continued below. Levels and a stope were started in two or three localities. The shaft is wider in one direction than in the other. It varies in size from sixteen to twenty-four feet, and near the bottom is about thirty feet wide, with mineralized ground all around it.

It is impossible to give the total value of the mine's product, as the former owner kept no books and did not preserve all his smelters' receipts. Those in existence show that from July 21, 1877, when work began, to June 2, 1879, 731 tons were sold for $145,144, averaging $199.92 per ton. The final yield of the ore was $186,654.27, or $255.34 per ton. Mr. Bassick claims to have sold more than double that amount during the time mentioned, and also to have sold $100,000 worth of ore between June 2 and August 1, 1879. The value of the low grade material on the dump, said to average $36.87 per ton, is estimated at $147,497. Production was not pushed in 1879, and for some time previous, owing to the driving of a tunnel, the construction of an underground chamber, retimbering the mine, and negotiations for a sale; otherwise the yield would have been larger. In July, 1879, the property was sold to New York parties, and the Bassick Mining Company was organized. In three months, to April 1, 1880, the ore shipped contained a total value of $79,800. A town has sprung up around the mine, called Querida, with a population of two hundred souls.

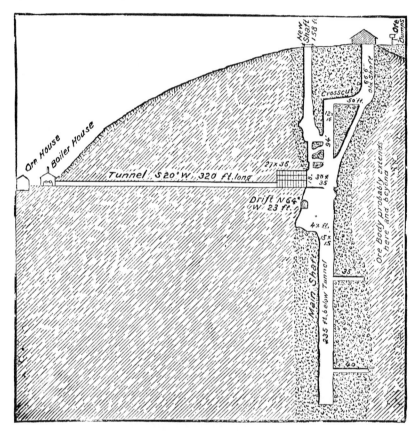

UNDERGROUND WORKINGS OF THE BASSICK MINE.

The first year's operations had left the mine in very bad shape, and this and the immense width of mineralized ground, rendered a new system of timbering and of work necessary. A tunnel was driven 320 feet to the shaft, where a huge chamber was excavated and timbered in the most substantial manner. Here the engine and hoisting works are located, and below, the fine three-compartment shaft extends in the old shaft and beneath. The company now has one of the best equipped shafts in the State. The shaft timbers and the walls of the mine are supported by "square sets," after the style of the Comstock. This superior underground work appears to be as nearly perfect as possible. The shaft was about 235 feet deeper than the tunnel chamber in June, 1880.

A concentrating mill is being erected to handle the low grade ore of which an immense amount has accumulated. This will enable the entire output of the mine to be made available. The underground developments are opening up a vast amount of paying ground. The drifts leading from the shaft are said to be looking finely. The shipping ore averages over $100 a ton. Some of it carries from two to six hundred dollars. Some rich telluride ores are being shipped. As depth is gained the rich scale or coating of the boulders carrying tellurides of gold and silver has been getting thicker, causing increased returns.

The formation of this section is trachyte, with granite to the northward. There appears to be a grand porphyry dike extending east and west, but it may be more properly termed trachyte. The boulders and pebbles in the great ore channel of the Maine are of the same material, and carry more or less mineral. They are cemented together with porphyry and other material, and coated over with mineral, and the entire filling is very rich in gold and silver as well as copper, the latter increasing as depth is gained. From sixty to seventy per cent. of the value obtained is in gold, and ten per cent. or more of the ore is copper. Down to the water line, or a depth of 150 feet or more, the boulders have a film or coating of rich mineral, varying in thickness from a knife blade to half an inch. Below that depth the ore is more in the shape of shells. While the boulders are mineralized, the filling between them carries chlorides, iron and copper pyrites, gray copper, tellurides, sylvanite, galena, zinc, carbonates, talc, native silver and free gold. In fact this hill comprises a conglomeration of nearly all kinds of mineral in almost unlimited quantity. The mineralized zone appears to have a width of over 100 feet.

MASS OF MINERALIZED BOULDERS.

The Bassick Mining Company has a capital stock of $10,000,000 and 100,000 shares. Its officers are Frank G. Brown, president, Dennis Ryan, vice-president, W. S. Hoyt, treasurer, Henry Cummins, secretary, and the same and Edmund C. Bassick, directors.

Silver Cliff is a new mining district, organized and settled within the past year. It is on the eastern slope of Wet Mountain Valley, and is mainly smooth prairie land, with occasional dome-shaped hills. It is seven miles west of Rosita, about the same distance east of the base of the Sangre de Cristo range, and thirty miles south or southwest of Cañon City and the railway. Wet Mountain valley had long been known as a fine stock-growing country, but few believed it possessed mineral resources of value.

Near Round Mountain a long sloping hill rises from the plain, but comes to an abrupt termination at one end. This was known as "the Cliff," and around it cattle had been grazing for years. A miner named Edwards passed along that way in the spring of 1878, and carelessly broke a piece of rock from the face of the cliff. With no expectation of its being rich in the precious metals, he had it assayed, and to his surprise it gave a return of 27 ounces of silver per ton. As that kind of silver ore would not pay expenses of treatment at smelting works, he paid no more attention to the place.

The next summer Edwards and a man named Powell mined among the hills toward Rosita. After working until August without making a dollar, it occurred to Edwards that the low grade assay of the "Cliff" rock was better than what they were getting. Acting on the suggestion of his partner, these men "broke camp" and moved over to the Cliff. The first assay they ordered went $1,700. This was good enough to tie to, and, taking a third party named Spoffard "in with them," they began work. They gave the locality the name of Silver Cliff, but kept their discovery a secret in order to be sure of a title and of more lodes in the future. It was not long, however, before the sight of some big bright silver buttons of theirs in a Rosita assay office caused a miner to follow up the clew until he discovered the owners and their mine. The Plata Verde and other claims were then located, and the reports of rich horn silver mines once noised abroad brought in scores of miners. Soon after the fame of the district attracted men from all parts of the State. The cattle were displaced from their old herding grounds by herds of men, busy and wild in their search for wealth, and the locality became a veritable staked plain.

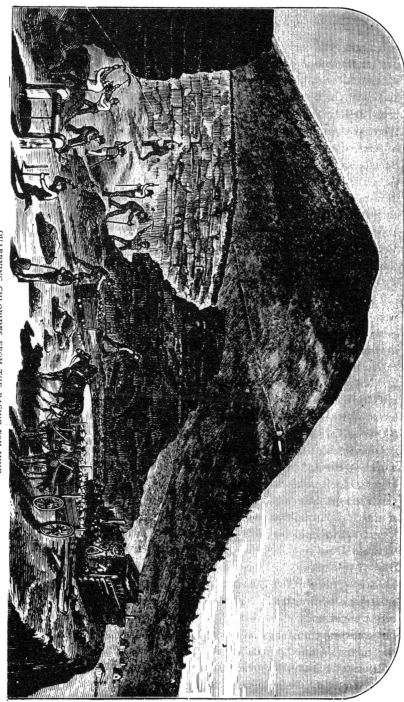

QUARRYING CHLORIDES FROM THE RACINE BOY MINE.

Among the early comers to the camp was J. W. Bailey, an old Pacific Slope and Black Hills mining operator and mill man. He purchased a large interest in the Racine Boy claims in August, and built the first house on the present site of Silver Cliff in September. Before the snows of November came a populous town was there, with stores, saloons, gambling-houses, and as great a medley of men of every class and description as one would wish to see. Specimens of horn silver were picked from the ashes or lava of the cliff that assayed ten and twenty thousand dollars, and chlorides in immense quantities were found in the Racine Boy, Plata Verde, and Horn Silver claims ; and this is the way that the Racine Boy mine and the town of Silver Cliff, now so famous, came to be located. Very soon after the discovery, and until the recent sale, this mine was owned by J. W. Bailey, who had nearly a half interest, and J. T. Beck, R. Curtis, and the original discoverer, Edwards.

The first car load of ore from the Racine Boy and Silver Cliff mines was sent to Omaha in September. Pending negotiations for the sale of the mine, and while the snows of winter obstructed work in the open cuts, little ore was shipped. Yet the yield was $70,074 up to April, 1879. The Cañon City works received 334 tons, containing $29,597, the Argo works, 183 tons, containing $22,121, and the Silver Cliff sampler 191 tons, yielding $18,356 ; average about $100 a ton. It cost but $12,000 to mine this ore. Eight tons brought $5,800 at Cañon City.

Quantities of the ore were treated at the Pennsylvania reduction works at Rosita, by raw amalgamation and shipments to Peublo and Denver smelters were discontinued. It was useless to ship and smelt the ores abroad at a cost of $50 a ton, when the erection of a stamp and pan mill at home would enable the silver contents to be secured at an expense of only five dollars to each ton of ore. There were no silver works of the required style in Colorado, because no ores of this nature had previously been mined in the state. The lodes of other parts of the mountains required costly smelting or some treatment by fire that was about as expensive. These Silver Cliff ores were already chloridized, and consequently needed no roasting, but could be transferred at once from the stamps to the pans where the silver is amalgamated. Like Gilpin County, Silver Cliff has millions of tons of low grade material that can be handled profitably by raw amalgamation, with the difference that gold is the main product in the first, and silver in the second locality.

In 1879 the Racine Boy and Silver Cliff mines were sold in New York, and the Silver Cliff Company organized, with a capital stock of $10,000,000 in 200,000 shares. James R. Keene, the famous New York speculator, is president, and I. Wormser, secretary.

In January, 1880, the company completed and set in operation its great stamp and pan mill. This is an immense affair, covering two acres of ground, and cost over $100,000, besides an outlay of $25,000 for bringing in water from Grape Creek. It contains 40 stamps, each weighing 750 pounds, 16 amalgamating pans, and 8 settlers or separating pans. To keep these stamps and pans in motion two tubular boilers of 100-horse power each have been provided, which furnish steam to drive the 200-horse-power Buckeye-Corliss engine. The fly-wheel measures 19 feet in diameter. To construct this mill 300 tons of machinery were required, 300,000 feet of lumber, 1,000 cubic yards of masonry, and 75,000 brick for the engine room, and yet there is talk of farther additions.

The method of treating the ores of the Silver Cliff Company is often called the Washoe process. It comprises dry crushing under stamps, and raw amalgamation in pans—no roasting or fire being needed, as the ore has already been chlorodized by nature.

The mill did not run steadily for some time after completion, owing to delays found necessary for changes and improvements. After milling began it was learned that the ore, being very porous and holding water almost like a sponge, required an enlargement of the drying capacity. Practice proved that the ore was "sluggish" in the pans, compelling their speed to be increased from 65 up to 85 revolutions per minute. This caused considerable delay and an entire change of the gearing of the mill.

A recent statement of the company says the mill treated 1,928 tons of ore between January 26 and April; that this had an average assay of $34 per ton and yielded silver bullion worth $49,880, showing a return of nearly $26 per ton. In 29 days of milling in March, 927 tons of ore were handled, yielding $27,572.12 in bullion, or over 72 per cent. of the $38,090.43 of original assay value. The average assay of the ore was 41.09 ounces of silver per ton. To get this $27,572.12 in bullion, $5,211.59 was expended in milling, $1,771.78 in mining, and other expenses made the total outlay $8 077.12, or $8.71 per ton. Better results were achieved in April, when over 35 tons were handled daily, with a saving of over 75 per cent. of the ore's contents. The remaining 25 per cent. is not lost because much of it can yet be reclaimed from the tailings. It is expected that the mill will soon treat 50 tons daily and that 90 per cent. of the silver can be saved in mill and tailings. This mill shows that ores can be mined and milled for eight or ten dollars a ton, and, as the district has vast beds and ledges of mineral carrying from fifteen to thirty dollars, the future of Silver Cliff seems assured.

A diamond drill has been sunk in five places, about one hundred feet, on the adjoining Belfast claim, on the same belt of mineral, proving a large body of profitable ore. Some of the drill cores assayed in the thousands. These results have caused the Silver Cliff Company to take steps for similar drill work, and to consider the subject of enlarging the mill.

Wet Mountain Valley is some thirty miles long from north to south and dips like an inclined floor easterly and westerly towards Grape creek, which flows northward to the Arkansas. On the eastern side of this creek extends the mineral belt of trachyte and porphyry strata in a granite country. Among the chloride mines obsidian dikes border some of the main ore channels. Carbonates have been found in the district, and galena veins and deposits are quite extensive a few miles north of Silver Cliff. The district centres in that city, and there and on Grape creek are located the reduction works and smelters. The situation could hardly be improved in a scenic point of view. To the west stretch the awful Sangre de Cristo mountains as far as the eye can reach. Changeless and immovable themselves, they present as a day rolls around a thousand different phases and colors. On their lofty summits slumber the snowfalls of ages and clouds repose there as if they sought rest from the fatigues of their wanderings. To the north is Pike's Peak, with its circling hills, and to the east are the rounded forms of the Sierra Mojada. The city of Silver Cliff is to be supplied with water from the Lake of the Clouds, located far up among the peaks of the snowy range. A railway is projected from Cañon.

The ore reducing mills of the district are as follows : Dillingham & Co's. ore sampling and shipping mill purchase hundreds of tons of ore monthly, which generally go to Omaha. The mills of the Silver Cliff and Plata Verde company are noted elsewhere. The Adelia mill on Grape creek began to work in March, on custom ores, with ten stamps, wet crushing and the necessary pans, etc. Additions are being made. A twenty-stamp will soon be in operation on this creek. Stacey, Knight & Co.'s Silver Cliff smelter has been at work on lead ores. A few miles north is Chambers & Co.'s smelter, which is supplied by the lead ores of Dora camp, the Bull-Domingo, and by ores of varied characters. The St. Joseph smelter is on Grape creek. The Mallett reduction works at Cañon City will be supplied with Custer County and other ores.

The Plata Verde mine, one of the most prominent in this part of the State, is located on Round Mountain, which rises several hundred feet above the plain on which Silver Cliff is situated. The town extends almost to the foot of the mountain, which is covered with mining locations from base to summit. W. J. Robinson, one of the pioneers of Rosita, discovered and located the Plata Verde on the second day of September, 1878. Although worked in an irregular manner, many lots of paying ore were shipped to Denver and elsewhere. At length the Plata Verde Silver Mining Company came into possession of the property. Since then mining has progressed, but little ore has been sold because it was deemed best to await the completion of a mill that would handle the product at one seventh of the cost. The company has the mill nearly completed, and will soon begin to draw upon this mountain of mineral.

Developments have proved the Plata Verde to be an enormous lode or deposit, carrying silver in paying quantities, interspersed with seams of exceedingly rich chlorides and horn silver. As yet only a small portion of the claim has been worked by means of open cuts and shafts. Large amounts of paying rock have been quarried from the sloping mountain side. Some lots of chlorides have milled as high as 260 ounces of silver per ton, and others taken without sorting have yielded 60 ounces, 72 ounces and similar figures. The various workings have also made the following returns: 160 ounces per ton, 71 ounces, 483 ounces, 53 ounces, 475 ounces, 412 ounces, 509 ounces, 1,956 and 1,047 ounces. There appear to be considerable quantities of mineral of such grades, along with an almost endless mass of poorer material capable of returning a profit in the mill. The unlimited quantity of available chlorides and the cheapness with which they can be mined and milled indicate a bright future for the mine.

The company's general manager in Colorado is George C. Munson, who formerly superintended the Bassick mine, which he left in

PLATA VERDE MINE AND MILL, ROUND MOUNTAIN.

good paying condition. Its interior workings and timbering planned by him have few equals. He is now engaged in pushing forward the Plata Verde Company's operations of opening the mine, erecting a mammoth mill, securing a water supply therefor, and driving a tunnel into Round Mountain.

The Plata Verde Mining Company has a capital stock of ten millions in one hundred thousand shares of a par value of one hundred dollars each. The officers are John R. Bartlett, president; George E. Cole, vice-president; Henry W. Ford, treasurer; John R. Lowther, secretary; and the above named and Hiram R. Crosby and Andrew W. Kent are trustees.

The Plata Verde mill is first class in every respect, and comprises a powerful engine and boilers, one rock breaker, an iron drying floor, 40 stamps with mortars and other attachments, 16 amalgamating pans, 8 settlers, a cleaning up pan, elevators and hoppers, two 14-inch retorts, and a double melting furnace. The 200-horse-power engine is of the Buckeye-Corliss pattern, and there are two great boilers each of 100-horse-power. The mortars of the stamps or batteries having been made with circular fronts permitting more ore to be crushed than would otherwise be the case. The capacity of the mill is placed at 80 tons of rock daily. The great mill building is nearly 120 feet by 96 in its longest and broadest parts. The room of the stamp department is 84 feet long by 45 wide; the pan room is 50 feet by 72; and the engine room is 50 feet square.

The method of treatment is dry crushing and pan amalgamation. The ore is conveyed from the mine and dumped on a heated iron drying floor at the upper end of the building. It is next broken in a rock-breaking machine and conducted by self feeders into the battery mortars, where it is crushed to powder by the ponderous 750-pound stamps, which rise and fall 80 times a minute. The pulverized material is conveyed in elevators to the hoppers standing over the amalgamating pans, and is dropped into the latter in the requisite quantities when wanted—generally once every six or seven hours. When the ore enters the pans, water is added, the pans are set in motion at the rate of nearly or quite 85 revolutions a minute and the pulp or thin mud constituting the charge is ground for two or three hours, when quicksilver and chemicals are introduced. Four hours more of grinding serves to amalgamate the silver, when the contents of these amalgamating pans are discharged into the settlers or separating pans below, each seven feet in diameter. Here the pulp is diluted with water, the amalgam settles, and the ore, now free from silver, is drawn off as tailings and run off in sluices. The amalgam is then strained, cleansed and retorted. Retorting volatilizes and condenses the quicksilver in the amalgam for future use, leaving the metallic silver in a spongy mass. The latter is then melted in melting furnaces and is ready to export to New York. The ore is handled entirely by machinery from the time crushing commences until the refuse passes out at the lower end of the mill, 120 feet distant. At the upper end of the mill a tunnel is being driven into the mountain through which the ore will pass by railway to the drying floor and stamps.

The entire surface of Round Mountain has been taken up with mining locations, and if many of them prove as valuable as the Richmond, Big Chief, and Horn Silver, not to speak of the Plata Verde, numerous mills will be required to handle their products. Several shafts and openings on the Richmond show ore milling from a few ounces up to hundreds. An Ingersoll drill has been used on the Big Chief.

The Buffalo Hunter and Boulder claims, near the Racine Boy, were developed by Halleck, Davidson & Co., and appear to be among the most valuable in the camp. Fifty-four tons of rock quarried out without assorting averaged $31\frac{1}{4}$ ounces of silver per ton. The amount of paying ore in these claims is immense. Prospecting drills in the Belfast and Fleetwood show them to be very valuable.

Further north are the Vanderbilt, Calumet, Last Chance, Iowa, Good Neighbor, Granite State, and other claims that show well. The first has yielded hundred-dollar ore in large quantities at a small cost for mining and assorting. Chlorides and horn silver are plentiful. The Gray Eagle has yielded very rich gold and silver ore. On what is known as the carbonate belt are the Lone Star, Song Bird, King of the Carbonates, Abandon and Rambler. The King of the Valley claim lies near the Silver Cliff.

The Bull-Domingo comprises two once conflicting claims, located in February, 1879. The owners after much trouble and litigation sold to Shaffer, Montgomery and others, who organized the Bull-Domingo Company thereon. The price is said to have been somewhere near a quarter of a million. Here is an immense deposit or vein composed of boulders covered with galena shells, with a filling of galena between the boulders. The latter resemble those of the Bassick mine, but silver and lead constitute the valuable metals. The deposit or vein has widened from 40 feet near the surface to 70 and 80 feet at depths of 90 and 150 feet. One well shaped excavation was carried down 30 feet wide to a depth of 90 feet. A new shaft is being sunk. The company have erected extensive ore and engine buildings and a concentrating mill—the latter to handle the lower grade material. The boulders appear to have no value, necessitating the handling of considerable waste material. In the few months of active operations by the old owners ore having an assay value of nearly $60,000 was shipped away—the lead and silver values being nearly equal. Some of the ore contains from 60 to 100 ounces in silver, and from 40 to 60 per cent. of lead. The product of this mine should be very large, for the amount of mineral is enormous.

The Bull-Domingo is stocked at $10,000,000. Ex-Senators W. H. Barnum and S. W. Dorsey are president and vice-president of the company, N. B. Stevens, secretary and treasurer, and among the directors are W. M. Lent, William Dorsheimer, and J. B. Dutcher. There are many other valuable mines in Custer county, which want of space forbids the mention of. Near Rosita, the Leviathan, Humboldt, Victoria, Ben. Franklin, Manhattan, and Fire King lodes have been shipping rich ore. The Humboldt sold about $82,000 worth of ore in 1879. Its shafts are 700 and 350 feet deep, respectively.

Verde district is on the lower slope of the Sangre de Cristo mountains, a few miles from Silver Cliff. Here is the Silver King, a lode of great value, recently developed by shafts and open cuts. The vein has an average width of two feet, yielding 150 ounces of silver, more or less, per ton, and carries quartz ore with gray copper and some galena, and azurite and malachite copper. One ton of ore yielded $680 at Stacy & Knight's smelter, and a large amount of various grades have been sold. The per cent. of copper is large. In Follet's Gulch is the Sangre de Cristo tunnel.

Iron and mica deposits are mined on Currant and Grape creeks.

CHAPTER XXIII.

SUMMIT COUNTY AND ITS MINES OF SILVER AND GOLD—THE LAND
BEYOND THE SNOWY RANGE—PAYING PLACERS OF 1860—ANNALS
OF THE GOLD HUNTERS—SOME BIG PLACER OPERATIONS OF THE
PRESENT TIME—BLUE RIVER, SNAKE RIVER, AND TEN MILE—
SUMMIT COUNTY'S YIELD OF GOLD, SILVER AND LEAD—THE EAGLE
—GUNNISON, ROUTT AND GRAND COUNTIES—THE NEW MINES.

Summit county extends from the crest of the Snowy Range westward to Utah, and lies entirely on the Pacific slope of the mountains.
Clear Creek and Park counties bound it on the east, Grand and
Routt on the north, and Lake and Gunnison on the south. It embraces a large amount of country adapted to farming and pastoral
purposes and is rich in silver lodes and gold placers. The yield of
the latter has been very great and that of the lode veins will evidently be immense in the near future. In the western portion are
coal measures of excellent quality.

Summit is a county of immense extent. It is larger than Delaware and Rhode Island combined, and has an area equal to that of
Connecticut. Its scenery is grand and magnificent. Mountain
ranges border and intersect it in almost all directions, and among
them are noble rivers, and hundreds of sparkling streams and dashing waterfalls. Vast forests of pine and spruce extend up the
mountain sides, and here and there are broad valleys green as emerald
and watered by the purest streams.

The first silver lode opened in Colorado was the Coaley in Summit county. Its discovery came about in this way: Some gulch
miners from the Blue River or Georgia Gulch were hunting for deer
in 1861, and getting out of bullets manufactured a few from the
outcroppings of what they called a lead vein. A year or two later
they were in Nevada, and found that the silver-bearing galena ores
of that section very much resembled the material which had supplied them with bullets in the Colorado mountains. They wrote to
an old friend in Empire and advised him to go over and locate the

lode. After some delay he did so, but never made a fortune from it. Yet it led to a great silver excitement and to the development of the Georgetown silver district.

That great natural barrier, the Snowy Range, has acted as a serious drawback to Summit county's progress and advancement. The heavy snows blockaded the entire region from the outside world in the winter season and the difficulty of crossing mountains from twelve to thirteen thousand feet high caused freighting and traveling to be slow and very expensive. Matters have assumed a different shape during the past few months. New wagon roads have been built at much lower elevations and on better grades, furnishing connection with Georgetown and Leadville. Railways are also projected and surveyed to both of these points. An extension of the Colorado Central Railroad is likely to be built through this county within a year. The leading towns of Summit are Kokomo, Carbonateville, and Summit City in the Ten Mile section—all founded within a few months—Montezuma and Saints John in the Snake river region, and Breckenridge in the Blue river placer country.

There are several important mining districts, old and new, that are attracting much attention. Of these the gold placers or alluvial deposits of the Blue and Swan rivers and their tributaries are the oldest. Extending north from these among the mountains is a belt of veins carrying silver and lead. The Snake river region contains both argentiferous galena and sulphuret and copper-bearing veins. There are some very rich veins in the vicinity of Montezuma, Saints John, Peru, Geneva, and Hall Valley—all located on the main range or some of its spurs. Near the headwaters of the Blue carbonates have lately been found.

The great excitement, however, at the present time is over the Ten Mile district. This locality has become famous during the past seven or eight months. Rich galena veins have been opened in the mountains west of Ten Mile River, and several thousand men have assembled there. The indications are good for one of the leading silver districts of the State. Further west valuable mineral discoveries are reported in the Eagle River region, but these were made this season, and of course sufficient time has not yet elapsed for their development. The fame of Ten Mile has brought in people enough to prospect the county very extensively, and there is no doubt but that its mineral wealth is of the first order.

The yield of Summit county mines from first to last was some-what as follows, the earlier years being estimated:

Gold from placers, 1860 to 1870.......	$5,500,000		$5,000,000
" " 1870.............	100,000		
" " 1871.............	70,000		
" " 1872.............	60,000		
" " 1873.............	101,000		
Silver and lead, 1869 to 1874.........	200,000		531,000
Gold from placers, 1874.............	76,408		
Silver and lead, 1874.............	50,000		126,408
Gold from placers, 1875.............	72,413		
Silver, 1875.............	50,000		152,413
Gold from placers, 1876.............	150,000		
Silver and lead, 1876.............	200,000		350,000
Gold from placers, 1877.............	150,000		
Silver and lead, 1877.............	40,000		190,000
Gold from placers, 1878.............	165,774		
Silver and lead, 1878.............	155,000		320,774

Total................................... $7,041,195

Total gold, $6,320,195 ; silver, $595,000 ; lead, $100,000.

In the early years of Colorado mining, the tributaries of the Blue River were among the most productive in the country. Mining fairly began in 1860, and for several summers the yield of gold in Georgia, French, and Humbug gulches, the Blue and Gold Run, was very great; there was a score of other localities, such as Illinois, McNulty, etc., but those named above were the most famous. It is claimed that a million a season was taken out at first, the years 1860–61 being the best; after that, many diggings had been more or less exhausted. The yield was very large, however, for years, and mining has been carried on there every summer since the first discoveries; the great placer enterprises that have lately been inaugurated promise to give a much more reliable and nearly as great an annual yield as when Georgia Gulch ranked next to California Gulch in the yield of the yellow metal. Many are the Aladdin-like tales of for-tunes made in that locality in the days of 1860–61, when men made from twenty to a hundred dollars a day.

The yield of the placer and gulch mines of the Blue River and tributaries in 1877 was as follows, some of the claims and localities being estimated:

Blue River—J. Bemrose, $3,500; L. Gorham, $800; A. McLeod, $2,000; Fuller & Krom, $10,000; H. Zingling, $800; A. Stahl, $1,000; J. E. Rankin, $1,500; R. Adams, $1,500; Nolan & Kromer, $3,500; G. Mumford, $1,000; T. Clague, $300; J. Izzard, $4,600; D. Schriven, $4,800; J. Bisly, $450; McMahon, $200.

Gold Run—L. S. Peabody, $8,500; S. Walker, $3,500.

Swan River—J. M. Riland, $3,000; A. Delaney, $500; D. Stogsdill, $8,000; Fuller Placer Co., $32,000; P. Iveson, $1,500; North Swan miners, $800.

French Gulch—Stillson Patch, $3,500; Badger Co., $3,000; Calvin Clark, $15,000; Ebert & Co., $8,000.

Ten Mile—Follett, L. S. Ballou and Tucker, $2,500; and miners of McNulty Gulch, $7,500.

Total yield of placer gold for the county, $150,000 in coin value. The expense of getting out this amount, exclusive of permanent improvements, is estimated at only 40 per cent. of the gross yield, leaving 60 per cent. of receipts as net gain. The average yield per cubic yard of placer ground was given at the handsome figure of 25 cents, while that of Izzard's claim was $1.45 per cubic yard.

The gold placer yield of 1878 was still larger and approximated as follows on the various streams and gulches. Some of these returns are exact and others are estimated:

Total, $165,774.

Blue River—J. B. Bemrose, $3,000; L. H. Gorham, $300; A. D. McLeod, $1,000; Fuller & Krom, $6,000; J. D. Rankin, in Corkscrew Gulch, $1,000; the Klack diggings, $500.

Blue Tributaries—Lomax Gulch—Ellis Stahl, $1,500; Picket & Downing, $1,000. Iowa Gulch—Adams & Engle, $2,600; Boston & Colorado P. M. Company, $500. Izzardville—A. Alexander, $6,000. Salt Lick Gulch—R. Schriven, $4,000. Ryan Gulch— Roby & Silverthorn, $800. Maryland Gulch—Blaisley & Albett, $1,000. Soda Gulch, $300; Yuba Dam, Nolan & Kroner, $3,000; other gulches, $5,000.

Swan River Tributaries—Gold Run—L. C. Barnard, $1,550; D. Peabody, 8,000; Silas Walker, $3,000; Barrett & Co., $1,000.

HYDRAULIC MINING, FRENCH GULCH.

Delaware Flats—Andy Delaine, $500.   Galena Gulch—D. Stogsdill, $6,000.   Brown Gulch—J. Cyphart, $1,000.

Bed of the Swan—Isaac Williams, $500; Eckhart & Co., $500.

Fuller Placer Company, including Georgia and other gulches, $36,000.

French Gulch—H. Farncomb, $8,000; T. Murphy, $500; George Clark, $20,000; Calvin Clark, $5,424; J. Sisler, $1,000; L. S. Ballou, $20,000; Goodman Steele, J. J. Cobb, etc., $500.

Illinois Gulch—Fuller Placer Company, $4,000.

Ten Mile River—Follett, $1,000.   McNulty Gulch—McNasser & Brandon, $5,000.   All others, $3,000.

The two great placer operations of the county are conducted by the Fuller Placer Company and by L. S. Ballou.   Their extensive lands have been brought into condition to produce largely, and hydraulics, flumes, and all necessary appliances are in use.   There are three requisites to successful placer mining—valuable ground, sufficient water, and sufficient "fall" or "dump."   No matter how much gold the ground contains, it cannot be extracted without water.

The Fuller Placer Company, possessing the most extensive appliances, and probably the most placer land of any one company east of California, possesses all of these requirements.   But water has been procured only at an outlay of a great deal of labor and money, and of no little display of engineering abilities.   The water supply was totally inadequate, and the necessary quantity could not be obtained without constructing long ditches and flumes, and in some places by carrying the latter at great elevations over ravines and along rugged mountain sides.   The placer lands were partially divided among many owners, and it took years to purchase and consolidate the vast amount of property now owned and controlled.

There was a vast tract of country known to be auriferous for which there seemed to be no possibility of obtaining water.   At length it was found that a pass in the main Continental Divide or watershed of the continent, 11,811 feet above sea level, was lower than a lake on the eastern slope, located among and fed by the eternal snows. The manager, with the eye of a true engineer, saw that this lake on the Atlantic slope could be made available for the Fuller placers on the Pacific side of the range by the construction of many miles of ditch and flume.   There were noble forests of pine at hand, and a saw-mill was soon set at work manufacturing the timber required for the great flume. At length the work was completed, and the waters turned from their natural course around Georgia Pass to eventually mingle with the waters of the Pacific.

The Fuller Placer Company's property embraces 3,000 acres of "pay gravel" patented and pre-empted, besides 30,000 acres controlled by its water. This land is on the western slope of the Rocky Mountains, around the headwaters of the Swan River, and some of the tributaries of the Blue, which is a tributary of the Grand. The property is classed as the Mayo and Georgia divisions. On this property are from twenty to thirty miles of flume and ditch, a score of buildings for the accommodation of workmen, and for a year's supplies. There is also a steam saw-mill, many hydraulics, tools, implements, and appliances for working the mines.

THE LONG FLUME.

These placers are worked about five and a-half months every year —that being the length of the warm season available for placer mining. Last year the gold product was reported at $42,000, and the expenses at $15,000. The yield of 1879, the present summer and fall, may reach $100,000, as everything is now in first-class condition. Six Little Giant hydraulics are at work in different gulches. There are altogether about 34,000,000 cubic yards of pay gravel, said to be capable of yielding at a low estimate twenty-five cents per cubic yard, indicating the total contents to exceed $8,000,000. The ground worked in American Gulch last season yielded one dollar per cubic yard. M. J. Cole is superintendent of this great enterprise, and Col. T. H. Fuller, president and treasurer.

The Mayo property embraces claims in Mayo, Negro, Dry, Boston, Pacific, and Illinois gulches, and Sargent and Page patches, and situated about two miles from Breckenridge. Its improvements consist of Mayo Ditch, six miles long, conveying water from Indiana Creek to all the mining claims of Mayo property, with a capacity of 600 inches of water. There is also a new ditch, 5,775 feet in length, to convey the excess of water in the spring season. There are two reservoirs in Illinois Gulch, with capacity of 500,000 gallons each, two in Mayo, one of 300,000 gallons capacity, and one of 600,000, the latter new and built last fall at head of Mayo, commanding a large amount of territory, and one reservoir in Negro, 100,000 gallons capacity. In these gulches are 1,200 feet of bed rock flume, riffled the whole distance, and 1,200 feet of iron pipe and one Little Giant hydraulic.

The Georgia property embraces many gulches, patches, and claims. The improvements consist of the Swan River and Georgia Gulch Mining, Ditching and Fluming Company, now belonging to Fuller Placer Mining Company, is 14 miles long, 48 inches on bottom and 70 on top, capacity 2,500 inches; also American Ditch, 6¼ miles long, with a capacity of 400 inches; Flume Extension Ditch, 3,465 feet long, 600 inches capacity, side ditches, 2,227½ feet; 5,445 feeding ditches to the great flume; ¼ interest in the Pollard Ditch, 2 miles long, 400 inches capacity, and the Stevens Flume, 8 miles long, 200 inches capacity; Mount Guyot Flume, 2 miles long, crossing Divide at Georgia Pass, 400 inches capacity, the only place on this continent where the waters of the Atlantic are diverted to the Pacific slope. On this property are 2,000 feet of bed-rock flume, riffled the whole distance; also 5,000 feet of iron pipe laid in the different gulches, and 2,000 feet of extra pipe on hand, and six Little Giants in different gulches.

On the same tract of land the Fuller Company owns many valuable lode veins, which, since the approach of the railway to Hall Valley and Fairplay, can be worked to advantage, and which may be still more profitable if the Colorado Central railway is extended as contemplated. Two of these lodes carry from $10 to $170 in silver, from $5 to $10 in gold, and from 24 to 68 per cent. in lead. Others contain gold in varying amounts up to as much as $120 per ton. These are all of great size and are more or less opened by shafts. Among them are the Emmet, Pacific, Washington, Bunker Hill, Independence, Uncle Sam, Etta, Bay State and Summit, 1, 2 and 3.

In February, 1880, and after the preceding pages of this chapter were written, the Fuller Placer Company sold its entire property to the Summit County Mining and Smelting Company, composed of about twenty capitalists of New York, Providence, Boston and San Francisco. M. J. Cole continues as general manager, and the principal owners of the five millions of stock are, W. H. Reynolds, G. D. Roberts, W. F. Shaffer, William Bond, J. Nelson Tappan, G. J. Forest, Abraham Avery, S. P. Wardwell, M. J. Cole, Elisha Riggs, G. S. Scott, Samuel Smith and T. H. Fuller.

During the past winter and spring, smelting works with three blast furnaces and 75 tons daily capacity were erected on the company mill site of fifteen acres at Breckenridge, and 3,000 tons of galena and other ores were taken out of the lode veins ready for treatment. A large portion of the ores are said to be carbonates. During the spring of 1880, the company's saw-mill, erected for turning out lumber for flumes and works, had its capacity taxed to the utmost in supplying lumber for the six hundred houses erected at Breckenridge. The company's six mines on Negro Hill are producing about 25 tons of ore daily and six other locations showing mineral are being developed. The Summit county company, with its hydraulic mining, diamond prospecting drill, lode mining and smelting, and heavy lumber operations, are among the chief promoters of the main industry of the county.

Breckenridge district is now the great point of excitement as far as Summit county is concerned. The interest in and immigration to that point are as great as Ten Mile enjoyed a year earlier. People are crowding in there by hundreds, and in a few short months Breckenridge has grown from a hamlet of a hundred inhabitants to a small city, with nearly a thousand houses and two or three times that number of people. Streets lined with stores or residences have been laid out on ground lately considered worthless, and lots are held at hundreds and even thousands of dollars. Even the history of Colorado affords few parallels to such rapid growth and sudden transformation. While more solid and enduring in character, the place is as lively and more populous than in the palmy days of placer mining in the summers of 1861-2. Years ago, when the more easily worked streams and gulches had been sluiced over, the miners departed for other localities and Breckenridge became almost deserted. What importance it retained was due to the fact of its being the county seat. This is the case no longer, for it is now the business centre of a flourishing mining district on which unlimited expectations are based. Chlorides and galena lodes and deposits are worked on every hand and the carbonates are reported in various localities. Hayden gives Breckenridge an elevation above the sea of 9,674 feet. Another measurement gives 9,200 feet.

Breckenridge can be reached from Georgetown by way of either Georgetown or Como. The former route embraces 55 miles of railway from Denver to Georgetown, thence 45 miles of staging by Nott's line. The other route includes 88¼ miles on the Denver and South Park Railway, and 17 miles of staging from Como by the Spottswood and Hogan line. The distance to Leadville is 43 miles. Railways are projected in various directions.

In the fall of 1878, Samuel Mishler, one of the original owners of the Caribou lode, and Hal Sayr, of Central City, made some important discoveries near Breckenridge, whose ores were pronounced genuine carbonates. From 25 to 333 ounces of silver per ton were smelted from this ore. One claim averaged 45 ounces in silver and 55 per cent. lead. Very high assays were obtained. Some prospecting was done by other parties, and a year after wonderful reports went abroad of discoveries made by a machine drill of the Fuller Placer Company. Prospectors and miners began to flock into the district in the beginning of 1880, while the snow yet lay many feet on the ground, and the discoveries of the previous fall were duplicated before summer came.

The most important mineral localities yet developed are Negro, Shock, Mineral, and Gibson hills. Here are many productive mines and numberless prospects that are evidently more or less valuable. A statement recently published places the yield of mill runs from the chloride claims at from 200 to 600 ounces of silver per ton, while the assays from galena and carbonate claims range from 15 to over 200 ounces. There are also free gold lodes in the district, and vast beds of iron—carrying some 60 per cent. of that metal, and from 15 to 30 ounces of silver. The Brooklyn Mining Company have shipped considerable ore, and may soon have a smelter at work.

In February, 1880, Kleinsmidt and Eckart started up their new 15 stamp quartz mill near Lincoln on ore from the Elephant, Helen, Poorman, Young America, and other gold-bearing lodes. The Elephant, on Wire Patch, was lately giving a daily yield of a ton of milling ore to each man employed and some smelting ore. The vein is of great size. The Helen, on the south side of French Gulch, is an immense lode, and has 395 feet of tunnels. The Poorman has heavy pyrites of iron.

The Gooding Smelter at Lincoln was started up and enlarged in the summers of 1878-9. The ores handled produced from $15 to $30 in silver, and 60 per cent. of lead, and came from the Cincinnati, Shamrock, Champion, and other lodes. Lincoln has increased its population many times over within a year.

Wonderfully rich ore in large quantities is found on Shock hill. George and Rufus Snyder, formerly part owners in the great Pelican mine of Georgetown, in company with T. W. Brooks, are operating several new but very valuable properties known as the Brooks and Snyder mines. These include the Fannie Barrett, showing remarkably rich gold-bearing ore, the Peerless gold lode, and the Illinois silver lode. The latter carries chlorides and horn silver, and has hundreds of tons of ore broken with much high grade material. The general appearance is that of a great quarry opening a huge body of ore. Mill returns have given over $200 in silver per ton, and a little gold. The Fannie Barrett is still more valuable. The Ohio mine, developed by A. and D. Shock, is similar to the Illinois, and is believed to be on the same vein or strata. The first lot of ore shipped, 2,000 pounds, netted $629, and the lowest returns were $154 a ton. Like the other claims mentioned, the main work has been done in open cuts made in the side of the hill. The Blue Danube is reported to carry iron and iron carbonates in a contact vein pitching downwards towards Ten Mile range. The Union mine on Mineral hill is producing high grade ore.

Further north is the Snake River mining region, including Montezuma, and Peru districts. On the opposite or eastern side of the same great mountain range are Hall, Geneva, and Argentine gulches. At the dividing line of Summit, Park, and Clear Creek counties is Geneva district, with the Brittanic, Leviathan and other tunnels, and the Revenue, Congress, Celtic, and Baltic and numberless lodes. The Herman, Belle East and Belle West locations, all on one lode of Glacier Mountain, are pretty well developed. The Cashier and

Champion are parts of the same vein, which has yielded from fifteen to thirty thousand dollars per annum. The Star of the West lode on Teller Mountain has high grade gold and silver ores, carrying more bismuth than any other vein in that section.

The Montezuma Silver Mining Company owns the Chatauqua, Erie, Radical, General Teller and several other lodes on Glacier and Teller mountains, which are being opened by shafts, levels and tunnels. Machine drills were used in the latter. The company has built a saw-mill and concentrating works. The North Star on Collier mountain carries much silver and lead.

Sts. John is the headquarters and settlement of the Boston Mining Company, which has been operating there for twelve years, and has spent large sums of money in smelting and other works, mills, machinery, tunnel work and mining. Ores were smelted and bullion shipped in 1870, in 1873–5--6--7 and in 1878, and thousands of tons of vein material have been mined. At present the company has over two miles of underground workings, such as tunnels, drifts and shafts, and a large amount of ore reserves. One hundred men and some-times more are employed in mining, smelting, teaming, burning char-coal, etc., when operations are in full blast. A splendid tunnel has been driven into Glacier mountain 1,800 feet. This has intersected ten lodes, of which number five is the best and number seven next best. Number five shows a vein of ore four feet wide, some of which is very valuable. Seventy-five tons of ore were shipped to Denver in 1879, at a cost of $17 a ton. The yield is reported at $200 a ton, from 30 to 50 per cent. of the ore being lead. Colonel William L. Candler is at the head of this enterprise, and Captain Ware is superintendent.

Peru or Snake river district was the scene of quite a mining excite-ment in the summer of 1879, and the settlement of Decatur was started at that time. While no very important discoveries were then made, considerable mining of a permanent character is being conducted on such old and valuable lodes as the Tariff, Peruvian, Delaware and other mines.

The Peruvian has been worked all winter and spring by fifteen men, and some of the ore is worth from one to two hundred dollars per ton. This lode is of great size and shows a good vein of galena mixed with gray and yellow copper.

The Delaware is an immense galena lode, said to show over seven feet of ore, much of which yields from $75 per ton up into the hundreds. Some of it assays from one to two thousand dollars. The yield is many tons daily. The Whale lode is also making a fine record, and the Aldrich, Mammoth, and Ruby Silver are worked.

The Tariff is one of the best lodes of this section, and has made a very good record whenever worked. It is located on and outcrops a thousand feet above the base of Cooper mountain, overlooking Decatur mining camp. Georgetown is about fifteen miles distant, and Montezuma five. Some time ago the Tariff Mining Company was organized in New York. Besides the Tariff and Mississippi lodes, this company has secured 28,500 feet of locations or veins, taking up a portion of one side of the mountain from a point above timber line down to its base, with fine timber land and a mill site.

The fact that the Tariff mine has paid largely notwithstanding the distance to an ore market and the cost of pack animal transportation are evidences of its value. It has been still further proven of late by the developments carried on by the superintendent, F. B. Gilbert. Ore mined within the past few months in the various shafts, drifts, and stopes carries from 26 ounces to 1,097 ounces of silver per ton, while 248 ounces seemed to be somewhere near the average. The width of the lode between walls is from three to fifteen feet, while the solid ore vein usually ranges from four to twelve inches in width. The main level usually has from six to eight inches of ore. Of past shipments to Georgetown, the first class ore yielded 445 ounces, second class 230, and third class 109; average value of all, $270 per ton. The vein is continuous, carries rich ruby silver, gray copper, and brittle silver, with argentiferous galena and iron and copper pyrites, and is free from zinc. The inclosing rock is soft and easily broken and solid enough to stand without timbers. The new road to Georgetown will permit of wagon transportation for the ore, which will cost but a fraction of that by pack animals. So far over 800 feet of shafts and drifts have been driven.

The greatest depth attained on the vein is about 300 feet. A tunnel has been driven toward the Tariff vein, a distance of 350 feet, and will reach it when 525 feet long at a depth of 360 feet. This will be valuable as an ore outlet and for drainage purposes. Another tunnel will be started near the base of the mountain. The mine's lower workings show the richest ore encountered for some time.

Nott's stages make daily trips from the railway terminus at Georgetown into Summit county, via Loveland Pass. At Frisco one line branches off to Breckenridge, ten miles distant, and the other continues to Kokomo and Leadville. Fisk's, on the north fork of the Snake, is the lay over station.

Ten Mile District comprises the converging slopes of two parallel ranges of mountains and the intervening valley of Ten Mile Creek. The settlements and mining camps are in the upper portion of this, and something like 11,000 feet above sea level. Most of the mines are on the Godey range west of and from 200 to 1,500 feet above the creek. Ten Mile range borders the valley on the east and has several peaks from 13,500 to over 14,000 feet high. These two ranges extend northward from the main divide on either side of a depression called Arkansas Pass, from whose slopes waters flow toward either ocean. Two miles west, Eagle river has its source in Tennessee Pass, the lowest of all passes on the Continental Divide.

McNulty gulch empties into Ten Mile creek near its source and at the new town of Carbonateville. Here are paying gold diggings, and a few thousand dollars are sluiced out every summer by Colonel James McNassar. The gulch was very productive in the summers of 1860–'1 –'2, and its total yield is said to exceed $300,000. Soon after its discovery five hundred men arrived from California gulch in a single day.

The Ten Mile region had been prospected at intervals for many years, but nothing very valuable was found until 1878. That summer George B. Robinson, a leading Leadville merchant, outfitted an old prospector named Charles Jones, who located a claim on the 16th of July, near the base of Sheep Mountain, which was called the Seventy-eight, and is now a part of the great Robinson mine. Jones' good fortune was evidently too much for him, for he died from excessive drinking a few months after. Captain J. W. Jacque, a veteran prospector, was one of the first arrivals. He located some of the same group of claims, now so immensely valuable. Among the important discoveries of the season were the Grand Union and Wheel of Fortune.

The value of these claims began to be noised abroad just as winter came on, but it did not deter people from moving in that direction.

Such was the excitement a little later, that claims were staked off on the surface of the snows. Leadville and Ten Mile have afforded a rich harvest for surveyors, and their services were in special request at the time referred to. In this elevated region, eleven or twelve thousand feet above the sea, snow falls deep and often, and there are usually five feet of it on the ground from January to April, but nothing could stop the fever of excitement that set in with the beginning of 1879. Men came in swarms, and over routes terrible to think of; trees were felled, cabins built, tents pitched on the top of the snow, and prospecting was carried on irrespective of the difficulties in the way.

The lack of surface indications was made up for by a super-abundance of faith. The miner would seek for unclaimed ground, clear away the snow from a chosen locality and then commence to sink in search of deposit or vein. This hazardous style of prospecting was occasionally successful, and some valuable discoveries were made on Sheep, Elk and Jack mountains, all of which greatly advertised the fame of Ten Mile and increased immigration. Town sites were laid out for miles down the valley, and the dull roar of the miner's blast or the echo of the woodman's axe could be heard at any time of the day in the previously uninhabited but stately forests of pine.

The embryo cities of Kokomo, Ten Mile, and Carbonateville presented a strange medley of log cabins, tents, and primitive habitations, and the prices of town lots compared in altitude with the places in which they were located. With the opening of summer Kokomo claimed a population of 1,500, and had an organized city government, a bank, hotels, stores, saloons, saw-mills, and the telegraph, where there was not a single settler a few months before. A newspaper and smelters came afterwards. The story is told of a miner who went out to dig a grave for a deceased comrade and "struck mineral before he had completed the job."

In the winter of 1879-80 the mines producing large amounts of ore good enough to ship away or to smelt were the Forest and the Tiger on Sheep Mountain, the Kokomo Giant on Gold Hill, the Mayflower on Jack Mountain, and the Reconstruction on Copper Mountain, besides the Robinson and White Quail. The Pittsburg smelter, now the property of the White Quail Company, was in operation a part of the fall and winter of 1879.

1 Robinson Cons. Mines.　2 Grand Union Mine.　3 Wheel of Fortune Mine.　4 Sheep Mtn.　5 Elk Mtn.　6 Jack Mtn.　7 Red Mtn.　8 McNulty Mtn.　9 Kokomo.　10 Carbonateville.

TEN MILE.

The Robinson Consolidated is the great mine of its section, and one of the leading mines of America. It has few superiors or equals at Leadville, or anywhere else. The property includes the Seventy-eight, Undine, G. B. Robinson, Big Giant, Windsor, Pirate, Checkmate, Ten Mile, and Rhone, and one-half of the Smuggler, all located in one group, and embracing about 48 acres of surface ground. The hillside is covered with splendid timber. The top or apex of the lode is in the Seventy-eight claim. Thence it dips under other claims to the northeast, at an angle of 22 degrees. The great size and high average value of the ore vein is extraordinary. So far it varies in thickness from three to twenty-two feet, and carries ore running in the hundreds, besides lower grades. In one part of the mine is a seam containing from $800 to $900 a ton, flanked by many feet of poorer, but very profitable material.

While George B. Robinson operated the mine in 1878-9, 650 tons of ore were sold in Leadville, besides a large amount of low and high grades, at the mine. Up to September, 1879, there were $226\frac{1488}{2000}$ tons of ore sold, of an assay value of $205.54 per ton, or $46,606.58 altogether. The average assay was $179\frac{1}{4}$ ounces of silver and 17.6 per cent. lead. The export of the mine previous to 1880 was probably valued at about $125,000. In February, 1880, between 700 and 800 tons of ore were shipped over the deep snows to Leadville, returning $40,000. Fifty tons sold for $15,000, and thus paid all costs of mining and transportation. Later still, one lot of fifty tons sold to the La Plata Smelting Company, gave an average yield of $300.60 per ton, or 262 ounces of silver and 14 per cent. lead. The lode was developed by inclines, side drifts and several shafts, showing immense quantities of ore. Hoisting machinery was procured, and the erection of a smelter began. The splendid pine timber with which the claims were covered affords all the lumber and mine timbers required for a generation.

On the 5th day of March, 1880, the Robinson Consolidated Mining Company came into possession of the property, and operations of a very extensive character were inaugurated. Machinery was procured powerful enough to drive the incline 1,000 feet. Roasting furnaces were constructed, buildings were erected capable of housing 2,000 tons of ore, pumps were set at work, and other improvements perfected. A tunnel has been driven from the base of the mountain, which will soon intersect the main incline, when the latter is down 425 feet.

This tunnel will be 750 feet long, and besides draining the lode, can serve as a main down grade ore outlet of the mine. It has been driven in ore from a point 260 feet from its mouth. The vein downward and eastward is over 400 feet long, with levels leading therefrom at intervals of 50 and 60 feet. Parallel with the main outlet are other inclines. The lower workings are as rich as those nearer the surface, and by far the largest ore body is located there. The vein has no gangue and very little waste. The foot wall, owing to the lime formation underneath, is wavy, and consequently the ore body varies greatly in thickness, but its continuous character, great average size and value, together with the fact that the vein can be followed downward indefinitely, assures the presence of millions. The present workings show an average thickness of solid ore, from a point 60 feet below the mouth of the main incline, of at least 5½ feet. Close examinations and tests, as well as smelting, show that about one-third of this carries an average value of over $200 a ton, and the remaining two-thirds about $70 a ton. There are thousands of tons of such ore standing blocked out in the mine between the inclines and levels. A large part of Sheep Mountain is evidently underlaid with this practically inexhaustible vein.

The Robinson is a contact vein, with dolomitic limestone for a foot wall. The predominating top rock is mainly of sandstone. The ores are iron pyrites, oxides of iron, galena, gray carbonates of lead, black sulphurets of silver, silver glance, and occasionally small quantities of zinc blende. The oxides and sulphurets are about equal in quantity. There is only a trace of gold and an average of ten per cent. of lead. The ores being sulphurets must be roasted before smelting unless mixed in small quantities with ores naturally oxidized. A smelter is being built.

The company has recently constructed a large number of roasting furnaces at the mine, so that the ore may be freed from sulphur where it can be done cheapest. The neighboring forests afford fuel for this purpose at the mere cost of cutting, so that the cost of roasting or desulphurization is but 75 cents a ton. A stone wall two and a half feet high, inclosing a space ten feet wide by twenty long, form the basis of these roasters. In these enclosures are placed floors of pine logs covered with finely split dry wood, and about forty-five tons of ore are piled thereon, after which the pine wood beneath is fired. Combustion continues for two weeks, when the sulphur and other refractory substances having been expelled by the fire, the ore is ready for smelting. Nearly 1,500 tons a month, or the regular product of the mine, will hereafter be handled in this manner daily. Open sheds have been built over the roasters.

The company sold 637 tons of ore in the month of March, 1880, for an average price of $100.18, or $61,814.66 altogether. The assay value must have been nearly one-fourth greater. In April a body of ore 19 feet thick was developed in one of the levels running north from the main incline. Here are large masses of mineral, averaging 360 ounces of silver per ton and 35 per cent. lead.

The Robinson Consolidated Mining Company has a capital stock of $10,000,000 in fifty-dollar shares. The officers are George D. Roberts, president, George B. Robinson, vice-president, S. V. White, treasurer, D. F. Verdenal, secretary, and the first three and Rufus Hatch, John D. Prince, A. P. K. Safford, and Jonas H. French, trustees. James C. Brown is general manager at the mines.

The White Quail consolidated group of mines, on Elk mountain, near Kokomo, ranks next to the Robinson in amount of production and extent of ore reserves. The vein is often from three to eight feet wide, averages from 50 to 60 per cent. lead and nearly 40 ounces of silver, and carries sand cemented together with cerusite. The vein dips with the hill, but at a sharper angle—22 degrees to the northeast. This was the main source of supply to the Pittsburg Company's smelter at Kokomo, in the latter part of 1879. The White Quail sent 460 tons of ore to those works, which returned 200 tons of bullion, worth $40,100—half of the value being silver and half lead. Ex-Senator A. McDonald has organized a company on these claims in New York, which has purchased the Pittsburg smelter of 30 or 40 tons capacity. The mine has shafts, drifts and tunnels, and a large force of men is employed.

The Wheel of Fortune mine is located on the summit of Sheep mountain, overlooking Ten Mile and Eagle river valleys. It embraces four claims located by Jacob Hecht in the summer of 1878. The first 300 feet of workings developed an immense body of ore. Quantities were sold in Leadville that smelted from $80 to $140 a ton. Galena and sulphurites carrying silver are the characteristics. The mine has not been worked steadily.

The Gold Hill Consolidated Mining and Smelting Company combines several groups of claims, embracing altogether twenty-one

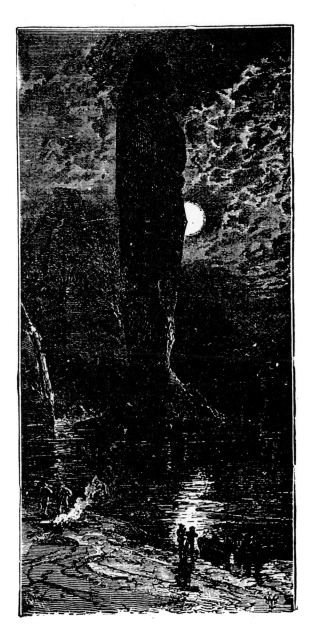

ISLAND OR SPECTRE MONUMENT—WESTERN COLORADO.

locations, mostly on Sheep Mountain and near the Robinson or Wheel of Fortune Mines. The property will be vigorously prospected and worked. It is claimed that nearly the whole of this slope of the mountain is underlaid with ore. Some of the claims show from 50 to 85 ounces of silver per ton.

The Grand Union or Lennon mine is on the main range and has proved among the most valuable of the district. There are said to be twelve feet of mineral, carrying from a few ounces of silver up to 200 per ton. One small lot milled at the rate of $1,000. On Sheep mountain are the Iron, Idalie, Champion, Comet, Seventy-nine, Silver Tip, Little Anna and Ready Cash, and many other claims, showing valuable ore. On Jack mountain are the Rising Sun and Racen lodes. Near the Robinson mine are the Leader, Globe and Commercial, all worked and in pay, and located in the centre of ten claims into which the same ore body undoubtedly extends.

On Gold Hill the Worcester claim shows a large body of valuable ore, and with a dozen adjoining claims has been purchased by F. Prentice & Co. of New York. The amount of mineral ground in this property is evidently very large.

The Reconstruction is the great mine of Copper mountain. It shows four feet of solid galena and quartz, is vigorously worked and is producing much paying ore. On Gold hill is the Kokomo Giant, which is producing paying ore. The Grand View, a gold and silver-bearing lode, and the Hook, Hymen and Pickwick, owned by George Goodwin, Peter Hook and others are valuable.

The ores of Ten Mile district are generally galena, and usually carry much iron and sulphur. There are large bodies of galena ores at the head of Clinton gulch and in two lodes of Mayflower gulch. There are gold-bearing veins near McNulty and Clinton gulches.

The Eagle river region came into prominence in 1879, when quite a stampede took place in that direction. Battle mountain was the scene of the greatest activity and of most of the discoveries. High up on its steep slopes is an outcropping limestone ledge which extends for miles, and dips downward and inward 20 degrees below the horizontal. For a distance of about a mile on the southwest slope many locations of value have been made, and carbonate deposits are found between the lime and porphyry. The vein matter is mainly hematite iron ore, which at the outcrop has the color of ochre. This carries silver, and is often mixed with lead ores—seams and bodies of different character lying side by side. The lead ore consists of galena, cerusite, etc. The deposit varies in thickness from a mere seam to ten or twelve feet, the limestone foot wall showing abrupt bends and waves.

Between the Ida May and Little Duke, about thirty claims have been located up and down the mountain and crossing the contact. Of those that have developed value, the Belden, Clinton, Silver Age, Indian Girl, Cora, Eagle Bird, Spirit, Iron Mask, May Queen, Kingfisher, Little Chief, Crown Point, and Little Ollie are the most prominent. The three first mentioned show large bodies of ore, the Belden being especially good. There are other mines and prospects on this mountain of which good reports are heard.

The town of Red Cliff has been built up at the base of Battle mountain. A smelter has been erected there. Another town called Coronado has been located in a beautiful park a few miles down the Eagle. Near it are several mining camps, such as Ore Creek and Horn Silver mountain. The Horn Silver has shipped ore that yielded from $1,000 to $1,500 per ton.

Summit county's mining product for 1879 was not far from the following:

Gold	$50,000
Silver	212,500
Lead	47,200
Total	$309,700

Of this product of $309,700, about $172,500 came from ores shipped out of the county, mainly from Ten Mile. The Pittsburg smelter at Kokomo exported 240 tons of lead bullion, worth $67,200. The Lincoln Smelter's shipments were less. The lack of water prevented the streams and gulches from producing largely. The summer's product is estimated at $50,000, or less than one-third of that of 1878.

Summit County's mining product up to 1880 may be approximately stated as follows:

Gold	$6,392,195	Lead	$147,200
Silver	807,500	Copper	2,000
Total			$7,348,895

The production of the present year will evidently be several times what has been known heretofore. Summit county will soon rival the best of its neighbors outside of Lake.

CHAPTER XXIV.

PARK COUNTY—GENERAL FORMATION—GOLD LODES AND PLACERS—
THE SILVER BELT OF THE MOSQUITO RANGE—MOUNTS LINCOLN
AND BROSS—MINING ABOVE THE CLOUDS—ETERNAL FROST AND
SNOW—THE MOOSE, DOLLY VARDEN, SACRAMENTO, AND OTHERS—
THE HIGHEST MINE IN NORTH AMERICA—THE BULLION PRODUCT
—THE PLACERS OF THE PLATTE—THE RAILWAY.

Park county occupies the South Park region and portions of the
surrounding ranges of mountains. It is east of Lake and Summit
counties, and west of the Snowy Range, south of Jefferson and
Clear Creek counties, and west of the Pike's Peak section. The
elevation of the park, which embraces nearly 1,000 square miles, is
9,000 to 10,000 feet above sea level. The outlaying mountains rise
some thousands of feet higher. The Mosquito range includes Mount
Lincoln, with an elevation of 14,297 feet above sea level, and in a
spur of the range to the northward are Mounts Evans and Rosalie,
14,330 and 14,340 respectively. The climate is cool but pleasant in
summer, but the winters are long and severe.

This region is rich in gold and silver. The placers have yielded
largely and are again doing so, but in a less degree. Up to the time
of the silver discoveries in 1871 the gold lodes and placers had produced $2,500,000, principally obtained prior to 1866. The silver
deposits are however of vastly greater value and extent. They did
not produce much until 1873, but have yielded over $3,000,000.

The argentiferous riches of the Mosquito range are found in limestone and sometimes porphyry formations—a different condition
from that existing among the northern mining districts of Colorado.
Instead of true fissure veins, deposits, chambers and pockets of
mineral are found often between two formations. These deposits
carry galena, gray copper, zinc blende, and a quartz gangue, when
located in the higher sandstone, and galena, gray copper and silver
glance, and usually a heavy spar gangue in the higher limestone
of Mount Lincoln. Far above timber line and vegetation, from

twelve to fourteen thousand feet above sea level, mining is successfully conducted in winter and summer.

The production of Park county, estimating the yield of the first thirteen years at two and a half millions of gold, was as follows:

1859–71 inclusive..	$2,500,000 00	1875	$716,258 62
1872..............	250,000 00	1876	550,044 84
1873..............	459,000 00	1877	616,459 32
1874..............	596,392 00	1878*...............	426,698 00

Total to 1879................................$6,114,852 78

Total gold, $3,050,200; silver, 3,014,652.78; copper, $36,500; lead, $13,500.

The first silver mine that attracted attention was the Moose in 1871. The fall of that year saw a small army of prospectors on Mounts Bross and Lincoln, and when the snows disappeared in the following summer this was the great centre of excitement. The villages of Alma and Dudleyville grew from the development of these silver mines, and smelting works were soon in operation at both places.

The active ore-treating works of Park county embrace the Moose chlorodizing-amalgamating establishment at Dudleyville, a stamp mill at Montgomery, and dressing works at Alma; there are sampling mills, such as Kendrick's, for the Golden works, and others. The Boston and Colorado Smelting Company do not smelt ores at Alma now, but buy, sample, and ship to Argo. Grose's wet concentrating works, built at Alma in 1876, dress 10 tons of ore daily. A quartz mill in the same building is running on ores from the Satisfaction, Phillips, and other lodes.

The Park mineral belt is about 35 miles long, and perhaps 14 wide. The following silver lodes of the Mosquito Range have been worked in recent years, some steadily and others at intervals: Sacramento, Moose, Dolly Varden, Russia, Ford, Security, Hiawatha, London, Lone Star, Guinea Pig, Ten-Forty, Silver Lake, North Star, Ocean Wave, D. H. Hill, Spring Cat, Danville, Buckskin, Mono, Hidden Treasure, Forest Queen, Keystone, Badger, Occi-

* Exclusive of this a large amount of ore awaited shipment at the close of the year at the B. & C. branch smelting works, which discontinued work early in the fall. The valuation will appear in the product of 1879.

dental, Lioness, Milwaukee, Danville (on Lincoln), Ford, **Musk Ox**, Buckeye, Mammoth (Mt. Lincoln), Schuyler, Kansas, Empress, Present Help, Gertrude, Hidden Treasure, Hunter, No End, Champaign, and Joe Chaffee; also, the Wheeler and other gold lodes near Montgomery, the Nova Zembla on Quandary Mountain, carrying gold and silver, and the Phillips, Orphan Boy, and other gold veins at Buckskin. Many other silver lodes have been worked.

The Moose has been the most productive mine in Park county. It was first opened in 1871, and yielded $21,768 in the first forty days. With the summer of 1872 mining was resumed and has been continued ever since. Dudley, Gill and McNab purchased the mine at an early date, and the Moose Mining Company was afterwards organized. The property consists of one hundred acres of surface ground, including twenty-one claims, mostly patented, and roasting and amalgamating works (with two furnaces) at Dudleyville. The capital stock is two millions, in ten dollar shares. The yield in 1872 was $105,000, and had exceeded $600,000 up to 1876. A company statement shows that the yield for the year ending March 31, 1877, was nearly 1,393 tons of ore, returning $164,425.62, with an assay coin value of $237,485; average assay of ore, 144 ounces; average price received $110.85. There were 650 tons of ore on hand. To get this 2,043 tons of ore, 6,898½ tons of rock were broken altogether, which included driving 2,122½ feet of levels or tunnels, and 333 fathoms of stopes. The Moose, like other mineral bodies of this section, is a series of deposits, some of them of great size. These are opened by tunnels, drifts, or stopes. From sixty to seventy men are usually employed, at $3 a day or by contract. The total yield of silver for less than eight years up to 1879 must have exceeded $1,150,000.

The Dolly Varden mine ranks next to the Moose in production and size of deposits, and often surpasses that mine in richness of ore. It was discovered in 1872, and has since then made a fortune for its owners, George W. Brunk and Assyria Hall, or the Hall and Brunk Silver Mining Company. The mine has paid from the time it was opened, and is remarkable for the large proportion of ore returning from three to seven hundred dollars a ton. The last reports from the mine show that the first-class ore averaged 624 ounces of silver per ton, the second class 313 ounces, and the third class 206 ounces.

The yield of the Dolly Varden in four years, up to June 27, 1878, was as follows :

YEAR.	TONS OF ORE SOLD.	PRODUCT IN OUNCES OF SILVER.	VALUE.
1874............................	$159\frac{1190}{2000}$	15,061	$18,173 00
1875............................	$233\frac{214}{2000}$	28,666	34,401 00
1876..........	461	61,801	74,161 00
1877 (six months)...............	$66\frac{1836}{2000}$	Receipts.	19,070 96
1877–8 (fiscal year).............	$299\frac{1071}{2000}$	Receipts.	80,624 41
Total.................	1,219	....	$226,430 37

The figures for 1877-8 represent receipts only. The actual yield would be $45 more per ton. Out of $80,624 received for the year ending June 27, 1878, the profits were $63,164.02. The expenses were: labor, $11,005.67; supplies, $2,807.30; ore hauling and packing, $1,147.96; hauling timber, wood and supplies up to the mine, $974.52; powder and fuse, $462.75; placer, claims, surveying, lumber and assaying, $1,062.19.

Product of 1879: $516\frac{1697}{2000}$ tons of ore, sold for $62,821.08.

Net profit for the year 1879, $34,888.93.

The actual yield at the smelter's for that year was probably $80,000.

The expenditures for 1879 were $22,115.84; for labor and contracts, $2,201.73; for hauling and packing ore, $1,813.90; for mining supplies, uphauling and packing supplies, timbers, lumber, wood etc., $694.49; powder and fuse, $669.60; wood etc., $436.59. The actual yield of the mine prior to 1880 was probably over $330,-000. The many claims making up this property comprise a large surface average. Where explored, it appears to be the richest part of Bross mountain, and has paid a profit ever since work began in 1872.

Mount Lincoln, that great natural monument, named in honor of President Lincoln, lies north of Mount Bross and in the Mosquito or Park range, just south of its point of union with the Continental Divide. Its summit is 14,297 feet above sea level, being one of the highest peaks in the country. The mountain is so situated regarding the various ranges and parks and valleys that the view is probably as fine as North America can afford. There are a large number of mines on Mount Lincoln, some of them paying handsomely. The ores are of lower average grade than on Mount Bross, but the Ford and Musk Ox have turned out very rich mineral. The ores carry galena, gray copper, sulphurets, brittle silver, and copper pyrites. The Russia has produced the most silver, and since it was well opened, early in 1876, it has yielded something like $50,000 per annum. The Danville, 1, 2, and 3, has been extensively and profitably worked for several years. The Gertrude, Mossvale, Present Help, and those mentioned above, are on the north spur of Mount Lincoln. The Present Help is 14,200 feet above the level of the sea, and is the highest mine in North America. In Montgomery district are the Chicago, Wheeler, and Atlantic. The last two have yielded a great deal of free milling gold quartz.

In Buckskin Gulch the Ten Forty and other mines are worked. In Mosquito district is the Forest Queen, in which a tunnel is driven from which ore is shipped that has milled as follows, per ton: 158 ounces, 221 ounces, 489 ounces, 541 ounces, 651 ounces, 690 ounces. The Champaign is another valuable lode. The Joe Chaffee, carrying silver and gold, is said to be paying well. The London mine is in this district. The Kansas is one of the leading mines of this section.

The Phillips, in Buckskin, is the great gold mine of this section. This was discovered in 1862, and in a few short years produced about $300,000. Stamp mills were in operation and a lively town was in existence, when the Phillips and Orphan Boy were yielding their thousands weekly. Some of the surface ores compared with the best in Gilpin county. When the decomposed material had been exhausted and solid iron and copper pyrites were reached, the crude mills of those days failed to save the gold, and work stopped. It was renewed occasionally since, but no important results were attained until the purchase of 1,200 feet of the lode by the Phillips Consolidated Gold Mining Company in 1880, of which A. J. Severance and J. Q. Rollins are leading members. The property is now worked on a most extensive scale. A mill will soon be completed, when the owners propose to make the Phillips one of the great producers of the State. The lode is proved to be from 25 to 40 feet wide.

The Orphan Boy is about a mile southwest, and is said to be on the same vein as the Phillips. In size, character, and past productiveness these lodes are much alike. J. W. Smith, of Denver, made his fortune here in 1862-3. The total yield of the Orphan Boy is reported at $250,000. Locations between this and the Phillips, claimed to be on the same vein, are now worked.

Hall Valley is in the northwest corner of Park county, and heads at the crest of the main range. The lower eight miles of the valley, including the steep mountain slopes on either side, are covered with splendid forests, and on the range itself are the great Whale and Leftwick silver mines. The Hall Valley Company operated these mines, and expended large sums of money in building smelting works, a connecting tramway, and in other ways.

Besides the Moose and Dolly Varden, with their great numbers of segregated claims and deposits, the following mines were worked on Mount Bross in the winter of 1879-80 : Ten Forty, Crescent, Mammoth, Criterion, Security, Gregory, Gilbert, Silver Saddle, Rising Sun, Everlasting, Sweet Home, and Colorado Springs. Other mines have since been reopened. The Criterion, long ago worked for gold, yields gold and silver and carbonates of lead. Further north, the Silver Gem, and on Mount Lincoln, the Russia, Danville, Bullion, Burnside and Present Help, are worked.

The placers of the Platte are said to have yielded $1,750,000 altogether, mostly in a few years succeeding 1859. The early mining camps of Fairplay, Tarryall, and Hamilton have already been referred to in the historical narrative. Thayer's placer operations in the Platte at Fairplay are the most extensive in the county. The Fairplay placer property embraces five miles of ground along the stream, with dams and miles of ditches and flumes. Nearly a hundred Chinamen are employed under the head man, Lin Sou, in Thayer's leased ground, and under his management.

The Tarryall placer claim of Hall, Barrett & Rische has a very rich streak in an old channel of the stream lately discovered. The twenty-five Chinamen working there are each making many dollars daily to the man. Mills, Hodges & Co. have worked a large placer claim on the Platte river at Alma for many summers, and have taken out nearly $100,000. The season of 1879 returned 1,100 ounces of gold dust, worth $17,930, at a trifling cost. If work was crowded, the yield could be trebled, but the owners consider their gravel bank as safe as any other bank, and take out the gold only as they want it.

Quite a mining revival has taken place in the old Montgomery gold district. Here are the Kansas, Nova Zembla, Pacific, Silver Lake, Atlantic, Buckeye, Peru, Columbia, Chicago, Magnolia, Ogden and Rip Van Winkle. The Nova Zembla, owned by G. W. Brunk, has a splendid body of ore, fully capable of supplying its quartz mill. Other stamp mills may soon be at work. The Wheeler, Pacific and Coaley carry gold, silver and copper to the value of from $30 to $350 a ton. The Washington is a very rich lode. All of the above are true fissure veins, and the same belt extends over the range to the head of McNulty and Ten Mile valleys. On the Summit county slope the Vandemoer lode is actively worked.

On Mosquito or Loveland mountain are the Good Samaritan, Kansas, Kansas Extension, U. P., Morrison, K. P., Legal Tender, Mountain King, Mountain Queen, Saint Mary's, Star, Powers, Centennial, Bell Front, Fanny Barrett, Ernest, Avalanche, Pharaoh, Rankin, Lizzie, Rosa Lee, Parole, Autocrat, Cock Robin, and Fair Damsel—the last three carrying both gold and silver.

Valuable discoveries were made on Mosquito mountain in 1880, which caused an influx of prospectors from all quarters. Claims were located all over that part of the range and down in Pennsylvania and other gulches. The result has been a general revival in mining and the development of properties that are destined to cut an important figure from this time on. During the past year three smelters have been completed, and there should be an excellent ore market.

The most important discovery of the year was the Fannie Barrett, so called by the locator, Henry Clements, after the daughter of the editor of the Rocky Mountain News. This is now embraced in the Loveland consolidated mines. Here is an immense ore body, which is being steadily developed and which promises to rival any mine in Park county. Large shipments of ore to Golden and elsewhere have returned good profits. The quantity of ore in sight should ensure a heavy production, now that the claims are extensively opened.

The Forest Queen mine, owned by John Z. Walker and R. A. Kirker, is situated on Loveland mountain in Mosquito Mining District. Here a very strong fissure vein connects with a contact. The dip of the fissure is 65 degrees, and of the contact 20 degrees. In one place is a body of ore four feet wide. The mine has given the remarkably high average for all ore sold of 317.47 ounces of silver per ton. Ores sold to Berdell & Witherell, A. R. Mcyer, St. Louis S. and R. works, and the Golden Smelting Company yielded as follows per ton : first class, 590½ ounces, 2,553½ ounces, 514 ounces, 651 and 690 ; second class, 381—317—428 ; third class, 216—180—232—226.

Pennsylvania gulch is the scene of considerable activity and valuable discoveries have been made, such as the Lone Star, Boss, Silver Jim, Cockeye, Bulger, Black Hawk, Elegant and Black Chief.

The London and Paris lodes, both on one vein, have lately been purchased by a company which is operating them on a large scale.

The Sacramento is comparatively a new mine, having been located in October, 1878, yet it has already shown value enough to take rank among the best mines in Park county. It is situated at the head of Sacramento gulch, about six hundred feet below timber line, six miles from Fairplay, and ten from the nearest station of the Denver and South Park railway. The property embraces seven mining claims, covering about 70 acres of mineral land. The ore body so far opened on only three of these claims has shown a width of from six inches to six feet, and a very high value.

The formation is limestone, dipping to the east at an angle of about sixteen degrees, and at this place carries a belt rich in sulphuret of silver. The richness and extent of the Sacramento induced crowds of prospectors to make their appearance in the vicinity and other good properties were located. The proved resources of the camp caused a party of moneyed men to erect a smelter near the mouth of the gulch and a few miles from Fairplay. Good roads of an extremely easy down grade extend from the mines down to these works, and also to the railway station.

The ore has generally been treated at Argo or Golden. The first lot sold from the mine comprised 9½ tons, and sold for $1,346. Since then the ores shipped have generally been richer. During the last half year, the ore sold in one month contained an average of 256 ounces of silver per ton, of another 275, another 340 and again 368. The total yield of the mine up to February 15, 1880, was about 190 tons of ore, averaging 274 ounces of silver per ton, or $53,471 altogether. This represents 254 pounds of mineral or $35.73 per running foot of workings. This has been obtained in drifting and sinking, and without encroaching on the ore reserves. In ten months 1,500 feet of rock drifts, 300 feet of tunnelling, and 150 feet of open cuts have been run, and 329 feet of shafts sunk. These have opened up a vast amount of paying ground, it being estimated that the ore in sight contains half a million in silver. All of the headings have paying mineral in sight. The first regular stoping done in the mine was in April. The ore carries galena, black sulphurets, chlorides of silver and carbonates of lead. There is plenty of timber and water near the mine, which is supplied with all the necessary ore houses and other buildings.

The Sacramento Mining Company has been organized on this mine, with a capital stock of $2,000,000 in 200,000 shares of a par value of ten dollars. The officers are W. B. Frue, president; Joseph Hobson, vice-president; R. G. Lay, secretary and treasurer, and the same and Hon. J. A. Hubbell and Charles W. Dwelle are directors. J. W. Plummer is superintendent of the mine. From this time forward, development and production will be pushed, and the immense reserves of rich ore should permit of princely revenues.

The Gold Placer Company, under the management of C. G. Hathaway, are taking steps to work its extensive placer lands.

Coal veins of an excellent lignite variety are mined near the railroad town of Como. It is said that this coal will coke successfully. If so the mining and smelting industries of Park county and of Leadville and other sections will be greatly benefited, for a vast saving can be effected in freights over what is now afforded from the distant El Moro mines. The Denver and South Park Company has two shafts on its extensive coal lands, one of which is equipped with steam machinery. The railway draws a portion of its fuel supply from this mine. Near by the Pittsburg Coal, Coke and Lime Company are mining coal for coking purposes. William Updike, of old time stage line celebrity, is working his coal claim in this vicinity. George W. Lechner was the first to develop coal veins in Park county. Coal has also been found at Jefferson.

In the southwestern portion of the South Park are saline springs of great strength and volume. Salt works were established there years ago by the owner, J. Q. A. Rollins. Now that the railway is in operation near by, these works can produce and ship to a market at living rates. These waters contain from 12 to 16 per cent. of salt.

The completion of the Denver and South Park railway has greatly benefited Park county. Freights and supplies have been so cheapened that the miner is enabled to sell his ore at much better figures than formerly, while smelting can be carried on to much greater advantage than ever before.

CHAPTER XXV.

THE SAN JUAN REGION—RIO GRANDE AND HINSDALE COUNTIES—
AMONG THE GREAT SOUTHERN MINES—LAKE CITY AND SUMMIT
DISTRICTS—BULLION STATISTICS OF THE SAN JUAN COUNTRY—
NARRATIVE OF GENERAL AND INDIVIDUAL OPERATIONS.

The San Juan country or region embraces the southwestern portion of Colorado. Under this name are included the mountainous counties of Hinsdale, Rio Grande, San Juan, La Plata, Conejos and Ouray; and San Luis Park, with the counties of Saguache and Costilla, are often classed under the same head. Here is an area of some 15,000 square miles, or more territory than is included in any one of the States of New Jersey, New Hampshire, or Vermont, with Delaware thrown in. West of San Luis Park is one mass of mountains, thrown together in the most chaotic confusion.

These mountains contain thousands of silver veins, many of them of huge size, and some of great richness. There are also gold lodes and placers. The Rocky Mountain range extends to the westward in this region. The silver belt is from twenty to forty miles wide, and perhaps eighty miles long in an air line. The rugged and almost impassable character of the mountains and their vast extent, and the heavy snows and long winters, have acted as serious drawbacks to growth and development. There is probably more country standing on edge in this section than anywhere else beneath the sun. Until recently no work was prosecuted in the winter season, except on a very few mines and on tunnels. It took years to build roads to the most important points—trails or foot-paths being the only thing previously afforded. The approach of the railway and the completion of many smelting works are bringing the San Juan country forward.

After the expulsion of the Baker expedition of 1860 by the Indians, few white men ventured among the San Juan mountains, and it remained a "terra incognita" for many years. Adnah French is considered the pioneer. After him came Miles T. Johnson, who dis-

covered the Little Giant gold mine in 1870, and others.   The outside world knew little of what these isolated prospectors were doing
until the Little Giant mine began to yield in 1872.   When Major
Hamilton was operating it in 1873, a great contest for possession
arose.   It yielded $22,000 in a few years.

MINERS' PACK TRAIN IN THE SAN JUAN MOUNTAINS.

Most of the San Juan region was formerly included in the county
of Conejos.   After several mining districts had been located and
settled, the counties of La Plata, Rio Grande, and Hinsdale were
created, and afterwards those of San Juan and Ouray.   As many of
the names of towns, rivers, and mountains in this section are of

Spanish origin, the pronunciation of some of them is given—the name appearing first and the pronunciation and definition immediately after; the Spanish i has the sound of the English e, and a the sound of ah; e is pronounced like a, and j like h.

Albuqueque, Albukerka; Conejos, Kon-à-hos, rabbits; Costilla, Kos-téel-ya or Cos-tée-ya, ribs; Rio Grande, Re-o Gránd-a, grand river; Hermosilla, Her-mos-eel-ya, beautiful; Heurfano, Whár-fan-oh, orphan; Las Vegas, Las Vagas; Rico, Re-co, rich; La Plata, Lah Plát-ah, the silver; Saguache, Sa-wash; San Juan, San Whón, Saint John; San Miguel, San Megéel, Saint Michael; San Luis, San Lú-e, Saint Louis; Santa Fe, San-ta Fa, Holy Faith; Ouray, Oo-rá; Ulé, Yu-lá; Uncompahgre, Un-com-pàr-gra; Veta Madre, Vatah Mad-rah, mother vein.

SAN JUAN MINING PRODUCT.

As near as can be ascertained, the San Juan region produced prior to 1880 as follows:

Silver, $1,015,052.19; gold, $387,925.06; lead, $158,546.27; total, $1,561,523.52.

The San Juan region yielded as follows in 1879:

Silver, $241,491.19; gold, $21,925.06; lead, $43,546.27; total, $306,972.52.

Of the product of 1879, the Crooke Smelter at Lake City gave $112,121.52, of which $85,498.19 was silver, $2,925.06 gold, and $23,698.27 lead; the Lee Smelter gave $3,000, the Gladstone works $5,000, the Norfolk and Ouray works about $30,000, the Windham Smelter $4,000. It is estimated that over $100,000 worth of ore was shipped out of the San Juan region for treatment. Summit district yielded but $11,000 in gold.

The gold yield prior to 1876 was about $102,000, and the silver yield over $75,000. Lake City shipments include some Silverton and Ouray ores. Below are the products of 1876-7-8.

1876.

San Juan County, Greene & Co. shipped lead bullion valued at............	$106,000
Hinsdale County, Crooke & Co. shipped silver ore, bought and concentrated	40,000
Gulch, bar, and lode gold and other silver ores shipped, La Plata, etc......	15,000
Rio Grande County, Summit mines, stamp mill gold......................	65,000
Gold ores shipped..	30,000
Sangre de Cristo range stamp mill and gulch gold, and elsewhere..........	10,000
Total.................	$266,000

1877.

	Tons Ore.	Tons Bullion.	Coin Value.
Gold from Summit district, Rio Grande County..........................	6,000	.....	$95,000
Gold from placers and veins elsewhere	....	...	10,000
Silver ore shipped from various districts.............................	....	....	15,000
Silver bars, Van Gieson, Hinsdale County...........................	400	....	35,000
SILVER LEAD BULLION.			
Crook's Smelters, Hinsdale County...	1,500	300	54,415
Ocean Wave Smelter...........	250	120	24,057
Greene's Silverton Smelter, San Juan County	1,400	400	141,000
Smelter, Ouray County.......	30	....	3,000
Total.....................	9,580	820	$377,472

1878.

Greene & Co.'s Smelter, Silverton, 350 tons bullion......................$142,256 00
Lixiviation Works, Cement Creek, San Juan...........................   3,000 00
Animas Mining and Smelting Works, Niegold Concentrating Works, 100
    tons, San Juan.. .... 15,000 00
Dacotah & San Juan Works, Animas Forks Conc. Works, San Juan.......   5,000 00
St. L. & S. J. Company, Ouray... 19,320 00
Windham Smelter, Ouray 11,430 00
Norfolk & Ouray Works, Ouray..... ....   8,000 00
Crooke Works, Lake City................................ .... 93,208 00
Van Gieson Works, Lake City...   6,400 00
Ocean Wave Smelter, Lake City... 56,483 00
Summit district, gold, Rio Grande..................................... 80,000 00
San Miguel & Sangre de Cristo placers.................................   9,000 00
Ores shipped elsewhere.. 85,000 00

Total...$534,089 00
Deduct for over estimates..$100,000 00

In the above is included a small amount of ore from the new silver mines of Spanish Peaks, 20 tons going in one shipment.

The lead yield, allowing an eastern price of $80 a ton, exceeded $20,000 prior to 1877. That year gave about $35,000 worth, and

1878 gave about $60,000 worth. Some of the figures given in the above tables are estimated.

Rio Grande County.

Rio Grande county is composed partly of plain and partly of mountain. Del Norte, the main town and county seat, is located on the Rio Grande where it leaves the mountains and enters the plains of San Luis Park. There are several mining districts, but the only one that has produced much is the gold-bearing portion of the Summit Mountains, which has yielded over $400,000 to date.

The richest gold district of Southern Colorado is that of South Mountain in the Summit Range, twenty-six miles south of Del Norte and nearly 12,000 feet above sea level. The great drawbacks are a severe climate, heavy snows, and the altitude—a divide of 13,000 feet must be crossed to reach Summit. The summers are short and the roads are almost impassable from snow or mud during most of the year. But the gold is there, and that has built a town and attracted miners, capitalists, and stamp mills.

In 1873 it began to be noised abroad that Peterson and Brandt had made a wonderful discovery in the far-off southern mountains, and the free gold quartz and nuggets they exhibited created no little excitement in Pueblo and Denver. In the short summers of 1874–5 hundreds of prospectors went there, and locations were made until the whole mountain was covered with pre-emptions—all in the endeavor to secure a piece, however small, of the precious ground. It appeared to be a vast mass of " float ore " or " slide," and for a time was considered one huge mountain of quartz. Subsequent developments show veins, and that it is not simply a deposit or a "blow out." The country rock is a kind of porphyry. The main lode runs diagonally across the mountain. As usual with prospectors, Peterson and Brandt had no money to build roads or stamp mills, and in the fall of 1874, transported ore on the backs of mules to Del Norte, thence by teams to Cañon, and by railway to Golden. The next summer the Crooke brothers sent a ten-stamp mill into the district, and became interested in the Little Annie. Some four years ago $\frac{281}{1500}$ of the property sold for $78,000. The discoverers still own $\frac{821}{1500}$, and P. J. Peterson is superintendent. Up to 1880 the Little Annie had yielded over $200,000 in gold, and the Summit district about $250,000, including the above. The Golden Queen mine

THE LITTLE ANNIE MINE.

and mill have yielded well at times.   Other mills were brought in, and a United States Signal Office was established.

In 27 months actual milling the company retorts of very fine gold gave $182,625.07; dividends paid, $46,282.56; average yield per ton, $33.73; cost of mining, 75 cents per ton; of tramming to mill, 17 to 20 cents; of milling, about $9; wages, $1 50 to $2 and board; cost of ten-stamp mill, $38,578.14; of automatic tramway from mine to mill, $6,691.90.   There are 615 feet of tunnels and shafts, and a depth of 200 feet has been attained.   The company placers have yielded the finest nuggets in Colorado; $365 worth of gold 980 fine was pounded out of one nugget weighing 5½ pounds.   These figures are from the report of treasurer C. E. Robins.

The Iowa and Colorado Cons. Company, General R. B. Smith, manager, owns forty locations, including the Golden Vault and Pay Roll, and is running a tunnel and a ten-stamp mill; twenty more stamps are coming.   An English company have sent J. Burrows into the district with a fifty-stamp mill for the Empire and other claims.   The Thomas M. Bowen tunnel has lately found rich ore on the San Juan Cons. claims.   These embrace a large part of South mountain, with an enormous amount of quartz, containing about $7 a ton.   Judge Bowen expects to make this pay with two mills and 54 stamps at work.

HINSDALE COUNTY.

Hinsdale county is the most easterly of the important silver districts of San Juan.   Its metropolis is Lake City, dating from 1874–5, located at the junction of Hensen Creek with the Lake Fork of the Gunnison.   Here are two smelting works in operation—Crooke & Co. and the Ocean Wave—the Crooke concentrating works and a chlorination and lixiviation mill—the latter not run steadily.   The location of the town is grand and beautiful and resembles that of Georgetown.   There are numberless silver lodes in the lofty mountains that rise almost perpendicularly for a half mile or a mile on every side—many of them worked extensively.

Promising as were the numerous discoveries of the San Juan country in 1873–4–5, they were generally of no immediate benefit to their owners, on account of the distance from an ore market, wagon roads and railways.   The region labored under peculiar disadvantages.   It was made up of almost inaccessible mountain ranges, and at that time was so remote from railways that capitalists and mill men were not inclined to investigate its mineral wealth. The pioneers who had been making discoveries of rich veins were too poor to build works for the extraction of the precious metals, and it cost too much to get ore to market to admit of attempting it,

LAKE CITY.

unless it was wonderfully rich and money was at hand to defray shipping expenses.

This was the condition of affairs when the Crooke brothers—the **first** eastern capitalists that showed their appreciation of the region by putting their money into it—began to buy mines and erect mills. They were conducting a smelting business in New York city, and inspection and contact with its ores begat that confidence in its worth that subsequent experience has in no wise abated. The results of their investments in the Little Annie and Golden Queen mines and mills in the Summit Mountain gold district induced them to look further.

An investigation of the Lake City silver district caused them to erect a concentrating mill there. This separated the silver-bearing mineral from the gangue, or waste rock of the ore. The miner then had his value in one ton of concentrates instead of having it distributed among five or ten tons as before. This was an important item where it cost more to get ore to a market than it did to treat it after it reached there.

The Ute and Ulé mines were purchased late in 1876 and the new owners then erected quarters for workmen and shaft and ore houses for the mine. The next spring contracts were let for sinking shafts and running drifts, and for the construction of works for the treatment of the ore. The stack furnace was not completed till near the close of the season, but 2,000 tons of ore had been mined and concentrated, and the dressed ore sent to New York. It yielded a net profit of twelve dollars per ton. The smelting works were completed so that reduction, parting and refining began in July, 1878. Up to this time Crooke & Co. had expended over $400,000 on their mines, works, and other property of this locality.

The Ute and Ulé overlook Hensen creek three miles above Lake City, the first being well up on the mountain, and the other near its base. Their great galena and gray copper veins, from one to seven feet wide, carry from $10 to $500 in silver per ton, $30 or $40 in lead, and from $3 to $10 in gold. Most of the ore yields only from 20 to 40 ounces in silver and requires concentration before smelting. The first 50 feet of shafting gave 450 tons of ore. The yield in 1879 probably ranged between $50,000 and $100,000. The officials of the Crooke Mining and Smelting Company owning these mines, are John N. Goodwin, ex-Governor of Arizona, president; Thomas F. Mason, vice-president; W. Hart Smith, secretary and treasurer; and the above and Lewis Crooke, E. J. Granger, William Spence and S. W. Hill, trustees. The concentrator and smelter at Crookeville, one mile from Lake City, have the finest water power in the state.

THE CROOKE SMELTING AND CONCENTRATING WORKS NEAR LAKE CITY.

A late report of the company shows that work is now confined to the Ulé, where 43 men are employed. In a few months' time 418 fathoms of ground were stoped, at an average cost of $34 per fathom, 302 feet of levels were driven, costing from $14 to $15 per linear foot, and 124 feet of shafting were sunk. The new workings show improvement in the vein. The Ute lode where last worked yielded only from 10 to 40 ounces of silver per ton and 30 per cent. of lead. The Ute mine has nearly 2,200 feet of levels, cross-cuts, winzes and shafts last winter, and the Ule nearly 1,700 feet.

In 1879 the Crooke Mining & Smelting Company's bullion product was $85,498.19 in silver, $23,698.27 lead, and $2,925.06 gold; total $112,121.52.

The California extension of the Ute, of which Morgan Draper is superintendent, is developed by a cross-cut tunnel, level and shaft.

The Belle of the West is one of the most famous lodes of this section. Its yield is reported at nearly or quite 60,000 ounces of silver, or $68,000, besides lead, which may have brought the total up to $80,000 or $100,000. One lessee paid 50 per cent. royalty. The average yield has been 100 ounces per ton. A good quantity of ore is reported in the two shafts and various levels, and the lode is likely to yield as largely as ever. The Belle of the East is an extension of the above. One mile distant is the Plutarch, which has yielded about $10,000. A few years ago the Hotchkiss yielded tellurides.

Several smelters are expected to be at work hereafter instead of one as in 1879. The Crooke works at Lake City and the Lee Smelter at Capitol will do an extensive business. The Palmetto company lixiviation works and the Ocean Wave smelter will start up soon. Some sixty lodes showing ore are mined, while as many more are worked to some extent. Most of the ore from Poughkeepsie gulch, Mineral Point and Animas Forks comes to Lake City for treatment. Among the producing mines of Hinsdale county are the Ule, California, Lightning Striker, Mountain Chief, Little Chief, Pueblo, Ocean Wave, Wave of the Ocean, Yellow Jacket, Big Casino, Pride of America, Joaquin, J. J. Crooke, Piute, El Paso, Silver Chord Extension, Yellow Medicine, Moose, Fairview, El Moro, St. Louis, Dolly Varden, the Copper Hill company's group of eight mines, the Palmetto, Ruby Queen, Frank Hough, Wyoming, Miners' Bank, First National, Polar Star, Syracuse Pride and others—along Hensen creek; the Rob Roy, Lone Star, Highland Mary, Dolphin, Cora,

RESIDENCE OF GEORGE S. LEE, CAPITOL CITY.

Belle of the East, Extension, Plutarch, Mayflower, Gladiator, Silver Coin and others—on the Lake Fork; the Black Wonder No. 2, Wolverine, George Washington, Salamanca, World's Wonder No. 2, Golden Chain, Cuba and others—about Sherman; the No. 1, Grand Central, Napoleon, Hoosier, General Hayes, Seward County, American Eagle and others in Park district.

The Ocean Wave mine is about five miles from Lake City. Its total product up to 1880 was about $100,000, including 75,000 ounces of silver. The largest yield was in 1877. In 1879, active work was prevented by the failure of parties in Kansas City who owned most of the property. The mine is now said to be in condition to yield as largely as ever. The lode carries about two tons of lead ore to one of gray copper, containing copper pyrites. Mill-runs range from 1,000 ounces down to 35. Much of the ore sold averaged $400 a ton. Second class ore treated at Lee's works yielded from 274 to 198 ounces, and third class 39 to 59 ounces. Two or three years ago the mine sold for $120,000. The Wave of the Ocean on the same vein has been opened but little.

Capitol City is located at the junction of the forks of Hensen Creek, nine miles above Lake City, where the almost perpendicular peaks and ranges open out into a level valley called Capitol Park, most of which is embraced in the Lee town site patent. All around this enclosure are numerous silver-bearing veins, and Capitol itself seems destined to be an important smelting centre. Paying ores are plentiful and so are lead, iron and other fluxing materials. And right here among these rugged mountains of far away San Juan, where one would least expect to find it, is the most elegantly furnished house in Southern Colorado. The handsome brick residence of George S. Lee and lady, distinguished for their hospitality, is a landmark of this locality. The scenic attractions, delightful atmosphere and the hunting, fishing, and boating facilities make this a popular summer resort, while the pleasure-seeker and traveler will find the best accommodations that San Juan affords. At either end of town is a smelter. The lower one was erected by Mr. Lee, and a trial run in 1879 gave $3,900 in bullion. The upper one has lately passed into the hands of a company organized by George S. Lee, who is superintendent of the works. The furnaces were fired up early in the season of 1880. The plant comprises roasting furnaces, a blast smelting furnace, crushers, rollers, and all sampling apparatus and machinery necessary to keep the mill at work. There is ample water-power, and a flume 1,000 feet long has been constructed. The ore is received at the upper side of the mill and passes successively through the furnaces, one below another, until the bullion is produced. Timber is abundant in this locality.

One of the great lodes of this section extends from Capitol City for several miles over the mountains, nearly parallel with Hensen Creek, and is known by the names Emperor, Fairview, Scotia, John J. Crooke and El Paso. Near the northern end the famous Ocean Wave comes in—a lode which has few equals in southwestern Colorado. The Lee tunnel will soon intersect the Fairview at great depth. On the opposite side of the creek from the Ocean Wave are the Big Casino and Red Rover lodes; the first having yielded about $10,000. Near Boulder gulch and Hensen Creek are the Moose and Argo properties of the Lee Mining and Smelting Company, and near Capitol is the Iron mine, so called from its iron ore. Copper Hill is on Hensen Creek, sixteen miles above Lake City, and near Rose's cabin. The Accidental and Copper Glance yield from $100 to $350 per ton in silver, and from 7 to 30 per cent. of copper. Total yield reported at $20,000. The Chipmunk has more than paid expenses since discovered. The Dolly Varden has yielded $9,000.

The Inez mine is in Park district, near the head of Cleveland gulch —said to be about 13,000 feet above sea level. At times it has produced as much as six tons daily of decomposed sulphuret ores, with an average yield of 150 ounces. There are 500 feet of tunnels, a shaft 200 feet deep and drifts leading therefrom. This is the property of the Inez Mining Company of New York. The Colorado, Morgan Draper, superintendent, said to be owned by H. B. Claflin and others of New York, is a high grade galena vein.

The Palmetto, located on the northern slope of Engineer mountain, came into prominence in 1879. The vein is from 10 to 30 inches wide, more or less, and carries ruby, brittle and wire silver in black stained quartz. The average of 40 tons of ore sold in the summer and fall of 1879 was 258 ounces of silver per ton—the highest run being 480 ounces—and the receipts were over $9,000. Fifteen men were employed at the mine last winter. Few properties in the county are as profitable or productive. Not long ago the owners, John S. Hough and George A. Smith, sold the mine to the Palmetto Company of Philadelphia—the lixiviation works at Lake City going with the mine.

CHAPTER XXVI.

THE MINES OF SAN JUAN COUNTY—HAZELTON, SULTAN, KING SOLOMON, ANIMAS FORKS, MINERAL POINT, AND POUGHKEEPSIE DISTRICTS—THE APPROACH OF THE D. & R. G. R. R.—A GREAT MINING AND SMELTING ENTERPRISE—INVESTMENTS OF EASTERN CAPITALISTS—WHAT HAS BEEN AND IS BEING DONE AMONG THE SAN JUAN MOUNTAINS.

San Juan county lies on the western slope of the Continental Divide, north of La Plata, and between that county and Hinsdale and Ouray. It contains many of the best mines of the San Juan mining region, galena ores predominating and promising the main support. Some lodes are of high grade and quite productive, while many galena veins are of great size, but too poor in silver to pay for transportation to distant works. Near the centre of the county is Baker's Park, which took its name from the first explorer, who led the disastrous San Juan gold-hunting stampede of 1860. This valley is several miles long and a mile wide at the broadest part, but it is too elevated for general farming purposes.

The leading mining camps of San Juan county are on Hazelton, King Solomon and Sultan mountains, in Cunningham gulch and vicinity, in the Animas Forks and Mineral Point section, and near the head of Poughkeepsie gulch. Some mining is also done at Eureka. Rugged and lofty mountains, rich in silver veins, enclose Baker Park, through which the Animas river flows southward on its way to the Rio San Juan. Ranges of mountains, divided by tributaries of the Animas, extend on every side. These are covered by forests of pine up to elevations where vegetation ceases. Most of the mineral veins are located above timber line, and mining camps have been started far up the water courses and on the crests of the snowy range. In order to prosecute work for the entire year the winter supplies are taken up to most of these mines before the first snows come, while the trails are yet passable. Baker's Park was naturally selected as the base of supplies. Here is Silverton, the county seat and metropolis of San Juan county, founded in 1873, in the time of the first silver prospecting excitement. Its elevation above the sea is 9,400 feet, while Sultan, Kendall and King Solomon mountains, rise abruptly on either hand over four thousand feet higher. For a long time pack animals and trails were the only freighting facilities. What few wagon roads have been constructed cost heavily, and, on the ranges, are snowed under for over half the year. Freighting supplies in, and ore and lead bullion out, has been very expensive. The costs of living and of packing to and from these elevated camps have discounted so much from the miner's receipts as to prevent work on all but the richer mines. From $40 to $50 per ton were required to get ore to a competing market in northern Colorado, with smelting charges to follow. As the San Juan silver region is too elevated to raise crops of any kind, provisions of every description and hay and grain were freighted in.

Better times are at hand however, for the Denver & Rio Grande Railway Company is extending its road to Silverton and Rico, and expects to reach those places by the close of the year. This should prove of incalculable benefit, and will so reduce the cost of freight transportation and supplies as to assure profitable operations where but partial success or total failure have been experienced heretofore. Cheap freights and the coal measures of the company at Animas City will aid to secure cheaper smelting, while rapid communication with the outside world at all seasons will ensure continuous mining and milling. The course of the road from Animas City to Silverton will be northward up the cañon of the Animas—a natural route soon to be blasted out by the railway construction force.

Greene & Co. started the first smelter used in this part of the State in Silverton, in 1875. The difficulties and costs of freighting the machinery over the roadless mountains and of putting up and operating works were very great. As the ores treated generally ran high in lead, the bullion turned out was from one third to one half as bulky as the ores it came from; and the cost of getting it to a railway necessitated the payment of low prices for ore. As the smelter possessed no steam power machinery, smelting was carried on only in those parts of the year when water power could be used—generally from June till some time in October. All of the above facts made smelting a costly operation, and owing to financial troubles the furnace was idle in 1879. Up to that time nearly $400,000 worth of

KENDALL MOUNTAIN.

SILVERTON.

SULTAN MOUNTAIN.

silver and lead had been exported from only about twelve months of actual work with a ten-ton furnance. A larger furnace was added in 1878, but never used.

Crooke & Co., of Lake City, and Mather & Geist, of Pueblo, had ore-buying agencies at Silverton in 1879. Joseph S. Reef, agent for the former, shipped about 500 tons of ore, averaging from 30 to 40 per cent. lead and worth altogether probably $60,000. Some of this came from Ouray county. Ingersoll & Sweet sent 185 tons of ore to Pueblo, averaging 23½ per cent. lead and containing $25,350, of which $4,347 was in lead.

The Greene smelter referred to above is now the property of the San Juan and New York Mining and Smelting Company, recently organized in New York, and which has also purchased the famous Hazelton group of mines, three miles from Silverton. The works and mines will be operated together, an engine and boiler having been procured for the former so as to furnish power for winter work. This is a strong company, a majority of its trustees being Denver & Rio Grande railway men. It will open up its lodes extensively before beginning to stope the ore reserves, and has ample funds to purchase ores to keep its smelter at work, as it starts in with a cash working capital of $150,000. The railway will afford such favorable rates for machinery, mine and smelter supplies, and bullion, that, when the works are operated the entire year, the cost of reducing the company's own ores will be but $24 per ton, while improvements made will cause the saving of a much higher per cent. of silver than before. It is said that the old prices of ores allowed a charge for smelting, for losses and profits of not far from $50 per ton. The S. J. and N. Y. Company will be enabled to handle all the ores that are likely to seek a market. Its own mines carry so high a percentage of lead that they will smelt to great advantage with less favorable mineral, while the purchase of extensive lime and iron beds near the furnaces will save outlays for fluxing material. The design is to build up a smelting business here which will be to San Juan what the Argo works are to other sections, and the Denver & Rio Grande railway will be a most efficient helper in the enterprise. In the figures given below silver is reckoned at $1.12½ an ounce, and lead at $80 a ton.

Hazelton mountain, situated about three miles northeast of Silverton, contains the most productive group of mines in San Juan county.

Here are the Aspen, Mammoth, Susquehanna, McGregor, Victor and Legal Tender, which, with the Ingersoll and J. L. P. intersecting tunnels, have been purchased by the S. J. and N. Y. Mining and Smelting Company. The veins, which are located on the easterly and northerly side of the mountain, dip towards and under its summit. The Ingersoll or upper tunnel is 1,300 feet long, and the veins it has intersected are believed to be the Victor, McGregor, Susquehanna and Aspen—the latter at a depth of 400 feet. The J. L. P. tunnel is about 400 feet lower down the mountain and on the northern slope. The Prospector vein, considered an extension of the Aspen, will be intersected 300 feet further in the mountain, and the Legal Tender is already intersected. When this work is completed these veins will have a drainage, ventilating and working outlet, with 400 feet of stoping ground above, or between the two tunnels. In driving the latter other valuable lodes will undoubtedly be discovered.

The Aspen was owned by Reese, Mulholland and others, and has been the largest silver producer in the San Juan. The old owners worked it steadily in 1876-7-8, and sold Greene & Co's. Silverton smelter 852 tons of ore, averaging 114 ounces of silver and 60 per cent. lead. This would give $109,657 worth of silver and $40,896 worth of lead. It is said some ore, probably $10,000 worth, had been sold elsewhere previous to 1879. In that year, lessees worked the mine in a small way, and sold about 100 tons of ore to the Crooke agency at Silverton. This was said to have yielded about 125 ounces of silver per ton and 50 per cent. of lead, making $18,-062 altogether. According to these figures, the total yield of the Aspen up to 1880 has been $178,558. Late in 1878 the mine contained very nearly 1,000 feet of levels, shafts and tunnels, and 1,768 fathoms of ground had been excavated, with an average return of $60 per fathom. The northerly extension of the Aspen is the Prospector, and the southerly extension the Gray Eagle. The vein is generally four feet wide, and the pay streak from two to eight inches, with frequent dislocations.

The Susquehanna is below and nearly parallel with the Aspen in present workings, but is supposed to come into the latter vein at another point. In 1876-7-8 there were 110 tons of ore smelted at Silverton, averaging about 60 per cent. in lead and 159 ounces in silver, taken from 63 fathoms of ground. Total yield of three years $24,972. Some ore went as high as $1,200 per ton. The Mammoth

HAZELTON MOUNTAIN.

is probably a feeder of the Aspen. Its outcrop is nearly 2,000 feet above Arastra gulch, or the base of the mountain. It is a large galena vein, but little developed. The McGregor has been worked but little; the ore mills from 40 to 379 ounces per ton. The Victor lode was intersected in 1877 by the Ingersoll tunnel 500 feet in and 300 feet below the surface. A level driven 60 feet east and 260 feet west on the vein has produced well and shows mineral scattered through a wide seam of ground. The Legal Tender is located on the northerly end or side of the mountain toward the Las Animas valley, with a direction at right angles to the other lodes excepting the McGregor. This lode has two shafts and levels and is intersected at a depth of 260 feet by the J. L. P. tunnel 465 feet from its mouth. It evidently drains the other veins, carries but little lead, and shows gray copper and wire silver; 156 tons of ore milled from 38 to 98 ounces of silver per ton. This group of mines has yielded altogether nearly a quarter of a million. Now that there is ample working capital with which to develop them in the most advantageous manner, their past product cannot compare with what is likely to come out in the future. The officials of the company are H. Amy, president; W. A. Bell, vice-president; Spencer Trask, treasurer; Geo. F. Peabody, secretary; and C. F. Woerishoffer, W. J. Palmer, T. E. Hambleton, Walter Hinchman, and Messrs. Amy, Bell and Trask are directors. J. A. Porter, once connected with the Silverton works, and lately superintendent of the K. K. mine at Eureka, Nevada, is superintending the mines and works of this company.

The difficulties and enormous expenses attending mining and smelting in the San Juan region heretofore, may be appreciated by the facts that Greene & Co., paid $60 a ton for transporting their base bullion to the nearest railway terminus in 1876, $56 for the same purpose in 1877, and $40 in 1878. The railway had approached a little nearer the last year. The bullion was conveyed on the backs of horses, mules, or burros over the main range to the nearest road, where wagons were employed. The low prices of lead and silver were drawbacks to success.

In 1878-9. Silverton for the first time had a wagon road over the range to the eastward. This enabled ore to be teamed out of San Juan for $30 a ton during the summer and early fall. In the same seasons of the year Brewster's mail line and passenger conveyances run to Silverton, and make daily connection at Antelope with the overland stage running between Lake City and the D. & R. G. railway terminus. Carrying the mails over these San Juan mountains is generally a perilous undertaking in winter when the snows are of immense depth. Several lives have been lost, and it has often been found impossible to face the terrible storms that prevail on these awful heights. Yet the mails go forward with commendable regularity.

The mountains containing heavy galena or lead veins are Sultan, Hazelton, King Solomon, Galena, Round, Tower, and others, in San Juan county, and Silver mountain, on Howard's Fork. Those sections whose lodes carry but little lead, or which contain what the smelters term " dry ores," embrace Poughkeepsie, Cement, Mineral, Animas Forks, Eureka, and Howard's Fork. The prevailing formation is trachyte.

Between the Animas River and Cunningham gulch, and near the junction of those streams, silver-ribbed King Solomon mountain rears its lofty summit. Of the numerous veins traceable for long distances on its face the North Star is apparently the mother lode. It will average forty feet wide, and this enormous mass of crevice-matter is composed of nearly vertical streaks of decomposed ferruginous quartz in contact with great seams and streaks of argentiferous mineral. It can be seen for a distance of two miles and has been traced for three miles. Some of the veins or seams of ore have a width in places of three feet of argentiferous galena, gray copper, and yellow sulphide of copper. The ore smelts readily, and yields from 40 to 500 ounces of silver per ton and a uniform per cent. of from 60 to 62 of lead. The direction is northeast and southwest and the dip 85 to 90 degrees northwest. Near by is the Royal Tiger lode. Both mines are owned by the North Star Company, of which McPherson Lemoyne is president; John N. Goodwin, vice-president; and Lewis Crooke, secretary and treasurer, and those gentlemen and John J. Crooke, F. Farrell, E. J. Granger, and N. A. Boynton, trustees.

The product of 1879 showed an average yield of 154 9-10 ounces of silver per ton for the North Star, and about 50 per cent. lead. The Royal Tiger averages 40 ounces of silver and 60 per cent. lead. There were sold from the North Star that year 105 tons and 723 pounds of ore, which yielded $18,360 in silver and $4,200 in lead, or

$22,560 altogether; average value per ton, $225.04. The three producing levels were then 95 feet, 130 and 165 feet long respectively. Work began about June 20 and ended October 15, when a heavy snow caused the miners to abandon work. ,

Recently a syndicate of twenty prominent New York capitalists and business men purchased three-fifths of the two millions of stock of the North Star Company for the sum of $500,000 in cash, of which $125,000 is to be placed in the company treasury as a working capital, to be expended in development and on smelting works. Among the subscribers are C. F. Woerishoffer, a leading director of the D. & R. G. R. R., Morris K. Jessup, Van Amberg & Atterbury, Dickinson Brothers, M. P. Bush, Ex-Lieutenant Governor Dorsheimer, Rev. Henry M. Field and others.

The Terrible adjoins and is a part of the same vein as the North Star, the outcropping extending the entire length of the claims. The Slide, 900 feet long, is the northwest extension of the Terrible and is also valuable. Both are owned by the Cordova Consolidated Mining Company of New York, capitalized at two millions. One-fourth of the stock has been set apart to provide means for developing the lodes. Work is being prosecuted on an extensive scale. The company officers and directors are General Adelbert Ames, president; Walter S. Carter, vice-president; Ben. I. Butler, secretary and treasurer; Lewis Crooke, Sherburne B. Eaton, E. J. Granger and E. R. Leland, trustees.

The Sinaloa and Eclipse on the divide between Arastra and Royal Tiger gulches, about twelve hundred feet south of the North Star and Terrible mines, are small but very rich veins, carrying gray copper averaging 167 ounces. Very high assays are obtained.

Southwest of Silverton rises Sultan mountain like a giant sentinel overlooking Baker's Park. The lower half of it is covered with immense forests of pine, and the upper portion, being above timber line, is a rough and rugged mass of rock, covered most of the year with deep snows. Many silver lodes have been discovered—most of them near the mountains base, and several tunnels have been driven for long distances. The most valuable and productive lode is the North Star. Many others have produced profitable ore however. These lodes are easy of access, enjoying a great advantage over most other San Juan mines.

The North Star was discovered in March, 1879, in a gulch on the northwesterly side of Sultan mountain. One of the owners, John Williams, leased it from the others, I. A. Ambold and W. Link.

SILVER VEINS IN THE SAN JUAN MOUNTAINS.

Levels or adits were driven in on the vein from the surface, and a splendid vein of galena was opened. As no smelter was at work in the county in 1879, and the ore was not of average high grade, it was deemed best to hold the product until such time as smelting could be done near by. For a long time Williams had been driving the Sultan tunnel (almost on the other side of the mountain) for prospecting purposes. This was quite expensive, and as no revenue could be derived from the North Star even after it was producing, Williams sold one-half of his lease on the latter, for $10,000, to Posey and Murdock, of Silverton. The lease had six months longer to run. This shows the good opinion held of the mine and its capacity. Within a few months it proved itself to be the equal of almost any property in the San Juan region. The Sultan tunnel was 500 feet long at that time. It is said to have since intersected the extension of the North Star 1,500 feet northeast of the mine workings.

The levels driven in on the vein of the North Star mine proper are hundreds of feet in length, and are connected by winzes, thus leaving blocks of ground ready for stoping. The lode is of great size and is very wet, a large stream of water issuing therefrom. The ore is galena, with some gray copper, and is found in almost continuous bunches and pockets, from one to three feet wide, flanked or surrounded with quartz and soft gouge of little or no value. Eight miners and a few timbermen were at work during the first six months of operations. In that time about five hundred tons of ore were on the dumps, supposed to carry over 40 ounces of silver and 50 per cent. of lead, or an assay value of $100 a ton. Work has since been prosecuted, until there must be one hundred thousand dollars' worth of ore broken. It is believed that the mine can supply a ten-ton smelter year after year, although but few properties can do this. There are now 1,500 tons of ore on the dump.

The Molas lode was located in July, 1876, by L. W. Pattison, A. Helphenstine and Samuel Bradbury. It is opened by two shafts, each about 50 feet deep, and two cross-cut tunnels, 80 or 90 feet long. The ore mined came from drifting for a distance of 75 feet, to a depth of 15 feet. This yielded about 10,000 ounces of silver. The pay vein is from one to three feet wide, composed of tetrahedrite, ruby, antimonial and chloride ores. The first-class ores milled about 200 ounces per ton, the second class, 110, and third class, 80

The Cleveland, Little Bertha and Gipsey, owned by Luesley, Herr and Hodges, have yielded ore containing from 600 to 1,266 ounces. Thirteen tons of ore from the Cleveland average 600 ounces. The vein is from three to seven inches wide. Twelve men have been at work in these lodes sinking shafts, drifting and tunneling.

The Diamond Tunnel has been driven about 500 feet into Sultan mountain, and has intersected several small veins. Discoveries of greater value are expected. The Cleveland–Bertha lode will soon be reached at great depth. The owners of the tunnel are Hyde, Campau & Co. Among other lodes on Sultan mountain, are the Jennie Parker, Empire and Tabor; all of which have produced more or less paying ore. The Tabor is owned by G. H. Bradford and J. L. Haynes; it carries gray copper and quartz, with ruby and brittle silver; the first-class ore averages 260 ounces of silver per ton.

The Empire is worked through a newly completed cross-cut tunnel and is said to be paying as well as ever. Its extensions are the Chief, Grand Central, Cashier, Teller and Victoria. Mill runs from the Victoria have averaged 81 ounces. This lode will soon be intersected 210 feet deep by the Montezuma tunnel. Among the lodes on Kendall mountain is the Bowery. Mill runs have averaged 87 ounces, and the vein is of immense size. Two tunnels have been driven 100 and 752 feet respectively, and another is projected from the mountain's base that is expected to run mainly on paying ore.

The Melville and Summerfield chlorination works are located in Baker's Park at the base of Sultan mountain and one mile from Silverton. They were completed late in 1879, and take the place of works on the same site whose process was impracticable.

Cunningham gulch lies between King Solomon mountain on the south and Green mountain on the north and comes down from the western slope of the main range to the Animas valley at Howardsville, a distance of about seven miles.

At the head of this gulch is the Highland Mary mine. Mr. Innis, who is at the head of this enterprise, has worked the mine for several years, and has expended a large amount of money in development work and permanent improvements. The lode comes down over this nearly perpendicular part of King Solomon mountain diagonally, and has been entered by running adits several hundred feet one above another. A tunnel has been driven over 500 feet at the base of the mountain, which intersects the vein and will afford the main ore and working outlet for the mine. Machine drills and air compressors are used. The buildings, machinery, and entire outfittings are first class. This mine is over 10,500 feet above sea level, and is one of the most elevated places in San Juan county where steam is used. The value of ore produced and sold in 1878 is said to have been $20,000. No shipments were made in 1879, the design being to await the completion of the tunnel. Superintendent Teal has a large force of men employed. The mine has produced some very high grade ore.

On the southerly side of Green mountain, which is considerably steeper than the roof of a house, are the Pride of the West, Philadelphia, and other lodes. The Pride of the West is one of the great mines of this region, and is of great size and evident value. It is owned by C. E. Schoelkoff, who opened it by a shaft, a short tunnel, and several drifts in 1877–8. A bond of the property prevented work in 1879. The lode has a total width between walls of about 28 feet, and has two large galena veins of ore, between which is vein matter carrying oxide of silver, native silver, silver glance, and pyrites of copper and iron. Portions of this are said to average 50 ounces in silver. The galena veins, each from two to four feet thick, contain more silver. They also carry about 60 per cent. of lead. On either wall are seams of ore showing brittle silver and silver glance. The lode contains some gray copper ore. In sinking a shaft 160 feet deep and 58 feet below the tunnel level, and in removing the ore to a height of ten feet in two levels about 50 feet long, over 500 tons of ore were obtained. While the main portion of the ore is of moderate grade, small amounts of it are said to yield over $200 per ton. This mine is evidently capable of turning out ten tons of ore daily. The Aquila and Oriental are locations on the same vein. A tunnel 575 feet long has recently intersected the Oriental about 400 feet below the surface.

The Philadelphia is located high up on Green mountain, nearly 1,800 feet above Cunningham gulch. The vein is not large, but carries from two to twelve inches of rich sulphuret ore, yielding from 200 to 800 ounces per ton. In 300 feet of levels and in stoping the ground above and for a short distance below, ore was obtained that yielded nearly $50,000. Work began in 1875. The vein carries some galena and gray copper. The adjacent and parallel Fannie lode is quite valuable, and has yielded considerable sulphuret, galena and gray copper ore. The owners are Niegold and Roedel, who have a concentrating mill in Cunningham gulch, and who are connected with the Midland Mining and Tunnel and other mining enterprises. The Green mountain lode has produced boulders of gray copper. On Galena mountain are many low grade veins, such as the Niegold, Pemberton, Ashurst, A. Begole, Roedel or Veta Madre and others. These will be intersected by the Roedel or Midland tunnel, which will pass from one to three thousand feet under the crest of the mountain.

Eureka is nearly midway between Howardsville and Animas Forks, and is surrounded by mountains ribbed with argentiferous galena veins. Most of these run low in silver, but considerable development work is being done. A Cincinnati company have recently erected reduction works. Between the Animas and Cement creek are the Belcher, Grand Central and other lodes, and the Silver Wing Company's property is in this district.

Animas Forks is the name of the settlement at the junction of the forks of Animas river, fourteen miles northward from Silverton. In this vicinity extensive mining operations are carried on. The Mineral Mountain Mining Company's dry concentrator, completed in 1879, by E. B. Greenleaf and C. H. McIntire, has been dressing ores from the Boston, Red Cloud, and other lodes. Still higher and just above timber line, and at an elevation of 11,400 feet, is the mining camp of Mineral City. Above this rises Mineral Point mountain, through which numerous silver-bearing veins take their course. Here are the Norris and its extensions, the Red Cloud, the Bill Young-Davenport, the Mastodon, Mineral Point, and Maid of the Mist, all nearly parallel lodes. The mineral is considerably scattered in most places so far explored, and concentration would evidently be of great assistance. It is hoped that more solid veins will be found a few hundred feet deeper. Most of these lodes are mainly of gray copper, quartz and sulphurets, but some carry considerable galena, and all have more or less zinc.

The Mineral Point or Bonanza tunnel is one of the leading enterprises of the county. It is driven for the purpose of intersecting at great depth the lodes mentioned above, as well as blind lodes, and has already cut one vein of great size, which is supposed to be the Norris. This tunnel has penetrated the mountain nearly 1,200 feet. Two machine drills and a sixty-horse-power engine have been used by Superintendent Savage to good advantage, although a high pressure is required at this great altitude. Colonel F. J. Pratt is president of the company. It is reported that twenty-two seams of mineral were cut in passing through the Norris or Burrows lode in a distance of 119 feet between walls. The ore assays from 15 ounces up into the hundreds. Among the mines operated by the same company or by parties connected therewith are the Red Cloud, Boston and Mastodon, all of which are producing ore. The Boston has a large amount of ore on the dump. Mill runs gave 98 ounces, 99 ounces and 120 ounces of silver per ton. A pump, steam engine and boiler have been procured for the main shaft. The Red Cloud is worked by three shafts and a tunnel, and has the most extensive developments and showing of ore of any lode opened on the surface of the mountain. There are said to be four feet of galena, gray copper pyrites and quartz.

The Norris, Yankton, Yankton Extension, and Big Giant locations are all on one vein of over a mile in length. Recent developments are said to be very encouraging. The Big Giant is owned by a company of the same name. The Bill Young has yielded some very rich ore and has large quantities of mineral on the dump.

The Davenport Consolidated Mining and Smelting Company owns the following locations of 1,500 feet each: the Wicker on the same vein as the Red Cloud, the Davenport on the same vein as the Bill Young, the Ashtabula on Houghton mountain, and the Palermo; all lodes of great size and evident value. These are being opened by shafts, and an adit is being driven on the first. The Wicker has a vein of solid argentiferous galena four feet wide. It is said that the entire Palermo vein, twenty inches wide, averages 60 ounces in silver, but some of it has assayed as high as 600 ounces. The Ashtabula pay vein is two feet wide. These three veins carry an average of 50 per cent. of lead. The Davenport has a vein of sulphurets three feet wide, carrying much gold as well as silver; also a little ruby silver, galena, and zinc. Work is being energetically pushed on all of these properties with excellent prospects of large returns. The company has a capital stock of one million in five-dollar shares. The officers are E. S. Douglas, president; R. D. A. Parrott, vice-president; Joseph C. Todd, treasurer; J. L. Cunningham, secretary; and Nathan Cornish, superintendent.

The Inter-Ocean Mining Company, of Chicago, is driving tunnels and working the Scotia lode. The Lake Park lode is one of the properties of the Buffalo Land and Mining Company, of which J. S. Buell is president. It is worked through shafts and tunnels, and is producing galena and gray copper ore. This yielded, at Lee's Capitol City works, 120 and 270 ounces of silver per ton.

On Engineer and Sigel mountains, which are a part of the dividing range between San Juan and Hinsdale counties, are several prominent mines. The Annie Wood is owned by J. J. Crooke and H. A. Wood; is extensively worked and carries considerable bismuth in its gray copper silver ores. Two tunnels have been driven, one of which is 450 feet long and into the vein. There are said to be two feet of ore in places from which mill runs of about 200 ounces have been obtained. In this locality are the Hidden Treasure, Mammoth, Humbolt, Ruby Silver, and Eighth Wonder.

The Mountain Queen is a galena vein of great size, but of rather low average grade. So far, the ore body has been found on the hanging wall, and is five feet wide and under, yielding from 30 to 75 ounces of silver per ton and 65 per cent. of lead. In 1878, F. B. Beaudry operated the mine, working from thirty to forty men. He sold 1,100 tons of ore and 400 remained on hand at the end of the season. The workings then comprised a shaft 104 feet deep and a few short drifts. The lode's capacity for production is very great. It is located on the divide between Mineral Point and Poughkeepsie gulch. The Mineral Mountain Mining Company, James Sowden, superintendent, is driving a tunnel to intersect the Red Cloud and other lodes. The Graham Silver Mining Company has expended a great deal of money on the E Pluribus Unum and other veins.

Poughkeepsie gulch slopes northward from the high range of mountains which divides the waters of the Animas from those of the Uncompahgre rivers. Poughkeepsie Pass is over 12,600 feet above the sea, and Hurricane Peak is a thousand feet higher. In going from Silverton to Ouray, one ascends 3,200 feet in a distance of thirteen miles and then descends very near 5,000 feet in seven miles. Poughkeepsie basin is circled about with a barren rocky range—a western spur of the continental divide. As the entire section is above timber line, provisions, tools, fire-wood, lumber, powder and everything needed has been conveyed to the mines on the backs of donkeys or pack animals. The materials that the many shaft houses, shaft timbers and cabins are composed of are teamed up Cement creek wagon road, and are then taken in by pack animals; there is no timber or vegetation up among these barren wilds. Beef has been obtained by driving the cattle up to the mines and slaughtering them there. Snow never disappears from the northern slope of this camp, and when winter fairly sets in, there is no further ingress or egress except at rare intervals by those accustomed to hazardous snow-shoe locomotion. A road was constructed from Silverton up Cement creek to the pass in 1879. From this, trails lead to the mines. The lodes of this section are quite numerous and are of the gray copper order. A majority of them seem to point in the direction of Lake Como, a body of water located in a deep basin at the base of Hurricane Peak and very near the head of the gulch.

The Gladstone chlorination and lixiviation works are located at Gladstone, in a well timbered and beautiful valley of Cement creek, nine miles from Silverton. A trial run was made in 1879, yielding over $5,000. The Augustin process is said to be the most favorable of any for 'oughkeepsie ores. These works are owned by the Gladstone Company, organized in England, of which W. Broderick Cloete is president and J. H. Ernest Waters superintendent.

On the summit of the pass are the Adelpheh and Alpha, on which work has been pushed steadily since their purchase by Tabor and others. On a mountain near by, are the Tribune and Columbia lodes, owned by the Gladstone Company. While worked in the summer and fall of 1879, each produced about 35 tons of ore, averaging 100 ounces of silver per ton. Twenty-five men were employed altogether. Drifting cost $12 a foot on the Tribune, and $18 on the other, and it cost from $26 to $30 a foot to sink a five by nine shaft. The poorest ore ran 40 ounces, and the highest 200. Each of these lodes shipped more ore in 1879 than any mines in Poughkeepsie gulch.

Among the lodes in Poughkeepsie gulch are the Alaska, Red Roger, Saxon, Pittsburg, Last Chance, Seven Thirty, Acapulca, Rollo, Bonanza, Gipsey King, and Alabama.

The Red Roger and Saxon are owned by H. A. W. Tabor and others, of Leadville, and J. F. Tabor—the latter superintending operations at the mine. The price paid is said to have been $55,600. The production had previously amounted to several thousand dollars, some of the ore running up in the hundreds. One lot of 9,316 pounds of ore from the Red Roger yielded at the rate of $74 a ton. This lode carries a great deal of spar. Tunnels and shafts are being driven on both lodes, and rich ore is mined, especially in the Saxon.

The Alaska is considered the most prominent vein of the district.

In 1879 it was purchased by H. A. W. Tabor and August Rische, along with the Adelpheh and others, for $125,000. Ore milling from $100 to $800 was mined previous to that time; 13,623 pounds of ore yielded at the rate of 113 ounces of silver per ton. The mine has been steadily developed by the new owners, and new buildings have been erected, including an ore house and quarters for the twenty-five men employed. Nathan Sloan is superintendent. The tunnel, shafts and diverging levels show over two feet of ore and a vein from three to six feet wide. It is estimated that a small proportion of the ore runs in the hundreds, while two-thirds of it may average $100 a ton. It consists of gray copper, carrying bismuth. So far hoisting has been done by horse power.

The Pittsburg and Last Chance lodes near the Alaska are owned by the Silver Mountain Gold and Silver Mining Company of Chicago, of which Colonel George Lewis is superintendent. Shaft houses were erected last fall, and development work was continued all winter by ten men. This opened fine bodies of ore, that in the Pittsburg being especially good. A vein of gray copper two feet wide, said to average 225 ounces per ton, was found in the five feet of lode material. The Last Chance adit shows 16 inches of gray copper ore. The same company owns the Protection, Rollo No. 2 and Champagne lodes, on the other side of Lake Como.

The Seven Thirty, Three Brothers and Canandaigua have been sold to what is called the British Consuls Silver Mining Company. These are rich veins carrying gray copper ore in spar and pyrites. A. Rapp has been developing the Saint Joe and other sulphuret lodes.

The Bonanza and six neighboring lodes and locations were purchased in 1879 by residents of Kalamazoo, Michigan, who have organized a company thereon. The Bonanza lode has been steadily worked for many months, in which time a shaft has been sunk 200 feet. A tunnel has intersected the shaft, and another one is being driven, which will enter and drain Lake Como, when 600 feet long. This and other lodes pass under the lake, and some believe they will be found richer there than elsewhere. The Bonanza does not partake of the nature of a true fissure vein as much as some. It carries gray copper, sulphurets, iron pyrites and a little galena. The average yield is not high, but a continuous daily output of five tons is predicted.

CHAPTER XXVII.

OURAY COUNTY—ITS SILVER MINES AND GOLD PLACERS—MOUNT
SNEFFELS, HOWARD'S FORK AND THE UPPER AND LOWER SAN
MIGUEL—THE NEW MINES OF RICO AND THE DOLORES—SMELTING
AND REDUCTION WORKS—TABULATED STATEMENTS—LA PLATA
COUNTY AND THE RUINS OF THE ANCIENT CLIFF CITIES.

Ouray County is fast coming into prominence as a mining region.
The progress and development of Mount Sneffels, Howard's Fork,
and the upper San Miguel districts as well as among the placers of
the San Miguel all helped to make it famous, but the discoveries on
the head-waters of the Dolores in 1879 caused such an excitement as
San Juan has not experienced for many years. The town of Ouray,
whose location could hardly be more beautiful, is the county seat.
It is situated in the narrow but attractive valley of the Uncompahgre,
above which tower the perpendicular walls of the river cañon for
thousands of feet. A railway is expected from Gunnison.

Ouray is on the Pacific slope of the range, and comprises the
northwestern portion of the San Juan region. Like its neighbors,
it is almost entirely composed of rugged and almost perpendicular
mountains and deeply cut ravines and river gorges, among which it
is generally an impossibility to build roads. The inaccessibility of
the section has retarded rapid growth, but reduction works having
at last been established, future advancement will be much more
rapid. A railway has been projected, and may be built within two
years, from Leadville or the Arkansas River through Marshall Pass.
Heretofore it has cost $25 a ton to pack the ore on burros from the
mines to Silverton, or to a wagon road, and as much more to get it
to Denver or Pueblo. The unusual value of the mineral is all that
enabled the miners to dispose of their products under such disadvantages. Last year the mines of Ouray county yielded $69,500, of
which $15,000 worth of ore was kept on hand. Ouray is the main
town and county seat.

The Norfolk and Ouray reduction works are supplied with ore

by the Begole " Mineral Farm," owned by the same company. Concentrating works were added this season to handle the low grade material from the same locality. The Windham Company smelter, with 20 tons daily capacity, started up not long ago with a large supply of ore on hand. One or two other works have been built, but the above, if operated steadily, will turn out a quarter of a million or more per annum.

The Begole "Mineral Farm" is one of the wonders of this part of the State. This is near the town of Ouray, and at about 800 feet greater elevation. It comprises forty acres of ground, being four claims 1,500 feet long by 300 wide, and was at first supposed to be a horizontal deposit of silver-bearing ore, but subsequent developments prove it to contain four mineral channels or lodes, from ten to twenty feet wide. One of these lodes has a streak of bright fine galena with heavy spar—the former carrying over 100 ounces of silver, and 40 per cent. of lead, and another streak of thirty-ounce galena with much antimony. Another lode has a very rich gray copper vein in a gangue of quartzite, and often milling from $400 to $700 a ton. A third lode carries sulphurets, and in places chlorides. This property was discovered and located in 1875, by Augustus Begole, an old Arizona miner, and by John Eckles. They had worked it in the summer seasons up to the fall of 1878, when they sold for $75,000 to the Norfolk and Ouray Reduction Company, who had built works at Ouray. Before that the principal work done was by quarrying or stripping the veins at and near the surface, and by sinking one or two short shafts. The new owners, having works near by, save enormous transportation and mill charges. They are mining large amounts of ore, concentrating the low grades and reducing the high grades and concentrates.

Cañon creek, near Ouray, is formed by the union of Imogene and Sneffels creeks ; the first coming down from Imogene basin and the other from Sneffels and Virginius basins. These deep cut valleys are enclosed by precipitous mountains, among which is Mount Sneffels, with an elevation of 14,158 feet.

The Virginius is as good a mine as there is in this region, and has been very profitable. It has been sold to eastern parties at a reported price of $100,000. It is badly situated for working, being in an almost inaccessible position, high up on a mountain nearly 12,300 feet above the sea. Its location has compelled the prosecution of work through the ground of its extension, the Monongahela, for which some compensation is said to be made. The vein of solid gray copper or heavy galena zinc ores is from six to twelve inches wide, and is very rich in silver. Allem & Co. worked the Virginius under lease for a time, and in nine months to July, 1879, shipped to Pueblo and sold 79 $\frac{1350}{2000}$ tons of ore for a little over $23,000, indicating an assay value of over $30,000. The shipments in pounds and the yield per ton in ounces of silver were as follows :

Pounds of ore.	Oz. of silver.	Pounds of ore.	Oz. of silver.
10,439	305	15,542	315
9,690	318	16,668	328
13,176	327	19,335	325
9,968	$310\frac{1}{5}$	17,363	335
10,000	$335\frac{9}{10}$	2,200	225
11,324	$310\frac{2}{10}$	2,614	781

21,031 pounds, 309 ounces.

The ore averaged 35 per cent. in lead, so that the average total value of all shipments must have exceeded $385 a ton. Thirteen men were at work, including the lessees and all hands about the mine, and five drills were employed. The Virginius had yielded previous to 1880 about $55,000.

The group of lodes in Sneffels basin, best known by the name of Yankee Boy, is one of the most valuable of San Juan properties. It includes the Yankee Boy and Dutch Boy locations on one vein, and the York State and Genesee on a parallel vein, all having similar characteristics, but with little development off of the first named. The Yankee Boy is a rich, strong, well defined vein, composed of gray copper, ruby and brittle silver, and a small quantity of galena. It is said the mine produced nearly $50,000 in 1877. In 1878 F. B. Beaudry leased the property and mined some 225 tons of ore, yielding $56,000—an average of $250 per ton—the largest receipts ever obtained from a San Juan silver mine in a single year, and the largest assay value, except on the Mountain Queen. The lowest mill run was 220 ounces, and the highest 1,704; 23 tons averaged 1,231 ounces. Ruby silver specimens assay up among the thousands. The death of one of the owners prevented steady work in 1879. The ore sold ranged from 181 to 396 ounces. There are nearly one thousand feet of workings, including two levels on the vein all the way in ore, 200 and 225 feet long respectively (connected by a winze 31 feet deep) and a tunnel 155 feet long, cutting the vein 265 feet from the surface. New levels will be driven from this tunnel. The mine is favorably located, and has not only paid for all outlays and expenses, but has yielded a large profit besides.

The Eldorado carries black sulphurets, chlorides, with some ruby and brittle silver, with considerable galena. The pay vein is from 12 to 18 inches wide. The last shipment embraced ten tons of ore, milling from 138 to 676 ounces per ton, with a little gold. There were from 75 to 100 tons remaining on the dump at the time.

The Trout and Fisherman group of mines on Cañon creek, near Ouray, includes the Trout, Fisherman, Gray Copper, Goodfroe, Johnny Bull and C. A. Weston lodes. The ores are mainly rich gray copper and galena, with some ruby silver and argentite. The first shipment from the Fisherman after its discovery in 1875 averaged 373 ounces of silver per ton. The average in 1876 was 406 ounces for first class and 287 for second class ore. Control assays in 1877 gave 688 ounces, 255 and 162 for the various grades, and in 1878 from 777 to 1,185. Three shipments to the Pueblo smelter in 1879 averaged 394 ounces of silver, one ounce of gold and three ounces of copper per ton. The total yield of the mine is said to have reached $50,000, at a cost of $8,000. The Trout, Fisherman and Gray Copper lodes each have from 125 to 200 feet of workings.

About four miles from Ouray, bordering the Uncompahgre river, is a group of veins owned by Governor Pitkin and William Sherman. The Royal Consort, Royal Albert and Duke of Edinburgh are upon one vein of immense size, carrying gray copper and copper pyrites, with some carbonate of copper. Prof. S. W. Hill after examination estimated the average yield of the outcrop for its entire length to be from 200 to 400 ounces of silver per ton. Samples have gone as high as 658 ounces. The Mickey Breen lode crosses the above, and carries gray copper mixed with galena. Two lots of the best ore assayed 430 and 524 ounces of silver respectively. The Mountain Monarch, parallel with the mother lode, carries from 70 to 76 per cent. lead, but runs low in silver. The Pioneer Lady is an offshoot of the principal vein. The Mother Kline lode is 18 feet thick, carrying an enormous quantity of galena. Assays have shown 81 per cent. of lead and about 17 ounces of silver. These veins can be seen cleaving the mountain for the height and distance of nearly a mile. They can be drained and worked to great advantage by tunnels, thus saving the expense of hoisting, while the varied character of the ores will be found to assist in fluxing, and in this way economize in smelting.

The Terrible mine in Sneffels district has lately been making a fine record. The vein is rich and of good size. The yield to the close of 1879 was about $10,000. The 600 feet of workings then showed some $50,000 worth of ore in sight.

Imogene basin and enclosing mountains, seven miles from Ouray, have many actively worked lodes, and several long veins on which are a number of locations. Here is the Millionaire-Deposit vein, and the lode containing the Chief Deposit, Mark Twain and Grand Trunk locations, which intersects the Monetizer, Wheel of Fortune and Potosi vein. Quinn and Richardson hold government titles for the Pocahontas, Imogene, Buckeye Girl, Highland Chief, Highland Lassie, Seven Thirty, Potosi, Circassian, Caribou and Chief Deposit. The latter has an eighteen-inch vein of ore that mills from $300 to $500 per ton. The Potosi is paying handsomely. Owing to difficulties among the owners, the Wheel of Fortune has not been worked steadily. It has yielded over $10,000. Most lodes of this section have the same direction, dip and characteristics, and a description of one group will give a general idea of all.

The company known as the "Allied Mines" recently purchased the Hidden Treasure, Gertrude, Norma, Talisman and Emily lodes— 1,500 feet on each—and secured half interests in the Crusader and Yellow Rose, with a prospect of buying the remainder. Twenty men have been employed in developing these lodes, which force will hereafter be increased to sixty. A smelter is being erected for the purpose of treating the ore product of the mines. The location is on one of the two mill sites of the company where water power is available in the summer and fall. All of these veins are true fissures in trachyte formation, dipping to the north with a trend nearly northeast and southwest. They carry much gray copper, with a vein filling of soft porphyry and clay gouge, and the matrix of the metals is a white crystalline quartz. The ore bodies are usually large and permanent, with galena as the base of the metals. The lower workings are said to show better mineral than was found at the surface. The elevations range from 10,300 to 11,400 feet above the sea; that of Ouray is 7,640.

The principal work has been done on the Hidden Treasure, which

WINTER AMONG THE MINES OF THE SAN JUAN MOUNTAINS.

makes a fine showing, but development is progressing rapidly on all the lodes since the snows of May disappeared. They are admirably situated for cheap working. All but the Gertrude cross the gulch and extend into the mountains on either side, thus permitting of the driving of adits or tunnels in on the veins. By this means hundreds of feet in depth are gained without hoisting or pumping machinery.

The Hidden Treasure has always been considered one of the prominent veins of the Sneffels district. There are nearly 300 feet of workings, showing an average width of ore body of from one to two feet of gray copper associated with galena. The ore, as far as handled, has carried from 98 to 540 ounces of silver per ton. The Pocahontas is an extension of the Hidden Treasure. The Norma, a parallel vein, is traceable on the surface for 6,000 feet. A tunnel 160 feet long shows bunches, seams, and chimneys of ore from one to three feet thick. The yield is from 40 to 226 ounces of silver, the latter being the character of the last mineral encountered. The Crusader is an extension of the Norma, and the Yellow Rose of the Millionaire, Deposit and Grand Trunk vein. An intersecting tunnel shows paying ore in the Gertrude 100 feet deep. On the surface is low grade galena and iron. It is evident that this group of mines can be made to yield largely, and, with the assistance of a smelter close by, dividends seem assured. The trustees of the company are Orrin Skinner, (president), H. M. Munsell, (vice-president), B. F. Ham, (secretary and treasurer), General Thomas Ewing, of Ohio, ex-Senator O. H. Browning, of Illinois, Senator P. B. Plumb, of Kansas, J. D. Ripley, George H. Bissell, and Thomas F. Wentworth. William Weston is general manager and mining engineer at the mines.

The Upper San Miguel district, lying west of Mount Sneffels, is an exceedingly rich and promising locality. Marshall basin contains numerous lodes of value. One vein has been pre-empted for a distance of a mile and a half, the locations from east to west being the Humboldt, Mendota, Sheridan, Smuggler, Union, Cleveland, and Cimarron. The Smuggler is the best developed. Fifteen tons of ore sold in 1879 gave from 300 to 350 ounces in silver and from 6 to $6\frac{7}{8}$ ounces of gold, or from $470 to $530 per ton. The Sheridan gave $18\frac{1}{2}$ tons, yielding from 129 to 508 ounces of silver per ton and from 1 to $3\frac{1}{4}$ ounces of gold. From the Cimarron $2\frac{1}{2}$ tons averaged 100 ounces of silver and $23\frac{1}{2}$ ounces of gold. The other properties are rich in silver, but show little gold.   The Sheridan and Smuggler are among the best of San Juan mines.   The Smuggler shaft, level and tunnel show an ore vein from 12 to 24 inches wide, carrying some wire and brittle silver.   In this district are the Shamrock, Pioneer, Grand Central, Gold and Silver Chief, Wade Hampton, Lone Star, Oriental, Ruby, Occidental, West Point, Eckland and other lodes.   The Boomerang, a mile east of San Miguel City, is a phenomenal deposit, said to resemble the Begole, near Ouray.   The great Pandora gold lode is a little below the Smuggler and is owned by Lothian and Medley.   A tunnel cutting the vein and 600 feet of levels have been driven at a cost of $20,000, exposing ore worth several times that sum.

Howard's Fork district has come into prominence during the past two years.   A town called Ophir has been started.   This is fifteen miles from Silverton.   The Snow Silver Smelting Company have a saw mill at Hoffman, and are building a twenty-stamp gold quartz mill and a smelter with three blast furnaces and an " Acme " furnace. Considerable gold is produced as well as silver.   Coal, said to be of the coking variety is found 7 miles distant and $2\frac{1}{2}$ miles from San Miguel lake.

Among the mines the Alta on Silver mountain, carrying silver and a little gold, is prominent.   This is crossed by the Summit.   The Valley View is also quite valuable.   All of these shipped ore in 1879.   In this section are the Sulphurets, Grand View, and Crown Jewel.   The Santa Cruz, Ida, and Crown Point are in Silver mountain.   At and near Turkey creek, are the Dixie, Gold King, Black, Warrior, Bessie, etc.   On Yellow mountain are the Nevada and What Cheer.   The latter has shipped ore.   Among the gold lodes are the Red Jacket, which is very rich, the Mocking Bird, the Powhattan, and the Osceola.   The latter has quartz treated in an arastra and the others ship ore.   The Gold King has gold alloyed with silver. Butler and Glass operate an arastra in Turkey creek.   The Montezuma, Parsons, and Idaho silver lodes have yielded largely.   The Missouri, Chance, A and B are large lodes.   The Missouri has sent over $6,000 worth of ore to Greene's smelter.   The ore generally runs from $76 to $200 per ton, but some has gone one or two thousand. The Alta has had mill runs of 265 and 290 ounces.   The Index is its extension.

In Upper San Miguel district are the Wasatch, Euclid Avenue,

Sylph, Louise, Crystal, Golden Shaft, Nettie and extension, the General Grant and the Amie.

So far it has cost $15 a ton to pack ore from Miguel and Sneffels districts down to Ouray, and $30 to team it to Alamosa and railroad it to Pueblo.

As near as can be ascertained, the mines of Howard's Fork shipped 20 tons of ore, containing about $4,000, in 1879. Two arastras on Turkey creek and elsewhere were at work, handling about 175 tons of surface gold-bearing quartz, with a probable yield of $5,000. Quartz from the Gold King did the best ; 111 pounds of this quartz sold for $500. The Yuba is another rich gold vein.

On Yellow mountain, near Ophir, is the Montezuma, discovered in 1878, and a third of it lately sold for $45,000. It has a high grade vein of galena, gray copper and chlorides. A party has contracted to sink 100 feet for the ore that may come out of the shaft. This indicates plenty of rich ore. The nearly parallel Parsons lode is quite valuable.

Probably no portion of the San Juan country is attracting as much attention at present as the Pioneer district, on the headwaters of the Rio Dolores. Its business metropolis is the town of Rico, which, although born no longer ago than August, 1879, already possesses hundreds of inhabitants, and all the accompaniments of a live mining camp. A newspaper was started before the town was six weeks old, and a bank soon after. Rico is 35 miles nearly southwest of Silverton, and about that distance northwesterly from Animas City. As soon as the D. & R. G. railway reaches the latter place, the company contemplate setting their construction forces at work on the route to Rico. A railway will advance the district's growth and prosperity greatly in the coming year.

Mineral deposits were known to exist there years ago, but it was not until Leadville became famous that prospectors believed them to be valuable. The first rich discovery—the Grand View lode—was made in the summer of 1879. The lucky owner at once began to send ore to Sweet and Ingersoll's sampling mill, at Silverton, where it found a ready market. It proved very remunerative, although packed over the mountains on burros. The ore was found to carry from $100 to $350 per ton in silver and $30 in gold. Other valuable discoveries were made before snow came, such as the Hope, Cross, Puzzle, and Newman, all of which were worked last winter. Most of the early locations were made on "Nigger Baby Hill," but since then, Expectation Hill and other places have shown themselves to be valuable. Senator J. P. Jones and J. W. Bailey were the first to invest heavily in the district. They purchased the Grand View, Phœnix and other claims, and organized the Grand View and Rico companies thereon. It is said that Sandy Campbell, the pioneer, received $100,000 for one claim.

Some very important discoveries are recorded since the disappearance of the snows. Many tons of ore can be seen at the mines, containing from 40 to 500 ounces in silver per ton. If late reports are correct, this district has mines capable of making money faster than anything in this part of the State. Nigger Baby Hill has the following formation: On top are alternate layers of white and red sandstone, dipping into the hill 30 degrees or less towards the mountain range, and up the creek, and from Rico basin. Beneath the sandstone, is a layer of limestone and silicate of lime for a base, underlaid with a strata of ore—zinc blende mixed with iron pyrites and a small quantity of copper pyrites—in other places bog iron takes the place of the zinc ore and pyrites.

Richard Gentry, superintendent for the Grand View company, is building a smelter of forty tons daily capacity. The freight from the end of the track at Alamosa, 240 miles distant, was 12½ cents a pound—the freighter having a little road building to do in one or two places. With this smelter at work and the mines opened into still better producing condition, a very large bullion export may be expected from the Rico and Grand View companies, and all of the best claims of Pioneer district. These two companies are officered alike, and by first-class men. Thompson Dean is president, L. M. Lawson, vice-president, and W. J. Osborn, secretary. The stock is owned from Maine to California. These pioneer companies will soon achieve the success they deserve in the remote but growing camp on the Dolores.

The Grand View company owns and works the mine of the same name, and the Major and other properties. The Rico company owns the Phœnix, Yellow Jacket, Pelican, and three other claims. The Grand View and Phœnix are being rapidly opened. Their veins, which seems to increase with size and depth, carry oxide of iron and black oxide of manganese—the latter containing the silver. At one time the average value was said to be 84 ounces, but since then a gain in both size of vein and value has been noted.

The Hope and Cross have over 400 feet of tunnels or inclines. One on the former will soon be 200 feet long. The Cross has been producing ore that runs up in the hundreds. The Hope is on the same contact as the Grand View, and has ore worth from $50 to $500. The Puzzle is one of the prominent mines, and adjoins the Minnie May. On Expectation Mountain are the Joner, O. G. Marston, Mabel Grey, Elgin Boy, Green Mountain and Green Mountain Boy.

The Newman lode on Dolores mountain was discovered by Harry Irving and is owned by him and Newman, Chestnut and Stephens. The first ore sold was packed on burros to Silverton in the fall of 1879. That shipment cleared more than money enough to pay the expenses of the previous summer and following winter. Some ore yielded $568 in silver and $112 in gold, 400 ounces of silver and 6 ounces of gold, 193 ounces of silver, and $122 in silver and $16 in gold. Bunches and streaks of vein matter occur in lime or porphyry, and show galena and what appear to be carbonates of various colors. In the middle level chlorides and ruby silver are found. There are three levels, the lowest in porphyry and lime, and altogether 300 feet of workings. Raymond & Co. have tunneled into an extension of the Newman.

Elliott's Trimountain mine, on Expectation Mountain close by Rico, is said to be steadily improving as work progresses. The ore body is nine feet thick in one place and the upper wall had not been found at the time. The vein material is so soft that the pick and shovel answer all purposes without the use of powder and drills. Among other lodes the Alice has had a mill run giving 169 ounces per ton. The Major, Eureka, Glasgow, Alameda Nos. 1 and 2, Frost, Alma Mater, Iron, Circassian Girl, Ellen, Black Imp, Independent, Snowbank, Zulu Chief, Melvina, Nile and Merrimac are all worked and some are paying. The last named is said to have ore worth from two to four hundred dollars. In this same district is the Aztec, which has a galena vein of ore. There are seven locations on the Alma Mater, several of them shipping ore. The Black Demon lode has yielded ore worth nearly $700 a ton. The Dolores, Mountain Queen and King Solomon run high in lead and low in silver.

The Rico Mining and Milling Company of Chicago, Colonel George Lewis, manager, will soon be mining and smelting extensively. It is erecting a 30-ton smelter and owns six valuable claims here, besides 320 acres of placer land on the San Miguel river.

San Miguel (Me-géel) mining district occupies the mountains and streams of a tract of country forty miles broad by some seventy miles long, and located west of Ouray and Mount Sneffels. Along the San Miguel river and its forks and tributaries are extensive gravel deposits, rich in gold. These, after much preparatory work in the way of flumes, hydraulics, etc., are being worked on a large scale by many companies and firms. The adjoining mountains are seamed with numberless gold and silver veins, some newly discovered and others already productive.

Extensive preparations have been and are being made to open up the immense placer deposits of the San Miguel river. Experts from the gravel deposits of California, after examining these, report very highly upon them. Several large companies that secured ground last year are now at work with hydraulics. Beginning at the upper part of the stream, the Keystone Hydraulic Company, near the south fork of the river, has been putting in all the latest appliances for saving gold and for moving gravel on a grand scale. Its gravel bank has 150 feet of face—flume capacity, 3,000 inches—1,000 feet of pipe, and 300 feet of pressure, with a No. 5 "Giant" hydraulic—move 2,000 cubic yards per day. D. T. Thompson is president of the company. The Red Cross Company, about ten miles below, has interested eastern capitalists and is preparing to work extensively.

The Wheeler and Kimball property, adjoining the Red Cross, has very rich and extensive claims that are worked to their full capacity. This comprises 400 acres in which the pay gravel lays in bars; average yield, fifty cents to the cubic yard; width of bottom, from 350 to 2,500 feet. Wheeler and Kimball began to construct a five-mile ditch to secure a water-supply in the fall of 1877, and brought the water on the bar last fall, but not in time to wash much gravel. They are now running in full blast with hydraulics—600 feet of iron pipe under pressure of 200 feet fall. Water is brought from the head of Alder Creek, comes in 1,000 feet above the mines and runs down the solid sandstone on to the pay ground and gravel. In washing away the ground, marble boulders of variegated colors and iron and granite are uncovered.

The Keithly Company have built a great flume high up around the perpendicular walls of the mountains for a distance of over three miles, which carries 1,200 inches of water—use No. 5 Giant

CAÑON OF THE UNCOMPAHGRE RIVER.

hydraulic, 200 feet pressure; have all the best appliances for work and several million yards of gravel to handle. This claim is ably managed by a Mr. Manly, an experienced placer miner from Dutch Flat, California. The Ware bar, owned by St. Louis men, will soon be in shape for work.

The "Montana Bar," owned by Greene & Co., of Keokuk, Iowa, a very large and rich deposit of gravel, is worked on a small scale by sending the gravel down a chute to the river where the sluices are located. Worked under such disadvantages, it more than pays wages. Immediately below is a series of bars extending several miles down the river, containing many millions of yards of pay gravel. Chief among them is the "Kansas City" claim, with several million yards of gravel, estimated from tests made to average $1 per yard. Such a property will not long remain without ditches and hydraulics. The product of San Miguel is usually what is known as "coarse gold," worth $17.50 per ounce, and the gravel deposits are all high bars, from 50 to 150 feet above the river.

Some idea of the value and extent of these grand deposits of an ancient river bed, from 50 to 150 feet above the present bed of the river, can be obtained from the fact that from $25,000 to $100,000 was expended to bring water upon them and to construct ditches and flumes. These immense deposits, like those of California, have been attracting the attention of capitalists, and it is safe to say that in a few years the yield of gold dust will be enormous.

LA PLATA COUNTY.

La Plata county is the extreme southwestern division of Colorado, bordering on New Mexico and Utah, and touching the corner of Arizona. This section is rich in coal, possesses silver veins, gold placers, and many fine fertile valleys; farming and stock-growing are especially successful. The county is settling up rapidly. The D. & R. G. railway will soon be completed to Animas City, from which extensions will lead to the Silverton and Rico mines.

The stock and agricultural resources and advantages of La Plata county and of its valleys along the San Juan river and tributaries have already been referred to in part third of this volume. The coal measures are deserving of especial mention, on account of their quality and enormous size. The area of coal land is estimated at over 600 square miles, and is cut or intersected by the Pinos, Florida, Animas, La Plata, and Mancos rivers, which flow southward into the San Juan. The thickness of the vein is reported at from 10 to 50 and 60 feet between floor and roof. There are two distinct beds of coal, separated only by four feet of iron shale. In some places the two beds are said to aggregate from 88 to 98 feet in thickness. Those who have tested this coal, pronounce it of a semi-bituminous character and of a better coking quality than any in the West except the Trinidad beds. In this same county are lodes carrying gold, silver, lead, copper, zinc, iron pyrites, tellurium, platina, etc.

In this extreme southwestern corner of Colorado, and far over among the mountains of the Pacific slope, are ancient ruins of towns and cities, built by an extinct race of people. These ruins are found at intervals over an area of 6,000 square miles, and are generally the remnants of stone structures. W. H. Holmes, in the Hayden Government Survey Reports, classes them under three heads: (1) Lowland or agricultural settlements, largely composed of rubble and adobe combined; (2) Cave dwellings; and (3) Cliff houses or fortresses. Those of the first class are on the low and fertile river bottoms; those of the second, near the agricultural lands, but built in low bluff faces, while the cliff houses are built high up in the inaccessible walls of cliffs and excavated therein. The latter must have been used only as a place of refuge and defence in times of war and invasion. Many of them are of massive character, and were built by a race totally distinct and far superior to the nomadic savages that occupied the country in more recent times.

CHAPTER XXVIII.

CHAFFEE COUNTY—THE SILVER MINES OF MONARCH AND ALPINE
DISTRICTS—GOLD MINING ON THE UPPER ARKANSAS—BUENA
VISTA AND THE RAILWAYS—NORTHWESTERN COLORADO—THE
PARKS, AND THE RABBIT EAR MINES—LARIMER, GRAND, AND
ROUTT COUNTIES.

Chaffee county was organized from the southern portion of Lake
county early in 1879. It embraces that part of the upper Arkansas
valley between Puncho Pass and a point a little north of Granite
and south of Leadville. On the east are the Park range and other
mountains, and the great Sawatch range or Continental Divide shuts
out the Gunnison region on the west. These mountains are of
greater average height than any others in the country, and embrace
Mount Elbert, Harvard, Yale, Princeton, Shavano, La Plata and
many peaks ranging from 14,000 to 14,386 feet above sea level.
Important mineral discoveries have been made among them; first
in what is now Alpine district, and later near the headwaters of the
South Arkansas, now known as Monarch district. Silver lodes are
being found along the entire slope of these mountains, between
Puncho and Tennessee passes. There are good grazing and farming
lands in the valley, where thousands of cattle are raised; also wheat
and vegetables.

The early gold seekers made their appearance along the Arkansas
in 1860, and the town of Granite became a prosperous, bustling
mining camp. The streams yielded considerable gold dust, and
some lode mining was done. Cash creek has ever been a paying
locality, and even in recent times has yielded $30,000 more or less
every summer. Wonderful were the stories of Lost Cañon, which
we are told the discoverers abandoned on the coming of the snows
and were unable to find ever after. Colorado creek was quite rich.
For fourteen years subsequent to 1864, the population and production were small. There was a temporary lode mining revival
in 1867-8.

In 1874 prospectors discovered silver lodes near the head of Chalk creek, and in time the district of Alpine was organized. No great progress was made until 1879, but some valuable silver lodes were worked, such as the Tilden, Riggins, Murphy, Hortense, Virginia, Deborah, Evening Star, Hartford, Anna and Black Swan. In 1878 Monarch mining camp was started, which has since developed into a famous and productive district. The coming of the railroads has given these districts cheap and rapid transportation to the best of ore markets, and will permit of cheaper mining as well as smelting near the seat of production. Near Chaffee and the Middle Fork the formation is generally contact—lime and porphyry or lime and quartzite, but ore is often found in the lime. Around the North Fork and at Alpine it is generally granite and porphyritic rock.

Chaffee county mines yielded about $70,000 in 1879, of which about $30,000 came from placers and gulches. The silver mines had hardly begun to produce then.

Buena Vista, the leading town of Chaffee county, is located at the crossing of the Denver and Rio Grande and the Denver & South Park railways; one leading to Leadville and the other to the Gunnison. On the advent of the last named road it became the transfer point for both localities. This road is now building on towards the Gunnison, via Alpine and Alpine pass tunnel. Barlow and Sanderson's stages make connection with all points in the Gunnison region, such as Pitkin, Gunnison, and the Elk Mountains.

Alpine is on the line of the Denver & South Park railroad, 20 miles west of Buena Vista, and 9,500 feet above sea level. Near by are Shavano and Princeton mountains and many silver mines. Ores can now be sent to the Denver smelters at the low figure of $7 a ton.

The Tilden, on Boulder mountain, opposite and two miles from Alpine, is the leading mine. It has been opened by inclines and tunnels for a length of 300 and depth of 200 feet, showing from one to four feet of ore—sulphuret of silver, silver glance, carbonate of lead, galena, and a little copper—said to aggregate 8,000 tons, containing $250,000 in silver, $200,000 in lead, and some gold. Fifty tons averaged silver $155, gold $20. The Tilden was recently sold in New York. It adjoins the Merrimac mine.

In Grizzly gulch, four miles from Alpine, many lodes are worked. The Chrysolite tunnel is being driven by the aid of a Burleigh steam drill, for the purpose of intersecting such promising lodes as the

Virginia, Morning Star, Great Eastern, Great Western, Rebecca, Bob Lee, Highland Lilly, and Quincy. Most of these show large veins and paying ore, and are being opened by levels and shafts. The Lilly level is over 200 feet long. Mill runs and assays vary from $80 to $500. The Virginia shows native and wire silver, and silver glance. The Brittenstine grant, as the group of mines is called, is expected to yield largely hereafter. The Independence shows ore carrying $90 in silver, $40 in gold and 55 per cent. of lead. The Alpine Silver Mining Company, of New York, owns and works the Yellow Jacket, Captain Jack, and ten other locations. A compressor and machine drills are employed, and a large force of men. The Lake View tunnel is 300 feet long. In Jay Gould gulch are the Continental, Blaine, and Jay Gould lodes.

Four Mile district is six miles from Buena Vista, and has several mines, such as the Storm King, Belle, etc. Cottonwood district is fast coming into notice and has some large veins.

Monarch Mining district is located around the headwaters of the South Arkansas river, in the southwestern corner of the county. Many of the lodes are above timber. A district as young as this that can show such proved and valuable mines as the Mountain Chief, Monarch, Smith and Gray, Song Bird, and Gulch, is sure to take a front rank now that the railway has reached the neighborhood. The towns of Monarch district are Maysville, Arbourville and Chaffee. The latter is up among the mines and the former is down nearer the base of the range, and seems to be the main business point. Maysville is 13 miles from the railroad at Cleora, 6 miles from Poncho Mineral Springs, and 8 miles below Monarch mountain and Chaffee. The Shavano Smelting Company has put up a blast furnace there.

Around the Middle Fork of the South Arkansas the ore is almost entirely carbonate of lead or galena, the former predominating. Fine specimens of chlorides and silver glance are not, however, wanting, and sometimes the ore is enriched by chlorides to such an extent that it would not be difficult to sort out considerable quantities that would mill over a thousand ounces per ton. Copper, in the form of carbonate, and antimony, in the form of both sulphide and oxide, are found in a few instances. No arsenic has been found, and sulphur, even in the galena, occurs in very small quantities. Some of the deposits occur as contacts. Most ores are low grade. On the North Fork are veins of galena.

VIEW ON D. & S. R. R., PLATTE CANON.

The famous Mountain Chief mine is located in Taylor's gulch, five miles northwest of Maysville, and is owned by Babcock, Follett & Company. It is a regular vein between lime and quartzite walls, and has an ore body from one to three feet thick of carbonates and galena, enriched by chlorides and some sulphurets of silver. A shaft nearly 200 feet deep, several drifts and an intersecting tunnel are being driven. The first fifteen tons of ore sent to Silver Cliff late in 1879 and early in 1880, yielded in different lots from 67 to 492 ounces of silver per ton, and from 11 to 45 per cent. of lead. Assays run up to $2,000. The mine produces largely. Near by are the Eagle Bird, Denver, Rainbow and Lilly Dale.

Over the divide to the northeast is Cree's camp, and the Song Bird, North Missouri, Legal Tender, Columbus, Pinion, Mark Twain, and Hunkidori lodes. The Song Bird ranks high and was one of the first found. The Pinafore's carbonates and galenas, between limestone and granite, yield from $20 to $100. Among other properties in the Middle Fork section are the Coal, Alpha and Beta, Mountaineer and Desdemona, and the Kansas City company's North Missouri, Legal Tender, Eureka and Arbor claims.

The Monarch, of Monarch mountain, is being systematically developed into a great mine, and has the material to make one of. It is opened by an incline several hundred feet long, run in at an angle of forty-five degrees. The vein widens to twelve feet in places, and contains rich galena and carbonate ores. So far shipments to Pueblo have yielded from 100 to 480 ounces of silver per ton. It is said that ten tons of ore are mined daily. The company owning the Monarch, Ben Bolt and Eclipse, all showing paying veins, have erected a smelter which these mines seem able to supply.

The Cherubim and Madonna or Smith and Gray mine is opened by several shafts, has plenty of ore and makes regular shipments. It is said to have been sold to eastern men for $60,000. The Fair Play, Little Charm and Paymaster are in this vicinity.

NORTHWESTERN COLORADO.

Grand, Larimer and Routt counties are all believed to be more or less rich in silver and gold, but the former visits of the Ute Indians deterred continuous prospecting and mining up to the present year. This is no longer the case in the parks and round about them.

GRAND COUNTY.

In the Rabbit Ear range, dividing Middle Park from North Park, some valuable developments are reported. Among the pioneers of this district were J. H. Stokes, Sandy Campbell, William Rodman, the Smart Brothers, L. Pollard, Nickerson and others. The Wolverine seems to be the great lode of this new silver district and carries a strong vein of high and low grade ore. Hundreds of feet of levels and tunnels are being driven and paying ore is being mined. A placer mine is worked in the park on Willow creek.

LARIMER COUNTY.

North Park is a large valley, from twenty to forty miles in either direction and enclosed by mountain ranges. The North Platte here takes its rise and helps to make a fine grazing country. This park has long held attractions for the venturesome prospector on account of the reputed presence of gold-bearing gravel deposits and gulches. Several white men have been killed there by the Indians, who were opposed to any intrusion on their old time hunting grounds. The value of the placer lands and gold and silver veins will be tested during the present season. The North Park, formerly thought to be in Grand or Routt counties, appears to be in Larimer. A wagon road has recently been constructed from near Fort Collins over a pass in the mountains 9,500 feet above sea level, which will afford an outlet to the park other than that into Wyoming Territory. Valuable coal veins have been discovered.

ROUTT COUNTY.

Routt county is the northwestern division of the State. It is composed of mountain ranges and spurs, divided by rivers and bordering valleys well adapted to grazing, and sometimes to farming. There are extensive placer lands on the headwaters of the Snake and Elk rivers, owned by companies and individuals. The principal of these is the International Company of Chicago, near Hanne's Peak, which has been making preparations for work on a large scale with great flumes and ditches, miles in length, and with hydraulics, which command an immense amount of paying gravel. About $10,000 in gold dust was produced one season. Hayden is the county seat. Steamboat Springs takes its name from its boiling hot springs, which at a distance sound like the puffing of a steamboat. Egeria Park is in this county. The western part of Routt, Summit, and Gunnison counties have heretofore been occupied by the Ute Indians.

CHAPTER XXIX.

THE GUNNISON REGION—EARLY EXPLORERS AND SUBSEQUENT HISTORY
—AN EMPIRE OF MINERAL WEALTH—THE GREAT SILVER BELT
OF THE ELK MOUNTAINS—THE ROARING FORK AND OTHER SEC-
TIONS—RUBY, GOTHIC, GUNNISON, PITKIN AND TIN CUP MINING
CAMPS—GOLD AND SILVER MINES—THE GREATEST MINING EX-
CITEMENT OF THE TIMES—A TIDAL WAVE OF PROSPECTORS.

The Gunnison country, to which the great tide of immigration is
drifting with irresistible force, has until recently been an unknown
land to the world at large and even to the people of Colorado. Over
thirty years ago the intrepid Fremont led his small but devoted band
of explorers over these mountain wilds. Previous to 1847–8, Mexico
possessed the country as far north as the 37th parallel from the Rocky
mountains to the Pacific. There were no white settlers (save a
few trappers) between the Missouri river and the western slope of the
Sierra Nevadas until the Mormons arrived at Great Salt Lake in
1845-6, and Colorado was the abode of Indians only. In 1853 Lieutenant Gunnison of the regular army was sent with a small force to
explore the Rocky Mountain country. He eventually fell a victim to
hostile Indians, and from him the noble Gunnison river took its name.

After mining began in California gulch, a few venturesome pioneers crossed the great mountains and worked the streams for gold,
but none remained permanently. In 1861, seven miners, coming from
Arizona towards the Colorado settlements, were surrounded and attacked by a large band of Piute Indians in a gulch leading into Taylor river. They fought with the desperation of men who knew that
death by the bullet was preferable to capture by such a foe. The
defence was maintained for three days and nights, until, worn
out and exhausted, the last of the brave little band were shot down,
fighting as they fell. Not one lived to tell the tale, but a Piute related the whole story to Kit Carson, saying that twenty of his comrades were slain in the encounter. The remains of men, mules and
equipage were subsequently seen by prospectors, and the locality

was ever afterwards known as Deadman's gulch. The fate of these men made the whites more cautious, and for many years the Gunnison region was seldom visited.

Benjamin Graham made a trip over into the Gunnison region in 1866. Four years after, R. A. Kirker, Benjamin Graham, William Gant, Samuel McMillen, Louis Brant, James Brennand and C. M. Defabauch, formed an exploring association, and, taking a summer's supplies along, prospected among the Elk Mountains and their western slopes in the Ute Indian reservation. They discovered many galena lodes, carrying cerussite in limestone formation. A coal vein was found on Rock creek, specimens from which good authorities analyzed and pronounced genuine anthracite coal. These discoveries of silver and coal veins were made during five summers.

A log fort was built as a place of refuge in case the Indians became hostile, and this was the main camp of the party. In 1874 the Utes burned the camp and drove the prospectors out of the country. The latter lost everything except what they had on their persons, and were obliged to travel one hundred miles before reaching the first white settlement, procuring a scanty subsistence on the way by shooting game. They had always been well armed with breech-loading rifles, but the Indians were too many for them. A. Thornton, now of Rosita, prospected in the Elk mountains about this time.

In 1873 the government scientific and geological exploring expedition, under Professor Hayden, passed the summer in the Gunnison region. This embraced probably as fine a corps of that description as was ever gathered together. The researches, maps and published reports of Hayden, Endlich, Peal, Taggett, Gannett and others in and for the entire Rocky Mountain region have been of inestimable service to Colorado. Further work of that character has since been conducted by R. A. Kirker, of Park county, relating more especially to the Park range, Leadville and neighboring counties.

Gunnison is probably the largest county·in the State, and embraces more than 10,000 square miles of territory. North of it is Summit county ; on the east the Sawatch mountains divide it from Lake and Chaffee, on the south is the San Juan region, and to the west is Utah. The Ute Indian reservation embraces the western two-thirds, or all of it lying west of a north and south line, fifteen miles east of the 107th meridian. Noble rivers and countless streams flow from and between its mountains, which occupy almost the entire country. Yet there is considerable grazing and some tillable land along the streams —more of it being on the reservation than elsewhere. There is some prospect of the Indians being removed by the Government, and a still greater prospect of their being expelled by the invading army of prospectors, should they conclude to oppose manifest destiny.

There is a gradual slope westward from the Sawatch range until the Utah line is reached. The river valleys for nearly a hundred miles east of that line are from four to six thousand feet only above sea level. Excellent wheat and other crops can be raised there, and grass grows luxuriantly as high as one's head. These valleys when peopled by the whites, will help to furnish supplies for the mining camps, for their farming and stock-growing capacities are first class.

In 1877 the county of Guanison was set off from Lake. The present destination of so many thousands of adventurers is generally termed the Gunnison country—almost an empire in extent and natural resources.

This until recently unknown land beyond the great mountains of the Continental divide has been and still is the scene of a mining excitement such as the world has seldom witnessed. The rumors of rich carbonate deposits and of huge fissure veins began to be noised abroad two years ago. These and the remoteness of the locality and difficulty of reaching it were sufficient fascinations to start people in that direction. Prospectors began to flock in from Leadville, and the reports they brought back caused a stampede for the new mines while the snows were yet deep on the intervening Sawatch range. These lofty mountains must necessarily be crossed in going to the new Eldorado, filled as their passes were with gigantic snow banks. In one place an immense deposit of snow was tunneled that the land of promise might be reached before the coming of summer would permit of succeeding arrivals. This was in the month of May, 1879. That season there were hundreds of men prospecting on the head-waters of Roaring Fork, Taylor and East rivers, and other hundreds roamed over the Elk mountains. They founded the mining camps of Hillerton, Tin Cup, Pitkin, Virginia, Gothic and Irwin.

But all previous accessions of population were trifling in numbers compared with the human " tidal wave " that came with the spring and summer of 1880. All winter the excitement over this inland empire had been growing in the east as well as in Colorado, and long before the snows were off the mountains multitudes of people were

AT THE MOUTH OF THE LITTLE COLORADO.

moving in that direction.   Long wagon trains took the circuitous routes by way of Marshall and Cochetopa passes, but hundreds of men, unencumbered with teams, crossed the snow-covered mountains further north.   The winter and spring had been a severe one, and thousands of emigrants after reaching the Gunnison, were obliged to await the departure of the snows.   It is claimed that nearly forty thousand people will summer in this Gunnison region, where but a few hundred passed the preceding winter.

Mining camps have been organized over a tract of country some fifty miles wide and one hundred long.   On the western slope of the Sawatch range, Tin Cup and its tributaries, and the Roaring Fork river flow northwesterly to the Grand river, and further south Taylor river, Ohio creek, and Tomichi aid to swell the waters of the Gunnison.   From the Elk Mountains, East and Slate rivers flow southward to the same destination.   Waters from the Elk Mountains flow easterly and northerly into the Roaring Fork, and westerly and southerly to the Gunnison.   Among the mountains around these streams are countless mineral veins.   The Indian reservation is believed to contain more mineral wealth than the more thoroughly prospected portion of the county

As far as explored the Gunnison region appears to have a formation similar to that extending from Leadville to the South Park. The mineral deposits of Gunnison are more extensive, however, and have more of a sulphide than a carbonate character.   While the outcroppings are enormous in quantity and sometimes rich, the grade is generally low.   Immense masses carry only from five to fifty ounces of silver per ton.   It is not unlikely, however, that a better average will be found as development progresses.   The formation of the Roaring Fork and Frying Pan region is limestone and quartzite, except around the heads of the creeks and gulches, where the country rock is of the metamorphic granite system of the main range.

The quantity of mineral is enormous.   Near Rock creek and elsewhere blocks of low grade galena, several feet square, have been rolled down the mountain sides.   In Ruby, Crested Butte and Gothic districts, limestone and quartzites abound, and some granite. Many veins of very high grade are worked, generally of the gray copper order, sometimes varied with galena and pyrites.   The same localities also have many great veins carrying galena alone, but of lower average grade than the others.   The Elk mountains extend in a southeasterly and northwesterly course through the eastern and northern parts of Gunnison county.

Coal measures have been found along Rock, Anthracite, Slate and Ohio creeks. Those on Ohio creek or tributaries are of bituminous character. The others are pronounced by competent investigators anthracite coals. These vast measures of coal will prove invaluable for Gunnison county as well as the State at large. The coal of Rock creek is in carboniferous measures above the belt of Devonian limestone. The veins are nearly horizontal and from 4 to 10 feet thick. Analyses made at the Smithsonian Institute and at other responsible places gave as high as 92 of fixed carbon and never less than 91, comparing with those of Pennsylvania, which are acknowledged the best in the world, and which carry from 85 to 93 per cent.

Gunnison City is the county seat and central business point of the Gunnison country. This will be the terminus of the Denver, South Park & Pacific railway for some time, or until a fresh start is made southward to Lake City or Ouray, and northward to the Elk Mountains. The town is growing with great rapidity, and has secured a newspaper, bank, hotels and many mercantile houses since the opening of spring. The town has an elevation of 7,500 feet, and is located in a narrow valley, skirting the Gunnison river. Just below, Tomichi river joins the Gunnison, and a mile above, Ohio creek comes in. To the east, north and west are the mining camps of Ohio creek, Pitkin, Tomichi, Copper creek, Taylor river, Washington gulch, Rock creek, Ruby and Gothic, all to be connected by telegraph and stage or railway.

Mines are worked near Tomichi and Quartz creeks, among the mountains around and east of Pitkin City. That place, named after the present popular governor of Colorado, has grown to be a lively and populous mining town in a few short months, and boasts of a bank, a newspaper and other institutions of civilization. It is the first settlement on the line of the D. & S. P. road, on the western slope of the main range, being 42 miles from Buena Vista, 12 from Alpine Pass railroad tunnel, and 25 east of Gunnison. The formation of the surrounding country is generally porphyry, quartzite and limestone, or decomposed granite. Among noteworthy mineral veins are the Fairview the Silver Islet, Silver Age, Terrible, Old Dominion, the Green Mountain group of lodes, and the Silver Queen, Silver King, Western Hemisphere, Black Cloud, Merrimac, and Silver

Point. The first two make a remarkable showing for the small amount of development.

The Fairview is four miles from Pitkin, and is opened by two shafts of no great depth. The vein is nearly vertical, with a foot wall of lime and hanging wall of porphyry, and is composed of black sulphurets, galena, carbonates of lead and pyrites of iron. A report on the lode indicated four feet of ore, averaging 160 ounces of silver per ton, and 38 per cent. of lead, with a large amount of ore containing 450 ounces.

The Silver Islet is two miles from Pitkin, and has a wagon road leading thereto. This is a large, strong vein, with a perfect slickenside foot wall of quartzite, and is nearly vertical. The ores are pyrites of copper and iron, blue and gray copper and silver glance. Sample assays from all parts of the mine, made by Cecil Morgan, showed as follows: five pieces of dressed mineral averaged 450 ounces of silver and $27\frac{1}{2}$ per cent. copper; undressed mineral gave 275 ounces of silver and 25 per cent. of copper; vein matter on the foot wall 53 ounces. Seven feet across the vein from the foot wall gouge and crevice gave 252 ounces. Before much work had been done on this lode C. C. Puffer sold it for $30,000.

The Green Mountain group of five lodes occupies a plat of ground 1,500 feet by 1,500, and is located at the head of Quartz creek, and ten miles above Pitkin. Morgan's report shows average assays of 69 ounces of silver and 14 per cent. of lead in the Nathaniel Slaght lode, from 81 to 117 ounces of silver and $12\frac{1}{2}$ per cent. of copper in the Green mountain lode, and 66 ounces and 20 per cent. of copper in the Blue Bird vein. The country rock is granite. The ore is gray copper and pyrites of copper and iron.

The Red Jacket lode has a vein about four feet wide. It is said to have been bought by ex-Governor Routt and others for $20,000.

Ohio City is a new settlement in a beautiful little park at the junction of Quartz and Little Ohio creeks. Near the latter are such lodes as the Ohio, Dodson, Grand View, Ontario, Gold Point, Humboldt, Tornado, Parole, Camp, and Gold Link. Many have free milling quartz. Rock showing native gold has been knocked off by the hammer from projecting ledges. While the surface ores show much gold, silver predominates below. Gulch mining was once carried on here.

The Taylor river section attracted many settlers in 1879. Here the rival towns of Hillerton and Virginia were located in a river valley and but two miles distant one from another. The Willow creek smelter near Virginia made a trial run in the fall of 1879, and then shut down for the winter. Among the many lodes of this section, the Prince, on Gold hill, is said to have five feet of carbonates carrying paying quantities of silver and traces of gold. One mill return gave 272 ounces. The Royal Oak Mining Company of New York is working properties in this section.

Tin Cup district was among the first organized after the Gunnison excitement began. Among the prominent mines are the Gold Cup, Tin Cup, Silver Cup, Golden Queen, Hirbie Lee, Allentown, Anna Dedricka, Mayflower, Red Lion, Thompson, Little Anna, and Big Galena, the last six on Mount Anna. The Golden Queen is said to be one of the few true fissure veins of its vicinity. Its vein assays about $60 a ton, mostly in gold, and shows cube galena. The Hirbie Lee and Allentown are in this locality.

The Tin Cup, Gold Cup, and Silver Cup mines are on one vein or deposit on the western slope of the main range near Chrysolite peak, and within two miles of Virginia City. Inclines running nearly 20 degrees below the horizontal are being driven on ore. These properties are owned and worked by the Bald Mountain Mining Company. The mineral is found in the limestone. The whole cap of the mountain is composed of porphyry underlaid with limestone. The ores are carbonates with some iron. Some of them are of very high grade. The main value is in silver. Southwest of this are a number of fissure veins in granite formation.

The Roaring Fork region is receiving an immense immigration, and is making a good record. Highland mining district is between the Roaring Fork and Castle creek. A belt of limestone about eighteen miles long and three miles wide extends north and south between these streams up to the Elk mountain range. In this belt an immense quantity of mineral is found.

The Monarch lode crops out of the ground to a height of twenty feet and is twenty-five feet wide. It is claimed that the average of a large part of this is 60 ounces of silver per ton. Shipments have been made that yielded $100. At the base of Aspen mountain is the Smuggler, showing carbonates. The Spar claim is considered a deposit, and seems to average about 60 ounces of silver per ton. The Ophir has a vein from three to four feet wide. The ore has yielded $500 a ton.　The Richmond, one of Stevens & Leiter's properties, yields ore worth from $70 to $100.

　Near Aspen City, and at the base of Aspen mountain, is the

SUMMIT OF ITALIAN MOUNTAIN.

Smuggler, the oldest location in camp.　This shows an immense outcrop, and carries from 70 to 100 ounces of silver per ton.　The Spar is one of the best properties in the district.　The ore is a heavy baryta, with chunks of copper and chlorides, yielding hundreds of dollars a ton. The average of the ore body is said to be 60 ounces. The Silver Bill lode shows native silver and has milled 94 ounces. The Galena lode is similar to the Monarch. The Little Russell mine is above timber line and shows an immense amount of ore on and near the surface. It has had mill runs of over $300 a ton.

The towns of the Roaring Fork section are Highland City, Aspen, and Roaring Fork. Smelters will soon be at work.

Massive City is the name of a new settlement on Frying Pan creek on the route of the projected Leadville and Gunnison railway, and in the centre of a great carbonate belt. Near it are mineral springs of unsurpassed value.

There are mines on Hunter's creek, a tributary of Roaring Fork, which starts in the range west of Leadville. Independence gulch is on the western slope of the Sawatch range, and only 35 miles from Leadville by the Twin Lakes pass. It has gold-bearing veins of iron and copper pyrites.

Ruby mining district is situated around Coal creek, a tributary of Slate river. This has been considered the richest of all the Gunnison camps, and is thought to be at the point of convergence of three mineral belts. Among the prominent mines are the Last Chance, Forest Queen, Lead Chief, Independence, Bullion King, Monte Cristo, Ruby Chief, Little Minnie, Silver Hill, Crystal, Zume, Justice, Bobtail, Hopewell, Pickwick, Fourth of July, Eureka, and Old Missouri. The seven first mentioned are extremely rich and valuable, and are producing largely. Their ore is said to yield from $200 to $2,000 per ton. Work is going forward at a lively rate all over the mountains and gulches. The main town is Irwin or Ruby City, the former being the post office title. This is 28 miles north from Gunnison City, soon to be the Denver & South Park Railway terminus, and about 80 miles from Buena Vista or Leadville.

Smelting and reduction works are being erected at Ruby, for which an ample ore supply is predicted. The Good Enough Smelting Company are building a great chlorodizing and amalgamating mill, similar to the Caribou. The machinery was shipped from New York and occupied twenty-five railway cars. The plant comprises rock breakers, drying floors, 20 stamps, 4 revolving roasting cylinders, and a full complement of amalgamating pans, elevating and conveying machinery. Connected with this enterprise are W.

H. Webb, J. R. T. Lindley, S. L. Townsend, and M. B. C. Wright.

The Lead Chief' is one of the great veins of this section. Locations known as Lead Chief, Little Chief, and Annie have been made, and work is going forward at a lively rate. The ore runs from among the hundreds down to the low grades. The Lead Chief is owned by Denver & Rio Grande railway officials, including Woerishoffer. Near by are the Fireside, Ruby, Equator, Morning Star, and Dictator. The Capitol, Hunkidori, and Hub join the Lead Chief on the east. The Ruby Chief is said to be the first location in this district. James Brennan was the discoverer. It is 12 feet wide, and often carries ruby mineral for a width of from 6 to 12 inches. It is owned by the Iowa Smelting Company. The Bullion King, supposed to be an extension of the Lead Chief, although half a mile distant, is another vein of surpassing value. Its vein shows a large seam of ruby silver ore. The Monte Cristo and George Washington are producing ore worth from $200 to $500 a ton. Among the galena and lower grade ores the Betsy and Jersey Blue are prominent. The Minnie, one mile north of Ruby Camp, has a vein of one-hundred-dollar ore four feet wide. J. H. Haverly, of theatrical fame, and others have purchased the Native Silver, Rustler, Ruby, and Giant lodes.

Among the mill runs of Ruby district are the following : Silvanite lode, ore sold at Pueblo, brought $1,919 per ton ; Forest Queen, sold at Denver, $1,209 ; Lead Chief, treated at Crested Butte, $543 ; George Washington, to same place, $236 ; Bullion King, sent to Denver, $903.

The Forest Queen created more excitement than any other property in the summer of 1879, by reason of its shipments to Denver and Pueblo of extremely rich ore—much of it of the ruby silver order. Richard Irwin & Co. worked the mine under lease at that time. They shipped 24 tons of ore that yielded over $10,000, the average being over $450 a ton, the lowest $350, and the highest $1,209 a ton. That was the lode's first production.

The Last Chance is on the same vein as the Forest Queen and is evidently just as valuable and profitable. It is partly owned by Richard Irwin, who visited the Gunnison region in 1878-9 and long before. Starting in when a boy, "Dick" has roamed over almost every part of the Colorado mountains, and has pioneered it from Salt Lake and the Black Hills to Mexico. This most famous of Colorado prospectors made the first Rosita discovery; was among the fortunate ones in the first Georgetown silver excitement, and was chased out of the San Juan mountains by the Indians twelve years ago. From him the twin peak with Gray took its name, as well as the chief town of Ruby district. Fortune seems to have favored him again in his Last Chance, and in his coal veins.

The Independence is an immense galena lode of size sufficient to keep a smelter occupied. The per cent. of lead is high, and enough silver is generally present to constitute paying ore. The lode is from ten to twenty feet wide. The Tabor Independence Silver Mining Company paid $112,000 for the mine and then stocked it in New York at $200,000 in one-dollar shares. This unusually low capitalization, amounting at the par value to little more than purchase money and working capital, is a very strong indication of a property of high value. Mines of small producing capacity or of no producing capacity at all are generally stocked in the millions when the average New York operator is at the helm—the more worthless the lode the higher the capitalization. The Independence is being rapidly opened in a systematic manner, and is expected to cut an important figure hereafter. This vein has several separate properties of 1,500 feet each. Among the stockholders is Senator James G. Blaine, who is also interested in Ouray and Park counties and in Leadville.

Crested Butte is eight miles from Ruby, seven miles from Gothic, nine miles from Washington gulch quartz mines, thirteen miles from Rock creek smelter, eight miles from Poverty gulch mines, and seven miles from Cement creek carbonates. A smelter was erected there in 1879 which will probably be steadily employed hereafter.

Gothic district is located around Copper creek and East river, and Gothic mountain. Gothic City, the main business point, is located at the foot of Gothic mountain, at a point where Copper creek empties into East river, and five miles from the head of the latter. Crested Butte is eight miles, Ruby or Irwin fifteen miles, and Gunnison thirty-five miles to the southward, and Cottonwood Pass is sixty miles to the east. Among the leading mines are the Independent, Silver Spence, Rensselaer, Vermont, Jenny Lind, Keno, Wolverine and Triumph. The Silver Queen vein carries several feet of gray copper, some of which contain as much as 350 ounces per ton. This mine is owned by Goodwin & Co. The Independent carries pyrites, gray copper, and galena. The Silver Spence has a vein 4 to 20 inches thick of galena, antimonial silver, native and ruby silver and sulphurets. The Rensselaer carries galena and gray copper, and is opened by two tunnels.

The Silvanite lode on Copper creek is one of the best properties in the county. It is owned by a Chicago company which expects a heavy yield hereafter. The Native Silver is its southwest extension.

The Evening Star lode is located on the east side of Copper creek, five miles from Gothic City. The vein is from $3\frac{1}{4}$ to 4 feet wide, of fine-grained galena ore, intimately intermixed with white feldspar. Samples of ore have assayed from $100 to $130 in gold, $130 to $190 in silver, and about 28 per cent. or $28 in lead. This is a newly opened property belonging to the Evening Star Silver Mining Company of New York, of which Calvin Goddard is president, Lewis Leland, vice-president, and J. A. Barker, secretary and treasurer. A good market will be afforded the ores of this district by the four smelters now being erected within a radius of ten miles.

On Rock creek are many argentiferous galena veins. The Silver Reef has a pay vein three feet wide. It has been bought by Tim Foley, of Leadville, E. B. Craven, of Cañon, and others, who talk of erecting a smelter. The Rock Creek Company's smelter will soon be ready for business.

East river and Washington gulch empty into Slate river, which flows southward from the Elk mountains into the Gunnison. In Washington gulch gold has been obtained by sluicing and panning, and by quartz mining.

Defiance mining camp, at the head of Grizzly creek, thirty miles into the Indian reservation, has lately been organized. Rich discoveries are reported.

Here ends this brief and inadequate description of the Gunnison country—a region where prospecting has but fairly begun and where mining is in its infancy, but whose future bids fair to be as bright and glorious as that of any land the sun shines upon.

CHAPTER XXX.

COAL—THE LIGNITES OF COLORADO—FACTS AND STATISTICS CONCERNING THE COAL MINES AND THEIR PRODUCT—THE COKING COAL OF TRINIDAD AND EL MORO—BOULDER, JEFFERSON AND FREMONT—COLORADO COKE MANUFACTURE—THE GUNNISON ANTHRACITES.

Colorado is rich in coal of a superior lignite quality: in some sections, like the Trinidad district, the veins take up with the character of bituminous coals to such an extent that they are often referred to as such. The coal-bearing lands embrace many thousand square miles of the State's area; the bulk of these so far located extend along the plains east of the foot hills, from Weld county in the north to the New Mexican line in the south. The coal lands of the mountains and parks are also very extensive, but have been worked but little, owing to their remoteness from railways and markets. The veins of La Plata county and White River are of superior quality and very extensive, those of North and South Park are excellent lignites, and those of the Gunnison are considered anthracite of a very inferior quality to that of Pennsylvania. The coal mines of Boulder, Weld, and Jefferson counties, on the plains and borders of the foot hills of northern Colorado, are very extensive and embrace many mines; there are other deposits near Colorado Springs. Coal Creek or Fremont county, Walsenburg, and the Trinidad section contain the best qualities of Colorado coal that are now mined extensively; the Trinidad coals are the only ones so far thoroughly tested that coke well, and they are said to be equal to those of Connellsville, Pennsylvania. The coking interests of El Moro and Trinidad are growing steadily in importance, and the product finds a continually increasing demand from the smelters of Leadville, Pueblo, San Juan and elsewhere. After the advent of the Pacific railways in Colorado, and the building of local roads, there was a heavy demand for Colorado coal, which caused the opening of many veins, horizontal and vertical; the production soon exceeded 100,000 tons per annum, and as the demands of Denver and other towns increased, and the coal began to be used extensively in Gilpin and Clear Creek mining districts, the yield became much larger. In 1877 the product was about 160,000 tons, worth, probably, $600,000; in 1878, 200,630 tons were mined, worth some $800,000.

The tonnage of coal produced in Colorado for 1878 was as follows:

LOCALITY AND NAME OF MINE.	Tons of Coal Mined.	LOCALITY AND NAME OF MINE.	Tons of Coal Mined.
BOULDER COUNTY—		JEFFERSON COUNTY—	
Marshall	13,965	Colorado Company	11,599
Welch	12,939	Pittsburg (Nichols)	2,000
Star (Canfield)	11,500	Rocky Mountain (E. Jones)	1,130
Boulder Valley	12,000	White Ash (Hall & Jones)	2,500
Other Erie Mines, Dietz, etc.	18,000	Murphy	800
Total	68,404	Total	17,229

Total given above	85,633
Weld and El Paso Counties	2,192
Huerfano County—Walsenburg	7,608
Fremont County—Coal Creek or Cañon	73,137
Las Animas County—Trinidad, etc.	32,060
Total tonnage produced in 1878	200,630

Two or three companies are engaged in manufacturing coke near Trinidad. The Trinidad Coal and Coke Company had increased its capacity to 36 ovens at the close of the year, and to 70 afterwards. In 1878 there were 6,042 tons of coke exported.

The most productive mine along the line of the Colorado Central Railway in northern Colorado is the Welch, which has been extensively opened within a year. Its product at last accounts, was 25 cars or 250 tons of coal daily. Some Colorado coal banks are vertical and others horizontal. They vary in thickness from six to fifteen feet. The Marshall is an immense vein of very good quality. The town of Erie is built among some of the leading coal banks, such as the Boulder Valley. The bed of the Coal creek mines near Cañon is about ten miles long by four wide. The product is unsurpassed if equaled for fuel purposes in the West. The mine contains over three miles of entry ways and drifts. Now that the D. & S. P. Railway has entered the South Park, the Lechner coal bank will have a ready market.

The rapidly increasing demands of railways, furnaces, mines, mills, and towns and cities for coal caused a large increase in the product in 1879, as compared with former years. The yield, as near as can be ascertained, was about as follows :

LOCALITY AND NAME OF MINE.	Tons of Coal Mined.	LOCALITY AND NAME OF MINE.	Tons of Coal Mined.
BOULDER COUNTY—		JEFFERSON COUNTY—	
Marshall	34,095	Colorado, Pittsburg, Rocky	
Welch	50,000	Mt., White Ash, Murphy	
White Rock, etc.	5,000	and Prout Mines	33,435
Star (Canfield)	20,000	HUERFANO COUNTY—	
WELD COUNTY—		Walsenburg	10,876
Boulder Valley Co.	25,100	LAS ANIMAS—	
Stuart, Mitchell, Superior and		Colo. C. & I. Co., El Moro	38,579
other Erie Mines	15,000	Trinidad coal mines	20,000
FREMONT COUNTY—		El Paso, Park, and other	
Canon Mine	70,647	counties	5,000

The total tonnage of 1879 was................................. 327,732

Value from.. $1,000,000 to $1,300,000

Boulder produced 109,095 tons, Weld 40,100, Jefferson 33,435, Fremont 70,647, Huerfano 10,876, and Las Animas 58,579.

The newly opened coal measures of South Park are said to be of the requisite description for coking as well as for steam, gas and fuel purposes. If these coals produce coke equal to that now furnished the Leadville market, they will cut a very important figure in smelting—for the proximity of these coal banks of the D. & S. P. railway will permit of cheaper transportation than from El Moro. It is proposed to erect coking ovens at Como at once.

The Welch mine in Boulder county has been opened with shafts and long levels for distances horizontally of a quarter of a mile underground. Between one and two hundred men are employed and a village called Louisville has grown up about the mine. The export now varies from 5,000 to 9,000 tons of coal per month.

The Marshall mine was opened many years ago before the railways were built all around it. It now has a railway connecting with Boulder and other points, and is turning out thousands of tons of very superior coal monthly for Denver, Central and Georgetown. The various mines at and near Erie, chief among which are the Boulder Valley and Star, continue to produce largely. The Golden mines are getting opened so as to show a steady gain in production.

The newly opened anthracite coal veins of Gunnison county contain from 90 to 92 per cent. of fixed carbon.

It is evident that the immense coal measures of the great parks and of western and southwestern Colorado will yet prove of incal-

culable benefit to the mining camps and cities growing up around
them.   Their value is already apparent in the South Park, Gunnison
and San Juan mining regions. A fine coal vein 18 feet thick has
been found in the North Park.   An enterprise involving the development of great coal, iron, and other resources is described below.

The Colorado Coal and Iron Company has absorbed the Central
Colorado Improvement, the Southern Colorado Coal and Iron, and
the Colorado Coal and Steel Works companies.   It owns 13,571
acres of coal lands and 83,748 acres of agricultural and town lands
along the Denver and Rio Grande railway, and 1,057 acres on what is
called the Iron Mountain south of Cañon City.

The Southern Colorado coals are the best of their class in the State
so far developed, and the only coals yet mined that can be successfully
used for iron manufacture and metallurgical purposes.   The El
Moro is a true coking coal.

The C. C. and I. company owns 8,121 acres of land at El Moro,
has 100 coke ovens in operation, having just erected 30, and is constructing as fast as possible 150 more.   This coke is supplied to
Leadville, Pueblo and all smelting works in the State, aggregating
150 tons daily, and still increasing.   The coal for the manufacture
of this coke is all crushed by machinery.   In quality it equals the
best Connellsville, Pa., coke.   With the Utah demand heretofore supplied by Pennsylvania, 1,400 miles further eastward, El Moro must
require 400 ovens capable of producing 500 tons of coke daily.   A
ton of coal makes about six-tenths of a ton of coke.

The C. C. and I. company's coal product in 1879, present number
of miners employed, and present producing capacity are as follows:

Name.	Number acres coal lands.	1879. Yield in tons.	No. men employed.	Present daily capacity.
Cañon mine.........	3,260	70,647	150	700
Cucharas...........	2,190	10,876	50	400
El Moro	8,121	38,579	150	1,200
Totals.........	13,571	120,102	350	2,300

The amount of coke manufactured at El Moro was 10,786 tons.
El Moro coal is especially adapted to manufacturing illuminating
gas, and is used by all Colorado gas works, while the present black-
smith supply throughout the State is El Moro " slack."   The great
Boston and Colorado smelting works at Argo use equal quantities of
Cañon and El Moro coal for fuel, consuming about 60 tons daily.

During the first four months of 1880, the C. C. and I. Company produced 22,851 tons of coal from its El Moro mine, and shipped 7,345 tons of coke. Out of 5,395 tons of coal mined in April, 3,344 went to the seventy coke ovens then in operation. Four or five firms and coal mines at Trinidad are producing coal.

The following analyses show the comparative qualities of Colorado and Pennsylvania coke : El Moro coke, fixed carbon, 87.47 ; ash, 10.68 ; sulphur, 0.8 ; Connellsville coke, fixed carbon, 87.26 ; ash, 11.99 ; sulphur, 0.75. Of non-coking coals those at Cucharas give 3.23 per cent. of water, 40.93 of volatile matter, 49.54 of carbon and 6.30 of ash ; sulphur, .62.

The Colorado Coal and Iron Company is erecting " bosh " furnaces at South Pueblo for manufacturing pig iron from iron ores from along the Arkansas valley and further south, some of the largest deposits being owned by this organization. It is also erecting a machine shop, foundry and rail mill for manufacturing bar iron and rails for railway use—the first furnace to be at work in November, 1880. It is proposed to erect a Bessemer steel plant in connection with these works. The company will soon begin to purchase 50 tons of iron ore daily from the Breece Iron mine of Leadville, which the railway will convey to South Pueblo. General W. J. Palmer is president, and Charles B. Lamborn vice-president of this company, which is an outgrowth of the Denver & Rio Grande railway.

Colorado has extensive deposits of iron, mica, lime and other valuable materials. Outside of the Breece Iron mine at Leadville, vast quantities of iron ore abound in southern Colorado. Mica of excellent quality is found in several places.

The Soltiel Mica and Porcelain Company of Colorado owns an extensive and superior mica mine on Current creek, Fremont county, comprising six claims. The mica occurs in extensive veins of quartz and feldspar—large pieces and leaves being found in abundance. Several car loads of good mica have been shipped to Saint Louis. There is every indication that this property will produce more and better mica at less cost than any similar mine in America. Ground mica is in great demand for steam packing, for lubricating purposes, the manufacture of mica bronze, and by railways for packing journal boxes, and the mine as yet is unable to supply the needs of the latter.

In this volume the author has endeavored to record the progress and achievements of Colorado and its miners and people from the days of the pioneers to the present time. The attention of the reader has been called to all important points from Wyoming to Arizona, and from the handsome plains metropolis to the newly built frontier cabin of the prospector. The " end of track " having long been passed and the extreme limit of civilization reached, calling a halt seems the one thing left to do. The rich discoveries and enormous profits of many mines have caused the investment of much eastern capital during the past year, and the creation of numerous stock companies; but most of Colorado's mineral veins are still operated by individual owners or lessees. In this extended description and history the design has been to show how profitable the search for the precious metals has been, and, while the cause of this great industry is advocated, that of the stock company industry is not, except in deserving instances—for the system often leaves very poor chances to the last man. Some mining stocks yield larger revenues than can be expected from anything else. Others are moderately profitable, but the majority of eastern companies are never likely to pay dividends. Many highly capitalized properties could give fair profits to industrious miners, but cannot afford such luxuries as stock companies, while others are so poor that a hard-working man would starve to death on them. The general attention lately given to mining is shown by the fact that stock and mine holders embrace men of all grades and circumstances. Leading government officials, merchants, railroad and professional men, and people from almost every calling have made their investments. So great an interest arises mainly from the knowledge of splendid results attained. Chief among these is the transformation, within a few short years, of a rugged wilderness into the world's most prosperous state and largest bullion producer. With the exception of a statistical and political appendix, this work on Colorado closes here.

APPENDIX.

COLORADO MINES.

PROMINENT MINES.

THEIR YIELD PRIOR TO 1880—ALSO LOCATION, CHARACTER, DATE OF DISCOVERY—ESTIMATED NUMBER OF YEARS OF WORK FOR AN ENTIRE LODE—AND DEPTH OF DEEPEST SHAFTS.

The yields given for a majority of mines are close estimates in coin value—not currency, as was the former custom. This list embraces all mines in Colorado whose product had exceeded a quarter of a million prior to January, 1880, and but very few whose yield was less than that. Gilpin and Clear Creek counties have many lodes that yielded from one to two hundred thousand dollars, but they don't think a mine prominent in those counties unless its yield exceeds such figures. Most lodes in Gilpin have several distinct mines on them, but each lode is combined here. Leadville has new mines now producing largely that did not appear below, and many of those mentioned have doubled their product since January 1, 1880. So that in this comparison the new Leadville mines do not appear to the advantage that they will another year.

NAME OF MINE.	County.	Character.	When Discovered.	Years of Active Work.	Total Yield to 1880
Chrysolite.........	Lake.....	Silver.....	1878	1¼	$2,100,000 00
Little Pittsburg...	"	"	1878	1½	3,800,000 00
Little Chief.......	"	"	1878	1½	2,056,292 00
Iron-Silver.......	"	"	1877	2½	700,000 00
Morning Star Cons.	"	"	1877	2	600,000 00
Robert E. Lee.....	"	"	1878	½	600,000 00
Leadville.........	"	"	....	2	450,000 00
Argentine.........	"	"	....	3	300,000 00
Glass-Pendery.....	"	"	....	½	250,000 00
Amie...............	"	"	....	1½	300,000 00
Climax...........	"	"	....	1½	200,000 00
Printer Boy.......	"	Gold......	..	5	300,000 00
Pocahontas--Humbolt.............	Custer.....	Silver.....	1874	5	723,929 51
Bassick...........	"	G. and S..	1877	2½	350,000 00
Little Annie	Rio Grande	Gold......	1873	4	200,000 00

NAME.	COUNTY.	Character.	When Discovered.	Est'd No. Years of Work for Entire Lode.	Depth in Feet of Deepest Shaft.	Total Yield from Discovery to January, 1880.
Caribou and No Name	Boulder	Silver	1869	10	812	$1,368,000
Native Silver	"	"	1873	6	580	250,000
Smuggler	"	G. and S.	1876	4	240	300,000
Melvina	"	"	1875	5½	500	310,000
Columbia Lode	"	Gold	1859	14	540	350,000
Gregory	Gilpin	"	1859	16	940	6,970,354
Bobtail	"	"	1859	16	920	5,138,837
Gunnell	"	"	1859	15	800	2,300,000
California Gardner, Hidden Treasure Lode	"	"	1859	15	1,100	2,150,000
Kansas	"	"	1859	15	1,150	2,000,000
Burroughs	"	"	1859	14	1,000	1,250,000
Rollins Mines	"	"	1860	7	450	1,000,000
Wyandotte Cons.	"	"	1859	14	300	800,000
Buell	"	"	1859	7	550	650,000
Bates	"	"	1859	9	450	600,000
Kent County	"	"	1859	15	800	550,000
Prize, Suderburg	"	"	1859	9	450	650,000
Fisk	"	"	1859	15	650	500,000
Forks	"	"	1860	10	700	450,000
Flack	"	"	1860	10	650	400,000
Rhoderick Dhu, Borton, etc.	"	"	1860	7	550	400,000
Alps	"	"	1860	9	550	300,000
Illinois	"	"	1860	7	260	300,000
American Flag	"	"	1860	8	450	300,000
Pewabic	"	"	1860	7	300	250,000
Pelican, Dives	Clear Creek	Silver	1871	8½	460	2,711,253
Terrible Group, Brown, etc.	"	"	1868	11	700	1,900,000
Colorado Central, Cons.	"	"	1868-72	9	350	900,000
Red Elephant, Cons.	"	"	1876-7	3	460	650,000
Dunderberg--East Terrible	"	"	1868	6	400	608,000
Hukill	"	G. and S.	1871	9	300	525,000
Pay Rock	"	Silver	1872	8	350	450,000
Baxter	"	"	1871	8	350	360,000
Freeland	"	G. and S.	1861	4	700	350,000
Maine-Phœnix	"	Silver	1871	6	300	300,000
Junction Group	"	"	1872	6	400	350,000
Equator	"	"	1867	7	450	300,000
Kirtley	"	"	1877	2¼	300	225,000
Roe-Hercules	"	"	1871	8	300	250,000
Snow Drift	"	"	1868	8	250	200,000
Silver Plume	"	"	1868	8	250	200,000
Seaton	"	"	1861	8	250	200,000
Saco	"	"	1871	5	...	200,000
Boston Co. Mines	Summit	"	1868	11	Tunnel.	500,000
Moose	Park	"	1871	9	Tunnels.	900,000
Dolly Varden	"	"	1872	8	"	340,000
Phillips	"	Gold	1862	5	150	300,000

The sections west of the Missouri river gave the following yield of the valuable metals in 1879. The figures are John J. Valentine's, of Wells, Fargo & Company, excepting for Colorado:

Nevada	$21,997,714	Arizona	$1,942,403
California	18,190,973	Oregon	1,037,961
Colorado	17,014,204	New Mexico	622,800
Utah	5,458,879	British Columbia	976,742
Montana	3,629,020	Mexico (West Coast)	1,683,871
Dakota	3,208,987		
Idaho	2,091,300	Grand total	$77,950,190

Total gold, $32,539,920; silver, $38,613,823; lead, $4,185,769.

The author estimates that the yield of the three leading States for 1880 will not vary a million from the following:

Colorado, $25,000,000; California, $18,500,000; Nevada, $16,000,000.

Colorado produced $7,006,087.10 more in 1879 than in 1878, and $10,797,920.47 more in 1879 than in 1876.

Nevada produced $13,184,235 less in 1879 than in 1878, and over 27,000,000 less in 1879 than in 1877.

California's product has shown little change for many years.

The silver production in the United States for the five years ending with the thirty-first of December, 1874, footed up $113,712,000, giving an average product of $22,742,300 per annum. For the next five years, including 1879, the product was $181,055,000, giving an average annual product of $36,211,000.

The gold product of the country for the five years ending with 1874 footed up $205,500,000, giving an annual average of $41,400,000. For the following five years the gold product amounted to $214,389,920, giving an average annual product of $42,867,984.

If silver had the same value as before the government demonetized it in 1873, Colorado's silver product of 1879 would have brought the producers $2,000,000, or over 16 per cent. more than it did. After a fair trial nearly all leading European countries feel the evils of the single gold standard—a currency very satisfactory to the small money-lending classes, but ruinous to everybody else. Silver should have the same advantages it always possessed previous to seven years ago—the same free coinage facilities as gold. These are likely to be afforded soon, not only in America but in Germany. A return to the old valuation of $1.29 an ounce may then be expected instead of $1 as in 1876, $1.12½ as in 1879, or $1.14 as in 1880.

The number of Colorado mines whose annual production exceeded $100,000 has been steadily growing larger. In 1879 there were 21 mines or lodes of such character; name, and yield for the year given below:

In Boulder county the Caribou Silver mine, $210,513.98.

In Gilpin county (gold) the Bobtail, $502,562.17; Gregory, $240,000; California, $160,000; Hidden Treasure, $160,000.

In Clear Creek (silver), Terrible Cons., $140,000; Pelican-Dives, $140,000; Freeland (gold and silver), $115,000; Red Elephant Cons., $100,000; Colorado Central, $100,000.

In Summit (silver), the Robinson, $130,000.

In Custer, the Bassick, gold and silver, $120,000.

In Leadville (silver), the Little Pittsburg, $2,600,000; Chrysolite, $1,850,000; Little Chief, $1,871,912; Morning Star, $600,000; R. E. Lee, $600,000; Amie, $400,000; Leadville, $280,000; Glass-Pendery, $250,000; Iron-Silver, $250,000; Climax, $175,000.

All of the Leadville mines except the Little Pittsburg and Leadville had not then got into their present producing condition. Some of the above represent two or three mines in one consolidation or on one lode. Some Leadville mines produce from $100,000 to $250,000 a month in 1880.

WAGES.

Outside of Leadville, mining is more generally carried on at so much per foot or fathom of ground broken, this being what is known as contract work. Where miners are employed by the day, the following are the usual wages in various sections, ten hours constituting a day in most counties, and eight in most Leadville mines.

Boulder county, $2 to $2.50 and sometimes $3; Gilpin, $2 to $2.50; Clear Creek, $2 to $3; Park, Summit, and Chaffee counties, $3 to $3.50; Leadville, $3; Custer, $2.50 to $3; San Juan region, $3.50 to $4; Gunnison, $3 to $4. Surface men and engineers usually work ten or twelve hours.

Mechanics receive from $3 to $4 in the plains and older mining towns and a little more in Leadville and the newer settlements.

COLORADO CENSUSES FOR THE YEARS 1860 AND 1870.

UNITED STATES OFFICIAL DECENNIAL CENSUSES.

The following statistics of the population of Colorado will be found interesting as showing the growth of counties, movements of population and the number of and the increase of either sex according to the national census. These can be compared in turn with the estimates of population given in the tabulated statement on page 156.

In 1860 all of what is now Colorado that was settled by white men was included in the county of Arapahoe, which then formed a part of the Territory of Kansas. This was the year after the first rush to the "Pike's Peak Gold Mines," so called.

Total population in 1860, 34,277; number of males, 32,654; females, 1,577. Indians not counted.

In 1861 the males had decreased to 20,798 and the females had increased to 4,484.

As to the nativity of the 34,277 pioneers of 1860, Ohio is credited with the largest number, 4,125; New York with 3,942, Illinois with 3,620, Missouri with 3,312, Indiana, 2,587, and other states with smaller numbers.

Of the total, 31,611 were Americans and 2,666 were foreigners.

The census of 1860 gave the following returns for leading settlements:

	NUMBER OF MALES.	NUMBER OF FEMALES.	TOTAL.	IN PRESENT COUNTY OF—
Denver.	4,140	609	4,749	Arapahoe.
Golden.	893	121	1,014	Jefferson.
South Clear Creek.	5,888	78	5,966	Clear Creek.
Central	526	72	598	Gilpin.
Eureka Gulch.	146	14	160	"
Enterprise District.	284	36	320	"
Mountain City.	737	102	839	"
Spring Gulch.	125	16	141	"
Missouri City.	528	69	597	"
Nevada Gulch.	755	123	879	"
Leavenworth Gulch.	220	20	240	"
Lake Gulch.	379	59	438	"
Russell Gulch.	432	48	480	"
Russell and part of Idaho.	232	23	255	"
South Park.	10,519	91	10,610	Park.
Tarryall and South Park	987	13	1,000	"
Valley of the Platte.	3,704	10	3,714	"
California Gulch.	2,000	36	2,036	Lake.

The census of 1870 made the following showing:

COUNTIES.	TOTAL, 1870.	NUMBER OF MALES.	NUMBER OF FEMALES.
Arapahoe	6,829	4,406	2,423
Bent	592	439	153
Boulder	1,939	1,180	759
Clear Creek	1,596	1,077	519
Conejos	2,504	1,303	1,201
Costilla	1,779	912	867
Douglas	1,388	1,005	383
El Paso	987	637	350
Fremont	1,064	637	427
Gilpin	5,490	3,539	1,951
Greenwood	510	417	93
Huerfano	2,250	1,205	1,045
Jefferson	2,390	1,521	839
Lake	522	387	135
Larimer	838	539	299
Las Animas	4,276	2,363	1,913
Park	447	317	130
Pueblo	2,265	1,471	794
Saguache	304	189	115
Summit	258	217	41
Weld	1,636	1,059	577
Totals	39,864	24,820	15,044

In Denver there were 2,800 males and 1,959 females.

It is believed that the census of 1880 will return a population for Colorado of between 200,000 and 250,000. More people emigrated to Colorado in the first five months of 1880 than the territory contained in 1870.

During the two months that have passed since compiling the populations of towns, given on page 157, several small settlements have grown into places of great importance. Breckenridge now claims 3,000 inhabitants, Gunnison 1,500, Pitkin nearly 1,000, and Leadville over 25,000.

UNITED STATES SENATORS FROM COLORADO.

Henry M. Teller, of Central City; term from 1877 to 1883.

N. P. Hill, of Denver; term from 1879 to 1885.

Jerome B. Chaffee was senator from December, 1876, to March, 1879, and Henry M. Teller from December, 1876, to March, 1877.

COLORADO—STATE OFFICIALS, 1879-80.

Governor—Frederick W. Pitkin. *Lieutenant Governor*—Horace A. W. Tabor. *Secretary of State*—Norman H. Meldrum. *State Treasurer*—Nathan S. Culver. *Auditor of State*—Eugene K. Stimson. *Attorney General*—Chas. W. Wright. *Superintendent of Public Instruction*—Joseph C. Shattuck.

SUPREME JUDGES.

Chief Justice—S. H. Elbert. *Associate Justices*—Wilbur F. Stone, W. E. Beck.

DISTRICT JUDGES.

First District—Mitchell, Georgetown. *Second District*—Victor A. Elliott, Denver. *Third District*—John W. Henry, Pueblo. *Fourth District*—T. M. Bowen, Leadville.

DISTRICT ATTORNEYS.

First District—H. M. Orahood, Central. *Second District*—D. B. Graham, Denver. *Third District*—J. M. Waldron, Huerfano. *Fourth District*—C. W. Burris, Rio Grande.

U. S. OFFICIALS FOR COLORADO.

U. S. District Judge—Moses Hallet. *U. S. Attorney*—W. S. Decker. *U. S. Marshall*—P. P. Wilcox. *Assayer, U. S. Mint*—Herman Silver. *Surveyor General*—Albert Johnson. *Collector Internal Revenue*—J. S. Wolfe.

United States Land Offices are located at Denver, Central, Leadville, Pueblo, Del Norte, and Lake City. These issue mining and mineral titles as well as land titles.

STATE JUDICIAL DISTRICTS.

First Judicial District is composed of the counties of Boulder, Jefferson, Gilpin, Clear Creek, Summit, Grand, and Routt.

Second Judicial District is composed of the counties of Weld, Arapahoe, Douglas, Elbert, and Larimer.

Third Judicial District is composed of the counties of Park, El Paso, Fremont, Pueblo, Bent, Las Animas, and Huerfano.

Fourth Judicial District is composed of the counties of Costilla, Conejos, Rio Grande, San Juan, La Plata, Hinsdale, Saguache, Custer, Lake, Ouray, Chaffee, and Gunnison.

COLORADO.

FIRST TWO STATE AND CONGRESSIONAL ELECTIONS.
Judicial Election of 1879.

COUNTIES. (30.)	GOVERNOR, 1878.			GOVERNOR, 1876.	
	REPUBLI-CAN.	DEMO-CRAT.	GREEN-BACK.	REPUBLI-CAN.	DEMO-CRAT.
	Pitkin.	Loveland.	Bucking-ham.	Routt.	Hughes.
Arapahoe	2,218	1,450	328	2,173	1,795
Bent	193	221	6	250	439
Boulder	998	627	654	1,539	1,096
Clear Creek	1,062	815	269	1,072	1,031
Conejos	400	478	14	341	218
Costilla	339	244	...	351	173
Custer	240	219	10	New	county.
Douglas	259	205	30	282	333
Elbert	153	160	21	84	117
El Paso	884	340	22	713	397
Fremont	339	222	82	522	531
Gilpin	1,037	633	280	1,005	763
Grand	33	42	1	73	147
Gunnison	88	49	...	New	county.
Hinsdale	319	283	56	420	382
Huerfano	438	496	4	410	614
Jefferson	425	614	210	537	596
Lake	977	953	160	229	234
La Plata	142	137	...	50	108
Larimer	362	354	132	374	300
Las Animas	641	977	33	669	1,271
Ouray	413	258	31	New	county.
Park	311	242	7	465	423
Pueblo	507	584	21	543	739
Rio Grande	255	151	3	364	362
Routt	21	29	...	New	county.
Saguache	235	154	2	306	189
San Juan	308	238	71	393	410
Summit	191	106	10	201	185
Weld	618	291	300	788	468
Total	14,396	11,573	2.784	14,154	13,316
Per cent	50.06	40.24	9.70	......	......

Pitkin over Loveland, 2,823 ; over all, 39. Routt over Hughes, 838. Total vote, 28.759 in 1878, and 27,470 in 1876.

In 1878 W. A. H. Loveland ran for governor on the Democratic ticket; Thomas M. Fields, for lieutenant-governor ; John S. Wheeler, for secretary of state ; Nelson Hallock, for treasurer ; and O. J. Goldrick, for superintendent of public instruction.

In 1879, for Supreme Judge, Beck (Republican) had 16,920 ; Richmond (Democrat), 12,702 ; and Saulsbury (Greenback), 1,246. Republican majority, 2,969. Total vote, 30,868.

REPRESENTATIVE IN CONGRESS.

1878.			1876.	
BELFORD.	PATTERSON.	CHILDS.	BELFORD.	PATTERSON.
Republican.	Democrat.	National.	Republican.	Democrat.
14,294	12,003	2,329	13,438	12,584

For 46th Congress—Belford over Patterson, 2,329; Patterson and Childs combined over Belford, 38. For 44th Congress—James G. Belford over Patterson, 854. Thomas M. Patterson was representative in the 45th Congress.

LEGISLATURE OF 1879–80.

The Senate has 19 Republicans, and 7 Democrats; the House, 36 Republicans, 12 Democrats, and 1 Greenbacker. The State government was inaugurated January 10, 1879. State officers and legislatures are elected biennially. The Senators hold office for four years, one-half being elected at each biennial election.

COLORADO STATE OFFICIALS, 1876–8.

The following were the Colorado State officials in 1876–8, all republicans, and the majorities by which they were elected at the general election:

Governor, John L. Routt, 837; *lieut-governor*, Lafayette Head, 1,098; *secretary of state*, William M. Clark, 1,728; *auditor*, D. C. Crawford, 863; *treasurer*, George C. Corning, 491; *attorney general*, A. J. Sampson, 541; *supt. of public instruction*, J. C. Shattuck, 1,323.

The above, with the first state government, were inaugurated November 3, 1876. The first state legislature stood politically as follows: Senate, 19 republicans, 7 democrats; House, 31 republicans and 18 democrats.

The democratic state ticket in 1876 was as follows: For governor, Bela M. Hughes; lieut-governor, Michael Beshoar; secretary of state, James T. Smith; auditor, J. F. Benedict; treasurer, Thomas M. Field; attorney general, G. Q. Richmond; superintendent public instruction, J. B. Groesbeck.

TERRITORIAL OFFICIALS OF COLORADO.

From 1861 to 1876, inclusive.

Governors of Colorado.—Wm. Gilpin, qualified July 8, 1861 ; John Evans, April 11, 1862 ; Alexander Cummings, October 19, 1865 ; A. C. Hunt, May 27, 1867 ; E. M. McCook, June 15, 1869 ; S. H. Elbert, 1873 ; E. M. McCook, August, 1874 ; John L. Routt, March 29, 1875.

Secretaries of State.—L. L. Weld, qualified July 8, 1861 ; S. H. Elbert, April 19, 1862 ; Frank Hall, May 24, 1866 ; June 15, 1869 ; June 18, 1873 ; J. W. Jenkins, appointed February 12, 1874 ; John Taffe, August 19, 1875.

Treasurers.—George T. Clark, qualified November 12, 1861 ; A. W. Atkins, March 17, 1864 ; A. C. Hunt, January 26, 1866 ; John Wanless, September 5, 1866 ; Columbus Nuckolls, December 16, 1867 ; reappointed March 17, 1868 ; George T. Clark, February 14, 1870 ; February 17, 1872 ; D. H. Moffat, January 26, 1874 ; F. Z. Solomon, February 12, 1876.

Auditors.—M. M. Delano, qualified November 12, 1861 ; R. E. Whitsett, March 10, 1864, January 26, 1866 ; H. J. Graham, December 13, 1866 ; N. T. Cheesman, January 7, 1868 ; James B. Thompson, February 15, 1870 ; February 14, 1872 ; L. C. Charles, January 26, 1874 ; February 12, 1876.

Justices Supreme Court and District Judges.—B. F. Hall, Chief Justice, S. N. Pettis, Chas. Lee Armour, July 9, 1861 ; A. A. Bradford, July 5, 1862 ; S. S. Harding, C. J., September 17, 1863 ; C. F. Holly, January 22, 1866 ; W. M. Gale, February 10, 1866 ; Moses Hallett, C. J., June 19, 1866 ; W. R. Gorsline, June 21, 1866 ; C. S. Eyster, November 26, 1866 ; Moses Hallett, reappointed, C. J., April 30, 1870 ; J. B. Belford, July 26, 1870 ; E. T. Wells, March 6, 1870 ; A. W. Stone, March 13, 1875 ; A. W. Brazee, 1875.

United States Marshals.—C. Townsend, 1861 ; A. C. Hunt, 1862 ; U. B. Holloway, 1866 ; M. A. Schaffenburg, 1868 ; C. C. Tompkins, April, 1875.

Colorado Mines, 1860-1880

594

Half-Way House claim—435
Hamburg Gulch placers—482
Hamill—359,397
Hard Cash—456
Hardin lode—394
Hard Money—350,352
Hardscrabble mining district—466
Harkaway—339
Harsh vein—342
Hartford lode—559
Hawley-Gardner claim—333
Hazeltime lode—318,323
Hecla lode—277
Hector lode—466
Helen lode—490
Helmer lode—318
Helvetia lode—440
Henriette claim—431,436
Henry lode—402
Hercules lode—398,584
Hercules-Roe-Seven-Thirty lode—
  397,584
Herman lode—490
Hiawatha lode—503
Hibernia—459
Hidden Treasure lode—324,503,504;
  mine, 329-30,540,547,549,584,586
Highland Chief lode—420,437,439,443,
  547
Highland Lassie lode—547
Highland Lilly lode—560
Highland Mary—521,536-37
Himmala—430
Hirbie Lee—571
Homestake lode—407
Hook lode—500
Hoosier lode—254; mine, 256,523
Hope lode—551,553
Hopewell lode—394,573
Horn Silver claim—472,478,501
Hortense lode—559
Hotchkiss lode—521
Hub lode—574
Hubert lode—323
Hugo lode—378
Hukill lode—368-70; mill, 363,364;
  mines, 244,356,360,367,368,
  375,584
Humbolt lode—282,283,351,462,570;
  mine, 238,385,462-63,466,479,
  540,549
Hunkidori lode—562
Hunter lode—131,288,503
Hymen lode—500

Ida—550
Idaho—262,270,550
Idalie—500
Ida May—501

Illinois lode—132,287,288,337-38,
  348,490,584; mill,296
Illinois Gulch placers—482,483,487
Imogene lode—547
Independence lode—439,440,488,553,560,
  573,575
Indiana lode—324,329,330
Indian Girl—501
Inez—524
Ingersoll—529
International—355,399
Iowa claim—478
Irene—339
Irish Flag lode—328
Iron—427,428,429,444,524
Iron Hill claim—410,420,427; mine,
  411,413,420,430
Iron Mask claim—501
Iron Silver—428-29,442,443,447,500,
  583,586
Iszard claim—440

J. Alden Smith lode—277
James B. claim—440
James Guthrie lode—389
Jay Gould lode—560
Jennie Blanche lode—318
Jennie Parker lode—536
Jenny Lind—575
Jersey Blue lode—574
Jessie—337
Jessie C.—440
J. L. P.—529,531
Joaquin—521
Joe Chaffee lode—504,506
Joe Reynolds vein—351,378
John D. Long lode—378
John J. Crooke—521,524
John Jay lode—254,273,277,278
Johnny Bull—546
Joner—553
Jones lode—288,322
Josephine claim—430
Junction-Galie lode—387
Junction lode—387,388,584
Justice—573

Kangaroo lode—380
Kansas City placer—556
Kansas Extension lode—508
Kansas lode—131,285,287,288,298,324-
  29,334,335,349; mines, 328,504,
  506,508,584
Keno—575
Kent County lode—132,287,324,328,338,
  584
Keystone lode—254,273,281,282,411,429,
  503; mine, 258,438
Keystone Picket lode—386

Index
for
FOSSETT'S COLORADO
It's Gold and Silver Mines,

622

To my esteemed friend

Robert Sheridan Miller

In appreciation of your many
able and helpful contributions to
Protestant Christianity and your
invaluable services to the Community and

With Congratulatory and Best
Wishes on the occasion of your Tenth
Anniversary as pastor of the Unitarian
Church in Burlington Vermont

John P. Gregory

December 4, 1956

Signs & Symbols in Christian Art

Giovanni Battista Tiepolo: *Madonna of the Goldfinch*. National Gallery of Art, Washington

SIGNS & SYMBOLS
IN
CHRISTIAN ART

BY GEORGE FERGUSON

With Illustrations from Paintings of the Renaissance

Published by
OXFORD UNIVERSITY PRESS
New York

The typography and format were by Richard Ellis and the text composed in his private cutting of Goudy Deepdene type by Westcott & Thomson, Philadelphia. The full-page illustrations were printed in England under the direction of Dr Horovitz of the Phaidon Press Ltd, London. Text printing and binding by The Plimpton Press, Norwood, Massachusetts, United States of America

FIRST EDITION, NOVEMBER 1954

SECOND EDITION, 1955

This Book is *Affectionately* Dedicated to

RUSH · H · KRESS

CONTENTS

THE REASON WHY

My seven-year-old daughter was looking at a color reproduction of Tiepolo's Madonna and the Goldfinch. It had just been sent to me by Col. H. A. McBride, Administrator of the National Gallery of Art in Washington. She asked, "What does the goldfinch in the child's hand mean?"

This question, which my daughter asked several years ago, was the beginning of this book. It began a search for the sources of information from which one could find simple and adequate meanings to aid in the understanding of the symbols which were so widely used in religious paintings.

We discovered that there had been a great deal written on religious symbolism, particularly of the Renaissance period. There was one obvious difficulty; the information was widely scattered. No thorough work which included the entire field of religious symbolism had been attempted for many years. After consultation with many persons having an interest in and knowledge of Christian art, we decided that a fresh approach might prove of great interest and help. We then determined to provide this study of religious symbolism and illustrate it with Renaissance paintings of religious subjects.

This book is the result of our exciting adventure in this field during the past five years. We commend it to you with the comments of its first reviewer. We asked a girl of twelve to read the manuscript. Her comment expresses far better than anything we could write the feeling we hope will be shared by every reader.

"Symbolism and its meaning in Christian art is a subject on which few books have been written. This book is very simple to read and to anyone who is interested in art it will be a great asset to their library. I found this book extremely interesting and charmingly written. The choice of words and the charming descriptions make it extremely enjoyable. I like the section about animals and birds best. I also like the wonderful descriptions of different symbols of animals, birds, and butterflies, also insects. Another lovely section was written on flowers and another on the Old Testament. I shall be very interested to see this book when it comes out because it seems so unique and is so interesting."

I wish to express my extreme appreciation to the author, the Reverend George Ferguson, Rector of Saint Philip's In The Hills, Tucson, Arizona. He has given the readers a fresh and unique presentation of the story of symbolism in Christian art. It is hoped that your interest will bring you a renewed insight into the universality of the Christian religion. We who are the children of the Christian heritage should be grateful that our religion can, as in previous ages, stimulate our thoughts, words, and daily actions.

RUSH H. KRESS

AN INTRODUCTION

The Christian asserts that man is created in the image of God. He declares that God has given man a soul, capable of reaching up into Heaven itself and inspiring the human mind to its noblest achievement, the quest after God.

It is this spiritual aspiration that lifts man to his greatest heights. No words have ever been found that are adequate to give it satisfactory expression. There is a reason for this. God has given the soul the privilege of enjoying a continuous awareness of the realities of life. These realities may be described as the never-ending experiences man has with truth, beauty, and goodness. These experiences are so vital and moving that man has a constant urge to impart them to others. It is in this act of sharing them that he gives witness to the truth that he is indeed made in the image of God.

There is a language for these experiences. It is a very simple and beautiful language which man has known and used since the beginning of time. It is called the language of the sign and the symbol, the outward and visible form through which is revealed the inward and invisible reality that moves and directs the soul of a man. Let us take one simple example. Are there any words that truly express human love? Yet the touch of a hand, the light of the eyes, the radiance of a face—these symbols of love are far more expressive than any words. Or sorrow—how can its depths be made known? A single tear coursing down the cheek reveals what words could never express. Then again, goodness—can anyone adequately describe it? Of course not. We know it as an act, or a hundred acts, a bent of the soul that has ruled a mind to think and a body to labor in kindness and gentleness and in sacrifice of self in the service of others. These are symbols that men have always understood. There are no words for them. Because the experiences of the soul with life's deepest realities are made known through them, they are a truly universal language. These signs and symbols are the language of the soul.

We have stated that inward realities are made known by the use of the sign and the symbol. In common practice they are used interchangeably. A sign is a symbol; a symbol is a sign. However, without becoming technical, there is a distinction that should be made between them which may be of assistance. A sign *represents*. It points to something, and takes its character from what is done with it. The cross represents the Christian faith and points to Christ's Crucifixion. A symbol *resembles*. It has acquired a deeper meaning than the sign, because it is more completely identified with what it represents, and its character is derived from what is known by it. The lamb, the sacrificial animal of the Jewish faith, was offered upon the altar as a propitiation for sin. Christ was identified as the Lamb of God because the offering of Himself upon the Cross resembled this act of atonement. The Cross symbolizes God's love for man in the sacrifice of His Son for the sins of the world.

It is in Christian symbolism that the universality of this unspoken language reaches its fullness. We can understand its development as the natural response of the Christian to his world. Christian man, in his quest after God, attaches to well-known words, actions, or things, a mystical and spiritual meaning. In this manner divine truth is recognized and a deeper insight is given to

xii

man's ability to understand God's presence in all creation. It was because the Christian Church believed the Christ to be the Saviour of all men that she used the universal language of the sign and the symbol. She was convinced that it was her task to redeem the world, and all men, under God's plan as it was now revealed in His Son. Therefore, she did not hesitate to borrow from every available source in her effort to further this commission. The sign and the symbol, particularly those most common in the realm of human experience, were given a Christian and spiritual meaning.

This book does not attempt to go beyond the age of the Renaissance in its description of religious symbolism. We have only gathered together the most generally and commonly recognized signs and symbols of this great age which, by the very nature of the religious art of the Renaissance, gave them a definitive form from which there has been little deviation. The artists of the Renaissance, under the patronage of the Church, introduced little that was new. They crystallized and ordered Christian symbolism as it had been known and experienced through the entire Christian era. It has come down to us chiefly because it was the perfecting in art form of the common experience of Christian man.

The early Christian saw God in everything. In God he "lived and moved and had his being." It followed quite naturally that, in his eyes, everything was symbolical of God. How the Christian attached religious and spiritual meaning to all that he observed is the story that this book seeks to tell. It was for this reason that we decided to include several sections that do not belong, strictly speaking, under the heading of signs and symbols, particularly those on The Old Testament, St. John the Baptist, The Virgin

Mary, and Jesus Christ. The material included in these sections is that which was most commonly portrayed by the Renaissance painters. In selecting the scenes of highest imagery for their portrayals, they broadened the scope of the field in which the signs and the symbols naturally emerged in definitive form. In other instances, such as the sections on Religious Dress, Religious Objects, and Artifacts, the symbolism was not inherent in the things described. It emerged through the use and association and identification in the mind of the Christian, as he attributed symbolical meaning to these things.

This is "The Reason Why," as Mr. Rush H. Kress has expressed the motive in his foreword. His interest and enthusiasm have been constant and happy companions in the writing of this book. I am grateful for his consent that the illustrations for this volume should be from the extensive Samuel H. Kress Collection of Renaissance art. All Biblical quotations are from the Authorized King James Version.

The assistance that has been accorded me by the staff of the Kress Foundation has been invaluable. Mr. John Walker, Chief Curator of the National Gallery of Art, Washington, D. C., has been a constant friend and advisor. The co-operation of his staff has been unfailing. Mr. Andreas Andersen, Professor of Art at the University of Arizona, was a valued colleague during the years of preparation. Mr. Mark Voris, Assistant Professor of Art at the University of Arizona, and Miss Enid Bell executed the line drawings. I wish to express my thanks to Miss Jean Card for her assistance in the preparation of this book.

GEORGE FERGUSON

Signs & Symbols in Christian Art

Section i

Animals, Birds, and Insects

¶In Christian art, the figure of the ape has been used to symbolize sin, malice, cunning, and lust. It may also symbolize the slothful soul of man: blind, greedy, sinful. Satan is sometimes portrayed in the form of an ape, and, when he is shown as an ape in chains, the idea of sin conquered by faith and virtue is conveyed. The ape sometimes appears, together with other animals, in the scenes of the Visitation of the Magi.

Ape

¶The ass is frequently portrayed in Renaissance painting, particularly in pictures of the Sacrifice of Isaac, the Nativity, the Flight into Egypt, and the Entry of Christ into Jerusalem. The most familiar portrayal is in the Nativity scenes, where the ass regularly appears. The ass and the ox symbolize that the humblest and least of the animal creation were present when Jesus was born and that they recognized Him as the Son of God. Their presence at the birth of Christ refers to the prophecy of Isaiah 1: 3, " the ox knoweth his owner, and the ass his

Ass

3

master's crib." A legend of St. Anthony of Padua may perhaps be connected with this interpretation. The saint had tried in vain to convert a Jew. He finally lost his patience and exclaimed that it would be easier to make a wild ass kneel before the Sacrament than to make the Jew see the truth of his argument. The Jew then challenged him to make the experiment. To the wonder of the people present, the wild ass did kneel, and a number of the Jews and unbelievers were converted to Christianity.

As a domestic animal, the ass appears in other legends of the saints. A typical legend, to be found in the life of St. Jerome, tells of the donkey that carried wood for the monastery.

Basilisk

⁋The basilisk is a fabulous animal, half cock and half snake. And according to legend, the basilisk could kill merely by its glance. In early symbolism, the basilisk was commonly accepted as the symbol of the Devil or the Antichrist, an interpretation based upon a passage from Psalm 91: 13, which reads in the Douay version: ". . . thou shalt tread upon the adder and the basilisk and trample under foot the lion and the dragon." These four animals were interpreted by St. Augustine as four aspects of the Devil, who was trodden down by the triumphing Christ. Though a well-established symbol, and often represented in the Middle Ages, the basilisk rarely appears in Italian paintings of the Renaissance.

I. Giovanni Antonio Bazzi, called Sodoma: *St. George and the Dragon*. National Gallery of Art, Washington

Bear

❡The bear, as a wild animal, has symbolized cruelty and evil influence. In the Old Testament it is used to represent the Kingdom of Persia, which brought death and corruption into the world, and was finally destroyed by God (Daniel 7: 5). Two bears are said to have appeared from the woods and eaten the children who mocked the prophet Elisha because of his baldness (II Kings 2: 24).

Bear cubs were believed to be born shapeless, their form being given to them by the mother bear. This legendary act became a symbol of Christianity, which reforms and regenerates heathen people. It is in this sense that a number of legends concerning the taming of a bear by a saint may be interpreted. Typical is the story of St. Euphemia, who, when thrown to the wild animals in the arena, was worshiped, rather than eaten, by the bear.

Bee

❡The bee, because of its industrious habits, has become the symbol of activity, diligence, work, and good order. Also, because the bee produces honey, it has come to be accepted as a symbol of sweetness and religious eloquence. Thus, the beehive is a recognized attribute of St. Ambrose and of St. Bernard de Clairvaux, for their eloquence is said to have been as sweet as honey. The beehive is similarly the symbol of a pious and unified community. St. Ambrose compared the Church to a beehive, and the Christian to the bee,

5

working ardently and forever true to the hive. As a producer of honey, which is a symbol of Christ, and for the virtue of its habits, the bee has been used to symbolize the virginity of Mary.

Since, according to ancient legend, the bee never sleeps, it is occasionally used to suggest Christian vigilance and zeal in acquiring virtue. (See Beehive, in Section XIV)

Birds ⁋In the earliest days of Christian art, birds were used as symbols of the "winged soul." Long before any attempt was made by the artist to identify birds according to species, the bird form was employed to suggest the spiritual, as opposed to the material. The representation of the soul by a bird goes back to the art of ancient Egypt. This symbolism may be implied in the pictures of the Christ Child holding a bird in His hand or holding one tied to a string. St. Francis of Assisi is represented preaching to the birds.

Blackbird ⁋The black feathers and the melodious song of the blackbird made it a symbol of the darkness of sin and the alluring temptations of the flesh. In this sense, it is often seen in scenes in the life of St. Benedict, who had to make such a great struggle against the temptations of the flesh. Legend relates that one day, while St. Benedict was at prayer, the Devil appeared to him in the form of a blackbird, seeking to divert his attention

from his devotions. The saint, however, recognized the bird as the Devil and vanquished him with the sign of the Cross.

Bull

⫿The bull, indicating mere brute strength, is sometimes shown kneeling at the feet of St. Sylvester, who performed the miracle of bringing a dead bull back to life. A bull of brass is the attribute of St. Eustace, who was martyred with his family by being incarcerated in a brazen bull under which a great fire was lighted. (See Ox)

Butterfly

⫿The butterfly is sometimes seen in paintings of the Virgin and Child, and is usually in the Child's hand. It is a symbol of the Resurrection of Christ. In a more general sense, the butterfly may symbolize the resurrection of all men. This meaning is derived from the three stages in its life as represented by the caterpillar, the chrysalis, and the butterfly, which are clearly symbols of life, death, and resurrection.

Camel

⫿This animal came to symbolize temperance, probably because the camel could go without drinking for such long periods of time. The camel, as the means of travel in the Orient, was not only a beast of burden but the sign of royalty and dignity. The trappings with which he was harnessed were often rich and costly. The camel was, therefore, commonly used in Renais-

7

sance art to help provide Oriental settings for Biblical themes. This was especially true in scenes depicting the Visit of the Wise Men at the Manger in Bethlehem. Camel's hair is the invariable symbol of John the Baptist, from the Biblical description of his dress, "And John was clothed with camel's hair, and with a girdle of a skin about his loins . . ." (Mark 1: 6).

Cat

❡ The cat, because of its habits, was taken as a symbol of laziness and lust. There is also the legend about the "cat of the Madonna" (*gatta della Madonna*), which tells that at the birth of Christ a cat gave birth to a litter of kittens in the same stable. This cat is usually shown with a cross-shaped marking on her back.

Centaur

❡ This fabled creature had the body of a horse and the head and bust of a human being. The figure has been used in Christian art to symbolize savage passions and excesses, especially the sin of adultery. The beast has also been used to represent brute force and vengeance; to symbolize the heretic; and to show man divided against himself, torn between good and evil. The centaur was sometimes depicted carrying a bow and arrow to symbolize the fiery darts of the wicked. The centaur frequently appears in paintings of the life of St. Anthony Abbot because, according to legend, this fabulous animal pointed out to the saint the way to reach St. Paul the Hermit in the desert.

8

Cock

The cock, because of its crowing early in the morning, is used as an emblem of watchfulness and vigilance. In paintings when the cock stands near the figure of St. Peter, it expresses his denial and subsequent repentance. In this connection, the cock also has become one of the symbols of the Passion. This is based upon Christ's response to Peter's avowal of loyalty, "Verily, verily, I say unto thee, the cock shall not crow till thou hast denied me thrice . . ." (John 13: 38).

Crane

The crane is a symbol of vigilance, loyalty, good life and works, and good order in the monastic life. All these favorable meanings are derived from the legendary habits of this bird. It is supposed that each night the cranes gather in a circle around their king. Certain cranes are selected to keep watch, and must, at all cost, avoid falling asleep. To this end, each guardian crane stands on one foot, while raising the other. In the raised foot it holds a stone which, should the crane fall asleep, would drop on the other foot and so awaken it.

Dog

The dog, because of his watchfulness and fidelity, has been accepted as the symbol of these virtues. There are many examples of the faithful dog, such as the dog of Tobias, and the dog of St. Roch, who brought bread to the saint and remained at his side. As a symbol of faithfulness in marriage, the dog is often shown at the feet or in the lap of married women. A dog with a

9

flaming torch in its mouth is a symbol of St. Dominic. Black-and-white dogs were sometimes used as symbols of the Dominicans (Domini canes, "dogs of the Lord"), who wore black-and-white habits.

Dolphin

❡The dolphin is portrayed in Christian art more frequently than any other fish. Generally, it has come to symbolize resurrection and salvation. Considered to be the strongest and swiftest of the fishes, it was often shown bearing the souls of the dead across the waters to the world beyond. Depicted with an anchor or a boat, it symbolized the Christian soul, or the Church, being guided toward salvation by Christ. It frequently represented the whale in the story of Jonah. This, in turn, led to the use of the dolphin as a symbol of the Resurrection and also, though more rarely, as a symbol of Christ.

Dove

❡The dove, in ancient and Christian art, has been the symbol of purity and peace. In the story of the flood, the dove, sent out from the ark by Noah, brought back an olive branch to show that the waters had receded and that God had made peace with man (Genesis 8).

In the law of Moses, the dove was declared to be pure and for this reason was used as an offering for purification after the birth of a child. Often Joseph carries two white doves in a basket in scenes of the Presentation of Christ in the Temple. "And when the days of her purification according to the law of Moses were accomplished, they brought him to Jerusalem, to present him to the Lord . . . And to offer a sacrifice according to that which is said in the law of the Lord, A pair of turtledoves, or two young pigeons" (Luke 2: 22, 24). As an emblem of purity the dove sometimes appears on top of Joseph's rod to show that he was chosen to be the husband of the Virgin Mary. The dove was seen by the father of St. Catherine of Siena above her head while she was in prayer.

The most important use of the dove in Christian art, however, is as the symbol of the Holy Ghost. This symbolism first appears in the story of the baptism of Christ. "And John bare record, saying, I saw the Spirit descending from heaven like a dove, and it abode upon him" (John 1: 32). The dove, symbolic of the Holy Ghost, is present in representations of the Trinity, the Baptism, and the Annunciation to Mary. Seven doves are used to represent the seven spirits of God or the Holy Spirit in its sevenfold gifts of Grace. This refers to the prophecy of Isaiah 11: 1, "And there shall come forth a rod out of the stem of Jesse, and a branch shall grow out of his roots: and the spirit of the Lord shall rest upon him, the spirit of wisdom and understanding, the spirit of counsel and might, the spirit of knowledge and of the fear of the Lord."

The dove is also connected with the lives of several saints. It is the attribute of St. Benedict because he saw the soul of his dead sister Scholastica fly up to Heaven in the shape of a white dove. The dove is also used as an attribute of St. Gregory the Great, for the dove of the Holy Spirit perched upon St. Gregory's shoulder while he wrote.

Dragon (Serpent)

❡The dragon, or serpent, was selected by the painters of the Renaissance to symbolize the Devil. The dragon as the enemy of God is vividly portrayed in Revelation 12: 7 – 9, "And there was war in heaven: Michael and his angels fought against the dragon; and the dragon fought and his angels, and prevailed not; neither was their place found anymore in heaven. And the great dragon was cast out, that old serpent, called the Devil, and Satan, which deceiveth the whole world: he was cast out into the earth, and his angels were cast out with him." The dragon, expelled from Heaven, continues his war against God. Thus, he is depicted as the devouring monster who angrily destroys his victims.

The dragon is the attribute of St. Margaret and of St. Martha, both of whom are said to have fought, and vanquished, a dragon. It is also the attribute of a number of other saints, including St. George of Cappadocia, who slew the dragon "through the power of Jesus Christ." The dragon appears with the Apostle Philip, St. Sylvester, and the Archangel Michael, who is often shown with a dragon under foot, in token of his victory over the powers of darkness.

12

The serpent, symbolizing the Devil and Satan, is depicted as the tempter of Adam and Eve. "And the Lord God said unto the Woman, What is this that thou hast done? And the woman said, The serpent beguiled me, and I did eat" (Genesis 3: 13). Thus, the serpent represents in general the wily tempter that betrays man into sin. The serpent is sometimes portrayed at the foot of the Cross to signify that the evil power responsible for man's fall has been overcome by the power of Christ, who died that man might be redeemed. (See Adam and Eve, in Section V)

⟨The eagle may generally be interpreted as a symbol of the Resurrection. This is based upon the early belief that the eagle, unlike other birds, periodically renewed its plumage and its youth by flying near the sun and then plunging into the water. This interpretation is further borne out by Psalm 103: 5, ". . . thy youth is renewed like the eagle's."

Eagle

The eagle is also used to represent the new life begun at the baptismal font and the Christian soul strengthened by grace. "But they that wait upon the Lord shall renew their strength; they shall mount up with wings as eagles. . ." (Isaiah 40: 31). The eagle is said to have the ability to soar until it is lost to sight, and still retain its ability to gaze into the blazing mid-day sun. For this reason, it has come to symbolize Christ. In a more general sense, it symbolizes those who are just; or stands for the virtues of courage, faith, and contemplation. More rarely, when it is depicted as a bird of prey, the eagle suggests the demon who ravishes souls, or the sins of pride and worldly power.

The eagle also symbolizes generosity. It was believed that the eagle, no matter how great its hunger, always left half its prey to the birds that followed.

The eagle is the particular attribute of St. John the Evangelist. The vision of Ezekiel 1: 5, 10, ". . . out of the midst thereof came the likeness of four living creatures . . . as for the likeness of their faces, they four had the face of a man, and the face of a lion . . . the face of an ox . . . the face of an eagle," was interpreted as referring to the four evangelists. Because St. John, in his Gospel, soared upward in his contemplation of the divine nature of the Saviour, the eagle became his symbol. In a more general sense, the eagle came to represent the inspiration of the gospels. It is from this symbolic interpretation that the lectern, from which the gospels are read, is often given the form of a winged eagle.

Egg ⁋The egg is the symbol of hope and resurrection. This meaning is derived from the manner in which the small chick breaks from the egg at its birth.

Ermine ⁋This small animal, because of the whiteness of its fur and the legend that it preferred death to impurity, is used to symbolize purity.

Falcon

¶ There are two kinds of falcons in religious symbolism: the wild and the domestic. The wild falcon symbolized evil thought or action, while the domestic falcon represented the holy man, or the Gentile converted to the Christian faith. As the favorite hunting bird, the domestic falcon was often represented during the Renaissance in pageants and courtly scenes, and was often held by a page in the company of the Magi.

Fish

¶ The most frequent use of the fish is as a symbol of Christ. This is because the five Greek letters forming the word "fish" are the initial letters of the five words: "Jesus Christ God's Son Saviour" ('Ιχθύς). In this sense, the fish symbol was frequently used in Early Christian art and literature. The fish is also used as a symbol of baptism, for, just as the fish cannot live except in water, the true Christian cannot live save through the waters of baptism.

In Renaissance imagery, the fish is given as an attribute to Tobias because the gall of a fish restored the sight of his father Tobit; it is also given as an attribute to St. Peter, an allusion to his being a fisherman; and to St. Anthony of Padua, who preached to the fish.

Fly

¶ The fly has long been considered a bearer of evil or pestilence. In Christian symbolism the fly is a symbol of sin. It sometimes appears in pictures of the Virgin and Child to convey the idea of sin and redemption.

The fly as a bringer of disease was sometimes shown with the goldfinch, a "saviour-bird" against disease.

Fox  ⁋Traditionally the symbol of cunning and guile, the fox also symbolized the Devil. Though it was shown frequently in sculpture during the Middle Ages, it was for the most part confined to book illustration during the Renaissance.

Frog  ⁋Because of his continuous croaking and the fact that a rain of frogs was one of the plagues of Egypt (Exodus 8), the frog has been given a devilish significance, and has sometimes been likened to heretics. Usually in paintings it conveys the repulsive aspect of sin. More loosely, it is interpreted as a symbol of those who snatch at life's fleeting pleasures; hence it represents worldly things in general.

Giraffe ⁋In the Renaissance the giraffe was depicted more because of its strange appearance and its rarity among animals in Europe than for any symbolic meaning.

Goat  ⁋In Early Christian art, the goat was taken as a symbol of the damned in the Last Judgment. This interpretation is based upon a long passage in the Bible (Matthew 25: 31-46) which relates how Christ, upon His coming, shall separate the believing from the unbelieving, as the shepherd separates the sheep from the goats.

16

In the Renaissance the goat was usually shown in order to distinguish the sinners from the righteous.

¶The goldfinch is fond of eating thistles and thorns, and since all thorny plants have been accepted as an allusion to Christ's crown of thorns, the goldfinch has become an accepted symbol of the Passion of Christ. In this sense, it frequently appears with the Christ Child, showing the close connection between the Incarnation and the Passion.

Goldfinch

¶Since the time of the Romans, the goose has been a symbol of providence and vigilance. The legend of the Capitoline geese that saved Rome from the invasion of the Gauls is well known. In Christian art the goose is sometimes given as an attribute to St. Martin of Tours, because a goose is supposed to have revealed his hiding place to the inhabitants of Tours, who had come to call the saint to be their bishop.

Goose

¶The grasshopper, or locust, was one of the plagues visited upon the Egyptians because the Pharaoh's heart was hardened against the Word of the Lord. Accordingly, the grasshopper when held by the Christ Child is a symbol of the conversion of nations to Christianity. This meaning is also derived from Proverbs 30: 27, " The locusts have no king, yet go they forth all of them by bands," a passage early interpreted as referring

Grasshopper
(Locust)

to the nations formerly without Christ for their King. St. John the Baptist was said to have fed on locusts.

Griffin

⁋This fabulous creature, usually depicted with the head and wings of an eagle and the body of a lion, is used with two different and opposite meanings: on the one hand to represent the Saviour; on the other, because it is a combination of the preying of the eagle and the fierceness of the lion, to symbolize those who oppress and persecute the Christians.

Hare
(Rabbit)

⁋The hare, itself defenseless, is a symbol of men who put the hope of their salvation in the Christ and His Passion. It is also a well-known symbol of lust and fecundity. A white hare is sometimes placed at the feet of the Virgin Mary to indicate her triumph over lust.

Hog

⁋The hog is used to represent the demon of sensuality and gluttony. The hog is frequently shown as one of the attributes of Anthony Abbot, for he is reputed to have vanquished this demon.

Horse

⁋In ancient mythology the horse was the emblem of the sun, as the ox was that of the moon. In the Renaissance, however, the horse was most often depicted as a symbol of lust. This interpretation is based on Jeremiah 5: 8, "They were as fed horses in the morning: every one neighed after his neighbor's wife."

18

Lamb

⟨The lamb, as a symbol of Christ, is one of the favorite, and most frequently used, symbols in all periods of Christian art. Many scriptural passages give authority for this symbolism. A typical reference is John 1: 29, "The next day John seeth Jesus coming unto him, and saith, Behold the Lamb of God, which taketh away the sin of the world!" The Holy Lamb is often depicted with a nimbus, standing upon a small hill from which four streams of water flow (Revelation 14: 1). The hill represents the Church of Christ, the mountain of God's house. The streams represent the four Holy Gospels, the four rivers of Paradise, ever flowing and refreshing the pastures of the Church on earth.

In pictures where Christ is shown as the rescuing shepherd, the lamb is also used to symbolize the sinner. This subject, usually called the Good Shepherd, is very frequent in Early Christian art, but was seldom used in the Renaissance.

During the Renaissance the lamb was often depicted in representations of the Holy Family with the Infant St. John. Here, the lamb alludes to St. John's mission as the forerunner of Christ, and his recognition of Christ as the Lamb of God at the time of His Baptism. This meaning is indicated by the portrayal of St. John the Baptist pointing to a lamb which he usually holds in his left hand. The lamb (Latin, *agnus*) is given as an attribute to St. Agnes, who was martyred because she declared herself to be the bride of Christ and refused to marry. It is also found as an attribute of St. Clement, who was guided by a lamb to the spot where he found water.

Lark ❡ The lark, because it flies high and sings only when in flight toward Heaven, has been taken as the symbol of the humility of priesthood.

Leopard  ❡ The leopard is a symbol of sin, cruelty, the Devil, and the Antichrist. It sometimes appears in representations of the Adoration of the Magi to show that the Incarnation of Christ was necessary for redemption from sin.

Lion ❡ The lion is used in Renaissance art with various meanings, depending upon the circumstances. In general, the lion is emblematic of strength, majesty, courage, and fortitude. Legendary natural history states that young lions are born dead, but come to life three days after birth when breathed upon by their sire. Thus, the lion has become associated with the Resurrection, and is the symbol of Christ, the Lord of Life.

The lion is one of the four animals that appear in the prophecy of Ezekiel. He is the symbol of the Evangelist Mark because St. Mark in his Gospel dwells most fully upon the Resurrection of Christ and proclaims with great emphasis the royal dignity of Christ. The winged lion is invariably the attribute of St. Mark, and it appears also as the emblem of Venice, because this city

was under the protection of St. Mark. St. Jerome is also closely identified with the lion. It is said that the saint removed a painful thorn from the paw of a lion, who thereupon became his close and faithful friend.

It was a medieval belief that the lion slept with its eyes open. For this reason, he also became a symbol of watchfulness. In rarer instances the lion, because of its pride and fierceness, was used as a symbol of the Prince of Darkness, this interpretation being supported by Psalm 91: 13, "Thou shalt tread upon the lion and adder . . ." This passage is interpreted as Christ triumphing over the Devil. In addition, lions appear as attributes of St. Mary of Egypt, St. Euphemia, St. Onuphrius, and St. Paul the Hermit.

Owl

❡ The owl, since it hides in darkness and fears the light, has come to symbolize Satan, the Prince of Darkness. As Satan deceives humanity, so the owl is said to trick other birds, causing them to fall into the snares set by hunters. The owl also symbolizes solitude and, in this sense, appears in scenes of hermits at prayer. Its most ancient gift, however, is that of wisdom, and, with this meaning, it is sometimes shown with St. Jerome.

In another sense, the owl is an attribute of Christ, who sacrificed Himself to save mankind, "To give light to them that sit in darkness and in the shadow of death . . ." (Luke 1: 79). This explains the presence of the owl in scenes of the Crucifixion.

21

Ox

❡The ox, a sacrificial animal of the Jews, was often used in Renaissance painting to represent the Jewish nation. It is also used as a symbol of patience and strength. Almost invariably, the ox and the ass appear together in paintings of the Nativity. (See Ass)

In the writings of some of the early Christian fathers, the ox is accepted as a symbol of Christ, the true sacrifice. The symbol is similarly used to represent all who patiently bear their yoke while laboring in silence for the good of others. The winged ox is the attribute of St. Luke because of his emphasis upon the sacrificial aspects of our Lord's atonement as well as upon His divine priesthood.

Partridge

❡In a good sense, the partridge is used as a symbol of the Church and of truth; but it is ordinarily symbolic of deceit and theft, and in a more general sense, of the Devil: "As the partridge sitteth on eggs, and hatcheth them not; so he that getteth riches, and not by right, shall leave them in the midst of his days, and at his end shall be a fool" (Jeremiah 17: 11).

Peacock

❡In Christian art the peacock is used as the symbol of immortality. This symbolism is derived from the legendary belief that the flesh of the peacock does not decay. It is with this meaning that it appears in scenes of the Nativity. The "hundred eyes" in the peacock's tail are sometimes used to symbolize the "all-seeing" Church.

The peacock's habit of strutting and displaying the beauty of its feathers has caused it also to become a symbol of worldly pride and vanity. A peacock's feather is often an attribute of St. Barbara, in reference to Heliopolis, the city of her birth.

Pelican

⟨According to legend, the pelican, which has the greatest love of all creatures for its offspring, pierces its breast to feed them with its own blood. It is on the basis of this legend that the pelican came to symbolize Christ's sacrifice on the Cross, because of His love for all mankind. In this sense, it also symbolizes the Eucharistic Sacrament. This interpretation is supported by Psalm 102:6, "I am like a pelican of the wilderness," which is an accepted allusion to Christ. The pelican is sometimes shown nesting on the top of the Cross.

Phoenix

⟨The phoenix was a mythical bird of great beauty which lived in the Arabian wilderness. Its life span was said to be between three hundred and five hundred years. Periodically, it burned itself upon a funeral pyre; whereupon, it would rise from its own ashes, restored to all the freshness of youth, and would enter upon another cycle of life.

The phoenix was introduced into Christian symbolism as early as the first century, when the legend of this bird was related by St. Clement in his first Epistle to the Corinthians. In Early Christian art, the phoenix

23

constantly appears on funeral stones, its particular meaning being the resurrection of the dead and the triumph of eternal life over death. The phoenix later became a symbol of the Resurrection of Christ, and commonly appears in connection with the Crucifixion. In another sense, the phoenix stands for faith and constancy. Though popular in the art of the Middle Ages, the phoenix is rare in Italian Renaissance paintings.

Ram

❡Because the ram is the leader of the herd, sometimes it was used as a symbol for Christ. Also, in the same way that the ram fights with the wolf and vanquishes him, so Christ battles with Satan and is victorious. The ram, the animal God caused to be placed in a thorny bush so that Abraham might sacrifice it in place of his son Isaac, represents Christ crowned with thorns and sacrificed for mankind. In a general sense, the ram is used as a symbol for strength.

Rat
(Mouse)

❡The rat, or the mouse, because of its destructiveness, is symbolic of evil. It is rarely seen in Renaissance art, except as an attribute of St. Fina.

Raven

❡According to a Jewish legend, the raven was originally white, but its feathers turned black when it failed to return to the ark, from which Noah had sent it to find out if the flood had abated. Because of the blackness of its plumage, its supposed habit of devouring the eyes and the brain of the dead, and its liking for spoiled flesh, the raven was selected as a symbol of the Devil, who throws the soul into darkness, invades the intelligence, and is gratified by corruption. The raven appears in a more favorable light in relation to certain saints. It is the attribute of St. Vincent because God sent a raven to guard his sacred remains. The raven is also the attribute of St. Anthony Abbot and St. Paul the Hermit because it brought them a loaf of bread each day when they lived together in the desert. The raven, as symbolizing solitude, is associated with these hermit saints.

⁋ The scorpion is one of the symbols of evil. The sting of the tail of the scorpion is poisonous and causes great agony to a person who is stung. It is often mentioned in the Bible, ". . . and their torment was the torment of a scorpion, when it striketh a man" (Revelation 9: 5). Because of the treachery of its bite, the scorpion became a symbol of Judas. As a symbol of treachery, the scorpion appears on the flags and shields held by the soldiers who assisted at the Crucifixion of Christ.

Scorpion

⁋ The shell, notably the cockleshell, or the scallop shell, is generally used in Christian art to signify pilgrimage. The scallop shell is used specifically as an attribute of St. James the Great. It is generally supposed to allude to the countless pilgrimages that were made to his celebrated shrine at Compostella in Spain. St. Roch is

Shell

25

customarily painted in the dress of a pilgrim with a cockleshell in his hat.

Snail ⟨The snail was believed to be born from the mud, and to feed upon it. It was, therefore, interpreted as the symbol of the sinner, and of laziness, because it made no effort to seek food, but ate what it found at hand.

Sparrow ⟨Considered to be the lowliest among all birds, the sparrow came to be used as a symbol of the lowly, the least among all people, who were, nevertheless, under the protection of God the Father; for even the sparrow came to earth only through the will of God, and received from Him its means of life.

Spider ⟨The spider is used symbolically, first, to represent the miser, for it bleeds the fly as the miser bleeds the poor; second, to represent the Devil, for the Devil prepares his traps as the spider does its web; and third, to represent the malice of evil-doers whose webs will perish like those of the spider. The cobweb is a symbol of human frailty.

Stag ⟨The stag takes its symbolic significance from Psalm 42: 1, "As the hart panteth after the water brooks, so panteth my soul after thee, O God." Thus, the stag has come to typify piety and religious aspiration. Similarly, because the stag seeks freedom and refuge in the high mountains, it has been used to symbolize solitude and purity of life.

The stag, as the attribute of St. Eustace and St. Hubert, is shown with a crucifix between its horns. The stag without the crucifix is an attribute of St. Julian the Hospitator.

❡The stork is a symbol of prudence and vigilance, piety, and chastity. It was associated with the Annunciation because, as the stork announces the coming of spring, the Annunciation to Mary indicated the Advent of Christ. It is possible that the present north European tradition that new born babies are carried to their mothers by storks may be derived from the association of this bird with the Annunciation.

Stork

❡In the Renaissance the swallow was a symbol of the Incarnation of Christ. For this reason, it appears in scenes of the Annunciation and of the Nativity, nestling under the eaves or in holes in the wall. It was thought that the swallow hibernated in the mud during the winter, and its advent in the spring was looked upon as a rebirth from the death-like state of winter. For this reason it also became a symbol of resurrection.

Swallow

❡The unicorn, according to the myth, was a small animal, similar in size to a kid, but surprisingly fierce and swift, with a very sharp, single horn in the center of its

Unicorn

forehead. Supposedly no hunter could capture the animal by force, but it could be taken by means of a trick. The hunter was required to lead a virgin to the spot frequented by the unicorn and to leave her alone there. The unicorn, sensing the purity of the maiden, would run to her, lay its head in her lap, and fall asleep. Thus its capture would be effected. For obvious reasons the unicorn was early accepted as the symbol of purity in general and of feminine chastity in particular. The legend was interpreted by Christian writers as an allegory of the Annunciation and the Incarnation of Christ, born of a Virgin.

Thus, the unicorn is usually an attribute of the Virgin Mary, but also of St. Justina of Padua and of St. Justina of Antioch, who retained their purity under great temptation.

Whale

⟨According to ancient legend, the huge body of the whale was often mistaken by mariners for an island, and ships anchored to its side were dragged down to destruction by a sudden plunge of the great creature. In this way, the whale came to be used as a symbol of the Devil and of his cunning, and the whale's open mouth was often depicted to represent the open gates of Hell.

The whale also appears in the Biblical story of Jonah, who was swallowed by a whale and disgorged three days later. Allegorically, the experience of Jonah is likened to Christ in the sepulchre and His Resurrection after three days. Unfamiliarity with the appearance and habits of the whale, and even with the identification of the Biblical sea-monster as such, prevented the artists of the Italian Renaissance from painting naturalistic whales. Rather, Jonah's monster was, to them, either something in the way of a dragon, a great shaggy fish, or a dolphin.

Wolf

¶The wolf is sometimes used as an attribute of St. Francis of Assisi. This is based on the famous story of the wolf of Gubbio. A wolf that had been doing great damage was being hunted by the people of Gubbio, when St. Francis encountered it. He addressed it as "Brother Wolf," and protected it as a fellow creature who knew no better, and set about to reform it.

Woodpecker

¶The woodpecker is usually symbolic of the Devil, or of heresy, which undermines human nature and leads man to damnation.

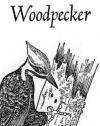

Section ii

Flowers, Trees, and Plants

❡The acacia is a symbol of the immortality of the soul.

❡The almond is a symbol of divine approval or favor. This symbolism is based upon Numbers 17: 1-8, in which it is told how Aaron was chosen to be the priest of the Lord through the miracle of his budding rod: ". . . and, behold, the rod of Aaron for the house of Levi was budded, and brought forth buds, and bloomed blossoms, and yielded almonds." It is with reference to this passage that the almond became a symbol of the Virgin Mary. (See Mandorla, in Section XI)

Almond

❡In pagan mythology, the anemone was a symbol of sorrow and death. Such a belief was based upon the legend of Adonis, who is believed to have died on a bed of anemones, which then turned from white to red. Christian symbolism has also attributed to the anemone the suggestion of illness. The anemone may be depicted in scenes of the Crucifixion, or in conjunction with the Virgin Mary to show her sorrow for the Passion of Christ. The red spots on the petals symbolize the blood

Anemone

31

of Christ, for it is said that anemones sprang up on Calvary the evening of the Crucifixion. In the early days of the Church, the triple leaf of this plant was used to symbolize the Trinity.

Apple

¶In Latin, the word for apple and the word for evil, *malum*, are identical. It is for this reason that the legend has grown up that the Tree of Knowledge in the Garden of Eden, the fruit of which Adam and Eve were forbidden to eat, was an apple tree (Genesis 3: 3). In pictures of the tempting of Eve by the serpent in the Garden of Eden, Eve is generally shown with an apple in her hand, offering it to Adam. The apple may also be symbolic of Christ, the new Adam, who took upon himself the burden of man's sin. For this reason, when the apple appears in the hands of Adam it means sin, but when it is in the hands of Christ, it symbolizes the fruit of salvation. Such interpretation is based upon the Song of Solomon 2: 3, "As the apple tree among the trees of the wood, so is my beloved among the sons. I sat down under his shadow with great delight, and his fruit was sweet to my taste." This passage has been interpreted as an allusion to Christ.

As Christ is the new Adam, so, in tradition, the Virgin Mary is considered to be the new Eve and, for this reason, an apple placed in the hands of Mary is also considered an allusion to salvation. Three apples are an attribute of St. Dorothea.

II. Carlo Crivelli: *Madonna and Child*. National Gallery of Art, Washington

in Christian Art

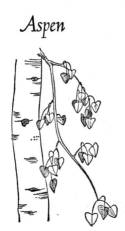

Aspen

❡ There are two early legends about the aspen tree. One relates that the Cross was made from the aspen, and that, when the tree realized the purpose for which it was being used, its leaves began to tremble with horror and have never ceased. The other legend is that, as Christ died on the Cross, all the trees bowed in sorrow except the aspen. Because of its pride and sinful arrogance, the leaves of the aspen were doomed to continual trembling.

Bramble

❡ The bramble was believed to be the burning bush in which the angel of the Lord appeared to Moses, ". . . the bush burned with fire, and the bush was not consumed" (Exodus 3: 2). The bramble has become a symbol of the purity of the Virgin Mary, who bore the flames of divine love without being consumed by lust.

Bulrush

❡ The bulrush is a lowly, thickly clustered, common plant, growing near the water. Because of these characteristics, it has become a symbol for the multitude of the faithful who lead a humble life and abide by the teaching of the Church, the source of living waters. This explanation found support in Job 8: 11, "Can the rush grow up without mire? Can the flag grow without water?" Also, since the infant Moses (and Moses is taken as the forerunner of Christ) was found in the bulrushes, they have come to be connected with the place whence salvation came.

Carnation

❡The red carnation is a symbol of pure love. According to a Flemish custom, a variety of carnation, the pink, was worn by the bride upon the day of her wedding, and the groom was supposed to search her and find it. From this custom, the pink has become a symbol of marriage. Newlyweds are often shown carrying a pink in their hands.

Cedar

❡The cedar tree, particularly the cedar of Lebanon, is a symbol of Christ: ". . . his countenance is as Lebanon, excellent as the cedars" (Song of Solomon 5:15). The stately form of the cedar caused it to be identified with the concepts of beauty and majesty. The prophet Ezekiel used the cedar as a symbol of the Messiah and His Kingdom. ". . . I will also take of the highest branch of the high cedar . . . and will plant it upon an high mountain and eminent" (Ezekiel 17:22).

Cherry

❡The red, sweet fruit of the cherry symbolizes the sweetness of character which is derived from good works. It is often called the Fruit of Paradise. A cherry, held in the hand of the Christ Child, suggests the delights of the blessed.

Chestnut

❡The chestnut in its husk is surrounded by thorns, but is unharmed by them. For this reason it is a symbol of chastity, because this virtue is a triumph over the temptations of the flesh, symbolized by the thorns.

34

¶The clover, with its three leaves, is an obvious symbol of the Trinity. According to legend, clover was given as an example of the Trinity by St. Patrick when he evangelized Ireland, and thus the clover, or shamrock, has become the emblem of Ireland. Another name for the three-leafed clover is "trefoil."

Clover

¶The cockle is a common weed that often invades the tilled fields and intermingles with the planted grain. It symbolizes wickedness invading the good field of the Church. "Let thistles grow instead of wheat and cockle instead of barley" (Job 31: 40).

Cockle

¶The form of this flower has been likened to a white dove, and, for this reason, columbine has been used to symbolize the Holy Ghost. Columbine is derived from the Latin word for dove, *columba*. Seven blooms on a stalk were symbolic of the seven gifts of the Spirit, according to the prophecy of Isaiah 11: 2, "And the spirit of the Lord shall rest upon him, the spirit of wisdom and understanding, the spirit of counsel and might, the spirit of knowledge and of the fear of the Lord."

Columbine

¶This plant was early dedicated to the Virgin Mary. The red spot at the heart of the flower signifies the bleeding sorrow in Mary's heart. The cyclamen is sometimes called "bleeding nun."

Cyclamen

35

Cypress ❡The cypress, even in pagan times, was associated with death. It is found in many cemeteries, both Christian and pagan. Carvings depicting the cypress are found on many Christian tombs. There were several reasons for associating the cypress with death; for example, it has dark foliage and, once cut, it never springs up again from its roots.

Daisy ❡Toward the end of the fifteenth century the daisy came to be used in paintings of the "Adoration" as a symbol of the innocence of the Christ Child. Apparently, the sweet simplicity of the daisy was felt to be a better symbol of His innocence than the tall, stately lily.

Dandelion ❡One of the "bitter herbs," the dandelion, was used as a symbol of the Passion, and as such appears, among other flowers, in paintings of the Madonna and Child, and of the Crucifixion.

Elm ❡The elm alludes to the dignity of life. Its all-encompassing growth and the spreading of its great branches in every direction symbolizes the strength which is derived by the devout from their faith in the Scriptures.

Fern ❡The fern conceals its grace, delicacy, and beauty in the shadowed glens of the forest. Because the charm of this plant is seen only by the honest searcher, the fern symbolizes solitary humility, frankness, and sincerity.

36

¶ The fig tree is sometimes used, instead of the apple tree, as the Tree of Knowledge in the Garden of Eden. The leaf of the fig tree appears in the story of the Fall in Genesis 3: 7, "And the eyes of them both were opened, and they knew that they were naked; and they sewed fig leaves together and made themselves aprons." From this allusion to its leaf, the fig has become a symbol of lust. Its many seeds have made it also a symbol of fertility.

Fig

¶ The fir tree is a symbol of the elect in Heaven, who despise lowly desires. It also symbolizes people who excel in the virtue of patience.

Fir

¶ Fruit is often used to suggest the twelve fruits of the Spirit: love, joy, peace, long-suffering, gentleness, goodness, faith, meekness, patience, modesty, temperance, and chastity.

Fruit

¶ The gourd is prominent in the story of Jonah, and, because of this association with him, has come to symbolize the Resurrection (Jonah 4). When painted together with an apple, the gourd, as the symbol of the Resurrection, is the antidote for the apple, the symbol of evil, or death.

The gourd was used by pilgrims as a flask to carry water. It is the special attribute of St. James the Great, and of the Archangel Raphael, and is sometimes given

Gourd

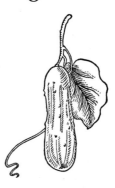

to Christ, who, dressed as a pilgrim, joined the two Apostles on their way to Emmaus. Frequently, in art the gourd resembles a cucumber.

Grain   ⸿Wheat, a well-known Eucharistic symbol, is used to suggest the human nature of Christ. This interpretation is based upon John 12: 24, "Verily, verily, I say unto you, except a corn of wheat fall into the ground and die, it abideth alone; but if it die, it bringeth forth much fruit." Ears of grain and bunches of grapes are used to symbolize the bread and wine of Holy Communion.

Grapes   ⸿Bunches of grapes with ears of grain were some-times used to symbolize the wine and bread of Holy Communion. In general, the grape, like the Eucharistic wine, is a symbol of the Blood of Christ. Representations of labor in the vineyard sometimes signify the work of good Christians in the vineyard of the Lord; the grape vine or leaf is used as an emblem of the Saviour, the "true vine." (See Vine)

Hyacinth   ⸿The hyacinth is sometimes regarded as a symbol of Christian prudence, peace of mind, and the desire for Heaven. Its symbolism is derived from pagan mythology, being based upon the legend of the beautiful youth, Hyacinthus, who was accidentally killed by Apollo, while playing with the discus. Apollo then caused the hyacinth to spring from the youth's blood.

38

¶This plant, which grows in solitary places among stones, is used to symbolize penitence and humility. Due to its purgative qualities, it is also taken to symbolize innocence regained and, hence, baptism. "Purge me with hyssop, and I shall be clean: wash me, and I shall be whiter than snow" (Psalm 51: 7).

Hyssop

¶The ilex, or holly oak, is an evergreen which, because of its thorny leaves, is regarded as a symbol of Christ's crown of thorns. It is also said to have been the tree of the Cross and, therefore, is symbolic of the Passion of Christ. A legend relates that all the trees, when they heard that Christ was to be crucified, agreed not to allow their wood to be defiled for this purpose. When the axe touched them, they all splintered into a thousand fragments. Only the ilex remained whole and permitted itself to be used as the instrument of the Passion. It is often found in paintings of St. Jerome meditating on the Passion, or of St. John the Baptist, who, by acclaiming Christ the Lamb of God, foretold His Passion.

Ilex
(Holly)

¶The iris, a rival of the lily as the flower of the Virgin, first appears as a religious symbol in the works of the early Flemish masters, where it both accompanies and replaces the lily in pictures of the Virgin. This symbolism stems from the fact that the name "iris" means "sword lily," which was taken as an allusion to the sorrow of the Virgin at the Passion of Christ.

Iris

Spanish painters adopted the iris as the attribute of the Queen of Heaven and also as an attribute of the Immaculate Conception. (See Lily)

Ivy ⁋Symbolically, the ivy has always been closely identified with death and immortality. Because it is forever green, it is a symbol of fidelity and eternal life. The ivy, which clings to its support, is also a symbol of attachment and undying affection.

Jasmine ⁋The white color and sweet scent of the jasmine make it a symbol of the Virgin Mary. As a secondary meaning, it may signify grace, elegance, and amiability.

Lady's Bed-Straw ⁋This lowly plant received its common name from the legend that some pieces of it were mingled with the straw in the manger where the Infant Christ was laid.

Laurel ⁋The laurel symbolizes triumph, eternity, and chastity. The victor in ancient contests was crowned with a wreath of laurel. St. Paul contrasts this wreath with the imperishable wreath with which the victorious Christian is crowned (I Corinthians 9: 24 - 27). This, with the fact that laurel leaves never wilt but preserve their green foliage, makes it symbolic of eternity. Its association with chastity is probably derived from the pagan symbolism that the laurel was consecrated to the Vestal Virgins, who vowed perpetual chastity.

40

¶The lemon is a symbol of fidelity in love, and, as such, is often associated with the Virgin Mary.

Lemon

¶The lily is a symbol of purity, and has become the flower of the Virgin. Originally, in Christian symbolism, the lily was used as the attribute of the virgin saints. The lily among thorns has become a symbol of the Immaculate Conception of the Virgin, in token of the purity she preserved amid the sins of the world. One incident in the life of the Virgin, the Annunciation, is particularly associated with lilies. In many of the scenes of the Annunciation painted during the Renaissance, the Archangel Gabriel holds a lily, or a lily is placed in a vase between the Virgin and the Announcing Angel. Because of this, the lily has become an attribute of the Archangel Gabriel.

Lily

Occasionally, the Infant Christ is represented offering a spray of lilies to a saint. Here the lily symbolizes the virtue of chastity. As a symbol of chastity, the lily is the attribute of several saints, among them St. Dominic, St. Francis, St. Anthony of Padua, St. Clare, and St. Joseph.

The fleur-de-lis, a variety of lily, is the emblem of royalty. The fleur-de-lis was chosen by King Clovis as an emblem of his purification through baptism, and this flower has since become the emblem of the kings of France. For this reason, the flower is an attribute of St. Louis of France and St. Louis of Toulouse, both of them members of the royal house of France. The fleur-de-lis was also the emblem of the city of Florence. As an attribute of royalty, the fleur-de-lis appears on crowns and sceptres of kingly saints, and is given to the Virgin Mary as Queen of Heaven.

Lily of the Valley

¶The lily of the valley is one of the first flowers of the year and announces the return of spring. For this reason it has become a symbol of the Advent of Christ. For the whiteness of its flowers and the sweetness of its scent it is a symbol of the Virgin Mary, especially of her Immaculate Conception. The latter meaning is based upon Song of Solomon 2: 1, " I am the rose of Sharon, and the lily of the valleys."

Myrtle

¶The evergreen myrtle has from very early times been used as the symbol of love. In Roman mythology the myrtle was considered sacred to Venus, the goddess of love. In Christian symbolism the myrtle is an allusion to the Gentiles who were converted by Christ. This interpretation is based upon Zechariah 1: 8, "I saw by night, and behold a man riding upon a red horse, and he stood among the myrtle trees that were in the bottom; and behind him were there red horses, speckled, and white." This passage was interpreted as showing Christ, the man riding upon the red horse amid the Gentiles and followed by the hierarchies of martyrs and confessors.

42

Narcissus

⁋The symbolism of the narcissus, which represents self-ishness and self-love, coldness, and indifference, refers to the Greek legend of the youth Narcissus, who fell in love with his own image when he saw it in the water and drowned while trying to embrace it. After his death, the youth was changed into a flower, the nar-cissus. This flower is sometimes depicted in scenes of the Annunciation or of Paradise to show the triumph of divine love, sacrifice, and eternal life over death, selfishness, and sin.

Oak

⁋Long before the Christian era, the ancient Celtic cult of the Druids worshiped the oak. As was often the case with pagan superstitions, the veneration of the oak tree was absorbed into Christian symbolism and its mean-ing changed into a symbol of Christ or the Virgin Mary. The oak was one of the several species of trees that were looked upon as the tree from which the Cross was made. (See Ilex, Aspen)

Because of its solidity and endurance, the oak is also a symbol of the strength of faith and virtue, and of the endurance of the Christian against adversity.

Olive

⁋The olive is a true Biblical tree, a tree "full of fatness" which yields great quantities of oil. Its rich yield sym-bolized the providence of God toward His children. " The trees went forth . . . to anoint a king over them; and they said unto the olive tree, Reign thou over us.

43

But the olive tree said unto them, Should I leave my fatness, wherewith by me they honour God and man . . .?" (Judges 9: 8 - 9).

The olive branch has always been regarded as a symbol of peace, and appears as such in allegorical paintings of Peace. It will be recalled that when Noah was in the ark during the flood, he sent forth a dove to find out whether the waters had receded from the earth. "And the dove came in to him in the evening; and, lo, in her mouth was an olive leaf plucked off: so Noah knew that the waters were abated from off the earth" (Genesis 8: 11). In this passage, the olive branch is symbolic of the peace God made with men. A dove with an olive twig in its beak is often used to indicate that the souls of the deceased have departed in the peace of God. As a token of peace, an olive branch is carried by the Archangel Gabriel to the Virgin Mary in scenes of the Annunciation. This symbolism was especially favored by painters of the Sienese school; they wished to avoid the representation of the lily, the customary symbol of the Annunciation, because it was also the emblem of Florence, the declared enemy of Siena.

Orange ❡The orange tree is regarded as a symbol of purity, chastity, and generosity. Thus, it is occasionally depicted in paintings of the Virgin Mary. The orange tree was sometimes used instead of the apple tree or the fig tree in scenes showing the fall of man. When it is seen

44

in representations of Paradise, it alludes to the fall of man and his redemption. The white flower is also used to suggest purity, and for this reason orange blossoms are the traditional adornment of brides.

℧ Among the Romans, the palm frond was traditionally the symbol of victory. This meaning was carried into Christian symbolism, where the palm branch was used to suggest the martyr's triumph over death. Martyrs are often depicted with the palm either in place of or in addition to the instruments of their martyrdom. Christ is often shown bearing the palm branch as a symbol of His triumph over sin and death. More often, it is associated with His triumphant entry into Jerusalem. "On the next day much people that were come to the feast, where they heard that Jesus was coming to Jerusalem, took branches of palm trees, and went forth to meet him, and cried, Hosanna; Blessed is the King of Israel that cometh in the name of the Lord" (John 12: 12 - 13).

Palm

A palm-tree staff is the attribute of St. Christopher, in reference to the legend that he uprooted a palm tree to support himself on his travels. After carrying Christ across the river, he thrust the staff into the ground, whereupon it took root and bore fruit. A dress made of palm leaves is an attribute of St. Paul the Hermit.

℧ Though rarely depicted in the Renaissance, the pansy is a symbol of remembrance and meditation.

Pansy

Peach ⁋The peach is symbolic of the silence of virtue and of a virtuous heart and tongue. Sometimes it appears in paintings of the Virgin and Child, in place of the apple, to symbolize the fruit of salvation.

Pear ⁋The pear frequently appears in connection with the Incarnate Christ, in allusion to His love for mankind.

Plane Tree ⁋The plane tree, which spreads its branches high and wide, has become a symbol of charity, firmness of character, and moral superiority. It is more specifically a symbol of the charity of Christ.

Plantain ⁋The plantain, often seen in Renaissance paintings, is a common and lowly plant which thrives along roads and pathways. It became known as "way bread" and a symbol of the "well-trodden path" of the multitude that seek the path to Christ.

Plum ⁋The plum is symbolic of fidelity and independence. However, it was most frequently used in Renaissance painting for decorative purposes.

Pomegranate ⁋In Christian symbolism, the pomegranate as a rule alludes to the Church because of the inner unity of countless seeds in one and the same fruit.

In pagan mythology, it was an attribute of Proserpina and symbolized her periodical return to earth in

the spring. From this pagan symbolism of the return of spring and rejuvenation of the earth was derived the second symbolism of the pomegranate in Christian art, that of hope in immortality and of resurrection.

The pomegranate, because of its many seeds, was also a symbol of fertility.

Poppy

❡The poppy is a symbol of fertility, sleep, ignorance, extravagance, and indifference. It is sometimes depicted in allusion to the Passion of Christ because of its blood-red color and its meaning of sleep and death.

Reed

❡The reed is one of the symbols of the Passion, for, on the Cross, Christ was tendered a sponge soaked in vinegar on the end of a reed. It thus symbolizes the humiliation of greatness. It is also sometimes used to represent the just, who dwell on the banks of the waters of grace. The small cross carried by St. John the Baptist is commonly made of reeds.

Rose

❡Traditionally, among the ancient Romans, the rose was the symbol of victory, pride, and triumphant love. It was the flower of Venus, goddess of love.

In Christian symbolism, the red rose is a symbol of martyrdom, while the white rose is a symbol of purity. This interpretation has been current since the earliest years of Christianity. St. Ambrose relates how the rose came to have thorns. Before it became one of the flowers of the earth, the rose grew in Paradise without thorns. Only after the fall of man did the rose take on its thorns to remind man of the sins he had committed and his fall from grace; whereas its fragrance and beauty continued to remind him of the splendor of Paradise. It is probably in reference to this legend that the Virgin Mary is called a "rose without thorns," because of the tradition that she was exempt from the consequences of original sin.

In Renaissance art, a garland of roses is often an allusion to the rosary of the Blessed Virgin. (See Rosary, in Section XIII)

Wreaths of roses worn by angels, saints, or by human souls who have entered into heavenly bliss are indicative of heavenly joy.

In accordance with a very ancient custom dating as far back as the time of Pope Gregory I, the sending of a golden rose by the Pope to people of distinction is a symbol of special papal benediction.

An apron full of roses is an attribute of St. Elisabeth of Hungary, while a basket of roses and apples is used to identify St. Dorothea of Cappadocia.

Strawberry

¶The strawberry is the symbol of perfect righteousness, or the emblem of the righteous man whose fruits are good works. When shown with other fruits and flowers, it represents the good works of the righteous or the fruits of the spirit. It is in line with this meaning

48

III. Francesco Pesellino: *The Crucifixion with St. Jerome and St. Francis.*
National Gallery of Art, Washington

that the Virgin is sometimes shown clad in a dress decorated with clusters of strawberries. The strawberry is occasionally shown accompanied by violets to suggest that the truly spiritual are always humble.

Thistle

¶The thistle is the symbol of earthly sorrow and sin because of the curse pronounced against Adam by God, in Genesis 3: 17 - 18, ". . . cursed is the ground for thy sake; in sorrow shalt thou eat of it all the days of thy life; thorns also and thistles shall it bring forth to thee; and thou shalt eat the herb of the field." The thistle is a thorny plant, and because of its connection with thorns in the passages quoted above, it has also become one of the symbols of the Passion of Christ, and particularly of His crowning with thorns. (See Thorn)

Thorn

¶Thorns and thorn branches signify grief, tribulation, and sin. According to St. Thomas Aquinas, thorn bushes suggest the minor sins, and growing briars, or brambles, the greater ones. The crown of thorns with which the soldiers crowned Christ before the Crucifixion was a parody of the Roman emperor's festal crown of roses. The tonsure of the priest is a reverent allusion to this thorny crown.

The crown of thorns, when shown in connection with saints, is a symbol of their martyrdom. St. Catherine of Siena is often depicted with the stigmata and the crown of thorns which she received from Christ.

Tree   ¶The tree has played an important part in Christian symbolism. In general, the tree is a symbol of either life or death, depending upon whether it is healthy and strong, or poorly nourished and withered. Genesis 2: 9 describes how the Lord planted the Garden of Eden: "And out of the ground made the Lord God to grow every tree that is pleasant to the sight, and good for food; the tree of life also in the midst of the garden, and the tree of knowledge of good and evil." Genesis continues to relate that the fall of man resulted from Adam's partaking of the fruit of the Tree of Knowledge. There is a legend that, after the death of Adam, the Archangel Michael instructed Eve to plant a branch of the Tree of Knowledge on his grave. From this branch grew the tree which Solomon moved to the Temple garden. It was later discarded and thrown into the pool of Bethesda. There it remained until it was taken out to be fashioned into the Cross. (See Solomon and the Queen of Sheba, in Section V)

The flowering tree is used as an attribute of St. Zenobius, with reference to the legend of the dead tree that burst into leaf at the touch of the saint's dead hand.

Tree of Jesse   ¶The genealogy of Christ, according to the Gospel of St. Matthew, is frequently shown in the form of a tree which springs from Jesse, the father of David, and bears, as its fruit, the various ancestors of Christ. Usually the tree culminates with the figure of the Virgin bearing her

50

Divine Son in her arms. The representation of the Tree
of Jesse is based upon the prophecy of Isaiah 11: 1 - 2,
"And there shall come forth a rod out of the stem of
Jesse, and a Branch shall grow out of his roots: And the
spirit of the Lord shall rest upon him . . ." The presence
of the Crucified Christ in the Tree of Jesse is based on
a medieval tradition that the dead tree of life may only
become green again if the Crucified Christ is grafted
upon it and revives it with His blood. The presence of
the Virgin Mary alone at the top of the Tree of Jesse,
alludes to her Immaculate Conception. In place of a tree,
sometimes the vine, a Eucharistic symbol, can be found.

¶The vine is one of the most vivid symbols in the Bible
and is used to express the relationship between God and
His people. The vine sometimes refers to the vineyard
as being the protected place where the children of God
(the vines) flourish under the tender care of God (the
Keeper of the Vineyard). "For the vineyard of the Lord
of hosts is the house of Israel, and the men of Judah his
pleasant plant" (Isaiah 5: 7). The vine was used as the
symbol of the Church of God, in which, alone, this
relationship exists.

Vine

The vine as the emblem of Christ follows from His
words expressing the new relation between God
and man through Him. "I am the true vine, and my
Father is the husbandman . . . I am the vine, ye are the
branches: He that abideth in me, and I in him, the same

bringeth forth much fruit: for without me ye can do nothing . . . Herein is my Father glorified, that ye bear much fruit; so shall ye be my disciples" (John 15:1, 5, 8).

Violet ❡The violet is a symbol of humility. St. Bernard describes the Virgin Mary as the "violet of humility." It is also used to denote the humility of the Son of God in assuming human form. White violets are an attribute of St. Fina, whose resting place, after her death, was found covered by these flowers. (See Strawberry)

Wheat ❡Wheat is used not only to suggest the bounty of the earth but, in relation to Holy Communion, it symbolizes the bread of the Eucharist. (See Grain)

Willow ❡The willow continues to flourish and to remain whole, no matter how many of its branches are cut. Therefore, it has come to be a symbol of the gospel of Christ, which remains intact, no matter how widely it is distributed among the peoples of the world.

Section iii

Earth and Sky

❡In Christian symbolism, ashes are the symbol of penitence. On Ash Wednesday, the first day of Lent, ashes placed on the forehead express the penitential nature of the season. The ashes are from the palms of the previous Palm Sunday. Ashes also represent the death of the human body and symbolize the shortness of earthly life.

Ashes

❡The deep blood red of the carbuncle is significant of blood and suffering, hence the stone is considered to be symbolic of Christ's Passion and of martyrdom. Five carbuncles are sometimes shown on the Cross to symbolize the five wounds received by Christ during the Crucifixion.

Carbuncle

❡Clouds in the heavens are the natural veil of the blue sky, and are, therefore, used as the symbol of the unseen God. A hand emerging from a cloud is the most common symbol of Divine Omnipotence.

Clouds

❡Coral was used as a charm against the "evil eye," and, as such, was commonly hung about the neck of children. In pictures of the Christ Child it denotes protection against evil.

Coral

53

Darkness ⟨Physical darkness is the symbol of spiritual darkness. The Devil is the Prince of Darkness. In his realm, all is dark; while in the realm of God, all is light.

Dawn

⟨Dawn is the symbol of the Blood of Christ. Through the shedding of His Blood, the darkness of sin was overcome, and the dawn of eternal salvation made the world light. It is with this meaning that, in paintings of the Resurrection, Christ sometimes appears clothed in the rose color of dawn. Dawn is also the symbol of the Advent of Christ.

Earth

⟨The earth, which produces plants and trees and furnishes a habitation for man, is often used as a symbol for the Church, which feeds man with spiritual faith and offers him shelter. Thus, the earth, in which the Cross was planted, sometimes conveys this symbolic meaning.

East ⟨East, being the direction in which the sunrise appears, is symbolic of Christ, the Sun of the Universe.

Fire and Flames 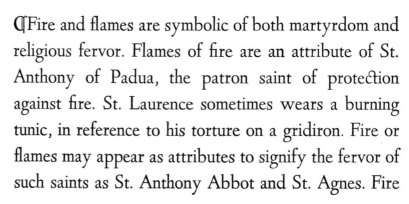 ⟨Fire and flames are symbolic of both martyrdom and religious fervor. Flames of fire are an attribute of St. Anthony of Padua, the patron saint of protection against fire. St. Laurence sometimes wears a burning tunic, in reference to his torture on a gridiron. Fire or flames may appear as attributes to signify the fervor of such saints as St. Anthony Abbot and St. Agnes. Fire itself is sometimes personified as a monster vomiting flames; or by a salamander, which, according to legend, can live in fire without being burned. In paintings of Pentecost, flames on the heads of the Apostles signify the presence of the Holy Ghost. They also signify the torments of Hell. (See Heart, in Section IV)

Fountain

❡The fountain is one of the attributes of the Virgin Mary, who was regarded as "the fountain of living waters." This interpretation is based on the famous passage in Song of Solomon 4: 12ff., and upon Psalm 36: 9, which reads, "For with thee is the fountain of life: in thy light shall we see light." The fountain is also the attribute of St. Clement, who miraculously found water in the desert for his followers.

Garden

❡The enclosed garden is a symbol of the Immaculate Conception of the Virgin Mary. The symbol is borrowed from the Song of Solomon 4: 12, "A garden inclosed is my sister, my spouse; a spring shut up, a fountain sealed."

Gold

❡The precious metal, gold, is used as the symbol of pure light, the heavenly element in which God lives. It is also used as a symbol of worldly wealth and idolatry. This is based on the story of Aaron (Exodus 32), who, in the absence of Moses, fashioned a golden calf which was to be worshiped instead of the true God.

55

Harbor ❡The harbor, according to some authorities, is a symbol of eternal life, and the ships making for the harbor are likened to souls in search of Heaven.

Honey

❡The purity and sweetness of honey have made it a symbol of the work of God and the ministry of Christ. Paradise, the reward of the faithful in their labors for Christ, is known as "the land of milk and honey."

Ivory ❡Ivory has two outstanding qualities: the whiteness of its color and the firmness of its texture. From these qualities come the symbols of purity and moral fortitude. Ivory is, on occasion, a symbol of Christ, in reference to the incorruptibility of His body in the tomb. This is in all probability the origin of the custom of carving crucifixes from ivory.

Light ❡Light is symbolic of Christ, in reference to His words in John 8: 12, " Then spake Jesus again unto them, saying, I am the light of the world: he that followeth me shall not walk in darkness, but shall have the light of life."

North ❡North has always been considered as the region of cold and night. In the early centuries of the Church, the barbarians lived to the north. The reading of the gospel from the north end of the altar symbolized the Church's desire to convert the barbarians to Christ.

¶Oil is the symbol of the Grace of God. It is used in the Church in the sacraments of baptism, confirmation, ordination, and unction.

Oil

¶The pearl, as the "most precious jewel," is used as a symbol of salvation, which is worth more than all the treasures of earth. "The Kingdom of Heaven," said Christ, according to Matthew 13: 45, "is like unto a merchant man, seeking goodly pearls; who, when he had found one pearl of great price, went and sold all that he had, and bought it." Elsewhere in Matthew the pearl represents the word of God: "Give not that which is holy unto the dogs, neither cast ye your pearls before swine, lest they trample them under their feet . . ." (Matthew 7: 6).

Pearl

¶Pitch, because of its color and clinging quality, is a symbol of evil. "Black as pitch" is a familiar phrase used to denote a sinful state or condition.

Pitch

¶The rainbow is a symbol of union and, because it appeared after the Flood, it is also the symbol of pardon and of the reconciliation given to the human race by God. In art, the rainbow is used as the Lord's throne, and in representations of the Last Judgment, Christ is often seated upon it. ". . . behold, a throne was set in heaven, and one sat on the throne . . . and there was a rainbow round about the throne" (Revelation 4: 2, 3).

Rainbow

Rivers ⟨ According to ancient tradition, there were four sacred rivers: the Pison, the Gihon, the Tigris, and the Euphrates. These rivers were believed to be the four rivers of Paradise, flowing from a single rock, and as such were used as symbols of the four gospels flowing from Christ.

Rocks

⟨ Rocks are a symbol of the Lord. This meaning is derived from the story of Moses, who smote the rock from which a spring burst forth to refresh his people. Christ is often referred to as a rock from which flow the pure rivers of the gospel. St. Peter, too, is referred to as a rock, the cornerstone of the Church, because of Christ's statement: " . . . that thou art Peter, and upon this rock I will build my church . . . " (Matthew 16: 18).

Salt ⟨ Salt is the symbol of strength and superiority. Christ, in the Sermon on the Mount, called His disciples "the salt of the earth" (Matthew 5: 13). Since salt protects food from decay, it is sometimes used as a symbol of protection against evil and, in this context, is sometimes placed in the mouth of the child being baptized.

Silver ⟨ Because of its whiteness and because it is a precious metal tested by fire, silver has become the symbol of purity and chastity. Silver also is symbolic of the eloquence of the evangelist. These concepts are based upon Psalm 12: 6, which states: "The words of the Lord are pure words: as silver tried in a furnace of earth, purified seven times." (See Coins and Money, in Section XIV)

❡ Smoke has come to suggest vanity and all that is fleeting because it rises into the air only to disappear. Symbolically, it is a reminder of the shortness of this life and the futility of seeking earthly glory. The anger and wrath of God were ofttimes indicated by smoke. "O God, why hast thou cast us off for ever? Why doth thine anger smoke against the sheep of thy pasture?" (Psalm 74: 1).

Smoke

❡ South, as one of the cardinal points, is the seat of light and warmth; it is therefore associated with the New Testament, especially the Epistles.

South

❡ The star, lighting the darkness of the heavens at night, is a symbol of divine guidance or favor. The Star of the East, often seen in pictures of the Magi, was the star that guided the wise men to Bethlehem and stood in the sky over the manger where Christ was born. Twelve stars may symbolize the twelve tribes of Israel and the twelve Apostles. The Virgin of the Immaculate Conception and the Queen of Heaven is crowned with twelve stars (Revelation 12: 1). One star is a symbol of the Virgin in her title " Stella Maris," Star of the Sea. A star on the forehead is one of the attributes given to St. Dominic, while a star on the breast is an attribute of St. Nicholas of Tolentino.

Star

59

Stones ❡Stones are symbols of firmness. They are used as an attribute of St. Stephen, who was stoned to death. St. Jerome is frequently portrayed at prayer beating his breast with a stone.

Sun and Moon

❡The sun is symbolic of Christ, this interpretation being based on the prophecy of Malachi 4: 2, "But unto you that fear my name shall the sun of righteousness arise with healing in his wings." The sun and moon are used as attributes of the Virgin Mary, referring to the "woman clothed with the sun, and the moon under her feet" (Revelation 12: 1). The sun and moon are often represented in scenes of the Crucifixion to indicate the sorrow of all creation at the death of Christ. St. Thomas Aquinas is sometimes depicted with a sun on his breast.

Time ❡In Renaissance art, Father Time, the personification of time, is generally represented as a nude figure with wings. His most common attributes are the scythe or sickle, but sometimes an hourglass, a snake or dragon biting its tail, or the zodiac is substituted. In many cases, the figure walks with crutches to suggest extreme age.

Water ❡Water is a symbol of cleansing and purifying. In this sense it is used in the sacrament of baptism, symbolizing the washing away of sin and the rising to newness of life. It also denotes innocence, as when Pilate publicly washed his hands, saying, "I am innocent of the blood of this just person" (Matthew 27: 24). More rarely, water suggests trouble or tribulation: "Save me, O God; for the waters are come into my soul . . . I am come into deep waters, where the floods overflow me" (Psalm 69:1, 2). The water, mixed with wine, in the Eucharist has come to denote Christ's humanity, the wine representing His divinity.

Well

℘The well or fountain is the symbol of baptism, of life and rebirth. The flowing fountain symbolizes the waters of eternal life. The sealed well or fountain is a symbol of the virginity of Mary. (See Fountain)

West

℘As one of the four cardinal points, the west signifies the seat of darkness and the abode of demons. To those sitting in the darkness, the rose window high up on the western end of the church was said to make the light of the gospel visible.

Wings

℘Wings are the symbol of divine mission. That is why the angels, archangels, seraphim, and cherubim are painted with wings. The emblems of the four evangelists, the lion of St. Mark, the ox of St. Luke, the man of St. Matthew, and the eagle of St. John, are all depicted as winged creatures.

Section iv

The Human Body

By its very nature, blood is the symbol of life and of the human soul. Christ, the Son of God, shed His blood upon the Cross to redeem mankind from its sins. "And he took the cup, and gave thanks, and gave it to them, saying, Drink ye all of it; for this is my blood of the New Testament, which is shed for many for the remission of sins" (Matthew 26:27-28). Red, the color of blood, has become the common attribute of all those martyrs who died rather than deny Christ.

Blood

The female breasts are the symbol of motherhood, and its attributes of love, nourishment, and protection. The Virgin as mother gives her breast to the Child. Two breasts on a platter are used as an attribute of St. Agatha, who, as part of her martyrdom, had her breasts torn by pincers or shears.

Breasts

The human ear has come to be one of the symbols of the betrayal of Christ and thus of the Passion. Related in John 18:10, at Christ's arrest by the servants of Caiaphas, ". . . Simon Peter having a sword drew it, and smote the high priest's servant and cut off his right ear."

Ear

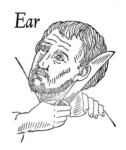

63

Eye

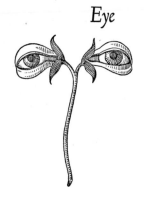

¶Because of the many scriptural references to the eye of God, the eye has come to symbolize the all-knowing and ever-present God. "The eyes of the Lord are over the righteous, and his ears are open to their prayers" (I Peter 3: 12). In Proverbs 22: 12, it is written: "The eyes of the Lord preserve knowledge, and he overthroweth the words of the transgressor." In the later period of Renaissance painting, the Eye of God surrounded by a triangle is used to symbolize the Holy Trinity. The eye within the triangle, surrounded by a circle and radiating rays of light, is used to suggest the infinite holiness of the Triune God. A pair of eyes, often on a platter, are the attribute of St. Lucy.

Foot

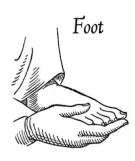

¶The human foot, because it touches the dust of the earth, is used to symbolize humility and willing servitude. The woman in the house of the Pharisee who washed Christ's feet with her tears did so as a token of her humility and penitence, and her sins were forgiven (Luke 7: 38). Christ Himself washed the feet of His disciples at the Last Supper (John 13: 5). It is on the basis of this act that it has become the tradition for bishops to perform the ceremony of washing feet on Maundy Thursday.

Hair

¶Loose, flowing hair is a symbol of penitence. Its origin is closely allied to the episode related in Luke 7: 37 - 38, "And, behold, a woman in the city, which was a

64

IV. Amico Aspertini: *St. Sebastian*. National Gallery of Art, Washington

sinner, when she knew that Jesus sat at meat in the Pharisee's house . . . ſtood at his feet behind him weeping, and began to wash his feet with tears, and did wipe them with the hairs of her head . . ." This Biblical ſtory led to the cuſtom of the hermits, and all those doing penance, of letting their hair grow long.

In ancient times, unmarried women wore their hair loose and long. This is the reason that the virgin saints are frequently portrayed with long, flowing hair. Long hair worn by men may sometimes symbolize ſtrength, an allusion to the ſtory of Samson.

Hand

¶ In the early days of Chriſtian art, Chriſtians hesitated to depict the countenance of their God, but the presence of the Almighty was frequently indicated by a hand issuing from a cloud that hid the awe-inspiring and glorious majeſty of God, which "no man could behold and live" (Exodus 33: 20). The origin of this symbol reſts in the frequent scriptural references to the hand and the arm of the Lord, symbols of His almighty power and will. The hand is sometimes shown closed or grasping some object, but is often shown open with three fingers extended, the symbol of the Trinity, with rays of light issuing from it. The hand is frequently, but not always, inveſted with the nimbus. The hand raised, palm outward, is symbolical of the blessing of God.

The hand also plays an important role in the Passion of Christ. The open hand recalls the mocking of

65

Christ in the Common Hall, for He was slapped in the face there. The hand closed over straws recalls the tradition that lots were drawn to see whether Christ or Barabbas should be released.

A hand pouring money into another hand, or a hand holding a bag of money, is an allusion to the betrayal by Judas. Finally, hands over a basin allude to the episode of Pilate's washing his hands of responsibility for Christ's Crucifixion. The clasping of hands, as in the marriage ceremony, has the symbolic meaning of union.

Head

℃The head, as the uppermost and chief part of the body, is sometimes used to represent the whole man. It also represents the seat of life and, being the chief member of the body, has rule and control over all of the other members. Thus Christ is the spiritual head of His Church not only in eminence and influence but in that He communicates life and strength to every believer.

The head is used as a symbol in relation to a number of Biblical persons. A severed head in the hands or at the feet of a male figure is an attribute of David, who, after striking down Goliath the Philistine with a stone from his sling, struck off the Philistine's head with a sword. Judith is portrayed with a severed head in her hands, in allusion to her killing of Holofernes. Salome is frequently depicted carrying the head, often haloed, of John the Baptist on a platter. A head on a platter is sometimes employed as an attribute of St. John the Baptist.

66

❡The heart was considered to be the source of understanding, love, courage, devotion, sorrow, and joy. Its deep religious meaning is expressed in I Samuel 16: 7, "But the Lord said unto Samuel, Look not on his countenance, or on the height of his stature . . . for the Lord seeth not as man seeth; for man looketh on the outward appearance, but the Lord looketh on the heart."

The human heart, when carried by a saint, is symbolic of love and piety. The flaming heart suggests the utmost religious fervor. The heart pierced by an arrow symbolizes contrition, deep repentance, and devotion under conditions of extreme trial. The flaming heart and, occasionally, the pierced heart are used as attributes of St. Augustine, symbolizing God's guidance of his zeal. The heart with a cross is an attribute of St. Catherine of Siena, with reference to the legend that, in response to her prayers, the Saviour one day appeared to her and replaced her heart with His own. The heart is also used as an attribute of St. Bernardino of Siena.

Nudity

❡The portrayal of the human body in its nakedness had great teaching to support its various representations. At the time of the Renaissance, there were four clearly defined, symbolic types of nudity.

Nuditas naturalis: The natural state of man as he is born into the world. "For we brought nothing into this world, and it is certain we can carry nothing out" (I Timothy 6: 7). Man's recognition of this fact should lead him to ". . . follow after righteousness, godliness, faith, love, patience, meekness" (I Timothy 6: 11).

Nuditas temporalis: The lack of worldly goods and possessions. While this is the natural state of man at his birth, it can also be the result of the trials and difficulties of life which cause a man to live in a condition of poverty. This lack of worldly goods can be voluntary, however, and assumed "to the glory of God," as in the case of those who have willingly surrendered all temporal things in order to serve God completely.

Nuditas virtualis: This is the use of nudity as the symbol of purity and innocence. It represents those in this world who, though engaged in the activities of life, nevertheless are not overcome by the evil and temptation which surround them. It represents the high and the desirable quality of the virtuous life.

Nuditas criminalis: This use of nudity is the opposite of *nuditas virtualis*. It is symbolic of lust, vanity, and the absence of all virtues.

The difference between these last two types of nudity might be explained as the quest for Eternal Bliss as opposed to the pursuit after Transient Bliss. Titian's picture of "Sacred and Profane Love" is said by some to point out this contrast. Eternal Bliss, *nuditas virtualis*, is personified by a woman whose nudity denotes her contempt for perishable, earthly things. A flame in her right hand symbolizes the love of God. Transient Bliss, *nuditas criminalis*, is depicted by a woman richly clothed

68

and adorned with glittering jewels. In her hands she holds a vessel of gold and gems, symbolizing vanity and the love of riches and pleasures of this world.

In portraying truth as a virtue, it is usually represented by the figure of a naked woman.

¶The human skeleton is, for obvious reasons, used as a symbol of death. Frequently, the skeleton is shown bearing in one hand a scythe, a symbol of the cutting short of life, and in the other hand an hourglass, a symbol of the swift passage of time.

Skeleton

¶The skull is used as a symbol of the transitory nature of life on earth. It suggests, therefore, the useless vanity of earthly things. The skull is sometimes used as an attribute of penitent saints, such as St. Mary Magdalene, St. Paul, St. Jerome, and St. Francis of Assisi. Hermits are usually shown with a skull to suggest their contemplation of death. When a cross is represented with the skull, it suggests their meditation upon eternal life after death. In some Renaissance pictures, the Cross is shown with a skull and crossbones at its foot, referring to the Cross on Golgotha, "the place of a skull." There is a legend that the Cross rested upon the skull and bones of Adam, suggesting that through the Cross all men may rise to eternal life. "And so it is written, The first man Adam was made a living soul; the last Adam was made a quickening spirit" (1 Corinthians 15:45).

Skull

69

Stigmata

❡The word "stigmata" is the plural of the word "stigma," which means a mark, usually of disgrace or infamy. Stigmata are marks said to have been supernaturally impressed upon certain persons of high religious character in the semblance of the five wounds suffered by Christ upon the Cross. In Christian art, the stigmata are used particularly as the attribute of St. Catherine of Siena and St. Francis of Assisi, because marks are reported to have appeared on both of them.

Section v.

The Old Testament

❡The great interest of the Renaissance painters was centered in Christ, the Virgin, and the saints of the Church. The belief that the events and personalities of the Old Testament foreshadowed events in the life of Christ led, however, to many representations of Old Testament scenes and episodes. The natural appeal of the dramatic quality of the Old Testament stories had encouraged the use of the more familiar themes. The portrayal of the great Old Testament characters who, in their offices, were considered as the forerunners of the Christian revelation was a part of the witness of the action of God in human events and human history which had its fulfillment in Christ. In Renaissance art, the following Old Testament themes were most popular.

The Creation

❡Many subjects which portrayed the story of Creation were found in the first chapters of Genesis. "And the earth was without form, and void; and darkness was upon the face of the deep. And the Spirit of God moved

71

upon the face of the waters" (Genesis 1: 2). On the first day, God created light and divided the light from darkness, thus creating Day and Night. On the second day, God divided the waters and created the firmament, which He called Heaven. On the third day, He created the land, which He called Earth, and endowed it with plants, flowers, and trees. On the fourth day, God created the lights of Heaven, including the sun, the moon, and the stars. On the fifth day, He created the birds of the air and creatures that inhabit the waters. Finally, on the sixth day, God created the beasts of the earth and Man himself. "And God said, Let us make man in our image, after our likeness . . ." (Genesis 1: 26). "And on the seventh day God ended his work which he had made; and he rested on the seventh day from all his work which he had made. And God blessed the seventh day, and sanctified it" (Genesis 2: 2, 3).

Adam and Eve ⁋The most common scenes from the story of Adam and Eve are the following:

The Creation of Adam: The creation of Adam, the first man, is thus described in Genesis 2: 7, "And the Lord God formed man of the dust of the ground, and breathed into his nostrils the breath of life; and man became a living soul."

The Creation of Eve: After God had created Adam, He decided that man needed a helpmeet in addition to the birds and the beasts. He therefore "caused a deep

72

1. Fra Bartolommeo della Porta: *The Creation of Eve*. Seattle Art Museum, Seattle, Washington

2. Albrecht Altdorfer: *Adam and Eve*. Centre panel of the triptych 'The Fall of Man'.
National Gallery of Art, Washington

3. Giovanni di Paolo: *The Expulsion of Adam and Eve*. Detail from 'The Annunciation'.
National Gallery of Art, Washington

4. Bernardo Cavallino: *Noah's Sacrifice*. Museum of Fine Arts, Houston, Texas

5. School of Antonello da Messina: *Abraham visited by the Angels.* Denver Art Museum, Denver, Colorado

6. Albrecht Dürer: *Lot and his Daughters*. Reverse of 'Madonna and Child'.
National Gallery of Art, Washington

7. Paolo Veronese: *Rebecca at the Well*. National Gallery of Art, Washington

8. Italian School, 17th Century: *Joseph's Brothers bring his Bloody Coat to Jacob.* Kress Collection, New York

sleep to fall upon Adam . . . and he took one of his ribs, and closed up the flesh instead thereof; and the rib, which the Lord had taken from man, made he a woman, and brought her unto the man. And Adam said, This is now bone of my bones and flesh of my flesh: she shall be called Woman, because she was taken out of Man" (Genesis 2: 21ff.).

The Temptation of Eve: In the Garden of Eden, where God had placed Adam and Eve, He had planted "the tree of the knowledge of good and evil," and He warned Adam on penalty of death not to eat the fruit of this tree. But the serpent, "more subtil than any beast of the field," came to the woman Eve and tempted her to eat of the fruit of the tree, telling her that if she did so her eyes would be opened and she would be like the gods, knowing good and evil (Genesis 3: 1ff.). Being tempted, Eve ate the forbidden fruit and gave some also to Adam, her husband. "And the eyes of them both were opened, and they knew that they were naked; and they sewed fig leaves together, and made themselves aprons" (Genesis 3: 7).

The Expulsion of Adam and Eve: Because Adam and Eve had disobeyed His command, and fearing that they might now eat also the fruit of the Tree of Life that grew in the Garden of Eden and become as gods, the Lord laid certain punishments upon Adam and Eve and banished them from the Garden of Eden. Because of the sin of Eve, He decreed that thereafter all women should bear their children in pain and should be subject to man. Because Adam had likewise sinned, the Lord decreed that henceforth man should earn his bread by the sweat of his brow. And He declared to Adam: ". . . dust thou art, and unto dust shalt thou return" (Genesis 3: 19).

Adam and Eve Toiling on Earth: A common representation of Adam and Eve shows them after their expulsion from the Garden of Eden toiling on earth in fulfillment of the Lord's decree that man shall earn his bread by the sweat of his brow.

The Sacrifice of Abel: The first child born to Adam and Eve was Cain, who became a tiller of the soil. His younger brother Abel, however, became a shepherd. And it was Abel who brought one of the first offspring of his flock as an offering to the Lord, ". . . and the Lord had respect unto Abel and to his offering" (Genesis 4: 4). This sacrifice by Abel was thought to foretell the Crucifixion, since Jesus, "the Lamb of God," was similarly sacrificed.

The Killing of Abel by Cain: Cain also made an offering to the Lord, "But unto Cain and to his offering he [the Lord] had not respect. And Cain was very wroth, and his countenance fell" (Genesis 4: 5). In his anger, Cain came upon his brother Abel in the field and slew him. In punishment for this foul crime, the Lord made Cain a fugitive and a vagabond and set a mark upon him so that all should know him.

74

❡The prophet Noah was a direct descendant of Adam and Eve through their third son, Seth. In the days of Noah, " God saw that the wickedness of man was great in the earth," and He determined to destroy man, whom He had created (Genesis 6: 5ff.). Noah alone found grace in the eyes of the Lord. So the Lord instructed Noah to build an ark, ". . . and thou shalt come into the ark, thou, and thy sons, and thy wife, and thy sons' wives with thee. And of every living thing of all flesh, two of every sort shalt thou bring into the ark, to keep them alive with thee; they shall be male and female" (Genesis 6: 18, 19).

The Building of the Ark: Often represented in art is the scene in which Noah is building the ark in accordance with the specific instructions given to him by God. "The length of the ark shall be three hundred cubits, the breadth of it fifty cubits, and the height of it thirty cubits. A window shalt thou make to the ark . . . and the door of the ark shalt thou set in the side thereof; with lower, second, and third stories shalt thou make it" (Genesis 6: 15, 16).

The Flood: Also frequently portrayed is the great flood itself which the Lord loosed upon the earth and which "prevailed upon the earth for an hundred and fifty days." Noah and his family and the animals that he had taken with him rode out the flood safely in the ark. And the Lord at last felt that His cleansing of the earth had been accomplished and He caused the rains to cease

75

and the waters to subside. When the waters fell, the ark of Noah came to rest upon the mountains of Ararat. To discover whether the earth was again habitable, Noah sent forth a raven, which did not return. He then sent forth a dove, which at first found no resting place. On being sent forth a second time, it returned bearing an olive leaf in its beak (Genesis 8: 11). So Noah knew that the flood was subsiding. This experience of Noah in the ark has been compared to the baptism of Christ.

The Sacrifice of Noah: In thankfulness for being saved from the flood, "Noah built an altar unto the Lord; and took of every clean beast, and of every clean fowl, and offered burnt offerings on the altar" (Genesis 8: 20).

The Drunkenness of Noah: Another scene from the life of Noah frequently represented depicts the unworthy action of his youngest son Ham, who spied upon his father in his tent after Noah had partaken too generously of wine. He thus dishonored his parent by gazing upon his nakedness. When Noah awoke and learned what his son had done, he cursed him, saying: ". . . a servant of servants shall he be unto his brethren" (Genesis 9: 25).

Abraham ¶Of the descendants of Noah, it was Abraham who was chosen by the Lord to depart from the place of his birth and to go forth into the land of Canaan (Genesis 12: 1ff.). The events in the life of Abraham most commonly portrayed are:

76

Hagar and Ishmael: Sarah, the wife of Abraham, finding that she was unable to bear a child, told her husband to take as another wife her handmaiden, Hagar, that he might have children (Genesis 16). Of this union a son was born who was named Ishmael.

The Apparition of the Three Angels: When he was far advanced in years, Abraham received a visitation from the Lord, who announced that Abraham and Sarah should at last be blessed with a son of their own. At first Abraham would not believe this, thinking that both he and his wife were too old. Some time later, as Abraham sat in the door of his tent, three men appeared before him. Perceiving that they were angels of the Lord, he hastened to do them honor. They, too, prophesied that he and his wife would be granted a son (Genesis 18: 2ff.). At the appointed time the Lord appeared to Sarah, as He had promised, and she bore a son to Abraham who was named Isaac (Genesis 21: 1 - 3). Since, on the occasion of the visitation of the three angels, Abraham addressed them in the singular, this scene has been considered an allusion to the Trinity.

Abraham and Melchizedek: Some time after Abraham had established himself in the land of Canaan, he learned that his nephew Lot, who resided in the city of Sodom, had been taken prisoner and all his goods had been seized in an attack upon that city. Upon hearing this news, Abraham armed his followers and pursued the raiders. When he caught up with them, he attacked them by night and defeated them, bringing back all the captives and the goods that had been stolen. When Abraham returned triumphant, Melchizedek, king of Salem and high priest, came out to meet the victor, bringing him bread and wine. And Melchizedek blessed Abraham, saying: "Blessed be Abraham of the most high God, possessor of heaven and earth." Abraham, in turn, paid one-tenth of the spoils of battle as tithes to Melchizedek. The writer of the Epistle to the Hebrews (Hebrews 7: 1ff.) relates this episode to the sacrifices of Christ and to Christ's priesthood.

The Sacrifice of Isaac: The scene from the life of Abraham most commonly portrayed concerns the story of how he, being tested by the Lord, would have sacrificed his son Isaac at the Lord's behest. At the crucial moment, when Abraham was about to slay his son, the Lord intervened, saying: "Lay not thine hand upon the lad, neither do thou anything unto him: for now I know that thou fearest God, seeing thou hast not withheld thy son, thine only son from me" (Genesis 22). This episode has been interpreted in the light of Christ's Passion; for just as Abraham was prepared to sacrifice his son to obey the will of God, so Christ sacrificed Himself at the behest of His Father. And as Isaac carried the wood for his pyre to the place of his intended sacrifice, so Christ bore His Cross to Golgotha.

Lot, his Wife, and Daughters: The Lord had determined to destroy the wicked cities of Sodom and Gomorrah.

78

But, because of Lot's goodness, the Lord decided to save Lot, his wife, and two daughters. "When the morning arose, then the angels hastened to Lot, saying, Arise, take thy wife, and thy two daughters, which are here; lest thou be consumed in the iniquity of the city . . . look not behind thee . . . lest thou be consumed . . . but his wife looked back from behind him, and she became a pillar of salt" (Genesis 19). After this tragedy to his wife, Lot went to dwell with his two daughters in a mountain cave. There, because there were no men for them to marry and because Lot himself was without a wife, the daughters conspired together to seduce their father. By plying him with wine, they were able to bemuse him so that, without realizing what he was doing, he received them each in turn into his bed, and they bore him sons, Moab and Ammon.

Isaac and Rebekah: Abraham, being far advanced in years, was anxious that his son Isaac should marry and should take as wife, not a daughter of the land of Canaan, but a woman of the land of his birth, which was Chaldea. Accordingly, Abraham sent a trusted servant to select a wife for Isaac. Approaching the city of Nahor, the servant prayed for guidance in his choice of a proper wife for Isaac, that she be the one who gave him and his camels drink. The prayer was answered and the servant selected the damsel Rebekah, whom he brought back to Canaan. Isaac, meditating in the fields at eventide, saw the camels approach. "And Rebekah lifted up her eyes, and when she saw Isaac, she lighted off the camel. For she had said unto the servant, What man is this who walketh in the field to meet us? And the servant had said, It is my master; therefore she took a vail, and covered herself . . . And Isaac brought her into his mother Sarah's tent, and took Rebekah, and she became his wife" (Genesis 24: 64ff.).

Jacob

¶ Of her marriage with Isaac, twin sons were born to Rebekah, Jacob and Esau. Esau was a great hunter and the favorite of his father. Jacob, "a plain man, dwelling in tents," was his mother's favorite.

The Blessing of Jacob: Isaac, now old, his eyesight failing, sensed that death was near. He called Esau to him, saying: "Take me some venison; and make me savoury meat, such as I love, and bring it to me that I may eat; that my soul may bless thee before I die." But Rebekah, overhearing, sought means by which her favorite, Jacob, might receive his father's blessing, rather than Esau. In Esau's absence, she dressed Jacob in Esau's clothes and covered Jacob's hands and neck with goat skin, for Esau was "a hairy man." Then she prepared savory meat and sent Jacob with it to his father. Isaac, in his blindness, was uncertain who had come. "The voice is Jacob's voice," he said, "but the hands are the hands of Esau." Deceived because the hands he touched were hairy, Isaac blessed Jacob, giving him authority over his brother and all their tribe (Genesis 27).

V. Giovanni Battista Gaulli, called Bacciccio: *The Sacrifice of Isaac*. Kress Collection, New York

in Christian Art

The Dream of Jacob: Often represented in paintings of the Renaissance is the dream that came to Jacob on his journey to Haran in search of a wife. Stopping at night along the roadside, he took stones for his pillow and lay down to sleep. "And he dreamed, and behold a ladder set up on the earth, and the top of it reached to heaven: and behold the angels of God ascending and descending on it" (Genesis 28: 12). Then the Lord addressed Jacob, saying: "I am the Lord God of Abraham thy father, and the God of Isaac: the land whereupon thou liest, to thee will I give it, and to thy seed." When Jacob awoke, he realized that the Lord had been with him, and he took the stones of his pillow and constructed a pillar and, pouring oil upon it, called the place Bethel. Moreover, he made a vow that, if God remained with him, "this stone, which I have set for a pillar, shall be God's house: and of all that thou shalt give me I will surely give the tenth unto thee" (Genesis 28: 22).

Jacob Wrestling with the Angel: Jacob had further evidence of God's favor toward him on the occasion of his journey to meet Esau, his estranged brother. Retiring for the night, "Jacob was left alone; and there wrestled a man with him until the breaking of the day." The angel did not prevail over Jacob. "And he said, Let me go, for the day breaketh. And he said, I will not let thee go, except thou bless me. And he said unto him, What is thy name? And he said, Jacob. And he said, Thy name shall be called no more Jacob, but Israel: for as a prince hast thou power with God and with men, and hast prevailed. And Jacob asked him, and said, Tell me, I pray thee, thy name, and he said, Wherefore is it that thou dost ask after my name? And he blessed him there. And Jacob called the name of the place Peniel: for I have seen God face to face, and my life is preserved" (Genesis 32: 24 – 32).

Joseph ⰓJoseph was the son of Jacob and his favorite wife, Rachel. Jacob " loved Joseph more than all his children, because he was the son of his old age: and he made him a coat of many colours." This coat was meant to show that Joseph, unlike his brothers, who were workmen for their father, was permitted to remain in his father's house and enjoy special privileges. "And when his brethren saw their father loved him [Joseph] more than all his brethren, they hated him, and could not speak peaceably unto him." One day Jacob sent Joseph to see whether all went well with his brothers and the flocks they were tending. "And when they saw him afar off, even before he came near unto them, they conspired against him to slay him. . . And it came to pass, when Joseph was come unto his brethren, that they ſtripped Joseph out of his coat, his coat of many colours that was on him; and they took him, and cast him into a pit . . . and they drew and lifted up Joseph out of the pit, and sold Joseph to the Ishmeelites for twenty pieces of silver: and they brought Joseph into Egypt . . . [his brothers⌉ took Joseph's coat, and killed a kid of the goats, and dipped the coat in the blood . . . and they brought it to their father. . . And he knew it, and said, It is my son's coat. . . And Jacob rent his clothes . . . and mourned for his son many days" (Genesis 37). The sale of Joseph to the Ishmeelites by his brothers has been compared to the Betrayal of Christ by Judas, who sold his Master for thirty pieces of silver.

Of the later events in the life of Joseph, those most frequently represented in art are the following:

Joseph and Potiphar's Wife: Joseph was taken into Egypt, where he became a servant to Potiphar, a captain in the guard of Pharaoh. He worked so faithfully that he was made overseer of his master's estate. But Potiphar's wife fell in love with Joseph and would have tempted him to sin. One day, Joseph was forced to escape from her approaches by slipping out of his coat and leaving it in her hands. Angry at Joseph's disregard of her, Potiphar's wife used his coat as evidence that he had made improper advances to her (Genesis 39).

Pharoah's Dream: Joseph was cast into prison by Potiphar because of false charges by his wife. While there, Joseph helped one of the servants of Pharaoh by interpreting his dreams. Some two years later Pharaoh himself had a dream which troubled him. He dreamed first that he saw seven fine fat cattle come down to a stream and drink. These were followed by seven lean, half-starved cattle that ate up the seven fat cattle. Again, he dreamed that he saw seven fine ears of corn spring up on one stalk. Thereafter, seven poor ears sprang up and they devoured the seven fat ears. When Pharaoh could obtain no satisfactory explanation of this dream from those around him, his servant persuaded him to send for Joseph, who interpreted the dream to mean that there would be seven years of plenty in the land of Egypt, which would be followed by seven years of famine. As a result of Joseph's advice, the harvests of the seven good years were stored against the ensuing famine, and the people of Egypt were saved from disaster (Genesis 40 and 41).

Joseph and His Brethren: The famine that afflicted Egypt affected also the land of Canaan, where Joseph was born. Jacob, Joseph's father, sent his sons to Egypt to buy corn in order that his people might not starve. Meanwhile, Joseph had been made governor of all Egypt. When his brothers appeared before him they failed to recognize him. The meeting of Joseph and his brothers and their eventual reunion has frequently been depicted (Genesis 42-47).

Moses ¶After the death of Joseph, the Israelites multiplied greatly and became powerful in the land of Egypt. Fearful of the growing strength of the Israelites, the king of Egypt ordered that all male children of the tribe should be put to death at infancy. But one of the Israelite women was determined to save her son. After three months,

84

when it was no longer possible to hide him in her home, she placed him in a wicker basket and left it "in the flags by the river's brink" (Exodus 2: 3). The child's aunt then stationed herself near the spot to see what would take place. She saw the daughter of Pharaoh come down to bathe and discover the infant. The princess realized that the baby was a child of the Israelites but, because he wept, she had compassion on him. The child's aunt seized the opportunity to approach the princess, and offered to find a woman to nurse the baby. In this way, the child's mother was permitted to take care of her own son. "And the child grew, and she brought him unto Pharaoh's daughter, and he became her son. And she called his name Moses" (Exodus 2: 10).

Many other scenes from the life of Moses have been subjects of Renaissance paintings. Among them are the following:

Moses and the Crown of Gold: While Moses, as a child, was still living in the court of Pharaoh, the king one day playfully set a crown upon his head. There was an idol in the center of the crown and the child threw the crown to the floor. The wise men of the court were called upon to interpret this omen. Some thought it signified that Moses would eventually overthrow the king. For this reason, they urged that the child be put to death. Others, however, saw in the incident merely a childish whim. To settle the question, it was decided to subject the child to a test. Two platters were placed before him;

one heaped with burning coals, and the other with cherries. It was agreed that, if Moses chose the hot embers, he should be saved. Guided by the Lord, Moses seized a handful of the burning coals and, screaming, put his hand into his mouth. Legend says that as a consequence his tongue was burned, and that thereafter he had speech difficulties. This story, based on a Hebrew legend, was often illustrated by Italian painters.

Moses and the Midianites: As a young man, Moses became increasingly aware of the cruel oppression of the Israelites by the Egyptians. In defending one of his people he killed an Egyptian overseer. Fleeing to save his life, he found refuge in the land of Midian. One day, as Moses sat by a well, the seven daughters of the priest of Midian came to water their father's sheep. When some local shepherds tried to drive the girls away, Moses helped them and saw that their sheep were properly watered. Hearing of this, the priest took Moses into his home. Moses later married one of his daughters, Zipporah (Exodus 2: 11ff.).

Moses and the Burning Bush: One day, while Moses was tending the sheep of his father-in-law Jethro, he chanced to come to Horeb, the mountain of God. "And the angel of the Lord appeared unto him in a flame of fire out of the midst of a bush: and he looked, and, behold, the bush burned with fire, and the bush was not consumed" (Exodus 3: 2). When Moses paused to see why the fire did not consume it, God called to him

86

out of the midst of the bush. It was then that the Lord told Moses that he was chosen to return to the land of Pharaoh and "bring forth my people the children of Israel out of Egypt."

The Plagues of Egypt: In accordance with the will of the Lord, Moses, together with Aaron, returned to Egypt and pleaded with Pharaoh to release the people of Israel from their bondage. But the heart of Pharaoh was hardened, and, instead of releasing the Israelites, he increased their burdens (Exodus 5: 7ff.). Then Moses, with the help of the Lord, brought upon Egypt a series of disasters. Moses first smote the waters of the rivers of Egypt with his rod. The rivers were turned to blood and the fish died. He next caused the land to be overrun by a plague of frogs. Next Moses smote the dust and turned it into a plague of lice that afflicted man and beast. When Pharoah still refused to relent, Moses caused a plague of flies to swarm over the land. Next he brought a pestilence upon the cattle of Egypt, and all cattle except that of the Israelites died in the fields. As this failed to move the king, Moses caused a plague of boils to afflict the Egyptians and, following this, a great storm of hail and lightning to destroy the crops in the fields. But Pharaoh still refused to bow before the will of God, so Moses set upon Egypt a plague of locusts which devoured everything that was green in the land. Then Moses stretched forth his hand and for three days the land of Egypt was enveloped in darkness. Finally,

Moses warned Pharaoh that if he would not free the people of Israel, the firstborn child of every Egyptian family would be struck dead. But Pharaoh still refused to listen, so the Lord ". . . smote all the firstborn in the land of Egypt, from the firstborn of Pharaoh that sat on his throne unto the firstborn of the captive that was in the dungeon; and all the firstborn of cattle" (Exodus 12: 29). But children of the people of Israel were spared, for the Lord ". . . passed over the houses of the children of Israel in Egypt, when he smote the Egyptians . . ." (Exodus 12: 27). As the result of this ultimate disaster, Pharaoh permitted the people of Israel to leave Egypt.

The Passage of the Red Sea: Even though Pharaoh at last permitted the people of Israel to depart from Egypt, his pride would not suffer them to go freely, and he gathered together his warriors and chariots to pursue them. The army of the Egyptians came upon the Israelites on the shores of the Red Sea. The people of Israel were very much afraid. "And Moses stretched out his hand over the sea; and the Lord caused the sea to go back by a strong east wind all that night, and made the sea dry land, and the waters were divided. And the children of Israel went into the midst of the sea upon the dry ground: and the waters were a wall unto them on their right hand, and on their left" (Exodus 14: 21, 22).

The Destruction of Pharaoh and His Army: When the army of Pharaoh, still in pursuit, sought to follow the Israelites across the Red Sea, Moses again stretched

88

9. Sebastien Bourdon: *The Finding of Moses.* M. H. de Young Memorial Museum, San Francisco, California

10. Florentine School, end of 15th Century: *Scenes from the Life of Moses*. Kress Collection, New York

11. Florentine School, end of 15th Century: *The Submersion of Pharaoh's Army.* Kress Collection, New York

12. Francesco Ubertini, called Bacchiacca: *The Gathering of Manna*. National Gallery of Art, Washington

13. Andrea Verrocchio: *David*. Terracotta. National Gallery of Art, Washington

14. Francesco Polazzo: *Elijah taken up in a Chariot of Fire*. National Gallery of Art, Washington

15. Filippino Lippi: *Tobias and the Angel*. National Gallery of Art, Washington

16. Matteo di Giovanni: *Judith with the Head of Holofernes*. Kress Collection, New York

forth his hand over the sea, "And the waters returned, and covered the chariots, and the horsemen, and all the host of Pharaoh that came into the sea after them; there remained not so much as one of them" (Exodus 14: 28). " Thus the Lord saved Israel that day out of the hand of the Egyptians; and Israel saw the Egyptians dead upon the sea shore" (Exodus 14: 30).

The Gathering of Manna: During the wanderings of the children of Israel after their escape from Egypt, they found themselves lost in the wilderness and without food. But the Lord gave help. ". . . in the morning the dew lay round about the host. And when the dew that lay was gone up, behold, upon the face of the wilderness there lay a small round thing, as small as the hoar frost on the ground. And when the children of Israel saw it, they said one to another, it is manna: for they wist not what it was. And Moses said unto them, This is the bread which the Lord hath given you to eat" (Exodus 16: 13ff.). The Israelites gathered the manna and were fed, and it was on manna that they subsisted during the forty years that they wandered before coming to the land of Canaan.

Moses and the Rock of Horeb: After the children of Israel had come out of the wilderness, they first pitched their tents in a place called Rephidim, but there was no water and they were very thirsty. When Moses called upon the Lord for help, the Lord said: " Go on before the people, and take with thee of the elders of Israel;

and thy rod, wherewith thou smotest the river, take in thine hand, and go. Behold, I will stand before thee there upon the rock in Horeb; and thou shalt smite the rock, and there shall come water out of it, that the people may drink. And Moses did so in the sight of the elders of Israel" (Exodus 17: 5, 6).

Moses Receiving the Ten Commandments: One of the most famous and most frequently represented scenes from the life of Moses is the one in which Moses, at the command of the Lord, ascended Mt. Sinai and there received from the Lord the two tablets of stone, upon which His commandments were written (Exodus 31: 18).

Moses and the Golden Calf: While Moses was absent upon Mt.Sinai receiving the commandments of the Lord, the people of Israel came to Aaron, saying, ". . . make us gods, which shall go before us; for as for this Moses, the man who brought us up out of this land of Egypt, we wot not what is become of him" (Exodus 32: 1). So Aaron gathered together the jewelry of the people and fashioned from it a golden calf which he gave to the people to worship. But when Moses, returning from Mt. Sinai, saw the golden idol, he was enraged and cast the tablets of the Lord upon the ground and broke them. Then he seized the golden calf and destroyed it (Exodus 32: 20).

Moses and the Brazen Serpent: During the course of their wanderings, the people of Israel came to the land of Edom. They were much discouraged because of the long and difficult way that they had traveled. There were murmurings against God and against Moses and, in punishment, the Lord sent a scourge of fiery serpents that bit the people, and many of them died. But Moses prayed for the people, and the Lord said: "... make thee a fiery serpent, and set it upon a pole: and it shall come to pass, that every one that is bitten, when he looketh upon it, shall live. And Moses made a serpent of brass, and put it upon a pole, and it came to pass, that if a serpent had bitten any man, when he beheld the serpent of brass, he lived" (Numbers 21: 8). In this way the faith of the children of Israel was restored.

¶Following the death of Moses, Joshua became leader of all the people of Israel. Under his command they crossed the River Jordan into the land of Gilead, the land "flowing with milk and honey" which the Lord had promised them. From the military exploits of Joshua the Renaissance painters singled out for special attention the story of Jericho.

The Fall of Jericho: Having crossed the Jordan, the Israelites found themselves before the walls of the city of Jericho, which they besieged. The Lord appeared to Joshua and told him how the city might be taken. Each day, for six days, the Israelites marched silently once around the walls of the city, bearing with them the Ark of the Covenant. On the seventh day, following

Joshua

91

the Lord's command, they circled the city seven times: "And it came to pass at the seventh time, when the prieſts blew with the trumpets, Joshua said unto the people, Shout; for the Lord hath given you the city . . . So the people shouted when the prieſts blew with the trumpets: and it came to pass, when the people heard the sound of the trumpet, and the people shouted with a great shout, that the wall fell down flat, so that the people went up into the city, every man ſtraight before him, and they took the city" (Joshua 6: 16ff.).

Samson

⟨During the years following the death of Joshua, the Israelites ſlipped from the paths of virtue. In punishment, the Lord delivered them first into the hands of the Midianites and then into the hands of the Philiſtines. At last, however, the Lord relented and ordained that there should be born to one of the women of Israel a son, who "shall begin to deliver Israel out of the hands of the Philiſtines" (Judges 13: 5). The boy was named Samson, and he was of great ſtrength. It is told how Samson in his youth slew a lion with his bare hands and how, later, in conflict with the Philiſtines, he ſlew a thousand of them with the jawbone of an ass. The following scenes from the life of Samson are most commonly portrayed:

Samson and Delilah: It chanced that Samson fell very much in love with a woman of the Philiſtines named Delilah. Hearing of this, the leaders among the Philiſtines urged Delilah to use her wiles; to discover from

Samson the secret of his great strength, so that he might be deprived of it and overcome. Thrice Delilah, with words of love, sought to beguile Samson into revealing his secret. It was not until the third attempt that Samson finally confessed that the source of his mighty strength lay in his hair which, since birth, had never been cut. Causing Samson to sleep, Delilah "called for a man, and she caused him to shave off the seven locks of his head; and she began to afflict him, and his strength went from him" (Judges 16: 19). Thus was Samson delivered into the hands of the Philistines.

Death of Samson: The Philistines, who had seized Samson, first blinded him, then placed fetters upon him, and finally imprisoned him at Gaza. They forgot, however, that Samson's hair would grow again. Some time later, Samson was haled from his prison cell to a great gathering of the Philistines, who wished to make sport of him. Because he was blinded, Samson was led into the house by a youth. Samson asked the lad to lead him to the pillars supporting the roof, in order that he might have something to lean against. Feeling the pillars under his hand, Samson, with a great effort, tore them down and the roof of the building collapsed upon all who were present. Samson himself was killed and ". . . the dead which he slew at his death were more than they which he slew in his life" (Judges 16: 30). The allegorical figure of Fortitude is sometimes portrayed with a column or pillar, in reference to this act of Samson's.

Ruth   ❡Well known in Renaissance art is the figure of Ruth, the woman of Moab, who, when her husband and her father-in-law both died, insisted upon remaining with her mother-in-law, Naomi, saying: ". . . intreat me not to leave thee, or to return from following after thee: for whither thou goest, I will go; and where thou lodgest, I will lodge: thy people shall be my people, and thy God my God" (Ruth 1: 16).

Ruth and Boaz: When Naomi returned to Bethlehem, the town of her birth, Ruth accompanied her. In order that they might have food, Ruth went into the field to glean the grain which remained after the reapers had passed. The field to which she went belonged to Boaz, a man of great wealth and of the same family as Naomi. Seeing Ruth standing in the field, Boaz fell in love with her and did her great kindness. That night Ruth came to Boaz on the threshing floor, after the threshing was over, and made herself known to him. Boaz then determined to exercise his right as her kinsman to claim her. This he did, and of their marriage was born a son, Obed, who was the father of Jesse, who in turn became the father of David the King.

David   ❡In the days following the death of Samson, while the Israelites were still embattled against the Philistines, Samuel, son of Hannah, came to be recognized as a true prophet of the Lord. The people of Israel appealed to Samuel that he appoint one of their people to be their king. The first to be chosen by Samuel as king of the Israelites was the great warrior, Saul. He fought mightily against the enemies of Israel, but because of his idolatries, the Lord turned against him and rejected him as king of the Israelites. It was then that the Lord directed Samuel how he should find David, son of Jesse, and make him king over all Israel. The events in the life of David most commonly depicted in Renaissance painting include the following:

The Anointing of David: Having rejected Saul as king of Israel, the Lord instructed the prophet Samuel to fill his horn with oil ". . . and go, I will send thee to Jesse the Bethlehemite: for I have provided me a king among his sons" (I Samuel 16: 1). At Bethlehem, Jesse brought forth each of his sons, in turn, and presented them to Samuel; each was rejected. Finally, David, the youngest, was brought from the field where he had been guarding the sheep. Then the Lord said to Samuel, ". . . Arise, anoint him: for this is he. Then Samuel took the horn of oil, and anointed him in the midst of his brethren: and the Spirit of the Lord came upon David from that day forward . . ." (I Samuel 16: 12, 13).

David Playing the Harp: This scene is based upon the passage in I Samuel 16: 23, which reads: "And it came to pass, when the evil spirit from God was upon Saul, that David took an harp, and played with his hand: so Saul was refreshed, and was well, and the evil spirit departed from him."

95

David and Goliath: The heroic battle between David and Goliath, the champion of the Philistines, is described at length in I Samuel 17. The account concludes: "And David put his hand into his bag, and took thence a stone, and slang it, and smote the Philistine in his forehead, that the stone sunk into his forehead; and he fell upon his face to the earth. So David prevailed over the Philistine with a sling and with a stone, and smote the Philistine, and slew him; but there was no sword in the hand of David. Therefore David ran, and stood upon the Philistine, and took his sword, and drew it out of the sheath thereof, and slew him, and cut off his head therewith. And when the Philistines saw their champion was dead, they fled" (I Samuel 17: 49ff.).

The Triumphs of David: Two triumphal scenes from the life of David are frequently portrayed in art. The first depicts the return of David and Saul after their victory over the Philistines and is based on the passage from I Samuel 18: 6ff., which reads: "And it came to pass as they came, when David was returned from the slaughter of the Philistine, that the women came out of all cities of Israel, singing and dancing, to meet king Saul, with tabrets, with joy, and with instruments of musick. And the women answered one another as they played, and said, Saul hath slain his thousands, and David his ten thousands. And Saul was very wroth . . ." Because of jealousy, Saul, thereafter, was set against David.

The second scene of triumph occurred after the death

of Saul and after David had been chosen king by all the tribes of Israel. Soon after he became king, David was again forced to fight the Philistines, whom he defeated in two great battles. He then gathered together his chosen followers and went to Judah to recapture the Ark of God, which had been in the hands of the Philistines. This he brought back triumphantly to Jerusalem, which he had made both the political and the religious capital of the state (II Samuel 6). The entrance of David himself into Jerusalem has been interpreted as foretelling Christ's entry into that city prior to the Passion.

David Dancing before the Ark: In describing the passage of the Ark of God into Jerusalem, it is recounted that "David went and brought the ark of God from the house of Obededom into the city of David with gladness. And it was so, that when they that bare the ark of the Lord had gone six paces, he sacrificed oxen and fatlings. And David danced before the Lord with all his might . . ." (II Samuel 6: 12ff.).

David and Bathsheba: Bathsheba, whom David first saw from the roof of his palace and coveted, was the wife of another, and it was not until David had contrived to have her husband killed in battle that he was able to marry her. And, as the Old Testament states, ". . . the thing that David had done displeased the Lord" (II Samuel 11: 27).

The Penitence of David: In punishment for having caused the death of Uriah the Hittite, the husband of

97

Bathsheba, and for marrying his widow, the Lord caused the first-born child of David and Bathsheba to fall mortally ill. In great repentance for his act, David admitted that he had sinned against the Lord. He was forgiven, but the child died. Following his repentance, a second child was born to David and Bathsheba, who was named Solomon (II Samuel 12).

Solomon

❡Solomon, the son of David and Bathsheba, who succeeded David as king of Israel, was renowned for his great wisdom. Among the episodes of his life that have been the subject of art, the best known are the following:

The Judgment of Solomon: Two women came to Solomon in dispute over a child, each claiming that the child belonged to her. To settle the dispute Solomon called for a sword and said, ". . . divide the living child in two, and give half to the one, and half to the other" (I Kings 3: 25). Then the true mother of the child, because she loved the infant so much and did not wish to see it die, said, "O my lord, give her the living child, and in no wise slay it. But the other said, Let it be neither mine nor thine, but divide it." From these words, Solomon was able to identify the real mother of the child and to restore it to its true parent.

Solomon and the Queen of Sheba: So famous did Solomon become for his wisdom that the Queen of Sheba came to Jerusalem, with a great train of followers, to put

98

his wisdom to the test. She asked him many questions, and to each Solomon gave a sound and accurate answer. Greatly impressed, the Queen departed after giving Solomon many precious gifts. Solomon, in turn, ". . . gave unto the queen of Sheba all her desire, whatsoever she asked, beside that which Solomon gave her of his royal bounty" (I Kings 10: 13).

There is a legend that on the occasion of the Queen of Sheba's visit to Jerusalem, she was confronted with a wooden bridge across a stream. She became immediately aware of the miraculous quality of the wood, and knelt before it. It seems that when Adam died, his son, Seth, planted a branch on the grave of his father. This branch grew into a mighty tree and was still flourishing at the time of Solomon. (See Tree, Section II) Solomon admired its beauty and ordered that it should be used as a pillar in the Temple. But the wood was not suitable in size. When it was discarded, it was thrown across a brook as a bridge. Legend further states that the Queen of Sheba warned Solomon that from this wood would be built the cross that would destroy the people of Israel. To prevent this, Solomon had the wood buried deep below the ground. But, in subsequent years, a well was dug at this self-same spot, and the waters of it became miraculously endowed because of their contact with the wood. At the time of Christ, the wood floated to the top of the water and was used to build the Cross on which Christ was crucified.

Esther ⊄Esther was the Hebrew maiden who, through the efforts of her cousin, Mordecai, was chosen as queen by the great king Ahasuerus, who reigned "from India even unto Ethiopia, over an hundred and seven and twenty provinces." The story of Esther and Mordecai is told in the Book of Esther, and several scenes from this account were used in Renaissance painting.

The Affliction of Mordecai: Mordecai aroused the anger of one Haman, a favorite of King Ahasuerus, with the result that Haman persuaded the king to issue an edict commanding the death of all Jews within his territories. To this the king agreed, not aware that Esther, his queen, was a Jewess. When Mordecai heard of the king's edict, he ". . . rent his clothes, and put on sackcloth with ashes, and went out into the midst of the city, and cried with a loud and a bitter cry" (Esther 4: 1).

Esther and Ahasuerus: Hearing from Mordecai what the king had decreed with respect to the Jews, Esther went to Ahasuerus to intercede on behalf of her people. "And it was so, when the king saw Esther the queen standing in the court, that she obtained favour in his sight: and the king held out to Esther the golden sceptre that was in his hand. So Esther drew near, and touched the top of the sceptre. Then said the king unto her, What wilt thou, queen Esther? and what is thy request? it shall be even given thee to the half of the kingdom" (Esther 5: 2, 3). In the Apocryphal expansion of the Book of Esther (Esther 15: 10ff.) it is indicated that, in touching Esther with his sceptre, Ahasuerus freed Esther from his decree, that anyone who dared to come into his royal presence without being summoned should be condemned to death.

Mordecai Honored by Ahasuerus: In examining the records of his reign, Ahasuerus discovered the great service that Mordecai had rendered him and realized that Mordecai had not been properly rewarded. It so chanced that Haman, Mordecai's enemy, was present at the court, and the king asked him, ". . . What shall be done unto the man whom the king delighteth to honour?" Haman, believing that it was he himself whom the king wished to honor, replied, ". . . Let the royal apparel be brought which the king useth to wear, and the horse that the king rideth upon, and the royal crown which is set upon his head: And let this apparel and horse be delivered to the hand of one of the king's most noble princes, that they may array the man withal whom the king delighteth to honour, and bring him on horseback through the street of the city, and proclaim before him, Thus shall it be done to the man whom the King delighteth to honour." And the king said, ". . . do even so to Mordecai the Jew . . ." and Haman did as the king instructed (Esther 6: 6ff.).

Jonah

¶It was Jonah who was chosen by the Lord to go down to the city of Nineveh to preach against the wickedness of the people. But Jonah was afraid and sought to flee from the presence of the Lord. Of the story of Jonah the following scenes are most frequently represented in art:

Jonah Cast into the Sea: In his flight, Jonah took ship at Joppa, hoping to reach Tarshish. "But the Lord sent out a great wind into the sea, and there was a mighty tempest in the sea, so that the ship was like to be broken" (Jonah 1: 4). To the others on the vessel, Jonah finally confessed that it was because of the anger of the Lord against him that the storm had come upon them, and he counseled them to cast him into the sea. When at last they did so, "the sea ceased from her raging."

Jonah Preserved from the Sea: The Lord did not intend that Jonah should drown and ". . . had prepared a great fish to swallow up Jonah. And Jonah was in the belly of the fish three days and three nights" (Jonah 1: 17). From the belly of the fish, Jonah, in his extremity, prayed to the Lord, declaring his willingness to bow to the Lord's will. "And the Lord spake unto the fish, and it vomited out Jonah upon the dry land" (Jonah 2: 10). This is the basis for assigning to Jonah, as a pictorial attribute, a great fish or whale.

Jonah and the Gourd: In compliance with the bidding of the Lord, Jonah went to the city of Nineveh. There he warned the people that because of their wickedness the city would be destroyed within forty days. In repentance the king of Nineveh declared a great fast, and the people of the city clad themselves in sackcloth and covered themselves with ashes. Seeing this, the Lord

102

forgave Nineveh, but Jonah was angry because the Lord did not fulfill his prophecy. After Jonah had stationed himself outside the city to see what would take place, the Lord caused a great gourd to grow so that Jonah would be shaded from the sun, and Jonah was greatly pleased. But in the night the Lord sent a worm to destroy the gourd, and again Jonah was overcome with anger. "Then said the Lord, Thou hast had pity on the gourd, for the which thou hast not laboured, neither madest it grow; which came up in a night, and perished in a night: And should not I spare Nineveh, that great city, wherein are more than sixscore thousand persons that cannot discern between their right hand and their left hand; and also much cattle?" (Jonah 4:10, 11). Jonah is often represented resting in the shadow of the gourd.

¶ In addition to the scenes from the Old Testament already described, which were an inspiration for many paintings of the Renaissance, the artistic representations of that period also include several well-known scenes from the Old Testament Apocrypha, which formed a part of the sacred literature of the Alexandrian Jews. Most commonly depicted are the following scenes:

Stories from the Apocrypha

Tobias and the Angel: Tobit, an upright man, and suffering from a severe affliction of his eyes, was making preparations for his death. He asked his son, Tobias, to journey into Media to collect certain moneys due him. Accompanied by his faithful dog, Tobias set forth. Un-

103

certain of the way, he sought a companion who could guide him. He chanced to meet the Archangel Raphael who, unrecognized by Tobias, agreed to accompany him on his journey. During their travels they came to the river Tigris. Tobias went down to the river to bathe, whereupon ". . . a fish leaped out of the river, and would have devoured him. Then the angel said unto him, Take the fish. And the young man laid hold of the fish, and drew it to land " (Tobit 6: 2, 3). Following the instructions of the angel, Tobias then roasted the fish that they might eat, but saved the heart, the liver, and the gall, for, said the angel, ". . . touching the heart and the liver, if a devil or an evil spirit trouble any, we must make a smoke thereof before the man or the woman, and the party shall be no more vexed. As for the gall, it is good to anoint a man that hath whiteness in his eyes, and he shall be healed." Tobias' journey, under the continual guidance of Raphael, was a happy one. He collected the money due his father. He cured Sara, with whom he had fallen in love and married, of an evil spirit. Upon returning home he restored his father's sight. It was not until the joy of this deeply religious family was complete that the Archangel Raphael revealed himself. ". . . by the will of our God I came; wherefore praise him forever. . . Now therefore give God thanks: for I go up to him that sent me; but write all these things which are done in a book. And when they arose, they saw him no more" (Tobit 12: 18, 20, 21).

in Christian Art

Judith and Holofernes: In the days when Nebuchadnezzar, king of Babylonia, ruled in the city of Nineveh, he determined upon a great conquest and called to him Holofernes, chief captain of his armies. " Thou shalt go against all the west country, because they disobeyed my command," said the king, and Holofernes "mustered the chosen men for the battle, as his lord had commanded him" (Judith 2: 6ff.). In due course, the army of the Babylonians came to the land of Israel, but the people of Israel had been warned of the invasion and had fortified themselves to resist. First of the citadels of the Israelites to be besieged was the city of Bethulia. Rather than take the city by assault, Holofernes decided to overcome it by cutting off its water supply. Soon the people in the city were in despair and were preparing to surrender. But a beautiful widow of the city named Judith asked permission of the city governors to save them all. After praying to the Lord for help, she decked herself in her finest raiment and went out to deliver herself to the Babylonians. In their camp, she demanded to be brought to Holofernes, for she declared that she knew of a way by which the city might be taken. Holofernes was impressed by her beauty and her intelligence, and for three days she was permitted to remain in the camp, going out at night to pray. On the fourth day, Holofernes prepared a great banquet for his officers, and Judith was invited to attend. As the evening progressed, Holofernes became more and more overcome by wine. At last all his guests and servants departed, leaving him alone in his tent with Judith. Stupefied by the wine, Holofernes became unconscious. Then Judith seized his sword and ". . . approached to his bed, and took hold of the hair of his head, and said, Strengthen me, O Lord God of Israel, this day. And she smote twice upon his neck with all her might, and she took away his head from him" (Judith 13: 7). Because the Babylonians were accustomed to seeing her leave the camp at night, she was able to depart, taking with her the head of the great captain. In the morning, when the death of Holofernes was discovered, the Babylonians were dismayed, and the warriors of Israel were able to defeat them utterly.

Susanna and the Elders: According to the Apocryphal story, Susanna was the beautiful wife of a citizen of Babylon. She was as good as she was beautiful, but because of her beauty, two elders of the community fell in love with her and determined to possess her. Together they hid in her garden and, as she was about to bathe, unattended even by her maid servants, they sprang out of hiding and demanded that she give herself to them. They threatened that if she refused they would bear false witness against her and swear that they had discovered her in the act of adultery. In spite of their threats Susanna repulsed them, whereupon the two elders cried out against her. She was brought to the place of judgment and condemned to death for her sin. But as she was being led away to her execution, a youth by the name of

Daniel "cried with a loud voice" and insisted that she had not been given a fair trial. The trial was resumed, and Daniel, by separating the two witnesses against her caused them to give conflicting evidence, thus proving that both were lying. As a result, Susanna was exonerated, and the two elders were condemned to suffer the fate they had sought to bring upon their innocent victim.

VI. Benozzo Gozzoli: *Dance of Salome and Beheading of St. John the Baptist. National Gallery of Art, Washington*

Section vi

St. John the Baptist

John the Baptist, as the forerunner of Christ, was one of the most frequently depicted saints in Renaissance painting. According to St. Mark, "John did baptize in the wilderness, and preach the baptism of repentance for the remission of sins" (Mark 1: 4). Mark also states that "John was clothed with camel's hair, and with a girdle of a skin about his loins; and he did eat locusts and wild honey." The following events from the story of John the Baptist are the most familiar.

¶In the days when Herod was king in Judea there lived a certain priest of the Israelite faith whose name was Zacharias and whose wife was named Elisabeth. Both these righteous people were distressed because they were childless and, since they were advanced in years, they had little hope that a child would be given to them. But one day, as Zacharias was burning incense in the temple, the Archangel Gabriel appeared to him saying, ". . . Fear not, Zacharias: for thy prayer is heard; and thy wife Elisabeth shall bear thee a son, and thou shalt call his name John" (Luke 1: 13). Zacharias could not at first believe the message of the angel. He asked for a sign as proof and was temporarily struck dumb.

Zacharias
in the Temple

109

The Birth and Naming of John

⁋As Gabriel had foretold, Elisabeth became pregnant with child. While she still was carrying the infant John she received a visit from her cousin, Mary of Nazareth, who had learned through the Annunciation Angel of Elisabeth's good fortune. The scene of the meeting of the two prospective mothers is commonly known as the *Visitation*. (See The Virgin Mary, in Section VII) In due course, Elisabeth's son was born. Her family and neighbors would have named the child after his father, but Elisabeth insisted that the infant be called John. To settle the matter, they appealed to Zacharias, the father, who, because he was dumb, ". . . asked for a writing table, and wrote, saying, His name is John. And they marvelled all" (Luke 1: 63). Thus did John the Baptist come by his name, and at the same instant his father regained his speech and praised the Lord. Renaissance artists often combined the Birth of St. John and the Naming into one composition.

St. John in the Wilderness

⁋According to legend, St. John took leave of his parents as a mere child and went to dwell in the desert. We have some representations of Christ and St. John meeting as children in the wilderness. As a young man sojourning in the wilderness, John one day experienced a divine revelation, urging him to become a preacher of the gospel of baptism for the remission of sins. "These things were done in Bethabara beyond Jordan, where John was baptizing" (John 1: 28).

110

in Christian Art

⓵After his revelation, John came into the country near the River Jordan preaching, "As it is written in the book of the words of Esaias the prophet, saying, The voice of one crying in the wilderness, Prepare ye the way of the Lord, make his paths ſtraight" (Luke 3: 4). The power of his message of the need of repentance for sin caused many of the people to receive baptism at the hands of John. But when some queſtioned whether John himself was the Christ, the Redeemer, whose coming had been foretold, "John answered, saying unto them all, I indeed baptize you with water; but one mightier than I cometh, the latchet of whose shoes I am not worthy to unloose: he ſhall baptize you with the Holy Ghost and with fire" (Luke 3: 16). Subsequently, Jesus Himself came to John and was baptized by him. This scene is a major composition in all representations of the St. John cycle, as it is for that of Christ's ministry. (See The Baptism of Christ, in Section VIII)

⓵Because of his preaching and, above all, because he had publicly dared to reproach Herod, the king, for his sins, John was seized by the soldiers of Herod and cast into prison. While in prison, John heard of some of the miracles that Jesus had performed and sent two of his disciples to ask whether Jesus was the true Christ. It was then that Jesus said of John, "This is he, of whom it is written, Behold, I send my messenger before thy face, which ſhall preparc thy way before thee. Among

111

those that are born of women there is not a greater prophet than John the Baptist. . ." (Luke 7: 27, 28).

The Feast of Herod

⸿The major sin which John had charged against Herod was that, contrary to the law, he had married Herodias, the wife of his deceased brother. Herodias would have had John put to death at once, but Herod was afraid, realizing that John was a just and holy man. Some time after John had been imprisoned, Herod held a great feast on the occasion of his birthday to which he asked all the dignitaries of his court. To entertain his guests, Salome, daughter of Herodias, came in and danced before them. So much did Salome and her dancing please Herod and the assembled company that he promised to make her a gift of whatever she might ask. "And she went forth, and said unto her mother, What shall I ask? And she said, The head of John the Baptist" (Mark 6: 24).

The Beheading of John the Baptist

⸿In accordance with the promise that he had made to Salome, ". . . the king sent an executioner, and commanded his head to be brought: and he went and beheaded him in the prison, And brought his head in a charger, and gave it to the damsel: and the damsel gave it to her mother" (Mark 6: 27, 28). Pictures of Salome bearing the head of John the Baptist are distinguishable from pictures of Judith bearing the head of Holofernes by the charger in the former, and by the halo with which the head of John is almost invariably crowned.

112

17. Master of the Life of St. John the Baptist: *Birth, Naming and Circumcision of St. John the Baptist.*
National Gallery of Art, Washington

18. Domenico Veneziano: *St. John in the Desert*. National Gallery of Art, Washington

19. Benedetto Bembo: *St. John Preaching*. Columbia Museum of Art, Columbia, South Carolina

20. Benozzo Gozzoli: *The Beheading of St. John*.
Detail from 'Dance of Salome and Beheading of St. John the Baptist'.
National Gallery of Art, Washington (see Pl. VI.)

in Christian Art

⁊The final scene in the cycle of John the Baptist is his burial. When his disciples heard of the execution of John, they came and took his body and laid it in a tomb (Mark 6: 29). (See The Saints, in Section X)

The Burial of John the Baptist

Section VII

The Virgin Mary

No other figure, except that of Christ Himself, was so often portrayed in Renaissance art as the Virgin Mary. Broadly speaking, representations of the Virgin fall into two major categories. On the one hand are the large number of pictures that use as subject matter the life of the Virgin. These are basically narrative. Their sources are the New Testament record and the rich tradition which centered about her who, as the mother of the Saviour, was "blessed among women." Distinct from this group are those paintings of the Virgin which may be termed devotional. (See The Trinity, the Madonna, and Angels; Section IX) The paintings of this second group were created to emphasize the outstanding characteristics of Mary as the Divine Mother. The events in the life of the Virgin Mary most commonly represented are the following.

The Legend of Joachim and Anna

¶Joachim and Anna were the parents of the Virgin Mary. They were of the royal house of David. Their one great sorrow was that they were childless. On a certain feast day, Joachim brought double offerings to the temple, which the high priest refused to accept. According to the law, Joachim was not permitted to make

115

these sacrifices because he had not fathered a child in Israel. Sorrowfully he went out into the wilderness and fasted for forty days and nights. Anna remained at home and, on the last day of the religious festival, went into her garden to pray. There an angel appeared to her, telling her that her prayer had been heard and that she would give birth to a child who would become blessed throughout the world. Meanwhile, another angel had come to Joachim, as he was tending his sheep in the mountains, and comforted him with promises. When Joachim returned home it befell as the angels had promised. Anna gave birth to a daughter, whom she named Mary. That Mary was conceived by divine intervention is connected with the religious concept of Immaculate Conception, which holds that Mary was herself free from original sin and, therefore, worthy to be the mother of the Saviour. Among the scenes from this legend frequently represented are those in which Joachim, with a sacrificial lamb in his arms, is rejected at the temple; Anna receiving the message of the angel; and Joachim being advised by the angel that he will become a father.

The Nativity of the Virgin

⁋ The scene of the birth of Mary generally shows Anna, the mother of the child, reclining in bed, receiving the ministrations of her handmaidens and the congratulations of her friends and neighbors. The bedchamber is usually richly decorated in keeping with the reputed wealth of the family.

116

VII. Master of the Barberini Panels: *The Annunciation*. National Gallery of Art, Washington

¶When Anna, mother of Mary, prayed in her garden for a child, she promised that if her prayer was answered she would dedicate her child to the service of God. In keeping with this promise, when the child Mary was three or four years old, Anna took her to the temple to begin her service to the Lord. Legend states: "And being placed before the altar, she danced with her feet, so that all the house of Israel rejoiced with her, and loved her."

The Presentation of the Virgin

¶Mary remained in the temple until she was fourteen years of age. Various pictures have been painted of her life during those years. She is sometimes represented teaching her companions to spin or to embroider and is sometimes attended by angels.

The Childhood of Mary

¶When the Virgin Mary was fourteen years old and having lived for some ten years in the temple, she was informed by the priests that she should be married. She replied that this was impossible because her life was dedicated to God. But the high priest, Zacharias, declared that he had received a revelation from an angel, who told him to assemble the marriageable men and to have each bring to the temple his rod or staff. These were to be left in the temple overnight when, it was promised, a sign would be given to indicate which of the suitors for Mary's hand was favored by the Lord. All was done according to the directions of the angel, and in the morning it was found that the staff of Joseph,

The Marriage of the Virgin

the carpenter of Nazareth, had blossomed. He was, therefore, chosen as the husband of Mary. Several of the episodes in this story appear in art.

The marriage ceremony itself is often depicted in front of the temple, with many people present. The priest, standing in the middle, joins the hands of the bride and groom. Mary generally stands at his right, attended by a group of maidens. Joseph stands at his left, and behind Joseph is the crowd of rejected suitors. At times Joseph is shown putting a ring on Mary's finger.

The Annunciation

⁋The Annunciation is the title of those pictures that depict the Archangel Gabriel coming to the Virgin Mary to announce to her that she will give birth to Christ. The scene is described in the Gospel according to St. Luke: "And the angel came in unto her, and said, Hail, thou that art highly favored, the Lord is with thee: blessed art thou among women . . . thou shalt conceive in thy womb, and bring forth a son, and shalt call his name Jesus" (Luke 1: 28ff.). The scene is usually laid in Mary's house. The Virgin frequently holds a book and appears to have been interrupted in her reading. In other portrayals, the Virgin is kneeling in prayer when Gabriel appears. In earlier Renaissance paintings, Gabriel carries the wand, or sceptre, as the herald of God. In later representations he carries the lily, as the symbol of the purity of the Virgin. The presence of God the Holy Ghost is symbolized by the dove.

118

¶ Joseph, the husband of Mary, when he found that she was with child, was greatly disturbed. But, ". . . being a just man, and not willing to make her a publick example, was minded to put her away privily. But while he thought on these things, behold, the angel of the Lord appeared unto him in a dream, saying, Joseph, thou son of David, fear not to take unto thee Mary thy wife: for that which is conceived in her is of the Holy Ghost. And she shall bring forth a son, and thou shalt call his name Jesus: for he shall save his people from their sins" (Matthew 1: 19ff.).

The Dream of Joseph

¶ This is the title given to those paintings that depict the visit of the Virgin Mary, who was already with child, to her cousin, Elisabeth, who had been advised through the Archangel Gabriel that she would give birth to John the Baptist. It was Elisabeth who first perceived the true character of Jesus, for she said to Mary: "And whence is this to me, that the Mother of my Lord should come to me?" (Luke 1: 43). In these pictures, Elisabeth can easily be distinguished from Mary, for she is much older, and she is usually shown making a gesture of welcome. Sometimes they are painted embracing each other.

The Visitation

¶ The Nativity is the scene of the birth of Christ (Luke 2). The time is midnight, as a rule, and the place a stable in the town of Bethlehem, there being no room available at the local inn. The figures usually included in paintings

The Nativity

119

of the Nativity are the Virgin Mary, the Infant Jesus, Joseph, an ox, and an ass. The ox and ass are depicted on the basis of the passage from the first chapter of Isaiah, which reads, "The ox knoweth his owner, and the ass his master's crib." Often the Annunciation to the Shepherds appears in the background of pictures of the Nativity.

The Purification ⸿According to the religious law of the people of Israel, it was ordained that, after giving birth to a man-child, a mother must go through a period of purification for thirty-three days. ". . . she shall touch no hallowed thing, nor come into the sanctuary, until the days of her purifying be fulfilled" (Leviticus 12: 4). Mary, the mother of Christ, being of the Israelite faith, obeyed the law. "And when the days of her purification according to the law of Moses were accomplished, they brought him to Jerusalem, to present him to the Lord; and to offer sacrifice according to that which is said in the law of the Lord, A pair of turtle doves, or two young pigeons" (Luke 2: 22, 24). This scene is sometimes called "Purification of the Virgin." Usually however, the emphasis in this scene is placed upon Jesus, rather than upon His mother, and the scene is then entitled "Presentation in the Temple."

Pentecost ⸿One of the last scenes in which the Virgin Mary appeared was on the occasion of the Feast of Pentecost,

120

21. Andrea di Bartolo: *The Nativity of the Virgin*. National Gallery of Art, Washington

22. Andrea di Bartolo: *The Presentation in the Temple*. National Gallery of Art, Washington

23. Bernart van Orley: *The Marriage of the Virgin*. National Gallery of Art, Washington

24. Hispano-Flemish Master: *The Annunciation.*
M. H. de Young Memorial Museum, San Francisco, California

25. Piero di Cosimo: *The Visitation with two Saints*;
in the background, right, *The Massacre of the Innocents*, left, *The Adoration of the Child*.
National Gallery of Art, Washington

26. Paolo di Giovanni Fei: *The Assumption of the Virgin*. National Gallery of Art, Washington

27. Agnolo Gaddi: *The Coronation of the Virgin*.
National Gallery of Art, Washington

28. Filippino Lippi: *The Coronation of the Virgin*. National Gallery of Art, Washington

following Christ's Ascension. There were gathered together in Jerusalem a number of Christ's followers, including the Apostles, Mary the mother of Jesus, and other women. While they were all together, "suddenly there came a sound from heaven as of a rushing mighty wind, and it filled all the house where they were sitting. And there appeared unto them cloven tongues like as of fire, and it sat upon each of them. And they were all filled with the Holy Ghost, and began to speak with other tongues, as the Spirit gave them utterance" (Acts 2: 2-4). (See Holy Ghost, in Section IX)

The Dormition (Death) and Assumption of the Virgin

¶These two episodes are so frequently portrayed together that they are presented under one heading. Legend states that after the Crucifixion of Christ, His mother lived with the Apostle John, though she revisited many of the places associated with the life of her Son. Finally, in her loneliness, she prayed to be delivered from life. She was visited by an angel who promised that within three days she should enter Paradise where her Son awaited her. The angel then presented her with a palm branch which she in turn handed to St. John with the request that it be borne before her at her burial. Mary also requested of the angel that all the Apostles be present at her death, and this wish was granted. Paintings of the death of Mary therefore usually show the Apostles gathered about her deathbed, with Peter at the head of the bed and John at its foot.

121

The account of Mary's death further states that, in the night, the house was suddenly filled with a great sound, whereupon Jesus Himself appeared, accompanied by a host of angels. The soul of Mary then left her body and was received into the arms of her Son, Who carried it into Heaven. Mary's body remained on earth and was buried by the Apostles. Three days later, however, Jesus decreed that the soul of His mother should be reunited with her body, and that both should be transported to Heaven. The full story of the Death and Assumption of the Virgin calls for at least six pictorial representations: first, the scene in which the angel announces her death and presents her with the palm branch; second, Mary saying farewell to the Apostles; third, Mary's death and the assumption of her soul into Heaven; fourth, bearing her body to the sepulchre; fifth, the entombment; and, sixth, the assumption of Mary's reunited body and soul.

St. Thomas and the Virgin's Girdle

¶This legend relates that the Apostle, St. Thomas, was absent when the Virgin's body and soul were reunited and transported to Heaven, and he refused to believe in her bodily assumption. He demanded that her grave be opened so that he might see whether her body still remained within. Finding the grave empty, he looked toward Heaven and there beheld the Virgin in her bodily form, slowly being transported upward. To convince him of her assumption, Mary flung down to Thomas the belt, or girdle, from her dress.

in Christian Art

⸿ The last scene in the cycle of the Virgin Mary is that in which she is received into Heaven by her Divine Son, and is crowned by Him as Queen of Heaven. The Coronation of the Virgin was believed to have been foreshadowed by that episode in the life of Solomon in which, after the death of David and the coronation of Solomon as king of the Israelites, his mother, Bathsheba, came to him to ask a favor. "And the king rose up to meet her, and bowed himself unto her, and sat down on his throne, and caused a seat to be set for the king's mother; and she sat at his right hand" (I Kings 2: 19). Narrative pictures of the Coronation of the Virgin may often be distinguished from allegorical pictures of the Queen of Heaven by the appearance in them of events from the last days of the Virgin on earth, including the deathbed, the tomb, and the Apostles and friends on earth weeping for her.

Section viii

Jesus Christ

As in the case of the Virgin Mary, a distinction should be made between those paintings of the Renaissance period which portray the events in the life of Christ from a narrative standpoint and the very large number of paintings of the Saviour that are of devotional character. The life cycle of Jesus, as recounted in the gospels of St. Matthew, St. Mark, St. Luke, and St. John, was presented in pictorial form by the great artists of the Renaissance, time and time again. In addition, many thousands of pictures of Christ were painted that had no narrative significance, but were intended to convey the spiritual quality and significance of the Son of God as the Saviour of Mankind. Of the narrative scenes from the life of Christ, those commonly depicted are described below.

¶Paintings which portray the birth of Jesus are almost without number. The Nativity portrays the Holy Family in the stable at Bethlehem. The Christ Child is lying in a manger or upon the straw. The Virgin kneels in adoration before Him. Joseph, in his wonderment, stands at one side. The ox and the ass, in the background, gaze quietly at the scene before them.

The Nativity

125

The Annunciation to, and the Adoration of, the Shepherds

❡In the story of the birth of Christ, as told by St. Luke, it is recounted that there were in the fields near Bethlehem certain shepherds who were watching their flocks. On the night when Christ was born, "... lo, the angel of the Lord came upon them, and the glory of the Lord shone round about them: and they were sore afraid. And the angel said unto them, Fear not: for, behold, I bring you good tidings of great joy ... For unto you is born this day in the city of David a Saviour, which is Christ the Lord. And this shall be a sign unto you; Ye shall find the babe wrapped in swaddling clothes, lying in a manger. And suddenly there was with the angel a multitude of the heavenly host praising God, and saying, Glory to God in the highest, and on earth peace, good will toward men" (Luke 2: 9ff.). This scene has been depicted frequently, and it is usually entitled "Annunciation to the Shepherds." Following the Annunciation, the shepherds went into the town of Bethlehem and there found Jesus lying in a manger, as the angel had predicted. The pictures showing the shepherds worshiping the Christ Child in the stable are commonly entitled "Adoration of the Shepherds."

The Presentation at the Temple, and the Circumcision

❡After Jesus was born, all the requirements of the law of Moses with respect to an infant son were fulfilled, including His Presentation at the Temple and His Circumcision (Luke 2). At the Circumcision, which took place eight days after birth, the Virgin Mary would not be present. In the Renaissance this scene is frequently shown together with the Purification of the Virgin. The scene in which Mary and Joseph bring the Infant Jesus to the temple is depicted often in Renaissance art, and is called "Presentation in the Temple." It is recounted that, in the temple, when Jesus was brought there by His parents, there was a man of Jerusalem named Simeon, to whom it had been revealed that he would not die until he had seen the Lord's Christ. Upon seeing Jesus, Simeon took the Child in his arms and said, "Lord, now lettest thou thy servant depart in peace, according to thy word: For mine eyes have seen thy salvation" (Luke 2: 29, 30). Also present in the temple was ". . . one Anna, a prophetess . . . and she coming in that instant gave thanks likewise unto the Lord . . ." (Luke 2: 36, 38).

¶St. Matthew in his version of the Gospel tells of the wise men from the East who came to Jerusalem at the time of Christ's birth and inquired for Him who had been born King of the Jews. Herod, the king of Judea, sent them to seek Jesus in Bethlehem, and a star went before them showing them the way. Pictures portraying the rich caravan of the three wise men, or Magi, journeying toward Bethlehem are commonly entitled "Journey of the Magi." When the wise men found Mary with her Son, in Bethlehem, they fell down and worshiped Him and presented Him with gifts of gold, frankincense, and

The Magi

myrrh. The scene in which the wise men worship the Infant Christ is called "Adoration of the Magi." The three Magi are sometimes represented as kings because of the passage from the Psalms which reads, " The kings of Tarshish and of the isles shall bring presents . . . all kings shall fall down before him: all nations shall serve him" (Psalm 72: 10, 11).

The Church's season celebrating the Visitation of the Magi is Epiphany, which means the Manifestation of Christ to the Gentiles. This signifies the spreading of Christianity to all lands, to all peoples, for all ages. Thus the Magi, to whom tradition has given the names Caspar, Melchior, and Balthasar, are frequently represented as youth, middle age, and old age. One of them is usually dark-skinned. Their gifts to the Christ Child have a symbolic meaning: gold to a King, frankincense to One Divine, myrrh, the emblem of death, to a Sufferer. To the Christian, these gifts represent the offering to Christ of wealth and energy, adoration, and self-sacrifice.

The Flight into Egypt and the Massacre of the Innocents

⟨When Herod, the king, heard that a child had been born who would become King of the Jews, he was angry, and sought to find the child in order that it might be destroyed. But an angel appeared to Joseph, the husband of Mary, and warned him to take the Infant Jesus and flee into Egypt to escape from Herod (Matthew 2: 13). This Joseph did, and the scene depicting the jour-

128

VIII. Fra Angelico and **Fra** Filippo Lippi: *The Adoration of the Magi.*
National Gallery of Art, Washington

ney of the Holy Family is termed "Flight into Egypt." Paintings of this scene generally show the Virgin Mary riding upon an ass, with the Infant Jesus in her arms, while Joseph leads the ass. Sometimes the Holy Family is shown resting by the side of the road during the long journey into Egypt. Occasionally, they are shown leaving Bethlehem while the massacre of the young children, decreed by Herod in order to destroy the Christ Child, is taking place. This slaughter is known as the "Massacre of the Innocents" (Matthew 2: 16).

¶The Holy Family remained in Egypt for several years. After the death of King Herod, an angel appeared to Joseph, telling him that it was now safe for him to return with Jesus to Israel (Matthew 2: 19). Paintings of the return journey are entitled the "Return from Egypt." Usually these pictures are easily distinguished from those of the "Flight into Egypt" because Jesus is depicted as a small boy instead of an infant.

The Return from Egypt

¶After the return from Egypt, the Holy Family lived in the village of Nazareth. When Christ was twelve years old, His family took Him to Jerusalem for the feast of the Passover. As the family was on the return journey, they found that Christ was not with them. Hurrying back to Jerusalem, they found Jesus in the temple, surrounded by several doctors, or Jewish Rabbis, with whom he was in deep discussion (Luke 2: 41ff.). This

The Dispute in the Temple

scene is usually called the "Dispute in the Temple," or "Christ among the Doctors."

| The Baptism of Christ | ¶John the Baptist was preaching in the wilderness of Judea, prophesying the coming of the Saviour. Many came out to him from Jerusalem and other places in Judea and were baptized by him in the River Jordan. "Then cometh Jesus from Galilee to Jordan unto John, to be baptized of him. But John forbad him, saying, I have need to be baptized of thee, and comest thou to me? And Jesus answering said unto him, Suffer it to be so now: for thus it becometh us to fulfil all right-eousness. Then he suffered him. And Jesus, when he was baptized, went up straightway out of the water: and, lo, the heavens were opened unto him, and he saw the Spirit of God descending like a dove, and lighting upon him: And lo a voice from heaven, saying, This is my beloved Son, in whom I am well pleased" (Matthew 3: 13ff.). |

| The Temptation | ¶After Jesus had been baptized by John the Baptist, He went into the wilderness, where He prayed and fasted for forty days and forty nights. As a result of His fast He was very hungry, and at this moment the Devil ap-peared to Him, saying, ". . . If thou be the Son of God, command that these stones be made bread." But Jesus replied, ". . . Man shall not live by bread alone, but by every word that proceedeth out of the mouth of God." |

130

Again the Devil sought to tempt Him, this time by taking Him to the top of the temple in the holy city. There he urged Jesus to cast Himself down, assuring Him that if He were indeed the Son of God, the Lord would send angels to see that Jesus was not hurt. Again, however, Jesus resisted, saying, ". . . Thou shalt not tempt the Lord thy God." Finally, the Devil took Jesus to the top of a high mountain and there showed Him all the wealth of the world, which he offered as a bribe if Christ would forsake God and worship Satan. To this Jesus replied, ". . . Get thee hence, Satan: for it is written, Thou shalt worship the Lord thy God, and him only shalt thou serve" (Matthew 4: 1 - 11). Paintings of the Temptation may show any one of these three scenes.

¶Frequently portrayed in art is the episode in which Christ called His first disciples. "And Jesus, walking by the sea of Galilee, saw two brethren, Simon called Peter, and Andrew his brother, casting a net into the sea: for they were fishers. And he said unto them, Follow me, and I will make you fishers of men. And they straightway left their nets and followed him" (Matthew 4: 18ff.).

The Calling of the First Two Apostles

¶During His ministry in Judea, Christ came to the city of Jerusalem and taught in the temple. This aroused the anger of the priests, who set spies upon Jesus and sought to convict Him of treason through His own words.

The Tribute Money

131

In an effort to trap Him, the spies asked Jesus if it were lawful for them to pay tribute to Caesar. In answer, Jesus asked them to show Him a penny and inquired whose image the penny bore. When the spies confirmed that the penny bore the image of Caesar, Jesus replied in His memorable words, ". . . Render therefore unto Caesar the things which be Caesar's, and unto God the things which be God's" (Luke 20: 25). On the basis of these words, no charge could be placed against Jesus and His enemies were discomfited. On another occasion, when Christ and His disciples came to Capernaum, they that received tribute money came to Peter and asked him if his Master paid tribute. Knowing of this, Christ instructed Peter, and told him, ". . . go thou to the sea, and cast an hook, and take up the fish that first cometh up; and when thou hast opened his mouth, thou shalt find a piece of money: that take, and give unto them for me and thee" (Matthew 17: 27).

The Sermon on the Mount
 ¶After Christ had begun His ministry, the fame of His preaching spread and there were many who came to listen to His words. One of the most famous occasions of Christ's preaching to the multitudes was the time He went into the mountain to address them (Matthew 5ff.). This scene is entitled "The Sermon on the Mount."

Supper in the House of Simon
 ¶In the city of Capernaum, Jesus was asked by a Pharisee, named Simon, to enter his house and eat.

29. Giorgione: *The Holy Family*. National Gallery of Art, Washington

30. Giorgione: *The Adoration of the Shepherds*. National Gallery of Art, Washington

31. Master of the Life of St. John the Baptist: *The Baptism of Christ*.
National Gallery of Art, Washington

32. Duccio di Buoninsegna: *The Calling of the Apostles Peter and Andrew*.
National Gallery of Art, Washington

While Jesus sat at meat, a woman of the city entered and began to wash His feet with her tears, to wipe them with her hair, and to kiss them. Simon the Pharisee was astounded, for he believed that if Jesus were a true prophet, He would realize that the woman was of low character and would refuse her touch. But Jesus said, "Her sins, which are many, are forgiven; for she loved much: but to whom little is forgiven, the same loveth little." To the woman Jesus said, "Thy faith hath saved thee; go in peace" (Luke 7: 36ff.).

¶Also in the city of Capernaum, Jesus had supper one night in the house of Levi, a collector of customs. Many of the publicans and sinners who had followed Him came in and sat down at the table with Him. Seeing this, the scribes and Pharisees inquired of His disciples why He was willing to sit at table with people of such bad character. Hearing their question, Jesus replied, ". . . They that are whole have no need of the physician, but they that are sick: I come not to call the righteous, but sinners to repentance" (Mark 2: 17).

Supper in the House of Levi

¶St. John describes in his Gospel (2: 13ff.) the famous scene when Jesus drove the money changers and merchants from the temple in Jerusalem. ". . . And Jesus went up to Jerusalem, and found in the temple those that sold oxen and sheep and doves, and the changers of money sitting: and when he had made a scourge of

Cleansing of the Temple

small cords, he drove them all out of the temple, and the sheep, and the oxen; and poured out the changers' money, and overthrew the tables; And said unto them that sold doves, Take these things hence; make not my Father's house an house of merchandise."

Christ and the Woman of Samaria

¶During a journey from Judea to Galilee, Jesus came to a city of Samaria and paused to refresh Himself at a well. "There cometh a woman of Samaria to draw water: Jesus saith unto her, Give me to drink . . . Then saith the woman of Samaria unto him, How is it that thou, being a Jew, asketh drink of me, which am a woman of Samaria? for the Jews have no dealings with the Samaritans" (John 4: 7, 9). As a result of their conversation, she recognized Him as the Messiah and brought many of the Samaritans from the city to see Him. Christ remained with them for two days, and many of the citizens were converted to faith in Him.

The Woman Taken in Adultery

¶While Christ was preaching in the temple, the scribes and the Pharisees brought to Him a woman who had sinned greatly. They said that, according to the law of Moses, the woman should be stoned, but they asked Jesus what was His opinion. In this manner they sought to trap Him in order that He might be accused before the Law. At first Jesus, seeming not to have heard them, stooped down and wrote with His finger upon the ground. When the question was repeated, however,

134

Jesus replied, "He that is without sin among you, let him first cast a stone at her . . . And they which heard it, being convicted by their own conscience, went out one by one . . . and Jesus was left alone, and the woman standing in the midst . . . he said unto her, Woman, where are those thine accusers? hath no man condemned thee? She said, No man, Lord. And Jesus said unto her, Neither do I condemn thee: go, and sin no more" (John 8: 7ff.).

¶This parable, one of the most famous Biblical stories and a favorite subject of artistic interpretation, is told in the words of Christ Himself, as reported by St. Luke. It seems that a certain lawyer questioned Jesus, asking how he might assure himself of eternal life. It was his understanding, he said, that to achieve eternity one must love God with all one's heart and soul, and must love one's neighbor like one's self. But, he asked, how is one to identify one's neighbor? To this Jesus replied in the form of a parable, saying, ". . . A certain man went down from Jerusalem to Jericho, and fell among thieves, which stripped him of his raiment, and wounded him, and departed, leaving him half dead. And by chance there came down a certain priest that way: and when he saw him, he passed by on the other side. And likewise a Levite, when he was at the place, came and looked on him, and passed by on the other side. But a certain Samaritan, as he journeyed, came where he was:

*The Parable of
the Good Samaritan*

and when he saw him, he had compassion on him, And went to him, and bound up his wounds, pouring in oil and wine, and set him on his own beast, and brought him to an inn, and took care of him. And on the morrow when he departed, he took out two pence, and gave them to the host, and said unto him, Take care of him; and whatsoever thou spendest more, when I come again, I will repay thee. Which now of these three, thinkest thou, was neighbor unto him that fell among the thieves? And he said, He that shewed mercy on him. Then said Jesus unto him, Go, and do thou likewise" (Luke 10: 30ff.).

The Parable of the Prodigal Son

¶Another of the familiar parables of Christ is that of the son who asked his father to give him outright his portion of the family estate. When the father acceded to his request, the son took his portion and, journeying in distant lands, squandered everything he had. Later, in poverty and humiliation, the son repented and returned to his father, saying, ". . . Father, I have sinned against heaven, and in thy sight, and am no more worthy to be called thy son." But the father embraced him and, clothing him in fine raiment, ordered that a feast be held and a fatted calf killed, in rejoicing for his return. The boy's elder brother, who had stayed at home working faithfully for his father, protested over the generous treatment accorded to his brother, who, he declared, had done nothing to deserve it. To this the father replied,

"... Son, thou art ever with me, and all that I have is thine. It was meet that we should make merry, and be glad: for this thy brother was dead, and is alive again; and was lost, and is found" (Luke 15: 11ff.).

This parable was Christ's answer to the scribes and Pharisees who were shocked that Christ had been willing to share His meal with the publicans and sinners who had come to listen to Him.

¶The first miracle performed by Christ was at a wedding in the town of Cana to which He and His mother, Mary, and His disciples were invited. "And when they wanted wine, the mother of Jesus saith unto him, They have no wine" (John 2: 3). Jesus then gave instructions that six waterpots of stone be filled with water and that these be carried to the governor of the feast. When the governor tasted the contents of the waterpots, he discovered that all were filled with the finest wine.

The Marriage at Cana

¶St. Luke gives a somewhat different version from St. Matthew and St. Mark of the calling of Simon Peter, the first Apostle. According to St. Luke, Jesus was preaching to the people beside the lake of Gennesaret when, to escape the pressure of the crowd, He stepped into one of the local fishing boats which happened to belong to Simon Peter. After Jesus had stopped preaching, He told Simon Peter to push off from land and let down his net. Simon protested that no one had

The Draught of Fishes

137

caught any fish that day but, nonetheless, complied with Christ's request. To his astonishment, the net came up so filled with fish that Simon had to call upon his partners, James and John, and the other fishermen, to help him bring the catch ashore. Simon Peter was astonished at this miracle and fell on his knees before Jesus, Who said, ". . . Fear not; from henceforth thou shalt catch men. And when they had brought their ships to land, they forsook all, and followed him" (Luke 5: 1 - 11). Another "Miraculous Draught of Fishes" took place when, after His Resurrection, Christ appeared to His disciples after they had fished in vain throughout the night in the sea of Tiberias (John 21).

The Healing at the Pool of Bethesda

¶In the city of Jerusalem there was a famous pool, called the pool of Bethesda, which was reputed to have healing powers for the blind, the lame, and those otherwise afflicted. One day, as He stood beside the pool, Jesus observed an old man, an invalid for many years. Jesus asked the suffering man if he did not wish to be cured. The man replied, ". . . Sir, I have no man, when the water is troubled, to put me into the pool: but while I am coming, another steppeth down before me. Jesus saith unto him, Rise, take up thy bed, and walk. And immediately the man was made whole and took up his bed, and walked" (John 5: 7 - 9). Because this incident took place on the Jewish Sabbath, the Jews were aroused against Jesus and sought to kill him.

138

in Christian Art

❡Jesus went up into a mountain near the Sea of Galilee, and a great crowd followed Him. Among them were many lame, blind, dumb, and maimed, who cast themselves at Jesus' feet and were cured. Then Jesus called His disciples to Him and said, ". . . I have compassion on the multitude, because they continue with me now three days, and have nothing to eat: and I will not send them away fasting, lest they faint in the way" (Matthew 15: 32). When the disciples asked how so large a gathering was to be fed, since all the food available was seven loaves and a few little fishes, Jesus commanded the crowd to sit on the ground. He then broke the loaves and the fishes into pieces which He handed to the disciples and which they, in turn, passed to the hungry multitude. By this means, some four thousand men, women, and children were fed.

The Loaves and the Fishes

❡One evening, Christ ordered His disciples to cross over the Sea of Galilee before Him. A great wind arose that threatened to swamp the boat. Late in the night ". . . Jesus went unto them, walking on the sea . . . the disciples . . . cried out for fear . . . Jesus spake unto them, saying, Be of good cheer, it is I, be not afraid" (Matthew 14: 25ff.). When Jesus came into the ship the wind ceased.

St. Matthew adds the further detail that, having received permission, Peter attempted to walk out toward Christ but, losing courage, he began to sink. Immedi-

Christ Walking upon the Water

139

ately Jesus ſtretched out His hand and saved him. The scene with this addition is known as "The Navicella."

The Raising of Lazarus

⸿While Jesus was on a journey, His friend Lazarus, brother of Mary and Martha, was taken ill. Word of the illness was sent to Jesus, but He did not at once return to Bethany, where Lazarus lived. After several days, however, He sensed that Lazarus had died, and, when He returned to Bethany, this truth was confirmed to Him by Mary and Martha. To them Jesus said that, if they would have faith, their brother would be reſtored to them. He then asked to be taken to the grave where Lazarus was buried. After the grave had been opened, Jesus called upon God and then, in a loud voice, said, "Lazarus, come forth." At these words, Lazarus emerged from the grave, ſtill wrapped in graveclothes. Jesus said, "Loose him, and let him go." This was done, and Lazarus was reſtored to life. By this means, many of the Jews who had witnessed the miracle were converted to belief in Christ (John 11). A figure frequently portrayed in paintings of the raising of Lazarus is that of a man who holds his hand to his nose. This figure is to recall the warning of Martha, "Lord, by this time he ſtinketh: for he hath been dead four days."

The Transfiguration

⸿After the return of the disciples from their first missionary journey and their recognition of Jesus as the Son of God, He took Peter, John, and James up into a

33. Vincenzo Catena: *Christ and the Samaritan Woman*. Honolulu Academy of Arts, Honolulu, Hawaii

34. Jacopo Tintoretto: *Christ at the Sea of Galilee*. National Gallery of Art, Washington

35. Sebastiano Ricci: *The Last Supper*. National Gallery of Art, Washington

36. Benvenuto di Giovanni: *The Agony in the Garden*. From the predella 'The Passion of Our Lord'.
National Gallery of Art, Washington

mountain to pray. There, before their eyes, Christ was transfigured. His garments became shining white with a heavenly radiance, and there appeared and talked with Him the prophets Moses and Elias. Then Peter offered to build on that site three shrines: one for Jesus, one for Moses, and one for Elias. But, as Peter spoke, ". . . there came a cloud, and overshadowed them . . . and there came a voice out of the cloud, saying, This is my beloved Son: hear him" (Luke 9: 34ff.).

Christ's Passion

⊄The last events of Christ's earthly life, from His entry into Jerusalem to His burial, are collectively called The Passion. The Passion scenes most frequently depicted include the following:

The Entry into Jerusalem: After journeying through Judea, preaching to the people, Christ came at last to the Mount of Olives, just outside Jerusalem. He had already told His disciples that He would be seized in Jerusalem and be put to death. But this knowledge did not cause Him to hold back, and He made His preparations to enter the city. He instructed two of the disciples to go into Jerusalem and to bring an ass that they would find there. When the ass was brought to Christ, the disciples spread their garments on its back and Christ mounted and rode toward the city. The people came out to meet Him, spreading palm branches before Him and crying out, ". . . Blessed is he that cometh in the name of the Lord . . . Hosanna in the highest" (Mark 11: 9ff.).

In paintings of Christ's entry into Jerusalem, it is common to find the figure of a man who has climbed a tree, obviously for the purpose of seeing over the heads of the crowd. The figure is intended to represent Zacchaeus, the publican, who did in fact climb a tree to see Jesus " because he was little of stature." Historically, this incident is inaccurate in relation to the entry into Jerusalem, for, according to St. Luke, it took place in Jericho when Jesus was passing through that town just prior to His entry into Jerusalem.

Christ Washes the Feet of the Disciples: Christ entered into Jerusalem a few days before the feast of the Passover. Christ realized that His time had come and that He would be betrayed by Judas Iscariot. After the Last Supper with His disciples, He rose from the table, "and laid aside his garments; and took a towel, and girded himself. After that he poureth water into a bason, and began to wash the disciples' feet, and to wipe them with the towel wherewith he was girded " (John 13: 4ff.). Christ then explained to the disciples that He had set them an example of humility which they should follow, for, "Verily, verily, I say unto you, The servant is not greater than his lord; neither he that is sent greater than he that sent him" (John 13: 16).

The Last Supper: This famous scene depicts the last meal that Christ had with His disciples before His betrayal by Judas Iscariot. It was at this meal that Christ broke bread and handed it to His disciples. "And as they were eating, Jesus took bread, and blessed it, and brake it, and gave it to the disciples, and said, Take, eat; this is my body. And he took the cup, and gave thanks, and gave it to them, saying, Drink ye all of it; For this is my blood of the new testament, which is shed for many for the remission of sins" (Matthew 26: 26ff.). This ceremony, as instituted by Christ, in anticipation of His death, is the basis for the Christian rite of Communion.

In paintings of the Last Supper, the traitor Judas Iscariot is generally shown sitting apart from the other disciples, or springing up from the table, as Christ says, "But, behold, the hand of him that betrayeth me is with me on the table" (Luke 22: 21). John, who sits at Christ's right hand, is frequently shown with his head resting on the table, or sometimes against Christ, because he is identified with the unnamed disciple "whom Jesus loved," described in John 13: 23.

The Agony in the Garden: After the Last Supper, Christ, knowing of the betrayal by Judas, retired with His disciples to a place called Gethsemane. There He took Peter, James, and John a little apart with Him. He asked them to wait for Him and watch, while He went by Himself to commune with God. After He prayed, He returned to find the three disciples asleep and said, ". . . What, could ye not watch with me one hour?" (Matthew 26: 40). Twice more, Christ left the disciples to watch while He reconciled His soul to death, and each time, when He returned, He found the disciples sleeping. When He returned the third time, He said, ". . . Sleep on now, and take your rest: behold, the hour is at hand, and the Son of man is betrayed into the hands of sinners" (Matthew 26: 36). Paintings of the Agony in the Garden almost always show the figures of the three sleeping disciples. St. Luke adds that while He was praying, "there appeared an angel unto him from Heaven, strengthening him" (Luke 22: 43). The angel is sometimes included in paintings of this scene.

The Betrayal: As Christ and His disciples were leaving the garden of Gethsemane, a multitude appeared, armed with swords and staves. To betray his Master, Judas identified Him to the servants of the priests by kissing Him (Mark 14: 44ff.). To protect Jesus, Simon Peter drew his sword and smote off the ear of Malchus, a servant of the high priest. But Christ said, ". . . Put up thy sword into the sheath: the cup which my Father hath given me, shall I not drink it?" (John 18: 10ff.).

Christ before Caiaphas: After his seizure, Christ was taken before the high priest, Caiaphas, where the scribes and the elders were assembled. There He was accused of speaking blasphemy (Mark 14: 53ff.).

The Denial of Peter: After Christ had been seized by the servants of the high priest, He was brought to the palace, and there the council sought to find witnesses against Him, in order that He might be put to death. Meanwhile, Peter had followed at a distance and was

IX. Master of the St. Lucy Legend: *Mary, Queen of Heaven*. National Gallery of Art, Washington

in the palace of the high priest, sitting with the servants while Christ was being accused. As Peter sat there, first a maid, then others in the palace recognized him and accused him of being a follower of Jesus. But, as Christ had foretold, ". . . Verily, I say unto thee, That this day, even in this night, before the cock crow twice, thou shalt deny me thrice" (Mark 14: 30). Peter three times declared that he did not know the man who had been taken prisoner. Then, upon hearing a cock crow for the second time, Peter remembered the words of Christ and wept, realizing that he had been unfaithful to his beloved Master.

Christ before Pilate: The morning after Christ had been accused before Caiaphas, the high priest, He was bound and brought before the governor, Pontius Pilate. Here He was accused by the chief priests and elders, who wished Him put to death. It was the custom, in connection with the Passover, for the governor to release one prisoner at the request of the people. Pilate asked whether he should release Christ. The priests and elders persuaded the people to ask for the release of another prisoner, Barabbas. When Pilate asked what should be done with Christ, the crowd demanded He be crucified. "When Pilate saw that he could prevail nothing, but that rather a tumult was made, he took water, and washed his hands before the multitude, saying, I am innocent of the blood of this just person: see ye to it" (Matthew 27: 24).

145

The Flagellation: After Pilate had reluctantly bowed to the demands of the mob and had released Barabbas, he delivered Jesus to the soldiers to be scourged and crucified (Matthew 27: 26).

The Mocking of Christ: After Christ had been scourged, He was taken by soldiers into the Common Hall, where His garments were stripped from Him. The soldiers then threw a scarlet (or purple) robe about Him, crowned Him with a crown of thorns, put a reed in His hand as a mock symbol of power, and jeered at Him, saying: "Hail, King of the Jews" (Mark 15: 15ff.).

"Ecce Homo": Very famous among the paintings of The Passion is that which is entitled "Ecce Homo" (Behold the Man). After the mocking of Christ in the Common Hall, Pilate had Him brought forth before the people, ". . . and saith unto them, Behold, I bring him forth to you, that ye may know that I find no fault in him. Then came Christ forth, wearing the crown of thorns, and the purple robe. And Pilate saith unto them, Behold the man!" (John 19: 4, 5).

The Road to Calvary: The Evangelists Matthew, Mark, and Luke relate that, as Christ was led away to be crucified, ". . . as they came out, they found a man of Cyrene, Simon by name: him they compelled to bear his cross" (Matthew 27: 32). It is only the Evangelist John who says that Christ was compelled to bear His own Cross. "And he bearing his cross went forth into a place called the place of a skull, which is called in the

Hebrew Golgotha" (John 19:17). The general portrayal of The Road to Calvary, following the version of St. John, shows Christ bearing His Cross on His shoulders.

The Stations of the Cross: In religious art, Christ's journey to Calvary is usually divided into fourteen scenes or Stations. These are:

1. Jesus is condemned to Death
2. Jesus receives His Cross
3. Jesus falls the First Time under His Cross
4. Jesus meets His Afflicted Mother
5. Simon of Cyrene helps Jesus to carry His Cross
6. Veronica wipes the Face of Jesus
7. Jesus falls the Second Time
8. Jesus speaks to the Women of Jerusalem
9. Jesus falls the Third Time
10. Jesus is stripped of His Garments
11. Jesus is nailed to the Cross
12. Jesus dies on the Cross
13. Jesus is taken down from the Cross
14. Jesus is laid in the Sepulchre

The Crucifixion: All four versions of the Gospel describe the crucifying of Christ, but these accounts vary considerably in detail. In paintings of the Crucifixion, therefore, it is not unnatural that a number of different aspects and variations of the scene should be represented. In general, it is agreed that after Christ had been brought to Golgotha (Calvary), He was stripped of

His clothes and crucified, His Cross being erected between those of two thieves who were crucified at the same time. Then Pilate caused a sign to be made which read, "Jesus of Nazareth The King of the Jews," and this was affixed to Christ's Cross. After the Crucifixion, the soldiers present cast lots for Christ's coat that ". . . was without seam, woven from the top throughout." While Christ was on the Cross, the crowd mocked Him, asking why, if He were King of Israel, He could not save Himself. Both St. Matthew and St. Mark say that the thieves who were crucified with Christ likewise cursed Him. St. Luke reports that one of them rebuked the other, saying, ". . . we receive the due reward of our deeds: but this man hath done nothing amiss." He then said to Christ, ". . . Lord, remember me when thou comest into thy kingdom." After Christ had been hanging on the Cross for many hours, He was thirsty. Thereupon, one of those present filled a sponge with vinegar and placed it on a reed and held it to Christ's mouth. The Gospels all agree that a number of women were present at the Crucifixion, among whom Mary, the mother of Christ, Mary, the mother of St. James the Less, and Mary Magdalene are named. St. John alone indicates that he, too, was present and that, just before Christ died, He commended His mother to John's care. It was after Christ's death on the Cross that one of the soldiers pierced the side of the Saviour with a spear and ". . . forthwith came there out blood

37. Umbrian School, about 1505 (possibly Raphael): *The Flagellation of Christ.*
National Gallery of Art, Washington

38. Guidoccio Cozzarelli: *The Crucifixion*. University of Arizona, Tucson, Arizona

39. Francesco del Cossa: *The Crucifixion*. National Gallery of Art, Washington

40. Fra Angelico: *The Entombment*. National Gallery of Art, Washington

and water." This soldier is commonly identified with the centurion who, on witnessing the Crucifixion, became convinced of Christ's divinity. And when he ". . . saw that he so cried out and gave up the ghost, he said, Truly this man was the Son of God." In Christian tradition, this centurion has been given the name St. Longinus.

The Descent from the Cross: All four of the Evangelists have described how Christ's body was taken down from the Cross and how Joseph of Arimathea, a wealthy lawyer, went to Pilate and begged for Christ's body, a request which was granted. St. John alone, however, mentions the presence of Nicodemus, who joined with Joseph in wrapping the body of Christ in linen, together with spices of myrrh and aloes, ". . . as the manner of the Jews is to bury" (John 19: 40). This scene is frequently called "The Deposition."

The Pietà: This is the title commonly given to representations of the Virgin, Mary Magdalene, and others lamenting over the body of Christ after the Crucifixion.

The Entombment: This scene describes the actual burial of Christ by Joseph of Arimathea. Some versions also show Nicodemus present at the burial, in accordance with the Gospel of St. John. The place of burial was a new tomb, hewn out of rock. St. Matthew states that it was a tomb that Joseph had prepared in anticipation of his own death. After the entombment, the sepulchre was closed by a great stone, which sealed it.

149

The Resurrection ❡ The Gospels do not describe the actual Resurrection of Christ from the tomb, but it is abundantly illustrated in art. Christ is arrayed in a white or golden garment. He often carries the banner of the Resurrection. The soldiers guarding the tomb have fallen into a deep sleep. Angels may be present. The soldiers set to guard the tomb and the question of their sleeping are discussed by St. Matthew (Matthew 27: 62ff.; 28: 11ff.). The Gospels vary as to who it was that first discovered that the Resurrection of Christ had taken place. St. Matthew states that it was Mary Magdalene and Mary, the mother of James, who came to the sepulchre early in the morning and there were told by an angel that Christ had risen. St. Mark states that these two, together with the girl Salome, came to the tomb and found the great stone that sealed it already rolled away. Entering the sepulchre, they found an angel, who told them that Christ had risen. In the same connection, St. Luke mentions the two Marys and several other women. St. John specifically states that it was Mary Magdalene who came at an early hour to the tomb, and was astonished to find that the stone which closed the sepulchre had been removed. She then hastened to Peter and John to tell them that the body of Christ had been taken away. Both disciples rushed to the tomb and found that the sepulchre was indeed empty. All of them departed, with the exception of Mary Magdalene. Weeping, she alone remained at the tomb. Finally, bending down,

150

she looked into the sepulchre. Two angels, clothed in white, were sitting there; one, where the head of Christ had been; the other, at the place of His feet. Then, suddenly, Mary saw the figure of Christ standing beside her. However, she did not recognize Him until after He had spoken her name.

¶According to the Gospels, Christ appeared several times to His disciples and others after the Resurrection, and these appearances have been the subject of many important paintings of the Renaissance. The Appearances most frequently portrayed are the following:

Noli Me Tangere (Touch Me Not): The first person to whom Christ is reported to have appeared is Mary Magdalene, when she went to His tomb. She did not recognize Jesus, whom she supposed to be the gardener, until He spoke her name. "Jesus saith unto her, Mary. She turned herself, and saith unto him, Rabboni; which is to say, Master. Jesus saith unto her, Touch me not; for I am not yet ascended to my Father" (John 20: 16, 17).

The Road to Emmaus: St. Luke tells how two of the disciples on the day of the Resurrection went to the village of Emmaus. As they journeyed ". . . they talked together of all these things which had happened. And it came to pass, that, while they communed together and reasoned, Jesus himself drew near, and went with them. But their eyes were holden that they should not know him" (Luke 24: 14ff.).

The Appearances

151

The Supper at Emmaus: When the two disciples and Jesus, whom they had not recognized, approached the village of Emmaus, He indicated that He would continue on the way. "But they constrained him, saying, Abide with us: for it is toward evening and the day is far spent. And he went in to tarry with them. And it came to pass, as he sat at meat with them, he took bread, and blessed it, and brake, and gave to them. And their eyes were opened, and they knew him; and he vanished out of their sight" (Luke 24: 28ff.).

The Incredulity of Thomas: According to St. John, Christ appeared to the disciples on the evening of the Resurrection, the first day of the week. Thomas was absent. When later he returned and was told of Christ's appearance, he said, ". . . Except I shall see in his hands the print of the nails, and put my finger into the print of the nails, and thrust my hand into his side, I will not believe." Thomas was present when, eight days later, Jesus again appeared to the disciples. "Then saith he to Thomas, Reach hither thy finger, and behold my hands; and reach hither thy hand, and thrust it into my side: and be not faithless but believing. And Thomas answered and said unto him, My Lord and my God" (John 21: 25ff.).

The Ascension

⁋St. Luke, in his Gospel and in The Acts of the Apostles, gives accounts of the Ascension of Christ. It was largely from these accounts that Renaissance artists

152

drew their inspiration for paintings of this scene. "And he led them out as far as Bethany, and he lifted up his hands, and blessed them. And it came to pass, while he blessed them, he was parted from them, and carried up into heaven" (Luke 24: 50, 51). "And while they looked stedfastly toward heaven as he went up, behold, two men stood by them in white apparel; Which also said, Ye men of Galilee, why stand ye gazing up into heaven? this same Jesus, which is taken up from you into heaven, shall so come in like manner as ye have seen him go into heaven" (Acts 1:10, 11). "And they worshipped him, and returned to Jerusalem with great joy: And were continually in the temple, praising and blessing God. Amen" (Luke 24: 52, 53).

¶The Church's teaching about the four last things: Death, Judgment, Heaven, and Hell, was quite widely portrayed by Renaissance painters. The themes most commonly used were the following:

The World Beyond

Christ in Limbo or the Descent into Hell: According to the Christian Creeds, after the Crucifixion and Burial of Christ, He descended into Hell. Hell, or Limbo, is portrayed in Renaissance painting as a cavelike place, crowded with those who await His coming. When its gates are shown, they are being trampled beneath Christ's feet. When the Devil is represented, he is a small, black, and cowering figure. In contrast, Christ is large and commanding, dressed in gleaming garments

153

and carrying the banner of the Resurrection. Adam, the first man, stands at the entrance to greet Him. Next to him stands Eve, and among the crowd behind them can usually be seen the crowned figures of David, Moses, and St. John the Baptist.

The Last Judgment: The Nicene Creed, the statement of Christian belief, asserts that Christ shall return in glory to judge both the living and the dead. In art, the Last Judgment has been shown, from the simple Biblical scene of the separation of the sheep and the goats, to the highly imaginative interpretations of the later Renaissance painters. In the latter, Christ is shown as the Presiding Judge. Frequently, the Virgin Mary is shown at His right, and St. John the Baptist at His left. In the upper part of the scene are the angelic hosts and the blessed company of saints and martyrs. Below, the graves yield up their dead at the sound of the trumpets borne by angels. Michael, the Archangel of the Last Judgment, balances the good and the evil in his scales, or sounds the trumpet of the Last Judgment. Often, other angels hover near Christ, bearing the instruments of His Passion. At His right hand, the elect are rising to their reward in Heaven; and at His left hand, the damned are being cast down into Hell.

Christ, with a radiance about Him, is usually seated upon a throne or rainbow. He shows His wounds, the mantle He wears leaving His right side uncovered. His appearance is expressive of His role as Judge. He may

154

turn away from the damned; His right hand, with palm upward, extends welcome to the elect; His left hand, with palm downward, rejects the damned. St. Peter, with his keys, often stands near by to admit the elect into Heaven. The scene of the Last Judgment may be shown in a single composition. Frequently, however, Heaven and Hell are shown as separate compositions.

Heaven: The three Renaissance concepts of Heaven: namely, the Realm beyond the Skies, the Garden of Paradise, and the Heavenly City, have the first two more frequently shown. Seated upon banks of clouds, the ranks of the elect are introduced to the everlasting happiness of eternal life in a richly flowered garden. Frequently, the Garden of Paradise is shown beyond the gates of Heaven.

Hell: The imagination of the Renaissance painters gave many concepts to the representation of Hell. Sometimes it was indicated as a dragon's mouth into which demons and lost souls were entering. Again, the Devil and a few of his host sufficed to convey the idea. At other times the Infernal City was shown filled with fire and smoke. Most elaborate are the pictures which represent, on a terraced mountain, the seven successive circles of damnation.

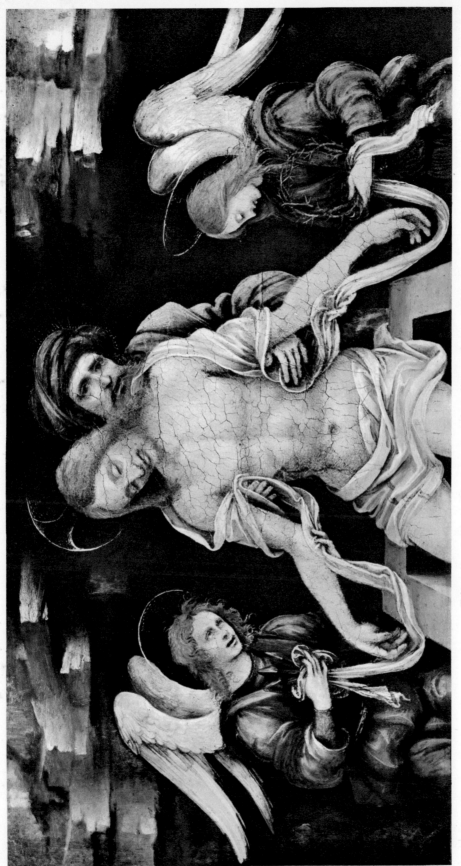

41. Filippino Lippi: *Pietà*. National Gallery of Art, Washington

42. Benvenuto di Giovanni: *The Descent into Limbo*. From the predella 'The Passion of Our Lord'.
National Gallery of Art, Washington

43. Ambrogio Borgognone: *The Resurrection*. National Gallery of Art, Washington

44. Leandro da Ponte da Bassano: *The Last Judgement*. Kress Collection, New York

Section ix

The Trinity, the Madonna, and Angels

In Renaissance painting, God may be represented in two principal ways. The Unity of the Godhead may be stressed or the Three Persons of the Trinity may be depicted. In the latter representations, the Father, the Son, and the Holy Ghost may appear together or separately, depending upon the subject portrayed. Generally, the activity of the Person of the Godhead is emphasized: God the Father presides over the creation of the world, the Son endures the Passion, and the Holy Ghost illumines the Church, the society of the redeemed.

¶In obedience to the second commandment, pictorial representations of God the Father had been avoided by early painters. Gradually, however, the feeling of sacrilege involved in the portrayal of the Almighty was overcome. At first, only the hand of God emerging from a cloud as a sign of His power came to be portrayed. Later His head was shown, then His bust, and finally His whole figure. By the time of the Renaissance, the representations of God the Father were used freely. Previously, when the whole figure of God was shown it stood for the Trinity rather than for the Father alone, but by the time of the Renaissance this distinction had

God the Father

157

been lost. The distinctive attributes of God the Father, by which He may be identified in Renaissance art in contrast to the other Persons of the Trinity, are His age and often the triangular halo. He may hold the globe or a book, though these attributes He shares with other personalities. He may be clad in papal dress and wear the papal tiara, although this attire is more frequent in Northern painting than in the Italian Renaissance.

God the Son ¶Representations of Christ as the Son of God appear not only in scenes of His earthly life but also in His continuing activity as the Son of God: seated at the right hand of the Father; the Judge of the living and the dead. In these, Christ is portrayed in a manner appropriate to the scene. (See Jesus Christ, in Section VIII)

In devotional pictures, Christ is usually depicted as younger than His Father. He may be represented in His maturity, bearded, bearing the wounds, and with bare feet; or He may appear as a child, either in company with His mother or, more rarely, alone. The Christ Child always stands for the Incarnation, but He may carry the symbols of His Passion to emphasize the relationship between His Incarnation and His sacrifice on behalf of mankind.

Instead of being shown in His human nature, Christ may also be represented as a lamb, with reference to the words of St. John the Baptist (John 1: 29), ". . . Behold the Lamb of God, which taketh away the sin of the

158

world," and also with reference to the vision in Revelation 5: 6, "And I beheld, and, lo, in the midst of the throne and of the four beasts, and in the midst of the elders, stood a Lamb as it had been slain, having seven horns and seven eyes, which are the seven Spirits of God sent forth into all the earth."

Less frequently Christ is represented as a lion. The fish, His very common symbol in Early Christian art, seems to have become obsolete by the Renaissance.

Other representations widely portrayed are:

The Crucified Christ: Christ upon the Cross, usually with the crosses of the two thieves on either side, with the Virgin and St. John the Evangelist standing at the foot of His Cross.

The Descent from the Cross: Christ being tenderly taken down from the Cross. This scene is also known as "The Deposition."

The Entombment: The Christ is frequently portrayed, after His death, being placed in the tomb. He may be erect, or sitting upright, showing His wounds and supported by angels. With Him may be the Virgin Mary, St. John the Evangelist, and the other two Marys.

Pietà: The dead Christ is shown in the arms of the Virgin Mary.

The Man of Sorrows: The Christ, living but showing His five wounds, and often accompanied by the instruments of His Passion.

Salvator Mundi (*Saviour of the World*): Christ holding the globe, crowned with thorns and sometimes carrying the Cross.

Noli Me Tangere and the *Road to Emmaus*: Both of these are Resurrection appearances which may depict the Christ as a gardener or pilgrim.

The specific attributes of Christ customary in Renaissance art are the cruciform halo, the cross, the stigmata, and the book. The book may have an inscription written upon it. Inscriptions most often used were "Pax vobis" (Peace be unto you), "Ego sum via, veritas, et vita" (I am the way, the truth, and the life), "Ego sum lux mundi" (I am the light of the world), "Ego sum resurrectio" (I am the resurrection), and "Qui vidit me videt et Patrem" (Whoever seeth me, seeth the Father). Various monograms are also used as symbols of Christ. Greek alphabetical letters, such as alpha and omega (the first and the last), or chi and rho, the first two letters of "Christos" (Christ) in Greek, frequently appear in representations of Christ. (See Cross, in Section XIII; Monograms, in Section XI)

God the Holy Ghost

❡The Holy Ghost is usually depicted as a white dove. When seen together with the other Persons of the Trinity, He may be depicted in human form, either identical with the other Persons or of a considerably younger age. On Pentecost, in accordance with the promise of Christ that He would send the Holy Ghost to dwell in

His Church, the Apostles were gathered in one place, and "suddenly there came a sound from heaven as of a rushing mighty wind, and it filled all the house where they were sitting. And there appeared unto them cloven tongues like as of fire, and it sat upon each of them. And they were all filled with the Holy Ghost..." (Acts 2: 2 - 4). In the paintings of Pentecost the Holy Ghost appears in the form of rays of light or flames.

¶ There are various ways of depicting the Trinity. When the idea of the Oneness or the Unity of God is being stressed, one figure, or three identical figures, may be shown. Otherwise, the three Persons are distinguished by Their individual attributes. God the Father is represented as a white-bearded older man; the Son, younger, bears the Cross or is nailed to it; and the Holy Ghost is depicted in the form of a dove. More rarely, the Trinity is represented by three persons of different ages.

The Trinity

¶ With the exception of Christ, no other figure is so frequently portrayed in Renaissance art as the Virgin Mary. Basically, Mary is the personification of grace and purity. She is the merciful mother, gathering together in her nature all the sweetness of womanhood. In art, many different symbols and attributes are used to identify her and to emphasize her outstanding characteristics. Most common among the devotional and idealized representations of Mary are:

The Virgin Mary

161

The *Madonna Adoring the Christ Child*: Such pictures show Mary kneeling before the Infant Christ in worship and adoration. This concept is sometimes combined with representations of the Nativity.

The *Mater Amabilis* (*Mother Worthy of Love*): Mary holds the Divine Child. She is usually standing, but is often seated on a throne.

The *Madonna of Humility*: Such pictures show Mary seated on the ground with the Christ Child.

The *Virgin in Glory*, wherein Mary is usually shown standing in the sky, surrounded by a radiance and supported, or surrounded, by the heads of cherubs.

The *Queen of Heaven*, wherein Mary is portrayed standing on the crescent moon, crowned as a queen. Frequently the crown bears the twelve stars of the apocalyptical vision (Revelation 12:1).

The *Majesty of the Madonna*, which shows Mary as a celestial monarch enthroned amid a retinue of angels.

Madonna del Misericordia (*Mother of Mercy*), wherein Mary is shown standing and gathering under her mantle kneeling crowds of the faithful whom she is protecting. Sometimes, when such devotional pictures were commissioned by monastic orders or religious brotherhoods, the kneeling crowds wear the habit of the particular order or brotherhood for which the painting was done.

The *Madonna del Soccorso* (*Mother of Succor*), closely connected with the Mother of Mercy, is a particular

162

form of devotion to the Virgin as the protector of children. The Virgin as protector is commonly shown carrying a club and chasing away an ugly devil which is trying to frighten a child. This type of image seems to be peculiar to the Renaissance and was used for the most part in central Italy.

The *Mater Dolorosa* (*Mother of Sorrow*) shows the Virgin sorrowing for the Passion of her Son, with hands clasped, tears running down her face, and sometimes wearing the crown of thorns over her veil.

The *Virgin of the Immaculate Conception*, wherein, during the Renaissance period, she is shown either in connection with her parents Joachim and Anna or with the Godhead (Father, Son, Holy Ghost). The attributes which most frequently identify the Virgin of the Immaculate Conception are:

1. the sun and moon (see Sun and Moon, in Section III)
2. the lily (see Lily, in Section II)
3. the rose without thorns (see Rose, in Section II)
4. the enclosed garden (see Garden, in Section III)
5. the sealed fountain (see Fountain, in Section III)
6. the cedar of Lebanon (see Cedar, in Section II)
7. the tree of Jesse (see Tree, in Section II)
8. the closed gate (see Gate, in Section XIV)
9. the spotless mirror (see Mirror, in Section XIV)
10. the tower of David (see Tower, in Section XIV)
11. the twelve stars (see Star, in Section III)

The Virgin of the Rosary was particularly favored by the Dominicans because, according to legend, the Virgin appeared to St. Dominic, founder of the order, and gave him a rosary. In paintings of this type, the central figure of the Virgin, holding a rosary, is often accompanied by her three types of mysteries: the joyful, the sorrowful, and the glorious. (See Rosary, in Section XIII)

Votive images of the Virgin may be connected with a particular occasion, or with a specific church for which the Virgin is said to have performed some miracle or evidenced a special favor. Some of the best known among these are:

The Madonna del Carmine, which portrays the Virgin as the founder of the Carmelite Order.

The Madonna di Loreto, which alludes to the miraculous transportation of the house of Nazareth to Loreto in Italy after the Holy Land was conquered by the infidel Saracens. In paintings of this type, the Virgin holds in her hand a building, which often has the appearance of a church. This represents the Sanctuary of Loreto, built over the original small chapel to protect it.

The Santa Maria della Neve, which refers to the miraculous building of the Church of Santa Maria Maggiore in Rome. According to legend, the Virgin indicated the plan of the church by a miraculous snowfall in August, which marked the site for the church as well as its future contours.

The Santa Maria della Vittoria, which depicts the image of the Virgin invoked in battle. She is usually represented in the sky with an army or fighting ships below. She may be represented enthroned with the victors in adoration.

The Madonna della Peste, a devotional image of the Virgin invoked against the plague. Here the Virgin is shown either hovering over a plague-stricken city or surrounded by the saints customarily invoked against the plague, such as St. Sebastian, St. Roch, and the Physician saints, Cosmas and Damian. Local patron saints may also appear in the picture, such as St. Petronio for Bologna, or St. Rosalie for Palermo.

In addition to the attributes mentioned above to identify the Virgin, others frequently used are the star, the rose, the sealed book, and the girdle (see individual listings).

⸿The word "angel" means a messenger, a "bringer of tidings." Mention of the angels and their office as "messengers and ministers from God" is so frequent in the Scriptures that belief in their existence is embedded in the Christian tradition. In this tradition the angelic host is divided into three tiers, or hierarchies, and each of these is in turn divided into three choirs. The most commonly accepted division and order of the angelic host is that established by Pseudo-Dionysius the Areopagite, as follows:

Angels and Archangels

165

First Hierarchy : Seraphim, Cherubim, Thrones.

Second Hierarchy : Dominations, Virtues, Powers.

Third Hierarchy : Princedoms, Archangels, Angels.

In the *First Hierarchy* the Seraphim are absorbed in perpetual love and adoration immediately around the throne of God. Seraphim, as representatives of Divine Love, are usually painted in red color and sometimes hold burning candles. The Cherubim know God and worship Him. Cherubim, representing Divine Wisdom, are portrayed in golden yellow or in blue. They are sometimes shown holding books. The Thrones sustain His Seat. Thrones represent Divine Justice. Frequently they wear the robes of judges and carry the staff of authority in their hands. They are believed to receive their glory directly from God and to bestow it upon the Second Hierarchy.

The *Second Hierarchy*, composed of the Dominations, Virtues, and Powers, is made up of the regents and the governors of the stars and the elements. They, in turn, illuminate the Third Hierarchy with the glory which they have received. Dominations are crowned, carry sceptres, and sometimes orbs, as emblems of authority. They represent the Power of God. Virtues carry white lilies, or sometimes red roses as symbols of Christ's Passion. Powers are often dressed in full armor as victorious warriors against the hordes of evil devils.

It is through the *Third Hierarchy*, the Princedoms, Archangels, and Angels, that the heavenly contact is

166

maintained with the created universe and with man, for these are the executors of the Will of God.

In relation to man the Princedoms are the dispensers of the fate of nations; the Archangels are the warriors of heaven; the Angels are the guardians of the innocent and the just. Both Archangels and Angels are the messengers of God to man.

In addition to the functions that are already listed, the angelic hosts act as the choristers of heaven.

⁋In spite of the fact that angels are almost universally represented in Renaissance art, only the archangels have assumed an individual form with definite character and attributes. Revelation 8: 2 mentions "the seven angels which stood before God," but they are not acknowledged by name in the Church. Seven great angels are occasionally introduced as being in attendance at the Crucifixion, in scenes of the Last Judgment, and in the Pieta. More often, they are used as decorative figures.

Archangels

The four archangels mentioned in the Scriptures are Michael, Gabriel, Raphael, and Uriel. According to the Hebrew tradition, these four archangels sustain the throne of God. Of these four, only the first three are given distinct personalities and have been accorded the title of saint. As the heavenly messengers, guides, and protectors of the church militant on earth, their gracious beauty, divine prowess, and lofty relations with mortal man have made them most prominent in Christian art.

167

St. Michael   ⫷The name of the Archangel Michael means " like unto God." Chriſtian tradition describes him as the Captain-General of the hoſts of heaven, the Protector of the Jewish nation who became, after the Chriſtian revelation, the Protector of the Church Militant in Chriſtendom. God has beſtowed upon Michael many and great privileges. It is he who will sound the last trumpet at the general resurrection; " In a moment, in the twinkling of an eye, at the last trump: for the trumpet ſhall sound and the dead ſhall be raised incorruptible, and we ſhall be changed " (I Corinthians 15: 52). It is his office to receive the immortal spirits when they are released from death and to weigh them in a balance; " Thou art weighed in the balances, and art found wanting" (Daniel 5: 27). His office of Protector of the Hebrew nation led him to become the guardian of the redeemed in Chriſtendom against his old adversary, the Prince of Hell.

The representations of St. Michael the Archangel in the Renaissance era were many. He is invariably depicted as young and beautiful, and most often clothed in a dazzling coat of mail with sword, spear, and shield. Resplendent wings rise from his shoulders. He sometimes wears a jeweled crown. Most frequently he is doing battle with Satan, who is represented as a serpent, dragon, or demon. This refers to the dramatic description in Revelation 12: 7-9, "And there was war in heaven: Michael and his angels fought against

45. Jacopo Tintoretto: *The Trinity adored by the Heavenly Choir*. Columbia Museum of Art, Columbia, S.C.

46. Sandro Botticelli: *The Virgin adoring her Child*. National Gallery of Art, Washington

47. Moretto da Brescia: *Pietà*. National Gallery of Art, Washington

48. Giotto and Assistants:
The Peruzzi Altarpiece.
National Gallery of Art, Washington

PRVD ENZA · IVST ITIA · FI DES · CHAR ITAS·

49. Francesco Pesellino: *The Seven Virtues.*
The William Rockhill Nelson Gallery of Art,
Kansas City, Missouri

50. Master of the Franciscan Crucifix: *The Mourning Madonna*.
National Gallery of Art, Washington

51. Domenico Ghirlandaio: *St. Michael*. Portland Art Museum, Portland, Oregon

52. Master of the St. Lucy Legend: *Angels with Musical Instruments*. Detail from 'Mary, Queen of Heaven'. National Gallery of Art, Washington (see Pl. IX)

the dragon; and the dragon fought and his angels, and prevailed not; neither was there place found any more in heaven. And the great dragon was cast out, that old serpent, called the Devil, and Satan, which deceiveth the whole world: he was cast out into the earth, and his angels were cast out with him." When Michael is represented carrying scales, or balances, in his hand he is acting in his office as the weigher of souls.

St. Michael frequently appears in Old Testament paintings, such as the Sacrifice of Isaac, Moses and the Burning Bush, with Joshua at Jericho, and at the Rebuking of David. He plays an important part in the legends of the Virgin, and it was Michael who was sent to announce to the Virgin her approaching death.

St. Gabriel

⧉The Archangel Gabriel, together with Michael and Raphael, is given the title saint in the Christian Church. His name means "God is my strength." He is the guardian of the celestial treasury, the Angel of Redemption, and the Chief Messenger of God. It is in this latter office that he figures so prominently in the Christian tradition.

It is Gabriel who is sent to Daniel to announce the return of the Jews from their captivity. He foretells the birth of Samson in the likeness of a "man of God with the countenance of an angel" (Judges 13). It is Gabriel who appears to Zacharias in the temple and tells him that his wife Elisabeth shall bear a son who shall be called John. He is the Angel of the Annunciation; "And in the sixth month the angel Gabriel was sent from God unto a city of Galilee, named Nazareth, to a virgin espoused to a man whose name was Joseph, of the house of David; and the virgin's name was Mary. And the angel came in unto her, and said, Hail, thou that art highly favoured, the Lord is with thee: blessed art thou among women" (Luke 1: 26 - 28). As the Angel of the Annunciation, Gabriel usually bears in his hand a lily or sceptre; in the other he carries a scroll upon which is inscribed *Ave Maria, Gratia Plena* (Hail Mary, full of grace).

In the earlier paintings of the Annunciation, Gabriel is usually shown as a majestic figure and richly robed. He wears a crown and bears a sceptre to indicate sovereignty. His wings are large and many-colored. His right hand is extended in salutation and benediction. He is the principal figure, while the Virgin is represented as receiving the angel with the utmost submission and in deep humility. It is to be noted in representations of this scene after the fourteenth century that a change in the importance of the Virgin and Gabriel takes place. The Virgin becomes the more prominent person and the superior being. She is portrayed as the Queen of the Angels. Gabriel no longer carries the sceptre, but he bears a lily as the symbol of the purity of the Virgin. He is usually shown in a kneeling position with his hands folded on his breast.

in Christian Art

⁋The Archangel Raphael, whose name means "the Medicine of God," is chief of the guardian angels and the guardian angel of all humanity. He is represented as the benign friend of those he serves. He is usually shown as the protector of Tobias on his journey to Gabael in Media. (See Tobias, The Old Testament, in Section V) It is from this ancient Hebrew romance that the attributes of Raphael are gathered and portrayed. Raphael is the protector of the young and the innocent. Especially does he watch over and protect the pilgrim and the wayfarer.

He is usually pictured as a kind, mild, and loving person. His dress is that of a pilgrim or traveler: he wears sandals, and his hair is bound with a diadem. He carries a staff in his hand, and there is sometimes a gourd of water or a wallet slung to his belt. When he is portrayed as a guardian spirit, however, he is richly dressed and a casket or wallet held by a golden belt is slung over his shoulder. He bears a sword in one hand, and the other is raised in the attitude of a warning gesture, as though to say, "Take heed."

Christian tradition relates that it was Raphael, in his office of guardian angel, who appeared to the shepherds on Christmas night with the message: "Fear not: for behold, I bring you good tidings of great joy, which shall be to all people. For unto you is born this day in the city of David a Saviour, which is Christ the Lord" (Luke 2: 10-11).

171

Uriel ⁣⁣ ❡Uriel is portrayed in art much less frequently than are Gabriel and Michael. The name Uriel signifies "the Light of God" and, in Milton's "Paradise Lost," the archangel is represented as the regent of the sun. Early legend states that it was Uriel who, as ambassador of Christ, appeared to the disciples at Emmaus. (See Jesus Christ, in Section VIII)

In art, Uriel is usually represented carrying a scroll and a book indicating his role as interpreter of judgments and prophecies.

Prophets ⁣⁣ ❡At the time of the Renaissance the general belief was that the Old Testament was to be understood as a record of God's preparing men, in their lives and thinking, for the coming of Christ. The events of the Old Testament were seen as anticipating that which had now come to pass in the Christian era. As the great patriarchs, kings, and leaders of the Old Testament were seen in their similarities to Christ, so the Prophets were honored because by their words they had predicted His coming.

In art, the Prophets were the embodiment of a symbol rather than portraits of actual human beings. For this reason no special attempt was made at characterization. The Prophets are usually a counterpart of the four Evangelists and the twelve Apostles, so that their number may be as many as sixteen, but their selection varies a great deal, and often patriarchs and kings were included with them without discrimination. The Prophets most frequently represented are Isaiah, Jeremiah, Daniel, Ezekiel, and Jonah. Only Jonah has an attribute which is distinctive: the whale. The other Prophets are usually recognized by a book or scroll upon which their prophecy is written. Besides the Jonah story, there are other illustrations from the books of the Prophets in Italian Renaissance art, notably the Vision of Ezekiel based on Ezekiel 1. The best-known examples, of course, are those of Michelangelo on the ceiling of the Sistine Chapel.

Sibyls

ⒻThe Sibyls are the counterpart of the Prophets. As the Prophets connect the Jewish world with Christianity, so the Sibyls connect the Greek and Roman world with the Christian era. The Sibyls had considerable prominence in antiquity. Varro, who lived in the first century before Christ, says that they were ten in number. To these were later added two more. The attributes of the Sibyls vary, just as there is no agreement concerning their prophecies. The most commonly represented in the Middle Ages were the Erythrean, who is supposed to have foretold the Annunciation, and the Tiburtine. The Latin adjectives indicating the geographical associations of the various Sibyls are as follows: Persica, Libyca, Erythrea, Delphica, Samia, Cumena, Cimmeria, Hellespontina, Phrygia, Tiburtina, Agrippa, or Hebraica, and Europa. These are often

173

inscribed beside the representations of the Sibyls in Renaissance art. Portrayals of the Sibyls are frequent in the Renaissance, either isolated or as a group.

Virtues and Vices, and Liberal Arts

⸿ Among the abstract personalities that are frequently represented in Renaissance art are those of the Seven Virtues, the Seven Vices, and the Liberal Arts. The Seven Virtues, all female, are usually as follows:

Faith is represented as a woman with a chalice or a cross, or both. At her feet is St. Peter.

Hope is a winged woman who raises her hands toward heaven. Her standard attribute is the anchor. St. James the Great is at her feet.

Charity usually has children around her and is nursing one of them. Sometimes she holds flames or a heart. St. John the Evangelist is seated at her feet.

Temperance holds a sword or two vases. At her feet is Scipio Africanus.

Prudence may have two heads, and she holds a mirror and a serpent. At her feet is Solon.

Fortitude may have a sword, a club, a shield, a globe, and a lionskin, or a column, in allusion to Samson's destruction of the Philistine temple. At her feet is Samson.

Justice holds scales and a sword. The Emperor Trajan is at her feet.

The first three of these are called the Theological Virtues, while the last four are known as the Cardinal Virtues.

To the Seven Virtues are opposed the Seven Vices, as follows: pride, covetousness, lust, anger, gluttony, envy, and sloth. Their attributes are not clearly defined.

In Renaissance painting, the Seven Virtues are sometimes accompanied by the seven Liberal Arts: grammar, logic, rhetoric, arithmetic, music, geometry, and astronomy. Their attributes are not clearly defined.

Section x

The Saints

¶St. Agatha of Sicily was a beautiful Christian girl who consecrated her body and soul to the Saviour. Quintianus, at that time the governor of Sicily, heard of Agatha's beauty and had her brought to his palace. In spite of every offer, however, Agatha refused to deny Christ, declaring that she belonged to her Heavenly Bridegroom. Enraged by her refusal to give herself to him, Quintianus resolved to punish her by subjecting her to the most cruel tortures. He had Agatha's breasts torn with shears and ordered that she was to be thrown into a great fire. Divine help saved her. Her wounded breasts were healed during the night by St. Peter and an accompanying angel, while an earthquake saved her from the fire. At last, the weary saint prayed that she might be released from her pain by death, and her prayer was granted.

About a year after her death, the city of Catania was threatened with destruction by a stream of molten lava which poured down from Mt. Etna. The people of the city rushed to the tomb of St. Agatha and, taking her silken veil, carried it upon a lance to meet the advancing river of fire. When the stream of lava met the sacred relic it turned aside, and the town was saved. Many were converted to Christianity by this miracle.

Agatha
Third Century

177

St. Agatha is usually painted carrying in one hand a palm branch as a symbol of victory and in the other a dish or salver bearing two female breasts, in allusion to her martyrdom. The shears, or pincers, instruments of her martyrdom, are sometimes shown in her hand or beside her. She is generally wearing a long veil, with reference to the miracle that saved Catania from the eruption of Mt. Etna.

Agnes (Inez)
Third Century

⁋St. Agnes, the child saint of Salerno and Rome, was only thirteen when she consecrated her life to Christianity. She declared herself the Bride of Christ and refused to marry the son of the prefect of Rome, who greatly loved her. The boy's father tried to shake her resolve, first by persuasion and then by shame. He caused her to be brought to a house of ill repute, where she was stripped of her garments. But as she prayed that her body, consecrated to Christ, might be kept pure for His sake, her hair grew to great length and covered her, and a bright and shining robe was sent to her from Heaven. Thereupon the prefect said that she was to be burned, but she stood unharmed in the midst of the flames. Finally, one of the soldiers standing by was told to strike off her head with his sword. After her burial many Christians came to worship at her grave, and on one occasion she is said to have appeared before them radiant with heavenly glory and with a lamb, symbol of purity, at her side.

178

In art, St. Agnes is easily recognizable by her attribute, the lamb. She may have a sword or flames at her feet in token of her martyrdom. She is sometimes shown covered by her long hair or by a long robe.

¶St. Ambrose is one of the four Latin Fathers of the Church. The son of a Roman prefect, he was born in Treves, in Gaul, and educated at Rome. He himself became a prefect of two Roman provinces and, in this capacity, went to Milan to restore peace in a dispute with the Arians which arose during the election of a new bishop.

Ambrose
Fourth Century

Legend states that he was addressing the people in Milan one day when a child's voice was heard to declare, "Ambrose shall be Bishop." This was taken as a sign from Heaven, and Ambrose was forthwith elected to the post, although he was not at that time even baptized. He devoted himself, however, to his new duties and proved to be a great statesman, theologian, and religious poet. He was responsible for raising Church services to a new dignity and impressiveness, and he originated the Ambrosian chant, a mode of intoning the liturgy.

St. Ambrose is painted in the dress of a bishop with mitre and crosier and holding a book. Sometimes he carries a scourge, which refers to his part in driving the Arians out of Italy. He is also shown with a beehive, a reference to the legend that, when he was an infant, a swarm of bees alighted on his mouth, thus foretelling his future eloquence.

Andrew, Apostle ¶ St. Andrew the Apostle, brother of Simon Peter, the fisherman of Bethsaida in Galilee, was one of the first disciples of Christ. According to tradition, when the Apostles were each allotted a part of the world to evangelize, Andrew was given the country to the north as far as southern Russia. His preaching converted so many people to the Christian faith that the Roman governor of Patrae in Greece feared a popular uprising. He had Andrew arrested and, after subjecting him to all kinds of tortures, had him bound to a cross in order to prolong his sufferings. The cross to which he was tied is believed to have been in the shape of an X, although very early representations of the saint show him tied to the straight cross or to one of the shape of a Y. The attribute of St. Andrew is the X cross, instrument of his martyrdom. He is a patron saint of Scotland.

Anna ¶ St. Anna, according to tradition, mother of the Virgin Mary, appears in many Renaissance works of art. She is shown in scenes of the life of the Virgin, such as the Meeting at the Golden Gate, teaching her child to read, or in the Presentation of the Virgin in the Temple. She also appears in pictures of the Holy Family with the Christ Child. (See The Virgin Mary, in Section VII)

Her chief emblems are the green mantle and red

dress, symbols of immortality and divine love. She may also be depicted holding a book.

¶ St. Ansanus, born of a noble Roman family, was secretly baptized when he was a child by his nurse Maxima, and brought up a Christian. At nineteen, in spite of the persecution of the Christians under the Emperor Diocletian, Ansanus openly declared his faith, and he and Maxima were subjected to the scourge. Maxima died, but Ansanus recovered and was taken as a prisoner to the city of Siena. There he preached the gospel and made many converts. Because of this, he was beheaded by order of the Emperor.

Ansanus was known as the Apostle of Siena and was adopted as a patron saint of that city. His customary attributes are a banner with the Cross and the fountain or baptismal cup.

Ansanus
Third Century

¶ Anthony the Great, or Anthony Abbot, is one of the figures most frequently portrayed in Renaissance painting. He was born in Upper Egypt of noble and wealthy Christian parents. After their death, when Anthony was eighteen, his spirit was suddenly awakened. He distributed all his worldly goods among the poor and, staff in hand, joined a band of hermits in the desert. His whole future life was devoted to self-denial and spiritual growth. For twenty years he lived alone in a ruin near the Nile, where he strove to overcome all

Anthony Abbot
Fourth Century

181

weakness of the flesh and to live for God alone. His struggles with temptations, which he called his "demons," have been the subject of many works of art. When he reappeared from his solitude, he had acquired such spiritual strength that many came to live near him in order to be under his guidance. At the age of ninety, he believed that no man had lived so long as he in solitude and self-denial. But he heard a voice saying, "There is one holier than thou, for Paul the Hermit, has served God in solitude and penance for ninety years." Anthony, therefore, went in search of the Hermit Paul.

On his way he met many wonders and temptations. A centaur and a satyr pointed out the way to him, while an ingot of gold was placed on his path by the Devil to stop him. But the saint dispelled all temptations with the sign of the Cross, and finally reached the cave where Paul was living. When they met, Paul told how each day for sixty years a raven had brought him half a loaf of bread. The two old men started to live together in the desert, and the raven thereafter brought, every day, a whole loaf of bread. After Paul's death, Anthony returned to his own dwelling, where he remained for fourteen years, until his own death at the age of one hundred and five.

St. Anthony is regarded as the father of monasticism. He is, therefore, usually represented in the hood and robe of a monk. On his left shoulder is a blue T, originally a theta, the first letter of the word "Theos,"

182

which means "God" in Greek. He bears a crutch, significant of his great age, and carries a bell, either in his hand or suspended from his crutch. The significance of this attribute is explained in different ways. The most common belief is that it symbolizes the ability of the saint to exorcise demons and evil spirits. A hog, representative of the demon of sensuality and gluttony, often accompanies St. Anthony as an indication of the saint's triumph over sin.

As a reminder that a vision of the flames of hell killed in St. Anthony the desires of the flesh, the saint is sometimes represented with flames under his feet.

⁋ St. Anthony of Padua was born in Lisbon and brought up in the cathedral school of that city. He first joined the Order of St. Augustine but, having heard much of the holiness of St. Francis, he sought out the founder of the Franciscans in Assisi. St. Francis at first thought Anthony was a simple, well-meaning youth, but after Anthony had had an opportunity to preach, St. Francis appreciated the young man's oratorical ability and entrusted to him much of the educational work of the Order. Anthony soon became the favorite disciple and close friend of Francis. He developed a wonderful gift of preaching and was greatly beloved by the people. He taught divinity at Bologna, Montpellier, Toulouse, and Padua, where he died at the early age of thirty-six.

Several legends are told about this saint. Among

Anthony of Padua
Thirteenth Century

183

them is the story of the heretic of Toulouse who refused to believe in the presence of Christ in the Eucharist unless his ass left its stable and knelt before the Sacrament. A few days later, when St. Anthony was leaving the church to carry the Eucharist to a dying man, the ass met him at the steps and knelt before the Sacrament.

Because of this legend, St. Anthony is frequently portrayed with a kneeling ass. He is generally painted in the robe of the Franciscan Order. In his hands are often seen his other attributes in art: the lily, the flowered Cross, the fish, a book, and fire. Especially after the Renaissance he came to be represented carrying the Christ Child. He is the patron saint of Padua.

Apollonia
Third Century

It is said that in Alexandria there was a magician who was held in great esteem by the pagan population. He ordered a general persecution of the Christians because they despised and destroyed the gods he worshiped. Many Christians left the city to avoid death, but Apollonia, a deaconess of the Church, remained in the city to comfort the few who were left there. She awaited her martyrdom with joy, preaching the Christian faith and making many converts. For this she was arrested by the authorities and ordered to sacrifice to the gods of the city. The saint, however, made the sign of the Cross before the idols she was ordered to worship, and the statues broke into a thousand fragments. As punishment she was bound to a column and her teeth

184

53. Pupil of Pietro Lorenzetti: *St. Andrew the Apostle.* Kress Collection, New York

54. Giovanni da Milano: *St. Anthony Abbot*.
Kress Collection, New York

55. Vincenzo Foppa: *St. Anthony of Padua*.
National Gallery of Art, Washington

56. Piero della Francesca: *St. Apollonia*. National Gallery of Art, Washington

were pulled out by pincers. She was then taken out-side the city, where a great fire had been prepared for her death. But Apollonia, far from being afraid of the flames, cast herself into the fire and offered her body to Christ.

Her attributes are the palm of martyrdom and a pair of pincers holding a tooth. She is the patron saint of dentists.

¶St. Augustine, one of the four Latin Fathers of the Church, was born in Numidia and educated in Car-thage. He then went to Rome, where he studied law and became noteworthy for his learning. His mother, Mon-ica, was a Christian and sought to have him follow the doctrine of the Church. Augustine, however, having previously embraced the Manichean teaching, refused her plea, although he became increasingly aware of a great moral struggle within himself. His argument for rejecting the Christian faith was that it was too simple and valuable only for simple minds. It was not until he came to Milan, as professor of rhetoric, that he was attracted to Christianity. It was the influence of St. Ambrose, then Bishop of Milan, that finally led him to accept the Christian faith. He made a public confession and received baptism. It was on this occasion that the *Te Deum* was sung for the first time. Augustine later be-came Bishop of Hippo, in Africa, where he remained for the rest of his life, and where he died of fever at

Augustine
Fifth Century

185

the age of seventy-six during the siege of the city by the Vandals. He had a tremendous influence on the Christian religion, both through his writings and his spiritual example. In his famous literary work, his *Confessions*, he told the story of his spiritual life.

St. Augustine is generally painted in the habit of a bishop bearing a book and pen, in reference to his writings. His special attribute, however, is a flaming heart, sometimes pierced by an arrow, suggestive of his flaming piety and love of God. One episode of his life has been frequently represented. The story is that while walking along the seashore St. Augustine came upon a small boy who was apparently trying to empty the entire ocean into a hole in the sand. The saint remarked to the youngster that he was seemingly attempting the impossible. To this the boy replied, "No more so than for thee to explain the mysteries on which thou art meditating."

Barbara
Third Century

⁋ St. Barbara was born either at Heliopolis in Egypt or at Nicomedia in Asia Minor. She was brought up by her father, a rich heathen, who loved her very much and was fearful some man would marry her and take her away. According to the legend, he therefore built for her a high tower, richly furnished, where she was jealously guarded from the world. Hearing of Christianity, she became interested and arranged to receive a Christian disciple disguised as a physician. She was

186

converted and baptized. One day, during her father's absence, realizing that her tower had but two windows, she commanded the workmen to make a third. On her father's return, she confessed her new faith to him and explained that the soul received its light through three windows: the Father, Son, and Holy Ghost. Enraged at her conversion to Christianity, the girl's father gave her up to the authorities, who ordered her to be tortured. Finally, at his own request, her father was permitted to strike off her head. As he returned home after committing this awful deed, the father was killed by a bolt of lightning, which struck him down in the midst of a great crash of thunder. Because of this thunderous punishment, St. Barbara has become the patron saint of artillery and hence of soldiers, gunsmiths, and fire fighters. She is invoked against accidents and sudden death.

Her invariable attribute is the tower, generally with three windows. She also sometimes carries the sacramental cup and wafer, and is the only female saint who bears this attribute. She does so in reference to her last wish. At the moment of her death, the saint requested the grace of the Sacrament for all who would honor her martyrdom. A peacock's feather, which is also her attribute, refers to Heliopolis, the city of her birth. This city was said to be the place in which the fabulous phoenix rejuvenated itself. Since the phoenix was unknown in the West, a peacock was substituted in its place as emblem of the city.

Bartholomew, Apostle

¶ St. Bartholomew is one of Christ's disciples about whom little is known. The tradition is that he traveled east as far as India. While preaching in Armenia, on his return journey, he was seized by the heathens, flayed alive, and then crucified. Thus, his invariable attribute is a large knife of peculiar shape, the instrument of his martyrdom. He is occasionally portrayed bearing a human skin over one arm, which indicates his flaying.

Benedict

Sixth Century

¶ St. Benedict, founder of the Benedictine Order, was born near Spoleto at Norcia, in what is now Umbria. At an early age, he became a hermit and attracted many disciples because of the holiness of his life. In order to provide a rule of life for his followers, he established them in twelve monasteries, with a Superior in charge of each. At Monte Cassino he established the great monastery that became the headquarters of his Order, and there he wrote the basic rules that have served as a guide for most of Western monasticism. His sister, Scholastica, became the head of the first community of Benedictine nuns.

St. Benedict is usually shown with a flowing beard, often white, and dressed in the habit of a Benedictine abbot, wearing either the black robe of the original habit of the Order or the white robe of the Reformed Order. Several attributes are given to him, each referring to some well-known episode in his life. A dove represents the soul of his sister Scholastica, which he

188

saw ascending to Heaven at her death. A crystal glass with a serpent or a broken glass with wine running from it recalls the poisoned wine that was once offered to him in an attempt upon his life. A raven recalls the bird that he fed when, as a hermit, he was living in a cave. The index finger sometimes shown across his lips is an allusion to the rule of silence which he gave to his Order. A broken vessel is given to him in reference to the legend of the miracle he once performed in joining together the fragments of a pot broken by his nurse. A luminous ladder refers to the ladder on which he is said to have ascended to Heaven. He is also sometimes represented as a naked youth rolling in a thorny bush to punish his flesh for the sin of lust. A blackbird, referring to his temptation by the Devil, is shown frequently. He is often painted in company with two youths, Maurus and Placidus, who were his close friends and are among the important saints honored by the Benedictine Order. A famous legend tells how on one occasion Placidus left the monastery in which they were living to fetch a pail of water from a near-by lake. In so doing, he slipped and fell into the water and was in danger of drowning. Aware of the situation, Benedict called to Maurus to go to the assistance of their brother monk. Maurus ran toward Placidus and, seizing him by the hair, dragged him to safety. Only after he had returned to the shore of the lake did Maurus realize that he had actually walked upon the water.

Bernard

Twelfth Century

⸿St. Bernard, abbot of Clairvaux in France, was a descendant of one of the greatest families of Burgundy. He studied at the University of Paris and, at the age of twenty-three, entered the parent monastery of the Cistercian Order at Citeaux. His qualities of leadership were such that only two years after he had entered the monastery of Citeaux he was sent with twelve disciples to found a new monastery. The place chosen was Clairvaux. Here Bernard became the great spiritual leader of all Europe. Even the kings of England and France gave heed to his advice and moral persuasion. He was largely instrumental in influencing Louis VI of France to undertake the Second Crusade.

Bernard is usually represented in the white habit of the Cistercian Order with a book or pen in his hand, indicative of his position as head of his Order and of his quality of Doctor of the Church. He is sometimes shown with a demon in chains to represent his defeat of heresy; with three mitres at his feet in reference to the three bishoprics that he refused; or with a beehive in token of his eloquence. The Cross and the instruments of the Passion refer to his main mystic writing, the *Meditations*.

Bernardino

Fifteenth Century

⸿St. Bernardino, of Siena, was born of a patrician family of that city. As a youth, he built himself a small chapel outside the city where he devoted himself to a life of severe asceticism. He later studied law at Siena, where, in 1400, a terrible outbreak of the plague took place. For months Bernardino worked to help the stricken people. He then determined to join the Order of St. Francis and give away all his possessions. After he had been ordained a priest, he journeyed throughout Italy and became tremendously influential in both religious and public affairs. He was offered three bishoprics, which he refused in order to continue as a missionary. At one time, he was accused of heresy by Pope Martin V because of the tablet, inscribed with IHS, the Greek letters symbolizing the name of Jesus, which he used in preaching. At his trial in Rome, he was triumphantly acquitted, and he became known as the founder of the "cult of the devotion to the name of Jesus," which led to the public display of the Holy Name.

Bernardino is generally represented in the Franciscan habit bearing a tablet or sun inscribed with IHS, or a heart. In some paintings mitres, which are symbolic of the three bishoprics he refused, are depicted.

¶ St. Blaise, Bishop of Sebaste in Armenia, was a physician by profession. Moved by divine inspiration, he retired to a cave in the mountains where he lived in contemplation, surrounded by wild animals. Instead of attacking him, however, the savage beasts welcomed him and fawned upon him, and came to him when they were sick or wounded. Here, one day, he was

Blaise
Third Century

191

discovered by some of the emperor's huntsmen, who believed him to be a magician and took him prisoner. Brought before Licinius, he was sentenced to be tortured by having his flesh torn with iron combs and afterward to be thrown into a lake. The story continues that through divine help the saint's wounds were healed, and he walked upon the water, preaching to the multitudes. Thereafter he was beheaded.

In Renaissance painting, the saint is represented as an old man with a white beard, attired as a bishop. He holds an iron comb in allusion to his martyrdom, and a lighted candle in memory of his dying wish for the healing of the sick. He is a patron saint of wild animals. St. Blaise is invoked against sore throats because of the legend that he once saved a child from choking after it had swallowed a fish bone.

Bonaventura
Thirteenth Century

⟪According to legend, the name of this saint may be traced to his infancy when, seriously ill, he was taken by his mother and laid at the feet of St. Francis, who was asked to intervene to save the child's life. The child recovered and St. Francis exclaimed, "O buona ventura!" (Oh good fortune). The mother then dedicated her child to God under that name.

Born at Bagnorea in Tuscany in 1221, Bonaventura joined the Franciscan Order in 1251 and eventually became its Minister General. He was a profound student, theologian, and mystic, and is recognized as the great

192

X. Studio of the Master of Flémalle:

Madonna and Child in the Enclosed Garden, with Saints Catherine of Alexandria, John the Baptist, Barbara and Anthony Abbott.
Kress Collection, New York

scholar of the Franciscans, being called the Seraphic Doctor. Among his well-known writings, of particular interest is his life of St. Francis. He died in Lyons in 1274 while acting as secretary to Pope Gregory X.

According to legend, when the ambassadors of the Pope came to Bonaventura to make him a cardinal, they found him washing his dinner plate. He asked the emissaries to hang his cardinal's hat on the limb of a tree until he was ready to receive it. Therefore, Bonaventura is frequently painted with the cardinal's hat hanging beside him or at his feet. Another legend states that, on one occasion, Bonaventura was too humble in spirit to go to the altar to receive the Holy Sacrament, whereupon an angel brought it to him. An angel bearing the sacramental wafer is sometimes shown in paintings of the saint. Other attributes of the saint are the Cross and the chalice. He is usually portrayed in the habit of the Franciscans, sometimes as a cardinal, sometimes as a friar, but always clean-shaven.

¶This saint was born at Alexandria in Egypt, of a noble and illustrious family, some say of royal blood. The rich legend of this widely loved saint relates that before she was baptized she had a remarkable dream. In it she saw the Virgin Mary holding the Christ Child in her arms. The Virgin asked Jesus to take Catherine as a servant. But the Child averted His head and said that she was not beautiful enough. When she awoke,

Catherine of Alexandria
Third Century

193

Catherine, who was famous for her beauty and her learning, began to wonder how to please the Divine Child, and found no peace until she was baptized. After her baptism, Christ appeared to her again in a dream and took her as His celestial spouse. He put a ring on her finger, which the saint found upon awakening and which she kept for the rest of her life.

At this time Maximin II, who shared the imperial crown with Constantine the Great and Licinius, selected Alexandria as the capital of his part of the Empire. He had pledged himself to the persecution of all Christians and ordered the massacre of all who refused to sacrifice to the gods. Catherine, dedicated to preaching the Christian faith, determined to see the emperor and open his eyes to his cruelty. She delivered such a learned speech that the emperor was taken aback, and decided to gather the most famous philosophers of his realm to refute her teaching. Catherine accepted the challenge and, by her eloquence and intelligence, converted the philosophers to her faith. Enraged, the emperor had the wise men beheaded, and imprisoned Catherine in a dungeon, where he sought to starve her into submission. Angels, however, brought her food, and Catherine succeeded in converting the wife of the emperor and all her retinue. In blind fury, the monarch passed the death sentence on all Christians except Catherine. Overcome by her serene beauty, he offered to make Catherine his wife and empress of the world, but she indignantly refused him. In a final burst of disappointed rage, Maximin then ordered Catherine to be bound between four wheels, rimmed with spikes, and torn to death. As the sentence was being carried out, a great burst of flame from Heaven destroyed the wheels. Catherine was then beheaded.

As the spouse of Christ, and the patron saint of girls, St. Catherine was one of the favorite themes in Renaissance painting. The Marriage of St. Catherine to Christ was widely portrayed. St. Catherine's special and peculiar attribute is the spiked wheel. She is usually shown wearing a crown to signify royalty, bearing a palm in token of victory, and carrying a sword, the instrument of her martyrdom. Sometimes she holds a book, in reference to her great learning.

¶As a young girl, Catherine of Siena dedicated herself to a religious life and prayed that like Catherine of Alexandria she might have Christ as her Heavenly Bridegroom. Her devotion was at first opposed by her family, until one day her father found her kneeling in prayer with a white dove perched upon her head. Thereafter, he allowed her to join the convent of St. Dominic. There she remained for three years in solitude and prayer, and her soul became "enamoured of God's truth." It was following this period of religious seclusion that her Mystic Marriage to Christ is reputed to have taken place. She left the convent and devoted

Catherine of Siena
Fourteenth Century

195

her life to the care of the poor and the sick. Her fame became such that, when the people of Florence were excommunicated by Pope Gregory XI, they requested Catherine to intercede for them. She went to Avignon, where the Pope was in residence, and so impressed him with her intelligence and tact that he permitted her to arrange the terms upon which the Florentines might be reinstated into the Church. She told Gregory that one of the chief causes for the disobedience of the Florentines was the Pope's continued residence in Avignon instead of Rome. As the result of her persuasions, Gregory returned to Italy. Throughout her life, she was a personage of great influence, constantly working for the strengthening and the purification of the Papacy.

Many legends are told about St. Catherine. Among these is a religious experience that occurred at Pisa. One morning during her prayers she was carried away by her love of the Lord. When she regained consciousness she found, imprinted on her hands and feet and side, the stigmata; that is, the marks of the wounds suffered by Christ upon the Cross.

St. Catherine of Siena is represented in the habit of the Dominican Order, of which she is considered to be the greatest female saint, and is shown bearing the stigmata which she is said to have received at Pisa. She frequently holds a cross surmounted by a lily, or a heart. She often carries a rosary and wears a crown

196

57. Taddeo di Bartolo: *St. Augustine*.
Isaac Delgado Museum of Art, New Orleans, Louisiana

58. Studio of the Master of Flémalle: *St. Barbara*.
Detail from 'Madonna and Child in the Enclosed Garden, with Saints Catherine of Alexandria,
John the Baptist, Barbara and Anthony Abbot'. Kress Collection, New York

59. Pietro Perugino: *St. Bartholomew*. Birmingham Museum of Art, Birmingham, Alabama

60. Fra Filippo Lippi: *St. Benedict Orders St. Maurus to the Rescue of St. Placidus*. National Gallery of Art, Washington

of thorns. Her Mystic Marriage remained a popular subject, particularly as an incident in paintings of the Madonna and Child.

¶The popular legend of St. Cecilia says that she was the daughter of a Roman patrician who brought her up as a Christian. She was engaged to a nobleman named Valerian, but after their marriage she told him that she had taken a vow of chastity, which she begged him to respect. Valerian agreed on condition that he might see the angel who, she said, was watching over her. Cecilia sent her husband to St. Urban, who was working with the Christians in the catacombs, and there Valerian was himself converted. On his return to Cecilia he found, standing in her presence, an angel bearing two crowns of flowers. The crown of lilies he placed upon the head of Cecilia, and the crown of roses upon the head of Valerian. Through the ministrations of the angel, Valerian's brother, Tiburtius, was also converted to Christianity, and the two brothers undertook to preach the gospel of Christ. Hearing of this, the governor of Rome ordered them to desist and, when they refused, he had them executed. Cecilia was at first spared, for the governor wished to gain possession of her wealth. He ordered her to sacrifice to the gods. When she refused, he attempted to kill her by suffocation. She was miraculously unharmed, so the governor sent for an executioner to have her beheaded. The exe-

Cecilia

Third Century

cutioner made three attempts to slay her with his sword, but succeeded only in wounding her three times in the neck. Cecilia remained alive for three days, in which time she distributed her wealth to the poor.

During her lifetime Cecilia was reputed to be so close to Heaven that she could hear the singing of the angels; it was also said that she could play any musical instrument. These gifts, however, did not suffice to give expression to the flood of heavenly melody that filled her soul. She therefore invented the organ, which she consecrated to the service of God. She is, for this reason, the patron saint of music and musicians.

In painting, she is usually portrayed listening to music, singing, or playing some musical instrument. Her particular attribute is the organ. She is sometimes shown with three wounds in her neck. There is often a crown of white and red roses on her head, or somewhere near by.

Christopher
Third Century

⁋St. Christopher is a martyr whose story is probably woven about the Greek word, Christopher, meaning the Christ-Bearer. Christopher was reputed to be a man of huge stature and great strength, who resided in the land of Canaan. He wished to find the most powerful sovereign in the world, whom he could serve and obey. He first attached himself to a great king, but when one day a minstrel sang of Satan, the king crossed himself in fear. Christopher then realized that the Devil was even more powerful than the king. So he set out to find Satan, and came across him on a desert plain. They traveled together until they came to a crossroad where a cross stood. Satan was afraid to pass it, and Christopher again realized that he was not serving the most powerful monarch of all. He therefore left Satan to find Christ.

In his wanderings, Christopher came upon a holy hermit who sought to instruct him in Christianity, but Christopher refused to fast, lest he lose his strength, nor would he pray. The hermit at last sent him to a river much swollen by rain, and there Christopher, aided by a palm tree which he had uprooted to use as a staff, helped many people to cross the flooded stream. One night, as Christopher slept, a small child called to him and asked to be carried over the river. Christopher lifted the child on his shoulders and, taking his staff, entered the water. As he strode forward, the river became more and more turbulent and the child upon his shoulders seemed to become heavier and heavier. It was only with the greatest difficulty that Christopher succeeded in reaching the far bank. As he set his passenger down, he breathed deeply and said, "Who art thou, child, that hath placed me in such extreme peril? Had I borne the whole world upon my shoulders, the burden had not been heavier!" To this the child replied, "Christopher, do not be surprised, for thou hast not only borne all the world upon thee, but thou hast borne Him that created the world. I am Jesus Christ, the King." Christ then told Christopher that if he would plant his staff in the earth, in the morning it would bear flowers and fruit. Christopher did this and the miracle was performed. In this way he was converted to Christianity.

Later, at Samos, he was taken before the king, who asked to know who he was. "Formerly I was called Offero, the bearer," he replied, "but now I am called Christopher, for I have borne Christ." The king tried to break down his faith but Christopher stood firm; whereupon the king had him tortured and finally beheaded. As Christopher was being led to his death, he prayed that all who saw him and trusted in God might be saved from fire, storm, and earthquake. For this reason, many statues were erected to him so that all might see him and be protected.

Christopher is generally painted wading through the water with the Infant Christ on his shoulders. In his hand he invariably grasps his palm-tree staff. He is the patron saint of travelers.

Clare
Thirteenth Century

⁋St. Clare of Assisi early dedicated herself to a religious life, becoming a disciple of St. Francis of Assisi. In the year 1212, she went secretly to the mother church of the Franciscan Order, where she was received into the Order of St. Francis. Later she was permitted to establish an order of her own, which was known as the Order of the Poor Clares. Its principal work was the care and education of poor girls. There is a legend that once, when her convent was besieged by Saracens, she arose from her bed and placed the pyx containing the Host on the threshold. She then knelt and began to pray and sing. Seeing the Host, the infidels threw down their arms and fled.

Based upon this legend, St. Clare's attribute in art is the pyx containing the Host. She is usually shown wearing a gray tunic with a black veil and the cord of St. Francis. Other emblems frequently shown with her are the lily of purity, the palm of victory, and the True Cross.

⁋St. Clement of Rome, an Apostolic Father, was one of the earliest bishops of Rome. He was a disciple of St. Peter and St. Paul—which leads some historians to maintain that he was the immediate successor of St. Peter. He was one of the most celebrated early Christian writers and many legends are recounted of him. During the reign of the Roman Emperor Trajan, Clement is said to have been banished to the marble quarries of the Crimea because of his refusal to deny Christianity. Many of his converts followed him, and their sufferings were intense due to the lack of fresh water. As Clement prayed for help, a lamb appeared and led them to a certain spot. Clement struck the ground with a pick axe, and immediately a stream of water gushed

Clement

Second Century

forth. Enraged at this miracle, his persecutors tied an anchor about his neck and hurled him into the sea. Upon the prayers of his followers, however, the waters drew back, revealing a small temple where the body of the saint was found.

Because of these legends, Clement is usually portrayed with an anchor around his neck or beside him. Often he is shown with the lamb that guided him to the water, or the fountain that gushed forth from the earth. He is generally painted in papal robes.

Cosmas and Damian
Third Century

⸿According to legend, Cosmas and Damian were twin brothers of Arabian birth who were brought up in the Christian faith. They devoted their lives to medicine and surgery, of which they are patron saints, in order to help the sick and wounded. They are reputed to have performed various miracles of healing. On one occasion, they treated a man with a diseased leg by cutting off his leg and replacing it with the leg of a Negro who had just died. When the patient awoke from a deep sleep into which he had fallen, he found he had a white leg and a brown one. This dramatic operation was depicted by Fra Angelico, among other Renaissance artists. During the persecution of Christians under the Emperor Diocletian, Cosmas and Damian were seized and condemned to death. They were first cast into the sea, but were rescued by an angel. They were then thrown into a great fire, but the flames would not

202

touch them. Thereupon, they were bound to a cross and stoned, but the stones rebounded without hurting them and killed those who had hurled them. Finally, the two brothers were beheaded.

They are always represented together, generally attired in the physicians' habit of a long red gown and cap. They hold in one hand a box of ointment and in the other a surgical instrument, or a mortar and pestle. They were adopted as patron saints by the famous Medici family of Italy.

¶ St. Dominic, founder of the Dominican Order, was born at Calahorra, in Spain. He belonged to the noble family of Guzman, and was educated at the University of Palencia. At an early age he entered the service of the Church, and in 1215 he went to Rome to obtain papal sanction for his Order of Preachers. This was granted, and in the next few years his black-and-white-robed friars penetrated into every corner of Europe. In 1220, the Order adopted a vow of poverty and became a mendicant brotherhood. Dominic himself traveled constantly and preached wherever he went. He died at Bologna in 1221.

He is generally represented in the habit of his Order. His special attribute is the rosary, for it was he who instituted the devotion of the rosary. He is sometimes shown with a dog bearing a flaming torch in its mouth. Before his birth, his mother is said to have had

Dominic
Thirteenth Century

203

a dream that revealed she had given birth to a dog carrying a lighted torch. This dream came to symbolize the activities of St. Dominic and his Order in spreading the Gospel. A star on his forehead, or on his halo, is in remembrance of the star said to have appeared on his forehead when he was baptized. A loaf of bread refers to an episode that occurred one day during his life. When told that there was nothing to eat in the monastery, he ordered the bell to be rung for the meal and instructed the brothers to sit at table. When all the monks were seated and reciting their prayers, two angels appeared and gave each a loaf of bread. The lily, also an attribute of the saint, is indicative of purity.

Donatus
Fourth Century

¶St. Donatus of Arezzo was of noble birth and was brought up in the Christian faith, together with his foster brother Julian, who later became emperor. Julian, however, denied his faith and persecuted the Christians, including Donatus and his mother and father, who fled to Arezzo. There Donatus was credited with miraculous powers and was eventually chosen Bishop of Arezzo. A number of different legends are told about him and the miracles he performed. A certain tax collector of the city, while absent on a journey, entrusted his tax collections to his wife. To insure its safety, the wife buried the money, but unfortunately she died before her husband's return, so that the place of concealment was not known. The tax collector, ac-

204

61. Roman Painter, 15th Century: *St. Blaise.*
E. G. Crocker Art Gallery, Sacramento, California

62. Pietro Lorenzetti: *St. Catherine of Alexandria*. National Gallery of Art, Washington

63. Antonio da Correggio: *The Mystic Marriage of St. Catherine*. National Gallery of Art, Washington

64. Quentin Massys: *St. Christopher*. Kress Collection, New York

cused of having stolen the money, appealed to Donatus, who went to the wife's tomb and asked her to reveal the hiding place. A voice from the tomb answered, and the money was recovered. On another occasion, while Donatus was celebrating mass, local ruffians came into the church and broke the communion cup. Donatus put the pieces together so not a drop of the communion wine was spilt. The ruffians were thereupon converted to Christianity.

Donatus is generally painted in his bishop's robes. His customary attribute is the broken communion cup. The incident of the tax collector and his wife also is represented in art.

Dorothea
Third Century

⟨St. Dorothea of Cappadocia was a Christian girl famous for her beauty and piety. The renown of her saintly life reached Sapricius, governor of the province, and he ordered two sisters who had renounced Christianity to take charge of her and persuade her to abandon her religion. But Dorothea stood fast, and at last induced the sisters to return to the Church. Sapricius then ordered the two sisters to be burned, and forced Dorothea to witness the execution. The saint encouraged the martyrs in their suffering, and then she was condemned to torture and execution. Legend relates that as she was being led to the place of execution a young lawyer named Theophilus jeered at her and asked her to send him some flowers and fruit from the heavenly garden where she was going. When at the place of execution an angel, in the guise of a small boy, appeared bearing three roses and three apples wrapped in white linen, she commanded him to give these to Theophilus. It was February, and all the trees were covered with frost. Theophilus, surrounded by friends, was scoffing when he saw the boy with the fruit and flowers. At the sight of this miracle, the young man was immediately converted to the Christian faith and subsequently suffered martyrdom.

The usual attributes of St. Dorothea in painting are roses in the hand or on the head, or a basket with three roses and three apples held by an attendant angel. She is sometimes shown offering a basket of fruit and flowers to the Virgin or the Infant Christ. She is also sometimes shown tied to a stake, a burning torch being held at her side.

Elisabeth ❡Elisabeth, mother of John the Baptist, is frequently represented in paintings of the Visitation and of the Birth of John the Baptist, and as an elderly woman. She has no special attributes. (See The Virgin Mary in Section VII; St. John the Baptist in Section VI)

Elisabeth of Hungary
Thirteenth Century

❡Elisabeth of Hungary, daughter of Andreas II, King of Hungary, was born at Pressburg. As an infant, she was betrothed to Ludwig, son of the Landgrave of Thuringia and Hesse, and was taken to live with the family of her future husband. There she was badly treated by the ladies of the court, who were jealous of her beauty. In her loneliness she instinctively turned to religion, devoting her time and substance to the poor. Shortly after her marriage, her husband fell ill while on a Crusade and died. Elisabeth was turned out of her castle by her brother-in-law, who wished to assure his own son of the succession, and placed under the direction of an ascetic priest. Her children were taken from her and, at the age of twenty-four, she died as a result of her fasts and of her labors on behalf of the poor.

Her life of self-sacrifice filled the world with admiration and many legends are told about her. It is said that on one occasion, in the middle of winter, she left her castle with her apron filled with food for the poor. On her way she chanced to meet her husband, who asked what she was carrying. When he opened her apron, he found it filled with roses, and when he bent to kiss her, he saw that her face was transfigured with the radiance of Heaven. Another legend tells how she met a leper whom she took home and put to bed in her own bed. When her husband came home, his mother accused Elisabeth of sharing her bed with a vile stranger, but God opened Ludwig's eyes and, instead of the leper, upon the bed he saw the figure of the crucified Christ.

St. Elisabeth was received into the Franciscan Order in 1228, and is considered one of the great saints of that Order. She is frequently painted as a Franciscan nun. Her usual attribute is an apron full of roses, but she is sometimes shown with three crowns, indicative of her royal birth, her marriage estate, and her glorification in Heaven.

Euphemia
Third Century

⫸ St. Euphemia was a famous saint of the Greek Church. According to legend, she was persecuted for her faith, but fire failed to burn her and lions refused to devour her. She was finally beheaded.

She is represented with a lion or a bear, the palm of victory, and a sword, which was the instrument of her martyrdom.

Eustace
Second Century

⫸ St. Eustace, who was originally known as Placidus, was a captain of the guards of the Emperor Trajan. The legend about him states that one day, while hunting, he saw before him a white stag. Between its horns appeared a bright light which formed a cross. On the cross was the figure of Christ. Placidus fell on his knees at the apparition, and the figure on the cross spoke, saying, "Placidus, I am Christ whom thou hast hitherto served without knowing me. Dost thou not believe?" Placidus answered, "Lord, I believe." The vision then told him that he would suffer many tribulations, but that the Lord would not forsake him. As a result of this vision, Placidus, his wife, and two sons were baptized, Placidus taking the name of Eustace.

208

XI. Hans Memling: *St. Veronica*. National Gallery of Art, Washington

As Christ had foretold, Eustace experienced much suffering, for his wife was carried away by pirates, and his sons by wild beasts. Eustace fled to the desert to pray, and after fifteen years his family was miraculously reunited. When the family refused to give thanks to the Roman gods, they were condemned to death by the emperor. All four were shut up in a huge brass bull, under which a great fire was kindled, and thus they died.

Eustace is usually represented as a soldier or knight on horseback. His most usual attribute is the stag with the crucifix between its horns. He is frequently accompanied by hounds, and is sometimes shown with a brazen bull, the instrument of his martyrdom. Eustace is the patron saint of huntsmen.

¶ St. Fina, of the town of San Gimignano in Tuscany, became ill when she was a small child of ten and experienced five years of great suffering. She worked as long as she could, making garments for the poor, but finally was made helpless by paralysis. She then took a hard wooden board as her resting place, for she wished to make her sufferings as great as possible in order to be nearer to Christ. Her sufferings were increased because, as she lay alone on her board, rats came to attack her and she was powerless to drive them off. For that reason, her most common attribute in art is a rat. It is said that after her death, when her

Fina
Thirteenth Century

body was lifted from her board, the wood was found covered with white violets of great sweetness. These flowers are therefore also one of her emblems in art.

Florian
Third Century

⁋ St. Florian of Noricum (now Austria) became a soldier in the Roman army during the reign of the Emperor Galerius. He was converted to Christianity, and suffered martyrdom by being thrown into a river with a stone tied to his neck. He is credited with having performed a number of miracles, including extinguishing the flames of a burning city by throwing a single bucket of water on the conflagration. As a result, St. Florian is invoked for protection against fire.

In art, he is generally shown pouring water on a burning house or city, or with a millstone, the symbol of his martyrdom.

Francis
Thirteenth Century

⁋ St. Francis of Assisi was born Giovanni Bernardone in Assisi, in 1182. The story is that he acquired the name Francesco (meaning "the Frenchman") because he had learned French in his youth and loved to sing the Provençal ballads which were so popular at that time.

His particularly vivid personality is known to us through the excellence of his biographer, St. Bonaventura. This biography, begun in 1260, was the source for the famous series of Franciscan frescoes in the Upper Church of Assisi, which were executed at the end of the thirteenth century by Giotto.

210

in Christian Art

Francis was a chivalrous warrior and a gay young man. But, according to legend, his spiritual quality was apparent even before he dedicated himself to God, for a certain man of Assisi, obviously inspired, would spread his cloak before Francis whenever they met, in recognition of the greatness that was to come.

His actual decision to consecrate himself to God came when Francis was twenty-four. One day on his way to the city he met a poor soldier to whom, out of compassion, he gave his rich clothes. That night St. Francis had a vision. Christ appeared to him and, pointing out a beautiful building filled with arms and banners, declared that these were to belong to St. Francis and his soldiers. Francis at first interpreted this to mean that he should continue his life as a soldier. But the voice of the Lord was to change his plans. For when he was passing near the neglected church of St. Damian at Assisi, he went in to pray before the crucifix for guidance, and a voice from the crucifix cried, "Francis, go repair my house that thou seest is all in ruins." Full of this mission, the impulsive youth secretly sold some silks from his father's warehouse to finance the project, whereupon his father had him brought to justice. At the bishop's court, Francis stripped himself of his fine clothes and money and flung them at his angry parent, renouncing forever his life of wealth. The bishop then wrapped him in a cloak.

Gathering the stone blocks himself and begging

other necessary materials, St. Francis set himself to repairing the church of St. Damian. He went on to repair the abandoned Benedictine Chapel of the Portiuncula, known as St. Mary of the Angels. This became the mother house of the Franciscan Order, just as the church of St. Damian became the mother house for St. Clare and the Franciscan nuns, called the Poor Clares.

The words of St. Luke 9:3, "And he said unto them, Take nothing for your journey, neither staves, nor scrip, neither bread, neither money; neither have two coats apiece," inspired St. Francis to formulate the simple rules of his Order. They were chastity, humility, obedience, and absolute poverty: his Lady Poverty, as St. Francis was wont to say.

St. Francis went to Rome to obtain approval of his Order, and at first he met with opposition from Pope Innocent III, whose cardinals considered the rules of the Order too severe for human strength. The Pope is said to have had a vision, in which he beheld St. Francis supporting a toppling Lateran Church upon his shoulders. Soon thereafter, approval of the Franciscan Order, with permission to preach, was granted.

St. Francis called the members of his Order "Frati Minori," meaning the lesser brothers. Their humility gained them an immediate popularity. They were soon to be seen everywhere, and their preaching and dedicated living inspired great religious fervor among the people. Unable to appear in person before all his flock,

212

St. Francis would on occasion reveal himself to them in spirit. Thus he is said to have appeared, with his arms outstretched in the form of a cross, at a provincial chapter of the Order in Arles, during a sermon by St. Anthony of Padua. On another occasion, he appeared to his brethren in Assisi in the form of a dazzling light, suspended over a chariot of fire which was seen to pass three times through the house.

A companion told of a vision in which he saw many thrones in Heaven, one of which was much more beautiful than the rest. Then he heard a voice which declared that this throne, that was once the seat of a fallen angel, was now reserved for St. Francis: "that the humble shall be exalted to that excellent glory from which the proud shall be cast down," in the words of St. Bonaventura.

St. Francis traveled to Spain and North Africa, and finally to Syria, where the Crusaders were battling the Saracens. Unharmed, he was successful in penetrating the very palace of the Sultan. There St. Francis offered to test the strength of the Christian religion against that of Islam by walking through fire. The Sultan's priests refused the contest, and the Sultan himself, although he greatly admired the saint, declined conversion for fear his own people might rebel.

St. Francis always began his sermons with these words, "God give you peace." His fame became so great that he was asked to preach before Pope Honorius III.

In the Pope's presence, Francis forgot the words of his sermon, whereupon he was inspired by the Holy Ghost.

The sweetness of the Franciscan spirit is best exemplified not so much by the cures and other miracles that St. Francis is credited with having accomplished, such as causing the devils at Arezzo to be expelled; the miracle of the Christmas Mass at Greccio, when the Christ Child appeared in his arms; the prayer for water, answered by a spring; the death of the knight of Celano, according to his prediction; but by the many accounts of his love for, and power over, wild beasts and lesser creatures, culminating in his beautiful sermon to the birds.

The climax of the legend of St. Francis is reached in the forty days of fasting and prayer which he undertook in his mountain retreat. During this withdrawal from the world a seraph appeared and filled the sky with its wings. Central in this vision was the figure of the crucified Christ, from whom St. Francis received the marks of the stigmata. He bore these to the end of his life, indicating his spiritual identity with the Master, whom he followed in all humility. The simple, gentle, and indeed joyous humanity of St. Francis' life served to emphasize to the world the true humanity of the Saviour, which was in danger of being forgotten.

Two years after he received the stigmata, suffering from blindness and other ailments, St. Francis asked to be carried to the church of St. Mary of the Portiuncula.

There, on October 4, 1226, he died. It is said that a friar beheld the soul of the saint being borne to Heaven on a white cloud; while a certain doubter, named Jerome, is said to have been converted to Christianity by touching the holy marks on the body of the saint. St. Francis was canonized by Pope Gregory IX in 1228.

St. Francis is generally shown in the dark brown habit of his Order. In addition to the stigmata, his principal attributes are the skull, the lily, the crucifix, the wolf, and the lamb. The symbolic scenes of the saint's marriage to poverty, and his receiving the Infant Christ from the hands of Mary, are important features of his pictorial cycle.

¶St. Geminianus, a friend of St. Ambrose of Milan, was famous for his powers of healing. On one occasion, he was summoned by the Byzantine Emperor to Constantinople to cast out a demon that was troubling the emperor's daughter. It is also recounted that when Attila and his Huns were attacking the town of Modena, St. Geminianus appeared in a vision to Attila and drove the savage hordes away. After his death, the saint is said to have saved the town of Modena from destruction by floods.

St. Geminianus is occasionally shown with the demon from which he freed the emperor's daughter. Quite frequently he is also painted holding a mirror in which the reflection of the Virgin is visible.

Geminianus
Fifth Century

215

George
Second Century

¶St. George of Cappadocia was born of Christian parents before the reign of Constantine. He suffered martyrdom at Diospolis, in Palestine. Many different legends are related about his life, and he has come to represent the triumph of right over oppression and wickedness. One story, recited in the Golden Legend, relates that a terrible dragon was infesting the country around Selena, in Lydia, making its lair in a marsh. In order to please the dragon, human sacrifices were offered to the beast, and lots were drawn to determine the victims. On one occasion, the lot fell to Cleodolinda, the daughter of the king. The maiden, dressed as a bride, was led to the marsh and offered to the dragon. St. George, a tribune of the Roman army, chanced to ride by on his charger at the fatal moment and, in the name of Christ, turned to help the princess. Making the sign of the Cross, he engaged the dragon in mortal combat. He finally succeeded in pinning the dragon to the earth with his lance, whereupon he slew it with his sword. The king, and all his people, who had witnessed the struggle, were converted by this sign of the power of the Lord and were baptized into the Christian faith. St. George continued his journey to Palestine. There he defied the edict of the Emperor Diocletian against the Christians. He was seized and put to all manner of tortures, but was miraculously protected against injury. Finally he was beheaded.

St. George was one of the favorite subjects of the

216

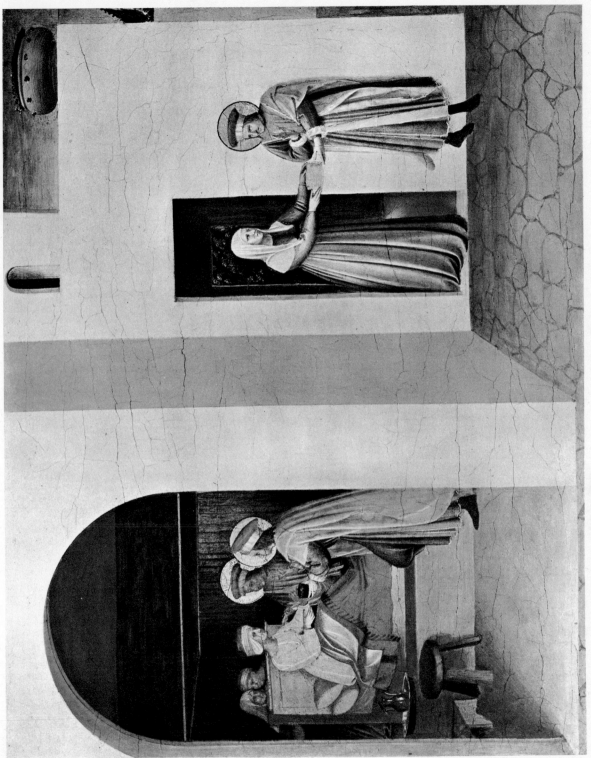

65. Fra Angelico: *The Healing of Palladia by St. Cosmas and St. Damian.* National Gallery of Art, Washington

66. Lippo Vanni: *St. Dominic.*
The William Rockhill Nelson Gallery of Art, Kansas City, Missouri

67. Lippo Vanni: *St. Elizabeth of Hungary*.
The William Rockhill Nelson Gallery of Art, Kansas City, Missouri

68. Vittore Crivelli: *St. Francis*. Kress Collection, New York

Renaissance artists, and pictures of him abound all over Italy. He is usually represented as a young knight clad in shining armor emblazoned with a red cross. Mounted on a charger, he is portrayed transfixing the dragon with his lance or in the act of slaying the dragon with his sword, the broken lance on the ground. St. George is the patron saint of England and, in Italy, of the cities of Venice and Ferrara. He is also the patron saint of all soldiers and armorers. In his portrayal as patron saint, he is clad in armor and holds a shield, lance, or broken lance and sword.

¶One of the four Latin Fathers of the Church, Pope Gregory I, known as Gregory the Great, was born in Rome of noble parentage. He rose to be the prefect of Rome. After the death of his father he came under the influence of the Benedictine Order and gave up his political life for that of service to the Church. He converted his palace into a monastery and lived there for seven years as a monk. Subsequently, he was made one of the deacons of Rome by Pope Benedict I. St. Gregory succeeded to the papacy after the death of Pelagius II in 590. He had a tremendous influence upon the affairs of the Church and upon the manners of his age. His breadth of activity and interest was remarkable. He worked to abolish slavery and to prevent war. He established the rule of celibacy for the clergy and made those special arrangements of church music that

Gregory
Sixth Century

217

have come to be known as Gregorian chants. He was a constant writer on religious subjects.

In art, Gregory is portrayed wearing the tiara of the Pope and bearing the crosier with the double cross. His special attribute is the dove, which refers to the legend that the Holy Ghost came in the form of a dove to dictate the words upon which Gregory's writings were based. He sometimes carries a church to signify the importance of his work in establishing the foundations of the Church.

Helena
Fourth Century

¶St. Helena, the mother of the Roman Emperor, Constantine the Great, was converted to Christianity after the victory of Constantine over his rival Maxentius. It was during this battle that Constantine is reported to have seen a vision of Christ bearing a banner inscribed with the Latin words, "In hoc signo vinces" (By this sign shalt thou conquer). Constantine, adopting this message as his motto, became a Christian. As a token of her piety, St. Helena ordered a number of churches to be built and, at the age of eighty, undertook a religious pilgrimage to the Holy City of Jerusalem. There she was particularly interested in the Mount of Calvary, where Christ had been crucified, and caused various excavations to be made. She is said, as a result, to have unearthed three crosses and the inscription, "Jesus of Nazareth, King of the Jews," which Pilate had commanded to be nailed upon the Cross of

218

Christ. To determine which of the three crosses was that upon which the Saviour died, St. Helena caused a man who was very ill to be placed on each of the crosses in turn. When he touched the True Cross, he was miraculously cured. During later excavations, at St. Helena's direction, some of the nails used to affix Christ to the Cross were discovered. When unearthed, they were "shining as gold." Two of these nails she gave to her son, Constantine. He used one as an emblem on the bridle of his horse; he wore the other upon his helmet.

St. Helena is usually represented wearing a royal crown and bearing a cross, together with hammer and nails. Sometimes she is shown with a model of the Holy Sepulchre in her hands; often with the Cross borne by angels who are appearing to her in a vision.

¶St. James the Great, brother of St. John, is reputed to have been closely related to Christ. The Gospels frequently mention Christ as calling aside Peter, James, and John, thus suggesting a more intimate relationship with these three Apostles. They were present at the Transfiguration and apart with Him during the Agony at Gethsemane.

James, Apostle

One of the Epistles in the New Testament is ascribed to St. James. Nothing is recorded of him after Christ's Ascension, except the fact that Herod slew him with the sword. The legend of St. James the Great is a rich one, however, and, as the military patron saint of Spain, he became one of the most renowned saints in Christendom, his common name becoming Santiago. It is said that on one of his most famous pilgrimages he arrived at Compostella in Spain, where he was the first to establish the Christian religion. It was upon his return to Judea that he was beheaded. His body was subsequently taken back to Spain, where, during the Saracen invasion of that country, it was lost. Recovered about the year 800, it was taken to Compostella. So many miracles took place at that shrine that St. James has become the patron saint of Spain.

Because he is said to have liberated Spain from the Moors, in Spanish art he is represented on horseback, bearing a banner. In Italy, he is usually portrayed with a pilgrim's staff, a scallop shell, or gourd, symbolic of his pilgrimage to Spain and, especially, to Compostella, a very famous goal of pilgrimages in the Middle Ages. As one of the Apostles, he sometimes bears a scroll in one hand with his text testifying to the Incarnation of Christ written upon it.

James the Less, Apostle ⁋There is some question about the identity of the Apostle St. James the Less. According to legend, he was a relative of Jesus and the first bishop of Jerusalem. His death occurred when, having survived being hurled from the roof of a temple, he was beaten to death by an enraged mob with a club or fuller's bat.

220

His attribute in painting is the club or bat which was the instrument of his martyrdom.

¶St. Jerome, one of the four Latin Fathers of the Church, was born at Stridona in Dalmatia. As a young man he came to Rome to study, and was baptized there. His great contribution to the Church was a new translation of most of the Old Testament into Latin (the Vulgate). His life was divided between scholarship and ascetic practices. In Rome he was ordained a priest, but his biting tongue made him many enemies and he had to leave. By way of Antioch and Alexandria he reached Bethlehem, and remained for the rest of his life.

Jerome
Fourth Century

St. Jerome was greatly aided by the arrival in Bethlehem of St. Paula and her daughter, St. Eustochium. After the death of her husband, St. Paula retired from Rome. Seeking the quiet of the religious life, she came to Bethlehem to settle near St. Jerome, who had been her confessor and director. Devoting her wealth to the Church, she erected a monastery for him and his followers, as well as a convent for women seeking the way of retirement. After her death, her daughter, St. Eustochium, carried on the work her mother had begun. It is said that they were tireless in their encouragement to St. Jerome as he engaged in the difficult task of translating the entire Bible into Latin. As Latin was the ordinary or vulgar speech of the common people, his work is known as the Vulgate.

An interesting legend is told that while he was living at his monastery in Bethlehem, a lion, limping grievously, suddenly appeared. The other monks fled, but St. Jerome, in complete confidence, examined the lion's paw and removed from it a deeply embedded thorn. The lion, to show his gratitude, became the constant companion of the saint. But the troubles of the lion had not yet ended. The monks of the convent petitioned St. Jerome that the lion should work to earn his daily food, as did everyone else in the convent. St. Jerome agreed, and ordered the lion to act as a guard for the ass of the convent on its trips to fetch wood. All went well for a time. One day the lion wandered off into the familiar desert, leaving the ass unguarded. Left alone, the ass was seized by robbers and sold to a caravan of merchants, who led it away. On his return, the lion could not find the ass, and went back to the convent alone, in great distress. The monks, seeing the lion's apparently guilty look, thought that he had eaten the ass. The lion was then ordered to do the work of the ass in atonement. The lion obeyed in perfect humility, but one day he saw the ass in a caravan, and triumphantly brought the whole caravan to the convent to prove his innocence.

In painting, St. Jerome is almost always accompanied by a lion. The saint is depicted as an old man, sometimes in the red hat and crimson robes of a cardinal, a contradiction explainable by the fact that in the early period of the Church, the priests of Rome had the functions that later fell to the cardinals. More often, St. Jerome is shown as a hermit in the desert, beating his breast with a stone and praying or writing, while a crucifix, a skull, and an owl are near by.

⟨St. Joachim, the father of the Virgin, often appears in scenes of her life, such as have already been mentioned in connection with the life of Anna, his wife. (See The Virgin Mary, in Section VII) His attributes are the lamb, lilies, and doves in a basket, in reference to his pious offerings at the temple.

Joachim

⟨St. John, the son of Elisabeth and Zacharias, is considered to be the last of the prophets of the Old Testament and the first of the saints of the New Testament. His story, of how he foretold the coming of Christ and baptized Him, and of how he was cast into prison by Herod and ultimately slain to please Salome, is familiar to all readers of the Bible. (See St. John the Baptist, in Section VI)

John the Baptist

In Renaissance art, there are innumerable paintings of John the Baptist, some devotional and others recounting his history and religious experiences. As patron saint of Florence, he is especially frequent in Florentine art. He is usually depicted as he was described by St. Matthew, who wrote, "And the same John had his raiment of camel's hair, and a leathern girdle about his loins; and his meat was locusts and wild honey" (Matthew 3:4). He is often richly dressed, however, when he is represented in Paradise, standing or seated on the left hand of Christ. He often bears in his arms a lamb and a scroll bearing the words "Ecce Agnus Dei" (Behold the Lamb of God) (John 1:36).

His attribute is the lamb. In addition, he is sometimes given a reed cross, or a banner with a reed cross. A dish or platter bearing his own head refers to his execution.

John, Apostle and Evangelist

⁋St. John, the Apostle and Evangelist, was the youngest of the twelve Apostles of Christ and the brother of St. James the Great. He is called "the disciple whom Jesus loved," and the gospel bearing his name refers to him as "leaning on Jesus' breast" at the Last Supper. John was present at the Crucifixion, together with the three Marys. Jesus said to his mother, "Woman, behold thy son!"; and to the disciple, "Behold thy mother!" (John 19:26,27). Tradition says that from this time on the Virgin Mary lived with John, in fulfillment of Christ's words. After the Virgin Mary's death, St. John traveled about Judea preaching the gospel with St. Peter. He is said to have journeyed into Asia Minor, where he founded the Seven Churches referred to in Revelation. Eventually, John went to live at Ephesus, where he endured persecution at the hands of the Emperor Domitian, who, according to legend, twice had

69. Sebastiano Ricci: *The Finding of the True Cross.*
National Gallery of Art, Washington

70. Simone Martini and Assistants: *St. James the Great*. National Gallery of Art, Washington

71. Master of St. Francis, 13th Century: *St. James the Less.*
National Gallery of Art, Washington

72. Giovanni Battista Cima da Conegliano: *St. Jerome in the Wilderness*. National Gallery of Art, Washington

73. Francisco Zurbaran: *St. Jerome, St. Paula and St. Eustochium*. National Gallery of Art, Washington

74. Piero di Cosimo: *St. John the Evangelist*. Kress Collection, New York

75. Andrea Bregno: *St. Jude*. Marble relief.
The William Rockhill Nelson Gallery of Art, Kansas City, Missouri

76. Florentine Painter, 15th Century: *Madonna and Child between St. Stephen and St. Lawrence.*
Kress Collection, New York

XII. Andrea di Giusto: *The Assumption of the Virgin, with St. Jerome and St. Francis.*
The Philbrook Art Center, Tulsa, Oklahoma

attempted taking his life. On one occasion, the emperor ordered him to drink a cup of poisoned wine; when John took up the cup to obey, the poison departed in the form of a snake. On another occasion, John was thrown into a cauldron of boiling oil, but emerged un-hurt. He was then exiled to the island of Patmos, the place of his Revelation. He is supposed to have died a natural death at Ephesus at a very advanced age. St. John is, of course, best known for the version of the Gospel which he wrote, for the three Epistles, and for the Revelation which bears his name.

He appears sometimes as an Evangelist, sometimes as an Apostle. His principal attributes are the eagle, symbol of the highest inspiration, and the book. He is also on occasion seen with the cauldron of oil or the cup with a snake, in reference to attempts upon his life.

⸿St. John Gualbert of Florence had a younger brother who was murdered on the eve of Good Friday. John pursued the assassin and would have slain him, but the man implored mercy in the name of Jesus Christ. John, in remembrance of Christ's sufferings, embraced the man instead of killing him. He then entered a near-by church to give thanks for having resisted the impulse to commit a crime and, as he prayed, the image of Christ on the crucifix appeared to incline its head toward him. This miracle led to John's forsaking the world and entering a Benedictine monastery. He later

John Gualbert
Eleventh Century

225

went to Vallombrosa, and lived as a solitary hermit. The fame of his holiness brought him many followers. To bring order into the community of his followers, John founded the Order of Vallombrosa in 1038 on rules similar to those of the Benedictines. When he died in 1073, twelve houses had been established and the Order had been approved by the Pope.

St. John Gualbert is painted in the gray habit of the Vallombrosans and is sometimes shown with a sword in his hand, or with a crucifix. In some cases, he is represented with the figure of Christ on the crucifix bending toward him.

Joseph ⁋ St. Joseph, husband of the Virgin Mary, was a carpenter of Nazareth. He frequently appears in paintings of the life of Christ, particularly in those of the birth of Jesus and in the other infancy narratives. (See The Virgin Mary, in Section VII; Jesus Christ, in Section VIII)

• He is frequently shown with a budded staff in his hand. This refers to the legend that, when the Virgin Mary was fourteen years old, each of her suitors left his staff at the temple, hoping for a sign to indicate which of them was most favored by God. In the morning, Joseph's staff was budding into leaf, and from it came a dove that flew up to Heaven. Other attributes of St. Joseph are a carpenter's plane, saw, and hatchet, and the lily, symbol of his purity. Often, in scenes of the Presentation, he carries two doves in a basket.

226

⟨ St. Jude is the reputed author of the last Epistle in the New Testament. Tradition says he was the brother of St. James the Less, and they are thought to have been relatives of the Virgin Mary. After the death of Christ, it is said that he traveled through Syria and Asia Minor with St. Simon Zelotes, preaching the gospel. In Persia, both were martyred for their faith, St. Jude being transfixed with a lance or beheaded with a halberd. For this reason, his attribute in art is the lance or the halberd.

Jude, Apostle

⟨ St. Julian the Hospitator is a legendary figure about whom little is known. The story is that Julian was a nobleman who spent much of his time in hunting. One day a stag that he was pursuing was brought to bay. The stag turned to him and said, " Thou that pursuest me to death shall cause the death of thy father and mother." Fearful that this prophecy might come true, Julian left home and journeyed into distant lands. There he met and married a beautiful girl named Basilissa. Julian's parents, overcome with grief at the loss of their son, set out in search of him. In due course, they found the place where Julian was living, but he was away from home. Basilissa, however, received them with joy and gave them her own bed in which to rest. Returning unexpectedly in the early morning, Julian was enraged to find two people in his wife's chamber and, drawing his sword, slew them both.

Julian
Ninth Century

When he learned the truth, Julian, in remorse, swore never to rest until Christ had forgiven him. In search of forgiveness, he and his wife set out upon a pilgrimage. They came at last to a dangerous river, and there Julian built a hospital for the poor as well as a penitential cell for himself. He spent his time ferrying travelers across the river. One night, in the midst of a storm, Julian saw on the other side of the river a leper who appeared to be dying from exposure. At the risk of his life, Julian crossed the river, brought the sick man back, and laid him in his own bed to recover. In the morning the leper had been transformed into an angel. He told Julian that he was the Lord's messenger sent to tell him that his penitence had been accepted. Soon after, well advanced in years, Julian and his wife found release from worldly cares in death.

Julian is generally painted as a huntsman with a stag by his side. Frequently, a river and a boat are shown in the background, in reference to his labors as a ferryman. Julian is the patron saint of travelers, ferrymen, and traveling minstrels.

Justina
Fourth Century

⟨St. Justina of Padua, the daughter of noble parents of the Christian faith, was left an orphan at the age of sixteen. One day Justina was traveling to Padua when she was stopped on the bridge crossing the River Po by some soldiers of the Emperor Maximianus. They forced her to alight from her chariot and follow them to the

77. Bernardo Strozzi: *St. Lawrence giving the Treasures of the Church to the Poor.* Kress Collection, New York

78. Bramantino: *The Raising of Lazarus*. Kress Collection, New York

local court of justice. Fearful for her innocence, Justina knelt upon the bridge and prayed God to preserve her from harm. It is said that the marks of her knees may still be seen in the stonework of the bridge. At her trial, the emperor ordered that she be stabbed in the throat with a sword.

Justina is represented holding the palm of martyrdom, with a unicorn, the emblem of purity, crouching at her feet; or with a sword piercing her throat, in reference to her martyrdom. She was frequently painted by artists of the Paduan and Venetian schools, and she is a patron saint of both Padua and Venice. It is sometimes difficult to distinguish St. Justina of Padua from St. Justina of Antioch, for both saints are given the same attributes.

¶ St. Laurence was born at Huesca in Spain and studied at Saragossa, where he met Pope Sixtus II. Sixtus was so impressed with the young man that he took him back to Rome and made him an archdeacon of the Church. In this capacity, Laurence was in charge of all the treasures of the Church. When Sixtus was seized by the prefect of Rome and condemned to die because of his religion, Laurence sought to die with him. Sixtus instructed him, however, to follow in three days, using the interval to distribute the wealth of the Church to the poor. After the execution of Sixtus, the prefect of Rome demanded that Laurence deliver to him the

Laurence
Third Century

Church's treasure. Laurence replied that he would show it to him in three days. By that time, Laurence had carried out the instructions of Sixtus and had gathered about him a great crowd of the poor and sick. Pointing to them, he told the prefect that these were indeed the treasures of the Church of Christ. Enraged at being thus outwitted, the prefect ordered Laurence to be executed by slow roasting on a gridiron. Defiant in the midst of his torment, Laurence shouted to the prefect, "I am roasted on one side. Now turn me over and eat!"

St. Laurence is generally shown in the dress of a deacon, bearing a palm, the symbol of his martyrdom. His special attribute is the gridiron upon which he was martyred. Sometimes, however, the gridiron is omitted and he carries in his hand a dish of gold and silver coins, in allusion to his distribution of the Church treasures. Occasionally he swings a censer or carries a cross; sometimes, he wears a tunic covered with flames.

Leonard
Sixth Century

St. Leonard is venerated throughout Europe as the patron saint of prisoners and captives. According to legend, Leonard was born in France, son of an official in the court of King Clovis. He was converted to Christianity and devoted himself to visiting prisoners. For many of them he interceded with the king, and paid their ransom himself. Later, Leonard abandoned the court to live as a hermit in a forest near Limoges. His death is said to have occurred in the year 546.

He is represented in painting as a deacon of the church, generally bearing broken fetters in his hand, or with prisoners kneeling at his feet.

¶ St. Liberalis is primarily known as one of the patron saints of Treviso. He became famous for his zeal in converting many residents of that city to Christianity.

In art, he is generally represented as a knight in armor, leaning on a spear or holding a banner.

¶ St. Longinus is the name given to the Roman centurion at Calvary. Tradition says it was he who pierced the side of Christ, and who cried out at His death, "Truly this man was the Son of God" (Mark 15: 39). Legend continues that he was baptized by the Apostles and retired to Caesarea, where he lived many years and converted great numbers to the Christian faith. His death came because of his refusal to sacrifice to the false gods. Anxious for martyrdom, he told the blind governor who condemned him that his sight would be restored only by putting him to death. After Longinus was beheaded, the governor's sight was immediately restored and he was converted. Relics supposed to be those of Longinus were brought to Mantua; consequently he is a patron saint of that city.

Longinus is pictured at the Crucifixion in one of two ways. He is afoot, sometimes lance in hand, gazing up at Christ in adoration. More often he is on horse-

Liberalis
Fourth Century

Longinus

back, clad as a Roman soldier, looking up and holding his helmet in his hands.

Louis of France
Thirteenth Century

¶Louis IX, King of France, was said to know how to "ally the majesty of the throne with the holiness of the Gospel." Born in 1215, he was trained for his great responsibility by a holy mother, Blanche of Castile. During an illness in 1244, Louis made a vow to go on a crusade. He returned to France bringing with him what were believed to be the crown of thorns and a part of the True Cross. On his second crusade, he contracted the plague and died.

His attributes are the crown of thorns, the cross, the kingly crown, the sword, and the fleur-de-lis.

Louis
Thirteenth Century

¶St. Louis of Toulouse had a saintly heritage. St. Louis of France was his great-uncle and St. Elisabeth of Hungary was his aunt. At the age of fourteen, he was sent to the King of Aragon as a hostage for his father. Released after seven years of captivity, he was offered the throne of Naples. He refused, and, renouncing all his royal rights, he made his profession as a member of the Order of St. Francis. He was made Bishop of Toulouse and was loved throughout his diocese for his zeal, charity, and holiness. He died in 1297, when he was only twenty-four years old.

In Renaissance paintings, he is represented as a beardless youth of gentle face. He is generally shown

in the costume of a bishop with the fleur-de-lis embroidered on his cope, or on some part of his dress.
The crown and sceptre, he renounced, lie at his feet.

¶According to legend, St. Lucy of Syracuse was the
daughter of a noble lady, Eutychia, who suffered from
a disease believed to be incurable. Lucy persuaded her
mother to make a pilgrimage to the shrine of St. Agatha
in Catania. There, St. Agatha appeared to Lucy in a
vision and told her that her mother would be cured,
but that she herself would suffer martyrdom. In gratitude for the healing of her mother, Lucy distributed all
her wealth among the poor. This angered the young
man to whom she was betrothed, and he denounced
her to the authorities as being a Christian. When she
persisted in her faith, soldiers were ordered to drag
her away, but she could not be moved, even though
she was bound with ropes and harnessed to a yoke of
oxen. The governor then ordered her to be burned, but
the flames did not touch her. Finally, one of the soldiers
stabbed her in the neck with a poniard and killed her.
Legend tells that one of her suitors was so smitten
with the beauty of her eyes that he could find no rest.
Fearing that her eyes were really causing harm to the
young man, Lucy tore them from her head and sent
them to him. He was overcome with remorse and so
impressed with the courage that Lucy evidenced
through her faith that he, too, became a Christian.

Lucy
Third Century

St. Lucy is sometimes represented with her eyes on a dish in her hand, or carried in some other manner. Other attributes of St. Lucy are a poniard and a wound in her neck, and a lamp, to suggest divine light and wisdom. As the name Lucy suggests light, the eyes and the lamp might also be attributed to her for this reason.

Luke, Evangelist ❧ St. Luke the Evangelist, born at Antioch in Syria, is well known to all readers of the Bible because of his Gospel and the book of The Acts of The Apostles. It is not known where Luke met Paul, but he became the constant companion of the famed Apostle and faithfully recorded the life of this great missionary. It is said that, after Paul's death, he continued preaching alone, and was crucified in Greece, although Greek tradition says that he died peacefully. He is called "the beloved physician" in reference to the medical profession, of which he was a practicing member. There is a legend to the effect that Luke was a painter, and that he did several portraits of the Virgin Mary and of Jesus. By showing these to his listeners, he is said to have made many converts to Christianity.

His most frequent attributes are the winged ox, presumably because in his Gospel he emphasizes the priesthood of Christ, and the ox is a symbol of sacrifice; the Gospel Book; and the portrait of the Virgin which he may be in the act of painting or holding in one hand. He is the patron saint of painters.

234

❡ St. Margaret of Antioch, the daughter of a pagan priest, is said to have been converted to Christianity by her nursemaid. One day the young girl was seen by the governor of Antioch, who was so struck by her beauty that he determined to marry her, but Margaret refused his offer of marriage, declaring that she was dedicated to Jesus Christ. The governor tried to shake her determination by torture, but Margaret stood firm. She was then dragged to a dungeon, where the Devil appeared to her as a dragon breathing fire, and sought to terrify her. Margaret fell upon her knees in prayer and made the sign of the Cross upon her breast. The dragon swallowed her, but the cross that Margaret had made grew larger and larger, until it split the body of the dragon in two, permitting Margaret to escape unharmed. Margaret's courage and constancy to her faith throughout her tortures so impressed the populace that thousands were converted to Christianity. To put a stop to this, the governor ordered that she be executed. On her way to the place of execution, St. Margaret, in memory of her escape from the body of the dragon, prayed that the memory of her might give help to those suffering the pains of childbirth. She has therefore become the patron saint of women in childbirth.

St. Margaret is invariably shown with a dragon which she is trampling under foot as she stands unharmed by his distended jaws. She often holds a cross and the crown and palm of martyrdom.

Mark, Evangelist

¶ St. Mark is a familiar figure as the author of one of the Gospels. His early history is obscure, but we know that he was the traveling companion of Paul and Barnabas on the first of Paul's missionary journeys. Tradition says that, after leaving Paul, he journeyed to Rome with Peter and, as Peter's secretary, wrote his Gospel, the material being given to him directly by Peter. Mark's Gospel is probably the earliest in existence, and is accepted as such by scholars today.

According to legend, while he was preaching along the shores of the Adriatic, the vessel in which he was traveling was caught in a great storm and was driven into the coastal islands and lagoons. Here an angel appeared to Mark, saying, " On this site, a great city will arise to your honor." (Four hundred years later, the people of the mainland, fleeing before Attila, the Hun, sought refuge among the islands where the city of Venice was established.) St. Mark is said to have then departed for Libya, where for twelve years he preached the Gospel. He journeyed to Alexandria and founded the Christian Church in that city, which was also the place of his martyrdom. Several centuries after his death, his body was carried off by Venetian sailors, who brought it back to Venice. St. Mark became the patron saint of Venice, which adopted his emblem, the lion, as its own; therefore, both the saint and the lion are very frequently represented in Venetian art.

His almost invariable attribute is the winged lion,

79. Francesco del Cossa: *St. Lucy*. National Gallery of Art, Washington

80. Giovanni di Paolo: *St. Luke the Evangelist*. Seattle Art Museum, Seattle, Washington

presumably because his Gospel emphasizes the royal dignity of Christ, the Lion of Judah. In his character of Evangelist and secretary of St. Peter, he is given a pen and the book of his Gospel.

⁋St. Martha was the sister of Mary (sometimes identified with Mary Magdalene) and of Lazarus. The Gospel account represents Martha as one who devoted herself to domestic affairs and to the running of the home, while her sister was more inclined to sociability. When their brother, Lazarus, was taken ill, the two sisters sent word to Jesus, asking him to come to their aid. When Jesus arrived in Bethany, it was Martha who went out to meet Him. It would appear that she was already a disciple of Christ, for she said to Him, "Lord, if thou hadst been here, my brother had not died. But I know, that even now, whatsoever thou wilt ask of God, God will give it thee." And it was to Martha that Jesus then spoke His famous words, "I am the resurrection, and the life: he that believeth in me, though he were dead, yet shall he live" (John 11: 21ff.). Some time later, before the feast of the Passover, Martha served Jesus a supper in their home at Bethany. It was on this occasion that Mary anointed the feet of Jesus. "Then took Mary a pound of ointment of spikenard, very costly, and anointed the feet of Jesus, and wiped his feet with her hair: and the house was filled with the odour of the ointment" (John 12: 3). It is said

Martha and Mary Her Sister

237

that the influence of Martha led to the eventual conversion of Mary Magdalene. According to legend, after the death of the Saviour, Martha was with Mary Magdalene and Lazarus in an open boat which miraculously landed at Marseilles, France. In France she converted the people of Aix and delivered them from a fearful dragon that was laying waste the countryside.

St. Martha is usually shown with a ladle or skimmer in her hand, or with a large bunch of keys attached to her girdle, in token of her housewifely qualities. Sometimes, however, she is shown with a dragon at her feet, together with the holy water and asperges with which she conquered the monster.

Martin
Fourth Century

⟨St. Martin was born in Hungary, called Pannonia at that time, during the reign of Constantine the Great. He was converted to Christianity as a child and ran away to a monastery, but his father, who was a military tribune, insisted that the boy take up the life of a soldier. Martin joined the imperial cavalry and was stationed in France. In Amiens, one cold winter day, he chanced to pass a beggar clad in only a few rags and suffering from the bitter weather. Martin took off his cloak and, cutting it in two with his sword, gave half of it to the beggar. That night, Christ appeared to him in a vision, saying, "What thou hast done for that poor man, thou hast done for me." Martin then determined to devote his life to religion, and asked to be released from military service. When the emperor accused him of being afraid to meet the enemy, Martin declared that he would gladly face the enemy armed only with the Cross. Before his courage could be put to this test, word was received that the enemy was seeking peace. It was believed that St. Martin's faith in God brought about this surrender. He was, therefore, allowed to retire from the army, whereupon he went to live a life of seclusion, first on an island in the Tyrrhenian Sea, then at Liguge, near Poitiers, in France, where he founded a monastery believed to be the first in France. While at Liguge, he learned that he had been appointed Bishop of Tours. Anxious to continue his life of religious solitude, he hid from the emissaries who came to take him back to Tours. According to one legend, his hiding place was disclosed by the quacking of a goose, and he was compelled to accept his new responsibilities. Another tradition relates that in order to overcome his resistance, a citizen of Tours told him that his wife was dying and begged Martin to come and administer the Sacrament to her. Martin hurried to the city, and, upon the insistence of the people, was consecrated bishop. He remained the Bishop of Tours for some thirty years.

In Renaissance paintings he is often shown in the raiment of a bishop, sometimes with a goose. In other pictures, he is in military attire on horseback, dividing his cloak with his sword to cover a naked beggar.

239

Mary of Egypt
Fifth Century

❡St. Mary of Egypt, according to legend, was an Egyptian girl of Alexandria who deliberately lived a life of sin. She joined a pilgrimage to Jerusalem, not for reasons of religious devotion but that she might seduce some of her fellow pilgrims. At Jerusalem, however, she had an impulse to enter a church with the others who had gone there to pray. A mysterious power prevented her from entering the church door, and she found that she was standing beside a statue of the Virgin. She was suddenly filled with remorse, and swore that she would sin no more. Purchasing three loaves of bread as her only source of sustenance, she went into the desert beyond the River Jordan, where she remained in solitude and prayer for many years. She was found there one day by a priest named Zosimus. She asked him to give her Holy Communion, but the priest was prevented from reaching her by the width of the River Jordan. Thereupon, Mary, aided by supernatural powers, passed dry-shod across the river and received her communion. Mary asked the priest to return at the same time the following year, that she might again receive the Sacrament. When he complied with her request, he found her dead, and written in the sand were these words: "O Father Zosimus, bury the body of the poor sinner, Mary of Egypt. Give earth to earth and dust to dust, for Christ's sake." Zosimus tried to bury her, but when his strength failed a lion appeared and helped to dig her grave with his paws.

240

XIII. Master of St. Gilles: *The Baptism of Clovis*. National Gallery of Art, Washington

Mary of Egypt is usually represented as a wasted old woman with long hair, holding three loaves of bread. Sometimes she has a lion beside her.

¶ St. Mary Magdalene (sometimes identified with the sister of Martha and Lazarus) has come to be accepted as the great example of the penitent sinner, absolved from sin through faith in Christ. She was one of the women who accompanied Jesus on his last journey to Calvary, and who stood weeping at the foot of the Cross. With that other Mary, mother of St. James the Less, she witnessed the burial of Jesus. The third day after the Crucifixion, the two Marys appeared at the Holy Sepulchre with the spices and ointment with which to anoint the body of the Saviour. There they discovered that the stone closing the Sepulchre had been rolled away, and that the body of Christ had vanished. Mary was thus the first to bring the news of Christ's Resurrection to His disciples. Later, as she was standing weeping by the grave, Jesus appeared to her and gave her comfort.

According to an account that identifies her with the Mary who was sister of Martha and Lazarus, she was later set adrift in an open boat with her brother and sister and a number of other Christians. These victims of persecution were saved by a favorable wind which brought them into the harbor that is now Marseilles, France. There, Mary converted many people.

241

Eventually she retired into a desert near the city, where she remained in solitude for thirty years. She had nothing to eat or drink, but, legend relates, she was refreshed by angels with celestial food.

Mary Magdalene was one of the favorite subjects of Renaissance painting, and pictures of her abound. Some are devotional, but many show scenes from the Gospel and from her legendary life. Her most common attribute is the alabaster box of ointment, in reference to her anointing the feet of Jesus: for she came to be regarded as the unnamed woman who anointed Jesus' feet, as St. Luke writes, "And, behold, a woman in the city, which was a sinner, when she knew that Jesus sat at meat in the Pharisee's house, brought an alabaster box of ointment. And stood at his feet behind him weeping, and began to wash his feet with tears, and did wipe them with the hairs of her head, and kissed his feet, and anointed them with the ointment" (Luke 7:37, 38). Sometimes she carries the box in her hand; other times it stands at her feet or is carried by an administering angel. She is often represented covered by her flowing hair, being carried by angels to receive refreshment in Heaven.

Matthew, Apostle and Evangelist

℧ St. Matthew is well known to all through his Gospel, the first book in the New Testament. Before he became one of Christ's disciples, he was a tax collector in the service of the Romans. The events of his life after the death of Christ are uncertain. He is supposed to have written his Gospel in Judea, and then to have preached in Ethiopia, where he died.

Matthew is portrayed in several ways. He is shown with a cherub, in human likeness, where he is pictured as recording the human ancestry of Christ. He appears with a winged man in reference to his detailed account of the Incarnation of Christ. He is also shown with a purse or a bag of money, in reference to his early profession, or with a book or pen, as writer of the Gospel. Sometimes an angel holds his inkhorn. An axe, the instrument of his martyrdom, is sometimes shown.

¶St. Monica is notable as the mother of St. Augustine and also because of her own saintly character. She devoted her whole life to her son, and, in his great book, "Confessions," St. Augustine pays magnificent tribute to his mother's sacrifices on his behalf. She followed St. Augustine to Italy; and, after he had been converted and baptized by St. Ambrose at Milan, she died at Ostia on the journey home to Africa.

Monica
Fourth Century

She is represented in the black or gray habit of a nun or widow, and is often shown in paintings of her famous son.

¶St. Nicholas of Myra is regarded by historians as a purely legendary character who is supposed to have lived in the fourth century. The universal tradition of

Nicholas of Myra or Bari
Fourth Century

Santa Claus (St. Claus), so loved by children, has its origin in the story of this saint. He was born in Asia Minor, of Christian parents, and very early dedicated his life to God. He was the nephew of the Archbishop of Myra, who, understanding the deep calling of Nicholas, ordained him to the priesthood. When his parents died, Nicholas distributed their great wealth among the poor. Several stories of his life are related. One of the best known is, that hearing of a certain nobleman of the city who had lost all his money, Nicholas provided a dowry for each of his three daughters by throwing a bag of gold for each daughter through the nobleman's window at night. He was discovered while throwing the third bag, but begged the nobleman not to reveal the truth.

Another story of the saint tells of a voyage he took to the Holy Land during which his vessel was almost wrecked by the heavy seas. St. Nicholas rebuked the waves, and they subsided. He became the patron saint of sailors and travelers, and his image is to be found in almost every seaport throughout the world.

Returning from Palestine, Nicholas went to Myra. The archbishop of that seaport, who had succeeded Nicholas' uncle, had just died, and the local clergy had decided that the first priest to enter the church on the following morning should be made bishop. Early that morning, Nicholas went to the church to pray, and, as a result, was elected to the post of bishop.

in Christian Art

One of the most famous legends of St. Nicholas tells of his visit to a certain inn, where he discovered that the wicked innkeeper was in the habit of stealing small children, killing them, and serving them to his guests as meat. Upon searching the establishment, Nicholas found the bodies of three children, hidden in a cask of brine. He made the sign of the Cross, and the three children were brought back to life. On the basis of this miracle, St. Nicholas was adopted as the protector and patron saint of little children.

Because the feast of the saint, December 6, falls near Christmas, and because his gift of the three purses was compared to the bringing of gifts to the Christ Child by the three Magi, the legend of St. Nicholas was gradually merged with the Christmas story, and he has become the familiar figure of Santa Claus.

St. Nicholas is usually represented as a bishop. His principal attribute is the three purses, or balls, in reference to his charity. He is often painted with an anchor or ship in the background, indicating his patronage of sailors. As the patron saint of children, he is sometimes shown with a small child kissing his hand. He is the chief patron saint of Russia.

¶ St. Nicholas was born at St. Angelo-in-Pontara and became a friar of the Order of St. Augustine. Because his parents had prayed to St. Nicholas of Myra for a son, he was given the saint's name. Nicholas was a

Nicholas of Tolentino
Thirteenth Century

245

man of great eloquence and saintly character. Many miracles are attributed to him.

Legend relates that, at his birth, a star flashed across the sky from his birthplace to Tolentino, where he was destined to spend much of his life. For this reason, he is frequently painted with a star on his breast. In recognition of the purity of his life, he is sometimes shown bearing a crucifix entwined with lilies. He is usually painted in the black habit of the Augustinian Order.

Onuphrius
Fourth Century

¶St. Onuphrius was a monk of Thebes, in Egypt, who lived in complete solitude in the desert for sixty years. According to legend, an angel brought him the Holy Eucharist each Sunday. He was eventually discovered by Paphnutius, Bishop of Upper Thebes, who remained with him until he died. When Paphnutius found the saint, he was naked except for his long hair and a garland of leaves about his loins. Upon the death of Onuphrius, two lions appeared and dug his grave.

Onuphrius is represented as a wild, unkempt figure covered with hair and wearing a girdle of leaves. Frequently shown with him are the two lions who supposedly helped to bury him.

Paul, Apostle

¶St. Paul is the most widely known of the first-century followers of Jesus, owing to St. Luke's Acts of The Apostles and the many Epistles of St. Paul in the New

246

Testament. He was born at Tarsus and was named Saul. His parents, though Jewish, were Roman citizens. He received careful instruction in Tarsus and was completing his studies at Jerusalem, under Gamaliel, when the first persecution of the Christians began. Saul officially witnessed the stoning of St. Stephen, the first deacon of the Church, and was on his way to Damascus with the commission to destroy the small community of Christians which had been formed there, when he was overcome by a great light from Heaven by which he was struck blind. He was felled to the earth and heard a voice saying, "Saul, Saul, why persecutest thou me?" Saul cried out, "Who art thou, Lord?" and the voice responded, "I am Jesus whom thou persecutest" (Acts 9: 3ff.). Saul's companions led him into Damascus. There he was visited by Ananias, who, by the laying on of hands, restored his sight. Saul arose and was baptized, and his Christian name became Paul. After a period of retirement in the desert, Paul joined with other disciples of Christ to become the greatest missionary of the Christian faith. He made three great missionary journeys throughout Asia Minor and Greece. His carrying the message of Christianity to the non-Jewish world brought him his title, "Missionary to the Gentiles." Eventually he was arrested in Palestine and, as a Roman citizen, appealed for a hearing before the Emperor Nero. He was sent to Rome and imprisoned. It was during this imprisonment that a number of his Epistles are supposed to have been written. Tradition says that Paul suffered martyrdom in Rome by the sword. St. Peter and St. Paul are considered to be the real founders of the Christian Church and, as such, are the subjects of innumerable religious paintings.

In art, St. Paul may be identified by the sword, with which he was beheaded, and the book or scroll of his Epistles.

Paul the Hermit
Fourth Century

¶ St. Paul the Hermit is considered to be the earliest of those who lived the life of the solitary hermit. As a young man, he lived in the city of Thebes, in Egypt. During the persecution of the Christians under the Emperor Decius, he sought refuge in the desert country. Living in a cave near a date tree and a well, he remained in the desert for ninety-eight years. Legend relates that during this time a raven came to him each day, bringing him half a loaf of bread. He was finally discovered in his desert solitude by St. Anthony Abbot, who lived with him until his death, when two lions came to help Anthony bury the body of the old man.

In Renaissance painting, Paul is represented as a very old man, with long white hair and a beard, clad only in palm leaves. The particular attributes by which St. Paul the Hermit may be recognized are the raven with the loaf of bread, a palm tree, and the lions that helped St. Anthony Abbot bury St. Paul.

248

81. Girolamo di Benvenuto: *St. Margaret of Antioch.*
The Isaac Delgado Museum of Art, New Orleans, Louisiana

·SCS· MATHEV·

82. Simone Martini and Assistants: *St. Matthew*. National Gallery of Art, Washington

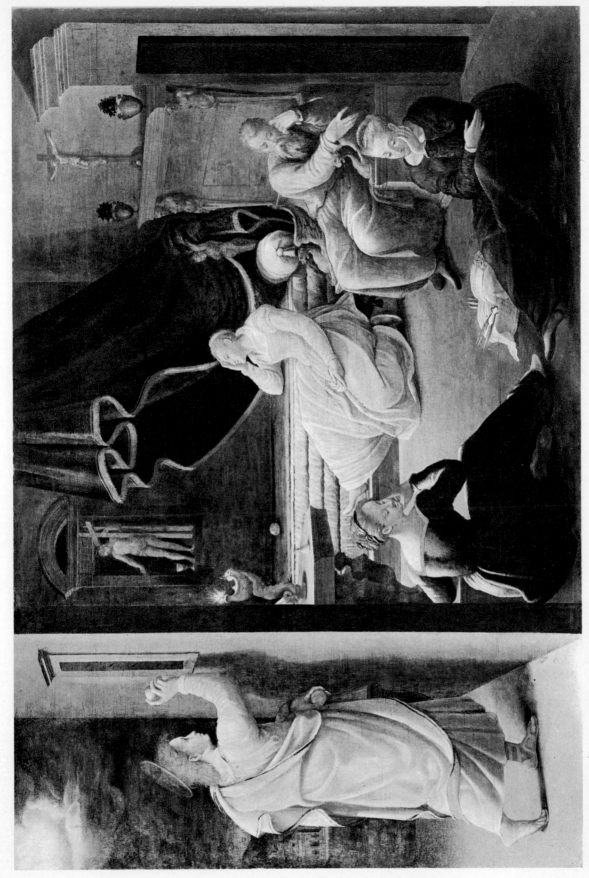

83. Florentine School, 16th Century: *A Scene from the Life of St. Nicholas.* Columbia Museum of Art, Columbia, South Carolina

84. Vincenzo Foppa: *St. Paul the Apostle.*
The Isaac Delgado Museum of Art, New Orleans, Louisiana

in Christian Art

¶ St. Peter, Apostle, was a fisherman in Galilee and the brother of Andrew. He, together with James and John, shared an inner intimacy with Christ. Peter's position among the Apostles seems to have been that of spokesman. St. Matthew, in his Gospel, relates how Peter and Andrew were called to the apostolate: "And Jesus, walking by the sea of Galilee, saw two brethren, Simon called Peter, and Andrew his brother, casting a net into the sea: for they were fishers. And he said unto them, Follow me, and I will make you fishers of men. And they straightway left their nets, and followed him" (Matthew 4: 18ff.). From the time of his calling, Peter is frequently mentioned in the Gospels. At Caesarea, it was Peter who answered Christ's question, ". . . whom say ye that I am," by giving the great declaration, "Thou art the Christ, the Son of the living God," to which Jesus replied, "Thou art Peter, and upon this rock I will build my church; and the gates of hell shall not prevail against it. And I will give unto thee the keys of the kingdom of heaven" (Matthew 16: 15ff.). In the scriptural accounts of the Passion, Peter's vow of loyalty followed closely by his denial and deep repentance are familiar to all. The life of Peter after the Ascension of Christ is related in The Acts of The Apostles. Peter carried the word of the Saviour throughout Asia Minor, centering his activities around Antioch. Subsequently, he came to Rome, where, it is believed, he formed the first Christian community

249

there. Tradition says that St. Peter carried on his work in Rome for some twenty-five years, until he was accused of having cast a spell over one of the favorites of the emperor. At the pleas of his Christian followers, the Apostle agreed to flee the city, but on his way he saw a vision of Christ. Peter asked, "Lord, whither goest thou?" (Domine, quo vadis?), to which Jesus answered, "To Rome, to be crucified anew." Taking this as a sign, Peter returned to Rome, where he was arrested and imprisoned. Condemned to death, he was eventually scourged and crucified head downward. This was done at his own wish, for he did not consider himself worthy to die in the same manner as Christ.

In most paintings of St. Peter, he is shown holding the keys to Heaven. Sometimes he holds a fish, to show he is the fisherman of souls. The cock is occasionally shown near by in reference to his denial. His mantle is bright yellow, symbolic of Revealed Faith.

Peter Martyr
Thirteenth Century

¶St. Peter Martyr is considered to be the most important saint of the Dominican Order, after St. Dominic. Born in Verona, Peter joined the Dominican Order upon hearing St. Dominic preach. He became a powerful preacher and was appointed Inquisitor-General by Pope Gregory IX. In this office he undertook to suppress heresy, acting so severely that the wrath of the people was raised against him. As a consequence, he was assassinated while on his way from Como to Milan.

Paintings of him generally represent him in the habit of the Dominican Order with a bleeding wound in his head. He is shown bearing the palm; and often a sword or a knife, the instrument of his martyrdom, is in his head or his hand.

⚓St. Petronius, one of the patron saints of Bologna, was born of noble Roman parents. He was converted to Christianity, entered the priesthood, and eventually became Bishop of Bologna. It was he who built the famous Church of San Stefano in that city. He is customarily shown in the vestments of a bishop, bearing a model of the city of Bologna in his hand.

Petronius
Fifth Century

⚓St. Philip appears infrequently in the Gospel narratives. He is associated chiefly with the account of the Feeding of the Five Thousand (John 6: 5), and as being present at the gathering of the disciples of Christ in Jerusalem after the Ascension (Acts 1: 13). Philip's later life is unknown, but he is supposed to have carried the Gospel to Scythia, where he remained for many years. There, according to legend, in the city of Hierapolis, he found the people worshiping a great serpent. Aided by the cross, Philip caused the serpent to disappear, but it left behind such a hideous stench that many people died of it. Among these was the son of the king. Again aided by the cross, Philip brought the youth back to life. The priests of the serpent were

Philip, Apostle

enraged by the overthrow of their god. Seizing Philip, they put him to death.

St. Philip is usually represented bearing a cross of the Latin type fastened to the top of a staff or reed, an allusion to his martyrdom. Sometimes the Tau cross is substituted for the Latin cross. The dragon may appear in remembrance of the miracle performed by St. Philip at Hierapolis.

Remigius (Remy)
Fifth Century

¶ St. Remigius was elected Bishop of Rheims at the age of twenty-two. He was not only a man of great knowledge and brilliance, but was well known and greatly admired for his sanctity. The Frankish King, Clovis, regarded him with great respect and afforded him constant protection in his work for the Church. In 496, as Clovis was facing a crushing defeat in battle, he sought the help of the God of his Christian queen, Clothild. The tide of battle turned and a victory was won. Fulfilling his promise, Clovis was brought to St. Remigius by Clothild. He was prepared for baptism and the ceremony was performed on Easter Even, 496. The conversion of the king greatly aided the work of St. Remigius. He directed a great deal of his activity against the Arians, and his gentleness of character and his wisdom of argument won many converts from this heresy. St. Remigius has been called the Founder of the Church of God in France. He died after having served as Bishop of Rheims for seventy-two years.

252

⊄St. Reparata, one of the patron saints of Florence, was a child of noble birth who lived in Caesarea, in Palestine. As a Christian, she was martyred at the age of twelve during the persecutions of the Emperor Decius. Legend relates that, after being tortured, she was killed by a stroke of the sword. As she died, her soul was seen rising to Heaven in the form of a dove. She is almost always represented with her spirit, in the form of a dove, flying from her mouth.

Reparata
Second Century

⊄St. Roch, the patron saint of those suffering from the plague, was born at Montpellier, in France. Because he had a birthmark in the shape of a cross, St. Roch believed he was consecrated to a religious life. After the death of his parents, he disposed of all his worldly goods and started on a pilgrimage to Rome. At the town of Aquapendente, he found the populace stricken by the plague. St. Roch immediately devoted himself to the care of the sick, and his nursing was so effective that many recovered. As a result of this experience, St. Roch came to believe that he had a special mission to help those stricken by the plague. He went from place to place, wherever the plague was raging, to aid its victims. After many years of this service, he was stricken by the plague in the town of Piacenza. Alone, he withdrew into the woods to die. His faithful dog refused to abandon him, and daily brought him a loaf of bread. At length, he recovered sufficiently to return to his native

Roch
Fourteenth Century

town of Montpellier. His illness had so changed him that no one recognized him. He was arrested as a spy and was brought before the magistrate, who happened to be his uncle. Not believing his story, his uncle sentenced him to prison. One morning, five years later, he was found dead in his prison cell, which was flooded with a heavenly light. Beside him was written this inscription: "All those who are stricken by plague and pray for help through the intercession of Roch, the servant of God, shall be healed." Many years later, the citizens of Venice succeeded in stealing his body and removing it to their city. The Franciscan monks built the Church of San Rocco as a shrine for the relics of the saint.

In Renaissance painting, St. Roch is usually shown in the habit of a pilgrim, with cockleshell, wallet, and staff, lifting his robe to exhibit a plague spot on his thigh. He is generally accompanied by his faithful dog.

Romuald
Eleventh Century

⸿St. Romuald, a citizen of Ravenna, joined the Order of St. Benedict to atone for his father's murder of a near relative. While in the monastery, he had a vision of St. Apollinaris, who told him to found a new Order in the service of God. Romuald, a man of great asceticism, was shocked at the laxity of many of those who professed to be living the religious life. None of the existing Orders was willing to accept the severity of the rule that Romuald wished to impose. So, in the year

254

975, he founded the Order of Camaldoli, whose members were vowed to perpetual silence and solitude. According to legend, when Romuald was looking for a place to build his monastery, he dreamed that he saw a ladder stretching from earth to Heaven, on which men in white raiment were ascending. Taking this as a sign, he decreed that the monks of his new Order should be dressed in white robes.

In paintings of the saint, his most common attribute is the ladder to Heaven. Sometimes he is shown with the Devil under his feet. He is usually depicted as an old man with a long beard and clad in the white habit of the Camaldoli Order.

¶St. Scholastica was the twin sister of St. Benedict. Like her brother, she dedicated her life to religion, and eventually founded a community of Benedictine nuns. It is said that at the time of her death her brother was praying in his cell. There, in a vision, he saw the soul of his sister in the likeness of a dove, ascending to Heaven. Thereupon, he announced her death to his monks and instructed that her body be brought to his abbey, where it was buried in a grave that he had prepared for himself. St. Scholastica is the chief female saint of the Benedictine Order.

St. Scholastica is generally represented holding a lily or a crucifix, with the dove of the legend either at her feet, pressed to her bosom, or flying toward Heaven.

Scholastica
Sixth Century

255

Sebastian
Third Century

⟨St. Sebastian was a young nobleman of Narbonne, in Gaul. He commanded a company of the Praetorian Guard, the special bodyguard of the Roman emperors. His secret belief in Christ was revealed when he encouraged two of his fellow officers, who were being tortured for their belief, to die rather than renounce their faith. Hearing of this, the Emperor Diocletian urged Sebastian to abandon his faith in Christ and return to the worship of the Roman gods. When Sebastian refused, Diocletian ordered that he be bound to a stake and shot to death with arrows. The order was carried out, and Sebastian was left for dead. The mother of one of his martyred friends discovered, however, that he was still alive. She dressed his wounds and, after they had healed, advised him to escape from Rome. Contrary to her advice, Sebastian determined to come forth openly and declare his faith. He stood on the steps of the emperor's palace, pleading for those who had been condemned, and reproaching the emperor for his intolerance. When Diocletian saw him, he was amazed and demanded, "Art thou not Sebastian?" To this the youth replied, "I am indeed Sebastian whom God hath delivered from thy hands that I might testify to the faith of Jesus Christ and plead for His servants." Diocletian then ordered that he should be taken to the arena and beaten to death with clubs. In order that his friends might not find it, Sebastian's body was thrown into the great sewer of Rome, but

85. Sebastiano Ricci: *The Death of St. Paul the Hermit.* Kress Collection. New York

86. Marco Zoppo: *St. Peter*. National Gallery of Art, Washington

87. Andrea Bregno: *St. Philip*. Marble relief.
The William Rockhill Nelson Gallery of Art, Kansas City, Missouri

88. The Master of St. Gilles, late 15th Century: *The Conversion of an Arian by St. Rémy.*
National Gallery of Art, Washington

89. Lorenzo Costa: *St. Roch* and *St. Julian*. Kress Collection, New York

90. Vittore Carpaccio:
St. Stephen. The William Rockhill Nelson Gallery of Art, Kansas City, Missouri.
St. Peter Martyr. The Philbrook Art Center, Tulsa, Oklahoma

91. Simone Martini and Assistants: *St. Simon*. National Gallery of Art, Washington

·SANTVS· TADEV

92. Simone Martini and Assistants: *St. Thaddeus*. National Gallery of Art, Washington

it was discovered, and was buried in the catacombs at the feet of St. Peter and St. Paul.

Sebastian is always shown as a young man whose body is transfixed by arrows. Often he is bound to a tree or stake. In ancient times, the plague was believed to have been brought by Apollo's arrows. Therefore, St. Sebastian became one of the chief saints invoked against that dread disease.

¶ St. Simon Zelotes is reputed to have been one of the shepherds to whom angels revealed the birth of Christ. After the Crucifixion, tradition says, he and St. Jude preached the gospel throughout Syria and Mesopotamia, and both were martyred in Persia. The instrument of their martyrdom is not known, and traditions vary. According to one legend, St. Simon was crucified; another relates that he was put to death by being sawed asunder. His attribute in art is a large saw or a cross.

Simon, Apostle

¶ St. Stephen was the first Christian deacon and the first martyr for the Faith. His story is told in the sixth and seventh chapters of The Acts of The Apostles, where it is stated that "Stephen, full of faith and power, did great wonders and miracles among the people." But those of the old faith in Jerusalem were angered by Stephen's words and by his influence over the people. They had him arrested and brought before the council, where, on the testimony of false witnesses, he was

Stephen
First Century

257

accused of having spoken blasphemous words against Moses and against God. In reply, Stephen preached his famous sermon (Acts 7: 2 - 53), which so aroused the authorities that he was taken out of the city and stoned to death. Saul, who later became the Apostle Paul, was present as a witness, and consented to Stephen's death. As he died, Stephen knelt down and cried, "Lord, lay not this sin to their charge." Legend states that some four hundred years after his death, a priest in Palestine by the name of Lucian had a vision in which the resting place of Stephen's body was revealed. As a result, the relics of the saint were taken up and eventually reburied in Rome beside the relics of St. Laurence. It is said that when the tomb of St. Laurence was opened to receive the body of St. Stephen, St. Laurence moved to one side and gave his hand to St. Stephen. This is the origin of the title of "the courteous Spaniard" which has been given to St. Laurence.

St. Stephen is represented as a young man in the costume of a deacon who bears the palm of martyrdom. His particular attributes are the stones which were the instruments of his martyrdom. Because of the legend of his burial, St. Stephen and St. Laurence are often portrayed together.

Sylvester
Fourth Century

St. Sylvester became the Bishop of Rome in the year 314, during the reign of the Emperor Constantine. Many legends are told of Sylvester, the most important being the story of his converting Constantine to Christianity. It is said that while stricken with leprosy, Constantine was visited in a vision by St. Peter and St. Paul, who told him to send for Sylvester. Recognizing the saints from pictures that Sylvester showed him, he accepted Sylvester's care. Sylvester took him to a pool and baptized him, whereupon the emperor was at once cured of his sickness. He then issued an order that Jesus Christ should be worshiped as the only true God throughout Rome. Another version of this legend places Constantine's baptism by Sylvester at the end of his life, when, in remorse for his many cruelties, he was cleansed of the leprosy of his sins by the waters of baptism. In a dispute with a group of learned doctors and magicians, Sylvester is said to have restored a dead bull to life, as proof that Christ was the God of Life.

St. Sylvester is generally represented in pontifical robes, wearing the mitre and the triple tiara, and bearing the crosier and a book. His particular attribute is the bull, which lies at his feet. Sometimes he is shown with a dragon, as a symbol that it was during his pontificate that the power of the pagan religions was broken in the Roman Empire.

⳩According to legend, St. Thecla was a young woman of Iconium who chanced to live in a house directly opposite that in which the Apostle Paul had his lodging. Sitting at her open window, she heard St. Paul preach-

Thecla

First Century

ing the word of Christ and thus became converted to Christianity. She became such a devoted follower of Paul that her rejected lover, Thamyrus, complained to the local governor. When he had Paul driven from the city, Thecla followed him. She survived many tortures, including the flames of fire and the wild beasts of the arena. In later life she retired to a mountain in Iconium, where she became famous for her powers of healing. The local doctors were jealous of her and, believing that her healing powers were derived from her chastity, they plotted to have her kidnaped and defiled. As St. Thecla fled, a rock opened to receive her, leaving only a piece of her veil in the hands of her pursuers.

In art, she is generally portrayed wearing a loose mantle of dark brown or gray, and holding the palm. Occasionally wild beasts appear with her.

Thomas, Apostle ¶St. Thomas, one of Christ's disciples, has often been called "doubting Thomas" because he refused to believe in the Resurrection of Christ until convinced by sight and touch. "Except I shall see in his hands the print of the nails, and put my fingers into the print of the nails, and thrust my hand into his side, I will not believe" (John 20: 25). In tradition, he has a similar role, doubting the Assumption of the Virgin. As Christ overcame Thomas' doubt by inviting him to thrust his hands in His side, the Virgin is said to have convinced Thomas by lowering her girdle to him from Heaven.

260

This doubt of Thomas does not mean that he did not possess great courage. When Christ insisted on returning to Judea in spite of the threats of the Jews to kill Him, it was Thomas who said to the other disciples, " Let us also go that we may die with Him." In the spreading of the gospel by the Apostles, Thomas is said to have gone to the east as far as India, where he established the Christian Church.

Legend recounts how he was asked by Gondophorus, King of the Indies, to build him a magnificent palace, but Thomas used the money given him for this purpose to distribute among the poor. The king was enraged and vowed vengeance. It so happened, however, that his brother, Gad, had just died. When Gad arrived in Heaven, he was asked by the angels where he would like to live. He pointed to a magnificent palace that stood near by, but the angels told him that he could not inhabit it, for it was the palace that a Christian had built in Heaven for his brother, Gondophorus. When Gad appeared to Gondophorus in a vision and told him this, the king set St. Thomas free. The Apostle then explained to the king that, by faith and charity in this world, it was possible to build up a store of wealth in Heaven. Because of this legend, the usual attribute of St. Thomas in art is the builder's rule or square.

¶ St. Thomas Aquinas was sent as a boy to the Benedictine school at Monte Cassino, but he later went to

Thomas Aquinas

Thirteenth Century

Naples, where, much against the wishes of his family, he joined the Order of St. Dominic. At this time, his manner was so heavy and apparently dull that his companions nicknamed him "the dumb ox." His tutor, however, was more perceptive and declared, "You may call him a dull ox, but he will give such a bellow in learning as will astonish the world." Thomas, in fact, soon became an outstanding theologian and teacher. He became a professor at the University of Naples, where he based his teaching of Christian doctrine on the philosophy of Aristotle. He spent his life lecturing, writing, and dealing with Church affairs. His major work, "Summa Theologica," is still the basis of much of the Roman Catholic doctrine. Thomas Aquinas has been called "the most saintly of the learned and the most learned of the saints."

In painting, his most common attributes are the ox, for which he was nicknamed; the sun, which appears on his breast; the chalice, because of his Eucharistic writings. He is generally represented in the Benedictine habit and carries a book or books, symbolizing his great learning.

Ursula
Fifth Century

⁋ St. Ursula was born in Brittany, and was the daughter of the Christian king, Theonestus. According to legend, she was endowed with great beauty and high intelligence. She had many suitors, but refused to marry until Agrippus, King of England, sent ambassadors to ask her hand in marriage to his only son, Conon. Ursula told the ambassadors that she would marry Conon, but only on three conditions. First, she insisted that she must have ten noble virgins as her companions, and that each of these must have a thousand maidens as attendants. She also required a thousand handmaidens for herself. Second, she insisted that before she was married, she should be allowed three years in which to visit the shrines of the Christian saints. Third, she insisted that Prince Conon and all his court must become Christians, for she refused to marry a heathen. These conditions were so extreme that Ursula believed they would be refused, but her beauty and wisdom had so impressed the ambassadors that Conon and his father accepted them all. Eleven thousand maidens were gathered together to form Ursula's retinue, and Conon himself decided to join her on her pilgrimage to Rome. On their return journey, they found the city of Cologne being besieged by the Huns. These heathen savages fell upon Ursula's party and slew them all. The leader of the Huns offered to spare Ursula if she would become his bride. When she refused, he drew his bow and drove three arrows through her body.

Ursula is generally represented as a crowned princess with an arrow, which is her attribute, and she is holding a pilgrim's staff surmounted by a white banner with a red cross. She is often surrounded by her many attendants who always accompany her.

Veronica ⁋The Apocryphal Gospels of Nicodemus tell the legend of St. Veronica. When Jesus was on His way to be crucified, she took pity on His sufferings and wiped the sweat from His brow with her veil, or handkerchief. Miraculously, the cloth retained the likeness of the Saviour.

In art, her attribute is the "veil of Veronica," Veronica's napkin, which bears the picture of Christ, wearing a crown of thorns. She appears in many pictures of the Road to Calvary.

Vincent
Fourth Century

⁋St. Vincent was a deacon of Saragossa, in Spain. During the reign of the Emperor Diocletian, Vincent was persecuted by the proconsul Dacian and was subjected to the most terrible tortures. Dacian, having tried in vain to shake St. Vincent's faith, then sought to tempt him by kindness and luxury. He prepared a fine bed of down, strewn with roses, upon which Vincent was lain. But Vincent had no sooner been placed upon the bed than he commended his spirit to God, and died. Dacian ordered the body to be thrown to wild animals, so that it might be devoured, but a raven came and protected it from all attacks. The body was then taken out to sea in a boat and thrown overboard, with a millstone tied to its neck. It was miraculously washed ashore, and the waves of the sea hollowed a tomb for St. Vincent in the sands. Many years later, his body was discovered and buried in Valencia.

93. Benozzo Gozzoli: *St. Ursula with Angels and Donor*. National Gallery of Art, Washington

94. Paolo Veronese: *Sacra Conversazione:* Madonna and Child surrounded by Saints Lawrence, Agnes and Anthony Abbot.
The Isaac Delgado Museum of Art, New Orleans, Louisiana

95. Biagio d'Antonio da Firenze: *Adoration of the Child with Saints and Donors.*
Left to right: Donor and his son, St. Dominic, St. John the Baptist, St. Nicholas of Tolentino,
St. Louis of Toulouse, the donor's wife. In the background, left, St. Christopher, right, St. Sebastian.
The Philbrook Art Center, Tulsa, Oklahoma

96. Master of Heiligenkreuz: *Death of a Nun* (probably St. Clare). The Virgin is holding the Nun's head. In front, with a lamb, is St. Agnes, or perhaps Blessed Agnes, St. Clare's sister. Left, with dragon, St. Margaret. Back, left to right: St. Dorothy with basket; St. Barbara with tower, and St. Catherine with wheel.

Kress Collection, New York

In painting, St. Vincent is represented as a beautiful young man, dressed in the habit of a deacon. He carries the palm of martyrdom, but his special attributes are two crows which accompanied the vessel that brought the relics of the saint from Cape St. Vincent to Lisbon, where they now lie. In reference to his martyrdom, he may have as attributes a whip, a chain, a grill with iron hooks, or a millstone.

¶According to legend, St. Zeno was a fisherman of Verona who became bishop. He was famous for his wisdom and kindness. He is said to have saved the city of Pistoia from destruction by flood by creating an exit for the waters of the two rivers, the Arno and Ombrone, through what is now known as the Gonfolina Pass.

St. Zeno is generally painted in the costume of a bishop, with a fish hanging from his crosier. He is the patron saint of Verona.

Zeno
Fourth Century

¶Born in Florence of noble birth, St. Zenobius was converted to Christianity by one of his tutors. He became a priest, and a friend of St. Ambrose of Milan, who recommended him to Pope Damasus I. After the death of that Pope, Zenobius returned to Florence, where he was chosen bishop. Many legends are told of the ability of Zenobius to restore the dead to life.

For this reason, he is frequently portrayed with a

Zenobius
Fourth Century

265

dead child or young man in his arms. Legend also
states that after his death, when his body was being
borne to the cathedral for burial, it chanced to touch a
withered elm tree that stood by the wayside. Forthwith, the dead tree burst into leaf. The flowering tree
is therefore another attribute of Zenobius.

Section xi

Radiances, Letters, Colors, and Numbers

A number of symbols have been used to suggest the divine nature or holiness of the persons portrayed in paintings of religious subjects. These symbols are used almost universally in representations of God, Christ, the Holy Ghost, the Virgin Mary, and the saints.

⁋The aureole is the symbol of divinity, therefore, of supreme power. Its use has been reserved for the representation of Divinity: the Father, the Son, and the Holy Ghost; or such symbols that represent the Persons of the Trinity. This use has been extended only to representations of the Blessed Virgin.

Aureole

The aureole consists of a field of radiance and splendor which encircles the whole body and appears to emerge from it. In some cases, the aureole follows the form of the body and clings closely to it, appearing as a fringe of light; in other instances, it is removed from the body and is composed of many luminous rays issuing from a central point. The aureole often appears to end in, or to consist of, pointed flames. It may be shaded off in the colors of the rainbow. The early aureoles were white, but by the Renaissance, gold was

267

generally used to give the impression of light. A blue aureole, indicating celestial glory, is occasionally seen.

The Mandorla, or Almond

❡The aureole obtained the Italian name *mandorla* from its almond shape. In the mandorla, the extended rays of the aureole are enclosed in an almond-shaped framework that surrounds the body of the person depicted. On rare occasions the mandorla may be composed of seven doves, indicating the seven gifts of the Holy Ghost. More rarely, a grouping of angels will be portrayed within the framework of the mandorla. The mandorla is frequently given to Christ in pictures of the Last Judgment, and, on certain occasions, to the Virgin Mary, as in representations of the Assumption.

Halo or Nimbus

❡The halo, or nimbus, is a zone of light, generally represented as a circle, square, or triangle. It is placed behind the heads of divine or sacred personages to identify their great dignity. The nimbus takes a variety of forms, depending upon the persons depicted. In portrayals of God the Father, of Christ, and of the Holy Ghost, the Trinity is often symbolized by three rays of light issuing from the head to form a rayed nimbus. The cross within a circle, the cruciform nimbus, refers to redemption through the Cross and is, therefore, used only in portrayals of Christ. The triangular nimbus is sometimes used in pictures of God the Father, and refers to the Trinity. The nimbus of the Virgin Mary is

268

always circular and is often elaborately decorated. The nimbus of saints, or of other sacred persons, is usually circular in form without much ornamentation.

A nimbus in the form of a square is used to distinguish living persons, such as donors, from the saints. The square has always been considered inferior to the circle, and hence was employed to symbolize the earth, whereas the circle expresses Heaven or eternal existence. The many-sided nimbus, usually hexagonal, is used in portrayals of persons imagined to represent the virtues or other allegorical figures.

¶The glory is a luminous glow that combines the nimbus surrounding the head and the aureole surrounding the body. It expresses the most exalted state of divinity and is, therefore, the attribute of God, the Supreme Lord of Heaven, and of Christ as Judge.

Glory

¶Various letters were used from early Christian times to identify Christ, or to stress the identity of some individual or object with Christ.

Letters

A and W: Alpha and Omega, the first and the last letters in the Greek alphabet, are frequently used on a plaque, shield, book, or elsewhere, as the symbol of God the Son. This usage is based upon Revelation 1: 8, which reads, "I am Alpha and Omega, the beginning and the ending, saith the Lord . . ."

T: This single Greek letter is explained as repre-

T senting the first letter of the Greek word Theos, meaning "God." The single letter T is used as an attribute of St. Anthony Abbot, generally being placed upon his left shoulder.

IHS, IHC: These letters are the first three letters of Ihsus, or Ihcuc, the name of Jesus in Greek. The S and the C are variant forms in the Greek alphabet. They have often been confused with the Latin phrase, "In hoc signo." This refers to the legend that Constantine, on the eve of battle and before his conversion, had a vision. In this vision he beheld a banner on which these words were inscribed: "In hoc signo vinces" (In this sign you will conquer). After victory in the battle, he is said to have embraced the Christian religion. Furthermore, these letters are sometimes misinterpreted as being an abbreviation of the Latin phrase, "Iesus Hominum Salvator" (Jesus Saviour of Men).

This monogram, inscribed in a sun, is the sign that appeared to St. Bernardino of Siena, and which that saint is often depicted carrying in his hand.

INRI: These represent the first four letters of the Latin words, "Jesus Nazarenus Rex Judaeorum," meaning "Jesus of Nazareth, King of the Jews." According to St. John 19:19, after Christ had been crucified, "Pilate wrote a title, and put it on the cross. And the writing was, Jesus of Nazareth, the King of the Jews." St. John goes on to say that this sign was written in Hebrew, Greek, and Latin.

in Christian Art

¶ A monogram is a character composed of two or more letters. The nature of the letters, together with various possible arrangements, may produce a beautiful and symbolic design. Frequently the letters are interwoven or combined with other symbols to represent God, or the Persons of the Godhead. By far the most common are the monograms representing Christ.

XP: The two Greek letters Chi and Rho, which most frequently appear in a monogram, are the first two letters of the Greek word for Christ, ΧΡΙΣΤΟΣ. The combination of these two letters readily gives the form of a cross. Furthermore, as Rho resembles "p" and Chi is similar to "x", the monogram could be read as the Latin word pax, meaning peace.

This was the ancient monogram symbolizing Christ the Conqueror. I and C are the first and last letters of the Greek word Ihcuc (Jesus); X and C are the first and last letters of Xpictoc (Christ); Nika is the Greek word for conqueror.

¶ Black: Black, as a symbol of death and of the underworld, was familiar before the days of Christianity. It was a pagan custom to sacrifice a black animal to propitiate the gods of the nether world.

In Christian symbolism, black is the color of the Prince of Darkness, and, in the Middle Ages, it was associated with witchcraft, the "black art." In general, black suggests mourning, sickness, negation, and death. Black and white together, however, symbolize humility and purity of life. In this sense black, or black and white, was used as the color of the habits of certain religious orders, such as the Augustinians, the original Benedictines, and the Dominicans. Black, as the traditional color of mourning, is the liturgical color for Good Friday, the day of Christ's Crucifixion.

Blue: Blue, the color of the sky, symbolizes Heaven and heavenly love. It is the color of truth, because blue always appears in the sky after the clouds are dispelled, suggesting the unveiling of truth. In paintings, both Christ and the Virgin Mary wear mantles of blue; Christ during His ministry on earth, and the Virgin when holding the Christ Child or shown with Him. In the Church, blue has become the traditional color of the Virgin Mary, and is used on days commemorating events in her life.

Brown: Brown is the color of spiritual death and degradation, and also of renunciation of the world. In this sense, it has been adopted by the Franciscan and the Capuchin Orders as the color of their habits.

Gold: (See *Yellow*)

Gray: Gray, the color of ashes, signifies mourning and humility. It is sometimes used as the Lenten color. Because gray symbolizes the death of the body and the immortality of the spirit, Christ is sometimes shown wearing gray in paintings of the Last Judgment. Gray is the color of the habit of the Vallombrosian Order of Benedictines.

Green: Green is the color of vegetation and of spring, and therefore symbolizes the triumph of spring over winter, or of life over death. Being a mixture of yellow and blue, it also suggests charity and the regeneration of the soul through good works. In pagan rites of initiation, green was the color of water; and it is as the symbol of spiritual initiation that St. John the Evangelist sometimes wears a green mantle. Green is the color of the Epiphany season in the Church, marking the Visitation of the Magi, and the initiation rites in the life of Christ.

Purple: Purple has always been associated with royalty, and is the accepted sign of imperial power. As such, it is sometimes used as a symbol of God the Father. Purple is also the color of sorrow and penitence. It is the liturgical color for Advent and Lent, the Church's seasons of preparation and penitence, when men are anticipating the joyous festivals of Christmas and Easter.

Red: Red is the color of blood, which is associated with the emotions, and is, therefore, symbolic of both love and hate. Red, the color of sovereign power among the Romans, has a similar meaning in the dress of the cardinals. St. John the Evangelist is clad in red to suggest his love of action. Red is the Church's color for martyred saints, because many of the early Christians suffered martyrdom in the Roman persecutions, or at the hands of the barbarians, rather than deny their faith in Christ. In a different sense, because red is the color of fire, it is used during the Church's season of Pentecost, which commemorates the coming of the Holy Ghost.

Violet: Violet symbolizes love and truth, or passion and suffering. It is the color worn by such penitents as Mary Magdalene, and sometimes is worn by the Virgin Mary after the Crucifixion.

White: White has always been accepted as symbolic of innocence of soul, of purity, and of holiness of life. Several references to white as the color of purity and innocence are found in the Bible. For example, "Wash me, and I shall be whiter than snow" (Psalm 51: 7). Christ in the Transfiguration is clad in a garment "as white as the light" (Matthew 17: 2). In describing the angel of the Lord who rolled back the stone from the door of Christ's sepulchre, St. Matthew wrote, "His countenance was like lightning, and his raiment white as snow" (Matthew 28: 3). White is worn by Christ after His Resurrection. It is also worn by the Virgin Mary in paintings of the Immaculate Conception, of her Presentation in the Temple, and, in general, in scenes prior to the Annunciation. The Roman vestal virgins wore white as a symbol of innocence and purity, and this custom has been perpetuated in the dress of brides, in the garments of those receiving their first communion, and in the garb for baptism. In the Early Christian period the clergy wore white, and this color has remained in liturgical use for such seasons as Christmas, Easter, and Ascension. White is the color of light, and is sometimes represented by silver.

Yellow: The color yellow may have either of two opposed symbolic meanings, depending on the way in which it is used. A golden yellow is the emblem of the sun, and of divinity. The backgrounds of many Renaissance paintings glow with a golden yellow, symbolizing the sacredness of that which is depicted. Both St. Joseph and St. Peter are sometimes painted in yellow dress. St. Peter wears a yellow mantle because yellow is the symbol of revealed truth. On the other hand, yellow is sometimes used to suggest infernal light, degradation, jealousy, treason, and deceit. Thus, the traitor Judas is frequently painted in a garment of dingy yellow. In the Middle Ages heretics were obliged to wear yellow. In periods of plague, yellow crosses were used to identify contagious areas, and this use established the custom of using yellow to indicate contagion.

Geometrical Figures

¶ *Circle*: The circle, or ring, has been universally accepted as the symbol of eternity and never-ending existence. As the monogram of God, it represents not only the perfection of God but the everlasting God, " Who was in the beginning, is now, and ever shall be, world without end." (See Ring, in Section XIV)

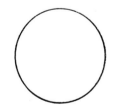

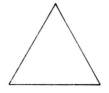

Triangle: The equilateral triangle is the symbol of the Trinity, suggesting three equal parts joined into one. The triangular nimbus is used only in representations of God the Father, or of the Trinity.

The triangle with three circles is the monogram of the Trinity: the Three Persons in the One God: the Father, the Son, and the Holy Ghost.

Square: The square, in contrast with the circle, is the emblem of the earth, and of earthly existence. In this sense it is used in painting as the nimbus of living persons. (See Halo or Nimbus)

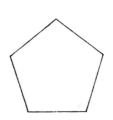

Pentagram: A pentagram is a five-pointed, star-shaped figure made by extending the sides of a regular pentagon until they meet. This geometrical figure has long had symbolic significance, having first been used by followers of Pythagoras, the Greek philosopher, mathematician, and religious reformer; and later by the magicians of the Middle Ages. In the secular sense, the pentagram was used as a protection against the evils of sorcery. In Christian symbolism, the figure suggests the five wounds suffered by Christ upon the Cross.

Numbers

℧ *One* is the symbol of unity.

Two suggests the two natures of Christ, the human and the divine.

Three was called by Pythagoras the number of completion, expressive of a beginning, a middle, and an end. In Christian symbolism, three became the divine number suggesting the Trinity, and also the three days that Christ spent in the tomb.

Four is ordinarily used in Christian art to suggest the four Evangelists.

Five is symbolic of the wounds of Christ.

Six is the number of creation, and perfection, symbolizing divine power, majesty, wisdom, love, mercy, and justice.

Seven is the number of charity, grace, and the Holy Spirit. It was also used by the early writers as the number of completion and perfection. Many instances of this use appear in Biblical writings. When the friends of Job came to comfort him, they "sat down with him upon the ground for seven days and seven nights" (Job 2: 13). Jacob, as a sign of perfect submission, bowed seven times before his brother. Again, there is reference to the sevenfold gifts of the Holy Spirit, the seven deadly sins, and the seven joys and the seven sorrows of the Virgin.

Eight is the number of Resurrection, for it was on the eighth day after His Entry into Jerusalem that Christ rose from the grave. Many baptismal fonts are octagonal in shape.

Nine is the angelic number, for the Bible refers to the nine choirs of angels.

Ten is the number of the Ten Commandments.

Twelve, as the number of the Apostles, has always been a favorite number in Christian symbolism. In a more extended meaning, it is occasionally used to represent the entire Church.

Thirteen is the number of faithlessness and betrayal. At the Last Supper there were thirteen persons at the table: Jesus and the twelve Apostles, including Judas, who had already agreed to betray his Master.

Forty is symbolic of a period of probation or trial. The Israelites wandered for forty years in the wilderness and, for a similar period of time were in bondage to the Philistines. Moses remained for forty days on Mount Sinai. The rain of the Flood lasted for forty days and forty nights. After Christ's baptism, He was forty days in the wilderness, being tempted by the Devil. The forty days of Lent commemorate this event. Forty is sometimes used as the symbol of the Church Militant.

One hundred is the number of plenitude.

One thousand was once regarded as the number signifying eternity, since the names of numbers which exceed one thousand were merely additions to, and multiplications of it.

Section xii

Religious Dress

¶The three orders of ministers in the medieval Church, namely, bishops, priests, and deacons, may be distinguished by the particular vestments and clothing they wear. Those in holy orders who do not belong to one of the religious communities are known as the secular clergy. In Renaissance art, it is usually members of the hierarchy; namely, bishops, cardinals, and the Pope, whom we find portrayed.

All seculars, regardless of their rank, wear a cassock which is a close-fitting, long-sleeved garment reaching to the ankles. Traditionally, it has thirty-three buttons, which are symbolical of the number of years of Christ's earthly life.

The regular clergy, as distinct from the secular, are those in holy orders who are joined under the common rule of the religious order to which they belong. They can be distinguished in two ways: first, by the color of the habit which is peculiar to the religious order of which they are members; and second, by the tonsure, or cut of the hair, which in Renaissance times was common to all those in monastic orders. The shape of the tonsure was often a distinguishing mark of the particular monastic order. The dress of the regulars is

279

called a habit. Usually, it is a long, loose gown, gathered about the waist by a leather belt or rope girdle, with wide sleeves and a hood. The hood, which is the most distinctive feature, is known as the cowl and may be drawn over the head. Some habits include a scapular and a mantle. The religious order of the wearer may be identified by the color of the habit.

Women also enter the religious life. Like the men, they live a communal life under the vows of poverty, chastity, and obedience. Their order is distinguishable by the habit which they wear. Though they take the monastic vows, they are not admitted to holy orders.

Liturgical Vestments   ❡When celebrating Mass, the priest wears over his cassock, or habit, the following vestments: amice, alb, stole, cincture, maniple, and chasuble. Bishops, and other members of the hierarchy, also wear the rochet under the alb, liturgical sandals and stockings, pontifical gloves and ring, pectoral cross, and mitre, and they carry the pastoral staff.

Alb   ❡The alb is a white linen tunic reaching to the feet. It alludes to the robe of mockery with which Herod caused Christ to be clothed, and symbolizes chastity, purity, and the eternal joy of those who have been redeemed by the Blood of the Saviour. In the Middle Ages, embroidery was on the sleeves, chest, and at the hem of the alb to symbolize the five wounds of Christ.

280

⁋The amice is the first vestment the priest puts on when vesting for Mass. It is an oblong piece of white linen upon which a cross is sewn or embroidered. It is an allusion to the cloth that covered the face of Christ during the mocking by the soldiers in the Praetorium.

Amice

⁋The biretta is a stiff, square hat with three or four ridges on the top. It may have a pompon attached at the center. It is worn by secular priests and members of the hierarchy. The color of the biretta may distinguish the ecclesiastical rank of the wearer: in general, black is worn by priests, purple by bishops, and scarlet by cardinals. Distinguished from the biretta is the cardinal's hat, having a broad brim, low crown, and two cords with fifteen tassels each. Its color is always red.

Biretta

In Renaissance painting, St. Jerome is sometimes depicted wearing the cardinal's red hat and robe, even though the ecclesiastical rank of cardinal was not known in his day. St. Bonaventura is upon occasion distinguished by a cardinal's hat hanging on a tree or lying on the ground beside him.

⁋The cassock is the everyday dress of the clergy, and signifies their devotion to Christ and the Church. In general the distinguishing colors of the cassock are white for the Pope, scarlet or red for cardinals, purple for bishops, and black for priests. However, several variations of these colors may occur. When a member

Cassock

of a religious order is raised to the hierarchy, he lays aside his habit and assumes a cassock. The color of the habit of his order, however, is retained in this cassock.

Chasuble

¶The chasuble is the last liturgical garment with which the celebrant is vested. It is the outer garment covering the other vestments, and the Latin origin of its name, *casula* (little house), aptly describes it. The chasuble may be white, red, rose, green, violet, black, gold, or silver, depending on the season of the Church's year or the feast that is being observed. It usually has a cross embroidered on the back, which is an allusion to the Passion of Christ. Symbolically, this vestment alludes to the purple dress that Pilate ordered to be placed on Christ as "King of the Jews." It also recalls Christ's seamless garment for which the soldiers, on Calvary, cast lots. Because the chasuble covers the other vestments, its symbolic meaning is Christian charity and protection; charity being the virtue that should supersede all others.

Cope

¶The cope, the richest and most magnificent of ecclesiastical vestments, is a large cape fashioned in the form of a half circle. A highly decorative deep collar, suspended from the shoulders, ornaments its back. The color of the cope is that of the Church's season. It is worn in processions and in services of great solemnity. Its symbolic meaning is innocence, purity, and dignity.

❡The cord, or cincture, is a linen rope (although it may be of wool or silk) worn around the waist, over the alb and the crossed stole of the celebrant. It is an allusion to the rope with which Christ was bound to the pillar during the Flagellation. Its symbolic meaning is chastity, temperance, and self-restraint.

Cord

❡The dalmatic is the traditional liturgical vestment of the deacon. It is a long-sleeved outer tunic which the deacon wears over the alb. Bishops and abbots may wear it under the chasuble at Solemn Pontifical Masses, and in Renaissance paintings bishops and abbots are often shown wearing both vestments. Its shape, which is the form of a cross, refers to the Passion of Christ. It symbolizes joy, salvation, and justice. The dalmatic is one of the attributes of St. Stephen and St. Laurence.

Dalmatic

❡The maniple is a narrow strip or band of silk worn over the alb on the left arm by the celebrant of the Mass. It is of the same material and color as the chasuble and stole. It is an allusion to the rope with which Christ was bound and led to Calvary, and is symbolic of good works, vigilance, and penitence.

Maniple

❡The mantelletta is a knee-length, sleeveless outer vestment, open in the front, worn by cardinals, archbishops, and bishops. Its color is determined by the ecclesiastical rank of the wearer. Cardinals wear a red

Mantelletta

mantelletta; bishops, a purple one. The vestment is worn as a sign of limited jurisdiction or authority.

Mitre

⟨The mitre in its modern form is a tall headdress with the top cleft crosswise, its outline resembling a pointed arch. It is a liturgical hat, and is worn by the Pope, cardinals, archbishops, and bishops and, with special permission, by some abbots. It is symbolic of their authority.

Mitres may be inlaid with precious stones, embroidered with orphreys, or unadorned and made with white linen or silk. Abbots wear only this latter type, except by special privilege.

The mitre is reminiscent of the pointed hat worn by the Jewish high priest as a symbol of authority, but it was not derived directly from that. The two horns of the mitre are an allusion to the two rays of light that issued from the head of Moses when he received the Ten Commandments. They are also symbolic of the Old and New Testaments. Attached to the back of the mitre, and falling over the shoulders of the wearer, are two flaps, or fanons, which are symbolic of the spirit and the letter of the Testaments. Three mitres are given as an attribute to both St. Bernard and St. Bernardino, in token of the three bishoprics that each man refused.

Morse (Brooch)

⟨The morse, or brooch, is a clasp used to fasten the front of the cope.

in Christian Art

Mozzetta

⁋The mozzetta is an elbow-length cape with an ornamental hood. It is a non-liturgical garment, and is not worn to administer the Sacraments. It is worn by the Pope, by cardinals when not in Rome, and by archbishops, bishops, and abbots within the limits of their jurisdiction.

Pallium

⁋The pallium is a narrow band of white wool worn around the shoulders. It has two short pendants, one hanging down the front, the other down the back, and is ornamented with six black crosses. It is a symbol of the papal authority, and may be given by the Pope to archbishops to indicate their participation in his authority. Its Y shape is symbolic of the Crucifixion.

Ring

⁋The ring worn by members of the hierarchy symbolizes not only spiritual marriage with the Church but also the ecclesiastical office of the wearer.

The papal ring is known as the Fisherman's Ring because it bears the image of St. Peter fishing. It is of plain gold. It is put on the finger of a new Pope at the time of his election. Since it bears his name, it is broken at his death. The Pope always wears a cameo; the privilege of wearing a carved gem is reserved for him.

The cardinal's ring is a sapphire, which he receives from the Pope at the time of his elevation. On the inside of this ring is engraved the coat of arms of the Pope who bestows it.

A bishop also wears a gemmed ring, and he may choose any stone he wishes except a sapphire, which is reserved for the exclusive use of cardinals.

Abbots and abbesses may also wear very simple gemmed rings.

A plain metal band, or a band in the form of a cross, may be worn by a nun to symbolize her marriage with Christ. This is represented pictorially in the many paintings of the Mystic Marriage of St. Catherine of Alexandria.

A ring is also used liturgically, and when it serves this function it is known as the Pontifical Ring. Such a ring is ornamented with a beautiful, large stone, and its band must be of a size which can easily fit over a gloved finger.

Rochet ❡The rochet is a knee-length, pleated tunic, of white linen with tight sleeves. The bottom, shoulder pieces, and ends of the sleeves are ornamented with lace lined with silk of a color that distinguishes the ecclesiastical rank of the wearer.

Scapular ❡The scapular, meaning shoulder, is a narrow length of cloth placed over the shoulders and extending to the hem of the garment, both in the front and in the back. It is a part of most monastic habits, and probably developed from some kind of large apron put on to protect the clothing. It is symbolic of the yoke of Christ.

¶The skull-cap is close-fitting and rimless. As with other ecclesiastical garments, its color is in accord with the rank of the wearer.

¶The stole is a narrow, embroidered vestment worn about the neck. When used as one of the Mass vestments, it is crossed over the breast and made secure by the cord. Its color matches that of the chasuble and maniple. It may have three crosses, one on each end and one in the middle. When worn for other liturgical offices it is not crossed. The deacon wears a broad stole over his left shoulder, across the breast, and fastened at the waist.

The stole is a sign of priestly dignity and power. It symbolizes the yoke of Christ and the Christian duty of working loyally for His Kingdom, and the hope of immortality.

¶The surplice is a knee-length, white linen tunic. Its large flowing sleeves and hem are usually trimmed with lace. Worn over the cassock, it is used during the administration of the Sacraments and for various other liturgical purposes. It is symbolic of man renewed in justice and in the holiness of truth.

¶The tiara, which is a circular headpiece consisting of three crowns, one above the other, surmounted by a cross, is worn only by the Pope. It has a long history,

but was first known in its present form in 1315. Its three crowns have numerous interpretations: they are symbolic of the Trinity, and also allude to the three estates of the Kingdom of God. In art, the tiara is an attribute of St. Gregory and St. Sylvester.

Tonsure

¶Tonsure was the custom of shaving the hair from the top of the head. This practice, during the Renaissance and in the early days of the Church, was adopted by the secular clergy and the monastic orders. It has a triple symbolism: the remembrance of the crown of thorns; the rejection of temporal things; and a reminder of the perfect life.

Tunicle

¶The tunicle is a short dalmatic and is worn by the subdeacon at High Mass. It is the symbol of joy and contentment of heart.

Veil

¶The veil, as a religious garment, is the outer covering of the headdress of a nun. It is symbolic of modesty and renunciation of the world.

Wimple

¶The wimple is a linen covering around the head, neck, and cheeks of a nun.

XIV. Franco-Rhenish Master, about 1440: *The Mass of St. Martin of Tours.*
Kress Collection, New York

Section xiii

Religious Objects

¶ The Christian altar is a table of stone or wood, and is usually beautifully carved. Situated in the center of the sanctuary, it is the chief focal point within the church. Liturgically, the altar faces the east and Jerusalem, the Holy Land of Christ's Passion and Death. This position is traditional and has scriptural authority in Ezekiel 43: 4, "And the glory of the Lord came into the house by the way of the gate whose prospect is toward the east." The altar, or holy table, symbolizes the presence of Christ in the Sacrament of the Eucharist.

Altar

¶ The altar cloth is of pure white linen, covering the top of the altar and extending downward on both sides. It is symbolic of the shroud that covered Christ.

Altar Cloth

¶ The altarpiece is a panel or panels attached to, or placed immediately behind, the altar. It takes many forms: a largen (single panel); the more common triptych (triple panel); or polytych (numerous panels); and it is richly ornamented. The central panel usually depicts the Crucifixion, although it may portray some other great event in the life of Christ. Often, the central panel is a representation of the Virgin and Child.

Altarpiece

289

The side panels portray events associated with Christ or the Virgin, or with the saints to whom the particular church or chapel is dedicated. These side panels are often hinged, so that they can be closed for penitential seasons or opened on special occasions.

Ampulla

⟨The ampulla is the vessel that contains the holy oil. The blessed oils are used in the Sacraments of Holy Baptism, Confirmation, Holy Orders, and Unction. They are also used in the ceremony of Coronation. The holy oil is symbolic of consecration.

Asperges
(Aspergillum)

⟨Asperges (thou shalt sprinkle) is the first word of the anthem, "Asperges me, Domine, hyssopo," which has come to designate the rite of sprinkling the altar, clergy, and people with holy water. It symbolizes the purification from and the expulsion of evil. "Purge me with hyssop, and I shall be clean: wash me, and I shall be whiter than snow" (Psalm 51: 7). Asperges has come to be used to designate the rite itself, as well as the aspergillum, which is used by the priest in performing the rite. The aspergillum is a brush, or a perforated globe holding a sponge, on a short handle. From its use, the aspergillum has acquired a very special significance as an instrument with which to exorcise evil. As such, it occurs as an attribute of St. Anthony Abbot, St. Benedict, St. Martha, and the other saints famed for their contests with the Devil.

290

in Christian Art

❡Bells in church towers and spires summon the faithful to worship. The sanctus bell at the altar announces the coming of Christ in the Eucharist. St. Anthony Abbot is frequently portrayed with a bell attached to his crutch as a warning to demons.

Candle

❡Candles play a great and varied role in churches, and according to their use and numbers the teaching of the Church is expressed symbolically. Examples of this are the six lights on the altar, representing the Church's constant round of prayer; the sanctuary lamp; the Eucharistic candles, symbolizing the coming of Christ in Communion; the Paschal candle, symbolical of the risen Christ during the Easter season. Candles are also symbolical when used in groupings: three candles represent the Trinity, or seven candles signify the Seven Sacraments. The Bishop's Candle is used when the bishop is pontificating, or is the celebrant of the Mass. The use of candles for devotional purposes, at shrines and in processions, is universal and frequently seen in Renaissance art. The candlestick, because of the symbolism attached to the candle, is usually a work of artistic beauty.

❡A cathedral is the official seat of a bishop, and is, therefore, the principal church of a diocese. It takes its name from the cathedra, or official chair or throne of the bishop, which is placed in the sanctuary.

Cathedral

291

Censer

¶A censer is the vessel in which incense is burned. It is cup-shaped, with a pierced cover, and is suspended by chains. In the Old Testament, the censer symbolized the pleas of the worshiper that his prayer would be acceptable to God. "Let my prayer be set forth before thee as incense; and the lifting up of my hands as the evening sacrifice" (Psalm 141:2). In Christian symbolism, the smoke of the incense symbolizes the prayers of the faithful ascending to Heaven. The censer is an attribute of St. Laurence and St. Stephen.

Chalice

¶A chalice is the cup from which the consecrated wine and water of the Eucharist are partaken at Holy Communion. It refers to the Last Supper and the sacrifice of Christ upon the Cross. "And he took the cup, and when he had given thanks, he gave it to them: and they all drank of it. And he said unto them, This is my blood of the new testament, which is shed for many" (Mark 14: 23, 24). Thus, the chalice is a symbol of the Christian faith. Its significance goes back to the Old Testament, where an allusion to the Eucharist may be found in Psalm 116: 13, "I will take the cup of salvation . . ." Also St. Paul conveys this idea in I Corinthians 10: 16, "The cup of blessing which we bless, is it not the communion of the blood of Christ?" The chalice with a serpent is the attribute of St. John the Evangelist. The chalice and wafer are attributes of St. Barbara; the broken chalice, of St. Donatus.

in Christian Art

⁋In Christian symbolism, the church has several meanings. In its basic sense, it means the House of God. It may also be used to signify the Body of Christ. Sometimes, the church is alluded to as the Ark, and in this sense means the salvation of all its members. In painting, a church placed in the hands of a saint signifies that he was the founder of a particular church or was its first bishop. In the hands of St. Jerome and St. Gregory, however, the church signifies no particular building, but the Church in general, of which they were great supporters and among the primitive fathers.

⁋The ciborium has two meanings. It is either a canopy erected over the altar and supported by four pillars, an allusion to the Ark of the Covenant, or it is a receptacle for the Reserved Host. In the latter sense, it symbolizes the Eucharist and the Last Supper.

⁋The corporal is a white linen cloth laid on the altar, upon which the elements of bread and wine are consecrated. At certain times during the service these elements may be covered with the corporal.

⁋The ancestor of the crosier is generally supposed to be the shepherd's crook; however, it may also be a descendant of the walking staff common in the days of the Apostles. Now, greatly enriched since its humbler days, it is the pastoral staff of a bishop, archbishop,

Church

Ciborium

Corporal

Crosier

abbot, or abbess. It is still common practice for an abbot's staff to bear a white pendant veil. The pennanted staff often appears in paintings. It is the symbol of authority and jurisdiction. The crosier bearing a double cross is the attribute of St. Gregory, and also of St. Sylvester. St. Zeno carries a crosier with a fish. The crosier is regarded as the symbol of mercy, firmness, and the correction of vices.

Cross

¶The cross is one of the oldest and most universal of all symbols. It is, of course, the perfect symbol of Christ because of His sacrifice upon the Cross. In a broader sense, however, the cross has become the mark or sign of the Christian religion, the emblem of atonement, and the symbol of salvation and redemption through Christianity.

There are many and varied forms of the cross. In Christian art, two major types, known respectively as the Latin cross and the Greek cross, are most commonly found.

The Latin cross has a longer upright than crossbar. The intersection of the two is usually such that the upper and the two horizontal arms are all of about equal length, but the lower arm is conspicuously longer. This cross is used to symbolize the Passion of Christ or the Atonement. Five red marks or jewels are sometimes placed on the face of the cross to represent the five wounds Christ suffered while being crucified. In addi-

294

tion, Christ's crown of thorns is frequently shown with the cross or hanging upon it. Tradition says that Christ was crucified on a Latin cross.

The Latin cross fastened to the top of a staff or reed is the attribute of St. Philip, who is also sometimes represented with a plain Latin cross in his hand or with a Tau cross on the end of his staff. The Latin cross, alone or in combination with other pictorial elements, is used as an attribute of numerous other saints. The plain Latin cross is borne by St. Reparata and St. Margaret. John the Baptist frequently bears a cross made of reeds. St. Helena is depicted with a cross with hammer and nails or with a cross borne by angels. St. Anthony of Padua has a flowered cross, while St. Catherine of Siena is given a cross with a lily. St. George of Cappadocia and St. Ursula are painted with a banner on which there is a red cross.

The Greek cross has four equal arms. This cross is used more often to suggest the Church of Christ than to symbolize Christ and His sacrifice for mankind.

Another well-known form of the cross is the St. Andrew cross, which consists of crossed arms which are not at right angles to each other, but diagonally placed in the shape of an X. The origin of this form is attributed to St. Andrew, who, when condemned to be crucified, requested that he be nailed to a cross of a different form than that upon which Christ was sacrificed. In true humility, St. Andrew believed that, even

in martyrdom, he was unworthy to approach the likeness of his Redeemer. The St. Andrew cross has, therefore, come to be a symbol of humility in suffering.

An older form of the cross is the Egyptian or Tau cross, which consists of three arms only, arranged in the shape of the letter T. This is known as the Old Testament cross. Tradition says that it was upon such a cross that Moses lifted up the serpent in the wilderness, foreshadowing the lifting up of Christ upon His Cross (John 3: 14). The Tau cross is occasionally one of the attributes of St. Philip because, according to one version of his martyrdom, he was crucified on a cross of this type. It is also one of the attributes of St. Anthony Abbot.

Two adaptations of the cross known as Ecclesiastical crosses are used to distinguish different ranks in the hierarchy of the Church. The double cross, that is, a cross with two crossbars, is used to signify patriarchs and archbishops, while the triple cross, with three crossbars, is used exclusively by the Pope.

Crown

℅The crown, from very early days, has been the mark of victory or distinction. From this, it came to be accepted as the mark of royalty. In Christian art, the crown, when on the head of the Madonna, indicates that she is the Queen of Heaven. When the crown is used as the attribute of a martyr, it signifies victory over sin and death, or denotes that the saint was of royal blood. The crown is sometimes merely a circlet, but it may be a chaplet of flowers or a magnificent circle of gold and jewels.

The Crown of Thorns is one of the emblems of the Passion and the Crucifixion of Christ. "And the soldiers . . . clothed him with purple and platted a crown of thorns, and put it about his head, and began to salute him, Hail King of the Jews!" (Mark 15: 16-18). Christ is usually pictured wearing the Crown of Thorns from this moment until He was taken down from the Cross. The tonsure of the monk, originally the sign of dedication to Divine service, is a reverential imitation of Christ's sacrificial Crown of Thorns.

The crown in various forms is used as an attribute of certain saints. The triple crown, for example, is an attribute of St. Elisabeth of Hungary. St. Catherine of Alexandria is given the royal crown because of her rank. St. Catherine of Siena wears the crown of thorns because of her stigmata. St. Louis of France has the crown of thorns, as well as the kingly crown, to commemorate his discovery of the Crown of Thorns in the Holy Land. St. Louis of Toulouse is painted with a royal crown and sceptre at his feet in token of his refusal of the royal succession. St. Cecilia is painted with a crown of roses. St. Veronica and St. Mary Magdalene are sometimes accorded the crown of thorns. The Pope wears a triple crown as an emblem of his triple royalty. (See Tiara, in Section XII)

**Crucifix
(Rood)**

❡The crucifix is a representation of Christ on the Cross. From the word *rood*, the alternate English name for crucifix, comes the designation of the screen at the entrance of the sanctuary of a church as the rood screen, for it was customary to erect a great crucifix upon it. A number of saints, including St. Anthony of Padua, are sometimes painted with a small crucifix in their hands. One of the attributes of St. Nicholas of Tolentino is a crucifix decorated with lilies. St. John Gualbert is sometimes painted kneeling before a large crucifix with the head of Christ bending toward him.

Cruet

❡The cruet is a small vessel that contains the wine or water of the Eucharist. It is symbolic of redemption.

Cup

❡The cup is the symbol of Christ's Agony in the Garden of Gethsemane. This is based on Christ's own words, when, in His prayer to God, He said, "O my Father, if this cup may not pass away from me, except I drink it, thy will be done" (Matthew 26: 42). Knowing that He had been betrayed by Judas and that His supreme sacrifice upon the Cross lay before Him, Christ thus accepted the burden which God had laid upon Him. (See Chalice)

Dossal

❡The dossal is a richly embroidered hanging placed behind the altar. It is usually a brocade of embroidered needlework on a cloth of gold. If the dossal is extended so that the sides of the altar are included, these extensions are known as riddles. (See Altarpiece)

⸿The ewer and basin are used for the washing of the celebrant's hands at the Eucharist, and at certain special offices of the Church. This washing of the hands is a symbolic act of innocency and purity. It refers to the act of Pilate when the multitude demanded that he condemn Jesus to death. "When Pilate saw that he could prevail nothing, but that rather a tumult was made, he took water, and washed his hands before the multitude, saying, I am innocent of the blood of this just person . . ." (Matthew 27: 24). In paintings of the Virgin Mary, the ewer is symbolic of purity.

Ewer and Basin

⸿The frontal is a decorative piece, usually movable, covering the front of the altar. This oblong panel was often richly figured with paintings or sculptural reliefs. In the Renaissance, the frontal was often of silk or brocade, frequently embroidered, and in the color of the Church season or feast.

Frontal

⸿The Host is the flat, round piece of unleavened bread which the celebrant consecrates at the Eucharist, or Mass. Its name is derived from the Latin word *hostia*, meaning victim or sacrifice. As such, and especially when shown with the chalice, it symbolizes the Sacrifice of Christ upon the Cross.

Host

Monstrance ⁌The monstrance, originally any receptacle in which sacred relics were exposed, is also a transparent container in which the consecrated Host is viewed. It is derived from the Latin word *monstro*, meaning show.

Pall ⁌The pall is a white linen cloth used to cover the chalice. It symbolizes the linen in which the body of Christ was enshrouded.

Paten ⁌The paten is a shallow plate for the bread of the Eucharist. It symbolizes the dish used at the Last Supper.

Purificator ⁌The purificator is a white linen cloth used to cleanse the chalice after the celebration of the Eucharist.

Pyx ⁌The word pyx is derived from the Latin word *pyxis*, meaning box. In earlier times the term was applied to all vessels used to hold the Eucharist. In ordinary usage it now refers to the vessel in which the Host is carried to the sick. In Christian art, the pyx is an attribute of St. Clare of Assisi, who, according to legend, placed a pyx containing the Host on the threshold of her convent, whereupon the infidels who were besieging it threw down their weapons and fled.

Reliquary ⁌The reliquary is a container for keeping or exhibiting a relic or relics. It may be of any form and material, but is often shaped in the form of the relic it contains.

300

❡The rosary is a form of devotion to the Virgin Mary. This devotion consists of a series of meditations and prayers centering about events in the life of Christ and of the Virgin. These meditations are known as mysteries, and are divided into three series: the Joyful, the Sorrowful, and the Glorious. The prayers of the rosary are counted on a string of beads. The rosary may be represented as a wreath of roses in which the color of the flowers; white, red, and yellow or gold, represents the mysteries.

    The rosary is an attribute of St. Dominic, for it was he who instituted the devotion of the rosary. It is also sometimes used as an attribute of St. Catherine of Siena, one of the great Dominican saints.

Rosary

❡The tabernacle is first mentioned in Exodus as a tent carried by the Israelites during their wanderings in the wilderness. It was used as the place of sacrifice and worship. In Christian usage, it denotes the receptacle in which is placed the pyx, or ciborium, containing the consecrated elements of the Eucharist. Three tabernacles are symbolic of the Transfiguration.

Tabernacle

❡The official throne or chair of the bishop, properly called a "cathedra," is a symbol of episcopal dignity which goes back to the very early days of the Church. It is located on the gospel, or left, side of the sanctuary, though in former times its position was behind the

Throne (Cathedra)

301

altar. This location is still retained in the Church of St. Peter in Rome. The cathedra was the chair of the teacher in ancient times, and from this it derives its name. The Bishop's church, which is the principal church of a diocese, is called a cathedral. This name originates from the fact that the cathedra (Bishop's throne) is located there as the symbol of his authority and jurisdiction.

Section xiv

Artifacts

¶ The anchor is the Christian symbol for hope and steadfastness. This symbolic meaning rests on the Epistle to the Hebrews 6: 19, which refers to the everlasting virtue of God's counsel in these words, "Which hope we have as an anchor of the soul, both sure and steadfast. . ." The symbol was frequently used in this sense in the catacombs of ancient Rome, and was carved on old Christian gems.

The anchor is the attribute of St. Clement, who was condemned to be cast into the sea bound to an anchor, and of St. Nicholas of Myra, patron saint of seamen.

¶ Armor is the symbol of chivalry. The warrior saints, of whom St. George is outstanding, are frequently shown in armor, as is the Archangel Michael. Armor also suggests the Christian faith as protection against evil. "Put on the whole armour of God," says St. Paul in his Epistle to the Ephesians, "that ye may be able to stand against the wiles of the devil . . . having on the breastplate of righteousness . . . the shield of faith . . . the helmet of salvation, and the sword of the Spirit, which is the word of God" (Ephesians 6: 11ff.).

Anchor

Armor

303

Arrow

⁋The arrow is generally used to suggest a spiritual weapon, dedicated to the service of God. The arrow as an instrument of war and death figures in the portrayals of many saints. St. Sebastian is usually depicted with his body pierced by arrows. St. Ursula is said to have survived torture by arrows. The arrow was also a symbol of the plague, and because St. Sebastian survived his ordeal of being shot by arrows, he became the one of the patron saints of all victims of the plague.

Balls

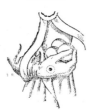

⁋Three balls, or purses, are one of the attributes of St. Nicholas of Myra, representing the three gifts of money which, according to legend, the saint threw into the window of the impoverished man with three marriageable daughters, to provide them with dowries.

Banner

⁋The banner, usually with a cross, is the symbol of victory. This alludes to the Emperor Constantine, who, seeing a cross in the clouds and thereupon being converted to Christianity, included it in the design of his flag. In Christian art, the Lamb of God often bears a banner with a cross symbolizing the victory over death won by the martyrdom of Christ. Christ Himself carries a banner only when rising from the grave, in the Descent into Hell, and in the Appearances on earth after the Resurrection and before the Ascension. St. John the Baptist is often represented with a banner, inscribed either with a cross or with the Latin words

XV. Jacopo del Sellaio: *Christ with the Symbols of the Passion.*
Birmingham Museum of Art, Birmingham, Alabama

Ecce Agnus Dei (Behold, the Lamb of God). It is also the attribute of military saints and of those who carried the gospel to foreign lands. A banner with a red cross is the attribute of St. George of Cappadocia and of St. Ansanus. St. Reparata and St. Ursula are the only female saints to whom a banner is attributed.

Beehive

❡The beehive has been used to symbolize great eloquence, as is suggested by the expression, "honeyed words." The beehive was given as an attribute to both St. Bernard of Clairvaux and St. Ambrose because "their eloquence was as sweet as honey." (See Bee, in Section I)

Book

❡The book, when used as a symbol in Renaissance painting, had a number of meanings, depending upon the person shown. The book in the hands of the Evangelists and Apostles represents the New Testament. In the hand of St. Stephen, it represents the Old Testament. In the hand of any other saint, it generally means that the saint was famous for his learning or his writings. It is so used in paintings of St. Catherine of Alexandria, the Doctors of the Church, St. Thomas Aquinas, and St. Bernard of Clairvaux. In paintings concerned with monastic orders, the book, accompanied by a pen or inkhorn, indicates that the individual was an author, and the book is sometimes lettered with the title of his work. The open book, in the hand of a founder of an

Order, is the symbol of his rule and is often lettered with the first sentence of the rule of the Order. A book with Alpha and Omega is an attribute of Christ. The sealed book is often placed in the hand of the Virgin Mary, in reference to the allusion of Psalm 139:16, "... in thy book all my members were written. . ." St. Augustine is frequently portrayed with book and pen, attributes sometimes given to the four Evangelists. St. Anthony of Padua is often shown with a book pierced by a sword.

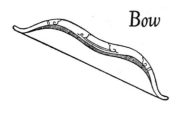

Bow ⁋The bow is the symbol of war and of worldly power: "Behold," said the Lord to the Prophet Jeremiah, "I will break the bow of Elam, the chief of their might" (Jeremiah 49:35).

Box of Ointment ⁋The box of ointment is most commonly used in Renaissance art as an attribute of St. Mary Magdalene. This refers, on the one hand, to the scene in the house of Lazarus after the conversion of Mary: "Then took Mary a pound of ointment of spikenard, very costly, and anointed the feet of Jesus, and wiped his feet with her hair..." (John 12:3).

It also refers to the scene at the sepulchre, after the Crucifixion: "And when the sabbath was past, Mary Magdalene, and Mary the mother of James, and Salome, had brought sweet spices, that they might come and anoint him" (Mark 16:1).

306

in Christian Art

The box of ointment is also used as an attribute of the brothers St. Cosmas and St. Damian, who, as physicians, are depicted holding a small box of ointment in one hand and a lancet, or some other surgical instrument, in the other.

❡Bread has always been a symbol of the means of sustaining life, hence the phrase, "Bread is the staff of life." In the Old Testament bread was the symbol of God's providence, care, and nurture of His people. He sent manna to the children of Israel in the wilderness. "And when the children of Israel saw it, they said one to another, It is manna: for they wist not what it was. And Moses said unto them, This is the bread which the Lord hath given you to eat" (Exodus 16: 15). Christ gave new meaning to this symbolism when He said, ". . . I am the bread of life: he that cometh to me shall never hunger . . ." (John 6: 35). At the Last Supper, Christ used bread as the symbol of His sacrifice upon the Cross. "And he took bread, and gave thanks and brake it, and gave unto them, saying, This is my body which is given for you: This do in remembrance of me" (Luke 22: 19).

Three loaves of bread are given to St. Mary of Egypt as an attribute, for she went forth into the desert to a life of solitude and prayer, bearing with her three loaves of bread. A raven bearing a loaf of bread is one of the attributes of St. Paul the Hermit, for the raven brought him bread during his many years in the wilderness. A loaf of bread is also used occasionally as an attribute of St. Dominic, on the basis of the legend of his obtaining bread for his monastery by divine intervention.

Cauldron of Oil

¶A cauldron of boiling oil is used as an attribute of St. John the Evangelist, who, according to legend, was hurled into a cauldron of boiling oil, but was miraculously saved from death.

Cloak or Coat

¶A cloak divided into halves by a sword is an attribute of St. Martin, who, in the midst of winter, befriended a poor man by giving him half of his own cloak. (See Robe)

Club
(Bat)

¶The club is one of the symbols of the betrayal of Christ. The club, or bat, is also the attribute of St. James the Less, for it was the instrument of his martyrdom. According to tradition, he was thrown to the ground from the top of the temple, but not being killed by the fall, he was afterward slain with a club, or a fuller's bat, as he rose to his knees to pray.

Coins

¶Thirty pieces of silver represent one of the symbols of the Passion, in reference to the betrayal of Christ by Judas Iscariot. "Judas Iscariot went unto the chief priests and said unto them, What will ye give me, and I

308

will deliver him unto you? And they covenanted with him for thirty pieces of silver" (Matthew 26: 14, 15).

St. Laurence is sometimes shown bearing in his hand a dish of gold and silver coins. This refers to his distribution of the wealth of the Church to the poor at the behest of Pope Sixtus II.

¶An iron comb is one of the attributes of St. Blaise, for, upon order of the Emperor Licinius, he was tortured by having his flesh torn by combs of iron, similar to the combs used for the carding of wool.

Comb

¶Crutches are frequently used as an attribute of St. Anthony to signify his age and feebleness after many years spent as a hermit in the desert. A bell is sometimes suspended from his crutch to symbolize his power to exorcise evil spirits.

Crutch

¶A dagger is one of the attributes of St. Lucy, who suffered martyrdom by being stabbed in the neck with a poniard.

Dagger

¶Dice are sometimes used as a symbol of the Passion, referring to the incident of the soldiers who, after the Crucifixion, cast lots for Christ's coat. "Now the coat was without seam, woven from the top throughout. They said therefore among themselves, Let us not rend it, but cast lots for it, whose it shall be" (John 19: 23, 24).

Dice

309

Dish CｰApart from the paten, the dish itself is not a symbol used in Chriſtian art, but a dish sometimes appears as part of a symbol or attribute. (See Paten, in Section XIII)

Dish Bearing Head: This is one of the attributes of St. John the Baptist. It refers to the slaying of John at the request of Salome.

Dish Bearing Eyes: According to legend, a suitor of St. Lucy was so moved by the beauty of her eyes that he left her no peace and complained that her beautiful eyes were a torture to him. Upon hearing this, St. Lucy tore out her eyes and sent them to the suitor on a dish. The dish bearing eyes has, therefore, come to be an attribute of St. Lucy.

Dish or Basket Bearing Roses: An attribute of St. Dorothea, who, at the place of her execution, received a gift of roses and apples from an angelic messenger.

Dish Bearing Money: This has come to be an attribute of St. Laurence, who was commanded by Sixtus, Bishop of Rome, to diſtribute the treasures of the Church to the poor.

Dish Bearing Female Breaſts: This is an attribute of St. Agatha, who, as a part of her martyrdom, had her breaſts torn by shears, or pincers.

Fetters (Chains) CｰFetters are one of the symbols of the Passion, referring to the Flagellation of Christ by the soldiers. St. Leonard is usually depicted bearing in his hand some

310

broken fetters, symbolic of his work on behalf of the prisoners of King Clovis of France, to whose court the saint was attached.

Gate

❡The gate has a number of symbolic meanings in Christian art. The gate may signify death and departure from life in this world. ". . . consider my trouble which I suffer of them that hate me, thou that liftest me up from the gates of death" (Psalm 9: 13). It may also represent the entrance into the heavenly Paradise. "Lift up your heads, O ye gates; and be ye lift up, ye everlasting doors. . ." (Psalm 24: 7). The gate carries both of these meanings in scenes of the Expulsion of Adam and Eve from the Garden of Eden. It also appears as the dividing barrier between the righteous and the damned in scenes of the Last Judgment. A gate is always a central feature in representations of the Descent into Hell. Christ has broken through it and its fragments lie strewn at His feet. The Virgin Mary is sometimes referred to as the Closed Gate, in reference to her unblemished virginity.

❡The girdle, or cincture, was worn over the other clothing and, in ancient costume, served as purse, protection, and ornament. Many symbolical meanings were attached to it. Christ used it to symbolize preparation for any service that God might require of His children. "Let your loins be girded about, and your lights burn-

Girdle (Cincture)

ing" (Luke 12: 35). St. Paul called the girdle the symbol of truth in the Christian's armor. "Stand therefore, having your loins girt about with truth . . ." (Ephesians 6: 14). When worn by the prophets, the girdle is the symbol of humility and contempt of the world, and is made of leather. The girdle of the monks, signifying their vows of poverty, chastity, and obedience, was probably developed from the prophetic meaning. The girdle is also symbolic of chastity. The Biblical origin of this meaning lies in the ancient practice of virtuous women, of making very beautiful girdles which became symbolic of their virtue and chastity (Proverbs 31).

The girdle, as an attribute of the Virgin Mary, signifies chastity. It also refers to the legend that she lowered her girdle from the sky to convince the unbelieving St. Thomas that she had actually ascended to Heaven.

Glass   ⸿Glass, being clear and transparent, is a symbol of purity. In this sense, it is often depicted in scenes of the life of the Virgin. In pictures of the Annunciation of the Virgin, the lily is often placed in a vase of transparent glass. It is also symbolic of the Immaculate Conception. In pictures of the Creation, God is sometimes shown holding a crystal ball, symbolic of the divine world of light before the creation of the earth.

A crystal glass containing a serpent, or a broken

312

crystal glass, is sometimes used as an attribute of St. Benedict, with reference to his miraculous escape from death by poisoning.

❡The globe is a symbol of power. As such, it is frequently shown as an attribute of God the Father. In the hands of Christ, the globe is an emblem of His sovereignty. In the hands of a man, the globe is the symbol of imperial dignity.

Globe

❡The gridiron is frequently used as an attribute of St. Laurence, who is said to have been tortured for his faith by being roasted upon a gridiron.

Gridiron

❡The halberd is the attribute of St. Jude, who, on his travels with St. Simon, is said to have been killed with a halberd.

Halberd

❡The hammer was used to nail Christ to the Cross, and so it is one of the instruments of the Passion and is a symbol of the Crucifixion.

Hammer

❡The harp is recognized as the attribute of King David. "And David and all Israel played before God with all their might, and with singing, and with harps . . ." (I Chronicles 13: 8). The harp has come to be the symbol of the Book of Psalms and of all songs and music in honor of God.

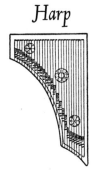

Harp

313

The harp as an instrument of divine music is referred to in Revelation 5: 8, which describes the twenty-four elders who surround the Throne of God as "having every one of them harps." St. Augustine, in his sermons, explains the Ten Commandments in terms of the ten strings of David's harp.

Hatchet
(Axe)

⁋The hatchet, or axe, is a symbol of destruction. The hatchet is also used as the attribute of several Biblical characters. It is an emblem of St. John the Baptist. In preaching to the people of Judea, he declared, "And now also the ax is laid unto the root of the trees: therefore every tree which bringeth not forth good fruit is hewn down" (Matthew 3: 10).

It is also an emblem of Joseph, in allusion to his trade as a carpenter. Since both St. Matthew and St. Matthias suffered martyrdom by beheading, the axe is one of their attributes.

Key

⁋Jesus said to St. Peter, according to St. Matthew 16: 19, "And I will give unto thee the keys of the kingdom of heaven: and whatsoever thou shalt bind on earth shall be bound in heaven . . ." Thus, St. Peter is regarded as the guardian of the Gate of Heaven and his attribute is a key, or a bunch of keys. St. Martha, patroness of feminine discretion and good housekeeping, is also frequently depicted with a large bunch of keys hanging from her girdle.

314

in Christian Art

❡A knife is most frequently shown as an instrument of martyrdom. St. Bartholomew is always shown with a large knife of a peculiar shape, and sometimes with a piece of human skin over his arm, which refers to his having been flayed alive. St. Peter Martyr is also given a knife, either in his head or in his hand, because it was also the instrument of his martyrdom.

❡The ladder is one of the instruments of the Passion and is frequently shown in scenes of the Descent from the Cross. It also refers to the vision of Jacob: "And he dreamed, and behold a ladder set up on the earth, and the top of it reached to heaven: and behold the angels of God ascending and descending on it" (Genesis 28: 12). In paintings of the patriarchs, the ladder is used as an attribute of Jacob. The ladder is similarly used as an attribute of St. Benedict, who, in a vision, saw the brethren of his Order ascend to Heaven on a ladder.

❡The lamp, because of the light it sheds, is used as a symbol of wisdom and piety. The Bible describes the Word of God as a lamp unto the faithful. In the parable of the wise and foolish virgins, a lighted lamp is used to indicate the wise ones. It is in this sense that the lamp has been given as an attribute to several saints, notably St. Lucy. The use of the lamp with St. Lucy refers to her vision of St. Agatha, who appeared to her and said, "Lucy, that art indeed a light."

Lance

⁋The lance, used to pierce the side of Christ on the Cross, is a symbol of the Passion. St. George of Cappadocia is frequently shown bearing in one hand a lance, often broken, because, according to legend, his lance being broken, he slew the dragon with his sword. The lance, or javelin, is also the attribute of St. Thomas, since it was the instrument of his martyrdom.

Millstone

⁋The millstone is used as an attribute for St. Florian and St. Vincent, because each was martyred by being thrown into the water with a millstone tied to his neck.

Mirror

⁋A mirror bearing the image of the Virgin is one of the attributes of St. Geminianus. The spotless mirror is a symbol of the Virgin Mary.

Money

⁋Two hands filled with money are sometimes used as a symbol of the Passion, in allusion to the betrayal by Judas. A bag of money is an attribute of St. Matthew the Apostle, who was a publican (tax collector) before he was converted to Christianity. Three bags of money are one of the attributes of St. Nicholas of Myra. A dish with money, or bags of money, may be used to identify St. Laurence, who distributed the treasures of the Church to the poor. Other saints notable for their charity may also be represented giving money to the poor. Among them is St. Elisabeth of Hungary.

⟪The mortar and pestle, instruments used by the apothecary in preparing medicines, are often attributes of the physician saints, Cosmas and Damian.

Mortar and Pestle

⟪Musical instruments, in addition to being one of the attributes of St. Cecilia, are frequently represented in the hands of angels shown in scenes of the Virgin and Child. Choirs of angels are portrayed playing musical instruments to symbolize their eternal praise to God.

Musical Instruments

⟪Nails, because of their use in the Crucifixion of Christ, are a symbol of the Passion. Early crucifixes show four nails piercing each of the hands and feet of Christ. On most crucifixes, there are only three nails, both feet being pierced by one nail. The number three was preferred when the nails were painted separately as instruments of the Passion, perhaps with symbolic reference to the Trinity.

Nails

⟪The organ is used to symbolize the praise that the Church is continually offering to the glory of God. It is an attribute of St. Cecilia, the patron saint of music. She is said to have invented the organ, in order that she might pour forth the flood of harmony with which her soul was filled.

Organ

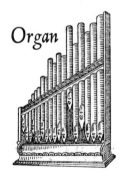

⟪A painting of the Virgin is one of the attributes given to St. Luke, who is often shown painting her portrait.

Painting

317

Pen ❧ The pen alone, or sometimes with an inkhorn, is given as an attribute to the Evangelists and Doctors of the Church. Notable among those to whom this attribute is applied are St. Augustine, St. Bernard, St. Mark, and St. Matthew.

Pillar

❧ The pillar to which Christ was bound during the Flagellation is used as one of the emblems of the Passion. The pillar is an attribute of Samson, who died tearing down the pillars of the palace of the Philistines. St. Sebastian is usually shown bound to a pillar, his body pierced with arrows.

Pincers (Shears)

❧ Pincers are an attribute of St. Agatha, who had her breasts torn with shears, or pincers. They are also an attribute of St. Apollonia of Alexandria, who, as a part of her martyrdom, is said to have had her teeth pulled out with pincers.

Plane

❧ The carpenter's plane is a customary attribute of St. Joseph, who followed the carpenter's trade in the village of Nazareth.

Ring ❧ The ring, or circlet, has been universally accepted as the symbol of eternity and never-ending existence. It is also the symbol of eternal union. The ring of a bishop suggests his union with the Church. Marriage rings are symbols of permanent union. Two rings linked, or two circles one above the other, are emblematic of the earth and sky. Three rings linked together signify the Holy Trinity. The bridal ring is the attribute of St. Catherine of Siena, who dedicated herself to a religious life and prayed that Christ would be her Bridegroom.

❡The scarlet or purple robe is one of the emblems of Christ's suffering while he was in the common hall, and is, therefore, one of the symbols of the Passion. " Then the soldiers of the governor took Jesus into the common hall, and gathered unto him the whole band of soldiers. And they stripped him, and put on him a scarlet robe. . . And after that they had mocked him, they took the robe off from him, and put his own raiment on him, and led him away to crucify him" (Matthew 27: 27–31).

Robe

The seamless robe is also one of the symbols of the Passion. " Then the soldiers, when they had crucified Jesus, took his garments, . . . and also his coat: now the coat was without seam, woven from the top throughout . . . They said . . . Let us not rend it, but cast lots for it. . ." (John 19: 23, 24).

❡The rope is one of the symbols of the betrayal of Jesus by Judas, for, according to John 18: 12, " Then the band and the captain and officers of the Jews took Jesus, and bound him, and led him away to Annas first; for he was father-in-law to Caiaphas, which was

Rope

the high priest that same year." St. John is the only one of the Evangelists to mention that Jesus was bound on this occasion, but Matthew and Mark mention that He was bound when taken to Pilate the next morning. According to tradition, it was with a rope that Judas hanged himself after the betrayal, in desperate repentance for his awful deed.

Rule ⬧A carpenter's rule is one of the customary attributes of the Apostle Thomas, builder of the heavenly palace of Gondophorus.

Saw ⬧The carpenter's saw, together with a plane and hatchet, is commonly used as an attribute of St. Joseph, who was a carpenter by trade. The saw is also the attribute of St. Simon Zelotes, who, according to legend, was martyred by being sawed asunder. It is also an attribute of certain sacred persons, notably St. Euphemia and Isaiah.

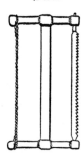

Scales ⬧The Archangel Michael is frequently portrayed bearing a pair of scales, for one of his responsibilities is to weigh the souls of the departed. In general, the scales symbolize equality and justice.

Sceptre ⬧The sceptre, or wand, carried in the hand is the symbol of authority. It is borne by princes of this earth and by the archangels, notably Gabriel.

in Christian Art

¶ The scourge is one of the symbols of the Passion. It is sometimes shown in combination with the pillar to which Christ was bound. In general, the scourge in the hands of a saint or at his feet suggests the penance which he inflicted on himself. In the hand of St. Ambrose, however, it is an allusion to his work in driving the Arians out of Italy.

Scourge

¶ A scroll, or rolled manuscript, is sometimes used in place of a book to suggest the gifts of an individual as a writer. This is particularly true of St. James the Great, who is frequently portrayed bearing a scroll in one hand. Scrolls, as the ancient type of book, are more often given to the Old Testament authors.

Scroll

¶ The scythe, like the sickle, symbolizes the cutting off of the strand of life and is, consequently, used as the attribute of Death. Death is frequently portrayed as a skeleton with a scythe in hand.

Scythe

¶ The seal is the mark, or signature, of God. "And I saw another angel ascending from the east, having the seal of the living God: and he cried with a loud voice to the four angels, to whom it was given to hurt the earth and the sea, saying, Hurt not the earth, neither the sea, nor the trees, till we have sealed the servants of our God in their foreheads" (Revelation 7 : 2, 3). This was known as the seal of the living God.

Seal

Ship ¶Through a number of different associations, the ship came to have a special meaning as symbolic of the Church of Christ. The ark of Noah, which floated safely in the midst of the deluge while everything else was overwhelmed, was an obvious symbol for the Church. St. Ambrose, in his writings, compares the Church to a ship, and the Cross to a ship's mast. The miracle of the Sea of Galilee, when Christ calmed the waves and saved the vessel of the Apostles from disaster, likewise served to give the ship a symbolic religious meaning. The ship is also the attribute of a few saints. The best known are St. Vincent and St. Nicholas of Myra. In paintings of St. Julian, a boat is frequently shown in the background, referring to his self-imposed task as a ferryman.

Spear ¶The spear, because it was used to pierce the side of Christ on the Cross, is one of the symbols of the Passion.

Sponge ¶The sponge is one of the emblems of the Crucifixion. This meaning is drawn from the scriptural story of the Crucifixion. "And straightway one of them ran, and took a spunge, and filled it with vinegar, and put it on a reed, and gave him to drink" (Matthew 27: 48).

Staff ¶The pilgrim's staff is used alone and in combination with various other objects as an attribute of numerous

saints who have been noteworthy for their travels and pilgrimages. The pilgrim's staff, together with a scroll and a scallop shell, are the customary attributes of St. James the Great.

The palm tree staff is always the attribute of St. Christopher, a man of great strength, who tore up a palm tree by the roots for his staff. After he had carried Christ, in the semblance of a child, across the river, he was told: "Plant thy staff in the ground and it shall put forth leaves and fruit." When this miracle took place, St. Christopher was converted to Christianity.

Other saints commonly given a pilgrim's staff as an attribute include St. John the Baptist and St. Jerome. St. Philip the Apostle is given a staff with a cross. St. Ursula frequently bears a staff with a banner on which the cross is inscribed. St. Roch is sometimes shown with a staff, cockleshell, and wallet.

¶ The stake, as the instrument of those who were tortured by fire, is used as an attribute of St. Dorothea, who was burned at the stake, and of St. Agnes, who was miraculously saved from a similar death.

Stake

Surgical Instruments

¶ These instruments are attributes of St. Cosmas and St. Damian, the physician brothers, who are customarily shown holding a lancet, or some other surgical instrument, in one hand. (See Box of Ointment and Mortar and Pestle)

323

Sword

❡The sword is used as an attribute of numerous saints who, according to tradition, suffered martyrdom at the sword's edge. Among these are St. Paul, who was beheaded; St. Euphemia, who was similarly beheaded after lions had refused to destroy her; St. Agnes, who met her fate in similar fashion; and St. Peter Martyr, who was assassinated. St. Justina is sometimes shown with a sword piercing her breast. The Archangel Michael is given the sword of the warrior, as is St. George of Cappadocia. St. John Gualbert is sometimes portrayed with a sword in hand, referring to his pursuit of the assassin of his brother. St. Martin is shown with a sword and the cloak which he divided, in order that he might share its warmth with a beggar.

Torch

❡The torch is one of the emblems of the Betrayal, and, therefore, of the Passion. This meaning is based upon John 18: 3, which describes the betrayal by Judas in these terms: "Judas then, having received a band of men and officers from the chief priests and Pharisees, cometh thither with lanterns and torches and weapons."

Christ as the Light of the World was sometimes portrayed by the torch in scenes of the Nativity.

The torch is also used as an attribute of certain martyrs. St. Dorothea, as an example, is sometimes shown with a torch at her side, for she was burned at the stake. A dog with a flaming torch in its mouth is an attribute of St. Dominic.

⟨A spotless towel is a symbol of purity, and is some-times used as an attribute of the Virgin Mary. A towel with a pitcher is sometimes employed as a symbol of the Passion of Christ, in reference to Pilate's washing his hands. (See Ewer and Basin, in Section XIII)

⟨The tower, generally with three windows, is the customary attribute of St. Barbara. This is an allusion to the legend that when her tower was being built she instructed that it should have three windows instead of two, the three windows signifying the Trinity.

Tower

⟨A vase holding a lily is one of the most frequently depicted objects in paintings of the Annunciation. The vase is very often of transparent glass; for glass, being clear and translucent, symbolizes the perfect purity of the Virgin.

Vase

In a general sense, the empty vase symbolizes the body separated from the soul. A vase with birds on its rim, quenching their thirst, is a symbol of eternal bliss.

⟨The veil, because it conceals the wearer, symbolizes modesty and chastity. The veil with the head of Christ depicted on it is the attribute of St. Veronica. This refers to a passage in the Apocryphal Gospel of Nico-demus, which relates that Veronica dried the sweat from the face of Christ on His way to Calvary with her veil, and that the imprint of His face remained on

Veil

it. It is also an attribute of St. Agatha, with reference to the legend that her veil ſtayed a flow of lava from Mt. Etna which had menaced the city of Catania.

Wheel

ℂRotating force is the symbol of divine power; hence the wheel, burning or otherwise, carries this meaning. It appears in the Expulsion of Adam and Eve from the Garden of Eden. The Throne of God is often shown borne upon flaming wheels with eyes and wings, an allusion to the vision of Ezekiel (Ezekiel 1: 1–28). The wheel is the special attribute of St. Catherine of Alexandria, who was tortured upon the wheel.

Winepress

ℂThe winepress is the symbol of the wrath of God. It takes this meaning from the passage in Isaiah 63: 3, " I have trodden the winepress alone; and of the people there was none with me; for I will tread them in mine anger and trample them in my fury. . ."

326

INDEX & BIBLIOGRAPHY

Corrigenda to the Captions

PLATE 1

Location should now read
Seattle Art Museum, Seattle, Washington

PLATE 29

Should now read
Giorgione : The Holy Family

PLATE 45

Should now read
Jacopo Tintoretto : The Trinity adored
by the Heavenly Choir

INDEX

☞ Plate references follow the text references and are indicated by italicized type

330

BIBLIOGRAPHY

The Holy Bible

The Apocryphal New Testament, *Translated by Montague Rhodes James*
Oxford, 1926

Audsley, W. and G.   Handbook of Christian Symbolism
London, Day and Son, Ltd. Preface dated 1865

Baring-Gould, S.   The Lives of the Saints
New and Revised Edition, 16 volumes. 1914

Les Benedictines de Saint Louis du Temple, Paris
Dictionnaire du Symbolisme   *Paris, (no date given)*

Benesch, Otto   The Art of the Renaissance in Northern Europe
Harvard University Press, Cambridge, Massachusetts, 1945

Berenson, Bernhard   The Central Italian Painters of the Renaissance
G. P. Putnam's Sons, New York and London, 1909

Berenson, Bernhard   The Italian Painters of the Renaissance
Clarendon Press, Oxford, 1930

Berenson, Bernhard   Italian Pictures of the Renaissance
Clarendon Press, Oxford, 1932

Berry, A. M.   Animals in Art   *London, 1929*

Braun, Joseph   Die Liturgische Gewandung
Freiburg im Breisgau, Herdersche Verlagshandlung, 1907

Corblet, J.   Précis de l'Histoire de l'art Chrétien
Revue de l'Art Chrétien Vol. 4, pp. 582–583, Paris, 1860

Didron, Adolphe Napoleon   Christian Iconography
Henry G. Bohn, London, 1851

Ditchfield, P. H.   Symbolism of the Saints
A. R. Mowbray and Co. Ltd., London, 1910

Doering, Oscar   Christliche Symbole   *Freiburg, 1933*

Duckett, Sir George F.   Monastic and Ecclesiastical Costume
Reprinted from Vol. 38 of the Sussex Archaeological Society's Collections, (no date)

343

Duffield, Mrs. William   The Art of Flower Painting   *New York, 1878*

Evans, E. P.   Animal Symbolism in Ecclesiastical Architecture
  Henry Holt and Co., New York, 1896

Faure, Elie   The Italian Renaissance
  Albert and Charles Boni, New York, 1929

Floerke, Hanns   Repräsentanten der Renaissance
  Georg Müller, München, 1924

Friedman, Herbert   The Symbolic Goldfinch   *New York, Copyright, 1946*

Goldsmith, Elizabeth   Sacred Symbols in Art
  G. P. Putnam & Sons, New York and London, 1912

Haig, Elizabeth   The Floral Symbolism of the Great Masters
  Kegan Paul, Trench, Trubner and Co. Ltd., London, 1913

Helyot, Pierre   Histoire des Ordres Monastiques Religieux et Militaires
  Nicholas Gosselin, Paris, 1714–1719

House, Homer D.   Wild Flowers   *Macmillan Co., 1935*

Howe, William Norton   Animal Life in Italian Painting   *London, 1912*

Huime, Edward F.   The History, Principles and Practice
  of Symbolism in Christian Art   *London, 1891*

Husenbeth, Frederick Charles   Emblems of Saints   *Norwich, 1882*

Jameson, Mrs. Anna Brownell Murphy   The History of our Lord as exemplified
  in Works of Art (continued and completed by Lady Eastlake)
  Longman, Green, Longman, Roberts and Green, London, 1865

Jameson, Mrs. Anna Brownell Murphy   Legends of the Madonna
  as represented in the Fine Arts
  Longmans, Brown, Green and Longmans, London, 1852

Jameson, Mrs. Anna Brownell Murphy   Sacred and Legendary Art
  Longmans, Green and Co., London, 1870

Jameson, Mrs. Anna Brownell Murphy   Legends of the Monastic Orders,
  as Represented in the Fine Arts
  Longmans, Green and Co., London, 1880

Jenner, Mrs. H.   Christian Symbolism
  Methuen and Co. Ltd., London, 1910

Knapp, Justina   Christian Symbols and How to Use Them
  The Bruce Publishing Company, Milwaukee, 1935

Loqemann, H.   The Fish and the Flower as Symbols in Medieval Manuscripts
    Modern Language Notes, Vol. 5; Baltimore, 1890

Mather, Frank Jewett, Jr.   History of Italian Paintings
    Henry Holt and Co., New York, 1923

Mather, Frank Jewett, Jr.   Western European Painting of the Renaissance
    Henry Holt and Co., New York, 1939

Menzel, Wolfgang   Christliche Symbolik (*2 volumes*)
    Regensburg, G. Joseph Manz, 1854

Odell, Shepard   The Lore of the Unicorn
    Houghton Mifflin Co., Boston, 1930

Panofsky, Erwin   Studies in Iconology   *New York, 1939*

Pastor, Ludwig Freiherr von   The History of the Popes (*volumes 1–12*)
    London, 1906–38

Pfeiffer, Harold A.   The Catholic Picture Dictionary
    Duell, Sloan and Pearce, New York, 1948

Picinellus, Philippus and Erath, Augustinus, Mundus Symbolicus   *Cologne, 1681*

The Pierpont Morgan Library   The Animal Kingdom   *New York, 1940–41*

Porteus, Alexander   Forest Folklore   *Macmillan Co., 1928*

Ripa, Caesar   Iconologia or Moral Emblems   *Tempest, London, 1709*

Schneider, Fred   La legende de la licorne ou du monocéros
    *Revue de L'Art Chrétien   Tome VI, (38 de la collection),
    31 ème Annee, 4e Série, Lille, Janvier 1888, pp. 16–22*

Suida, Wilhelm   Leonardo und sein Kreis   *F. Bruckmann, München, 1929*

Symonds, John Addington   Renaissance in Italy
    Smith, Elder and Co., London, 1898

Tiron, Abbé   Histoire et Costumes des Ordres Religieux,
    civils et militaires   *2 volumes (Illustrations)
    Bruxelles, Librairie Historique-Artistique, 1845*

Vasari, Giorgio   The Lives of the Most Eminent Painters,
    Sculptors and Architects (*10 volumes*)
    Phillip Lee Warner, Publisher to the Medici Society Ltd. London, 1912–1914

Venturi, Adolfo   North Italian Painting of the Quattrocento Pantheon, Firenze
    Harcourt, Brace & Co., New York, 1930

Verneuil, M. P.   Dictionnaire des symboles, emblèmes et attributs   *Paris, 1898*

345

Waters, Clara E. C. (Mrs. C.)   Angels in Art
    L. C. Page and Co., Boston, 1898

Waters, Clara E. C. (Mrs. C.)   A Handbook of Christian Symbols
    Ticknor and Company, Boston, 1886

Waters, Clara E. C. (Mrs. C.)   A Handbook of Legendary and Mythological Art
    Hurd and Houghton, New York, 1871

Webber, F. R.   Church Symbolism   *J. H. Jansen, Cleveland, 1927*

Wölfflin, H.   The Art of the Italian Renaissance
    G. P. Putnam's Sons, New York and London, 1913

Costumes of Religious Orders   60 Original drawings identified in manuscript
    No text, not dated, approx. 1800

The Catholic Encyclopedia   *15 volumes, 1909 Edition*

The Encyclopedia Britannica